THE LETTERS OF CASSIODORUS

HODGKIN

Oxford
PRINTED BY HORACE HART, PRINTER TO THE UNIVERSITY

THE
LETTERS OF CASSIODORUS

BEING

A CONDENSED TRANSLATION OF THE VARIAE EPISTOLAE
OF MAGNUS AURELIUS CASSIODORUS SENATOR

With an Introduction

BY

THOMAS HODGKIN

FELLOW OF UNIVERSITY COLLEGE, LONDON; HON. D.C.L. OF DURHAM UNIVERSITY
AUTHOR OF 'ITALY AND HER INVADERS'

LONDON: HENRY FROWDE

AMEN CORNER, PATERNOSTER ROW, E.C.

1886.

[*All rights reserved*]

PREFACE.

THE abstract of the 'Variae' of Cassiodorus which I now offer to the notice of historical students, belongs to that class of work which Professor Max Müller happily characterised when he entitled two of his volumes 'Chips from a German Workshop.' In the course of my preparatory reading, before beginning the composition of the third and fourth volumes of my book on 'Italy and Her Invaders,' I found it necessary to study very attentively the 'Various Letters' of Cassiodorus, our best and often our only source of information, for the character and the policy of the great Theodoric. The notes which in this process were accumulated upon my hands might, I hoped, be woven into one long chapter on the Ostrogothic government of Italy. When the materials were collected, however, they were so manifold, so perplexing, so full of curious and unexpected detail, that I quite despaired of ever succeeding in the attempt to group them into one harmonious and artistic picture. Frankly, therefore, renouncing a task which is beyond my powers, I offer my notes for the perusal of the few readers who may care to study the mutual reactions of the Roman and the Teutonic mind upon one another in the Sixth Century, and I ask these to accept the artist's assurance, 'The curtain is the picture.'

It will be seen that I only profess to give an abstract, not a full translation of the letters. There is so much repetition and such a lavish expenditure of words in the writings of Cassiodorus, that they lend themselves very readily to the work of the abbreviator. Of course the longer letters generally admit of greater relative reduction in quantity than the shorter ones, but I think it may be said that on an average the letters have lost at least half their bulk in my hands. On any important point the real student will of course refuse to accept my condensed rendering, and will go straight to the fountain-head. I hope, however, that even students may occasionally derive the same kind of assistance from my labours which an astronomer derives from the humble instrument called the 'finder' in a great observatory.

A few important letters have been translated, to the best of my ability, verbatim. In the not infrequent instances where I have been unable to extract any intelligible meaning, on grammatical principles, from the words of my author, I have put in the text the nearest approximation that I could discover to his meaning, and placed the unintelligible words in a note, hoping that my readers may be more fortunate in their interpretation than I have been.

With the usual ill-fortune of authors, just as my last sheet was passing through the press I received from

Italy a number of the 'Atti e Memorie della R. Deputazione di Storia Patria per le Provincie di Romagna' (to which I am a subscriber), containing an elaborate and scholarlike article by S. Augusto Gaudenzi, entitled 'L'Opera di Cassiodorio a Ravenna.' It is a satisfaction to me to see that in several instances S. Gaudenzi and I have reached practically the same conclusions; but I cannot but regret that his paper reached me too late to prevent my benefiting from it more fully. A few of the more important points in which I think S. Gaudenzi throws useful light on our common subject are noticed in the 'Additions and Corrections,' to which I beg to draw my readers' attention.

I may perhaps be allowed to add that the Index, the preparation of which has cost me no small amount of labour, ought (if I have not altogether failed in my endeavour) to be of considerable assistance to the historical enquirer. For instance, if he will refer to the heading *Sajo*, and consult the passages there referred to, he will find, I believe, all that Cassiodorus has to tell us concerning these interesting personages, the Sajones, who were almost the only representatives of the intrusive Gothic element in the fabric of Roman administration.

From textual criticism and the discussion of the authority of different MSS. I have felt myself entirely relieved by the announcement of the forthcoming critical edition of the 'Variae,' under the superintendence of Professor Meyer. The task to which an eminent German scholar has devoted the labour of several years, it would be quite useless for me, without appliances and without special training, to approach as an amateur; and I therefore simply help myself to the best reading that I can get from the printed texts, leaving to Professor Meyer to say which reading possesses the highest diplomatic authority. Simply as a a matter of curiosity I have spent some days in examining the MSS. of Cassiodorus in the British Museum. If they are at all fair representatives (which probably they are not) of the MSS. which Professor Meyer has consulted, I should say that though the titles of the letters have often got into great confusion through careless and unintelligent copying, the main text is not likely to show any very important variations from the editions of Nivellius and Garet.

I now commend this volume with all its imperfections to the indulgent criticism of the small class of historical students who alone will care to peruse it. The man of affairs and the practical politician will of course not condescend to turn over its pages; yet the anxious and for a time successful efforts of Theodoric and his Minister to preserve to Italy the blessings of *Civilitas* might perhaps teach useful lessons even to a modern statesman.

THOS. HODGKIN.

NOTE.

The following Note as to the MSS. at the British Museum may save a future enquirer a little trouble.

(1) 10 B. XV. is a MS. about 11 inches by 8, written in a fine bold hand, and fills 157 folios, of which 134 belong to the 'Variae' and 23 to the 'Institutiones Divinarum Litterarum.' There are also two folios at the end which I have not deciphered. The MS. is assigned to the Thirteenth Century. The title of the First Book is interesting, because it contains the description of Cassiodorus' official rank, 'Ex Magistri Officii,' which Mommsen seems to have looked for in the MSS. in vain. The MS. contains the first Three Books complete, but only 39 letters of the Fourth. Letters 40–51 of the Fourth Book, and the whole of the Fifth, Sixth, and Seventh Books, are missing. It then goes on to the Eighth Book (which it calls the Fifth), but omits the first five letters. The remaining 28 appear to be copied satisfactorily. The Ninth, Tenth, Eleventh, and Twelfth Books, which the transcriber calls the Sixth, Seventh, Eighth, and Ninth, seem to be on the whole correctly copied.

There seems to be a certain degree of correspondence between the readings of this MS. and those of the Leyden MS. of the Twelfth Century (formerly at Fulda) which are described by Ludwig Tross in his 'Symbolae Criticae' (Hammone, 1853).

(2) 8 B. XIX. is a MS. also of the Thirteenth Century, in a smaller hand than the foregoing. The margins are very large, but the Codex measures only $6\frac{3}{4}$ inches by $4\frac{1}{4}$. The rubricated titles are of somewhat later date than the body of the text. The initial letters are elaborately illuminated. This MS. contains, in a mutilated state and in a peculiar order, the books from the Eighth to the Twelfth. The following is the order in which the books are placed:

    IX. 8–25, folios 1–14.
    X. . . ,, 14–33.
    XI. . . ,, 33–63.
    XII. . . ,, 63–83.
    VIII. . . ,, 83–126.
    IX. 1–7, . ,, 126–134.

The amanuensis, who has evidently been a thoroughly dishonest worker, constantly omits whole letters, from which however he sometimes extracts a sentence or two, which he tacks on to the end of some preceding letter without regard to the sense. This process makes it exceedingly difficult to collate the MS. with the printed text. Owing to the Eighth Book being inserted after the Twelfth, it is erroneously labelled on the back, 'Cassiodori Senatoris Epistolae, Lib. X—XIII.'

(3) 10 B. IV. (also of the Thirteenth Century, and measuring 11 inches by 8) contains, in a tolerably complete state, the first Three Books of the 'Variae,' Book IV. 5-39, Book VIII. 1-12, and Books X—XII. The order, however, is transposed, Books IV. and VIII. coming after Book XII. These excerpts from Cassiodorus, which occupy folios 66 to 134 of the MS., are preceded by some collections relative to the Civil and Canon Law. The letters which are copied seem to be carefully and conscientiously done.

These three MSS. are all in the King's Library.

Besides these MSS. I have also glanced at No. 1,919 in the Bodleian Library at Oxford. Like those previously described it is, I believe, of the Thirteenth Century, and professes to contain the whole of the 'Variae;' but the letters are in an exceedingly mutilated form. On an average it seems to me that not more than one-third of each letter is copied. In this manner the 'Variae' are compressed into the otherwise impossible number of 33 folios (149-182).

All these MSS., even the best of them, give me the impression of being copied by very unintelligent scribes, who had but little idea of the meaning of the words which they were transcribing. In all, the superscription V. S. is expanded (wrongly, as I believe) into 'Viro Senatori;' for 'Praefecto Praetorio' we have the meaningless 'Praeposito;' and the Agapitus who is addressed in the 6th, 32nd, and 33rd letters of the First Book is turned, in defiance of chronology, into a Pope.

CONTENTS.

INTRODUCTION.

CHAPTER I.

LIFE OF CASSIODORUS.

	PAGE
Historical position of Cassiodorus	1
His ancestry	3-4
His name	5-6
His birthplace	6-9
Date of his birth	9-12
His education	12
Consiliarius to his father	12
Quaestor	14-16
Composition of the 'Variae'	16
Their style	17-19
Policy of Theodoric	20
Date of composition of the 'Variae'	23
Consulship	25
Patriciate	27
Composition of the 'Chronicon'	27
„ „ Gothic History	29-35
Relation of the work of Jordanes to this History	34
Master of the Offices	36
Praetorian Praefect	39
Sketch of history during his Praefecture	42-50
End of official career	50
Edits the 'Variae'	51
His treatise 'De Anima'	53
He retires to the cloister	54
His theological works	60-63
His literary works	64-66
His death	67
NOTE ON THE TOPOGRAPHY OF SQUILLACE	68-72

CHAPTER II.

THE 'ANECDOTON HOLDERI.'

	PAGE
Contents of the MS.	74–75
To whom addressed	76
Information as to life of Symmachus	77
" " " Boethius	79
Religious position of Boethius	81
Information as to life of Cassiodorus	84

CHAPTER III.

THE GRADATIONS OF OFFICIAL RANK IN THE LOWER EMPIRE.

Nobilissimi	85
Illustres	86–90
Spectabiles	90–91
Clarissimi	91
Perfectissimi	92
Egregii	92

CHAPTER IV.

ON THE OFFICIUM OF THE PRAEFECTUS PRAETORIO.

Military character of the Roman Civil Service	93
Sources of information	95
Princeps	96
Cornicularius	97–102
Adjutor	103
Commentariensis	104
Ab Actis	106
Numerarii	108
Inferior Officers	109–114

CHAPTER V.

BIBLIOGRAPHY.

Editions of the 'Variae'	115–118
Literature concerning the 'Variae'	118–121

CHAPTER VI.

CHRONOLOGY.

Consular Fasti	122
Indictions	123
Chronological Tables	126–130

CONTENTS. xiii

ABSTRACT OF THE 'VARIAE.'

PREFACE 133–140

BOOK I.

CONTAINING FORTY-SIX LETTERS WRITTEN BY CASSIODORUS IN THE NAME OF THEODORIC.

1. To EMPEROR ANASTASIUS. Persuasives to peace . . . 141
2. „ THEON. Manufacture of purple dye . . . 143
3. „ CASSIODORUS, father of the author. His praises . . . 144
4. „ SENATE. Great deeds of ancestors of Cassiodorus . . . 145
5. „ FLORIANUS. End of litigation 147
6. „ AGAPITUS. Mosaics for Ravenna . . . 147
7. „ FELIX. Inheritance of Plutianus . . . 148
8. „ AMABILIS. Prodigality of Neotherius . . . 149
9. „ BISHOP EUSTORGIUS. Offences of Ecclesiastics . . . 149
10. „ BOETIUS. Frauds of moneyers . . . 150
11. „ SERVATUS. Violence of Breones . . . 151
12. „ EUGENIUS. Appointment as Magister Officium . . . 151
13. „ SENATE. On the same 152
14. „ FAUSTUS. Collection of 'Tertiae' . . . 152
15. „ FESTUS. Interests of the absent . . . 153
16. „ JULIANUS. Remission of taxes . . . 153
17. „ GOTHIC AND ROMAN INHABITANTS OF DERTONA. Fortification of Camp 153
18. „ DOMITIANUS AND WILIAS. Statute of Limitations, &c. . 154
19. „ SATURNINUS AND VERBUSIUS. Rights of the Fiscus . 155
20. „ ALBINUS AND ALBIENUS. Circus quarrels . . . 155
21. „ MAXIMIAN AND ANDREAS. Embellishment of Rome . 156
22. „ MARCELLUS. His promotion to rank of Advocatus Fisci . 156
23. „ COELIANUS AND AGAPITUS. Litigation between Senators . 157
24. „ ALL THE GOTHS. Call to arms . . . 157
25. „ SABINIANUS. Repair of the walls of Rome . . . 158
26. „ FAUSTUS. Immunity of certain Church property . . 159
27. „ SPECIOSUS. Circus quarrels . . . 159
28. „ GOTHS AND ROMANS. Building of walls of Rome . . 160
29. „ THE LUCRISTANI ON RIVER SONTIUS. Postal Service . 160
30. „ SENATE. Injury to public peace from Circus rivalries . 161
31. „ THE ROMAN PEOPLE. Same subject . . . 161
32. „ AGAPITUS. Same subject . . . 162
33. „ „ Arrangements for Pantomime . . . 162

b

				PAGE
34.	To Faustus.	Exportation of corn		163
35.	,,	,, Unreasonable delays in transmission of corn		163
36.	,,	Theriolus. Guardianship of sons of Benedictus		164
37.	,,	Crispianus. Justifiable homicide		164
38.	,,	Baion. Hilarius to have possession of his property		165
39.	,,	Festus. Nephews of Filagrius to be detained in Rome		165
40.	,,	Assuin (or Assius). Inhabitants of Salona to be drilled		166
41.	,,	Agapitus. Enquiries into character of younger Faustus		166
42.	,,	Artemidorus. Appointment as Praefect of the City		167
43.	,,	Senate. Promotion of Artemidorus		167
44.	,,	the People of Rome. Same subject		168
45.	,,	Boetius. Water-clock and sundial for Burgundian King		168
46.	,,	Gundibad. Same subject		170

BOOK II.

CONTAINING FORTY-ONE LETTERS WRITTEN BY CASSIODORUS IN THE NAME OF THEODORIC.

1.	To Emperor Anastasius.	Consulship of Felix	171
2.	,, Felix.	Same subject	172
3.	,, Senate.	Same subject	173
4.	,, Ecdicius (or Benedictus).	Collection of *Siliquaticum*	173
5.	,, Faustus.	Soldiers' arrears	173
6.	,, Agapitus.	Embassy to Constantinople	174
7.	,, Sura (or Suna).	Embellishment of City	174
8.	,, Bishop Severus.	Compensation for damage by troops	175
9.	,, Faustus.	Allowance to retired charioteer	175
10.	,, Speciosus.	Abduction of Agapita	175
11.	,, Provinus (Probinus ?).	Gift unduly obtained from Agapita	176
12.	,, the Count of the Siliquatarii, and the Harbour Master (of Portus ?).	Prohibition of export of lard	177
13.	,, Fruinarith.	Dishonest conduct of Venantius	177
14.	,, Symmachus.	Romulus the parricide	178
15.	,, Venantius.	Appointment as Comes Domesticorum	178
16.	,, Senate.	Same subject. Panegyric on Liberius, father of Venantius	179
17.	,, Possessors, Defensors, and Curials of Tridentum (Trient).	Immunity from Tertiae enjoyed by lands granted by the King	180
18.	,, Bishop Gudila.	Ecclesiastics as Curiales	181
19.	,, Goths and Romans, and Keepers of Harbours and Mountain Fortresses.	Domestic treachery and murder	181
20.	,, Uniligis (or Wiligis).	Order for provision ships	182
21.	,, Joannes.	Drainage-concession too timidly acted upon	182
22.	,, Festus.	Ecdicius to be buried by his sons	183
23.	,, Ampelius, Despotius, and Theodulus.	Protection for owners of potteries	183

		PAGE
24. To SENATE. Arrears of taxation due from Senators	.	183
25. ,, SENATE. AN EDICT. Evasion of taxes by the rich	.	184
26. ,, FAUSTUS. Regulations for corn-traffic	.	185
27. ,, JEWS LIVING IN GENOA. Rebuilding of Synagogue	.	185
28. ,, STEPHANUS. Honours bestowed on retirement	.	186
29. ,, ADILA. Protection to dependents of the Church	.	186
30. ,, FAUSTUS. Privileges granted to Church of Milan	.	187
31. ,, THE DROMONARII [ROWERS IN EXPRESS-BOATS]. State Galleys on the Po	.	187
32. ,, SENATE. Drainage of marshes of Decennonium	.	188
33. ,, DECIUS. Same subject	.	189
34. ,, ARTEMIDORUS. Embezzlement of City building funds	.	189
35. ,, TANCILA. Theft of statue at Como	.	190
36. EDICT. Same subject	.	190
37. To FAUSTUS. Largesse to citizens of Spoleto	.	190
38. ,, ,, Immunity from taxation	.	191
39. ,, ALOISIUS. Hot springs of Aponum	.	191
40. ,, BOETIUS. Harper for King of the Franks	.	193
41. ,, LUDUIN [CLOVIS]. Victories over the Alamanni	.	194

BOOK III.

CONTAINING FIFTY-THREE LETTERS WRITTEN BY CASSIODORUS IN THE NAME OF THEODORIC.

1. To ALARIC. Dissuades from war with the Franks	.	196
2. ,, GUNDIBAD. Dissuades from war	.	197
3. ,, THE KINGS OF THE HERULI, WARNI (GUARNI), AND THURINGIANS. Attempt to form a Teutonic coalition	.	198
4. ,, LUDUIN (LUDWIG, or CLOVIS). To desist from war on Alaric	.	198
5. ,, IMPORTUNUS. Promotion to the Patriciate	.	199
6. ,, SENATE. Same subject	.	200
7. ,, JANUARIUS. Reproof for alleged extortion	.	201
8. ,, VENANTIUS. Remissness in collection of public revenue	.	201
9. ,, POSSESSORES, DEFENSORES, AND CURIALES OF AESTUNAE. Marbles for Ravenna	.	202
10. ,, FESTUS. Same subject	.	202
11. ,, ARGOLICUS. Appointment to Praefecture of the City	.	203
12. ,, SENATE. Same subject	.	203
13. ,, SUNHIVAD. Appointment as Governor of Samnium	.	204
14. ,, BISHOP AURIGENES. Accusations against servants of a Bishop	.	204
15. ,, THEODAHAD. Disposal of contumacious person	.	205
16. ,, GEMELLUS. Appointment as Governor of Gaulish Provinces	.	205
17. ,, GAULISH PROVINCIALS. Proclamation	.	206
18. ,, GEMELLUS. Re-patriation of Magnus	.	206

19. To Daniel. Supply of marble sarcophagi	.	207
20. „ Grimoda and Ferrocinctus. Oppression of Castorius by Faustus	.	207
21. „ Faustus. Disgrace and temporary exile	.	208
22. „ Artemidorus. Invitation to King's presence	.	209
23. „ Colossaeus. Appointment as Governor of Pannonia	.	209
24. „ Barbarians and Romans settled in Pannonia. Same subject		210
25. „ Simeon. Tax-collecting and iron-mining in Dalmatia	.	210
26. „ Osun. Simeon's journey to Dalmatia	.	211
27. „ Joannes. Protection against Praetorian Praefect	.	211
28. „ Cassiodorus (Senior). Invitation to Court	.	211
29. „ Argolicus. Repair of granaries in Rome	.	212
30. „ „ Repair of Cloacae „ „	.	212
31. „ Senate. Conservation of aqueducts and temples in Rome	.	213
32. „ Gemellus. Remission of taxes to citizens of Arles	.	214
33. „ Argolicus. Promotion of Armentarius and Superbus	.	214
34. „ Inhabitants of Massilia. Appointment of Governor	.	215
35. „ Romulus. Gifts not to be revoked	.	215
36. „ Arigern. Complaints against Venantius	.	216
37. „ Bishop Peter. Alleged injustice	.	216
38. „ Wandil [Vuandil]. Gothic troops not to molest citizens	.	217
39. „ Felix. Largesse to charioteers of Milan	.	217
40. „ Provincials settled in Gaul. Exemption from taxation	.	218
41. „ Gemellus. Corn for garrisons on the Durance	.	218
42. „ Provincials in Gaul. Exemption from military contributions		219
43. „ Unigis. Fugitive slaves to be restored to owners	.	219
44. „ Landowners (Possessores) of Arles. Repair of walls, &c.	.	220
45. „ Arigern. Dispute between Roman Church and Samaritans		220
46. „ Adeodatus. Further charges against Venantius	.	220
47. „ Faustus. Banishment of Jovinus to Vulcanian Islands	.	222
48. „ Goths and Romans living near Fort Verruca. Fortification		222
49. „ Possessores, Defensores, and Curiales of Catana. Repair of walls	.	224
50. „ Provincials of Noricum. Alamanni and Noricans to exchange cattle	.	225
51. „ Faustus. Stipend of charioteer. Description of Circus	.	226
52. „ Consularis. Roman land surveying	.	231
53. „ Apronianus. Water-finders	.	233

BOOK IV.

CONTAINING FIFTY-ONE LETTERS WRITTEN BY CASSIODORUS IN THE NAME OF THEODORIC.

1. To King of the Thuringians. Marriage with Theodoric's niece	235
2. „ King of the Heruli. Adoption as son	236
3. „ Senarius. Appointment as Comes Patrimonii	237

		PAGE
4. To SENATE. Same subject	.	237
5. ,, AMABILIS. Supply of provisions to Gaulish Provinces	.	238
6. ,, SYMMACHUS. Sons of Valerian to be detained in Rome	.	238
7. ,, SENARIUS. Losses by shipwreck to be refunded	.	239
8. ,, POSSESSORES AND CURIALES OF FORUM LIVII (FORLI). Transport of timber to Alsuanum	.	240
9. ,, OSUIN. 'Tuitio regii nominis'	.	240
10. ,, JOANNES. Repression of lawless custom of Pignoratio	.	240
11. ,, SENARIUS. Dispute between Possessores and Curiales	.	241
12. ,, MARABAD AND GEMELLUS. Complaint of Archotamia	.	241
13. ,, SENARIUS. Supplies for Colossaeus and suite	.	242
14. ,, GESILA. Evasion of land-tax by Goths	.	242
15. ,, BENENATUS. New rowers, and their qualifications	.	243
16. ,, SENATE. Arigern entrusted with charge of City of Rome	.	243
17. ,, IDA. Church possessions to be restored	.	244
18. ,, ANNAS. Enquiry concerning a priestly Ghoul	.	244
19. ,, GEMELLUS. Corn, wine, and oil to be exempt from the Siliquaticum	.	245
20. ,, GEBERICH. Church land to be restored	.	245
21. ,, GEMELLUS. Promptness and integrity required	.	245
22. ,, ARGOLICUS. } Accusation of magic against Roman Senators	.	246
23. ,, ARIGERN.		
24. ,, ELPIDIUS. Architectural restoration at Spoleto	.	247
25. ,, ARGOLICUS. Petrus to become Senator	.	247
26. ,, CITIZENS OF MARSEILLES. Remission of taxes	.	248
27. ,, TEZUTZAT. } Petrus assaulted by his Defensor	.	248
28. ,, DUDA.		
29. ,, ARGOLICUS. Official tardiness rebuked	.	249
30. ,, ALBINUS. Erection of workshops near Roman Forum	.	249
31. ,, AEMILIANUS. Aqueduct to be promptly finished	.	250
32. ,, DUDA. Crown rights to be asserted with moderation	.	250
33. ,, JEWS OF GENOA. Their privileges confirmed	.	251
34. ,, DUDA. Reclamation of buried treasure	.	252
35. ,, REPRESENTATIVES (ACTORES) OF ALBINUS. Extravagant minor	.	252
36. ,, FAUSTUS. Remission of taxes for Provincials	.	253
37. ,, THEODAGUNDA. To do justice to Renatus	.	253
38. ,, FAUSTUS. Taxes to be reduced	.	254
39. ,, THEODAHAD. His encroachments	.	254
40. ,, REPRESENTATIVES (ACTORES) OF PROBINUS. The affair of Agapita	.	255
41. ,, JOANNES. Unjust judgment reversed	.	255
42. ,, ARGOLICUS. Property to be restored to sons of Volusian	.	256
43. ,, SENATE. Punishment of incendiaries of Jewish Synagogue	.	256
44. ,, ANTONIUS. To do justice to Stephanus	.	257
45. ,, COMITES, DEFENSORES, AND CURIALES OF TICINUM (PAVIA). Heruli to be forwarded on their way to Ravenna	.	258
46. ,, MARABAD. Case of Liberius' wife to be reheard	.	258
47. ,, GUDISAL. Abuses of the Cursus Publicus	.	259

			PAGE
48. To Eusebius. His honourable retirement			260
49. „ Provincials and the Long-haired Men, the Defensores and Curiales residing in Suavia. Appointment of Governor, &c.			260
50. „ Faustus. Campanian taxes remitted. Eruption of Vesuvius			261
51. „ Symmachus. Restoration of Theatre of Pompey			263

BOOK V.

CONTAINING FORTY-FOUR LETTERS WRITTEN BY CASSIODORUS IN THE NAME OF THEODORIC.

1. To King of the Vandals. Thanking for presents	264
2. „ the Haesti. Their present of amber	265
3. „ Honoratus. } Promotion to Quaestorship, &c.	266
4. „ Senate.	
5. „ Mannila. Abuses of the Cursus Publicus	268
6. „ Stabularius. } Default in payments to Treasury	269
7. „ Joannes.	
8. „ Anastasius. Transport of marbles to Ravenna	270
9. „ Possessores of Feltria. New city to be built	270
10. „ Veranus. } Payment on march to Gaul	271
11. „ the Gepidae.	
12. „ Theodahad. His avarice and injustice	272
13. „ Eutropius and Acretius. Commissariat	272
14. „ Severi(a)nus. Financial abuses in Suavia	273
15. „ Possessores in Suavia. Same subject	274
16. „ Abundantius. Formation of navy	274
17. „ „ Same subject	275
18. „ Uvilias [Willias?]. } Same subject	276
19. „ Gudinand.	
20. „ Avilf.	
21. „ Capuanus. } Appointment as Rector Decuriarum	277
22. „ Senate.	
23. „ Abundantius. Archery drill	279
24. „ Epiphanius. Property of intestate claimed for the State	279
25. „ Bacauda. Appointment as Tribunus Voluptatum	280
26. „ Goths settled in Picenum and Samnium. Summons to the royal presence	280
27. „ Guduim. The same	280
28. „ Carinus. Invitation to Court	281
29. „ Neudes. Blind Gothic warrior enslaved	281
30. „ Gudui[m]. Servile tasks imposed on free Goths	281
31. „ Decoratus. Arrears of Siliquaticum to be enforced	282
32. „ Brandila. Assault of his wife on Regina	282
33. „ Wilitanch. Adulterous connection between Brandila and Regina	283
34. „ Abundantius. Frontosus compared to chameleon	284
35. „ Luvirit and Ampelius. Punishment of fraudulent shipowners	285

		PAGE
36. To Starcedius. Honourable discharge	. . .	285
37. „ Jews of Milan. Rights of Synagogue not to be invaded	.	286
38. „ All Cultivators. Shrubs obstructing aqueduct of Ravenna		286
39. „ Ampelius and Liveria. Abuses in administration of Spanish government	. . . . . .	287
40. „ Cyprian. ⎫ Promotion to the Comitiva Sacrarum Largitionum		289
41. „ Senate. ⎭		
42. „ Maximus. Rewards to performers in Amphitheatre	.	291
43. „ Transmund [Thrasamund]. Complains of protection given to Gesalic	. . . . .	292
44. „ Transmund [Thrasamund]. Reconciliation	. . .	293

BOOK VI.

CONTAINING TWENTY-FIVE FORMULAE.

1. Of the Consulship	. . . . .	294
2. „ „ Patriciate	. . . . .	296
3. „ „ Praetorian Praefecture	. . .	296
4. „ „ Praefecture of the City	. . .	299
5. „ „ Quaestorship	. . . . .	300
6. „ „ Magisterial Dignity, and its Excellency (Magistratus Officiorum)	. . . . .	302
7. „ „ Office of Comes Sacrarum Largitionum	. . .	303
8. „ „ „ „ „ Privatarum, and its Excellency	.	304
9. „ „ „ „ Count of the Patrimony, and its Excellency		305
10. For Promotion as Proceres per Codicillos Vacantes	. .	306
11. Conferring the Rank of an Illustris and Title of Comes Domesticorum, without Office	. . .	307
12. Bestowal of Countship of First Order, without Office	.	307
13. Bestowing the Honorary Rank of Master of the Bureau and Count of the First Order on an Officer of the Courts in Active Service	. . . . .	308
14. Bestowing Rank as a Senator	. . . .	309
15. Of the Vicarius of the City of Rome	. . .	310
16. „ „ Notaries	. . . . .	311
17. „ „ Referendarii	. . . . .	311
18. „ „ Praefectus Annonae, and his Excellency	. .	312
19. „ „ Count of the Chief Physicians	. . .	313
20. „ „ Office of a Consular, and its Excellency	. .	314
21. „ „ Governor (Rector) of a Province	. .	315
22. „ „ Count of the City of Syracuse	. . .	316
23. „ „ Count of Naples	. . . .	316
24. To the Gentlemen-Farmers and Common Councilmen of the City of Naples	. . . . .	317
25. 'De Comitiva Principis Militum' (?)	. . .	317

BOOK VII.

CONTAINING FORTY-SEVEN FORMULAE.

	PAGE
1. Of the Count of a Province	319
2. Of a Praeses	319
3. Of Count of the Goths in the Several Provinces	320
4. Of the Duke of Raetia	322
5. ,, ,, Palace Architect	323
6. ,, ,, Count of the Aqueducts	324
7. ,, ,, Praefect of the Watch of City of Rome	326
8. ,, ,, ,, ,, ,, ,, Ravenna	327
9. ,, ,, Count of Portus	327
10. ,, ,, Tribunus Voluptatum	327
11. ,, ,, Defensor of any City	328
12. ,, ,, Curator of a City	329
13. ,, ,, Count of Rome	329
14. ,, ,, ,, Ravenna	330
15. Addressed to the Praefect of the City on Appointment of an Architect	331
16. Of the Count of the Islands of Curritana and Celsina	331
17. Concerning the President of the Lime-kilns	332
18. Concerning Armourers	332
19. To the Praetorian Praefect concerning Armourers	333
20. } Relating to Collection of Bina and Terna	333
21. }	
22. Exhortation addressed to two Scriniarii	333
23. Of the Vicarius of Portus	334
24. ,, ,, Princeps of Dalmatia	334
25. Recommending the Princeps to the Comes	335
26. Of the Countship of Second Rank in divers Cities	336
27. Addressed to the Dignified Cultivators and Curiales	336
28. Announcing Appointment of a Comes to the Chief of his Staff	336
29. Concerning the Guard at the Gates of a City	337
30. Of the Tribunate in the Provinces	337
31. ,, ,, Princeps of the City of Rome	338
32. ,, ,, Master of the Mint	338
33. Respecting the Ambassadors of Various Nations	339
34. Of Summons to the King's Court (unsolicited)	339
35. Of Summons to the Court (solicited)	339
36. Granting temporary Leave of Absence	339
37. Conferring the Rank of a Spectabilis	340
38. ,, ,, ,, Clarissimus	340
39. Bestowing 'Police Protection'	340

CONTENTS. xxi

PAGE
40. FOR THE CONFIRMATION OF MARRIAGE AND THE LEGITIMATION OF OFFSPRING 341
41. CONFERRING THE RIGHTS OF FULL AGE 342
42. EDICT TO QUAESTOR, ORDERING PERSON WHO ASKS FOR PROTECTION OF SAJO TO GIVE BAIL 342
43. APPROVING THE APPOINTMENT OF A CLERK IN RECORD-OFFICE . 343
44. GRANT OF PUBLIC PROPERTY ON CONDITION OF IMPROVEMENT . 343
45. REMISSION OF TAXES WHERE TAXPAYER HAS ONLY ONE HOUSE, TOO HEAVILY ASSESSED 344
46. LEGITIMATING MARRIAGE WITH A FIRST COUSIN . . . 345
47. TO PRAETORIAN PRAEFECT, DIRECTING SALE OF THE PROPERTY OF A CURIALIS 345

BOOK VIII.

CONTAINING THIRTY-THREE LETTERS, ALL WRITTEN IN THE NAME OF ATHALARIC THE KING, EXCEPT THE ELEVENTH, WHICH IS WRITTEN IN THE NAME OF TULUM.

1. TO THE EMPEROR JUSTIN. Announcement of Athalaric's accession 347
2. „ „ SENATE. Same subject 348
3. „ „ ROMAN PEOPLE. Same subject 349
4. „ „ ROMANS SETTLED IN ITALY AND THE DALMATIAS. Same subject 350
5. „ „ GOTHS SETTLED IN ITALY. Same subject . . 350
6. „ LIBERIUS, GOVERNOR OF GAUL. „ „ . . 351
7. „ THE PROVINCIALS SETTLED IN GAUL. Same subject . 351
8. „ BISHOP VICTORINUS. Same subject . . . 352
9. „ TULUM. Raised to the Patriciate. His praises . . 352
10. „ SENATE. Same subject 354
11. TULUM'S ADDRESS TO SENATE. Elevation to the Patriciate . 356
12. TO ARATOR. Promotion to Count of the Domestics . 357
13. „ AMBROSIUS. Appointment to Quaestorship . . 358
14. „ SENATE. Same subject 359
15. „ „ Election of Pope Felix III (or IV) . . 360
16. „ OPILIO. Appointment as Count of the Sacred Largesses . 361
17. „ SENATE. Same subject 363
18. „ FELIX. Promotion to Quaestorship . . . 365
19. „ SENATE. Same subject 366
20. „ ALBIENUS. Appointment as Praetorian Praefect . 367
21. „ CYPRIAN. } Elevation to the Patriciate . . 368
22. „ SENATE.
23. „ BERGANTINUS. Gifts to Theodahad . . . 370
24. „ CLERGY OF THE ROMAN CHURCH. Ecclesiastical immunities . 371
25. „ JOANNES. Confirmation of Tulum's gift of property . 373

		PAGE
26.	To INHABITANTS OF REATE AND NURSIA. To obey their Prior	374
27.	„ DUMERIT AND FLORENTINUS. To suppress robbery at Faventia	375
28.	„ CUNIGAST. Enforced slavery of Possessores (or Coloni?)	376
29.	„ THE DIGNIFIED CULTIVATORS AND CURIALS OF PARMA. Necessity for sanitary measures	377
30.	„ GENESIUS. Same subject	377
31.	„ SEVERUS. Dissuasions from a country life, and praises of Bruttii	378
32.	„ „ Fountain of Arethusa	380
33.	„ „ Feast of St. Cyprian	381

BOOK IX.

CONTAINING TWENTY-FIVE LETTERS, WRITTEN IN THE NAME OF ATHALARIC THE KING.

1.	To HILDERIC. Murder of Amalafrida	384
2.	EDICT. Oppression of the Curiales	385
3.	To BERGANTINUS. Gold-mining in Italy	387
4.	„ ABUNDANTIUS. Curiales to become Possessores	388
5.	„ CERTAIN BISHOPS AND FUNCTIONARIES. Forestalling and regrating prohibited	389
6.	„ A CERTAIN PRIMISCRINIUS. Leave to visit Baiae	389
7.	„ REPARATUS. Appointment to Praefecture of City	390
8.	„ OSUIN (or OSUM). Promotion to Governorship of Dalmatia and Savia	391
9.	„ GOTHS AND ROMANS IN DALMATIA AND SAVIA. Same subject	392
10.	„ PROVINCIALS OF SYRACUSE. Remission of Augmentum	393
11.	„ GILDIAS. } Oppression by King's officers rebuked	394
12.	„ VICTOR AND WITIGISCLUS (or WIGISICLA). }	
13.	„ WILLIAS. Increase of emoluments of Domestici	394
14.	„ GILDIAS. Charge of oppression	395
15.	„ POPE JOHN II. Against Simony at Papal elections	398
16.	„ SALVANTIUS. Same subject	400
17.	„ „ Release of two Roman citizens	400
18.	EDICT. Offences against Civilitas	401
19.	To SENATE. Promulgation of Edict	405
20.	„ JUDGES OF PROVINCES. Same subject	405
21.	„ SENATE. Increase of Grammarians' salaries	406
22.	„ PAULINUS. Appointment as Consul	407
23.	„ SENATE. Same subject	408
24.	„ SENATOR [CASSIODORUS HIMSELF]. Appointment as Praetorian Praefect, &c.	408
25.	„ SENATE. Eulogy of Cassiodorus on his appointment. His Gothic History. His official career. His military services. His religious character	412–413

BOOK X.

CONTAINING THIRTY-FIVE LETTERS WRITTEN BY CASSIODORUS:

FOUR IN THE NAME OF QUEEN AMALASUENTHA;
TWENTY-TWO IN THAT OF KING THEODAHAD;
FOUR IN THAT OF HIS WIFE GUDELINA;
FIVE IN THAT OF KING WITIGIS.

		PAGE
1. QUEEN AMALASUENTHA TO EMPEROR JUSTINIAN. Association of Theodahad in the Sovereignty		415
2. KING THEODAHAD TO EMPEROR JUSTINIAN. Same subject		416
3. AMALASUENTHA TO SENATE. Same. Praises of Theodahad		416
4. THEODAHAD TO SENATE. Same. Praises of Amalasuentha		418
5. " " HIS MAN THEODOSIUS. Followers of new King to live justly		421
6. " " PATRICIUS. Appointment to Quaestorship		422
7. " " SENATE. Same subject		422
8. AMALASUENTHA TO JUSTINIAN. Acknowledging present of marbles		423
9. THEODAHAD TO JUSTINIAN. Same subject		423
10. AMALASUENTHA TO THEODORA. Salutation		424
11. THEODAHAD TO MAXIMUS. Appointment to office of Primicerius		424
12. " " SENATE. Same subject.		425
13. " " " Summons to Ravenna. Suspicions of Senators		426
14. " " THE ROMAN PEOPLE. Dissensions between citizens of Rome and Gothic troops		427
15. " " EMPEROR JUSTINIAN. Letter of introduction for Ecclesiastic		428
16. " " SENATE. Assurances of good-will		428
17. " " THE ROMAN PEOPLE. Same subject		429
18. " " SENATE. Gothic garrison for Rome		430
19. " " JUSTINIAN. Embassy of Peter		431
20. QUEEN GUDELINA TO THEODORA, AUGUSTA. Embassy of Rusticus		432
21. " " " " " Soliciting friendship		433
22. THEODAHAD TO JUSTINIAN. Entreaties for peace		434
23. GUDELINA TO THEODORA. Same subject		435
24. " . " JUSTINIAN. Same subject		436
25. THEODAHAD TO JUSTINIAN. Same subject		436
26. " " " Monastery too heavily taxed		437
27. " " SENATOR. Corn distributions in Liguria and Venetia		438
28. " " " Grant of monopolies		438
29. " " WINUSIAD. Old soldier gets leave to visit baths of Bormio		440
30. " " HONORIUS. Brazen elephants in the Via Sacra. Natural history of elephant		442
31. KING WITIGIS TO ALL THE GOTHS. On his elevation		444

				PAGE
32. King Witigis to Justinian. Overtures for peace				445
33. " " " the Master of the Offices (at Constantinople). Sending of embassy				447
34. " " " his Bishops. Same subject				448
35. " " " the Praefect of Thessalonica. Same subject				448

BOOK XI.

CONTAINING THIRTY-NINE LETTERS WRITTEN BY CASSIODORUS IN HIS OWN NAME AS PRAEFECTUS PRAETORIO, AND ONE ON BEHALF OF THE ROMAN SENATE.

Preface 449
1. To Senate. On his promotion to the Praefecture. Praises of Amalasuentha. Comparison to Placidia. Relations with the East. Expedition against Franks. League with Burgundians. Virtues of Amal Kings 452–457
2. " Pope John. Salutations 458
3. " divers Bishops. The same 459
4. " Ambrosius (his Deputy). Functions of Praefect's Deputy . 460
5. " the Same. Grain distributions for Rome . . . 461
6. " Joannes. Functions of the Cancellarius . . . 462
7. " Judges of the Provinces. Duties of tax-collectors . . 464
8. Edict published through the Provinces. Announcement of Cassiodorus' principles of administration . . . 465
9. To Judges of the Provinces. Exhortation to govern in conformity with Edict 467
10. " Beatus. Davus invalided to Mons Lactarius. The milk-cure for consumption 468–469
11. Edict. Concerning prices to be maintained at Ravenna . . 469
12. " Concerning prices along the Flaminian Way . . 470
13. The Senate to Emperor Justinian. Supplications of the Senate 471
14. To Gaudiosus. Praises of Como. Relief of its inhabitants . 474
15. " the Ligurians. Relief of their necessities . . 475
16. " the Same. Oppressions practised on them to be remedied . 476
17. " the Princeps (?). Promotions in Official Staff of Praetorian Praefect 477
18–35. Variously Addressed. [Documents, for the most part very short ones, relating to these promotions.] . . 477–480
36. To Anat(h)olius. Retirement of a Cornicularius on superannuation allowance justified on astronomical grounds . . 480
37. " Lucinus. Payment of retiring Primiscrinius . . 482
38. " Joannes. Praises of paper 483
39. " Vitalian. Payment of commuted cattle-tax . . 484
40. Indulgence [to Prisoners on some great Festival of the Church; probably Easter]. General Amnesty . . 485

BOOK XII.

CONTAINING TWENTY-EIGHT LETTERS WRITTEN BY CASSIODORUS IN HIS OWN NAME AS PRAETORIAN PRAEFECT.

		PAGE
1.	To THE VARIOUS CANCELLARII OF THE PROVINCES. General instructions	487
2.	,, ALL JUDGES OF THE PROVINCES. General instructions to Provincial Governors	488
3.	,, SAJONES ASSIGNED TO THE CANCELLARII. General instructions	489
4.	,, THE CANONICARIUS OF THE VENETIAE. Praise of *Acinaticium*	490
5.	,, VALERIAN. Measures for relief of Lucania and Bruttii	492
6.	,, ALL SUBORDINATE GOVERNORS OF THE PRAEFECTURE. General instructions	494
7.	,, THE TAX-COLLECTOR OF THE VENETIAN PROVINCE. Remission of taxes on account of invasion by Suevi	495
8.	,, THE CONSULARIS OF THE PROVINCE OF LIGURIA. Permission to pay taxes direct to Royal Treasury	495
9.	,, PASCHASIUS. Claim of an African to succeed to estate of intestate countryman	496
10.	,, DIVERS CANCELLARII. Taxes to be punctually enforced	497
11.	,, PETER, DISTRIBUTOR OF RELISHES. Their due distribution	498
12.	,, ANASTASIUS. Praise of the cheese and wine of Bruttii	499
13.	EDICT. Frauds committed by revenue-officers on Churches	500
14.	To ANASTASIUS. Plea for gentle treatment of citizens of Rhegium	501
15.	,, MAXIMUS. Praises of author's birthplace, Scyllacium	503
16.	,, A REVENUE OFFICER. Payment of Trina Illatio	506
17.	,, JOHN, SILIQUATARIUS OF RAVENNA. Defence of city	507
18.	,, CONSTANTIAN. Repair of Flaminian Way	507
19.	,, MAXIMUS. Bridge of boats across the Tiber	509
20.	,, THOMAS AND PETER. Sacred vessels mortgaged by Pope Agapetus to be restored to Papal See	510
21.	,, DEUSDEDIT. Duties of a Scribe	511
22.	,, PROVINCIALS OF ISTRIA. Requisition from Province of Istria	513
23.	,, LAURENTIUS. Same subject	515
24.	,, TRIBUNES OF THE MARITIME POPULATION. First historical notice of Venice	515
25.	,, AMBROSIUS, HIS DEPUTY. Famine in Italy	518
26.	,, PAULUS. Remission of taxes in consequence of famine	520
27.	,, DATIUS. Relief of famine-stricken citizens of Ticinum, &c.	521
28.	EDICT [ADDRESSED TO LIGURIANS]. Relief of inhabitants	523

ADDITIONS AND CORRECTIONS.

P. 6, l. 30, for 'Scylletium' read 'Scylletion.'

P. 24, n. 1, for 'Uterwerfung' read 'Unterwerfung.'

In the 'Note on the Topography of Squillace' (pp. 68–72), and the map illustrating it, for 'Scylacium' read 'Scyllacium.' (The line of Virgil, however, quoted on p. 6, shows that the name was sometimes spelt with only one 'l.')

Pp. 94 and 96, head line, dele 'the.'

P. 128 (Chronological Table, under heading 'Popes') for 'John III.' read 'John II.'

P. 146 (last line of text). S. Gaudenzi remarks that the addresses of the laws in the Code of Justinian forbid us to suppose that Heliodorus was Praetorian Praefect for eighteen years. He thinks that most likely the meaning of the words 'in illa republica nobis videntibus praefecturam bis novenis annis gessit eximie' is that twice in the space of nine years Heliodorus filled the office of Praefect.

P. 159, Letter 27 of Book I. The date of this letter is probably 509, as Importunus, who is therein mentioned as Consul, was Consul in that year.

P. 160, Letter 29 of Book I. S. Gaudenzi points out that a letter has probably dropped out here, as the title does not fit the contents of the letter, which seems to have been addressed to a Sajo.

In the titles of I. 14, 26, 34, 35, and II. 5 and 9, for 'Praepositus' read 'Praetorian Praefect.' The contraction used by the early amanuenses for Praefecto Praetorio has been misunderstood by their successors, and consequently many MSS. read 'Praeposito,' and this reading has been followed by Nivellius. There can be no doubt, however, that Garet is right in restoring 'Praefecto Praetorio.'

On the other hand, I have been misled by Garet's edition into quoting the following letters as addressed *Viro Senatori*: I. 38; II. 23, 28, 29, 35; III. 8, 13, 15, 16, 27, 32, 41; IV. 10, 12, 15, 18, 19, 20, 21, 28; V. 21, 24. Here, too, the only MSS. that I have examined read 'Viro Senatori;' but Nivellius preserves what is no doubt the earlier reading, 'V. S.,' which assuredly stands for 'Viro Spectabili.' Practically there is no great difference between the two readings, and the remarks made by me on II. 29, 35, &c., as to Senators with Gothic names may still stand; for as every Senator was (at least) a Clarissimus, it is not likely that any person who reached the higher dignity of a Spectabilis was not also a Senator. (See pp. 90 and 91.)

P. 181, Letter 13 of Book II. Here again, on account of the want of correspondence between the title and contents of the letter, S. Gaudenzi suggests that a letter has dropped out.

P. 182, title of Letter 20, for 'Unigilis' read 'Uniligis.'

P. 205, l. 6 from bottom, for 'Praefectum' read 'Praefectorum.'

P. 206, l. 1, for 'Provinces' read 'Provincials.'

P. 224 (marginal note), for 'amphitheatre' read 'walls.' Last line (text), for 'its' read 'their.'

P. 244, title of Letter 17, for 'Idae' some MSS. read 'Ibbae,' which is probably the right reading, Ibbas having commanded the Ostrogothic army in Gaul in 510.

P. 247, dele the last two lines. (The Peter who was Consul in 516 was an official of the Eastern Empire, the same who came on an embassy to Theodahad in 535.)

P. 253, l. 9, for '408' read '508.'

P. 255, ll. 9, 14, and in margin, for 'Agapeta' read 'Agapita.'

P. 256, ll. 16, 26, and in margin, for 'Velusian' read 'Volusian.'

P. 256, title of Letter 43. S. Gaudenzi thinks this letter was really addressed to Argolicus, Praefectus Urbis.

P. 269, l. 20, dele 'possibly Stabularius.'

P. 282, Letter 31 of Book V. (to Decoratus). As Decoratus is described in V. 3 and 4 as already dead, it is clear that the letters are not arranged in chronological order.

P. 282, l. 27, for 'upon' read 'before.'

P. 288, l. 25, for 'extortions' read 'extra horses.'

P. 291, l. 6, for 'Anomymus' read 'Anonymus.'

P. 308, l. 7. This is an important passage, as illustrating the nature of the office which Cassiodorus held as Consiliarius to his father.

P. 333, second marginal note, for 'aguntur' read 'agantur' (twice).

P. 398, title of Letter 15, for '532' read '533–535.'

P. 400, title of Letter 17, for 'between 532 and 534' read 'between 533 and 535.'

P. 450, l. 8. Probably, as suggested by S. Gaudenzi, Felix was Consiliarius to Cassiodorus.

INTRODUCTION.

CHAPTER I.

LIFE OF CASSIODORUS.

THE interest of the life of Cassiodorus is derived from his position rather than from his character. He was a statesman of considerable sagacity and of unblemished honour, a well-read scholar, and a devout Christian; but he was apt to crouch before the possessors of power however unworthy, and in the whole of his long and eventful life we never find him playing a part which can be called heroic.

His position, however, which was in more senses than one that of a borderer between two worlds, gives to the study of his writings an exceptional value. Born a few years after the overthrow of the Western Empire, a Roman noble by his ancestry, a rhetorician-philosopher by his training, he became what we should call the Prime Minister of the Ostrogothic King Theodoric; he toiled with his master at the construction of the new state, which was to unite the vigour of Germany and the culture of Rome; for a generation he saw this edifice stand, and when it fell beneath the blows of Belisarius he retired, perhaps well-nigh broken-hearted, from the political arena. The writings of such a man could hardly fail, at any rate they do not fail, to give us many

Position of Cassiodorus on the confines of the Ancient and the Modern.

interesting glimpses into the political life both of the Romans and the Barbarians. It is true that they throw more light backwards than forwards, that they teach us far more about the constitution of the Roman Empire than they do about the Teutonic customs from whence in due time Feudalism was to be born. Still, they do often illustrate these Teutonic usages; and when we remember that the writer to whom after Tacitus we are most deeply indebted for our knowledge of Teutonic antiquity, Jordanes, professedly compiled his ill-written pamphlet from the Twelve Books of the Gothic History of Cassiodorus, we see that indirectly his contribution to the history of the German factor in European civilisation is a most important one.

Thus then, as has been already said, Cassiodorus stood on the confines of two worlds, the Ancient and the Modern; indeed it is a noteworthy fact that the very word *modernus* occurs for the first time with any frequency in his writings. Or, if the ever-shifting boundary between Ancient and Modern be drawn elsewhere than in the fifth and sixth centuries, at any rate it is safe to say, that he stood on the boundary of two worlds, the Roman and the Teutonic.

Also on the confines of Politics and Religion.

But the statesman who, after spending thirty years at the Court of Theodoric and his daughter, spent thirty-three years more in the monastery which he had himself erected at Squillace, was a borderer in another sense than that already mentioned—a borderer between the two worlds of Politics and Religion; and in this capacity also, as the contemporary, perhaps the friend, certainly the imitator, of St. Benedict, and in some respects the improver upon his method, Cassiodorus largely helped to mould the destinies of mediaeval and therefore of modern Europe.

I shall now proceed to indicate the chief points in the life and career of Cassiodorus. Where, as is generally the case, our information comes from his own correspondence, I shall, to avoid repetition, not do much more than refer the reader to the passage in the following collection, where he will find the information given as nearly as may be in the words of the great Minister himself.

The ancestors of Cassiodorus for three generations, and their public employments, are enumerated for us in the letters (Var. i. 3-4) which in the name of Theodoric he wrote on his father's elevation to the Patriciate. From these letters we learn that— *His ancestors.*

(1) Cassiodorus, the writer's great grandfather, who held the rank of an Illustris, defended the shores of Sicily and Bruttii from the incursions of the Vandals. This was probably between 430 and 440, and, as we may suppose, towards the end of the life of this statesman, to whom we may conjecturally assign a date from 390 to 460. *Great grandfather.*

(2) His son and namesake, the grandfather of our Cassiodorus, was a Tribune (a military rank nearly corresponding to our 'Colonel') and Notarius under Valentinian III. He enjoyed the friendship of the great Aetius, and was sent with Carpilio the son of that statesman on an embassy to Attila, probably between the years 440 and 450. In this embassy, according to his grandson, he exerted an extraordinary influence over the mind of the Hunnish King. Soon after this he retired to his native Province of Bruttii, where he passed the remainder of his days. We may probably fix the limits of his life from about 420 to 490. *Grandfather.*

(3) His son, the third Cassiodorus, our author's father, served under Odovacar (therefore between 476 and 492), as Comes Privatarum Rerum and Comes Sacrarum Largitionum. These two offices, one of which nominally involved the care of the domains of the Sovereign and the other the regulation of his private charities, were in fact the two great financial offices of the Empire and of the barbarian royalties which modelled their system upon *Father.*

it. Upon the fall of the throne of Odovacar, Cassiodorus transferred his services to Theodoric, at the beginning of whose reign he acted as Governor (Consularis[1]) of Sicily. In this capacity he showed much tact and skill, and thereby succeeded in reconciling the somewhat suspicious and intractable Sicilians to the rule of their Ostrogothic master. He next administered (as Corrector[1]) his own native Province of 'Bruttii et Lucania[2].' Either in the year 500 or soon after, he received from Theodoric the highest mark of his confidence that the Sovereign could bestow, being raised to the great place of Praetorian Praefect, which still conferred a semi-regal splendour upon its holder, and which possibly under a Barbarian King may have involved yet more participation in the actual work of reigning than it had done under a Roman Emperor.

The Praefecture of this Cassiodorus probably lasted three or four years, and at its close he received the high honour of the Patriciate. We are not able to name the exact date of his retirement from office; but the important point for us is, that while he still held this splendid position his son was first introduced to public life. To that son's history we may now proceed, for we have no further information of importance as to the father's old age or death beyond the intimation (contained in Var. iii. 28) that Theodoric invited him, apparently in vain, to leave his beloved Bruttii and return to the Court of Ravenna.

MAGNUS AURELIUS CASSIODORUS SENATOR was born at Scyllacium (*Squillace*) about the year 480. His name, his birthplace, and his year of birth will each require a short notice.

---

[1] We get these titles from the Notitia Occidentis I.
[2] On the authority of a letter of Pope Gelasius, 'Philippo et Cassiodoro,' Usener fixes this governorship of Bruttii between the years 493 and 496 (p. 76).

(1) *Name.* Magnus (not Marcus, as it has been sometimes incorrectly printed) is the author's praenomen. Aurelius, the gentile name, connects him with a large gens, of which Q. Aurelius Memmius Symmachus was one of the most distinguished ornaments. As to the form of the cognomen there is a good deal of diversity of opinion, the majority of German scholars preferring Cassiodor*ius* to Cassiodorus. The argument in favour of the former spelling is derived from the fact that some of the MSS. of his works (not apparently the majority) write the name with the termination *rius*, and that while it is easy to understand how from the genitive form *ri* a nominative *rus* might be wrongly inferred instead of the real nominative *rius*, it is not easy to see why the opposite mistake should be made, and *rius* substituted for the genuine *rus*.

The question will probably be decided one way or the other by the critical edition of the 'Variae' which is to be published among the 'Monumenta Germaniae Historica;' but in the meantime it may be remarked that the correct Greek form of the name as shown by inscriptions appears to be Cassiodo*rus*, and that in a poem of Alcuin's[1] occurs the line

'Cassiodorus item Chrysostomus atque Johannes,'

showing that the termination *rus* was generally accepted as early as the eighth century. It is therefore to be hoped that this is the form which may finally prevail.

Senator, it is clear, was part of the original name of Cassiodorus, and not a title acquired by sitting in the Roman Senate. It seems a curious custom to give a title of this kind to an infant as part of his name, but the well-known instance of Patricius (St. Patrick) shows that this was sometimes done, and there are other instances

---

[1] De Pontificibus et Sanctis Ecclesiae Eboracensis, p. 843 of Migne's Second Volume of Alcuin's Works. I owe this quotation to Adolph Franz.

(collected by Thorbecke, p. 34) of this very title Senator being used as a proper name.

It is clear from Jordanes (who calls the Gothic History of Cassiodorus 'duodecem Senatoris volumina de origine actibusque Getarum[1]'), from Pope Vigilius (who speaks of 'religiosum virum filium nostrum Senatorem[2]'), from the titles of the letters written by Cassiodorus[3], and from his punning allusions to his own name and the love to the Senate which it had prophetically expressed, that Senator was a real name and not a title of honour.

<small>Birth-place, Scyllacium.</small> (2) Scyllacium, the modern Squillace, was, according to Cassiodorus, the first, either in age or in importance, of the cities of Bruttii, a Province which corresponds pretty closely with the modern Calabria. It is situated at the head of the gulf to which it gives its name, on the eastern side of Italy, and at the point where the peninsula is pinched in by the Tyrrhene and Ionian Seas to a width of only fifteen miles, the narrowest dimensions to which it is anywhere reduced. The Apennine chain comes here within a distance of about five miles of the sea, and upon one of its lower dependencies Scyllacium was placed. The slight promontory in front of the town earned for it from the author of the Aeneid the ominous name of 'Navifragum Scylaceum[4].' In the description which Cassiodorus himself gives of his birthplace (Var. xii. 15) we hear nothing of the danger to mariners which had attracted the attention of Virgil, possibly a somewhat timid sailor. The name, however, given to the place by the Greek colonists who founded it, *Scylletium*, is thought by some to contain an allusion to dangers of the coast similar to those which were

---

[1] Preface to Getica (Mommsen's Edition, p. 53).

[2] Epist. XIV. ad Rusticum et Sebastianum (Migne, p. 49).

[3] Nearly all the letters in the XIth and XIIth Books of the Variae are headed 'Senator Praefectus Praetorio.'

[4] 'Attollit se diva Lacinia contra,
Caulonisque arces, et navifragum Scylaceum.'
(iii. 552-3.)

typified by the barking dogs of the not far distant Scylla.

According to Cassiodorus, this Greek city was founded by Ulysses after the destruction of Troy. Strabo[1] attributes the foundation of it to the almost equally widespread energy of Menestheus. The form of the name makes it probable that the colonists were in any case of Ionian descent; but in historic times we find Scylletion subject to the domineering Achaian city of Crotona, from whose grasp it was wrested (B.C. 389) by the elder Dionysius. It no doubt shared in the general decay of the towns of this part of Magna Graecia consequent on the wars of Dionysius and Agathocles, and may very probably, like Crotona, have been taken and laid waste by the Bruttian banditti in the Second Punic War. During the latter part of this war Hannibal seems to have occupied a position near to, but not in, the already ruined city, and its port was known long after as Castra Hannibalis[2].

The Greek city.

[3]'A century before the end of the Republic, a city much more considerable than that which had existed in the past was again established near the point where the Greek Scylletion had existed. Among the colonies of Roman citizens founded B.C. 123 on the rogation of Caius Gracchus, was one sent to this part of Bruttii, under the name of Colonia Minervia Scolacium, a name parallel to those of Colonia Neptunia Tarentum and Colonia Junonia Karthago, decided on at the same time. *Scolacium* is the form that we meet with in Velleius Paterculus, and that is found in an extant Latin inscription of the time of Antoninus Pius. This is the old

The Roman colony.

---

[1] p. 375: ed. Oxon. 1807.
[2] Pliny (Hist. Nat. iii. 10) says: 'Dein sinus Scylacius et Scyllacium, Scylletium Atheniensibus, cum conderent, dictum: quem locum occurrens Terinaeus sinus peninsulam efficit: et in eâ portus qui vocatur Castra Annibalis, nusquam angustiore Italia XX millia passuum latitudo est.'
[3] I take the two following paragraphs from Lenormant's La Grande Grèce, pp. 342–3.

Latin form of the name of the town. *Scylacium*, which first appears as used by the writers of the first century of our era, is a purely literary form springing from the desire to get nearer to the Greek type *Scylletion*.

'Scolacium, or Scylacium, a town purely Roman by reason of the origin of its first colonists, was from its earliest days an important city, and remained such till the end of the Empire. Pomponius Mela, Strabo, Pliny, and Ptolemy speak of it as one of the principal cities of Bruttii. It had for its port Castra Hannibalis. Under Nero its population was strengthened by a new settlement of veterans as colonists. The city then took the names of Colonia Minervia Nervia Augusta Scolacium. We read these names in an inscription discovered in 1762 at 1,800 metres from the modern Squillace, between that city and the sea—an inscription which mentions the construction of an aqueduct bringing water to Scolacium, executed 143 A.D. at the cost of the Emperor Antoninus.'

Appearance of the city at the time of Cassiodorus.

For the appearance of this Roman colony in the seventh century of its existence the reader is referred to the letter of Cassiodorus before quoted (Var. xii. 15). The picture of the city, 'hanging like a cluster of grapes upon the hills, basking in the brightness of the sun all day long, yet cooled by the breezes from the sea, and looking at her leisure on the labours of the husbandman in the corn-fields, the vineyards, and the olive-groves around her,' is an attractive one, and shows that kind of appreciation of the gentler beauties of Nature which befits a countryman of Virgil.

This picture, however, is not distinctive enough to enable us from it alone to fix the exact site of the Roman city. Lenormant (pp. 360–370), while carefully distinguishing between the sites of the Greek Scylletion and the Latin Scolacium, and assigning the former with much apparent probability to the neighbourhood of the promontory and the Grotte di Stalletti, has been probably too hasty in his assertion that the modern city of Squillace incontestably covers the ground of the Latin Scolacium. Mr. Arthur J. Evans, after making a much more careful survey of the place and its neighbourhood than the French archaeologist had leisure for, has come to the conclusion that in this identification M. Lenormant is entirely wrong, and that the Roman city was not at Squillace, where there are no remains of earlier than mediaeval times, but at Roccella del Vescovo, five or six miles from Squillace in a north-easterly direction, where there are such remains as can only have belonged to a Roman provincial city of the first rank. For a further discussion of the question the reader is referred to the Note (and accompanying Map) at the end of this chapter.

We pass on from considering the place of Cassiodorus' birth to investigate the date of that event.

(3) The only positive statement that we possess as to the birth-year of Cassiodorus comes from a very late and somewhat unsatisfactory source. John Trittheim (or Trithemius), Abbot of the Benedictine Monastery of Spanheim, who died in 1516, was one of the ecclesiastical scholars of the Renaissance period, and composed, besides a multitude of other books, a treatise 'De Scriptoribus Ecclesiasticis,' in which is found this notice of Cassiodorus[1]:—

Date of birth.

'Claruit temporibus Justini senioris usque ad imperii Justini junioris paene finem, annos habens aetatis plus quam 95, Anno Domini 575.'

This notice is certainly not one to which we should attach much importance if it contradicted earlier and trustworthy authorities, or if there were any internal

[1] The reference is given by Köpke (Die Anfänge des Königthums, p. 88) as 'De scr. ecc. 212 Bibliotheca Ecclesiastica, ed. Fabricius, p. 58;' by Thorbecke (p. 8) as 'Catalogus seu liber scriptorum ecclesiasticorum, Coloniae 1546, p. 94.' Franz (p. 4) quotes from the same edition as Köpke, 'De script. eccl. c. 212 in Fabricii biblioth. eccl., Hamburgi 1728, iii. p. 58.'

evidence against it. But if this cannot be asserted, it is not desirable entirely to discard the assertion of a scholar who, in the age of the Renaissance and before the havoc wrought among the monasteries of Germany by the Thirty Years' War, may easily have had access to some sources which are now no longer available.

When we examine the information which is thus given us, we find it certainly somewhat vague. 'Cassiodorus was illustrious' (no doubt as a writer, since it is 'ecclesiastici scriptores' of whom Trittheim is speaking) 'in the time of Justin the Elder [518–527] down nearly to the end of the reign of Justin the Younger [565–578], attaining to more than 95 years of age in the year of our Lord 575.' But on reflection we see that the meaning must be that Cassiodorus died in 575 (which agrees well with the words 'paene finem imperii Justini junioris'), and that when he died he was some way on in his 96th year, or as we say colloquially 'ninety-five off.' The marvel of his attaining such an age is no doubt the reason for inserting the 'plus quam,' to show that he did not die immediately after his 95th birthday. If this notice be trustworthy, therefore, we may place the birth of Cassiodorus in 479 or 480.

Now upon examining all the facts in our possession as to his career as a statesman and an author, and especially our latest acquired information[1], we find that they do in a remarkable manner agree with Trittheim's date, while we have no positive statement by any author early or late which really conflicts with it.

The only shadow of an argument that has been advanced for a different and earlier date is so thin that it is difficult to state without confuting it. In some editions of the works of Cassiodorus there appears a very short anonymous tract on the method of determining Easter, called 'Computus Paschalis,' and composed in 562. In the 'Orthographia,' which was undoubtedly written by

---

[1] The Anecdoton Holderi.

Cassiodorus at the age of 93, and which contains a list of his previously published works, no mention is made of this 'Computus.' It must therefore, say the supporters of the theory, have been written after he was 93. He must have been at least 94 in 562, and the year of his birth must be put back at least to 468. In this argument there are two absolutely worthless links. There is no evidence to show that the 'Computus Paschalis' came from the pen of Cassiodorus at all, but much reason to think that Pithoeus, the editor who first published it under his name, was mistaken in doing so. And if it were his, a little memorandum like this—only two pages long, and with no literary pretension whatever—we may almost say with certainty would *not* be included by the veteran author in the enumeration of his theological works prefixed to his 'Orthographia.'

The reason why a theory founded on such an absurdly weak basis has held its ground at all, has probably been that it buttressed up another obvious fallacy. A whole school of biographers of Cassiodorus and commentators on his works has persisted, in spite of the plainest evidence of his letters, in identifying him with his father, who bore office under Odovacar (476-493). To do this it was necessary to get rid of the date 480 for the birth of Cassiodorus Senator, and to throw back that event as far as possible. And yet, not even by pushing it back to 468, do they make it reasonably probable that a person, who was only a child of eight years old at Odovacar's accession, could in the course of his short reign (the last four years of which were filled by his struggle with Theodoric) have held the various high offices which were really held during that reign by the father of Senator.

We assume therefore with some confidence the year 480 as the approximate date of the birth of our author; and while we observe that this date fits well with those which the course of history induces us to assign to his ancestors in the three preceding generations[1], we also note with interest that it was, as nearly as we can ascertain, the year of the birth of two of the most distinguished contemporaries of Cassiodorus—Boethius and Benedict.

Education of Cassiodorus.

Of the training and education of the young Senator we can only speak from their evident results as displayed in the 'Variae,' to which the reader is accordingly referred. It may be remarked, however, that though he evidently received the usual instruction in philosophy and rhetoric which was given to a young Roman noble aspiring to employment in the Civil Service, there are some indications that the bent of his own genius was towards Natural History, strange and often laughable as are the facts or fictions which this taste of his has caused him to accumulate.

Consiliarius to his father.

In the year 500[2], when Senator had just attained the age of twenty, his father, as we have already seen, received from Theodoric the high office of Praetorian Praefect. As a General might make an *Aide-de-camp* of his son, so the Praefect conferred upon the young Senator the post of *Consiliarius*, or Assessor in his Court[3]. The Consiliarius[4] had been in the time of the Republic an experienced jurist who sat beside the Praetor or the Consul (who might be a man quite unversed in the law) and advised him as to his judgments. From the time of Severus onwards he became a paid functionary of the Court, receiving a salary which varied from 12 to 72 solidi (£7 to £43). At the time which we are now describing it was customary for the Judge to choose his Consiliarius from among the ranks of young jurists who had just completed

---

[1] Cassiodorus the First, born about 390; the Second, about 420; the Third, about 450.

[2] Or possibly 501.

[3] This fact, and also the cause of Senator's promotion to the Quaestorship, we learn from the Anecdoton Holderi described in a following chapter.

[4] The terms *Adsessor*, *Consiliarius*, Πάρεδρος, Σύμβουλος, seem all to indicate the same office.

their studies. The great legal school of Berytus especially furnished a large number of Consiliarii to the Roman Governors. In order to prevent an officer in this position from obtaining an undue influence over the mind of his principal, the latter was forbidden by law to keep a Consiliarius, who was a native of the Province in which he was administering justice, more than four months in his employ[1]. This provision, of course, would not apply when the young Assessor, as in the case of Cassiodorus, came with his father from a distant Province: and in such a case, if the Magistrate died during his year of office, by a special enactment the fairly-earned pay of the Assessor was protected from unjust demands on the part of the Exchequer[2]. The functions thus exercised by Senator in his father's court at Rome, and the title which he bore, were somewhat similar to those which Procopius held in the camp of Belisarius, but doubtless required a more thorough legal training. In our own system, if we could imagine the Judge's Marshal invested with the responsibilities of a Registrar of the Court, we should perhaps get a pretty fair idea of the position and duties of a Roman Consiliarius[3].

It was while Cassiodorus was holding this agreeable but not important position, that the opportunity came to him, by his dexterous use of which he sprang at one bound into the foremost ranks of the official hierarchy. On some public occasion it fell to his lot to deliver an oration in praise of Theodoric[4], and he did this with such admirable eloquence—admirable according to the

Panegyric on Theodoric.

---

[1] Cod. Theod. i. 12. 1.

[2] This seems to be the meaning of Cod. Theod. i. 12. 2. The gains of the 'filii familias Assessores' were to be protected as if they were 'castrense peculium.'

[3] Some points in this description are taken from Bethmann Hollweg, Gerichtsverfassung der sinkenden Römischen Reichs, pp. 153-158.

[4] 'Cassiodorus Senator ... juvenis adeo, dum patris Cassiodori patricii et praefecti praetorii consiliarius fieret et laudes Theodorichi regis Gothorum facundissime recitasset, ab eo quaestor est factus' (Anecdoton Holderi, ap. Usener, p. 4).

depraved taste of the time—that Theodoric at once bestowed upon the orator, still in the first dawn of manhood[1], the 'Illustrious' office of Quaestor, giving him thereby what we should call Cabinet-rank, and placing him among the ten or eleven ministers of the highest class[2], by whom, under the King, the fortunes of the Gothic-Roman State were absolutely controlled.

Appointed Quaestor.

The Quaestor's duty required him to be beyond all other Ministers the mouthpiece of the Sovereign. In the 'Notitia[3]' the matters under his control are concisely stated to be 'Laws which are to be dictated, and Petitions.'

Nature of the Quaestor's office.

To him therefore was assigned the duty (which the British Parliament in its folly assigns to no one) of giving a final revision to the laws which received the Sovereign's signature, and seeing that they were consistent with one another and with previous enactments, and were clothed in fitting language. He replied in the Sovereign's name to the petitions which were presented to him. He also, as we learn from Cassiodorus, had audience with the ambassadors of foreign powers, to whom he addressed suitable and stately harangues, or through whom he forwarded written replies to the letters which they had brought, but always of course speaking or writing in the name of his master. In the performance of these duties he had chiefly to rely on his own intellectual resources as a trained jurist and rhetorician.

---

[1] He himself says, or rather makes Theodoric's grandson say to him, 'Quem *primaevum* recipiens ad quaestoris officium, mox reperit [Theodoricus] conscientiâ praeditum, et legum eruditione maturum' (Var. ix. 24).

[2] At this time the Illustres actually in office would probably be the Praefectus Praetorio Italiae (Cassiodorus the father), the Praefectus Urbis Romae, the two Magistri Militum in Praesenti, the Praepositus Sacri Cubiculi, the Magister Officiorum, the Quaestor, the Comes Sacrarum Largitionum, the Comes Rerum Privatarum, and the two Comites Domesticorum Equitum et Peditum.

[3] 'Sub dispositione viri illustris Quaestoris
        Leges dictandae
        Preces.
Officium non habet sed adjutores de scriniis quos voluerit.'

The large official staff which waited upon the nod of the other great Ministers of State was absent from his apartments[1]; bu' for the mere manual work of copying, filing correspondence, and the like, he could summon the needful number of clerks from the four great bureaux (scrinia) which were under the control of the Master of the Offices.

We have an interesting summary of the Quaestor's duties and privileges from the pen of Cassiodorus himself in the 'Variae' (vi. 5), under the title 'Formula Quaesturae,' and to this document I refer the reader who wishes to complete the picture of the occupations in which the busiest years of the life of Cassiodorus were passed.

Special utility of a Quaestor to Theodoric.

To a ruler in Theodoric's position the acquisition of such a Quaestor as Cassiodorus was a most fortunate event. He himself was doubtless unable to speak or to write Latin with fluency. According to the common story, which passes current on the authority of the 'Anonymus Valesii,' he never could learn to write, and had to 'stencil' his signature. I look upon this story with some suspicion, especially because it is also told of his contemporary, the Emperor Justin; but I have no doubt that such literary education as Theodoric ever received was Greek rather than Latin, being imparted during the ten years of his residence as a hostage at Constantinople. Years of marches and countermarches, of battle and foray, at the head of his Ostrogothic warriors, may well have effaced much of the knowledge thus acquired. At any rate, when he descended the Julian Alps, close upon forty years of age, and appeared for the first time in Italy to commence his long and terrible duel with Odovacar, it was too late to learn the language of her sons in such fashion that the first sentence spoken by him in the Hall of Audience should not betray him to his new subjects as an alien and a barbarian.

[1] Officium non habet.

Yet Theodoric was by no means indifferent to the power of well-spoken words, by no means unconcerned as to the opinion which his Latin-speaking subjects held concerning him. He was no Cambyses or Timour, ruling by the sword alone. His proud title was 'Gothorum Romanorumque Rex,' and the ideal of his hopes, successfully realised during the greater part of his long and tranquil reign, was to be equally the King of either people. He had been fortunate thus far in his Praetorian Praefects. Liberius, a man of whom history knows too little, had amid general applause steered the vessel of the State for the first seven years of the new reign. The elder Cassiodorus, who had succeeded him, seemed likely to follow the same course. But possibly Theodoric had begun to feel the necessity laid upon all rulers of men, not only to be, but also to seem, anxious for the welfare of their subjects. Possibly some dull, unsympathetic Quaestor had failed to present the generous thoughts of the King in a sufficiently attractive shape to the minds of the people. This much at all events we know, that when the young Consiliarius, high-born, fluent, and learned, poured forth his stream of panegyric on 'Our Lord Theodoric'—a panegyric which, to an extent unusual with these orations, reflected the real feelings of the speaker, and all the finest passages of which were the genuine outcome of his own enthusiasm—the great Ostrogoth recognised at once the man whom he was in want of to be the exponent of his thoughts to the people, and by one stroke of wise audacity turned the boyish and comparatively obscure Assessor into the Illustrious Quaestor, one of the great personages of his realm.

Composition of the VARIAE.

The monument of the official life of Cassiodorus is the correspondence styled the 'Variae,' of which an abstract is now submitted to the reader. There is no need to say much here, either as to the style or the thoughts of these letters; a perusal of a few pages of the abstract will give a better idea of both than an elaborate description. The style is undoubtedly a bad one, whether it be compared with the great works of Greek and Latin literature or with our own estimate of excellence in speech. Scarcely ever do we find a thought clothed in clear, precise, closely-fitting words, or a metaphor which really corresponds to the abstract idea that is represented by it. We take up sentence after sentence of verbose and flaccid Latin, analyse them with difficulty, and when at last we come to the central thought enshrouded in them, we too often find that it is the merest and most obvious commonplace, a piece of tinsel wrapped in endless folds of tissue paper. Perhaps from one point of view the study of the style of Cassiodorus might prove useful to a writer of English, as indicating the faults which he has in this age most carefully to avoid. Over and over again, when reading newspaper articles full of pompous words borrowed from Latin through French, when wearied with 'velleities' and 'solidarities' and 'altruisms' and 'homologators,' or when vainly endeavouring to discover the real meaning which lies hidden in a jungle of Parliamentary verbiage, I have said to myself, remembering my similar labour upon the 'Variae,' 'How like this is to Cassiodorus.' *Their style.*

Intellectually one of the chief deficiencies of our author—a deficiency in which perhaps his age and nation participated—was a lack of humour. It is difficult to think that anyone who possessed a keen sense of humour could have written letters so drolly unsuited to the character of Theodoric, their supposed author, as are some which we find in the 'Variae.' For instance, the King had reason to complain that Faustus, the Praetorian Praefect, was dawdling over the execution of an order which he had received for the shipment of corn from the regions of Calabria and Apulia to Rome. We find the literary Quaestor putting such words as these into the mouth of Theodoric, when reprimanding the *Lack of humour.*

The letter about the sucking-fish.

lazy official[1]: 'Why is there such great delay in sending your swift ships to traverse the tranquil seas? Though the south wind blows and the rowers are bending to their oars, has the sucking-fish[2] fixed its teeth into the hulls through the liquid waves; or have the shells of the Indian Sea, whose quiet touch is said to hold so firmly that the angry billows cannot loosen it, with like power fixed their lips into your keels? Idle stands the bark though winged by swelling sails; the wind favours her but she makes no way; she is fixed without an anchor, she is bound without a cable; and these tiny animals hinder more than all such prospering circumstances can help. Thus, though the loyal wave may be hastening its course, we are informed that the ship stands fixed on the surface of the sea, and by a strange paradox the swimmer [the ship] is made to remain immovable while the wave is hurried along by movements numberless. Or, to describe the nature of another kind of fish, perchance the sailors in the aforesaid ships have grown dull and torpid by the touch of the torpedo, by which such a deadly chill is struck into the right hand of him who attacks it, that even through the spear by which it is itself wounded, it gives a shock which causes the hand of the striker to remain, though still a living substance, senseless and immovable. I think some such misfortunes as these must have happened to men who are unable to move their own bodies. But I know that in their case the echeneis is corruption trading on delays; the bite of the Indian shell-fish is insatiable cupidity; the torpedo is fraudulent pretence. With perverted ingenuity they manufacture delays that they may seem to have met with a run of ill-luck. Wherefore let your Greatness, whom it specially concerns to look after such men as these, by a speedy rebuke bring them to a better mind. Else the famine which we fear, will be imputed not to the barrenness of the times but to

[1] Var. i. 35.   [2] Echeneis.

official negligence, whose true child it will manifestly appear.'

It is not likely that Theodoric ever read a letter like this before affixing to it his (perhaps stencilled) signature. If he did, he must surely have smiled to see his few angry Teutonic words transmuted into this wonderful rhapsody about sucking-fishes and torpedoes and shell-fish in the Indian Sea.

The French proverb 'Le style c'est l'homme,' is not altogether true as to the character of Cassiodorus. From his inflated and tawdry style we might have expected to find him an untrustworthy friend and an inefficient administrator. This, however, was not the case. As was before said, his character was not heroic; he was, perhaps, inclined to humble himself unduly before mere power and rank, and he had the fault, common to most rhetoricians, of over-estimating the power of words and thinking that a few fluent platitudes would heal inveterate discords and hide disastrous blunders. But when we have said this we have said the worst. He was, as far as we have any means of judging, a loyal subject, a faithful friend, a strenuous and successful administrator, and an exceptionally far-sighted statesman. His right to this last designation rests upon the part which he bore in the establishment of the Italian Kingdom 'of the Goths and Romans,' founded by the great Theodoric. *Character of Cassiodorus.*

Theodoric, it must always be remembered, had entered Italy not ostensibly as an invader but as a deliverer. He came in pursuance of a compact with the legitimate Emperor of the New Rome, to deliver the Elder Rome and the land of Italy from the dominion of 'the upstart King of Rugians and Turcilingians[1],' Odovacar. The compact, it is true, was loose and indefinite, and contained within itself the germs of that misunderstanding which, forty-seven years later, was developed into a terrible war. Still, for the present, Theodoric, King of *His work in seconding the policy of Theodoric.*

---
[1] Jordanes, De Rebus Geticis, lvii.

the Ostrogoths, was also in some undefined way legitimate representative of the Old Roman Empire within the borders of Italy. This double aspect of his rule was illustrated by that which (rather than the doubtful Rex Italiae) seems to have been his favourite title, 'Gothorum Romanorumque Rex.'

Theodoric's love of Civilitas.

The great need of Italy was peace. After a century of wars and rumours of wars; after Alaric, Attila, and Gaiseric had wasted her fields or sacked her capital; after she had been exhausting her strength in hopeless efforts to preserve the dominion of Gaul, Spain, and Africa; after she had groaned under the exactions of the insolent *foederati*, Roman soldiers only in name, who followed the standards of Ricimer or Odovacar, she needed peace and to be governed with a strong hand, in order to recover some small part of her old material prosperity. These two blessings, peace and a strong government, Theodoric's rule ensured to her. The theory of his government was this, that the two nations should dwell side by side, not fused into one, not subject either to the other, but the Romans labouring at the arts of peace, the Goths wielding for their defence the sword of war. Over all was to be the strong hand of the King of Goths and Romans, repressing the violence of the one nation, correcting the chicanery of the other, and from one and all exacting the strict observance of that which was the object of his daily and nightly cares, CIVILITAS. Of this civilitas—which we may sometimes translate 'good order,' sometimes 'civilisation,' sometimes 'the character of a law-abiding citizen,' but which no English word or phrase fully expresses—the reader of the following letters will hear, even to weariness. But though we may be tired of the phrase, we ought none the less to remember that the thing was that which Italy stood most in need of, that it was secured for her during forty years by the labours of Theodoric and Cassiodorus, and that happiness, such as she knew not again for many centuries, was the result.

But the theory of a warrior caste of Goths and a trading and labouring caste of Romans was not flattering to the national vanity of a people who, though they had lost all relish for fighting, could not forget the great deeds of their forefathers. This was no doubt the weak point of the new State-system, though one cannot say that it is a weakness which need have been fatal if time enough had been given for the working out of the great experiment, and for Roman and Goth to become in Italy, as they did become in Spain, one people. The grounds upon which the praise of far-seeing statesmanship may be claimed for Cassiodorus are, that notwithstanding the bitter taste which it must have had in his mouth, as in the mouth of every educated Roman, he perceived that here was the best medicine for the ills of Italy. All attempts to conjure with the great name of the Roman Empire could only end in subjection to the really alien rule of Byzantium. All attempts to rouse the religious passions of the Catholic against the heretical intruders were likely to benefit the Catholic but savage Frank. The cruel sufferings of the Italians at the hands of the Heruli of Belisarius and from the ravages of the Alamannic Brethren are sufficient justification of the soundness of Cassiodorus' view that Theodoric's State-system was the one point of hope for Italy. *Foresight of Cassiodorus in aiding this policy.*

Allusion has been made in the last paragraph to the religious differences which divided the Goths from the Italians. It is well known that Theodoric was an Arian, but an Arian of the most tolerant type, quite unlike the bitter persecutors who reigned at Toulouse and at Carthage. During the last few years of his reign, indeed, when his mind was perhaps in some degree failing, he was tempted by the persecuting policy of the Emperor Justin into retaliatory measures of persecution towards his Catholic subjects, but as a rule his *His religious tolerance.*

policy was eminently fair and even-handed towards the professors of the two hostile creeds, and even towards the generally proscribed nation of the Jews. So conspicuous to all the world was his desire to hold the balance perfectly even between the two communions, that it was said of him that he beheaded an orthodox deacon who was singularly dear to him, because he had professed the Arian faith in order to win his favour. But this story, though told by a nearly contemporary writer[1], is, it may be hoped, mere Saga.

This did not proceed from indifference.

The point which we may note is, that this policy of toleration or rather of absolute fairness between warring creeds, though not initiated by Cassiodorus, seems to have thoroughly commended itself to his reason and conscience. It is from his pen that we get those golden words which may well atone for many platitudes and some ill-judged display of learning: *Religionem imperare non possumus, quia nemo cogitur ut credat invitus*[2]. And this tolerant temper of mind is the more to be commended, because it did not proceed from any indifference on his part to the subjects of religious controversy. Cassiodorus was evidently a devout and loyal Catholic. Much the larger part of his writings is of a theological character, and the thirty-five years of his life which he passed in a monastery were evidently

'Bound each to each in natural piety'

with the earlier years passed at Court and in the Council-chamber.

Date of the commencement of the Variae.

We cannot trace as we should like to do the precise limits of time by which the official career of Cassiodorus was bounded. The 'Various Letters' are evidently not arranged in strict chronological order, and to but few

---

[1] Theodorus Lector (circa 550), Eccl. Hist. ii. 18. Both he and some later writers who borrow from him call the King Θεοδέριχος ὁ Ἄφρος; why, it is impossible to say.

[2] Var. ii. 27.

of them is it possible to affix an exact date. There are two or three, however, which require especial notice, because some authors have assigned them to a date previous to that at which, as I believe, the author entered the service of the Emperor.

The first letter of the whole series is addressed to the Emperor Anastasius. It has been sometimes connected with the embassy of Faustus in 493, or with that of Festus in 497, to the Court of Constantinople, the latter of which embassies resulted in the transmission to Theodoric of 'the ornaments of the palace' (that is probably the regal insignia) which Odovacar had surrendered to Zeno. But the language of the letter in question, which speaks of 'causas iracundiae,' does not harmonise well with either of these dates, since there was then, as far as we know, no quarrel between Ravenna and Constantinople. On the other hand, it would fit perfectly with the state of feeling between the two Courts in 505, after Sabinian the general of Anastasius had been defeated by the troops of Theodoric under Pitzias at the battle of Horrea Margi; or in 508, when the Byzantine ships had made a raid on Apulia and plundered Tarentum. To one of these dates it should probably be referred, its place at the beginning of the collection being due to the exalted rank of the receiver of the letter, not to considerations of chronology. *Letter to Anastasius.*

The fortieth and forty-first letters of the Second Book relate to the sending of a harper to Clovis, or, as Cassiodorus calls him, Luduin, King of the Franks. In the earlier letter Boethius is directed to procure such a harper (citharoedus), and to see that he is a first-rate performer. In the later, Theodoric congratulates his royal brother-in-law on his victory over the Alamanni, adjures him not to pursue the panic-stricken fugitives who have taken refuge within the Ostrogothic territory, and sends ambassadors to introduce the harper *Letters to Clovis.*

whom Boethius has provided. It used to be thought that these letters must be referred to 496, the year of the celebrated victory of Clovis over the Alamanni, commonly, but incorrectly, called the battle of Tulbiacum. But this was a most improbable theory, for it was difficult to understand how a boy of sixteen (and that was the age of Boethius in 496) should have attained such eminence as a musical connoisseur as to be entrusted with the task of selecting the citharoedus. And in a very recent monograph[1] Herr von Schubert has shown, I think convincingly, that the last victory of Clovis over the Alamanni, and their migration to Raetia within the borders of Theodoric's territory, occurred not in 496 but a few years later, probably about 503 or 504. It is true that Gregory of Tours (to whom the earlier battle is all-important, as being the event which brought about the conversion of Clovis) says nothing about this later campaign; but to those who know the fragmentary and incomplete character of this part of his history, such an omission will not appear an important argument.

Letters to Gaulish princes. The letters written in Theodoric's name to Clovis, to Alaric II, to Gundobad of Burgundy, and to other princes, in order to prevent the outbreak of a war between the Visigoths and the Franks, have been by some authors[2] assigned to a date some years before the war actually broke out; but though this cannot, perhaps, be disproved, it seems to me much more probable that they were written in the early part of 507 on the eve of the war between Clovis and Alaric, which they were powerless to avert.

Duration of Cassiodorus' office. More difficult than the question of the beginning of the Quaestorship of Cassiodorus is that of its duration and its close. It was an office which was in its nature

---

[1] Die Uterwerfung der Alamannen: Strassburg, 1884.
[2] Especially Binding, Geschichte des Burgundisch-Romanischen Königreichs, p. 181.

an annual one. At the commencement of each fresh year 'of the Indiction,' that is on the first of September of the calendar year, a Quæstor was appointed; but there does not seem to have been anything to prevent the previous holder of the office from being re-appointed. In the case of Cassiodorus, the Quaestor after Theodoric's own heart, his intimate friend and counsellor, this may have been done for several years running, or he may have apparently retired from office for a year and then resumed it. It is clear, that whether in or out of office he had always, as the King's friend, a large share in the direction of State affairs. He himself says, in a letter supposed to be addressed to himself after the death of Theodoric[1]: 'Non enim proprios fines sub te *ulla dignitas* custodivit;' and that this was the fact we cannot doubt. Whatever his nominal dignity might be, or if for the moment he possessed no ostensible office at all, he was still virtually what we should call the Prime Minister of the Ostrogothic King[2].

In the year 514 he received an honour which, notwithstanding that it was utterly divorced from all real authority, was still one of the highest objects of the ambition of every Roman noble: he was hailed as Consul Ordinarius, and gave his name to the year. For some reason which is not stated, possibly because the City of Constantinople was in that year menaced by the insurrection of Vitalian, no colleague in the East was nominated to share his dignity; and the entry in the Consular Calendars is therefore 'Senatore solo Consule.'

Consulship of Cassiodorus, 514.

In his own Chronicle, Cassiodorus adds the words, 'Me etiam Consule in vestrorum laude temporum, adunato clero vel [=et] populo, Romanae Ecclesiae rediit optata

---

[1] ix. 24.

[2] Thorbecke has pointed out (pp. 40–41) that we possess letters written by Cassiodorus to four Quaestors before the year 510, and that therefore the fact of others holding the nominal office of Quaestor did not circumscribe his activity as Secretary to Theodoric.

concordia.' This sentence no doubt relates to the dissensions which had agitated the Roman Church ever since the contested Papal election of Symmachus and Laurentius in the year 498. Victory had been assured to Symmachus by the Synod of 501, but evidently the feelings of hatred then aroused had still smouldered on, especially perhaps among the Senators and high nobles of Rome, who had for the most part adopted the candidature of Laurentius. Now, on the death of Symmachus (July 18, 514) the last embers of the controversy were extinguished, and the genial influence of Cassiodorus, Senator by name and Consul by office, was successfully exerted to induce nobles, clergy, and people to unite in electing a new Pope. After eight days Hormisdas the Campanian sat in the Chair of St. Peter, an undoubted Pontiff.

Deference to the Roman Senate. Not only in maintaining the dignity of the Consulship, but also in treating the Roman Senate with every outward show of deference and respect, did the Ostrogothic King follow and even improve upon the example of the Roman Emperors. The student of the following letters will observe the tone of deep respect which is almost always adopted towards the Senate; how every nomination of importance to an official post is communicated to them, almost as if their suffrages were solicited for the new candidate; what a show is made of consulting them in reference to peace and war; and what a reality there seems to be in the appeals made to their loyalty to the new King after the death of Theodoric. In all this, as in the whole relation of the Empire to the Senate during the five centuries of their joint existence, it is difficult to say where well-acted courtesy ended, and where the desire to secure such legal power as yet remained to a venerable assembly began. Perhaps when we remember that for many glorious centuries the Senate had been the real ruler of the Roman State, we may assert that the attitude and the language of the successors of Augustus towards the Conscript Fathers were similar to those used by a modern House of Commons towards the Crown, only that in the one case the individual supplanted the assembly, in the other the assembly supplanted the individual. But whatever the exact relations between King and Senate may have been, and though occasionally the former found it necessary to rebuke the latter pretty sharply for conduct unbecoming their high position, there can be no doubt that the general intention of Theodoric was to soothe the wounded pride and flatter the vanity of the Roman Senators by every means in his power: and for this purpose no one could be so well fitted as Cassiodorus, Senator by name and by office, descendant of many generations of Roman nobles, and master of such exuberant rhetoric that it was difficult then, as it is often impossible now, to extract any definite meaning from his sonorous periods.

It was possibly upon his laying down the Consulship, that Cassiodorus received the dignity of Patrician—a dignity only, for in itself it seems to have conferred neither wealth nor power. Yet a title which had been borne by Ricimer, Odovacar, and Theodoric himself might well excite the ambition of Theodoric's subject. If our conjecture be correct that it was conferred upon Cassiodorus in the year 515, he received it at an earlier age than his father, to whom only about ten or eleven years before he had written the letter announcing his elevation to this high dignity.

Cassiodorus Patrician.

Five years after his Consulate, Cassiodorus undertook a little piece of literary labour which he does not appear to have held in high account himself (since he does not include it in the list of his works), and which has certainly added but little to his fame. This was his 'Chronicon,' containing an abstract of the history of the world from the deluge down to A.D. 519, the year of the Consulship of the Emperor Justin, and of Theo-

The Chronicon.

doric's son-in-law Eutharic. This Chronicle is for the most part founded upon, or rather copied from, the well-known works of Eusebius and Prosper, the copying being unfortunately not correctly done. More than this, Cassiodorus has attempted with little judgment to combine the mode of reckoning by Consular years and by years of Emperors. As he is generally two or three years out in his reckoning of the former, this proceeding has the curious result of persistently throwing some Consulships of the reigning Emperor into the reign of his predecessor.[1] Thus Probus is Consul for two years under Aurelian, and for one year under Tacitus; both the two Consulships of Carus and the first of Diocletian are under Probus, while Diocletian's second Consulship is under Carinus and Numerianus; and so forth. It is wonderful that so intelligent a person as Cassiodorus did not see that combinations of this kind were false upon the face of them.

When the Chronicle gets nearer to the compiler's own times it becomes slightly more interesting, but also slightly less fair. Throughout the fourth century a few little remarks are interspersed in the dry list of names and dates, the general tendency of which is to praise up the Gothic nation or to extenuate their faults and reverses. The battle of Pollentia (402 [2]) is unhesitatingly claimed as a Gothic victory; the clemency of Alaric at the capture of Rome (410) is magnified; the valour of the Goths is made the cause of the defeat of Attila in the Catalaunian plains (451); the name of

---

[1] It need hardly be explained that, as a matter of compliment to the reigning Emperor, the first Consulship that fell vacant after his accession to the throne was (I believe invariably) filled by him, and that though he might sometimes have held the office of Consul before his assumption of the diadem, this was not often the case. Certainly, in the instances given above, Probus, Carus, and Diocletian held no Consulships till after they had been saluted as Emperors.

[2] Clinton's date for this battle, 403, differs from that assigned by Cassiodorus, and is, in my judgment, erroneous.

Gothic Eutharic is put before that of Byzantine Justin in the consular list; and so forth. Upon the whole, as has been already said, the work cannot be considered as adding to the reputation of its author; nor can it be defended from the terrible attack which has been made upon it by that scholar of our own day whose opinion upon such a subject stands the highest, Theodor Mommsen[1]. Only, when he makes this unfortunate Chronicle reflect suspicion on the other works of Cassiodorus, and especially on the Gothic History[2], the German scholar seems to me to chastise the busy Minister more harshly than he deserves.

I have just alluded to the Gothic History of Cassiodorus. It was apparently shortly after the composition of his Chronicle[3] that this, in some respects his most important work, was compiled and arranged according to his accustomed habit in twelve books. His own estimate—and it is not a low one—of the value of this performance is expressed in a letter which he makes his young Sovereign Athalaric address to the Senate on his promotion to the Praefecture[4]: 'He extended his labours even to our remote ancestry, learning by his reading that which scarcely the hoar memories of our forefathers retained. He drew forth from their hiding-place the Kings of the Goths, hidden by long forgetfulness. He restored the Amals to their proper place with the lustre of his own[5] lineage (?), evidently proving that up

The Gothic History.

---

[1] Abhandlungen der philologisch-historischen Klasse der Königlich Sächsischen Gesellschaft der Wissenschaften, iii. 547-696.

[2] 'Dass die ganze Procedur von der übelsten Art ist und den viel gefeierten gothischen Historiker in jeder weise compromittirt, bedarf keiner Ausaneindersetzung' (l. c. 564).

[3] It could not have been written, at any rate in its present shape, before 516, because Athalaric's birth is mentioned in it. I prefer Jordanes' date for this event, 516 or 517, to that given by Procopius, 518.) On the other hand, Usener proves (p. 74), from the reference to it in the Anecdoton Holderi, that it could not have been written after 521.

[4] Var. ix. 25.

[5] 'Iste Amalos cum generis *sui* claritate restituit.' Perhaps it is better to take 'sui' as equivalent to 'illorum,' and translate 'their lineage.'

to the seventeenth generation we have had kings for our ancestors. He made the origin of the Goths a part of Roman history, collecting as it were into one wreath all the flowery growth which had before been scattered through the plains of many books. Consider therefore what love he showed to you [the Senate] in praising us, he who showed that the nation of your Sovereign had been from antiquity a marvellous people; so that ye, who from the days of your forefathers have ever been deemed noble, are yet ruled over by the ancient progeny of Kings [1].'

Its purpose.

In reading this estimate by Cassiodorus of his own performance, we can see at once that it lacked that first of all conditions precedent for the attainment of absolute historic truth, complete impartiality [2]. Like Hume and like Macaulay Cassiodorus wrote his history with a purpose. We may describe that purpose as two-fold:

(1) To vindicate the claim of the Goths to rank among the historic nations of antiquity by bringing them into some sort of connection with Greece and Rome ('Originem Gothicam historiam fecit esse Romanam'); and (2) among the Goths, to exalt as highly as possible the family of the Amals, that family from which Theodoric had sprung, and to string as many regal names as possible upon the Amal chain ('Evidenter ostendens in decimam septimam progeniem stirpem nos habere regalem').

I have said that the possession of a purpose like this is unfavourable to the attainment of absolute historic truth; but the aim which Cassiodorus proposed to himself was a lofty one, being in fact the reconciliation of the past and the future of the world by showing to

---

[1] 'Ut sicut fuistis a majoribus vestris semper nobiles aestimati, ita vobis rerum antiqua progenies imperaret.' For 'rerum' we must surely read 'regum.'

[2] My meaning would be better expressed by the useful German word 'voraussetzungslosigkeit,' freedom from a foregone conclusion.

the outworn Latin race that the new blood which was being poured into it by the northern nations came, like its own, from a noble ancestry: and, for us, the labour to which it stimulated him has been full of profit, since to it we owe something like one half of our knowledge of the Teutonic ancestors of Modern Europe.

The much-desired object of 'making the origin of Gothic history Roman' was effected chiefly by attributing to the Goths all that Cassiodorus found written in classic authors concerning the Getae or the Scythians. The confusion between Goths and Getae, though modern ethnologists are nearly unanimous in pronouncing it to be a confusion between two utterly different nations, is not one for which Cassiodorus is responsible, since it had been made at least a hundred years before his time. When the Emperor Claudius II won his great victories over the Goths in the middle of the Third Century, he was hailed rightly enough by the surname of *Gothicus;* but when at the beginning of the Fifth Century the feeble Emperors Arcadius and Honorius wished to celebrate a victory which, as they vainly hoped, had effectually broken the power of the Goths, the words which they inscribed upon the Arch of Triumph were 'Quod *Getarum* nationem in omne aevum docuere extingui.' In the poems of Claudian, and generally in all the contemporary literature of the time, the regular word for the countrymen of Alaric is Getae.

Confusion between Goths and Getae.

The Greek historians, on the other hand, freely applied the general term Scythian—as they had done at any time since the Scythian campaign of Darius Hystaspis—to any barbarian nation living beyond the Danube and the Cimmerian Bosporus. With these two clues, or imaginary clues, in his hand, Cassiodorus could traverse a considerable part of the border-land of classical antiquity. The battles between the Scythians and the Egyptians, the story of the Amazons, Telephus son of Hercules and

The term Scythian.

nephew of Priam, the defeat of Cyrus by Tomyris, and the unsuccessful expedition of Darius—all were connected with Gothic history by means of that easily stretched word, Scythia. Then comes Sitalces, King of Thrace, who makes war on Perdiccas of Macedon; and then, 'in the time of Sylla,' a certain wise philosopher-king of Dacia, Diceneus by name, in whose character and history Cassiodorus perhaps outlined his own ideal of wisdom swaying brute force. With these and similar stories culled from classical authors Cassiodorus appears to have filled up the interval—which was to him of absolutely uncertain duration—between the Gothic migration from the Baltic to the Euxine and their appearance as conquerors and ravagers in the eastern half of the Roman Empire in the middle of the third century of the Christian era. Now, soothing as it may have been to the pride of a Roman subject of Theodoric to be informed that his master's ancestors had fought at the war of Troy and humbled the pride of Perdiccas, to a scientific historian these Scytho-Getic histories culled from Herodotus and Trogus are of little or no value, and his first step in the process of enquiry is to eliminate them from 'Gothica historia,' thus making it, as far as he can, *not* 'Romana.' The question then arises whether there was another truly Gothic element in the history of Cassiodorus, and if so, what value can be attached to it. Thus enquiring we soon find, both before and after this intrusive Scytho-Getic element, matter of quite a different kind, which has often much of the ring of the true Teutonic *Saga*. It is reasonable to believe that here Cassiodorus, whose mission it was to reconcile Roman and Goth, and who could not have achieved this end by altering the history of the less civilised people out of all possibility of recognition by its own chieftains and warriors, has really interwoven in his work some part of the songs and Sagas which were still current among the older men who had shared the wanderings of Theodoric. This legendary portion, which Cassiodorus himself perhaps half despised, as being gathered not from books but from the lips of rude minstrels, is in fact the only part of his work which has any scientific value.

In his glorification of the Amal line, Cassiodorus follows more closely these genuine national traditions than in his history of the Gothic people. References to Herodotus and Trogus would have been here obviously out of place, and he accordingly puts before us a pedigree fashioned on the same model as those which we find in the Saxon Chronicle, and therefore probably genuine. By genuine of course is meant a pedigree which was really current and accepted among the people over whom Theodoric ruled. How many of the links which form it represent real historical personages is a matter about which we may almost be said neither to know nor care. We see that it begins in the approved fashion with 'Non puri homines sed semidei id est Anses[1],' and that the first of these half-divine ancestors is named *Gaut*, evidently the eponymous hero of the Gothic people. Some of the later links—Amal, Ostrogotha, Athal—have the same appearance of names coined to embody facts of the national consciousness. At the end of the genealogy appear the undoubtedly historical names of the immediate ancestors of Theodoric. It is noteworthy that several, in fact the majority of the names of Kings who figure in early Gothic history, are not included in this genealogy. While this fact permits us to doubt whether Cassiodorus has not exaggerated the pre-eminence of the Amal race in early days, it must be admitted to be also an evidence of the good faith with which he preserved the national tradition on these points. Had he been merely inventing, it would have been easy to include every name of a distinguished Gothic King among the progenitors of his Sovereign.

The Amal pedigree.

---

[1] Jordanes, De Reb. Get. xiii.

Abstract by Jordanes.

Such then was the general purpose of the Gothic History of Cassiodorus. The book itself has perished—a tantalising loss when we consider how many treatises from the same pen have been preserved to us which we could well have spared. But we can speak, as will be seen from the preceding remarks, with considerable confidence as to its plan and purpose, because we possess in the well-known treatise of Jordanes 'On the Origin of the Goths[1]' an abbreviated copy, executed it is true by a very inferior hand, but still manifestly preserving some of the features of the original. It will not be necessary here to go into the difficult question as to the personality of this writer, which has been debated at considerable length and with much ingenuity by several German authors[2]. It is enough to say that Jordanes, who was, according to his own statement, 'agrammatus,' a man of Gothic descent, a notary, and then a monk[3], on the alleged request of his friend Castalius, 'compressed the twelve books of Senator, *de origine actibusque Getarum*, bringing down the history from olden times to our own days by kings and generations, into one little pamphlet.' Still, according to his statement, which there can be little doubt is here thoroughly false, he had the loan of the Gothic History for only three days from the steward of Cassiodorus, and wrote chiefly or entirely from his recollection of this hasty perusal[4]. He says that he

---

[1] 'De Rebus Geticis,' or 'De Gothorum Origine,' is the name by which this little treatise is usually known. It seems to be doubtful, however, what title, if any, Jordanes himself prefixed to it. Mommsen calls it simply 'Getica.'

[2] Especially Schirren, 'De Ratione quae inter Jordanem et Cassiodorum intercedat' (Dorpat, 1858); Sybel, 'De Fontibus Libri Jordanis' (Berlin, 1838); and Köpke, 'Die Anfänge des Königthums bei den Gothen' (Berlin, 1859).

[3] *Possibly* in the end Bishop of Crotona, or a Defensor of the Roman Church, since we find a Jordanes in each of these positions; but this is mere guesswork, and to me neither theory seems probable.

[4] 'Sed ut non mentiar, ad triduanam lectionem dispensatoris ejus

added some suitable passages from the Greek and Latin historians, but his own range of historical reading was evidently so narrow that we may fairly suspect these additions to have been of the slenderest possible dimensions. Upon the whole, there can be little doubt that it is a safe rule to attribute everything that is good or passable in this little treatise to Cassiodorus, and everything that is very bad, childish, and absurd in it to Jordanes.

The literary labours of Cassiodorus, of which the Gothic History was one of the fruits, were probably continued for two or three years after its completion[1]. At least there is reason to believe that he was not actively engaged in the service of the State during those terrible years (524 and 525) in which the failing intellect of Theodoric, goaded almost to madness by Justin's persecution of his Arian co-religionists, condescended to ignoble measures of retaliation, which brought him into collision with Senate and Pope, and in the end tarnished his fame by the judicial murder of Boethius and Symmachus. It was fortunate indeed for Cassiodorus if he was during this time, perhaps because of his unwillingness to help the King to his own hurt, enjoying an interval of literary retirement at Squillace. His honour must have suffered if he had abetted the intolerant policy of Theodoric; his life might have been forfeit if he had openly opposed it.

Temporary retirement from official life (?).

Whatever may have been the cause of the temporary obscuration of Cassiodorus, he was soon again shining in

beneficio libros ipsos antehac relegi.' Notwithstanding the 'ut non mentiar,' most of those who have enquired into the subject have come to the opinion which is bluntly expressed by Usener (p. 73), 'Die dreitägige Frist die Jordanes zur Benutzung der 12 Bücher gehabt haben will, *ist natürlich Schwindel.*' Even by an expert précis-writer a loan of three months would be much more probably needed for the purpose indicated by Jordanes than one of three days.

[1] This was probably 521 at latest.

<small>Cassiodorus as Master of the Offices, 526.</small>

all the splendour of official dignity; for when Theodoric died, his old and trusted minister was holding—probably not for the first time in his official career[1]—the great place of Master of the Offices.

The *Magister Officiorum*, whose relation to the other members of the Cabinet of the Sovereign was somewhat indefinite, and who was in fact constantly trying to enlarge the circle of his authority at their expense, was at the head of the Civil Service of the Roman Empire, and afterwards occupied a similar position in the Ostrogothic State. It was said of him by the Byzantine orator Priscus (himself a man who had been engaged in important embassies), 'Of all the counsels of the Emperor the Magister is a partaker, inasmuch as the messengers and interpreters and the soldiers employed on guard at the palace are ranged under him.' Quite in harmony with this general statement are the more precise indications of the 'Notitia.' There, 'under the disposition of the illustrious Magister Officiorum,' we find five *Scholae*, which seem to have been composed of household troops[2]. Then comes the great Schola of the *Agentes in rebus* and their deputies—a mighty army of 'king's messengers,' who swarmed through all the Provinces of the Empire, executing the orders of the Sovereign, and earning gold and hatred from the helpless Provincials among whom their errands lay. In addition to these the four great stationary bureaux—the Scrinium Memoriae, Scrinium Dispositionum, Scrinium Epistolarum, and Scrinium Libellorum—the offices whose duty it was to conduct the correspondence of the Sovereign with foreign powers, and to answer the petitions of his own subjects, all owned the Master of the Offices as their head. More-

---

[1] The language of Cassiodorus in Var. ix. 24 implies that he had held this office for a considerable time before the death of Theodoric. Usener thinks that he was made Magister Officiorum for the first time about the year 518.

[2] They are 'Scutariorum prima, secunda et tertia, armaturarum seniorum et gentilium seniorum' (Notitia Occidentis, cap. ix.).

over, the great arsenals (of which there were six in Italy, at Concordia, Verona, Mantua, Cremona, Ticinum, and Lucca) received their orders from the same official. An anomalous and too widely dispersed range of functions this seems according to our ideas, including something of the Secretaryship for Foreign Affairs, something of the Home Secretaryship, and something of the War Office and the Horse Guards. Yet, as if this were not enough, there was also transferred to him from the office of the Praetorian Praefect the superintendence of the Cursus Publicus, that excellent institution by which facilities for intercourse were provided between the capital and the most distant Provinces, relays of post-horses being kept at every town, available for use by those who bore properly signed 'letters of evection.' Thus to the multifarious duties of the Master of the Offices was added in effect the duty of Postmaster-General. It was found however in practice to be an inconvenient arrangement for the Master of the Offices to have the control of the services of the 'public horses,' while the Praetorian Praefect remained responsible for the supply of their food; and the charge of the *Cursus Publicus* was accordingly retransferred—at any rate in the Eastern Empire—to the office of the Praefect, though the letters of evection still required the counter-signature of the Master[1].

Such was the position of Cassiodorus when, on the 30th of August, 526, by the death of Theodoric, he lost the master whom he had served so long and so faithfully. The difficulties which beset the new reign are pretty clearly indicated in the letters which Cassiodorus published in the name of the young King Athalaric, Theodoric's grandson, and which are to be found in the

Death of Theodoric, Aug. 30, 526.

---

[1] This is the account of the matter given by Lydus (De Magistratibus ii. 10); but as the Notitia (Or. xi.) puts the 'Curiosus Cursus Publici Praesentalis' under the disposition of the Magister Officiorum, the retransfer had probably not then taken place. It would seem also from the Formula of Cassiodorus (Var. vi. 6) that in his time the Magister Officiorum still had the charge of the Cursus Publicus.

Eighth Book of the 'Variae.' Athalaric himself being only a boy of eight or ten years of age, supreme power was vested in his mother Amalasuentha, with what title we are unable to say, but apparently not with that of Queen. This Princess, a woman of great and varied accomplishments, perhaps once a pupil, certainly a friend, of Cassiodorus, ruled entirely in accordance with the maxims of his statesmanship, and endeavoured with female impulsiveness to carry into effect his darling scheme of Romanising the Goths. During the whole of her regency we may doubtless consider Cassiodorus as virtually her Prime Minister, and the eight years which it occupied were without doubt that portion of his life in which he exercised the most direct and unquestioned influence on State affairs.

Services of Cassiodorus to the Regent Amalasuentha.
His services at the commencement of the new reign will be best described in his own words: 'Nostris quoque principiis[1]' (the letter is written in Athalaric's name) 'quanto se labore concessit, cum novitas regni multa posceret ordinari? Erat solus ad universa sufficiens. Ipsum dictatio publica, ipsum consilia nostra poscebant; et labore ejus actum est ne laboraret imperium. *Reperimus eum quidem Magistrum sed implevit nobis Quaestoris officium:* et mercedes justissima devotione persolvens, cautelam, quam ab auctore nostro didicerat, libenter haeredis utilitatibus exhibebat[2].'

Fears of invasion.
Cassiodorus then goes on to describe how he laboured for his young Sovereign with the sword as well as with the pen. Some hostile invasion was dreaded, perhaps from the Franks, or, more probably, from the Vandals, whose relations with the Ostrogoths at that time were strained, owing to the murder of Theodoric's sister Amalafrida by Hilderic the Vandal King. Cassiodorus provided ships and equipped soldiers at his own expense,

---

[1] Variarum ix. 25.

[2] The meaning apparently is: 'The experience which he had gained in Theodoric's service was employed for the advantage of his grandson.'

probably for the defence of his beloved Province of Bruttii. The alarm of war passed away, but difficulties appear to have arisen owing to the sudden cancellation of the contracts which had been entered into when hostilities seemed imminent; and to these difficulties Cassiodorus tells us that he brought his trained experience as an administrator and a judge, resolving them so as to give satisfaction to all who were concerned.

Seven years of Amalasuentha's regency thus passed, and now at length, at fifty-three years of age, Cassiodorus was promoted (Sept. 1, 533) to the most distinguished place which a subject could occupy. He received from Amalasuentha the office of Praetorian Praefect. As thirty-three years had elapsed since his father was invested with the same dignity, we may fairly conjecture that father and son both climbed this eminence at the same period of their lives; yet, considering the extraordinary credit which the younger Cassiodorus enjoyed at Court, we might have expected that he would have been clothed with the Praefecture before he attained the fifty-third year of his age. And, in fact, he hints in the letter composed by him, in which he informs himself of his own elevation[1], that that elevation had been somewhat too long delayed, though the reason which he alleges for the delay (namely, that the people might greet the new Praefect the more heartily[2]) is upon the face of it not the true cause.

Cassiodorus as Praetorian Praefect, 533.

The majesty of the Praetorian Praefect's office is fully dwelt upon and its functions described in a letter in the following collection[3], to which the reader is referred. Originally only the chief officer of those Praetorian troops in Rome by whom the Emperor was guarded, until, as

Office of the Praetorian Praefect.

---

[1] Var. ix. 24.

[2] 'Diutius quidem differendo pro te cunctorum vota lassavimus, ut benevolentiam in te probaremus generalitatis, et cunctis desiderabilior advenires.'

[3] Var. vi. 3.

was so often the case, he was in some fit of petulance by the same pampered sentinels dethroned, the Praefectus Praetorio had gradually become more and more of a judge, less and less of a soldier. In the great changes wrought by Constantine the Praetorian guards disappeared—somewhat in the same fashion after which the Janissaries were removed by Sultan Mahmoud. The Praetorian Praefect's dignity, however, survived, and though he lost every shred of military command he became or continued to be the first civil servant of the Empire. Cassiodorus is fond of comparing him to Joseph at the Court of Pharaoh, nor is the comparison an inapt one. In the Constantinople of our own day the Grand Vizier holds a position not altogether unlike that which the Praefect held in the Court of Arcadius and Theodosius. 'The office of this Praefect,' said one who had spent his life as one of his subordinates[1], 'is like the Ocean, encircling all other offices and ministering to all their needs. The Consulate is indeed higher in rank than the Praefecture, but less in power. The Praefect wears a *mandye*, or woollen cloak, dyed with the purple of Cos, and differing from the Emperor's only in the fact that it reaches not to the feet but to the knees. Girt with his sword he takes his seat as President of the Senate. When that body has assembled, the chiefs of the army fall prostrate before the Praefect, who raises them and kisses each in turn, in order to express his desire to be on good terms with the military power. Nay, even the Emperor himself walks (or till lately used to walk) on foot from his palace to meet the Praefect as he moves slowly towards him at the head of the Senate. The insignia of the Praefect's office are his lofty chariot, his golden reed-case [pen-holder], weighing one hundred pounds, his massive silver inkstand, and silver bowl on a tripod of the same metal to receive the petitions of suitors. Three

---

[1] Joannes Lydus, De Dignitatibus ii. 7, 8, 9, 13, 14.

official yachts wait upon his orders, and convey him from the capital to the neighbouring Provinces.'

The personage thus highly placed had a share in the government of the State, a share which the Master of the Offices was for ever trying to diminish, but which, in the hands of one who like Cassiodorus was *persona grata* at the Court, might be made not only important but predominant[1]. The chief employment, however, of the ordinary Praefectus Praetorio consisted in hearing appeals from the Governors of the Provinces. When the magical words 'Provoco ad Caesarem' had been uttered, it was in most cases before the Praetorian Praefect that the appeal was practically heard; and when the Praetorian Praefect had pronounced his decision, no appeal from that was permitted, even to the Emperor himself[2].

The Praetorian Praefect as Judge of Appeal.

Cassiodorus held the post of Praetorian Praefect, amid various changes in the fortunes of the State, from 533 to 538, or perhaps a year or two longer. Of his activity in the domain of internal administration, the Eleventh and Twelfth Books of the 'Variae' give a vivid and interesting picture. Unfortunately, neither those books nor the Tenth Book of the same collection, which contains the letters written by him during the same time in the names of the successive Gothic Sovereigns, give any sufficient information as to the real course of public

Letters written during the Praefecture of Cassiodorus.

---

[1] Bethmann Hollweg (pp. 75, 76) enumerates the functions of the Praetorian Praefect thus: '(1) *Legislative.* He promulgated the Imperial laws, and issued edicts which had almost the force of laws. (2) *Financial.* The general tax (indictio, delegatio) ordered by the Emperor for the year, was proclaimed by each Praefect for his own Praefecture. Through his officials he took part in the levy of the tax, and had a special State-chest (arca praetoria) for the proceeds. (3) *Administrative.* The Praefect proposed the names of provincial governors, handed to them their salaries, had a general oversight of them, issued rescripts on the information furnished by them, and could as their ordinary Judge inflict punishments upon them, even depose them from their offices, and temporarily nominate substitutes to act in their places. (4) *Judicial*, as the highest Judge of Appeal.'

[2] See authorities quoted by Bethmann Hollweg, pp. 79, 80.

events. Great misfortunes, great crimes, and the movements of great armies are covered over in these documents by a veil of unmeaning platitudes and hypocritical compliments. In order to enable the student to 'read between the lines,' and to pierce through the verbiage of these letters to the facts which they were meant to hint at or to conceal, it will be necessary briefly to describe the political history of the period as we learn it from the narratives of Procopius and Jordanes—narratives which may be inaccurate in a few minor details but are doubtless correct in their main outlines.

Opposition to Romanising policy of Amalasuentha.

The Romanising policy of the cultivated but somewhat self-willed Princess Amalasuentha met with considerable opposition on the part of her Gothic subjects. Above all, they objected to the bookish education which she was giving to her son, the young King. They declared that it was entirely contrary to the maxims of Theodoric that a young Goth should be trembling before the strap of a pedagogue when he ought to be learning to look unfalteringly on spear and sword. These representations were so vigorously made, and by speakers of such high rank in the State, that Amalasuentha was compelled to listen to them, to remove her son from the society of his teachers, and to allow him to associate with companions of his own age, who, not being wisely chosen, soon initiated him in every kind of vice and dissipation.

Amalasuentha puts three Gothic nobles to death.

The Princess, who had not forgiven the leaders of the Gothic party for their presumptuously offered counsels, singled out three of the most powerful nobles who were at the head of that party and sent them into honourable banishment at the opposite ends of Italy. Finding, however, that they were still holding communication with one another, she sent to the Emperor Justinian to ask if he would give her an asylum in his dominions if she required it, and then gave orders for the secret assassination of the three noblemen. The *coup d'état* succeeded: she had no need to flee the country; and the ship bearing the royal treasure, which amounted to 40,000 pounds weight of gold, which she had sent to Dyrrhachium to await her possible flight, was ordered to return home.

Athalaric's health was now rapidly failing, owing to his licentious excesses, and Amalasuentha, fearing that after his death her own life might be in danger, began again secretly to negotiate with Justinian for the entire surrender of the kingdom of Italy into his hands, on receiving an assurance of shelter and maintenance at the Court of Byzantium. These negotiations were masked by others of a more public kind, in which Justinian claimed the Sicilian fortress of Lilybaeum, which had once belonged to the Vandals; insisted on the surrender of some Huns, deserters from the army of Africa; and demanded redress for the sack by the Goths of the Moesian city of Gratiana. These claims Amalasuentha met publicly with a reply as brave and uncompromising as her most patriotic subjects could desire, but in private, as has been already said, she was prepared, for an adequate assurance of personal safety, to barter away all the rights and liberties of her Italian subjects, Roman as well as Gothic, and to allow her father's hard-earned kingdom to sink into a mere dependency of Constantinople. *Embassies between Ravenna and Constantinople.*

Such was the position of affairs when on the 2nd October 534, little more than a year after Cassiodorus had donned the purple of the Praefect, Athalaric died, and by his death the whole attitude of the parties to the negotiations was changed. The power to rule, and with it the very power to make terms of any kind with the Emperor, was in danger of slipping from the hands of Amalasuentha. The principle of female sovereignty was barely accepted by any Teutonic tribe. Evidently the Ostrogoths had not accepted it, or Amalasuentha would have ruled as Queen in her own right instead of as Regent for her son. In order to strengthen her position, and ensure her acceptance *Death of Athalaric, Oct. 2, 534.*

as Sovereign by the Gothic warriors, she decided to associate with herself, not in matrimony, for he was already married, but in regal partnership, her cousin Theodahad, the nearest male heir of Theodoric, and to mount the throne together with him. Previously, however, to announcing this scheme in public, she sent for Theodahad and exacted from him 'tremendous oaths[1]' that if he were chosen King he would be satisfied with the mere name of royalty, leaving her as much of the actual substance of power as she possessed at that moment.

Amalasuentha associates Theodahad in the Sovereignty.

The partnership-royalty and the oath of self-abnegation were the desperate expedients of a woman who knew herself to have mighty enemies among her subjects, and who felt power slipping from her grasp. With one side of her character her new partner could sympathise; for Theodahad, though sprung from the loins of Gothic warriors, was a man of some literary culture, who preferred poring over the 'Republic' of Plato to heading a charge of the Gothic cavalry. But his acquaintance with Latin and Greek literature had done nothing to ennoble his temper or expand his heart. A cold, hard, avaricious soul, he had been entirely bent on adding field to field and removing his neighbour's landmark, until the vast possessions which he had received from the generosity of Theodoric should embrace the whole of the great Tuscan plain. It will be seen by referring to two letters in the following collection[2] that Theodoric himself had twice employed the pen of Cassiodorus to rebuke the rapacity of his nephew; and at a more recent date, since the beginning of Athalaric's illness, Amalasuentha had been compelled by the complaints of her Tuscan subjects to issue a commission of enquiry, which had found Theodahad guilty of the various acts of land-robbery which had been charged against him, and had compelled him to make restitution.

---

[1] ὅρκοις δεινοτάτοις.   [2] Variarum iv. 39 and v. 12.

The new Queen persuaded herself, and tried to persuade her cousin, that this ignominious sentence had in some way put the subject of it straight with the world, and had smoothed his pathway to the throne. She trusted to his gratitude and his tremendous oaths for her own undisturbed position at the helm of the State, but she found before many months of the joint reign had passed that the reed upon which she was leaning was about to pierce her hand. Only four letters, it will be seen, of the following collection were written by order of Amalasuentha after the commencement of the joint reign. Soon Theodahad felt himself strong enough to hurl from the throne the woman who had dared to compel him to draw back the boundary of his Tuscan *latifundium*. The relations of the three noblemen whom Amalasuentha had put to death gathered gladly round him, eager to work out the blood-feud; and by their help he slew many of the strongest supporters of the Queen, and shut her up in prison in a little lonely island upon the lake of Vulsinii. This event took place on the 30th of April, 535, not quite seven months after the death of Athalaric[1].

Amalasuentha is deposed and imprisoned by Theodahad, April 30, 535.

During all these later months there had been a perpetual flux and reflux of diplomatic communications between Ravenna and Constantinople. The different stages of the negotiations are marked, apparently with clearness, by Procopius; but it is not always easy to harmonise them with the letters published by Cassiodorus, who either did not write, or shrank from republishing, some of the most important letters to the Emperor. This remark applies to the missive which was probably taken by the Senators Liberius and Opilio, who were now sent by Theodahad to Justinian to apologise for the imprisonment of Amalasuentha, and

[1] The dates of the death of Athalaric and deposition of Amalasuentha are given by Agnellus in his Liber Pontificalis Ecclesiae Ravennatis, p. 322 (in the edition comprised in the Monumenta Germaniae Historica).

Embassy of Peter. to promise that she should receive no injury. Meanwhile Peter, a rhetorician and an ex-Consul, was travelling from Constantinople with a commission the character of which was being constantly changed by the rapid current of events. He started with instructions to complete the transaction with Amalasuentha as to the surrender of Italy, and to buy from Theodahad, who was still a private individual, his possessions in Tuscany. Soon after his departure he met the ambassadors, who told him of the death of Athalaric and the accession of Theodahad. On the shores of the Hadriatic he heard of Amalasuentha's captivity. He waited for further instructions from his master, and on his arrival at Ravenna he found that all was over. The letter which he was to have handed to the deposed Queen, assuring her of Justinian's protection, was already obsolete. The kinsmen of the three nobles had been permitted or encouraged by Theodahad to end the blood-feud bloodily. They had repaired to the Lake of Vulsinii and murdered Amalasuentha in her bath[1]. The Byzantine ambassador sought the presence of the King, boldly denounced his wicked deed, and declared on the part of his master a war which would be waged without truce or treaty till Amalasuentha was avenged. Thus began the eighteen years' war between Justinian and the Ostrogoths.

Death of Amalasuentha.

Why did Cassiodorus continue in the service of Theodahad? It might certainly have been expected that a statesman who had been honoured with the intimate friendship of Theodoric and his daughter, even if unable to avenge her death, would have refused to serve in the Cabinet of her murderer. It is accordingly with a feeling of painful surprise that we find Cassiodorus still holding the Secretary's pen, and writing letter after letter (they form the majority of the documents in the

---

[1] We do not seem to have the precise date of the death of Amalasuentha, but apparently it happened about the month of May, 535.

Tenth Book of the 'Variae') in the name of Theodahad and his wife Gudelina. Dangers no doubt were thickening round his beloved Italy. He may have thought that whoever wore the Gothic crown, Duty forbade him to quit the Secretum at Ravenna just when war with the Empire was becoming every day more imminent. On the other hand, the Praetorian Praefecture, the object of a life's ambition, was now his, but had been his only for two years. It was hard to lay aside the purple *mandye* while the first gloss was yet upon it; hard to have to fall back into the ranks of the ordinary senators, and no longer to receive the reverent salutations of the chiefs of the army when he entered the hall of meeting. Whether the public good or the private advantage swayed him most who shall say? There are times when patriotism calls for the costliest sacrifice which a statesman can make—the sacrifice, apparently, of his own honour. The man who has made such a sacrifice must be content to be misjudged by his fellow-men. Certainly, to us the one stain upon an otherwise pure reputation seems to be found in the service, the apparently willing service, which in the Tenth Book of his letters Cassiodorus renders to Theodahad.

Throughout the latter half of 535, Belisarius in Sicily and Mundus in Dalmatia were warring for Justinian against Theodahad. The rhetorician Peter, who had boldly rebuked the Gothic King for the murder of his benefactress, and had on his master's behalf denounced a truceless war against him, still lingered at his Court. Theodahad, who during part of the summer and autumn of 535 seems to have been at Rome, not at Ravenna, was more than half inclined to resume his old negotiations with the Emperor, and either to purchase peace by sinking into the condition of a tributary, or to sell his kingdom outright for a revenue of £48,000 a year and a high place among the nobles of the Empire. Pro-

Vacillation of Theodahad.

copius[1] gives us a vivid and detailed narrative of the manner in which these negotiations were conducted by Theodahad, who was perpetually wavering between arrogance and timidity; trembling at the successes of Belisarius, elated by any victory which his generals might win in Dalmatia; and who at length, upon receiving the tidings of the defeat and death of Mundus, broke off the negotiations altogether, and shut up Peter and his colleague Athanasius in prison.

Silence of the 'Variae' as to many of the negotiations between Theodahad and Justinian.

Here again, while not doubting the truth of the narrative of Procopius, I do not find it possible exactly to fit in the letters written by Cassiodorus for Theodahad with the various stages of the negotiation as described by him. Especially the striking letter of the King to the Emperor—striking by reason of its very abjectness—which is quoted by Procopius in the sixth chapter of his First Book, appears to be entirely unrepresented in the collection of Cassiodorus. Evidently all this part of the 'Variae' has been severely edited by its author, who has expunged all that seemed to reflect too great discredit on the Sovereign whom he had once served, and has preserved only some letters written to Justinian and Theodora by Theodahad and his wife, vaguely praising peace, and beseeching the Imperial pair to restore it to Italy; letters which, as it seems to me, may be applied with about equal fitness to any movement of the busy shuttle of diplomacy backwards and forwards between Ravenna and Constantinople.

Theodahad deposed, Witigis elected, Aug. 536.

The onward march of Belisarius trampled all the combinations of diplomatists into the dust. In the early part of July, 536, he had succeeded in capturing the important city of Neapolis, and had begun to threaten Rome. The Gothic warriors, disgusted at the incapacity of their King, and probably suspecting his disloyalty to the nation, met (August, 536) under arms upon the plain

---

[1] De Bello Gotthico, i. 6.

of Regeta[1], deposed Theodahad, and elected a veteran named Witigis as his successor. Witigis at once ordered Theodahad to be put to death, and being himself of somewhat obscure lineage, endeavoured to strengthen his title to the crown by marrying Matasuentha, the sister of Athalaric and the only surviving descendant of Theodoric.

Whether Cassiodorus had any hand in this revolution—which was pre-eminently a Gothic movement—we cannot tell; but certainly one of the best specimens of his letters is that written in the name of the new King[2], in which he makes Witigis thus speak, 'Universis Gothis'—not as Theodoric had so often spoken, 'Universis Gothis et Romanis:' *Letter on the elevation of Witigis.*

'Unde Auctori nostro Christo gratias humillimâ satisfactione referentes, indicamus parentes nostros Gothos inter procinctuales gladios, more majorum, scuto supposito, regalem nobis contulisse, praestante Deo, dignitatem, ut honorem arma darent, cujus opinionem bella pepererant. Non enim in cubilis angustis, sed in campis latè patentibus electum me esse noveritis: nec inter blandientium delicata colloquia, sed tubis concrepantibus sum quaesitus, ut tali fremitu concitatus desiderio virtutis ingenitae regem sibi Martium Geticus populus inveniret.'

We have only five letters written by Cassiodorus for Witigis (who reigned from August, 536, to May[3], 540). One has been already described. All the other four are concerned with negotiations for peace with Justinian, and may probably be referred to the early part of the new reign. *Letters written in name of Witigis.*

It will be seen that the letters written by Cassiodorus for the Sovereign during the five years following the death of Athalaric are few and somewhat unsatisfactory. *Share of Cassiodorus in the administration during the war.*

---

[1] The situation of this plain is unknown.
[2] Var. x. 31.
[3] We get this date only from Agnellus (loc. cit. p. 522).

But, on the other hand, it was just during these years that he wrote in his own name as Praetorian Praefect the letters which are comprised in the Eleventh and Twelfth Books of his collection, and which are in some respects the most interesting of the whole series. There is a strong probability that he was not present at the long siege of Rome (March, 537, to March, 538), nor is it likely that he, an elderly civilian, would take much part in any of the warlike operations that followed. Upon the whole, it seems probable that during the greater part of this time Cassiodorus was, to the best of his power, keeping the civil administration together by virtue of his own authority as Praetorian Praefect, without that constant reference to the wishes of the Sovereign which would have been necessary under Theodoric and his daughter. Perhaps, in the transitional state of things which then prevailed in Italy, with the power of the Gothic sceptre broken but the sway of the Roman Caesar not yet firmly established in its stead, men of all parties and both nationalities were willing that as much as possible of the routine of government should be carried on by a statesman who was Roman by birth and culture, but who had been the trusted counsellor of Gothic Kings.

Dates of later letters.

I have endeavoured as far as possible to fix the dates of these later letters. It will be seen that we have one[1] probably belonging to the year 536, five[2] to 537, and one[3] (possibly) to 538. These later letters refer chiefly to the terrible famine which followed in the train of the war, and of which Cassiodorus strenuously laboured to mitigate the severity.

End of Cassiodorus' official career.

It is possible that the Praefect may have continued to hold office down to the capture of Ravenna in May, 540, which made Witigis a prisoner, and seemed to bring the Ostrogothic monarchy to an end. Upon the whole,

---

[1] Var. xii. 20.   [2] Var. xii. 22, 23, 24, 27, 28.
[3] Var. xii. 25.

however, it is rather more probable that in the year 538 or 539 he finally retired from public life. The dates of his letters will show that there is nothing in them which forbids us to accept this conclusion; and the fact, if it be a fact, that in 540, when Belisarius, with his Secretary Procopius in his train, made his triumphal entry into Ravenna, the late Praefect was no longer there, but in his native Province of Bruttii, a little lessens the difficulty of that which still remains most difficult of comprehension, the entire omission from Procopius' History of the Gothic War of all mention of the name of Cassiodorus.

The closing years of the veteran statesman's tenure of office were years of some literary activity. It was in them that he was collecting, and to some extent probably revising, the letters which appear in the following collection. His motives for publishing this monument of his official life are sufficiently set forth in the two prefaces, one prefixed to the First Book and the other to the Eleventh. Much emphasis is laid on the entreaties of his friends, the regular excuse, in the sixth century as in the nineteenth, for an author or a politician doing the very thing which most pleases his own vanity. A worthier reason probably existed in the author's natural desire to vindicate his own consistency, by showing that the influence which for more than thirty years he had wielded in the councils of the Gothic Sovereigns had been uniformly exerted on the side of law and order and just government, directed equally to the repression of Teutonic barbarism and the punishment of Roman venality. *The Variae edited.*

The question how far the letters which now appear in the 'Variae' really reproduce the actual documents originally issued by Cassiodorus is one which has been a good deal discussed by scholars, but with no very definite result. It is, after all, a matter of conjecture; and every student who peruses the following letters is *What alterations were made in the letters.*

entitled to form his own conjecture—especially as to those marvellous digressions on matters of Natural History, Moral Philosophy, and the like—whether they were veritably included in the original letters that issued from the Royal Secretum, and were carried over Italy by the Cursus Publicus. My own conjecture is, that though they may have been a little amplified and elaborated, substantially they were to be found in those original documents. The age was pedantic and half-educated, and had lost both its poetic inspiration and its faculty of humour; and I fear that these marvellous letters were read by the officials to whom they were addressed with a kind of stolid admiration, provoking neither the smile of amusement nor the shrug of impatience which are their rightful meed.

'Illum atque Illum.'

The reader will observe that in many, in fact most of the letters, which were meant to serve as credentials to ambassadors or commissions to civil servants, no names are inserted, but we have instead only the tantalising formula, 'Illum atque Illum,' which I have generally translated, 'A and B.' This circumstance has also been much commented upon, but without our arriving at any very definite result. All that can be said is, that Cassiodorus must have formed his collection of State-papers either from rough drafts in his own possession, or from copies preserved in the public archives, and that, from whichsoever source he drew, the names in that source had not been preserved: a striking comment on the rhetorical unbusinesslike character of the Royal and Imperial Chanceries of that day, in which words were deemed of more importance than things, and the flowers of speech which were showered upon the performer of some piece of public business were preserved, while the name of the performer was forgotten.

Treatise 'De Animâ.'

As soon as he had finished the collection of the 'Variae,' the Praefect—again in obedience to the entreaties of his friends—composed a short philosophic treatise on the

Nature of the Soul ('De Animâ'). As he said, it seems an absurd thing to treat as a stranger and an unknown quantity the very centre of our being; to seek to understand the height of the air, the extent of the earth, the causes of storms and earthquakes, and the nature of the wandering winds, and yet to leave the faculty, by which we grasp all this knowledge, itself uncomprehended[1]. He therefore sets himself to enquire, in twelve chapters:

1. Why the Soul is called Anima?
2. What is the definition of the Soul?
3. What is its substantial quality?
4. If it is to be believed to have any shape?
5. What moral virtues it has which contribute to its glory and its adornment?
6. What are its natural virtues [or powers], given to enable it to hold together the framework of the body?
7. Concerning the origin of the Soul.
8. What is its especial seat, since it appears to be in a certain sense diffused over the whole body?
9. Concerning the form and composition of the body itself.
10. Sufficient signs by which we may discern what properties the souls of sinners possess.
11. Similar signs by which we may distinguish the souls of righteous men, since we cannot see them with our bodily eyes.
12. Concerning the Soul's state after death, and how it will be affected by the general resurrection.

---

[1] 'Cum jam suscepti operis optato fine gauderem, meque duodecim voluminibus jactatum quietis portus exciperet, ubi etsi non laudatus, certe liberatus adveneram, amicorum me suave collegium in salum rursus cogitationis expressit, postulans ut aliqua quae tam in libris sacris, quam in saecularibus abstrusa compereram de animae substantiâ, vel de ejus virtutibus aperirem, cui datum est tam ingentium rerum secreta reserare: addens nimis ineptum esse si eam per quam plura cognoscimus, quasi a nobis alienam ignorare patiamur, dum ad anima sit utile nosse qua sapimus' (De Animâ, Praefatio).

The treatise ends with a prayer to Christ to preserve the body in good health, that it may be in tune with the harmony of the soul; to give reason the ascendancy over the flesh; and to keep the mind in happy equipoise, neither so strong as to be puffed up with pride, nor so languid as to fail of its proper powers.

Cassiodorus retires to the cloister.

The line of thought indicated by the 'De Anima' led, in such a country as Italy, at such a time as the Gothic War, to one inevitable end—the cloister. It can have surprised none of the friends of Cassiodorus when the veteran statesman announced his intention of spending the remainder of his days in monastic retirement. He was now sixty years of age[1]; his wife, if he had ever married, was probably by this time dead; and we hear nothing of any children for whose sake he need have remained longer in the world. The Emperor would probably have received him gladly into his service, but Cassiodorus had now done with politics. The dream of his life had been to build up an independent Italian State, strong with the strength of the Goths, and wise with the wisdom of the Romans. That dream was now scattered to the winds. Providence had made it plain that not by this bridge was civilisation to pass over from the Old World to the New. Cassiodorus accepted the decision, and consecrated his old age to religious meditation and to a work even more important than any of his political labours (though one which must be lightly touched on here), the preservation by the pens of monastic copyists of the Christian Scriptures, and of the great works of classical antiquity.

He founds two monasteries at Scyllacium.

It was to his ancestral Scyllacium that Cassiodorus retired; and here, between the mountains of Aspromonte and the sea, he founded his monastery, or, more accurately, his two monasteries, one for the austere hermit, and the other for the less aspiring coenobite. The

---

[1] Fifty-eight, if the retirement was in 538.

former was situated among the 'sweet recesses of Mons Castellius[1],' the latter among the well-watered gardens which took their name from the Vivaria (fish-ponds) that Cassiodorus had constructed among them in connection with the river Pellena[2]. Baths, too, especially intended for the use of the sick, had been prepared on the banks of the stream[3]. Here in monastic simplicity, but not without comfort, Cassiodorus ordained that his monks should dwell. The Rule of the order—in so far as it had a written Rule—was drawn from the writings of Cassian, the great founder of Western Monachism, who had died about a century before the Vivarian monastery was founded. In commending the writings of Cassian to the study of his monks, Cassiodorus warns them against the bias shown in them towards the Semi-Pelagian heresy, and desires them to choose the good in those treatises and to refuse the evil. Whatever the reason may have been, it seems clear that Cassiodorus did not make the Rule of Benedict the law of his new monastery; and indeed, strange as the omission may appear, there is, I believe, no allusion to that great contemporary Saint, the 'Father of Monks,' in the whole of his writings.

[1] 'Nam si vos in monasterio Vivariensi divinâ gratia suffragante coenobiorum consuetudo competenter erudiat, et aliquid sublimius defaecatis animis optare contingat, habetis montis Castelli secreta suavia, ubi velut anachoritae (praestante Domino) feliciter esse possitis' (De Inst. Div. Litt. xxix.).

[2] 'Invitat vos locus Vivariensis monasterii ... quando habetis hortos irriguos, et piscosi amnis Pellenae fluenta vicina, qui nec magnitudine undarum suspectus habetur, nec exiguitate temnibilis. Influit vobis arte moderatus, ubicunque necessarius judicatur et hortis vestris sufficiens et molendinis.... Maria quoque vobis ita subjacent, ut piscationibus variis pateant; et captus piscis, cum libuerit, vivariis possit includi. Fecimus enim illic (juvante Deo) grata receptacula ubi sub claustro fideli vagetur piscium multitudo; ita consentanea montium speluncis, ut nullatenus se sentiat captum, cui libertas est escas sumere, et per solitas se cavernas abscondere.'

[3] 'Balnea quoque congruenter aegris praeparata corporibus jussimus aedificari, ubi fontium perspicuitas decenter illabitur, quae et potui gratissima cognoscitur et lavacris.'

Probably never Abbot.

Though the founder and patron of these two monasteries, it seems probable that Cassiodorus never formally assumed the office of Abbot in either of them[1]. He had probably still some duties to perform as a large landholder in Bruttii; but besides these he had also work to do for 'his monks' (as he affectionately called them)—work of a literary and educational kind—which perhaps made it undesirable that he should be burdened with the petty daily routine of an Abbot's duties. Some years before, he had endeavoured to induce Pope Agapetus[2] to found a School of Theology and Christian Literature at Rome, in imitation of the schools of Alexandria and Nisibis[3]. The clash of arms consequent on the invasion of Italy by Belisarius had prevented the fulfilment of this scheme; but the aged statesman now determined to devote the remainder of his days to the accomplishment of the same purpose in connection with the Vivarian convent.

In the earliest days of Monasticism men like the hermits of the Thebaid had thought of little else but mortifying the flesh by vigils and fastings, and withdrawing from all human voices to enjoy an ecstatic communion with their Maker. The life in common of monks like those of Nitria and Lerinum had chastened some of the extravagances of these lonely enthusiasts while still keeping their main ends in view.

---

[1] But the words of Trithemius (quoted by Migne, Patrologia lxix. 498), 'Hic post aliquot conversionis suae annos abbas electus est, et monasterio multo tempore utiliter praefuit,' *may* preserve a genuine and accurate tradition. Cassiodorus' mention of the two Abbots, Chalcedonius and Geruntius (De Inst. Div. Litt. cap. xxxii.) shows that at any rate in the infancy of his monasteries he was not Abbot of either of them.

[2] Agapetus was Pope in 535 and 536.

[3] 'Nisus sum ergo cum beatissimo Agapeto papa urbis Romae, ut sicut apud Alexandriam multo tempore fuisse traditur institutum, nunc etiam in Nisibi civitate Syrorum ab Hebraeis sedulo fertur exponi, collatis expensis in urbe Romana professos doctores scholae potius acciperent Christianae, unde et anima susciperet aeternam salutem, et casto atque purissimo eloquio fidelium lingua comeretur' (De Inst. Praefatio).

St. Jerome, in his cell at Bethlehem, had shown what great results might be obtained for the Church of all ages from the patient literary toil of one religious recluse. And finally St. Benedict, in that Rule of his which was to be the code of monastic Christendom for centuries, had sanctified Work as one of the most effectual preservatives of the bodily and spiritual health of the ascetic, bringing together *Laborare* and *Orare* in friendly union, and proclaiming anew for the monk as for the untonsured citizen the primal ordinance, 'In the sweat of thy brow thou shalt eat bread.'

The great merit of Cassiodorus, that which shows his deep insight into the needs of his age and entitles him to the eternal gratitude of Europe, was his determination to utilise the vast leisure of the convent for the preservation of Divine and human learning and for its transmission to after ages. In the miserable circumstances of the times Theology was in danger of becoming brutified and ignorant; the great treasures of Pagan literature were no longer being perpetuated by the slaves who had once acted as *librarii* to the Greek or Roman noble; and with every movement of the Ostrogothic armies, or of the yet more savage hordes who served under the Imperial standard, with every sacked city and with every ravaged villa, some Codex, it may be such as we should now deem priceless and irreplaceable, was perishing. This being the state of Italy, Cassiodorus resolved to make of his monastery not merely a place for pious meditation, but a theological school and a manufactory for the multiplication of copies, not only of the Scriptures, not only of the Fathers and the commentators on Scripture, but also of the great writers of pagan antiquity. In the chapter[1] which he devotes to the description of the *scriptorium* of his monastery he describes, with an enthusiasm which must have been con-

The father of literary Monasticism.

---

[1] The 30th of the De Institutione Div. Litt.

tagious, the noble work done there by the *antiquarius:* 'He may fill his mind with the Scriptures while copying the sayings of the Lord. With his fingers he gives life to men and arms them against the wiles of the devil. So many wounds does Satan receive as the *antiquarius* copies words of Christ. What he writes in his cell will be scattered far and wide over distant Provinces. Man multiplies the heavenly words, and by a striking figure—if I may dare so to speak— the three fingers of his hand express the utterances of the Holy Trinity. The fast-travelling reed writes down the holy words, and thus avenges the malice of the Wicked One, who caused a reed to be used to smite the head of the Saviour.'

It is true that the passage here quoted refers only to the work of the copyist of the Christian Scriptures, but it could easily be shown from other passages[1] that the literary activity of the monastery was not confined to these, but was also employed on secular literature.

Book-binding. Cassiodorus then goes on to describe the care which he has taken for the binding of the sacred Codices in covers worthy of the beauty of their contents, following the example of the householder in the parable, who provided wedding garments for all who came to the supper of his son. One pattern volume had been prepared, containing samples of various sorts of binding, that the amanuensis might choose that which pleased him best. *Mechanical appliances for the convent.* He had moreover provided, to help the nightly toil of the *scriptorium*, mechanical lamps of some wonderful construction, which appears to have made them self-trimming, and to have ensured their having always

---

[1] For instance, in cap. xv., after cautioning his copyists against rash corrections of apparent faults in the sacred MSS., he says: 'Ubicunque paragrammata in disertis hominibus [i. e. in classical authors] reperta fuerint, intrepidus vitiosa recorrigat.' And the greater part of cap. xxviii. is an argument against 'respuere saecularium litterarum studia.'

a sufficient supply of oil[1]. Sun-dials also for bright days, and water-clocks for cloudy days and the night-season, regulated their labour, and admonished them when it was time to unclose the three fingers, to lay down the reed, and to assemble with their brethren in the chapel of the convent for psalmody and prayer.

Upon the whole, though the idea of using the convent as a place of literary toil and theological training was not absolutely new, Cassiodorus seems certainly entitled to the praise of having first realised it systematically and on an extensive scale. It was entirely in harmony with the spirit of the Rule of St. Benedict, if it was not formally ordained in that document. At a very early date in the history of their order, the Benedictines, influenced probably by the example of the monastery of Vivaria, commenced that long series of services to the cause of literature which they have never wholly intermitted. Thus, instead of accepting the obsolete formula for which some scholars in the last age contended, 'Cassiodorus was a Benedictine,' we should perhaps be rather justified in maintaining that Benedict, or at least his immediate followers, were Cassiodorians. *Relation to the Benedictine Rule.*

In order to set an example of literary diligence to his monks, and to be able to sympathise with the difficulties of an amanuensis, Cassiodorus himself transcribed the Psalter, the Prophets, and the Epistles[2], no doubt from the translation of Jerome. This is not the place *Cassiodorus as a transcriber of the Scriptures.*

---

[1] Paravimus etiam nocturnis vigiliis mechanicas lucernas, conservatrices illuminantium flammarum, ipsas sibi nutrientes incendium, quae humano ministerio cessante, prolixe custodiant uberrimi luminis abundantissimam claritatem; ubi olei pinguedo non deficit, quamvis flammis ardentibus jugitor torreatur.

[2] 'In Psalterio et Prophetis et Epistolis apostolorum studium maximum laboris impendi. . . . Quos ego cunctos novem codices auctoritatis divinae (ut senex potui) sub collatione priscorum codicum amicis ante me legentibus, sedula lectione transivi' (De Inst. Praefatio). We should have expected 'tres' rather than 'novem,' as the Psalter, the Prophets, and the Epistles each formed one codex.

for enlarging on the merits of Cassiodorus as a custodian and transmitter of the sacred text. They were no doubt considerable; and the rules which he gives to his monks, to guide them in the work of transcription, show that he belonged to the Conservative school of critics, and was anxious to guard against hasty emendations of the text, however plausible. Practically, however, his MSS. of the Latin Scriptures, showing the Itala and the Vulgate in parallel columns, seem to have been answerable for some of that confusion between the two versions which to some extent spoiled the text of Jerome, without preserving to us in its purity the interesting translation of the earlier Church.

Besides his labours as a transcriber, Cassiodorus, both as an original author and a compiler, used his pen for the instruction of his fellow-inmates at Vivarium.

Commentary on the Psalms.

(1) He began and slowly completed a Commentary on the Psalms. This very diffuse performance (which occupies more than five hundred closely printed pages in Migne's edition) displays, in the opinion of those who have carefully studied it[1], a large amount of acquaintance with the writings of the Fathers, and was probably looked upon as a marvel of the human intellect by the Vivarian monks, for whose benefit it was composed, and to whom it revealed, in the Psalms which they were daily and nightly intoning, refutations of all the heresies that had ever racked the Church, and the rudiments of all the sciences that flourished in the world. It is impossible now for this or any future age to do aught but lament over so much wasted ingenuity, when we find the author maintaining that the whole of the one hundred and fifty Psalms were written by King David, and that Asaph, Heman, and Jeduthun have only a mystical meaning; that the first seventy represent the Old Testament, and the last eighty the New, because we celebrate the Resurrection of Christ

---

[1] I take my account of this treatise chiefly from Franz (pp. 93–100).

on the eighth day of the week, and so forth. A closer study of the book might perhaps discover in it some genuine additions to the sum of human knowledge; but it is difficult to repress a murmur at the misdirected industry which has preserved to us the whole of this ponderous futility, while it has allowed the History of the Goths to perish.

(2) The 'Complexiones in Epistolas Apostolorum' (first published by Maffei in 1721, from a MS. discovered by him at Verona) have at least the merit of being far shorter than the Commentary on the Psalms. Perhaps the only points of interest in them, even for theological scholars, are that Cassiodorus evidently attributes the Epistle to the Hebrews without hesitation to the Apostle Paul, and that he notices the celebrated passage concerning the Three Heavenly Witnesses (1 John v. 7) in a way which seems to imply that he found that passage in the text of the Vulgate, though on examination his language is seen to be consistent with the theory that these words are a gloss added by the commentator himself.

Commentary on the Epistles.

(3) In order to supply the want of any full Church History in the Latin tongue, a want which was probably felt not only by his own monks but throughout the Churches of the West, Cassiodorus induced his friend Epiphanius to translate from the Greek the ecclesiastical histories of Socrates, Sozomen, and Theodoret, and then himself fused these three narratives into one, the well-known 'Historia Tripartita,' which contains the story of the Church's fortunes from the accession of Constantine to the thirty-second year of the reign of Theodosius II (306–439). The fact that the numerous mistranslations of Epiphanius have passed uncorrected, probably indicates that Cassiodorus' own knowledge of Greek was but slight, and that he depended on his coadjutor entirely

Historia Tripartita.

for this part of the work. The 'Historia Tripartita' has probably had a larger circulation than any other of its author's works; but Cassiodorus himself thought so little of his share in it, that he does not include it in the list of his writings prefixed to the treatise 'De Orthographiâ.' And, in fact, the inartistic way in which the three narratives are soldered together, rather than recast into one symmetrical and harmonious whole, obliges us to admit that Cassiodorus' work at this book was little more than mechanical, and entitles him to scarcely any other praise than that of industry.

Institutiones Divinarum et Humanarum Lectionum.

(4) Of a different quality, though still partaking somewhat of the nature of a compilation, was his chief educational treatise, the 'Institutiones Divinarum et Humanarum Lectionum[1].' About the year 543, some three or four years after his retirement from public life, while he was slowly ploughing his way through the Commentary on the Psalms, twenty of which he had already interpreted, he seems to have laid it aside for a time in order to devote himself to this work, which aimed more at instruction than at religious edification. In the outset of this book he describes that unsuccessful attempt of his, to which allusion has already been made, for the establishment of a theological school in Rome, and continues that, 'as the rage of war and the turbulence of strife in the Italian realm[2] had prevented the fulfilment of this desire, he felt himself constrained by Divine charity to write for his monks' behoof these *libri introductorii*, in which, after the manner of a teacher, he would open to them the series

---

[1] Printed hitherto as two works, De Institutione Divinarum Litterarum, and De Artibus ac Disciplinis Liberalium Litterarum. But, as Ebert has shown (i. 477), the Preface to the Orthographia makes it probable that these two really formed one book, with a title like that given above.

[2] 'In Italico regno.' These words seem to favour the conjecture that Theodoric may have called himself King of Italy.

of the books of Holy Scripture, and would give them a compendious acquaintance with secular literature.' As the book is not written for the learned, he undertakes to abstain from 'affectata eloquentia,' and he does in the main keep his promise. The simple, straightforward style of the book, which occasionally rises into real and 'unaffected eloquence' where the subject inspires him to make an appeal to the hearts of his readers, presents a striking and favourable contrast to the obscure and turgid phraseology in which the perverted taste of the times caused him generally to shroud his meaning[1].

In the first part of this treatise (commonly called the 'De Institutione Divinarum Litterarum') Cassiodorus briefly describes the contents of the nine Codices[2] which made up the Scripture of the Old and New Testaments, and mentions the names of the chief commentators upon

---

[1] As a specimen of this better style of Cassiodorus, I may refer to his praises of the life of the literary monk, and his exhortation to him who is of duller brain to practise gardening: 'Quapropter toto nisu, toto labore, totis desideriis exquiramus ut ad tale tantumque munus, Domino largiente, pervenire mereamur. Hoc enim nobis est salutare, proficuum, gloriosum, perpetuum, quod nulla mors, nulla mobilitas, nulla possit separare oblivio; sed in illa suavitate patriae, cum Domino faciet aeterna exsultatione gaudere Quod si alicui fratrum, ut meminit Virgilius,

"Frigidus obstiterit circum praecordia sanguis,"

ut nec humanis nec divinis litteris perfecte possit erudiri, aliqua tamen scientiae mediocritate suffultus, eligat certe quod sequitur,

"Rura mihi et rigui placeant in vallibus amnes."

Quia nec ipsum est a monachis alienum hortos colere, agros exercere, et pomorum fecunditate gratulari; legitur enim in Psalmo centesimo vigesimo septimo, "Labores manuum tuarum manducabis; beatus es et bene ti erit."'

[2] 1. Octateuchus (Pentateuch, Joshua, Judges, Ruth).
2. Kings (Samuel and Kings, Chronicles).
3. Prophets (Four Major, including Daniel, and Twelve Minor).
4. Psalms.
5. Solomon (Proverbs, Ecclesiastes, Canticles, Wisdom, Ecclesiasticus).
6. Hagiographa (Tobias, Esther, Judith, Maccabees, Esdras).
7. Gospels.
8. Epistles of the Apostles (including that to the Hebrews).
9. Acts of the Apostles and Apocalypse.

each. After some important cautions as to the preservation of the purity of the sacred text and abstinence from plausible emendations, the author proceeds to enumerate the Christian historians—Eusebius, Orosius, Marcellinus, Prosper, and others[1]; and he then slightly sketches the characters of some of the principal Fathers—Hilary, Cyprian, Ambrose, Jerome, and Augustine. This part of the work contains an interesting allusion to 'Dionysius Monachus, Scytha natione, sed moribus omnino Romanus,' of whom Cassiodorus speaks as a colleague in his literary enterprises. This is the so-called Dionysius Exiguus, who fixed (erroneously, as it now appears) the era of the birth of Christ, and whose system of chronology founded on this event has been accepted by all the nations of Christendom. At the conclusion of this the first part of the treatise we find some general remarks on the nature of the monastic life, and some pictures of Vivarium and its neighbourhood, to which we are indebted for some of the information contained in the preceding pages. The book ends with a prayer, and contains thirty-three chapters, the same number, remarks Cassiodorus (who is addicted to this kind of moralising on numbers) that was reached by the years of the life of Christ on earth.

The second part of the treatise, commonly called 'De Artibus ac Disciplinis Liberalium Litterarum,' contains so much as the author thought that every monk should be acquainted with concerning the four liberal arts—Grammar, Rhetoric, Logic, Mathematics—the last

---

[1] The remarks on Marcellinus Comes and Prosper are worth transcribing: 'Hunc [Eusebium] subsecutus est suprascriptus Marcellinus Illyricianus, qui adhuc patricii Justiniani fertur egisse cancellos; sed meliore conditione devotus, a tempore Theodosii principis usque ad finem imperii triumphalis Augusti Justiniani opus suum, Domino juvante, perduxit; ut qui ante fuit in obsequio suscepto gratus, postea ipsius imperio copiose amantissimus appareret.' [The allusion to 'finem imperii Justiniani' was probably added in a later revision of the Institutiones.] 'Sanctus quoque Prosper Chronica ab Adam ad Genserici tempora et urbis Romae depraedationem usque perduxit.'

of which is divided into the four 'disciplines' of Arithmetic, Geometry, Music, and Astronomy. As illustrating the relative importance of these sciences (as we call them) as apprehended by Cassiodorus, it is curious to observe that while Geometry and Astronomy occupy only about one page, and Arithmetic and Music two pages each, Logic takes up eighteen pages, Grammar two, and Rhetoric six.

(5) Some other works, chiefly of a grammatical kind[1], which have now perished, together with the exegetical treatises already named, occupied the leisure hours of the old age of Cassiodorus. At length, in the ninety-third year of his age, the veteran statesman, nobleman, and judge crowned his life of useful service by writing for his beloved monks his still extant treatise 'De Orthographia[2].' He tells us that the monks suddenly exclaimed, 'What doth it profit us to study either those works which the ancients have composed or those which your Wisdom has caused to be added to the list, if we are altogether ignorant how we ought to write these things, and on the other hand cannot understand and accurately represent in speech the words which we find written?' In other words, 'Give us a treatise on spelling.' The venerable teacher gladly complied with the request, and compiled from twelve grammarians[3] various rules, the observance of which would prevent the student from committing the usual faults in spelling.

De Orthographia.

---

[1] They were a compilation from the 'Artes' of Donatus, from a book on Etymologies (perhaps also by Donatus), and from a treatise by Sacerdos on Schemata; and a short Table of Contents of the Books of Scripture, prepared in such a form as to be easily committed to memory.

[2] Ad amantissimos orthographos discutiendos anno aetatis meae nonagesimo tertio (Domino adjuvante) perveni.

[3] They were Donatus, Cn. Cornutus, Velius Longus, Curtius Valerianus, Papirianus, Adamantius Martyrius, Eutiches, Caesellius, Lucius Caecilius, and 'Priscianus grammaticus, qui nostro tempore Constantinopoli doctor fuit.' Two names seem to be omitted by Cassiodorus.

It is no doubt true[1] that this work is a mere collection of excerpts from other authors, not arranged on any systematic principle. Still, even as such a collection, it does great credit to the industry of a nonagenarian; and it seems to me that there is much in it which a person who was studying the transition of Latin into the Lingua Volgare might peruse with profit. To an epigraphist especially it must be interesting to see what were the mistakes which an imperfectly educated Italian in that age was most likely to commit. The confusion between *b* and *v* was evidently a great source of error, and their nice discrimination, to which Cassiodorus devotes four chapters, a very *crux* of accurate scholarship. We see also from a passage in the 'De Institutione Divinarum Litterarum[2]' that the practice of assimilating the last letter of the prefix in compound words, like i*l*luminatio, i*r*risio, i*m*probus, though it had been introduced, was as yet hardly universal; and similarly that the monks required to be instructed to write quicquam for euphony, instead of qui*d*quam.

Death of Cassiodorus, 575 (?).

The treatise 'De Orthographia' was the last product, as far as we know, of the industrious brain of Cassiodorus. Two years after its composition the aged statesman and scholar, in the ninety-sixth year of his age, entered into his well-earned rest[3]. The death of Cassiodorus occurred (as I believe) in the year 575, three years before the death of the Emperor Justin II, nephew and successor of Justinian. The period covered by his life had been one of vast changes. Born when the Kingdom of Odovacar was only four years old, he

---

[1] As stated by Ebert (p. 481).

[2] Cap. xv.

[3] In assigning the death of Cassiodorus to the ninety-sixth year of his age I rest upon the authority of Trittheim (as quoted in the earlier part of this chapter), who appears to me to have preserved the chronology which was generally accepted, before the question became entangled by the confusion between Cassiodorus and his father.

had as a young man seen that Kingdom overthrown by the arms of Theodoric; he had sat by the cradle of the Ostrogothic monarchy, and mourned over its grave; had seen the eunuch Narses supreme vicegerent of the Emperor; had heard the avalanche of the Lombard invasion thunder over Italy, and had outlived even the Lombard invader Alboin. Pope Leo, the tamer of Attila and the hero of Chalcedon, had not been dead twenty years when Cassiodorus was born. Pope Gregory the Great, the converter of England, was within fifteen years of his accession to the Pontificate when Cassiodorus died. The first great schism between the Eastern and Western Churches was begun in his boyhood and ended before he had reached old age. He saw the irretrievable ruin of Rome, such as Augustus and Trajan had known her; the extinction of the Roman Senate; the practical abolition of the Consulate; the close of the schools of philosophy at Athens.

Reverting to the line of thought with which this chapter opened, if one were asked to specify any single life which more than another was in contact both with the Ancient World and the Modern, none could be more suitably named than the life of Cassiodorus.

NOTE ON THE TOPOGRAPHY OF SQUILLACE.

THE chief conclusions which Mr. Evans came to after his two days' study of the country about Squillace are these:—

Position of Scylacium.

I. The Scylacium or Scolacium of Roman times, the city of Cassiodorus, is not to be looked for at the modern Squillace, but at the place called Roccella in the Italian military map, which Lenormant and Evans know as *La Roccelletta del Vescovo di Squillace*.

This place, which is about ten kilometres north-east of modern Squillace, is on a little hill immediately overhanging the sea, while Squillace is on a spur of the Apennines three or four miles distant from the sea. Mr. Evans' chief reasons for identifying Roccella with Scylacium are (1) its position, 'hanging like a cluster of grapes on hills not so high as to make the ascent of them a weariness, but high enough to command a delightful prospect over land and sea.' This description by Cassiodorus exactly suits Roccella, but does not suit Squillace, which is at the top of a conical hill, and is reached only by a very toilsome ascent. 'With its gradual southern and eastern slope and its freedom from overlooking heights (different in this respect from Squillace),' says Mr. Evans, 'Roccella was emphatically, as Cassiodorus describes it, "a city of the sun."'

(2) Its ruins. While no remains of a pre-mediaeval time have been discovered at Squillace, there is still standing at Roccella the shell of a splendid basilica, of which Mr. Evans has taken some plans and sketches, but which seems to have strangely escaped the notice of most preceding travellers. The total length of this building is 94 paces, the width of the nave 30, the extreme width of the transept 54. It has three fine apses at the eastern end, and is built in the form of a Latin cross. On either side of the nave was an exterior arcade, which apparently consisted originally of eleven window arches, six of them not being for the transmission of light. 'Altogether,' says Mr. Evans, 'this church, even in its dilapidated state, is one of the finest monuments of the kind anywhere existing. We

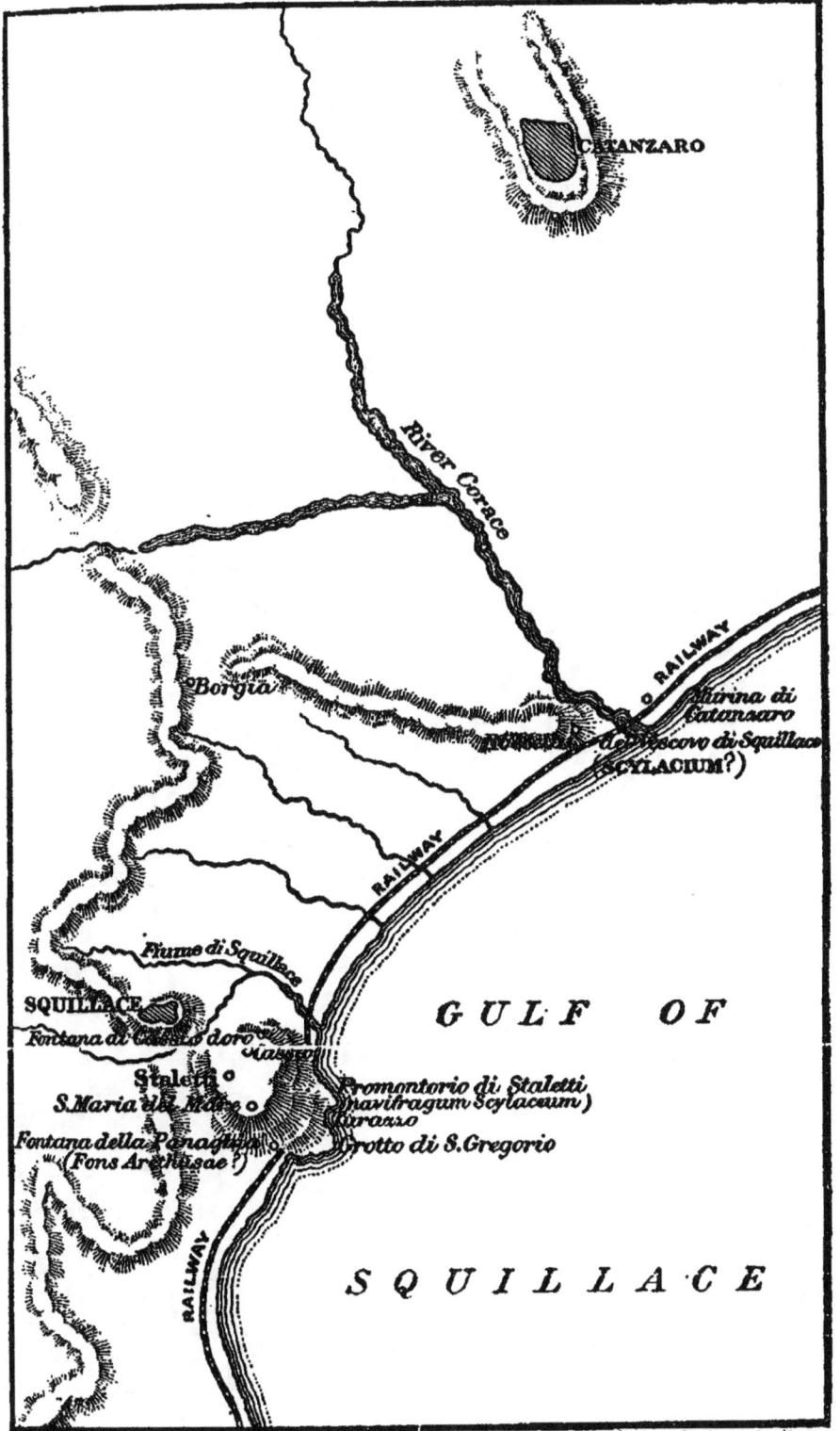

should have to go to Rome, to Ravenna, or to Thessalonica, to find its parallel; but I doubt whether, even at any of those places, there is to be seen a basilica with such fine exterior arcading. It is a great tribute to the strength of the original fabric that so much should have survived the repeated shocks of earthquake that have desolated Calabria, and scarcely left one stone upon another of her ancient cities.'

After a careful examination of the architectural peculiarities of this basilica, Mr. Evans is disposed to fix its erection somewhere about the time of the Emperor Justinian.

In addition to this fine building there are at Roccella the ruins of two smaller late Roman churches, mausolea, and endless foundations of buildings which must have formed very extensive suburbs.

More important than all, the massive walls of a considerable city can still be traced for nearly a mile in two parallel lines, with the transverse wall which unites them. Certainly all these indications seem to point to the existence at this spot of a great provincial city of the Empire, and to make Mr. Evans' conjecture more probable than that of M. Lenormant, who identified the ruins at Roccella with those of Castra Hannibalis, the seaport of Scylacium. It would seem probable, if Mr. Evans' theory be correct, that the city may have been removed to its present site in the early middle ages, in order to guard it against the incursions of the Saracens.

II. As to the situation of the *Vivarian Monastery* Mr. Evans comes to nearly the same conclusion as M. Lenormant. Both place it on the promontory of Squillace (eastward of Staletti), and, as Mr. Evans observes, 'only such a position can be reconciled, on the one hand, with the presence of an abundant stream and rich Campagna, on the other with the neighbourhood of caves and grottoes on the sea-shore.' But while M. Lenormant places it at a place called Coscia, almost immediately to the north of and under Staletti, Mr. Evans pleads for the site now occupied by the Church of S. Maria del Mare, on the cliff top, very near the sea, and about three kilometres south of Staletti. This church is itself of later date than Cassiodorus, and probably formed part of the work of restoration undertaken by Nicephorus Phocas in the Tenth Century; but there are signs of its having formerly joined on to a monastery, and some of the work about it looks as if materials taken from the Cassiodorian edifice had been used in the work of reconstruction.

The Fons Arethusae. III. The *Fountain of Arethusa* may possibly, according to Mr. Evans, be identified with the Fontana della Panaghia, a small fountain by the sea-shore at the south end of a little bay under the promontory of S. Gregorio. The so-called Fontana di Cassiodoro, near Coscia, has received its name and its present appearance in modern times, and is much too far from the sea to be the Fountain of Arethusa.

CHAPTER II.

THE ANECDOTON HOLDERI.

A FEW pages must be devoted to the MS. bearing the somewhat uncouth title of 'Anecdoton Holderi,' because it is the most recently opened source of information as to the life and works of Cassiodorus, and one which, if genuine, settles some questions which have been long and vigorously debated among scholars.

My information on the subject is derived from a pamphlet of 79 pages by Hermann Usener, printed at Bonn in 1877, and bearing the title 'Anecdoton Holderi: Ein Beitrag zur Geschichte Roms in Ostgothischer Zeit.' I am indebted to Mr. Bywater, of Exeter College, Oxford, for my introduction to this pamphlet, which, while strikingly confirming some conclusions which I had come to from my own independent study of the 'Variae,' has been of the greatest possible service to me in studying the lives of Cassiodorus and Boethius.

The 'Anecdoton' (which loses its right to that name by Usener's publication of it) was discovered by Alfred Holder in a MS. known as Codex Augiensis, No. CVI, which came from the Monastery of Reichenau and is now in the Grand-Ducal Library at Carlsruhe. The monks of the fertile island of Reichenau (Augia Dives), in the Lake of Constance, were celebrated in the ninth and tenth centuries for their zeal in the collection and transcription of manuscripts. The well-known Codex Augiensis (an uncial MS. of the Greek text of the New Testament, with the Vulgate version in parallel columns)

Description of the MS.

is referred by palaeographers to the ninth century[1]. The Codex Augiensis with which we are now concerned, and which is a copy of the 'Institutiones Humanarum Rerum' of Cassiodorus, is believed to have been written in the next succeeding century. On the last page of this MS. Holder discovered the fragment—not properly belonging to the 'Institutiones'—to which he has given his name, and which is as follows[2]:—

<small>Contents of the Anecdoton Holderi.</small>

'Excerpta ex libello Cassiodori Senatoris monachi servi Dei, ex-Patricio, ex-Consule Ordinario Quaestore et Magistro Officiorum, quem scripsit ad Rufum Petronium Nicomachum ex-Consule Ordinario Patricium et Magistrum Officiorum. Ordo generis Cassiodororum[3]: qui scriptores exstiterint ex eorum progenie vel ex civibus[4] eruditis.

'Symmachus Patricius et Consul Ordinarius, vir philosophus, qui antiqui Catonis fuit novellus imitator, sed virtutes veterum sanctissima religione transcendit. Dixit sententiam pro allecticiis in Senatu, parentesque suos imitatus historiam quoque Romanam septem libris edidit.

'Boethius dignitatibus summis excelluit. Utraque lingua peritissimus orator fuit. Qui regem Theodorichum in Senatu pro Consulatu filiorum luculenta oratione laudavit. Scripsit librum de Sancta Trinitate et capita quaedam dogmatica et librum contra Nestorium. Condidit et carmen bucolicum. Sed in opere artis logicae, id est dialecticae, trans-

---

[1] See Scrivener, Plain Introduction to the Criticism of the New Testament, pp. 133-4.

[2] I have adopted the emendations—most of them the corrections of obvious mistakes—which are suggested by Usener.

[3] In the original, 'Casiodorū.'

[4] In the original, 'ex quibus.'

ferendo ac mathematicis disciplinis talis fuit ut antiquos auctores aut aequiperaret aut vinceret.

'Cassiodorus Senator, vir eruditissimus et multis dignitatibus pollens. Juvenis adeo, dum patris Cassiodori Patricii et Praefecti Praetorii Consiliarius fieret et laudes Theodorichi regis Gothorum facundissime recitasset, ab eo Quaestor est factus. Patricius et Consul Ordinarius, postmodum dehinc Magister Officiorum [et praefuisset formulas dictionum, quas in duodecim libris ordinavit et Variarum titulum superposuit] scripsit praecipiente Theodoricho rege historiam Gothicam, originem eorum et loca moresque XII libris annuntians.'

This memorandum, for it is hardly more, is a vestige, and the only vestige now remaining, of a short tract by Cassiodorus on the literary history of his family and kinsmen. The 'Excerpta' have been made by some later hand—perhaps that of a monk in the Vivarian convent. To him undoubtedly we owe the words 'monachi servi Dei' as a description of Cassiodorus; probably also the 'ex-Patricio,' which is perhaps an incorrect designation. 'Vir eruditissimus,' in the last paragraph, is probably due to the same hand, as, with all his willingness to do justice to his own good qualities, Cassiodorus would hardly have spoken thus of himself in a work avowedly proceeding from his own pen. The clause which is placed in brackets [et ... superposuit] is probably also due to the copyist, anxious to supply what he deemed the imperfections of his memorandum. In short, it must be admitted that the fragment cannot consist of the very words of Cassiodorus in however abbreviated a form. Still it contains so much that is valuable, and that could hardly have been invented by any writer of a post-Cassiodorian age, that it is well worthy of the careful and, so

Date of the fragment.

to speak, microscopical examination to which it has been subjected by Usener.

The work from which these 'Excerpta' are taken was composed, according to Usener, in the year 522. This is proved by the facts that the receiver of the letter is spoken of as Magister Officiorum, a post which he apparently held from Sept. 1, 521, to Sept. 1, 522; and that the Consulship of the two sons of Boethius, which began on Jan. 1, 522, is also referred to. The name of the person to whom the letter is addressed is given as Rufius Petronius Nicomachus. Usener, however, shows good reason for thinking that his final name, the name by which he was known in the consular lists, is omitted, and that his full designation was Rufius Petronius Nicomachus Cethegus, Consul in 504, Magister Officiorum (as above stated) in 521–522, and Patrician. He was probably the same Cethegus whom Procopius mentions[1] as Princeps Senatus, and as withdrawing from Rome to Centumcellae in the year 545 because he was accused of treachery to the Imperial cause[2].

Persons to whom addressed.

Its object.

The object of the little treatise referred to evidently was to give an account of those members of the family to which Cassiodorus belonged who had distinguished themselves in literature. The words 'Ex genere Cassiodororum' are perhaps a gloss of the transcribers. At least it does not appear that they would correctly describe the descent of Symmachus and Boethius, though they were relations of Cassiodorus, being de-

---

[1] De Bello Gotthico iii. 13 (p. 328, ed. Bonn).

[2] If Usener be right (and he has worked up this point with great care), we can trace the following links in the pedigree of Cethegus (see pp. 6 and 11):

Rufius Petronius *Placidus*, Consul 481.
|
Rufius Petronius Anicius *Probinus*, Consul 489.
|
Rufius Petronius Nicomachus *Cethegus*, Consul 504, correspondent of Cassiodorus.

Probinus and Cethegus are referred to by Ennodius in his letter to Ambrosius and Beatus, otherwise called his Paraenesis (p. 409, ed. Hartel).

scended from or allied to the great house of the Aurelii from which he also sprang. Probably several other names may have been noticed in the original treatise, but the only three as to which the 'Anecdoton' informs us are the three as to whom information is most acceptable—Symmachus, Boethius, and Cassiodorus himself.

I. The name of Q. Aurelius Memmius *Symmachus* was already known to us as that of the friend, guardian, and father-in-law of Boethius, and his fellow-sufferer from the outburst of suspicious rage which disgraced the last years of Theodoric. That he was Consul in 485 (under the dominion of Odovacar), and that he had at the time of his fall attained the honoured position of Father of the Senate [1], we also know from the 'Consular Fasti' and the 'Anonymus Valesii.' This extract tells us that he had attained the rank of Patricius, which may perhaps have been bestowed upon him when he laid down the Consulship. He was 'a philosopher, and a modern imitator of the ancient Cato; but surpassed the virtues of the men of old by [his devotion to] our most holy religion.' This sentence quite accords with all that we hear of the character of Symmachus from our other authorities—the 'Anonymus Valesii,' Procopius, and Boethius. The blending of old Roman gravity and Christian piety in such a man's disposition is happily indicated in the words before us. It would be an interesting commentary upon them if we were to contrast the career of the Christian Symmachus, who suffered in some sense as a martyr for the Nicene Creed under Theodoric, with that of his ancestor the Pagan Symmachus, who, 143 years before, incurred the anger of Gratian by his protests against the removal of the

Information as to life of Symmachus.

---

[1] Caput Senati. This, not Caput Senatus, is the form which we find in Anon. Valesii. Usener suggests (p. 32) that Symmachus probably became Caput Senati on the death of Festus, who had held that position from 501 to 506.

Altar of Victory from the Senate House, and the curtailment of the grant to the Vestal Virgins.

The Symmachus with whom we are now concerned was also an orator; and we learn from this extract that he delivered a speech, evidently of some importance, in the Senate, 'pro allecticiis.' There seems much probability in Usener's contention that these 'allecticii' were men who had been 'allecti,' or admitted by co-optation into the Senate during the reign of Odovacar, and whom, on the downfall of that ruler, it had been proposed to strip of their recently acquired dignity—a proposal which seems to have been successfully resisted by Symmachus and his friends.

Lastly, we learn that Symmachus, 'in imitation of his ancestors,' put forth a Roman History in seven books. The expression for ancestors (parentes) here used is thought by Usener to refer chiefly to Virius Nicomachus Flavianus (Consul in 394[1]), whose granddaughter married Q. Fabius Memmius Symmachus, and was the grandmother of our Symmachus. This Flavianus, who was in his time one of the chief leaders of the heathen party in the Senate, is spoken of in one inscription as 'historicus disertissimus;' and in another, mention is made of the fact that he dedicated his annals to Theodosius.

Whether the elder Symmachus, the Pagan champion, was a historian as well as an orator is a matter about which there is a good deal of doubt. Jordanes twice quotes 'The History of Symmachus,' once as to the elevation of the Emperor Maximin, and once as to his death[2]. Usener thinks that the 'Anecdoton Holderi' authorises us henceforward to assign these quotations without doubt to the younger, Christian Symmachus,

---

[1] See Usener, p. 29. The Consules Ordinarii for that year were Arcadius and Honorius.

[2] Jordanis, Getica xv.: 'Nam, ut dicit Symmachus in quinto suae historiae libro, Maximinus ... ab exercitus effectus est imperator.' 'Occisus Aquileia a Puppione regnum reliquit Philippo; quod nos huic nostro opusculo de Symmachi hystoria [sic] mutuavimus.'

not to his Pagan ancestor. To me the allusion to *parentes* (in the plural), whose industry as historians the Symmachus there spoken of imitated, seems to make it at least as probable that the earlier, not the later member of the family composed the history which is here quoted by Jordanes.

II. We now pass on to consider the information furnished by this fragment as to the illustrious son-in-law of Symmachus, Anicius Manlius Severinus *Boethius*. Of the facts of his life we had already pretty full information, from the autobiographical sections of the 'Consolation of Philosophy' and other sources. He does not indeed mention the exact year of his birth, but the allusion to 'untimely gray hairs' which he makes in that work, written in 523 or 524, together with other indications[1] as to his age, entitle us to fix it at about 480, certainly not earlier than that year. The death of his father (who was Consul in 487) occurred while he was still a child. Symmachus, as has been already said, was the guardian of his youth and the friend of his manhood, and gave him his daughter Rusticiana to wife. That he received the honour of the Consulship in 510 we know from the 'Fasti Consulares;' but it is perplexing to find him even before that year spoken of[2] as Patricius, since this honour was generally bestowed only on those who had already sat in the curule chair of the Consul[3]. The high consideration in which he was held at the Court of Theodoric, and the value placed upon his scientific attainments, are sufficiently proved by the letters in the following collec-

Information as to life of Boethius.

---

[1] Chiefly derived from the Paraenesis of Ennodius (Opusc. vi.).

[2] In the Paraenesis.

[3] Usener's suggestion (pp. 38, 39) that he obtained this honour in consequence of having filled the place of *Comes Sacrarum Largitionum* seems to me only to land us in the further difficulty caused by the entire omission of all allusion to this fact both in the Paraenesis and in the Anecdoton Holderi.

tion, especially by those in which he is consulted about the frauds committed by the officers of the Mint, about the water-clock which is to be sent to Gundobad King of the Burgundians, and the harper who is to be provided for the King of the Franks[1]. In the year 522 his two sons, Symmachus and Boethius, though they had but just attained to man's estate, received the honour of the Consulship, upon which occasion the proud and happy father pronounced a panegyric upon Theodoric before the assembled Senate. Some of these facts in the life of Boethius are referred to in the extract before us, which, as was before said, appears to be taken from a treatise composed in this same year 522, the year of the Consulship of the young Boethii. Of their father's investiture with the office of *Magister Officiorum* on September 1, 522, of his sudden fall from the royal favour, of the charge of treason which was preferred against him before the end of that year, of his imprisonment during 523 and execution (probably in the early part of 524), we have of course no trace in this extract; and the fact that we have none is a strong argument for the genuineness and contemporary character of the treatise from which it is taken.

His theological treatises.
So far, then, we have in the 'Anecdoton Holderi' only a somewhat meagre reiteration of facts already known to us. But when we come to the statement of the literary labours of Boethius the case is entirely altered. It is well known that in the Middle Ages certain treatises on disputed points of Christian theology were attributed to him as their author. They are:—

1. A treatise 'De Sancta Trinitate.'
2. 'Ad Johannem Diaconum: Utrum Pater et Filius et Spiritus Sanctus de Divinitate substantialiter praedicentur.'
3. 'Ad eundem: Quomodo substantiae in eo quod sint bonae sint cum non sint substantialia bona.'

---

[1] See Var. i. 10 and 45; ii. 40.

4. 'De Fide Catholica.'
5. 'Contra Eutychen et Nestorium.'

It may be said at once that in the earlier MSS. the fourth treatise is not attributed to Boethius. It seems to have been included with the others by some mistake, and I shall therefore in the following remarks assume that it is not his, and shall confine my attention to the first three and the fifth.

Even as to these, notwithstanding the nearly unanimous voice of the early Middle Ages (as represented by MSS. of the Ninth, Tenth, and Eleventh Centuries) assigning them to Boethius as their author, scholars, especially recent scholars, have felt the gravest possible doubts of their being really his, doubts which have of late ripened into an almost complete certainty that he was not their author. The difficulty does not arise from anything in the diction or in the theology which points to a later age as the time of their composition, but from the startling contrast which they present to the religious atmosphere of the 'Consolation of Philosophy.' Here, in these theological treatises, we have the author entering cheerfully into the most abstruse points of the controversy concerning the Nature of Christ, without apparently one wavering thought as to the Deity of the Son of Mary. There, in the 'Consolation,' a book written in prison and in disgrace, with death at the executioner's hands impending over him—a book in which above all others we should have expected a man possessing the Christian faith to dwell upon the promises of Christianity—the name of Christ is never once mentioned, the tone, though religious and reverential, is that of a Theist only; and from beginning to end, except one or two sentences in which an obscure allusion may possibly be detected to the Christian revelation, there is nothing which might not have been written by a Greek philosopher ignorant of the very name of Christianity. Of the various attempts which

Difficulty as to religious position of Boethius.

have been made to solve this riddle perhaps the most ingenious is that of M. Charles Jourdain, who, in a monograph devoted to the subject [1], seeks to prove that the author of the theological treatises referred to was a certain Boethus, an African Bishop of the Byzacene Province, who was banished to Sardinia about the year 504 by the Vandal King Thrasamond.

Not thus, however, as it now appears, is the knot to be cut. And after all, M. Jourdain, in arguing, as he seems disposed to argue, against any external profession of Christianity on the part of Boethius, introduces contradictions greater than any that his theory would remove. To any person acquainted with the thoughts and words of the little coterie of Roman nobles to which Boethius belonged, it will seem absolutely impossible that the son-in-law of Symmachus, the receiver of the praises of Ennodius and Cassiodorus, should have been a professed votary of the old Paganism. It is not the theological treatises coming from a man in his position which are hard to account for; it is the apparently non-Christian tone of the 'Consolation.'

The fragment now before us shows that the old-fashioned belief in Boethius as a theologian was well founded. 'He wrote a book concerning the Holy Trinity, and certain dogmatic chapters, and a book against Nestorius.' That is a sufficiently accurate *resumé* of the four theological treatises enumerated above. Here Usener also observes—and I am inclined to agree with him—that there is a certain resemblance between the style of thought of these treatises and that of the 'Consolation' itself. They are, after all, philosophical rather than religious; one of the earliest samples of that kind of logical discussion of theological dogmas which the Schoolmen of the Middle Ages so delighted to indulge in. The young philosopher, hearing at his father-in-law's table the discussions between Chalce-

[1] De l'Origine des Traditions sur le Christianisme de Boèce (Paris, 1861.)

donian and Monophysite with which all Rome resounded, on account of the prolonged strife with the Church of Constantinople, set himself down to discuss the same topics which they were wrangling over by the light—to him so clear and precious—of the Greek philosophy. There was perhaps in this employment neither reverence nor irreverence. He had not St. Augustine's intense and almost passionate conviction of the truth of Christianity; but he was quite willing to accept it and to discourse upon it, as he discoursed on Arithmetic, Music, and Geometry.

But when premature old age, solitude, and the loss of liberty befell him, it was not to the highly elaborated Christian theology of the Sixth Century that he turned for support and consolation. Probably enough the very fact that he knew some of the pitfalls in the way deterred him from that dangerous journey, where the slightest deviation on either side landed him in some detested heresy, the heresy of Nestorius or of Eutyches. 'On revient toujours à ses premiers amours;' and even so Boethius, though undoubtedly professing himself a Christian, and about to die in full communion with the Catholic Church, turned for comfort in his dungeon to the philosophical studies of his youth, especially to the ethical writings of Plato and Aristotle.

After all, the title of the treatise is '*Philosophiae Consolatio*;' and however vigorous a literature of philosophy may in the course of centuries have grown up in the Christian domain, in the sixth century the remembrance of the old opposition between Christianity and Philosophy was perhaps still too strong for a writer to do anything more than stand neutral as to the distinctive claims of Christianity, when he had for the time donned the cloak of the philosopher.

We learn from the fragment before us that Boethius also wrote a 'Bucolic Poem.' This is an interesting fact, and helps to explain the facility with which he

The Bucolic Poem of Boethius.

breaks into song in the midst of the 'Consolation.' It may have been to this effort of the imagination that he alluded when he said at the beginning of that work—

'Carmina qui quondam studio florente peregi
Flebilis, heu, moestos cogor inire modos.'

We would gladly know something more of this 'Bucolic Poem' indited by the universal genius, Boethius.

Cassiodorus.

III. As for *Cassiodorus* himself, the additional information furnished by this fragment has been already discussed in the foregoing chapter. That he was *Consiliarius* to his father during his Praefecture, and that in that capacity he recited an eloquent panegyric on Theodoric, which was rewarded by his promotion to the high office of the Quaestorship, are facts which we learn from this fragment only; and they are of high importance, not only for the life of Cassiodorus but for the history of Europe at the beginning of the Sixth Century, because they make it impossible to assign to any letter in the 'Variae' an earlier date than 500.

CHAPTER III.

THE GRADATIONS OF OFFICIAL RANK IN THE LATER EMPIRE.

It is well known that Diocletian introduced and Constantine perfected an elaborate system of administration under which the titles, functions, order of precedence, and number of attendants of the various officers of the Civil Service as well as of the Imperial army were minutely and punctiliously regulated. This system, which, as forming the pattern upon which the nobility of mediaeval Europe was to a great extent modelled, perhaps deserves even more careful study than it has yet received, is admirably illustrated by the letters of Cassiodorus. The *Notitia Utriusque Imperii*, our copies of which must have been compiled in the early years of the Fifth Century, furnishes us with a picture of official life which, after we have made allowance for the fact that the Empire of the West has shrunk into the Ostrogothic Kingdom of Italy (with the addition of Dalmatia and some other portions of Illyricum), is almost precisely reproduced in the pages of the 'Various Letters.' In order that the student may understand the full significance of many passages in those letters, and especially of the superscriptions by which each letter is prefaced, it will be well to give a brief outline of the system which existed alike under Theodosius and Theodoric.

Official Hierarchy introduced by Diocletian.

In the first place, then, we come to what is rather a family than a class, the persons bearing the title *Nobilissimus*[1]. These were the nearest relatives of

Nobilissimi.

[1] The existence of this title is proved not only by the language of

the reigning Emperor; his brothers, sisters, sons, and daughters. The title therefore is not unlike that of Royal or Imperial Highness in modern monarchies. I am not sure whether any trace can be found of the survival of this title in the Ostrogothic Court. Theodahad, nephew of Theodoric, is addressed simply as 'Vir Senator[1],' and he is spoken of as 'praecelsus et amplissimus vir[2].' It is not so, however, in respect of the three great official classes which follow—the Illustres, Spectabiles, and Clarissimi—whose titles were rendered as punctiliously in the Italy of Theodoric as ever they were in the Italy of Diocletian and Constantine.

Illustres.   I. The *Illustres* were a small and select circle of men, the chief depositaries of power after the Sovereign, and they may with some truth be compared to the Cabinet Ministers of our own political system. The 'Notitia' mentions thirteen of them as bearing rule in the Western Empire. They are:

1. The Praetorian Praefect of Italy.
2. The Praetorian Praefect of the Gauls.
3. The Praefect of the City of Rome.
4. The Master of the Foot Guards (Magister Peditum in Praesenti).
5. The Master of the Horse Guards (Magister Equitum in Praesenti).
6. The Master of the Horse for the Gauls (per Gallias).
7. The Grand Chamberlain (Praepositus Sacri Cubiculi).
8. The Master of the Offices.
9. The Quaestor.

Arcadius in the Theodosian Code x. 25. 1, concerning 'Nobilissimae puellae, filiae meae,' but also by Zosimus (ii. 39), who says that Constantine bestowed the dignity of Nobilissimus on his brother Constantius and his nephew Hannibalianus (τῆς τοῦ λεγομένου ναβελισσίμου παρ' αὐτοῦ Κωνσταντίνου τυχόντες ἀξίας αἰδοῖ τῆς συγγενείας); and by Marcellinus Comes, s. a. 527, who says: 'Justinus Imperator Justinianum ex sorore suâ nepotem, jamdudum a se Nobilissimum designatum, participem quoque regni sui, successoremque creavit.' It is evident that the title did not come by right of birth, but that some sort of declaration of it was necessary.

[1] Var. iii. 15.   [2] Var. viii. 23.

10. The Count of Sacred Largesses.

11. The Count of the Private Domains (Comes Rerum Privatarum).

12. The Count of the Household Cavalry (Comes Domesticorum Equitum).

13. The Count of the Household Infantry (Comes Domesticorum Peditum).

Substantially these same titles were borne by the Illustres to whom Cassiodorus (himself one of them) addressed his 'Various Letters.' The second and the sixth (the Praetorian Praefect of the Gauls, and the Master of the Horse for the Gauls) may possibly have disappeared; and yet, in view of the fact that Theodoric was during the greater part of his reign ruler of a portion of Gaul, it is not necessary to assume even this change. Into the question of the military officers I will not enter, as I confess that I do not understand the relations (whether co-ordinate or subordinated one to another) of the two pairs of officers, Nos. 4 and 5 and Nos. 12 and 13.

The rank and duties of the Praetorian Praefect of Italy, the Master of the Offices, and the Quaestor have already been described in the first chapter. It will be well to say a few words as to the four remaining civil dignitaries, the Praefect of the City, the Grand Chamberlain, the Count of Sacred Largesses, and the Count of the Private Domains.

(a) The *Praefectus Urbis Romae* was by virtue of his office head of the Senate. He had the care of the Annona or corn-largesses to the people, the command of the City-watch, and the duty of keeping the aqueducts in proper repair. The shores and channel of the Tiber, the vast *cloacae* which carried off the refuse of the City, the quays and warehouses of Portus at the river's mouth were also under his authority. The officer who was charged with taking the census, the officers charged with levying the duties on wine, the masters of the markets, the superintendents of the granaries, the curators of

Praefect of the City.

the statues, baths, theatres, and the other public buildings with which the City was adorned, all owned the supreme control of the Urban Praefect. At the beginning of the Fifth Century the *Vicarius Urbis* (whom it is difficult not to think of as in some sort subject to the *Praefectus Urbis*), had jurisdiction over all central and southern Italy and Sicily. But if this was the arrangement then, it must have been altered before the time of Cassiodorus, who certainly appears as Praetorian Praefect to have wielded authority over the greater part of Italy. He states, however[1], that the Urban Praefect had, by an ancient law, jurisdiction, not only over Rome itself, but over all the district within 100 miles of the capital.

Grand Chamberlain.

(*b*) The *Praepositus Sacri Cubiculi* had under his orders the large staff of Grooms of the Bedchamber, at whose head stood the *Primicerius Cubiculariorum*, an officer of 'respectable' rank. The *Castrensis*, Butler or Seneschal, with his army of lacqueys and pages who attended to the spreading and serving of the royal table; the *Comes Sacrae Vestis*, who with similar assistance took charge of the royal wardrobe; the *Comes Domorum*, who perhaps superintended the needful repairs of the royal palace, all took their orders in the last resort from the Grand Chamberlain. So, too, did the three Decurions, officers with a splendid career of advancement before them, who marshalled the thirty brilliantly armed Silentiarii, that paced backwards and forwards before the purple veil guarding the slumbers of the Sovereign.

Count of Sacred Largesses.

(*c*) The *Comes Sacrarum Largitionum*, theoretically only the Grand Almoner of the Sovereign, discharged in practice many of the duties of Chancellor of the Exchequer. The mines, the mint, the Imperial linen factories, the receipt of the tribute of the Provinces, and many other departments of the public revenue were originally under the care of this functionary,

[1] Var. vi. 4.

whose office however, as we are expressly told by Cassiodorus, had lost part of its lustre, probably by a transfer of some of these duties to the Count of the Private Domains.

(*d*) This Minister, the *Comes Rerum Privatarum*, had the superintendence of the Imperial estates in Italy and the Provinces. Confiscations and the absorption by the State of the properties of defaulting tax-payers were probably always tending to increase the extent of these estates, and to make the office of Count of the Domain more important. The collection of the land-tax, far the most important item of the Imperial revenue, was also made subject to his authority. Finally, in order, as Cassiodorus quaintly observes[1], that his jurisdiction should not be exercised only over slaves (the cultivators of the State domains), some authority was given to him within the City, and by a curious division of labour all charges of incestuous crime, or of the spoliation of graves, were brought before the tribunal of the Comes Privatarum.

Count of Private Domains.

Besides the thirteen persons who, as acting Ministers of the highest class, were entitled to the designation of Illustris, there were also those whom we may call honorary members of the class: the persons who had received the dignity of the Patriciate—a dignity which was frequently bestowed on those who had filled the office of Consul, and which, unlike the others of which we have been speaking, was held for life.

It is a question on which I think we need further information, whether a person who had once filled an Illustrious office lost the right to be so addressed on vacating it. I am not sure that we have any clear case in the following collection of an ex-official holding this courtesy-rank; but it seems probable that such would be the case.

Considering also the great show of honour with which

[1] Var. vi. 8.

the Consulate, though now destitute of all real power, was still greeted, it seems probable that the Consuls for the year would rank as Illustres; but here, too, we seem to require fuller details.

Spectabiles.

II. We now come to the Second Class, the *Spectabiles*, which consists chiefly of the lieutenants and deputies of the Illustres.

For instance, every Praetorian Praefect had immediately under him a certain number of *Vicarii*, each of whom was a Spectabilis. The Praefecture included an extent of territory equivalent to two or three countries of Modern Europe (for instance, the Praefecture of the Gauls embraced Britain, Gaul, a considerable slice of Germany, Spain, and Morocco). This was divided into Dioceses (in the instance above referred to Britain formed one Diocese, Gaul another, and Spain with its attendant portion of Africa a third), and the Diocese was again divided into Provinces. The title of the ruler of the Diocese, who in his restricted but still ample domain wielded a similar authority to that of the Illustrious Praefect, was *Spectabilis Vicarius*.

But the Praefect and the Vicar controlled only the civil government of the territories over which they respectively bore sway. The military command of the Diocese was vested in a *Spectabilis Comes*, who was under the orders of the Illustrious Magister Militum. Subordinate in some way to the Comes was the *Dux*, who was also a Spectabilis, but whose precise relation to his superior the Comes is, to me at least, not yet clear[1].

[1] I think the usual account of the matter is that which I have given elsewhere (Italy and her Invaders, i. 227), that the Comes had military command in the Diocese and the Dux in the Province. But on closer examination I cannot find that the Notitia altogether bears out this view. It gives us for the Western Empire eight Comites and twelve Duces. The former pretty nearly correspond to the Dioceses, but the latter are far too few for the Provinces, which number forty-two, excluding all the Provinces of Italy. Besides, in some cases the jurisdiction appears to be the same. Thus we have both a Dux and a Comes Britanniarum,

Besides these three classes of dignitaries, the *Castrensis*, who was a kind of head steward in the Imperial household, and most of the Heads of Departments in the great administrative offices, such as the *Primicerius Notariorum* and the *Magistri Scriniorum*[1], bore the title of Spectabilis. We have perhaps hardly sufficient data for an exact calculation, but I conjecture that there would be as many as fifty or sixty Spectabiles in the Kingdom of Theodoric.

It appears to me that the epithet *Sublimis* (which is almost unknown to the Theodosian Code), when it occurs in the 'Variae' is used as synonymous with Spectabilis[2].

III. The *Clarissimi* were the third rank in the official hierarchy. To our minds it may appear strange that the 'most renowned' should come below 'the respectable,' but such was the Imperial pleasure. The title 'Clarissimus' had moreover its own value, for from the time of Constantine onwards it was conferred on all the members of the Senate, and was in fact identical with Senator[3]; and this was doubtless, as Usener points out[4], the reason why the letters Cl. were still appended to a Roman nobleman's name after he had risen higher in the official scale

Clarissimi.

and the Dux Mauritaniae Caesariensis must, one would think, have held command in a region as large or larger than the Comes Tingitaniae. Again, we have a Comes Argentoratensis and a Dux Moguntiacensis, two officers whose power, one would think, was pretty nearly equal. The same may perhaps be said of the Comes Litoris Saxonici in Britain and the Dux Tractus Armoricani et Nervicani in Gaul. While recognising a *general* inferiority of the Dux to the Comes, I do not think we can, with the Notitia before us, assert that the Provincial Duces were regularly subordinated to the Diocesan Comes, as the Provincial Consulares were to the Diocesan Vicarius. And the fact that both Comes and Dux were addressed as Spectabilis rather confirms this view.

[1] Probably, from the order in which they are mentioned by the Notitia.
[2] Sublimis occurs in the superscription of the following letters: i. 2; iv. 17; v. 25, 30, and 36; ix. 11 and 14; xii. 5.
[3] See Emil Kühn's Verfassung des Römischen Reichs i. 182, and the passages quoted there.
[4] p. 31.

and was entitled to be called Spectabilis or Illustris. The *Consulares* or *Correctores*, who administered the Provinces under the Vicarii, were called Clarissimi; and we shall observe in the collection before us many other cases in which the title is given to men in high, but not the highest, positions in the Civil Service of the State.

Besides the three classes above enumerated there were also:—

Perfectissimi.   IV. The *Perfectissimi*, to which some of the smaller provincial governors belonged, as well as some of the clerks in the Revenue Offices (Numerarii) who had seen long service, and even some veteran Decurions.

Below these again were:—

Egregii.   V. The *Egregii*, who were also Decurions who had earned a right to promotion, or even what we should call veteran non-commissioned officers in the army (Primipilares).

But of these two classes slight mention is made in the Theodosian Code, and none at all (I believe) in the 'Notitia' or the 'Letters of Cassiodorus.'

CHAPTER IV.

ON THE OFFICIUM OF THE PRAEFECTUS PRAETORIO[1].

THE official staff that served under the Roman governors of high rank was an elaborately organised body, with a carefully arranged system of promotion, and liberal superannuation allowances for those of its members who had attained a certain position in the office. *Military character of the Roman Civil Service.*

Although, in consequence of the changes introduced by Diocletian and Constantine, the civil and military functions had been for the most part divided from one another, and it was now unusual to see the same magistrate riding at the head of armies and hearing causes in the Praetorium, in theory the officers of the Courts of Justice were still military officers. Their service was spoken of as a *militia*; the type of their office was the *cingulum*, or military belt; and one of the leading officers of the court, as we shall see, was styled *Cornicularius*, or trumpeter.

The Praetorian Praefect, whose office had been at first a purely military one, had now for centuries been chiefly concerned in civil administration, and as Judge over the highest court of appeal in the Empire. His *Officium* (or staff of subordinates) was, at any rate in the Fifth Century, still the most complete and highly developed that served under any great functionary; and probably the career which it offered to its members was more brilliant than any that they could look for elsewhere. Accordingly, in studying the composition of this body we shall familiarise ourselves with the type to which

---

[1] To illustrate the Eleventh Book of the Variae, Letters 18 to 35.

NOTITIA.	CASSIODORUS (xi.).	LYDUS (iii. 3 and ii. 18.).
Princeps.		
Cornicularius.	Cornicularius.	Cornicularius.
Adjutor.	Primiscrinius.	II Primiscrinii.
Commentariensis.	Scriniarius Actorum.	
Ab Actis.	Cura Epistolarum.	
IV Numerarii.	Scriniarius Curae Militaris.	
Subadjuva.	Primicerius Exceptorum.	
Cura Epistolarum.	Sextus Scholarius.	
Regerendarius.	Praerogativarius.	
Exceptores.	Commentariensis.	II Commentarisii.
Adjutores.	Regendarius.	II Regendarii.
Singularii.	Primicerius Deputatorum.	II Curae Epistolarum Ponticae.
	Primicerius Augustalium.	
	Primicerius Singulariorum.	Singularii.

Lydus calls all the officers down to the Curae Ep. Ponticae Αἱ λογικαί λειτουργίαι (Officium Litteratum).

all the other *officia* throughout the Empire more or less closely approximated.

Our chief information as to this elaborate official hierarchy is derived from three sources [1]:— {Sources of information as to the Officium.}

(1) The *Notitia Dignitatum*, the great Official Gazetteer of the Empire [2], which in its existing shape appears to date from the reign of Arcadius and Honorius, early in the Fifth Century.

(2) The *De Magistratibus* of Joannes Lydus, composed by a civil servant of the Eastern Empire in the middle of the Sixth Century.

(3) The *Variae Epistolae* of Cassiodorus, the composition of which ranges from about 504 to 540.

The first of these authorities relates to the Eastern and Western Empires, the second to the Eastern alone, the third to the Western Empire as represented by the Ostrogothic Kingdom founded by Theodoric.

Much light is also thrown on the subject by the Codes of Theodosius and Justinian.

Godefroy's Commentary on the Theodosian Code, and Bethmann Hollweg's 'Gerichtsverfassung des sinkenden Römischen Reichs,' are the chief modern works which have treated of the subject.

We will follow the order in which the various offices are arranged by the 'Notitia,' which is most likely to correspond with that of official precedence. {The Officium as described in the Notitia.}

In the second chapter of the 'Notitia Orientis,' after an enumeration of the five Dioceses and forty-six Provinces which are 'sub dispositione viri illustris Praefecti Praetorio per Orientem,' we have this list, 'Officium viri illustris Praefecti Praetorio Orientis:'

> Princeps.
> Cornicularius.
> Adjutor.

[1] See Table, p. 94.
[2] To use a modern illustration, we might perhaps say that the Notitia Dignitatum = Whitaker's Almanac + the Army List.

>Commentariensis.
>Ab actis.
>Numerarii.
>Subadjuvae.
>Cura Epistolarum.
>Regerendarius.
>Exceptores.
>Adjutores.
>Singularii.

The lists of the officia of all the other Praetorian Praefects in the 'Notitia' are exactly the same as this, except that under the head 'Praefectus Praetorio per Illyricum' we have, instead of the simple entry 'Numerarii,'

'Numerarii quatuor: in his auri unus, operum alter;'
and the 'Praefectus Urbis Romae' had under his Numerarii, a

>'Primiscrinius,'

and between the 'Adjutores' and 'Singularii,'
>Censuales and
>Nomenculatores.

We will go through the offices enumerated above in order:

Princeps. (1) The PRINCEPS was the head of the whole official staff. In the case of the officium of the Praetorian Praefect, however, this officer seems, after the compilation of the 'Notitia,' to have disappeared, and his rights and privileges became vested in the Cornicularius.' It will be observed that in the letters of Cassiodorus to the members of his staff there is none addressed to the Princeps; and similarly there is no mention of a Princeps as serving under the Praetorian Praefect in the treatise of Lydus. This elimination of the Princeps, however, was not universally applicable to all the officia. Cassiodorus (xi. 35) mentions a *Princeps Augustorum*, who was, perhaps, Princeps of the *Agentes in Rebus;* and Lydus more distinctly ('De Mag.' iii. 24) speaks of a bargain made between the Cornicularius of the Praetorian Praefect and the Πρίγκιψ τῶν μαγιστριανῶν, who must be supposed to be Princeps in the officium of the *Magister Officiorum*, though no such officer appears in the 'Notitia[1].'

Speaking generally, however, we may perhaps say that the greater part of what we are about to hear concerning the rights and endowments of the Cornicularius in the Praefect's office might be truly asserted of the Princeps at the time when the 'Notitia' was compiled, before the two offices had been amalgamated.

(2) The *Cornicularius*. As to this officer we have a good many details in the pages of Joannes Lydus. The antiquarian and etymological part of his information must generally be received with caution; but as to the actual privileges of the office in the days of Justinian we may very safely speak after him, since it was an office which he himself held, and whose curtailed gains and privileges caused him bitter disappointment.

Cornicularius.

'The foremost in rank,' says he[2], 'of the Emperor's assistants (Adjutores) is even to this day called *Cornicularius*, that is to say *horned* (κερατης), or *fighting in the front rank*. For the place of the monarch or the Caesar was in the middle of the army, where he alone might direct the stress of battle. This being the Emperor's place, according to Frontinus, on the left wing was posted the Praefect or Master of the Horse, and on the right the Praetors or Legati, the latter being the officers left in charge of the army when their year of office was drawing to a close, to hold the command till the new Consul should come out to take it from them.

'Of the whole Legion then, amounting to 6,000 men, exclusive of cavalry and auxiliaries, as I before said, the *Cornicularius* took the foremost place; and for that reason he still presides over the whole [civil] service,

[1] See also Var. 24 and 28.   [2] De Mag. iii. 3, 4.

now that the Praefect, for reasons before stated, no longer goes forth to battle.

'Since, then, all the rest of the staff are called assistants (*Adjutores*), the Praefect gives an intimation under his own hand to him who is entering the service in what department (κατάλογος) he is ordered to take up his station[1]. And the following are the names of all the departments of the service. First the *Cornicularius*, resplendent in all the dignity of a so-called Count (κόμης; comes; companion), but having not yet laid aside his belt of office, nor received the honour of admission to the palace, or what they call brevet-rank (*codicilli vacantes*), which honour at the end of his term of service is given to him, and to none of the other chiefs of departments[2].

'And after the Cornicularius follow:—

 '2 Primiscrinii,
 '2 Commentarisii,
 '2 Regendarii,
 '2 Curae Epistolarum,
 '15 Scholae of Exceptores,

and then the "unlearned service" of the Singularii[3].'

Again, further on[4], Lydus, who delights to 'magnify his office,' gives us this further information as to the rank and functions of the Cornicularius:

'Now that, if I am not mistaken, we have described all the various official grades, it is meet to set forth the history of the Cornicularius, the venerable head of the Civil Service, the man who, as beginning and ending, sums up in himself the complete history of the whole official order. The mere antiquity of his office is

---

[1] Lydus here gives the Formula for the admission of assistants, 'et colloca eum in legione primâ adjutrice nostrâ,' which he proceeds to translate into Greek for the benefit of his readers (καὶ τάξειας αὐτὸν ἐν τῷ πρώτῳ τάγματι τῷ βοηθοῦντι ἡμῖν).

[2] I have slightly expanded a sentence here, but this is evidently the author's meaning.

[3] Condensed from Lydus, De Mag. iii. 4–7.   [4] Ib. iii. 22–24.

sufficient to establish his credit, seeing that he was the leader of his troop for 1,300 years, and made his appearance in the world at the same time with the sacred City of Rome itself: for the Cornicularius was, from the first, attendant on the Master of the Horse, and the Master of the Horse on the King, and thus the Cornicularius, if he retained nothing of his office but the name, would still be connected with the very beginnings of the Roman State.

'But from the time when Domitian appointed Fuscus to the office of Praefect of the Praetorians (an office which had been instituted by Augustus), and abolished the rank of Master of the Horse, taking upon himself the command of the army [1], everything was changed. Henceforward, therefore, all affairs that were transacted in the office of the Praefect were arranged by the Cornicularius alone, and he received the revenues arising from them for his own refreshment. This usage, which prevailed from the days of Domitian to our own Theodosius, was then changed, on account of the usurpation of Rufinus. For the Emperor Arcadius, fearing the overgrown power of the Praefectoral office, passed a law that the Princeps of the Magister [Officiorum]'s staff [2] ... should appear in the highest courts, and should busy himself with part of the Praefect's duties, and especially should enquire into the principle upon which orders for the Imperial post-horses (συνθήματα; *evectiones*) were granted [3]. ... This order of Arcadius was inscribed in the earlier editions of the Theodosian Code, but has been omitted in the later as superfluous.

'Thus, then, the Princeps of the Magistriani, being introduced into the highest courts, but possessing nothing there beyond his mere empty dignity, made a

---

[1] This seems to be the meaning of Lydus, but it is not clearly expressed.
[2] There is something wanting in the text here.
[3] See Cod. Theod. vi. 29. 8, which looks rather like the law alluded to by Lydus, notwithstanding his remark about its omission.

bargain with the Cornicularius of t e day, the object of which was to open up to him some portion of the business; and, having come to terms, the Princeps agreed to hand over to the Cornicularius one pound's weight of gold [£40] monthly, and to give instant gratuities to all his subordinates according to their rank in the service. In consequence of this compact the Cornicularius then in office, after receiving his 12 lbs. weight of gold without any abatement, with every show of honour conceded to his superior[1] (?) the preferential right of introducing "one-membered" cases (τὴν τῶν μονομερῶν ἐντυχιῶν εἰσαγωγήν), having reserved to himself, beside the fees paid for promotion in the office[2], and other sources of gain, especially the sole right of subscribing the *Acta* of the court, and thus provided for himself a yearly revenue of not less than 1,000 aurei [£600].'

I have endeavoured to translate as clearly as possible the obscure words of Lydus as to this bargain between the two court-officers. The complaint of Lydus appears to be that the Cornicularius of the day, by taking the money of the Princeps Magistrianorum, and conceding to him in return the preferential claim to manage 'one-membered' cases (or unopposed business), made a purse for himself, but prepared the way for the ruin of his successors. The monthly payment was, I think, to be made for twelve months only, and thus the whole amount which the Cornicularius received from this source was only £480, but from other sources—chiefly the sums paid for promotion by the subordinate members of the *officium*, and the fees charged by him for affixing his subscription to the *acta* of the court—he still remained in receipt of a yearly revenue of £600.

Jealousy between the Officia of the Praefect and the Magister.

The jealousy between the Officia of the Praetorian Praefect and the Magister Officiorum was intense. Almost every line in the treatise of Lydus testifies to it, and shows that the former office, in which he had the

---

[1] τῷ κρείττονι. [2] ἐκ τοῦ βαθμοῦ.

misfortune to serve, was being roughly shouldered out of the way by its younger and more unscrupulous competitor.

Lydus continues[1]: 'Now, what followed, like the Peleus of Euripides, I can never describe without tears. For on account of all these sources of revenue having been dried up, I myself have had to bear my part in the general misery of our time, since, though I have reached the highest grade of promotion in the service, I have derived nothing from it but the bare name. I do not blush to call Justice herself as a witness to the truth of what I say, when I affirm that I am not conscious of having received one obol from the Princeps, nor from the Letters Patent for promotions in the office[2]. For indeed whence should I have derived it, since it was the ancient custom that those who in any way appeared in the highest courts should pay to the *officium* seven and thirty *aurei* [£22] for a "one-membered" suit; but ever after this bargain was made there has been given only a very moderate sum of copper—not gold—in a beggarly way, as if one were buying a flask of oil, and that not regularly? Or how compel the Princeps to pay the ancient covenanted sum to the Cornicularius of the day, when he now scarcely remembered the bare name of that officer, as he never condescended to be present in the court when promotions were made from a lower grade to a higher? Bitterly do I regret that I was so late in coming to perceive for what a paltry price I was rendering my long services as assistant in the courts, receiving in fact nothing therefrom as my own *solatium*. It serves me right, however, for having chosen that line of employment, as I will explain, if the reader will allow me to recount to him my career from its commencement to the present time.'

---

[1] De Mag. iii. 25.
[2] ἀπὸ τῶν λεγομένων κομπλευσίμων, apparently the same source of revenue as the promotion-money (τὴν ἐκ τοῦ βαθμοῦ προνομίαν).

Lydus then goes on to describe his arrival at Constantinople (A.D. 511), his intention to enter the *Scrinium Memoriae* (in which he would have served under the Magister Officiorum), and his abandonment of this intention upon the pressing entreaties of his countryman Zoticus, who was at the time Praefectus Praetorio. This step Lydus looks upon as the fatal mistake of his life, though the consequences of it to him were in some degree mitigated by the marriage which Zoticus enabled him to make with a lady possessed of a fortune of 100 pounds' weight of gold (£4,000). Her property, her virtues (for 'she was superior to all women who have ever been admired for their moral excellence'), and the consolations of Philosophy and Literature, did much to soothe the disappointment of Lydus, who nevertheless felt, when he retired to his books after forty years of service, in which he had reached the unrewarded post of Cornicularius, that his official life had been a failure.

It has seemed worth while to give this sketch of the actual career of a Byzantine official, as it may illustrate in some points the lives of the functionaries to whom so many of the letters of Cassiodorus are addressed; though I know not whether we have any indications of such a rivalry at Ravenna as that which prevailed at Constantinople between the *officium* of the Praefect and that of the Magister. We now pass on to

Adjutor. (3) The *Adjutor*. Some of the uses of this term are very perplexing. It seems clear (from Lydus, 'De Mag.' iii. 3) that all the members of the officium were known by the generic name *Adjutores*. Here however we may perhaps safely assume that Adjutor means simply an assistant to the officer next above him, as we find, lower down in the list of the 'Notitia,' the Exceptores followed by their Adjutores. We may find a parallel to Adjutor in the word Lieutenant, which, for the same reason is applied to officers of such different rank as the Lord Lieutenant of Ireland, a Lieutenant-General, a Lieutenant-Colonel, and a simple Lieutenant in the Army or Navy. In the lists of Cassiodorus and Lydus we find no mention of an officer bearing the special name of Adjutor, but we meet instead with a *Primiscrinius*, Primiscrinius. of whom, according to Lydus, there were two. He says [1], 'After the Cornicularius are two Primiscrinii, whom the Greeks call first of the service [2].' And later on [3], when he is describing the course of business in the *secretum* of the Praefect, as it used to be in the good old days, he informs us that after judgment had been given, and the Secretarii had read to the litigant the decree prepared by the Assessors and carefully copied by one of the Cancellarii, and after an accurate digest of the case had been prepared in the Latin language by a Secretarius, in order to guard against future error or misrepresentation, the successful litigant passed on with the decree in his hand *to the Primiscrinii, who appointed an officer to execute the judgment of the Court* [4]. These men then put the decree into its final shape by means of the persons appointed to assist them [5] (men who could puzzle even the professors themselves in logical discussions), and endorsed it on the litigant's petition in characters which at once struck awe into the reader, and which seemed actually swollen with official importance [6]. The name and titles of the 'completing' officer were then subscribed.

If the suggestion that the Primiscrinii were considered as in some sense substitutes (Adjutores) for the Cornicularius be correct, we may perhaps account for there

---

[1] De Mag. iii. 4.
[2] μετὰ δὲ τὸν κορνικουλάριον πριμισκρίνιοι δύο, οὓς Ἕλληνες πρώτους τῆς τάξεως καλοῦσι.
[3] De Mag. iii. 11.
[4] παρῄει πρὸς τοὺς πριμισκρινίους τάξαντας ἐκβιβαστὴν τοῖς ἀποπεφασμένοις. Probably we should read τάξοντας for τάξαντας.
[5] ἐπλήρουν διὰ τῶν βοηθεῖν αὐτοῖς τεταγμένων (? Adjutores).
[6] ἐπὶ τοῦ νώτου τῆς ἐντυχίας γράμμασιν αἰδοῦς αὐτόθεν ἁπάσης καὶ ἐξουσίας ὄγκῳ σεσοβημένοις.

being two of them in the days of Lydus by the disappearance of the Princeps. The office of Cornicularius had swallowed up that of Princeps, and accordingly the single Adjutor, who was sufficient at the compilation of the 'Notitia,' had to be multiplied by two.

Commentariensis, or Commentarisius.

(4) The *Commentariensis*. Here we come again to an officer who is mentioned by all our three authorities, though in Cassiodorus he seems to be degraded some steps below his proper rank (but this may only be from an accidental transposition of the order of the letters), and though Lydus again gives us two of the name instead of one. The last-named authority inserts next after the Primiscrinii 'two Commentarisii—so the law calls those who are appointed to attend to the drawing up of indictments [1].'

The Commentariensis (or Commentarisius, as Lydus calls him [2]) was evidently the chief assistant of the Judge in all matters of criminal jurisdiction [3]. We have a remarkably full, and in the main clear account of his functions in the pages of Lydus (iii. 16–18), from which it appears that he was promoted from the ranks of the *Exceptores* (shorthand writers), and had six of his former colleagues serving under him as Adjutores [4]. Great was the power, and high the position in the Civil Service, of the Commentariensis. The whole tribe of process-servers, gaolers, lictors [5]—all that we now understand by the police force—waited subserviently on his nod. It rested with him, says Lydus, to establish the

---

[1] κομμενταρίσιοι δύο (οὕτω δὲ τοὺς ἐπὶ τῶν ὑπομνημάτων γραφῇ ταττομένους ὁ νόμος καλεῖ) (iii. 4). I accept the necessary emendation of the text proposed in the Bonn edition.

[2] To avoid confusion I will use the term 'Commentariensis' throughout.

[3] So Bethmann Hollweg (p. 179), 'Diess ist der Gehülfe des Magistrats bei Verwaltung der Criminaljustiz.' I compare him in the following translation of Cassiodorus to a 'magistrate's clerk.'

[4] See iii. 9 (p. 203, ed. Bonn), and combine with iii. 16. The *Augustales* referred to in the latter passage were a higher class of Exceptores.

[5] Applicitarii, Clavicularii, Lictores.

authority of the Court of Justice by means of the wholesome fear inspired by iron chains and scourges and the whole apparatus of torture[1]. Nay, not only did the subordinate magistrates execute their sentences by his agency, he had even the honour of being chosen by the Emperor himself to be the minister of vengeance against the persons who had incurred his anger or his suspicion. 'I myself remember,' says Lydus, 'when I was serving as Chartularius in the office of the Commentariensis, under the praefecture of Leontius (a man of the highest legal eminence), and when the wrath of Anastasius was kindled against Apion, a person of the most exalted rank, and one who had assisted in his elevation to the throne[2], at the same time when Kobad, King of Persia, blazed out into fury[3], that then all the confiscations and banishments which were ordered by the enraged Emperor were entrusted to no one else but to the Commentarienses serving under the Praefect. In this service they acquitted themselves so well, with such vigour, such harmonious energy, such entire clean-handedness and absence of all dishonest gain, as to move the admiration of the Emperor, who made use of them on all similar occasions that presented themselves in the remainder of his reign. They had even the honour of being employed against Macedonius, Patriarch of Constantinople, when that prelate had provoked the Emperor by suspending all intercourse with him as a heretic; and that, although Celer, one of the most intimate friends of Anastasius, was at that very time holding the rank of Magister Officiorum.'

An officer who was thus privileged to lay hands on Patriarch and Patrician in the name of Augustus was

---

[1] σιδηρέοις δεσμοῖς καὶ ποιναίων ὀργάνων καὶ πλήκτρων ποικιλίᾳ σαλευόντων τῷ φόβῳ τὸ δικαστήριον (iii. 16).

[2] καὶ κοινωνήσαντος αὐτῷ τῆς βασιλείας.

[3] ὅτε Καάδης ὁ Πέρσης ἐφλέγμαινε. The whole passage is mysterious, but we seem to have here an allusion to the outbreak of the Persian War (A.D. 502).

looked up to with awful reverence by all the lower members of the official hierarchy; and Lydus, with one graphic touch, brings before us the glow of gratified self-love with which, when he was a subordinate *Scriniarius*, he found himself honoured by the familiar conversation of so great a person as the Commentariensis[1]: 'I too am struck with somewhat of my old awe, recurring in memory to those who were then holders of the office. I remember what fear of the Commentarisii fell upon all who at all took the lead in the *Officium*, but especially on the Scriniarii; and how greatly he who was favoured with a chat with a Commentarisius passing by valued himself on the honour.' Lydus also describes to us how the Commentariensis, instructed by the Praefect, or perhaps even by the Emperor himself, would take with him one of his faithful servants, the Chartularii, would visit the abode of the suspected person (who might, as we have seen, be one of the very highest officers of the State), and would then in his presence dictate in solemn Latin words the indictment which was to be laid against him, the mere hearing of which sometimes brought the criminal to confess his guilt and throw himself on the mercy of the Emperor.

It was from this *commentum*, the equivalent of a French *acte d'accusation*, that the Commentariensis derived his title.

Ab Actis (Scriniarius Actorum?).

(5) The *Ab Actis*. The officer who bore this title (which is perhaps the same as the Scriniarius Actorum of Cassiodorus[2]) seems to have been exclusively concerned with civil cases, and perhaps held the same place in reference to them that the Commentarienses held in criminal matters[3]. Practically, his office appears to have been very much what we understand by that of *Chief Registrar* of the Court. He (or they, for in Lydus'

---

[1] iii. 17 (p. 210). [2] Var. xi. 22.
[3] This seems to be Bethmann Hollweg's view (p. 181).

time there were two *Ab Actis* as well as two Commentarienses[1]) was chosen from the select body of shorthand writers who were known as Augustales, and was assisted by six men of the same class, 'men of high character and intelligence and still in the vigour of their years[2].' His chief business—and in this he was served by the *Nomenclatores*, who shouted out in a loud voice the names of the litigants—was to introduce the plaintiff and defendant into the Court, or to make a brief statement of the nature of the case to the presiding magistrate. He then had to watch the course of the pleadings and listen to the Judge's decision, so as to be able to prepare a full statement of the case for the Registers or Journals[3] of the Court. These Registers—at least in the flourishing days of Roman jurisprudence—were most fully and accurately kept. Even the *Dies Nefasti* were marked upon them, and the reason for their being observed as legal holidays duly noted. Elaborate indices, prepared by the Chartularii, made search an easy matter to those who wished to ascertain what was the decision of the law upon every point; and the marginal notes, or *personalia*, prepared in Latin[4] by the Ab Actis or his assistants, were so excellent and so full that sometimes when the original entry in the Registers had been lost the whole case could be sufficiently reconstructed from them alone.

The question was already mooted at Constantinople in the sixth century whence the Ab Actis derived his somewhat elliptical name; and our archaeology-loving scribe was able to inform his readers that as the officer of the household who was called *A Pigmentis* had the care of

---

[1] This we learn from iii. 20. They are not mentioned in iii. 4, where we should have expected to find them.

[2] ἐξ ἄνδρες ἐραστοὶ καὶ νουνεχέστατοι καὶ σφριγῶντες ἔτι (Lydus iii. 20).

[3] ῥεγέστων ἢ κοττιδιανῶν (ἀντὶ τοῦ ἐφημέρων).

[4] Ἰταλιστί. Of course the emphasis laid on this point proceeds from the Greek nationality of our present authority.

the aromatic ointments of the Court; as the *A Sabanis*[1] had charge of the bathing towels of the baths; as the *A Secretis* (who was called Ad Secretis by vulgar Byzantines, ignorant of the niceties of Latin grammar) was concerned in keeping the secret counsels of his Sovereign: so the *Ab Actis* derived his title from the Acts of the Court which it was his duty to keep duly posted up and properly indexed.

Numerarii.

(6) The *Numerarii* (whose exact number is not stated in the 'Notitia'[2]) were the cashiers of the Praefect's office. Though frequently mentioned in the Theodosian Code, and though persons exercising this function must always have existed in a great Court of Justice like the Praefect's, we hear but little of them from Cassiodorus[3]; and Lydus' notices of the διαψηφισταί, who seem to correspond to the Numerarii[4], are scanty and imperfect. Our German commentator has collected the passages of the Theodosian Code which relate to this class of officers, and has shown that on account of their rapacity and extortion their office was subjected to a continual process of degradation. All the Numerarii, except those of the two highest classes of judges[5], were degraded into *Tabularii*, a name which had previously indicated the cashiers of a municipality as distinguished from those in the Imperial service; and the Numerarii, even of the Praetorian Praefect himself, were made subject to examination by torture. This was not only to be dreaded on account of the bodily

---

[1] σάβανον = a towel.

[2] Except, as before stated, those in the office of the Praetorian Praefect for Illyricum. These were four in number, and one of them had charge of 'gold,' another of '[public] works.' Further information is requisite to enable us to explain these entries.

[3] They are alluded to in Var. xii. 13. The Canonicarii (Tax-collectors) had plundered the Churches of Bruttii and Lucania in the name of 'sedis nostrae Numerarii;' but the Numerarii with holy horror declared that they had received no part of the spoils.

[4] See Bethmann Hollweg, 184.

[5] Illustres and Spectabiles.

suffering which it inflicted, but was also a mark of the humble condition of those to whom it was applied.

We may perhaps see in the *Scriniarius Curae Mili-* taris of Cassiodorus[1] one of these Numerarii detailed for service as paymaster to the soldiers who waited upon the orders of the Praefect.

Scriniarius Curae Militaris.

(7) The *Subadjuvae*. This is probably a somewhat vague term, like Adjutores, and indicates a second and lower class of cashiers who acted as deputies for the regular Numerarii.

Subadjuvae.

(8) *Cura Epistolarum*. The officer who bore this title appears to have had the duty of copying out all letters relating to fiscal matters[2]. This theory as to his office is confirmed by the words of Cassiodorus (Var. xi. 23): 'Let Constantinian on his promotion receive the care of the letters relating to the land-tax' (Hic itaque epistolarum *canonicarum* curam provectus accipiat).

Cura Epistolarum.

(9) *Regerendarius*, or *Regendarius*[3]. This officer had the charge of all contracts relating to the very important department of the *Cursus Publicus*, or Imperial Mail Service. At the time of the compilation of the 'Notitia' only one person appears to have acted in this capacity under each Praefect. When Lydus wrote, there were two Regendarii in each Praefecture, but, owing to the increasing influence of the Magister Officiorum over the Cursus Publicus[4], their office had become apparently

Regerendarius, or Regendarius.

---

[1] xi. 24.

[2] This is Bethmann Hollweg's interpretation of the words of Lydus, of τὰς μὲν ἐπὶ τοῖς δημοσίοις φοιτώσας ψήφους γράφουσι μόνον, τὸ λοιπὸν καταφρονούμενοι (iii. 21). In another passage (iii. 4, 5) Lydus appears to assign a reason for the fact that the Praefectus Urbis Constantinopolitanae, the Magister Militum, and the Magister Officiorum had no *Cura Epistolarum* on their staff; but the paragraph is to me hopelessly obscure. Curiously enough, too, while he avers that every department of the State (perhaps every diocese) had, as a rule, its own Curae Epistolarum, he limits the two in the Praetorian Praefect's office to the diocese of Pontica (κοῦρα ἐπιστολάρουμ Ποντικῆς δύο).

[3] The first form of the name is found in the Notitia, the second in Lydus and Cassiodorus.

[4] It is not easy to make out exactly what Lydus wishes us to understand

little more than an ill-paid sinecure. As we hear nothing of similar changes in the West, the Cursus Publicus was probably a part of the public service which was directly under the control of Cassiodorus when Praetorian Praefect, and was administered at his bidding by one or more Regendarii.

Exceptores.

(10) We now come to the *Exceptores*, or shorthand writers[1], a large and fluctuating body who stood on the lowest step of the official ladder[2] and formed the raw material out of which all its higher functionaries were fashioned in the regular order of promotion.

Augustales.

We are informed by Lydus[3], that in his time the Exceptores in the Eastern Empire were divided into two corps, the higher one called *Augustales*, who were limited in number to thirty, and the lower, of indefinite number and composing the rank and file of the profession. The Augustales only could aspire to the rank of Cornicularius; but in order that some prizes might still be left of possible attainment by the larger class, the rank of Primiscrinius was tenable by those who remained 'on the rolls of the Exceptores.' The reason for this change was that the unchecked application of the principle of seniority to so large a body of public servants was throwing all the more important offices in the Courts of Justice into the hands of old men. The principle of 'seniority tempered by selection' was therefore introduced, and the ablest and most learned members of the class of Exceptores were drafted off into this favoured section of Augustales, fifteen of the most experienced of

about the Cursus Publicus; but I think his statements amount to this, that it was taken by Arcadius from the Praetorian Praefect and given to the Magister Officiorum, was afterwards restored to the Praefect, and finally was in effect destroyed by the corrupt administration of John of Cappadocia. (See ii. 10; iii. 21, 61.)

[1] The ταχυγράφοι of Lydus.

[2] In making this statement I consider the Adjutores to be virtually another class of Exceptores, and I purposely omit the Singularii as not belonging to the *Militia Litterata*, which alone I am now considering.

[3] iii. 6, 9.

whom were appropriated to the special service of the Emperor, while the other fifteen filled the higher offices (with the exception of the Primiscriniate) in the Praefectoral Courts[1]. The first fifteen were called *Deputati*[2], the others were apparently known simply as Augustales.   *Deputati.*

The change thus described by Lydus appears to have been made in the West as well as in the East, since we hear in the 'Variae' of Cassiodorus (xi. 30) of the appointment of a certain Ursus to be Primicerius of the Deputati, and of Beatus to take the same place among the Augustales[3].

(11) The *Adjutores* of the 'Notitia' were probably a lower class of Exceptores, who may very likely have disappeared when the Augustales were formed out of them by the process of differentiation which has been described above.   *Adjutores.*

We have now gone through the whole of what was termed the 'Learned Service[4]' mentioned in the 'Notitia,' with one exception—the title of an officer, in himself humble and obscure, who has given his name to the highest functionaries of mediaeval and modern Europe.

(12) The *Cancellarius* appears in the 'Notitia' only   *Cancellarius.*

---

[1] I think this is a fair summary of Lydus iii. 9 and 10, but these paragraphs are very difficult and obscure.

[2] We should certainly have expected that the Augustales would be those writers who were specially appropriated to the Emperor's service, but the other conclusion necessarily follows from the language of Lydus (iii. 10): ὥστε καὶ πεντεκαίδεκα ἐξ αὐτῶν τῶν πεπανωτέρων πείρᾳ τε καὶ τῷ χρόνῳ κρειττόνων πρὸς ὑπογραφὴν τοῖς βασιλεῦσιν ἀφορισθῆναι, οὓς ἔτι καὶ νῦν δηπουτάτους καλοῦσιν, οἱ τοῦ τάγματος τῶν Αὐγουσταλίων πρωτεύουσιν.

[3] The form of the word must I think prevent us from applying the Princeps *Augustorum* of xi. 35 to the same class of officers.

[4] τοὺς ἐπὶ ταῖς λογικαῖς τεταγμένους λειτουργίαις (Lydus iii. 7). Πέρας μὲν ὧδε τῶν λογικῶν τῆς τάξεως συστημάτων (iii. 21). The 'Learned Service' may be taken as corresponding to 'a post fit for a gentleman,' in modern phraseology. In our present Official Directories the members of the λογικὴ τάξις appear to be all dignified with the title 'Esq.;' the others have only 'Mr.'

once[1], and then in connection not with the Praetorian Praefect, but with the Master of the Offices. At the very end of the Officium of this dignitary, after the six *Scholae* and four *Scrinia* of his subordinates, and after the *Admissionales*, whom we must look upon as the Ushers of the Court, comes the entry,

Cancellarii:

their very number not stated, the office being too obscure to make a few less or more a matter of importance.

After the compilation of the 'Notitia' the office of Cancellarius apparently rose somewhat in importance, and was introduced into other departments besides that of the Master of the Offices.

One Cancellarius appears attached to the Court of Cassiodorus as Praetorian Praefect, and from the admonitions addressed to him by his master[2], we see that he had it in his power considerably to aid the administration of justice by his integrity, or to hinder it by showing himself accessible to bribes.

In describing the Cancellarius, as in almost every other part of his treatise, Lydus has to tell a dismal story of ruin and decay[3]:

'Now the Scriniarii [subordinates of the Magister Officiorum] are made Cancellarii and Logothetes and purveyors of the Imperial table, whereas in old time the Cancellarius was chosen only from the ranks of Augustales and Exceptores who had served with credit. In those days the Judgment Hall [of the Praefect] recognised only two Cancellarii, who received an *aureus* apiece[4] per day from the Treasury. There was aforetime in the Court of Justice a fence separating the Magistrate from his subordinates, and this fence, being made of long splinters of wood placed diagonally, was called *cancellus*, from its likeness to network, the regular Latin word for

---

[1] Occidentis ix. 15.
[2] In Var. xi. 6, which see.
[3] iii. 36, 37.
[4] About twelve shillings.

a net being casses, and the diminutive cancellus¹. At this latticed barrier then stood two *Cancellarii*, by whom, since no one was allowed to approach the judgment-seat, paper was brought to the members of the staff and needful messages were delivered. But now that the office owing to the number of its holders² has fallen into disrepute, and that the Treasury no longer makes a special provision for their maintenance, almost all the hangers-on of the Courts of Law call themselves Cancellarii; and, not only in the capital but in the Provinces, they give themselves this title in order that they may be able more effectually to plunder the wealthy.'

This description by Lydus, while it aptly illustrates Cassiodorus' exhortations to his Cancellarii to keep their hands clean from bribes, shows how lowly their office was still considered; and indeed, but for his statement that it used to be filled by veteran Augustales, we might almost have doubted whether it is rightly classed among the 'Learned Services' at all.

Now at any rate we leave the ranks of the gentlemen of the Civil Service behind us, and come to the 'Militia Illiterata,' of whom the 'Notitia' enumerates only

End of the Militia Literata.

(13) The *Singularii*, a class of men of whose useful services Lydus speaks in terms of high praise, contrasting their modest efficiency with the pompous verbosity³ of the Magistriani (servants of the Master of the Offices) by whom they were being generally superseded in his day. They travelled through the Provinces, carrying the Praefect's orders, and riding in a post-chaise drawn by a single horse (veredus), from which circumstance, according to Lydus, they derived their name Singularii⁴.

Militia Illiterata: Singularii.

---

¹ This derivation from casses is, of course, absurd.
² Can this be the meaning of εἰς πλῆθος?
³ Κομποφακελλορρημοσύνη = Pomp-bundle-wordiness, an Aristophanic word.
⁴ De Dignitatibus iii. 7.

I

We observe that the letter of Cassiodorus[1] addressed to the retiring chief (Primicerius) of the Singularii informs him that he is promoted to a place among the King's Body-guard (Domestici et Protectores), a suitable reward for one who had not been a member of the 'Learned Services.'

After the Singularii Lydus mentions the *Mancipes*, the men who were either actually slaves or were at any rate engaged in servile occupations; as, for instance, the bakers at the public bakeries, the *Rationalii*, who distributed the rations to the receivers of the annona[2], the *Applicitarii* (officers of arrest), and *Clavicularii* (gaolers), who, as we before heard, obeyed the mandate of the Commentariensis. The Lictors, I think, are not mentioned by him. A corresponding class of men would probably be the *Apparitores*, who in the 'Notitia' appear almost exclusively attached to the service of the great Ministers of War[3].

Thus, it will be seen, from the well-paid and often highly-connected Princeps, who, no doubt, discussed the business of the court with the Praetorian Praefect on terms of friendly though respectful familiarity, down to the gaoler and the lictor and the lowest of the half-servile *mancipes*, there was a regular gradation of rank, which still preserved, in the staff of the highest court of justice in the land, all the traditions of subordination and discipline which had once characterised the military organisation out of which it originally sprang.

---

[1] Var. xi. 31.

[2] This seems a probable explanation of a rather obscure passage.

[3] See the following sections of the Notitia: Magister Militum Praesentatis (Oriens v. 74, vi. 77; Occidens v. 281, vi. 93); M. M. per Orientem (Or. vii. 67); M. M. per Thracias (Or. viii. 61); M. M. per Illyricum (Or. ix. 56); Magister Equitum per Gallias (Occ. vii. 117). The only civil officer who has Apparitores is the Proconsul Achaiae (Oriens xxi. 14).

CHAPTER V.

BIBLIOGRAPHY.

THE Ecclesiastical History ('Historia Tripartita') seems to have been the first of the works of Cassiodorus to attract the notice of printers at the revival of learning. The Editio Princeps of this book (folio) was printed by Johann Schuszler, at Augsburg, in 1472 [1]. *Editiones Principes.*

The Editio Princeps of the 'Chronicon' is contained in a collection of Chronicles published at Basel in 1529 by Joannes Sichardus (printer, Henricus Petrus). The contribution of Cassiodorus is prefaced by an appropriate Epistle Dedicatory to Sir Thos. More, in which a parallel is suggested between the lives of these two literary statesmen.

Next followed the Editio Princeps of the 'Variae,' published at Augsburg in 1533, by Mariangelus Accurtius.

In 1553, Joannes Cuspinianus, a counsellor of the Emperor Maximilian, published at Basel a series of Chronicles with which he interwove the Chronicle of Cassiodorus, and to which he prefixed a short life of our author.

The Editio Princeps of the collected works of Cassiodorus was published at Paris in 1579 by Sebastianus Nivellius; and other editions by the same publisher followed in 1584 and 1589. This edition does not contain the Tripartite History, the Exposition of the Psalter, or the 'Complexiones' on the Epistles. Some notes, not *Edition of Nivellius.*

---

[1] This edition is described by Dibdin (Bibliotheca Spenceriana iii. 244–5).

without merit, are added, which were compiled in 1578 by 'Gulielmus Fornerius, Parisiensis, Regius apud Aurelianenses Consiliarius et Antecessor.' The annotator says[1] that these notes had gradually accumulated on the margin of his copy of Cassiodorus, an author who had been a favourite of his from youth, and whom he had often quoted in his forensic speeches.

The edition of Nivellius, which is evidently prepared with a view to aid the historical rather than the theological study of the writings of Cassiodorus, contains also the Gothic history of Jordanus (sic), the 'Edictum Theoderici,' the letter of Sidonius describing the Court of Theodoric II *the Visigoth* (453-466), and the Panegyric of Ennodius on Theodoric the Great. The letter of Sidonius is evidently inserted owing to a confusion between the two Theodorics; and this error has led many later commentators astray. But the reprint of the 'Edictum Theoderici' is of great interest and value, because the MS. from which it was taken has since disappeared, and none other is known to be in existence. A letter is prefixed to the 'Edictum,' written by Pierre Pithou to Edouard Molé, Dec. 31, 1578, and describing his reasons for sending this document to the publisher who was printing the works of Cassiodorus. At the same time, 'that the West might not have cause to envy the East,' he sent a MS. of the 'Leges Wisigothorum,' with illustrative extracts from Isidore and Procopius, which is printed at the end of Nivellius' edition.

I express no opinion about the text of this edition; but it possesses the advantage of an Index to the 'Variae' only, which will be found at the end of the Panegyric of Ennodius. Garet's Index, which is in itself not so full, has the additional disadvantage of being muddled up with the utterly alien matter of the Tripartite History.

In 1588 appeared an edition in 4to. of the works of Cassiodorus (still excluding the Tripartite History and

---

[1] p. 492.

the Biblical Commentaries), published at Paris by Marc Orry. This was republished in 1600 in two volumes 12mo.

The 'Variae' and 'Chronicon' only, in 12mo. were published at Lyons by Jacques Chouet in 1595, and again by Pierre and Jacques Chouet at Geneva in 1609, and by their successors in 1650. These editions contain the notes of Pierre Brosse, Jurisconsult, as well as those of Fornerius.

In 1679 appeared, in two volumes folio, the great Rouen edition by François Jean Garet (of the Congregation of S. Maur), which has ever since been the standard edition of the works of Cassiodorus. Garet speaks of collating several MSS. of various ages for the text of this edition, especially mentioning 'Codex S. Audoeni' (deficient for Books 5, 6, and 7 of the 'Variae'), 'et antiquissimae membranae S. Remigii Remensis' (containing only the first four books of the same collection). A codex which once belonged to the jurist Cujacius, and which had been collated with Accurtius' text in 1575 by a certain Claude Grulart, seems to have given Garet some valuable readings by means of Grulart's notes, though the codex itself had disappeared. Garet's edition was re-issued at Venice in 1729, and more recently in Migne's 'Patrologia' (Paris, 1865), of which it forms vols. 69 and 70. *Edition of Garet.*

There can be little doubt, however, that all these editions will be rendered obsolete by the new edition which is expected to appear as a volume of the 'Auctores Antiquissimi' in the *Monumenta Germaniae Historica*. The editor is Professor Wilhelm Meyer, of Munich. The work has been for some years announced as near completion, but I have not been able to ascertain how soon it may be expected to appear. *Forthcoming Edition by Meyer.*

Finally, I must not omit to notice the fragments of an oration published by Baudi de Vesme in the Transactions of the Royal Academy of Sciences at Turin *Supposed fragment of orations.*

(1846). These fragments, which were found in a palimpsest MS. of the Acts of the Council of Chalcedon, were first published in 1822 by Angelo Mai, who was then disposed to attribute them to Symmachus (the elder), and to assign them to the early part of the fifth century. On reflection, however, he came to the conclusion that they were probably the work of Cassiodorus, and formed part of a panegyric addressed to Theodoric. This theory appears now to meet with general approval. The style is certainly very similar to that of Cassiodorus; but, as will be inferred from the doubt as to their origin, there is little or nothing in these scanty fragments which adds anything to our knowledge of the history of Theodoric.

Life by Garet. To the literature relating to Cassiodorus the most important contribution till recent times was the life by Garet prefixed to his edition of 1679. I cannot speak of this from a very minute investigation, but it seems to be a creditable performance, the work of one who had carefully studied the 'Variae,' but unfortunately quite misleading as to the whole framework of the life of Cassiodorus, from the confusion which it makes between him and his father, an error which Garet has probably done more than any other author to perpetuate.

Life by St. Marthe. The life by Garet was paraphrased in French by Denys de *Ste Marthe* ('Vie de Cassiodore,' Paris, 1695), whose work has enjoyed a reputation to which it was not entitled on the ground either of originality or accuracy, but which was probably due to the fact that the handy octavo volume written in French was accessible to a wider circle of readers than Garet's unwieldy folio in Latin. A more original performance was that of *Count Buat* (in the 'Abhandlungen der Kurfürstlichen Bairischen Akademie der Wissenschaften,' Munich, 1763); but this author, though he pointed out the cardinal error of Garet, his confusion between Senator and his father, introduced some further gratuitous entanglements of his own into the family history of the Cassiodori.

All these works, however, are rendered entirely obsolete by three excellent monographs which have recently been published in Germany on the life and writings of Cassiodorus. These are—

August *Thorbecke's* 'Cassiodorus Senator' (Heidelberg, 1867);

Adolph *Franz's* 'M. Aurelius Cassiodorius Senator' (Breslau, 1872); and

Hermann *Usener's* 'Anecdoton Holderi' (Bonn, 1877), described in the second chapter of this introduction.

Thorbecke discusses the political, and Franz the religious and literary aspects of the life of their common hero, and between them they leave no point of importance in obscurity. Usener, as we have already seen, brings an important contribution to our knowledge of the subject in presenting us with Holder's fragment; and his Commentary (of eighty pages) on this fragment is a model of patient and exhaustive research. It seems probable that these three authors have really said pretty nearly the last word about the life and writings of Cassiodorus. In addition to these authors many writers of historical works in Germany have of late years incidentally contributed to a more accurate understanding of the life and times of Cassiodorus.

Dahn, in the third section of his 'Könige der Germanen' (Würzburg, 1866), has written a treatise on the political system of the Ostrogoths which is almost a continuous commentary on the 'Variae,' and from which I have derived the greatest possible assistance.

Köpke, in his 'Anfänge des Königthums bei den Gothen' (Berlin, 1859), has condensed into a small compass a large amount of useful disquisition on Cassiodorus and his copyist Jordanes. The relation between these two writers was also elaborately discussed by *von Sybel* in his thesis 'De Fontibus Libri Jordanis' (Berlin, 1838), and by *Schirren*, in his monograph 'De Ratione quae inter Jordanem et Cassiodorum intercedat' (Dorpat, 1885). The latter, though upon the whole a creditable performance, is disfigured by one or two strange blunders, and not improved by some displays of irrelevant learning.

Von Schubert, in his 'Unterwerfung der Alamannen unter die Franken' (Strassburg, 1884), throws some useful light on the question of the date of the early letters in the 'Variae;' and *Binding*, in his 'Geschichte des Burgundisch-Romanischen Königreichs' (Leipzig, 1868), discusses the relations between Theodoric and the Sovereigns of Gaul, as disclosed by the same collection of letters, in a manner which I must admit to be forcible, though I do not accept all his conclusions.

Mommsen, in his paper 'Die Chronik des Cassiodorus Senator' (Vol. viii. of the 'Abhandlungen der Königlich Sächsischen Gesellschaft der Wissenschaften;' Leipzig, 1861), has said all that is to be said concerning the unfortunate 'Chronicon' of Cassiodorus, which he handles with merciless severity.

To say that *Ebert*, in his 'Allgemeine Geschichte der Litteratur des Mittelalters im Abendlande' (Leipzig, 1874), and *Wattenbach*, in his 'Deutschlands Geschichtsquellen im Mittelalter,' tell us with fullness and accuracy just what the student ought to wish to know concerning Cassiodorus as an author, is only to say that they are Ebert and Wattenbach. Every one who has had occasion to refer to these two books knows their merits.

Passing from German literature, I regret that I am prevented by ignorance of the Dutch language from forming an opinion as to the work of *Thijm* ('Iets over M. A. Cassiodorus en zijne eeuw;' Amsterdam, 1857), which is frequently quoted by my German authorities.

Gibbon of course quotes from the 'Variae,' and though he did not know them intimately, he has with his usual sagacity apprehended the true character of the book and of its author. But the best account of the 'Various Letters' in English, as far as I know, is unfortunately entombed in the pages of a periodical, being an article by Dean *Church*, contributed in July, 1880, to the 'Church Quarterly Review.' There is also a very good though necessarily brief notice of Cassiodorus in *Ugo Balzani*'s little volume on the 'Early Chroniclers of Italy,' published by the Christian Knowledge Society in 1883.

CHAPTER VI.

CHRONOLOGY.

In the following chronological table of the life of Cassiodorus I have, for convenience sake, assumed 480 as the year of his birth, and 575 as that of his death. It is now, I think, sufficiently proved that if these dates are not absolutely correct, they cannot be more than a year or two wrong in one direction or the other.

Consular Fasti. As dates were still reckoned by Consulships, at any rate through the greater part of the life of Cassiodorus, I have inserted the Consular Fasti for the period in question. It will be seen that several names of correspondents of Cassiodorus figure in this list. As a general though not universal practice, one of the two Consuls at this time was chosen from out of the Senate of Rome and the other from that of Constantinople. We can almost always tell whether a chronicler belongs to the Eastern or Western Empire by observing whether he puts the Eastern or Western Consul first. Thus, for A.D. 501, Marcellinus Comes, who was an official of the Eastern Empire, gives us 'Pompeius et Avienus, Coss.;' while Cassiodorus, in his 'Chronicon,' assigns the year to 'Avienus et Pompeius.' Pompeius was a nobleman of Constantinople, nephew of the Emperor Anastasius; while Avienus was a Roman Senator[1]. Again, in A.D. 490, Marcellinus gives the names of Longinus and Faustus, which Cassiodorus quotes as Faustus and Longinus. Longinus was a brother of the Emperor Zeno, and Faustus was for many years Praetorian Praefect under Theodoric, and was the receiver of many letters in the following collection.

[1] See Usener, p. 32.

I have endeavoured to give the priority always to the *Western* Consul in the list before us, except in those cases where an Emperor (who was of course an Eastern) condescended to assume the Consular *trabea*.

Another mode of reckoning the dates which the reader will continually meet with in the following pages is by *Indictions*. The Indiction, as is well known, was a cycle of fifteen years, during which, as we have reason to believe, the assessment for the taxes remained undisturbed, a fresh valuation being made all round when the cycle was ended. Traces of this quindecennial period may be found in the third century, but the formal adoption of the Indiction is generally assigned to the Emperor Constantine, and to the year 312[1]. The Indiction itself, and every one of the years composing it, began on the 1st of September of the calendar year. The reason for this period being chosen probably was that the harvests of the year being then gathered in, the collection of the tithes of the produce, which formed an important part of the Imperial revenue, could be at once proceeded with. What gives an especial importance to this method of dating by Indictions, for the reader of the following letters is, that most of the great offices of State changed hands at the beginning of the year of the Indiction (Sept. 1), not at the beginning of the Calendar year.

To make such a mode of dating the year at all satisfactory, it would seem to us necessary that the number of the cycle itself, as well as of the year in the cycle, should be given; for instance, that A.D. 313 should be called the first year of the first Indiction, and A.D. 351 the ninth year of the third Indiction. This practice, however, was not adopted till far on into the Middle Ages[2]. At the time we are speaking of, the word Indic-

---

[1] Compare Marquardt (Römische Staatsverwaltung ii. 237). He remarks that the Indiction seems to have been first adopted in Egypt, and did not come into universal use all over the Empire till the end of the Fourth Century.

[2] The Twelfth Century, according to Marquardt.

tion seems generally to have been given not to the cycle itself, but to the year in the cycle. Thus, 313 was the first Indiction, 314 the second Indiction, 315 the third Indiction, and so on. And thus we find a year, which from other sources we know to be 313, called the first Indiction, 351 the ninth Indiction, 537 the fifteenth Indiction, without any clue being given to guide us to the important point in what cycles these years held respectively the first, the ninth, and the fifteenth places.

As the Indiction began on the 1st of September a question arises whether the calendar year is to be named after the number of the Indiction which belongs to its beginning or its end; whether, to go back to the beginning, A.D. 312 or A.D. 313 is to be accounted the first Indiction. The practice of the chroniclers and of most writers on chronology appears to be in favour of the latter method, which is natural, inasmuch as nine months of the Indiction belong to the later date and only three to the earlier. Thus, for instance, Marcellinus Comes calls the year of the Consulship of Belisarius, which was undoubtedly 535, 'Indictio XIII:' the thirteenth Indiction of that cycle having begun Sept. 1, 534, and ended August 31, 535. But it is well that the student should be warned that our greatest English authority, Mr. Fynes Clinton, adopts the other method. In the very useful table of comparative chronology which he gives in his Fasti Romani[1] he assigns the Indiction to that year of the Christian era in which it had its beginning, and accordingly 534, not 535, is identified with the thirteenth Indiction.

In order to translate years of Indiction into years of the Christian era it is necessary first to add some

---

[1] Vol. ii. pp. 214-216. See his remarks, p. 210: 'The Indictions in Marcellinus and in the Tables of Du Fresnoy are compared with the Consulship and the Julian year in which they end. In the following Table they are compared with the year in which they begin, because the years of the Christian era are here made the measure of the rest, and contain the beginnings of all the other epochs.'

multiple of 15 (*what* multiple our knowledge of history must inform us) to 312. On the 1st of September of the year so obtained the Indiction cycle began; and for any other year of the same cycle we must of course add its own number minus one. Thus, when we find Cassiodorus as Praetorian Praefect writing a letter[1] informing Joannes of his appointment to the office of Cancellarius 'for the *twelfth* Indiction,' as we know within a little what date is wanted, we first of all add 14 × 15 (= 210) to 312, and so obtain 522. The first Indiction in that cycle ran from September 1, 522, to August 31, 523. The twelfth Indiction was therefore from September 1, 533, to August 31, 534, and that is the date we require.

On the other hand, when we find a letter written by Cassiodorus as Praetorian Praefect to the Provincials of Istria[2] as to the payment of tribute for the *first* Indiction, we know that we must now have entered upon a new cycle. We therefore add 15 × 15 (= 225) to 312, and get 537. As it happens to be the *first* Indiction that we require, our calculation ends here: September 1, 537, to August 31, 538, is the answer required.

If anyone objects that such a system of chronology is cumbrous, uncertain, and utterly unscientific, I can only say that I entirely agree with him, and that the system is worthy of the perverted ingenuity which produced the Nones and Ides of the Roman Calendar.

In the following tables I have not attempted to mark the years of the Indiction, on account of the confusion caused by the fact that two calendar years require the same number. But I have denoted by the abbreviation 'Ind.' the years in which each cycle of the Indictions *began*. These years are 492, 507, 522, 537, 552, and 567.

---

[1] Var. xi. 6. [2] Var. xii. 22.

Chronological Tables.

A.D.	Consuls.	Private Events.	Public Events.	Rulers of Italy.	Popes.	Emperors.
480	Basilius Junior.	Magnus Aurelius Cassiodorus Senator, born at Scyllacium (?).	Assassination of Nepos, formerly Emperor of the West.	ODOVACAR (from 476).	SIMPLICIUS (from 468).	ZENO (from 474).
481	Placidus.		Odovacar avenges the murder of Nepos. Death of Theodoricus Triarii. Accession of Clovis.			
482	Trocondus and Severinus.		Zeno issues the Henoticon.			
483	Faustus.				FELIX II (or III).	
484	Theodoricus and Venantius.		Illus revolts against Zeno. Schism between Eastern and Western Churches.			
485	Q. Aurelius Memmius Symmachus.					
486	Decius and Longinus.					
487	Boethius (father of the great Boethius).		War between Odovacar and the Rugians. Theodoric starts for Italy.			
488	Dynamius and Sifidius.		Death of Illus. Theodoric descends into Italy. Battles of the Isonzo and Verona.			
489	Anicius Probinus and Eusebius.					
490	Flavius Faustus Junior and Longinus (II).		Battle of the Adda.			
491	Olybrius Junior.		Battle of Ravenna.			ANASTASIUS.
492 (Ind.)	Flavius ANASTASIUS Augustus and Rufus.					
493	Eusebius (II) and Albinus.		Surrender of Ravenna. Death of Odovacar.	THEODORIC.	GELASIUS.	
494	Turcius Rufus Apronianus Asterius and Praesidius.					
495	Flavius Viator.					
496	Paulus.		Clovis defeats the Alamanni. His conversion.			
497	Flavius ANASTASIUS Aug. (II).				ANASTASIUS.	
498	Paulinus and Joannes Scytha.				SYMMACHUS (Antipope Laurentius).	
499	Joannes Gibbus.					

Chronological Tables.

A.D.	Consuls.	Private Events.	Public Events.	Rulers of Italy.	Popes.	Emperors.
500	Patricius and Hypatius.	Cassiodorus Senior, Patrician, Praefect. His son becomes his *Consiliarius*.	War between Gundobad and Clovis. Theodoric's visit to Rome. Conspiracy of Odoin.			
501	Rufus Magnus Faustus Avienus and Flavius Pompeius.	About this time Cassiodorus pronounces his panegyric on Theodoric, and is rewarded by being appointed Quaestor.	Synodus Palmaris at Rome. Symmachus confirmed in the Pontificate.			
502 503 504 505	Flavius Avienus Junior and Probus. Dexicrates and Volusianus. Cethegus. Theodorus and Sabinianus.		War of Sirmium. War between Theodoric and Anastasius (affair of Mundo). Battle of Horea Margi.			
506 507 (Ind.) 508	Messala and Areobinda. Flavius ANASTASIUS Aug. (III) and Venantius. Venantius and Celer.		Clovis defeats Alaric II at Campus Vogladensis. Tulum endeavours to raise siege of Arles. Byzantine raid on Apulia. Mammo invades Burgundy. Ibbas defeats Franks and Burgundians. Death of Clovis.			
509 510 511 512 513 514	Importunus. Anicius Manlius Severinus Boethius (*Author of the 'Consolation'*). Felix and Secundinus. Paulus and Muschianus. Probus and Clementinus. Senator, *solus Consul* (Cassiodorus).	Cassiodorus as Consul restores harmony between clergy and people of Rome.				
515	Florentius and Anthemius.	Cassiodorus receives the Patriciate (?).	Marriage of Eutharic and Amalasuentha.			
516 517	Petrus. Agapitus and Flavius Anastasius (*nephew of the Emperor*).				HORMISDAS.	

Chronological Tables.

A.D.	Consuls.	Private Events.	Public Events.	Rulers of Italy.	Popes.	Emperors.
518	Magnus.					JUSTIN I.
519	JUSTINUS Augustus and Eutharicus Cillica.	Composition of the 'Chronicon,' dedicated to Eutharic.	End of schism between Eastern and Western Churches.			
520	Rusticus and Vitalianus.	Composition of the Gothic History (?).				
521	Valerius and Flavius Justinianus.					
522	Symmachus and Boethius (sons of the great Boethius).		Franks invade Burgundy. Imprisonment of Boethius.		JOHN I.	
523 (Ind.)	Flavius Anicius Maximus.		Death of Boethius.			
524	Flavius JUSTINUS Aug. (II) and Opilio.		Death of Symmachus. Pope John's Mission to Constantinople.			
525	Anicius Probus Junior and Flavius Theodorus Philoxenus.					
526	Olybrius.	Cassiodorus Master of the Offices.	Pope John dies in prison (May 25). Death of Theodoric (Aug. 30).	ATHALARIC.	FELIX III (or IV).	
527	Vettius Agorius Basilius Mavortius.		Death of Amalafrida, Queen-dowager of the Vandals.			JUSTINIAN.
528	Flavius JUSTINIANUS Aug. (II).				BONIFACE II.	
529	Decius Junior.					
530	Flavius Lampadius and Orestes.					
531	Post Consulatum Lampadii et Orestis, Anno II.		Final invasion of Burgundy by the Franks.			
532	,, ,, ,,	Cassiodorus Praetorian Praefect (Sept. 1), which office he holds till he retires from public life.	The Vandal War of Justinian (June, 533–March, 534).		JOHN III.	
533	Flavius JUSTINIANUS Aug. (III).					
534	Flavius JUSTINIANUS Aug. (IV). and Flavius Theodorus Paulinus Junior.		Death of Athalaric (Oct. 2). Association of Theodahad with Amalasuentha.	AMALASUENTHA. THEODAHAD.		
535	Flavius Belisarius.		Death of Amalasuentha. The Gothic War begun.		AGAPETUS.	

Chronological Tables.

A.D.	Consuls.	Private Events.	Public Events.	Rulers of Italy.	Popes.	Emperors.
536	Post Consulatum Fl. Belisarii.		Belisarius takes Naples and enters Rome. Siege of Rome by Witigis.	WITIGIS.	SILVERIUS.	
537 (Ind.)	" Anno II.				VIGILIUS.	
538	Flavius Johannes (John of Cappadocia).	Collection of the 'Variae.' Composition of the 'De Anima.'	Siege of Rome raised.			
539	Flavius Appion.	Cassiodorus about this time lays down his office and retires to his birthplace (Scyllacium), where he founds the Monastery of Vivaria.	Mediolanum taken by the Goths. Belisarius takes Auximum.			
540	Flavius Justinus Junior.		Ravenna surrendered to Belisarius. Captivity of Witigis.	ILDIBAD.		
541	Flavius Basilius Junior.			EBARIC. BADUILA (TOTILA).		
542		He writes Commentary on the Psalms as far as Psalm 21.	Totila twice defeats the Imperial generals, and retrieves the fortune of the Ostrogoths.			
543		Composition of the 'Institutiones Divinarum et Humanarum Litterarum.'				
544	Years reckoned Post Consulatum Basilii.		Belisarius returns to Italy. Rome taken by Totila.			
545						
546			Rome re-occupied by Belisarius.			
547						
548		Continues and completes his Commentary on the Psalms.	Death of Empress Theodora.			
549			Rome again taken by Totila.			
550			Death of Germanus.			
551			Narses Commander of Italian Expedition.			

A.D.	Consuls.	Private Events.	Public Events.	Rulers of Italy.	Popes.	Emperors.
552 (Ind.) 553	Years reckoned Post Consulatum Basilii.		Narses defeats Totila near Tadinum. Teias defeated and slain near Mons Lactarius. The Ostrogoths leave Italy. Invasion of the Alamannic brethren.	TEIAS. NARSES, Governor of Italy under the Emperor.		
554 555 556 557 558 559		Writes the 'Complexiones in Epistolas Apostolorum,' and compiles the 'Historia Tripartita' (the precise date of these works unknown).			PELAGIUS.	
560 561 562 563			Belisarius defeats the Huns under Zabergan.			
564 565 566	Post Consulatum Basilii XXIV. Flavius JUSTINUS Augustus.		Disgrace of Belisarius. Belisarius restored to favour.		JOHN III.	
567 (Ind.)	Years reckoned Post Consulatum Justini.		Death of Belisarius and of Justinian. Narses recalled by Justin. Alleged invitation to the Lombards.			JUSTIN II.
568			The Lombards under Alboin enter Italy.	LONGINUS, Exarch.		
569			Milan taken by the Lombards.	ALBOIN, King of the Lombards.		
570 571			Ticinum taken by the Lombards.			
572 573		Composition of treatise 'De Orthographia,' in 93rd year of Cassiodorus.	Assassination of Alboin.	CLEPH, King of the Lombards. Death of Cleph.	Death of John III.	
574 575		Cassiodorus dies in his 95th year (?).			BENEDICT I.	

THE
LETTERS OF CASSIODORUS.

PREFACE[1].

LEARNED men, who had become my friends through conversations which we had had together, or benefits which I had bestowed upon them, sought to persuade me to draw together into one work the various utterances which it had been my duty to make, during my tenure of office, for the explanation of different affairs. They desired me to do this, in order that future generations might recognise the painful labours which I had undergone for the public good, and the workings of my own unbribed conscience. I then replied that their very kindness for me might turn out to my disadvantage, since the letters which their good-will found acceptable might to future readers seem insipid. I reminded them also of the words of Horace, warning us of the dangers of hasty publication. *[Reason for publication: entreaties of friends.]*

'You see,' said I, 'that all require from me a speedy reply to their petitions; and do you think that I couch those replies in words which leave me nothing to regret hereafter? Our diction must be somewhat rude when there is no sufficient delay to enable the speaker to choose words which shall rightly express the precise shade of his meaning. Speech is the common gift of all mankind: it is embellishment (ornatus) alone which distinguishes between the learned and unlearned. The author is told to keep his writings by him for nine years for reflection; but I have not as many hours, hardly as many moments. *[Difficulty of writing.]*

[1] Translated in full.

As soon as I begin the petitioner worries me with his clamours, and hurries me too much to prevent my finishing cautiously, even if I have so begun my task. One vexes me past endurance by his interruptions and innuendoes; another torments me with the doleful tale of his miseries; others surround me with the mad shouts of their seditious contentions [1]. In such circumstances how can you expect elegance of language, when we have scarcely opportunity to put words together in any fashion? Even at night indescribable cares are flitting round our couch [2], while we are harassed with fear lest the cities should lack their supplies of food—food which the common people insist upon more than anything else, caring more for their bellies than for the gratification of their ears by eloquence. This thought obliges us to wander in imagination through all the Provinces, and ever to enquire after the execution of our orders, since it is not enough to tell our staff what has to be done, but the diligent administrator must see that it is done [3]. Therefore, I pray you, spare us your harmful love. I must decline this persuasion of yours, which will bring me more of danger than of glory.'

So I pleaded; but they plied me all the more with such arguments as these:

The Praefecture.

'All men have known you as Praefect of the Praetorian throne, a dignity which all other public employments wait upon like lacqueys. For from this high office, ways and means for the army are demanded; from this, without any regard for the difficulty of the

---

[1] 'Alii furiosa contentionum seditione circumdant.' This is probably meant to describe turbulent Goths.

[2] οὐ χρὴ παννύχιον εὕδειν βουληφόρον ἄνδρα (Il. ii. 24).

[3] Quia non sufficit agenda militibus imperare, nisi haec Judicis assiduitas videatur exigere.

times, the food of the people is required; on this, a weight of judicial responsibility is thrown, which would be by itself a heavy burden. Now the law, which has thrown this immense load on the Praefect's office, has, on the other hand, honoured him by putting almost all things under his control. In truth, what interval of leisure could you snatch from your public labours, when into your single breast flowed every claim which could be made on behalf of the common good of all?

'We must add, moreover, that when you were on frequent occasions charged with the office of the Quaestorship, the leisure which you might have enjoyed was taken from you by your own constant thoughtfulness for the public good; and when you were thus bearing the weight of an honour which was not the highest, your Sovereigns used to lay upon you those duties, properly belonging to other offices, which their own holders were unable to discharge[1]. All these duties you discharged with absolute freedom from corruption, following your father's example in receiving, from those who hoped for your favour, nothing but the obligation to serve them, and bestowing on petitioners all that they had a right to ask for without traffic or reward.

The Quaestorship.

'Moreover, men know that the conversations which you were honoured by holding with the King occupied a large portion of your days, greatly to the public welfare[2], so that men of leisure have no right

Intimacy with Theodoric.

---

[1] 'Addimus etiam quod frequenter Quaesturae vicibus ingravato otii tempus adimit crebra cogitatio, et velut mediocribus fascibus insudanti, illa tibi de aliis honoribus principes videntur imponere, quae proprii Judices nequeunt explicare.' This is probably the clearest account that is anywhere given of the peculiar and somewhat undefined position held by Cassiodorus during the greater part of the reign of Theodoric.

[2] 'Regum quinetiam gloriosa colloquia pro magnâ diei parte in bonum publicum te occupare noverunt.' It is difficult to translate the expressive term, 'gloriosa colloquia.'

to expect that their requirements shall be met by you, whose day was thus occupied with continuous toil[1]. But in truth this will redound yet more to your glory, if amid so many and such severe labours you succeed in writing that which is worthy to be read. Besides, your work can without wounding their self-love instruct unlettered persons who are not prepared by any consciousness of eloquence for the service of the Republic[2]; and the experience which you have gained by being tossed to and fro on the waves of stormy altercation, they in their more tranquil lot may more fortunately make their own. Again (and here we make an appeal which your loyalty cannot resist), if you allow posterity to be ignorant of the numerous benefits conferred by your King, it is in vain that with benevolent eagerness he so often granted your requests. Do not, we pray, draw back once more into silence and obscurity those who, while you were sounding their eulogies, seemed worthy to receive illustrious dignities. For you then professed to describe them with true praises, and to paint their characters with the colours of history[3]. Now if you leave it to posterity to write the panegyric on these men, you take away as it were from those who die an honourable death the funeral oration to which, by the customs of our ancestors, they are entitled. Besides, in these letters you correct immorality with a ruler's authority; you break the insolence of the transgressor; you restore to the laws their reverence. Do you still hesitate about publishing that which, as you

---

[1] 'Ut fastidium sit otiosis exspectare quae tu continuo labore cognosceris sustinere.' I cannot translate this literally.

[2] 'Rudes viros et ad Rempublicam conscia facundia praeparatos.' Surely some negative has dropped out of the latter clause.

[3] 'Tu enim illos assumpsisti verā laude describere, et quodammodo historico colore depingere.'

know, satisfies so many needs? Will you conceal, if we may say so, the mirror of your own mind, in which all ages to come may behold your likeness? Often does it happen that a man begets a son unlike himself, but his writings are hardly ever found unequal to his character[1]. The progeny of his own will is his truest child; what is born in the secret recesses of his own heart is that by which posterity will know him best.

'You have often, amid universal acclamation, pronounced the praises of kings and queens. In twelve books you have compiled the History of the Goths, culling the story of their triumphs[2]. Since these works have had such favourable fortunes, and since you have thus served your first campaign in literature, why hesitate to give these productions of yours also to the public?' Gothic History.

So pleaded my friends, and to my shame I must own that I was conquered, and could no longer resist so many prayers; especially when I saw myself accused of want of affection. I have now only to crave my readers' pardon; and if they find rashness and presumption in my attempt, to blame my advisers rather than me, since my own judgment agrees with that of my severest critic. Cassiodorus consents to publish.

All the letters, therefore, which I have been able to find

---

[1] 'Contingit enim dissimilem filium plerumque generari, oratio dispar moribus vix potest inveniri.'

[2] 'Duodecim libris Gothorum historiam *defloratis prosperitatibus* condidisti.' By an extraordinary error this sentence has been interpreted to mean that Cassiodorus wrote his history of the Goths after their prosperity had faded; and some writers have accordingly laboured, quite hopelessly, to bring down the composition of the Gothic History to a late period in the reign of Athalaric. It is perfectly clear from many passages that Cassiodorus uses 'deflorare' in the sense of 'picking flowers,' 'culling a nosegay.' See Historia Tripartita, Preface (twice); De Instit. Divin. Litterarum, cap. xxx; and De Orthographiâ, cap. ii (title). I doubt not that careful search would discover many more instances. It is only strange to me that Cassiodorus should, by the words 'defloratis *prosperitatibus*,' so naïvely confess the one-sided character of his history.

in various public archives that had been dictated by me as Quaestor, as Magister [Officiorum], or as Praefect, are here collected and arranged in twelve books. By the variety of subjects touched upon, the attention of the reader will be aroused, and it will be maintained by the feeling that he is rapidly approaching the conclusion of the letter.

I have also wished to preserve others from those unpolished and hasty forms of speech into which I am conscious that I have often fallen in announcing the bestowal of dignities, a kind of document which is often asked for in such haste that there seems scarce time for the mere manual labour of writing it. I have therefore included in my Sixth and Seventh Books *Formulae* for the granting of all the dignities of the State, hoping thus to be of some service to myself, though at a late period of my career, and to help my successors who may be hard pressed for time. What I have thus written concerning the past will serve equally well for the future, since I have said nothing about the qualities of the individual office-holder, but have made such explanations as seemed suitable concerning the office.

Reason of the title Variarum. As for the title of all twelve books, the index of the work, the herald of its meaning, the expression in briefest compass of the whole performance, I have for this chosen the name VARIAE. And this, because it was necessary for me not always to use the same style, since I had undertaken to address various kinds of persons. One must speak in one way to men jaded with much reading; in another to those who skim lightly over the surface, tasting here and there; in another (if one would persuade them), to persons who are devoid of a taste for letters, since it is sometimes a proof of skill to avoid the very things which please the learned. In short, the definition given by our ancestors is a good one: 'To speak fitly is to persuade the hearers to accept your wishes for their own.' Nor was it at random that the prudence of Antiquity thus defined the three modes of speaking:—

(1) The *humble* style, which seems to creep along the ground in the very expression of its thought.

(2) The *middle* style, which is neither swollen with self-importance nor shrunk into littleness; but being placed between the two, and enriched by a peculiar elegance, is contained within its own true boundaries.

(3) The *supreme* style, which by exquisite phraseology is raised to the very highest pitch of oratory.

The three styles of composition.

The object of this distinction is that the various sorts and conditions of men may each receive their appropriate address, and that the thoughts which proceed from the same breast may nevertheless flow in divers channels. No man is entitled to the name of eloquent who is not prepared to do his duty manfully with the triple strength of these three styles, as one cause after another may arise. It must be added hereto that we have sometimes to speak to Kings, sometimes to the Officers of the Court, sometimes to the very humblest of the people. To the last we may allowably pour out our words with some degree of haste, but the other addresses should be deeply pondered before they are delivered. Deservedly therefore is a work entitled VARIAE, which is subject to so much diversity in its composition.

Would that, as we have received these maxims from those who have gone before us, so our own compositions could claim the praise f having reduced them into practice. In sooth we do with shamefacedness promise that the Humble style shall be found in us; we think we may without dishonesty covenant for the Middle style; but the Supreme style, which on account of its nobility is the fitting language of a royal Edict[1], we cannot hope that we have attained unto.

But since we are to be read, let us abstain from further unlawful canvassing for the votes of our readers. It is an incongruous thing for us to be thus piling up our own discourses about ourselves: we ought rather to wait for your judgment on our work.

---

[1] The editors waver between 'quod est in edicto' and 'quod est in edito (constitutum).'

BOOK I.

CONTAINING FORTY-SIX LETTERS WRITTEN BY CASSIODORUS IN THE NAME OF THEODORIC.

---

1. KING THEODORIC TO EMPEROR ANASTASIUS.

Persuasives to peace between Italy and Constantinople.

'It behoves us, most clement Emperor, to seek for peace, since there are no causes for anger between us.

'Peace by which the nations profit; Peace the fair mother of all liberal arts, the softener of manners, the replenisher of the generations of mankind. Peace ought certainly to be an object of desire to every kingdom.

'Therefore, most pious of princes, it accords with your power and your glory that we who have already profited by your affection [personally] should seek concord with your Empire. You are the fairest ornament of all realms; you are the healthful defence of the whole world, to which all other rulers rightfully look up with reverence[1], because they know that there is in you something which is unlike all others[2]: we above all, who by Divine help learned in your Republic the art of governing Romans with equity. Our royalty is an imitation of yours, modelled on your good purpose, a copy of the only Empire; and in so far as we follow you do we excel all other nations.

---

[1] 'Vos totius orbis salutare praesidium, quod caeteri dominantes jure suspiciunt quia in vobis singulare aliquid inesse cognoscunt.' 'Suspiciunt' seems to give a better sense than the other reading, 'suscipiunt.'

[2] 'Quia in vobis singulare aliquid inesse cognoscunt.'

'Often have you exhorted me to love the Senate, to accept cordially the laws of past Emperors, to join together in one all the members of Italy. How can you separate from your august alliance one whose character you thus try to make conformable to your own? There is moreover that noble sentiment, love for the City of Rome, from which two princes, both of whom govern in her name, should never be disjoined.

'We have thought fit therefore to send A and B[1] as ambassadors to your most serene Piety, that Peace, which has been broken, through a variety of causes, may, by the removal of all matters of dispute, be firmly restored between us. For we think you will not suffer that any discord should remain between two Republics, which are declared to have ever formed one body under their ancient princes[2], and which ought not to be joined by a mere sentiment of love, but actively to aid one another with all their powers. Let there be always one will, one purpose in the Roman Kingdom. Therefore, while greeting you with our respectful salutations, we humbly beg that you will not remove from us the high honour of your Mildness's affection[3], which we have a right to hope for if it were never granted to any others.

'The rest of their commission will be verbally conveyed to your Piety by the bearers of these letters[4].'

---

[1] 'Illum atque illum.' I shall always render this phrase (which shows that Cassiodorus had not preserved the names of the ambassadors) as above.

[2] 'Quia pati vos non credimus, inter utrasque Respublicas, quarum semper unum corpus sub antiquis principibus fuisse declaratur, aliquid discordiae permanere.'

[3] 'Pomâ mente deposcimus ne suspendatis a nobis mansuetudinis vestrae gloriosissimam caritatem.'

[4] For some remarks on the date of this letter, see Introduction, p. 23. The mention of interrupted peace, which evidently requires not mere estrangement but an actual state of war, points to the year 505, when Sabinian, the general of Anastasius, was defeated by the Ostrogoths and their allies at Horrea Margi; or to 508, when the Imperial fleet made a raid on the coast of Apulia, as probable dates for the composition of the letter. Its place at the beginning of the Variae does not

2. KING THEODORIC TO THEON, VIR SUBLIMIS.

[Sidenote: Manufacture of purple dye.]

'We are informed by Count Stephen that the work of preparing the purple for the sacred (*i.e.* royal) robes, which was put under your charge, has been interrupted through reprehensible negligence on your part. There must be neglect somewhere, or else the wool with its milk-white hairs would long before now have imbibed the precious quality of the adorable *murex*. If the diver in the waters of Hydruntum[1] had sought for these murex-shells at the proper season, that Neptunian harvest, mixed with an abundant supply of water, would already have generated the flame-bright liquid which dyes the robes that adorn the throne. The colour of that dye is gay[2] with too great beauty; 'tis a blushing obscurity, an ensanguined blackness, which distinguishes the wearer from all others, and makes it impossible for the human race not to know who is the king. It is marvellous that that substance after death should for so long a time exude an amount of gore which one would hardly find flowing from the wounds of a living creature. For even six months after they have been separated from the delights of the sea, these shell-fish are not offensive to the keenest nostrils, as if on purpose that that noble blood might inspire no disgust. Once this dye is imparted to the cloth, it remains there

---

at all imply priority in date to the letters which follow it. It was evidently Cassiodorus' method to put in the forefront of every book in his collection a letter to an Emperor or King, or other great personage.

As for the tone of the letter, and the exact character of the relation between the Courts of Ravenna and Constantinople which is indicated by it, there is room for a wide divergence of opinion. To me it does not seem to bear out Justinian's contention (recorded by Procopius, De Bello Gotthico ii. 6) that Theodoric ruled Italy as the Emperor's lieutenant. Under all the apparent deference and affectation of humility the language seems to me to be substantially that of one equal addressing another, older and with a somewhat more assured position, but still an equal.

[1] Otranto.   [2] Vernans.

for ever; the tissue may be destroyed sooner than part with it. If the murex has not changed its quality, if the press (torcular) is still there to receive its one vintage, it must be the fault of the labourers that the dye is not forthcoming. What are they doing, all those crowds of sailors, those families of rustics? And you who bear the name of Count, and were exalted high over your fellow-citizens on purpose that you might attend to this very thing, what sacrilegious negligence is this which you are manifesting in reference to the sacred vesture? If you have any care for your own safety come at once with the purple[1], which you have hitherto been accustomed to render up every year. If not, if you think to mock us by delay, we shall send you not a constrainer but an avenger.

'How easy was the discovery of this great branch of manufacture! A dog, keen with hunger, bounding along the Tyrian shore, crunched the shells which were cast up there. The purple gore dyed his jaws with a marvellous colour; and the men who saw it, after the sudden fashion of inventors, conceived the idea of making therewith a noble adornment for their kings. What Tyre is for the East, Hydron[2] is for Italy—the great cloth-factory of Courts, not keeping its old art (merely), but ever transmitting new improvements.'

3. KING THEODORIC TO CASSIODORUS, VIR ILLUSTRIS AND PATRICIAN[3].

Praises of the father of Cassiodorus.

Extols in high-flown language the merits of the minister who in the early and troublous days of Theodoric's reign conciliated the wavering affections of the suspicious Sicilians[4], governed them so justly that not even they

---

[1] Blatta.
[2] I presume the same as Hydruntum (Otranto).
[3] Father of the Author.
[4] 'In ipso quippe imperii nostri devotus exordio, cum adhuc fluctuantibus rebus provinciarum corda vagarentur, et negligi rudem dominum novitas ipsa pateretur.'

(addicted as they are, according to Cicero, to grumbling) could complain; then displayed equal rectitude in the government of his own native Province of Bruttii and Lucania (hard as it is to be perfectly just in the government of one's own native place); then administered the Praefecture in such a way as to earn the thanks of all Italy, even the taxes not being felt to be burdensome under his rule, because so justly levied; and now, finally, as a reward for all these services, is raised to the distinguished honour of the Patriciate.

4. KING THEODORIC TO THE SENATE OF THE CITY OF ROME.

[Introducing Cassiodorus (Senior) on his accession to the honours of the Patriciate.]

Compliments to the Senate, of which Theodoric wishes to increase the dignity by bestowing honours on its most eminent members. *Great deeds of the ancestors of Cassiodorus for three generations.*

Recital of the services and good qualities of Cassiodorus[1]:

(a) as 'Comes Privatarum;'
(b) as 'Comes Sacrarum Largitionum;'
(c) as Governor of Provinces.

(General reflections on the importance of a governor being himself a virtuous man).

'Having been trained thus to official life under the preceding King [Odovacar] he came with well-earned praises to our palace.'

(d) His eminent career as Praetorian Praefect and modest demeanour therein.

Services of previous members of his family. Fame seems to be always at home among the Cassiodori. They are of noble birth, equally celebrated among orators and warriors, healthy of body, and very tall.

His father, *Cassiodorus*[2], was 'Tribunus et Notarius'

---
[1] Father of Cassiodorus Senator.
[2] Grandfather of Cassiodorus Senator.

under Valentinian III. This last was a great honour, for only men of spotless life were associated with the Imperial 'Secretum.' A friendship, founded on likeness, drew him to the side of Aetius, whose labours for the State he shared.

Embassy to Attila. 'With the son of this Aetius, named Carpilio, he was sent on no vain embassy to Attila, the mighty in arms. He looked undaunted on the man before whom the Empire quailed. Calm in conscious strength, he despised all those terrible wrathful faces that scowled around him. He did not hesitate to meet the full force of the invectives of the madman who fancied himself about to grasp the Empire of the world. He found the King insolent; he left him pacified; and so ably did he argue down all his slanderous pretexts for dispute that though the Hun's interest was to quarrel with the richest Empire in the world, he nevertheless condescended to seek its favour. The firmness of the orator roused the fainting courage of his countrymen, and men felt that Rome could not be pronounced defenceless while she was armed with such ambassadors. Thus did he bring back the peace which men had despaired of; and as earnestly as they had prayed for his success, so thankfully did they welcome his return.'

He was offered honours and revenues, but preferred to seek the pleasant retirement of Bruttii in the land which his exertions had freed from the terror of the stranger.

His father, Cassiodorus[1], an 'Illustris,' defended the coasts of Sicily and Bruttii from the Vandals, thus averting from those regions the ruin which afterwards fell upon Rome from the same quarter.

In the East, Heliodorus, a cousin of the Cassiodori, has brilliantly discharged the office of Praefect for eighteen years, as Theodoric himself can testify. Thus

---
[1] Great-grandfather of Cassiodorus Senator.

the family, conspicuous both in the Eastern and Western World, has two eyes with which it shines with equal brilliancy in each Senate.

Cassiodorus is so wealthy that his herds of horses surpass those of the King, to whom he makes presents of some of them in order to avoid envy. 'Hence it arises that our present candidate [for patrician honours] mounts the armies of the Goths; and having even improved upon his education, generously administers the wealth which he received from his parents.

'Now, Conscript Fathers, welcome and honour the new Patrician, who is so well worthy of a high place among you.'

5. KING THEODORIC TO FLORIANUS, VIR SPECTABILIS.

'Lawsuits must not be dragged on for ever. There must be some possibility of reaching a quiet haven. Wherefore, if the petitioners have rightly informed us that the controversy as to the farm at Mazenes has been decided in due course of law by Count Annas, and there is no reasonable ground for appeal[1], let that sentence be held final and irreversible. We must sometimes save a litigious man from himself, as a good doctor will not allow a patient to take that which is injurious to him.' *Interest reipublicae ut sit finis litium.*

6. KING THEODORIC TO AGAPITUS, PRAEFECTUS URBIS.

[One of the MSS. reads *Pontifici*, but this is clearly wrong. The language is not at all suitable to be addressed to a Pope, and there was no Pope Agapetus till 535, nine years after the death of Theodoric.]

'I am going to build a great Basilica of Hercules at Ravenna, for I wish my age to match preceding ones *Mosaics ordered for Ravenna.*

---

[1] 'Nec aliqua probatur appellatione suspensa.'

in the beauty of its buildings, as it does in the happiness of the lives of my subjects.

'Send me therefore skilful workers in Mosaic' [of which kind of work we have a very good description as follows].

(*Cassiodorus on Mosaic*).

'Send us from your city some of your most skilful marble-workers, who may join together those pieces which have been exquisitely divided, and, connecting together their different veins of colour, may admirably represent the natural appearance[1]. From Art proceeds this gift, which conquers Nature. And thus the discoloured surface of the marble is woven into the loveliest variety of pictures; the value of the work, now as always, being increased by the minute labour which has to be expended on the production of the Beautiful.'

7. KING THEODORIC TO FELIX, VIR CLARISSIMUS.

This letter will be best understood by a reference to the following pedigree:

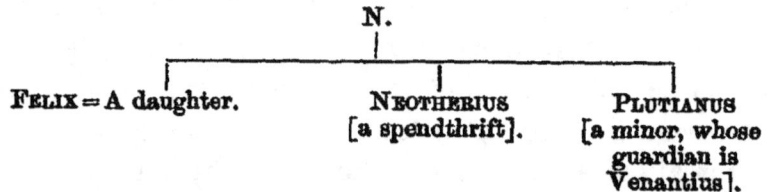

The inheritance of Plutianus.

Apparently Felix is accused by Venantius, the guardian of his young brother-in-law Plutianus, of having, on behalf of his wife, made an unfair division of the family property (which had been originally given to the father of these lads by Theodoric, as a reward for his services). In doing this he has availed himself of the spendthrift character of Neotherius, the elder brother, who was probably already of age.

Felix is severely blamed, and ordered to hand over

---

[1] 'Et venis colludentibus illigata naturalem faciem laudabiliter mentiantur.'

what he has fraudulently appropriated to the official, who is charged with the execution of this mandate.

Both are summoned to the 'Comitatus' of the King, that a fair division may there be made between them.

8. KING THEODORIC TO AMABILIS, THE COLLECTOR (EXSECUTOR).

In reference to this same matter of the wasted property of Plutianus. It appears from this letter that Neotherius has been not merely a spendthrift, but has been actuated by motives of passionate hatred to his younger brother[1]. The King enlarges on his obligation to protect the weak, and orders the officer to see that justice is done according to the representations of Venantius, unless the other side have any counter plea to allege, in which case 'ad nostrum venire deproperet comitatum.'

The prodigality of Neotherius.

9. KING THEODORIC TO EUSTORGIUS, BISHOP OF MILAN.

'You will be glad to hear that we are satisfied that the Bishop of Augusta [Turin or Aosta] has been falsely accused of betrayal of his country. He is therefore to be restored to his previous rank. His accusers, as they are themselves of the clerical order, are not punished by us, but sent to your Holiness to be dealt with according to the ecclesiastical tradition.'

Offences charged against Ecclesiastics.

[The reflections in this letter about the impropriety of believing readily accusations against a Bishop[2], and the course adopted of handing over the clerical false accusers to be dealt with by their Bishop, have an

---

[1] ' Neotherium fratrem suum, affectum germanitatis oblitum, *bona parvuli hostili furore lacerasse.*'

[2] 'Nihil enim in tali honore temeraria cogitatione praesumendum est, ubi si proposito creditur, etiam tacitus ab excessibus excusatur. Manifesta proinde crimina in talibus vix capiunt fidem. Quidquid autem ex invidia dicitur, veritas non putatur.'

obvious bearing on the great Hildebrandic controversy. But as Dahn ('Könige der Germanen' iii. 191) points out, there is no abandonment by the King of the ultimate right to punish an ecclesiastic.]

10. KING THEODORIC TO BOETIUS[1], VIR ILLUSTRIS AND PATRICIAN.

Frauds of the moneyers.

The Horse and Foot Guards[2] seem to have complained that after their severe labours they were not paid in solidi of full weight by the 'Arcarius Praefectorum.'

Cassiodorus gives—

(1) Some sublime reflections in the true Cassiodorian vein on the nature of Arithmetic, by which earth and the heavens are ruled.

(2) Some excellent practical remarks on the wickedness of clipping and depreciating the currency.

The most interesting but most puzzling sentence in this letter is that in which he says that 'the ancients wished that the *solidus* should consist of 6,000 *denarii*, in order that the golden coin like a golden sun might represent the 6,000 years which are the appointed age of the world.' But how can we reconcile this with any known solidus or any known denarius? The solidus of Constantine (72 to the lb.) was worth about twelve shillings. The reduced denarius of Diocletian was probably worth one penny. At the very lowest (and most improbable) computation it was worth at least a farthing, and even thus one would only get 576 to a solidus. The earlier denarius, worth about eightpence, clearly will not do; and the matter is made more difficult by the fact that Cassiodorus is talking about the an-

---

[1] If the MSS. are correctly represented in the printed editions, the name of the author of the Consolation of Philosophy was spelt Boetius in the Variae. There can be little doubt however that Boethius is the more correct form, and this is the form given us in the Anecdoton Holderi.

[2] Why are these called 'Domestici patres equitum et peditum?'

cients (veteres), whereas the solidus was a comparatively modern coin. It seems that either Cassiodorus has some entirely wrong information as to the early currency of Rome, or else that we have not yet got the clue to his meaning.

This passage is quoted by Finlay ('Greece under the Romans,' p. 536, ed. 1857), but the difficulty is not removed by his remarks.

11. KING THEODORIC TO SERVATUS, DUKE OF THE RAETIAS.

Violence of the Breones.

'It is your duty to repress all violence and injustice in the Provinces over which you preside. Maniarius complains that his slaves (mancipia) have been without any cause taken away from him by the *Breones* [a Raetian tribe dwelling near the pass of the Brenner], who are continuing in peace the habits and maxims of war.

'If this proves to be a true complaint, see that justice is done, and speedily.'

12. KING THEODORIC TO EUGENIUS (OR EUGENITES)[1], VIR ILLUSTRIS, MAGISTER OFFICIORUM.

Bestowal of dignity of Magister Officiorum.

'It is the glory of our reign to confer office on those who deserve it.

'You are a learned man, and arrived long ago at the dignity of the Quaestorship as a reward for your creditable exertions as an Advocate.

'One office leads to another: the tree of the fasces puts forth fresh fasces; and we therefore have great pleasure in calling you now to the dignity of Magister, bestowing upon you all the privileges which have belonged to your predecessors in that office. Justify our choice by your actions. You know, as one of our counsellors,

---

[1] Perhaps the name really was Eugenes, -etis. See Var. viii. 19, and Ennodii, Epist. iv. 26.

what our standard of righteousness is. A sort of religious holiness is required from those who hold office under a righteous king[1].'

13. KING THEODORIC TO THE SENATE OF THE CITY OF ROME.

On the same subject.

Announces the elevation of Eugenius (or Eugenites) to the post of Master of the Offices, and recapitulates his past services and character in nearly the same terms as the preceding letter. He is to go from one office to another, 'even as the sun having shone one day, rises in order to shine again on another. Even horses are stimulated to greater speed by the shouts of men. But man is an animal peculiarly fond of approbation. Do you therefore stimulate the new Master to all noble deeds.'

[Notice this sentence about the Senate: 'Whatever is the flower of the human race, the Senate ought to possess it: and as the citadel is the crown of the city, so should your order be the ornament of all other ranks.']

14. KING THEODORIC TO FAUSTUS, PRAEPOSITUS.

Collection of 'Tertiae.'

'We have no objection to grant the petition of the inhabitants of Cathalia(?), that their "Tertiae" shall be collected at the same time as the ordinary tribute. What does it matter under what name the "possessor" pays his contribution, so long as he pays it without deduction? Thus they will get rid of the suspected name of "Tertiae," and our mildness will not be worried by their importunity.'

[See Dahn ('Könige der Germanen' iii. 143), who decides that the 'Tertiae' was the pecuniary equivalent paid by the Roman possessor for that portion of

---

[1] 'Pio principi sub quodam sacerdotio serviatur.' Cf. Claudian, 'Nunquam libertas gratior exstat quam *sub rege pio*.'

the *Sors Barbarica* (the Gothic third of the lands of Italy) which, for convenience sake, was left in the actual occupation of Romans.]

15. King Theodoric to Festus, Vir Illustris and Patrician.

Looking after the interests of the absent.

'We are glad to see that our good opinion of you is shared by your neighbours, and that the Patrician Agnellus, going to Africa on our business, has chosen you to defend his interests in his absence. No one can give a higher proof of confidence than this. Look well after the trust committed to you. There seems to be a peculiar temptation to neglect the interests of the absent.'

16. King Theodoric to Julianus, Comes Patrimonii [probably 508].

Remission of taxes. Hostile incursions.

'It is an excellent investment to do a generous thing to our subjects. The Apulian "Conductores" [farmers of the Royal domain] have represented to us with tears that their crops have been burned by hostile invaders [Byzantines?]. We therefore authorise you to deduct at the next Indiction what shall seem the right proportion for these losses from the amount due to us[1]. See, however, that our revenue sustains no unnecessary loss. We are touched by the losses of the suppliants, but we ought on the other hand to share their profits.'

17. King Theodoric to all the Gothic and Roman Inhabitants of Dertona (Tortona).

Fortification of camp near Dertona.

'We have decided that the camp near you shall at once be fortified. It is expedient to execute works of this kind in peace rather than in war.

---

[1] 'Ut quantum eos minus vendidisse constiterit, de reliquis primae indictionis habita moderatione detrahatis.'

'The true meaning of *expeditio* shows that the leader of a military expedition should have an unencumbered mind.

'Do you therefore second our efforts by building good private houses, in which you will be sheltered, while the enemy (whenever he comes) will be in the worst possible quarters[1], and exposed to all the severity of the weather.'

18. KING THEODORIC TO DOMITIANUS AND WILIAS.

Statute of Limitations.

'It is right that you, who are administering justice to the nations, should learn and practise it yourselves. We therefore hasten to reply to the question which you have asked [concerning the length of time that is required to bestow a title by prescription]. If any Barbarian usurper have taken possession of a Roman farm since the time when we, through God's grace, crossed the streams of the Isonzo, when first the Empire of Italy received us[2], and if he have no documents of title [sine delegatoris cujusquam pyctacio] to show that he is the rightful holder, then let him without delay restore the property to its former owner. But if he shall be found to have entered upon the property before the aforesaid time, since the principle of the thirty years' prescription comes in, we order that the petition of the plaintiff shall be dropped.

Crimes of violence.

'The assailant, as well as the murderer, of his brother, is to be driven forth from the kingdom, that the serenity of our Commonwealth may not be troubled with any such dark spots.'

[Theodoric crossed the Isonzo, August, 489, and as I understand this letter, it was written somewhere about 518, and he therefore lays down a convenient practical

---

[1] 'Durissimae mansiones.'

[2] 'Ex quo, Deo propitio, Sonti fluenta transmisimus ubi primum Italiae nos suscepit imperium.'

rule: 'No dispossession which occurred before I crossed the Isonzo shall be enquired into; any which have happened since, may.' But the letter is a very difficult one, and I am bound to say that Dahn's interpretation ('Könige der Germanen' iii. 11, 12) does not agree with mine.]

19. KING THEODORIC TO SATURNINUS AND VERBUSIUS, VIRI SUBLIMES.

'The *Fiscus* is to have its rights, but we do not wish to oppress our people. Let moderation be observed in all things.

The rights of the Fiscus.

'When you receive the petition of the Curiales of Adriana, if anyone who is able to pay, stubbornly and impudently refuses to contribute to the *Fiscus Gothorum*, you are to compel him to do so. But let off the really poor man who is unable to contribute.'

20. KING THEODORIC TO ALBINUS AND ALBIENUS, VIRI ILLUSTRES AND PATRICIANS.

'Notwithstanding our greater cares for the Republic, we are willing to provide also for the amusement of our subjects. For it is the strongest possible proof of the success of our labours that the multitude knows itself to be again at leisure [1].

Circus quarrels. Patronage of the Greens. Rivalry between Helladius and Theodorus.

'The petition of the Green party in the circus informs us that they are oppressed, and that the factions of the circus are fatal to public tranquillity. We therefore order you to assume the patronage of the Green party, which our father of glorious memory paid for [2].

---

[1] 'Illud enim, propitiante Deo, labores nostros asserit quod se *otiosam* generalitas esse cognoscit.'

[2] 'Quapropter illustris magnitudo vestra praesenti jussione commonita, patrocinium partis Prasini, quod gloriosae recordationis pater noster impendit, dignanter assumat.' This passage probably alludes to Theodoric's adoption by Zeno. But one reading is 'pater *vester*.'

So let the spectators be assembled, and let them choose between Helladius and Theodorus which is fittest to be Pantomimist of the Greens, whose salary we will pay.'

Then follows a digression on pantomimes.

21. KING THEODORIC TO MAXIMIAN, VIR ILLUSTRIS; AND ANDREAS, VIR SPECTABILIS.

Embellishment of Rome.
'If the people of Rome will beautify their City we will help them.

'Institute a strict audit (of which no one need be ashamed) of the money given by us to the different workmen for the beautification of the City. See that we are receiving money's worth for the money spent. If there is embezzlement anywhere, cause the funds so embezzled to be disgorged. We expect the Romans to help from their own resources in this patriotic work, and certainly not to intercept our contributions for the purpose.

'The wandering birds love their own nests; the beasts haste to their own lodgings in the brake; the voluptuous fish, roaming the fields of ocean, returns to its own well-known cavern. How much more should Rome be loved by her children!'

22. KING THEODORIC TO MARCELLUS, VIR SPECTABILIS, ADVOCATUS FISCI.

Promotion of Marcellus.
After some rather vapid praise of the eloquence and good qualities of Marcellus, Theodoric promotes him from the rank of a Private Advocate to that of an *Advocatus Fisci*, and gives him some excellent counsels about not pressing the claims of the Crown too far. 'We shall not enquire how many causes you have gained, but how you have gained them. Let there sometimes be a bad cause for the Fiscus, that the Sovereign may be seen to be good.'

23. KING THEODORIC TO COELIANUS AND AGAPITUS, VIRI ILLUSTRES AND PATRICIANS.

[Sidenote: Litigation between Senators.]

'The concord and harmony of subjects redound to the praise of their prince.

'We desire that Festus and Symmachus (Patricians and Magnifici) should prosecute the causes for action which they say they have against Paulinus (Illustris and Patrician) in your Court. Let Paulinus bring before you any counter-claim which he may assert himself to possess. Let justice be rendered speedily. Show yourselves worthy of this high trust. It is a matter of great moment to end lawsuits between men of such eminence in the State as these.'

24. KING THEODORIC TO ALL THE GOTHS.

[Sidenote: A call to arms for the invasion of Gaul.]

'To the Goths a hint of war rather than persuasion to the strife is needed, since a warlike race such as ours delights to prove its courage. In truth, he shuns no labour who hungers for the renown of valour. Therefore with the help of God, whose blessing alone brings prosperity, we design to send our army to the Gauls for the common benefit of all, that you may have an opportunity of promotion, and we the power of testing your merits; for in time of peace the courage which we admire lies hidden, and when men have no chance of showing what is in them, their relative merits are concealed. We have therefore given our Sajo[1], Nandius, instructions to warn you that, on the eighth day before the kalends of next July, you move forward to the campaign in the name of God, sufficiently equipped, according to your old custom, with horses, arms, and every requisite for war. Thus will ye at the same time show that the old valour of your sires yet dwells in your hearts, and also successfully perform

---

[1] See for the office of the Sajo, note on ii. 13.

your King's command. Bring forth your young men for the discipline of Mars. Let them see you do deeds which they may love to tell of to their children. For an art not learned in youth is an art missing in our riper years. The very hawk, whose food is plunder, thrusts her still weak and tender young ones out of the nest, that they may not become accustomed to soft repose. She strikes the lingerers with her wings; she forces her callow young to fly, that they may prove to be such in the future as her maternal fondness can be proud of. Do you therefore, lofty by nature, and stimulated yet more by the love of fame, study to leave such sons behind you as your fathers have left in leaving you.'

[We can hardly be wrong in referring this stirring proclamation to the year 508, when Theodoric sent troops into Gaul to save the remnants of the Visigothic Monarchy from the grasp of Clovis. The first sentence recalls the expression 'certaminis gaudia,' which Jordanes no doubt borrowed from Cassiodorus. For the simile at the end of the letter, cf. Deuteronomy xxxii. 11, 'As an eagle stirreth up her nest'.]

25. KING THEODORIC TO SABINIANUS, VIR SPECTABILIS.

Repair of the walls of Rome.
'It is important to preserve as well as to create. We are earnestly anxious to keep the walls of Rome in good repair, and have therefore ordered the Lucrine port[1] to furnish 25,000 tiles annually for this purpose. See that this is done, that the cavities which have been formed by the fall of stones may be roofed over with tiles, and so preserved, and that thus we may deserve the thanks of ancient kings, to whose works we have given immortal youth.'

[1] I presume that 'portum Lucini' is an error for the Lucrine harbour; but there is an allusion which I do not understand in the following passage: 'Simul etiam portubus junctis, qui ad illa loca antiquitus pertinebant, et nunc diversorum usurpatione suggeruntur invasi?'

26. King Theodoric to Faustus, Praepositus.

Immunity of Church property from taxation.

In the time of Cassiodorus the Patrician (a man of tried integrity and pure fidelity[1]), a grant of freedom from taxation[2] was made to the Church of Vercelli. Since that time other property has been conveyed to the same Church, apparently by a soldier. An attempt is made to represent this after-acquired property as also tax-free. 'No,' says the King. 'It would be very wrong in us to recall our gift; but it is equally wrong in you to try to stretch it to something which it never included. Private persons must not make grants to the injury of our treasury. Tribute belongs to the purple, not to the military cloak[3]. Your newly acquired possessions must pay taxes along with those of other owners.'

27. King Theodoric to Speciosus.

Circus quarrels.

'If we are moderating under our laws the character of foreign nations, if the Roman law is supreme over all that is in alliance with Italy, how much more doth it become the Senate of the seat of civilisation itself to have a surpassing reverence for law, that by the example of their moderation the beauty of their dignities may shine forth more eminently. For where shall we look for moderation, if violence stains Patricians? The Green party complain that they have been truculently assaulted by the Patrician Theodoric and the "Illustris and Consul Importunus," and that one life has been lost in the fray. We wish the matter to be at once brought before the Illustres Coelianus and Agapitus and examined into by them[4].

'As to their counter-complaints of rudeness against the mob, you must distinguish between deliberate inso-

---

[1] This is evidently the writer's father.
[2] 'Onera indictorum titulorum.'
[3] 'Tributa sunt purpurae, non lacernae.'
[4] See i. 23, from which it appears that these two men had special jurisdiction in cases affecting Patricians.

lence and the licence of the theatre. Who expects seriousness of character at the spectacles? It is not exactly a congregation of Catos that comes together at the circus. The place excuses some excesses. And besides, it is the *beaten* party which vents its rage in insulting cries. Do not let the Patricians complain of clamour that is really the result of a victory for their own side, which they greatly desired.'

[The mention of 'the Patrician Theodoric' is a difficulty, as we know of no namesake of the King among the Roman nobility. Perhaps we ought to read (with the Remensian MS.) 'Theodoro,' as we know from 'Anon. Valesii' 68 that there was a Theodorus, son of Basilius, who perhaps succeeded Liberius, Praef. Praetorio.]

28. King Theodoric to all the Goths and Romans.

The walls of Rome.

'Most worthy of Royal attention is the rebuilding of ancient cities, an adornment in time of peace, a precaution for time of war.

'Therefore, if anyone have in his fields stones suitable for the building of the walls, let him cheerfully and promptly produce them. Even though he should be paid at a low rate, he will have his reward as a member of the community, which will benefit thereby.'

29. King Theodoric to all the Lucristani (Lustriani?) on the River Sontius (Isonzo).

The Postal Service.

'The post (*Cursus Publicus*) is evidently an institution of great public utility, tending to the rapid promulgation of our decrees.

'Care must therefore be taken that the horses are not allowed to get out of condition, lest they break down under their work, and lest the journey, which should be rapid, become tediously slow.

'Also any lands formerly appropriated to the *muta-*

tiones [places for changing horses] which have fallen into private hands must be reclaimed for the public service, the owners being sufficiently indemnified for their loss.'

30. KING THEODORIC TO THE SENATE OF THE CITY OF ROME.

On the injury to public peace arising from the Circus rivalries.

The Senators are exhorted not to allow their menials to embroil themselves with the populace, and thus bring their good name into disgrace. Any slave accused of the murder of a free-born citizen is to be at once given up, under penalty of a fine of 10lbs. of gold (£400), and the King's severe displeasure for the master who disobeys this command.

'And do not you, oh Senators, be too severe in marking every idle word which the mob may utter amidst the general rejoicing. If there is any insult which requires notice, bring it before the "Praefectus Urbis"—a far better and safer course than taking the law into your own hands.'

[This letter, a very interesting and sensible one, is somewhat spoilt by a characteristic Cassiodorian sentence at the end:—

'Men in old time used always to fight with their fists, whence the word *pugna*, "a pugnis." Afterwards iron was introduced by King Belus, and hence came *bellum*, "a Belo."']

31. KING THEODORIC TO THE ROMAN PEOPLE.

On the same subject.

Gives similar good advice to that contained in the previous letter to the Senate.

'The Circus, in which the King spends so much money, is meant to be for public delight, not for stirring up wrath. Instead of uttering howls and insults like other nations [the populace of Byzantium?], whom they have despised for doing so, let them tune their voices, so that their applause shall sound like the notes of some vast organ, and even the brute creation delight to hear it.

'Anyone uttering outrageous reproaches against any Senator will be dealt with by the Praefectus Urbis.'

32. KING THEODORIC TO AGAPITUS, VIR ILLUSTRIS, PRAEFECTUS URBIS.

On the same subject.

'The ruler of the city ought to keep the peace, and justify my choice of him. Your highest praise is a quiet people.

'We have issued our "oracles" to the "amplissimus ordo" (Senate) and to the people, that the custom of insulting persons in the Circus is to be put under some restraint; on the other hand, any Senator who shall be provoked to kill a free-born person shall pay a fine. The games are meant to make people happy, not to stir them up to deadly rage. Helladius[1] is to come forth into the midst and afford the people pleasure [as a pantomimist], and he is to receive his monthly allowance (menstruum) with the other actors of the Green Faction. His partisans are to be allowed to sit where they please.'

[Was there not some division in the Green Faction itself concerning the merits of Helladius and his rival Theodorus?]

33. KING THEODORIC TO AGAPITUS, VIR ILLUSTRIS, PRAEFECTUS URBIS.

Arrangements for the Pantomime.

'Our Serenity is not going to change the arrangements which we have once made for the public good. We told Albinus and Albienus[2] to choose the most fitting person they could find as Pantomimist of the Greens. They have done so [choosing probably Helladius]. He shall have his monthly allowance, and let there be peace.'

---

[1] See Letter i. 20. [2] Ibid.

34. KING THEODORIC TO FAUSTUS, PRAEPOSITUS.

Only the surplus of corn to be exported.

'It should be only the surplus of the crops of any Province, beyond what is needed for the supply of its own wants, that should be exported. Station persons in the harbours to see that foreign ships do not take away produce to foreign shores until the Public Providers[1] have got all that they require.'

35. KING THEODORIC TO FAUSTUS, PRAEPOSITUS.

Unreasonable delays. The sucking-fish and torpedo.

'This extraordinarily dry season having ruined the hopes of our harvest, it is more than ever necessary that the produce should be brought forward promptly. We are therefore exceedingly annoyed at finding that the crops which are generally sent forward by your Chancellor from the coasts of Calabria and Apulia in summer have not yet arrived, though it is near autumn and the time is at hand when the sun, entering the southern signs (which are all named from showers), will send us storm and tempest.

'What are you waiting for? Why are your ships not spreading their sails to the breeze? With a favourable wind and with bending oarsmen, are you perhaps delayed by the *echeneis* (Remora, or sucking-fish)? or by the shell-fish of the Indian Ocean? or by the torpedo, whose touch paralyses the hand? No; the echeneis in this case is entangling venality; the bites of the shell-fish, insatiable avarice; the torpedo, fraudulent pretence.

'The merchants are making delays in order that they may seem to have fallen on adverse weather.

'Let your Magnitude put all this to rights promptly, otherwise our famine will be imputed, not to bad seasons, but to negligence[2].'

---

[1] 'Expensae publicae' perhaps = curatores annonae.
[2] For a fuller translation of this marvellous letter, see Introd. p. 18.

36. KING THEODORIC TO THERIOLUS, VIR SPECTABILIS.

Guardianship of children of Benedictus.

'We wish you to take the place of the late Benedictus in the city of Pedon.

'As we never forget the services of the dead, we wish you to undertake officially the guardianship of the sons of the said Benedictus.

'We always pay back to our faithful servants more than we have received from them, and thus we do not go on the principle "equality is equity," because we think it just to make them *more* than an equal recompence.'

37. KING THEODORIC TO CRISPIANUS.

Justifiable homicide.

'Murder is abominable, but it is right to take into account the circumstances which may have provoked to homicide. If the slain man was trying to violate the rights of wedlock, his blood be on his own head. For even brute beasts vindicate their conjugal rights by force: how much more man, who is so deeply dishonoured by the adulterer!

'Therefore, if it be true that the man whom you slew had wronged you as a husband, we do not agree to the punishment of exile which has been inflicted upon you. Nor will we uphold the action of the *Vicarius* or of his *Officium*, who, as you say, have impounded the money paid by your *fidei-jussor* (guarantor) Agnellus. Also, we will protect you against the hostile assaults of Candax [next of kin to the murdered man?] in future. But your allegation as to the provocation must be fully established by legal process.'

[It may be remarked that Candac, King of the Alani in Moesia, is mentioned in the pedigree of Jordanes ('Getica,' cap. 4).]

38. KING THEODORIC TO BAION, A SENATOR[1].

The young Hilarius to be allowed to enter on possession of his property.

'We are told that you are keeping in your own hands the administration of the property of your young nephew [or grandson] Hilarius against his will, and not for his good, but yours. Restore it at once. Let him dispose of it as he likes. He seems to be quite able to enter upon the lordship of his own. The eagle feeds her callow young with food which she has procured for them, till their wings grow. Then, when their flight is strong and their nails sharp, she trains them to strike their own prey. So with our young Goths: when they are fit for soldiership we cannot bear that they should be deemed incapable of managing their own concerns. "To the Goths valour makes full age. And he who is strong enough to stab his enemy to the heart should be allowed to vindicate himself from every accusation of incapacity."'

[Notwithstanding his Roman name, Hilarius is evidently a Goth].

39. KING THEODORIC TO FESTUS, VIR ILLUSTRIS AND PATRICIAN.

The nephews of Filagrius to be detained in Rome.

'We are always delighted to grant just requests.

'Filagrius (Vir Spectabilis), who has been long absent from his home on our business, seeks to return to Syracuse, but at the same time asks that his brother's sons may be kept for their education's sake at Rome. Do you attend to this petition, and do not let the lads go till we send you a second order to that effect. No one ought to murmur at being detained in Rome, which is every-

---

[1] See remarks on this letter in Dahn, Könige der Germanen iv. 147-8. Some MSS. read Coion or Goinon, as the name of the Senator to whom it is addressed.

one's country, the fruitful mother of eloquence, the wide temple of all virtues. Ulysses would very likely never have become famous if he had lingered on at home; but Homer's noble poem most chiefly proclaims his wisdom in this fact, that he roamed among many cities and nations.'

40. KING THEODORIC TO ASSUIN (OR ASSIUS), VIR ILLUSTRIS AND COMES.

The inhabitants of Salona to be drilled.

'War needs rehearsal and preparation. Therefore let your Illustrious Sublimity provide the inhabitants of Salona with arms, and let them practise themselves in the use of them; for the surest safeguard of the Republic is an armed defender.'

The necessity of drill and practice is shown by the early combats of bullocks, the play-huntings of puppies, the necessity of first kindling a fire with very little sticks, and so forth.

41. KING THEODORIC TO AGAPITUS, VIR ILLUSTRIS, PRAEFECTUS URBIS.

Enquiries into character of the younger Faustus.

'The dignity of the Senate makes it necessary to be unusually careful who is admitted into that body. Let other orders receive middling men: the Senate must receive none but those who are of proved excellence.

'Therefore let your Illustrious Magnificence cause those enquiries to be made concerning Faustus, the grown-up son of the Illustrious Faustus, which the Senate hath ordered to be made concerning all persons who are to be enrolled in its council[1]. In thus confirming and ratifying the proceedings of the Senate we are in no degree trenching on the accustomed authority of that sacred order.'

[1] 'Quae circa referendos curiae priscus ordo designavit.'

42. King Theodoric to Artemidorus, Vir Illustris and Patrician [509 or 524].

Artemidorus to be Praefect of the City.

'We are especially bound to reward merit. Everyone who does us a service makes a very good investment. You have long had what was formerly considered more precious than great dignity—near access to our person. Much as we loved you, we somewhat retarded your advance in order that you might be the more richly adorned with all virtues when you came to honour. Your birthplace, your lineage, your merit, all declare you worthy of the promotion which we now bestow upon you, declaring you for this third Indiction[1] *Praefectus Urbis*. You will thus have the function of presiding over the Senate, a far higher office than that of ruling the Palace or arranging private houses. The value of the object committed to a person's care increases the dignity of the post. It is much more honourable to be caretaker of a diadem than of a wine-cellar. Judge of our esteem for you by the preciousness of the body over which we are thus calling you to preside.'

43. King Theodoric to the Senate of the City of Rome.

[Announcing the elevation of Artemidorus to the post of Praefectus Urbis.]

Promotion of Artemidorus.

'Artemidorus, though entitled from his relationship to the Emperor Zeno to expect great promotion at the Court of Constantinople, has preferred to share the fortunes and attach himself to the person of Theodoric, who has often been refreshed after the cares of State by an hour of his charming converse. Though he might have aspired to the highest dignities of the Court, he has hitherto been satisfied with the comparatively humble post of Superintendent of the Public Spectacles

---

[1] Either 509-510 or 524-525; more probably the former.

[as Tribunus Voluptatum?]. Now, as Praefectus Urbis, he is to preside over and become a member of your body. Welcome him.'

44. KING THEODORIC TO THE PEOPLE OF ROME.

On the same subject.

[On the same subject as 42 and 43, the elevation of Artemidorus to the Urban Praefecture.]

Rebukes the commonalty sharply for their recent disturbances, which defile with illicit seditions the blessings of peace, earned under God's blessing by their Prince. The newly-appointed Praefectus Urbanus, Artemidorus, long devoted to the service of Theodoric, will attest the innocence of the good, and sharply punish the errors of the bad, both by his own inherent prerogative and by a special commission entrusted to him for that purpose by the King.

45. KING THEODORIC TO BOETIUS, VIR ILLUSTRIS AND PATRICIAN.

The water-clock and sundial destined for the Burgundian King.

'It is important to oblige our royal neighbours even in trifles, for none can tell what great matters may be aided thereby. Often what arms cannot obtain the offices of kindness bring to pass. Thus let even our unbending be for the benefit of the Republic. For our object in seeking pleasure is that we may thereby discharge the serious duties of life.

'The Lord of the Burgundians has earnestly requested that we would send him a clock which is regulated by water flowing under a modulus, and one which is marked by embracing the illumination of the immense sun[1].'

---

[1] An unintelligible translation doubtless, but is the original clearer? 'Burgundionum dominus a nobis magnopere postulavit ut horologium quod aquis sub modulo fluentibus temperatur et quod solis immensi comprehensa illuminatione distinguitur ... ei transmittere deberemus.' It is pretty clear that the first request of the Burgundian King was for a clepsydra of some kind. The second must be for some kind of sundial, but the description is very obscure.

[I transcribe, and do not attempt to translate, the further description of the two machines, the order of which is now changed.]

'*Primum* sit, ubi stylus diei index, per umbram exiguam horas consuevit ostendere. Radius itaque immobilis, et parvus, peragens quod tam miranda magnitudo solis discurrit, et fugam solis aequiparat quod modum semper ignorat. [This must be the sundial.] Inviderent talibus, si astra sentirent: et meatum suum fortasse deflecterent, ne tali ludibrio subjacerent. Ubi est illud horarum de lumine venientium singulare miraculum, si has et umbra demonstrat? Ubi praedicabilis indefecta roratio, si hoc et metalla peragunt, quae situ perpetuo continentur? O artis inaestimabilis virtus quae dum se dicit ludere, naturae praevalet secreta vulgare.

'*Secundum* sit [the clepsydra] ubi praeter solis radios hora dignoscitur, noctes in partes dividens: quod ut nihil deberet astris, rationem coeli ad aquarum potius fluenta convertit, quorum motibus ostendit, quod coelum volvitur; et audaci praesumptione concepta, ars elementis confert quod originis conditio denegavit.'

'It will be a great gain to us that the Burgundians should daily look upon something sent by us which will appear to them little short of miraculous. Exert yourself therefore, oh Boetius, to get this thing put in hand. You have thoroughly imbued yourself with Greek philosophy[1]. You have translated Pythagoras the musician, Ptolemy the astronomer, Nicomachus the arithmetician, Euclid the geometer, Plato the theologian, Aristotle the logician, and have given back the mechanician Archimedes to his own Sicilian countrymen (who now speak Latin). You know the whole science of Mathematics, and the marvels wrought thereby. A machine [perhaps something like a modern orrery] has been

---

[1] Evidently 'sic enim Atheniensium scholas longe positus introisti' does not mean that Boethius actually visited Athens, but that he became thoroughly at home in the works of Athenian philosophers.

made to exhibit the courses of the planets and the causes of eclipses. What a wonderful art is Mechanics! The mechanician, if we may say so, is almost Nature's comrade, opening her secrets, changing her manifestations, sporting with miracles, feigning so beautifully, that what we know to be an illusion is accepted by us as truth.'

46. KING THEODORIC TO GUNDIBAD [SIC], KING OF THE BURGUNDIANS.

On the same subject.

Sends the two clocks, or rather perhaps the celestial globe and the water-clock.

'Have therefore in your country what you have often seen in Rome. It is right that we should send you presents, because you are connected with us by affinity. It is said that under you "Burgundia" looks into the most subtle things, and praises the discoveries of the ancients. Through you she lays aside her "Gentile" (barbarous) nature, and imitating the prudence of her King, rightly desires to possess the inventions of sages. Let her arrange her daily actions by the movements of God's great lights; let her nicely adjust the moments of each hour. In mere confusion passes the order of life when this accurate division of time is unknown. Men are like the beasts, if they only know the passage of the hours by the pangs of hunger, and have no greater certainty as to the flight of time than such as is afforded them by their bellies. For certainty is undoubtedly meant to be entwined in human actions.'

BOOK II.

CONTAINING FORTY-ONE LETTERS WRITTEN BY CASSIODORUS IN THE NAME OF THEODORIC.

---

1. KING THEODORIC TO ANASTASIUS, MOST PIOUS EMPEROR. A.D. 511.

'By excellent ordinance of the ancients the year is named from the Consul. Let the happy year take its title from our new Consul, *Felix* [Consul with Secundinus, A.D. 511 [1]]. *Consulship of Felix.*

'It is most suitable that Rome should gather back her children to her bosom, and in her venerable Senate should enrol a son of Gaul.

'Felix showed his excellent disposition first in this, that while still a young man he hastened to "the native land of all the virtues" [Rome]. Success followed his choice; we promoted him as he deserved. While still a young man, deprived of his father's care, he showed the rare gift of continence; he subdued avarice, the enemy of wisdom; he despised the blandishments of vice; he trampled under foot the vanities of pride.

'We have now determined to reward him with the Consulship. Do you who can with indiscriminate pleasure rejoice in both the blessings of the Republic [in the Consuls of the East and West] join your favouring vote. He who is worthy of so high an office as

---

[1] 'Portamque dierum tali nomine dicatus annus, tempus introeat.' The figure here used seems borrowed from Claudian, In Primum Cons. Stilichonis ii. 425-476.

the Consulship may well be chosen by the judgment of both' [Emperor and King].

[An important letter, as showing the extent to which concurrent choice of Consuls was vested in Rome, or rather Ravenna, and Constantinople.]

2. KING THEODORIC TO FELIX, VIR ILLUSTRIS, CONSUL ORDINARIUS, A.D. 511 (4TH OF THE INDICTION).

On the same subject.

An address on his elevation to the Consulship, touching on nearly the same topics as the preceding.

Theodoric delights in bestowing larger favours on those whom he has once honoured [a favourite topic with Cassiodorus].

Felix has come back from Gaul to the old fatherland[1]. Thus the Consulship has returned to a Transalpine family, and green laurels are seen on a brown stock.

Felix has shown an early maturity of character. He has made a wise use of his father's wealth. The honour which other men often acquire by prodigality he has acquired by saving. Cassiodorus evidently has a little fear that the new Consul may carry his parsimony too far, and tells him that this office of the Consulship is one in which liberality, almost extravagance, earns praise[2]; in which it is a kind of virtue not to love one's own possessions; and in which one gains in good opinion all that one loses in wealth.

'See the sacred City all white with your *vota* (?). See yourself borne upon the shoulders of all, and your name flitting through their mouths, and manifest yourself such that you may be deemed worthy of your race, worthy of the City, worthy of our choice, worthy of the Consular *trabea*.'

[The letter makes one suspect a certain narrowness and coldness of heart in the subject of its praise.]

---

[1] 'Cum soli genitalis fortunâ relictâ, velut quodam postliminio in antiquam patriam commeasses.'

[2] 'Ubi praeconium meretur effusio.'

3. KING THEODORIC TO THE SENATE. A.D. 511.

On the same subject.

Recommends Felix for the Consulship, going over again the topics mentioned in the two last letters. It appears that it was the father of Felix who emerged, after a temporary eclipse of the family fortunes, and then showed himself 'the Cato of our times, abstaining from vice himself, and forming the characters of others; imbued also with all Greek philosophy, he glutted himself with the honey of the Cecropian doctrine.'

Mention is made of the Consulship of an earlier Felix, A.D. 428, the happy renown of which still lingered in the memories of men.

The young Felix is praised for the qualities described in the two previous letters, and also for his power of conciliating the friendship of older men, especially the excellent Patrician Paulinus.

4. KING THEODORIC TO ECDICIUS (OR BENEDICTUS), VIR HONESTUS.

Collection of Siliquaticum.

'We wish always to observe long-established rules in fiscal matters, the best guarantee against extortion. Therefore, whatever dues in the way of *Siliquaticum* appertained to Antiochus are now transferred to you by the present authority, and the Sajo is charged to support your claims herein; only the contention must not be mixed up with any private matters of your own.'

[The *Siliquaticum* was a tax of one twenty-fourth—the *siliqua* being the twenty-fourth of a *solidus*—payable on all sales in market overt by buyer and seller together.]

5. KING THEODORIC TO FAUSTUS, PRAEPOSITUS.

Soldiers' arrears.

'We are always generous, and sometimes out of clemency we bestow our gifts on persons who have no claim upon us. How much more fitting is it then that the servants of the State should receive our gifts promptly! Wherefore, pray let your Magnificence see to it that the sixty soldiers who are keeping guard in the fastnesses of Aosta receive their *annonae* without delay. Think what a life of hardship the soldier leads in those frontier forts for the general peace, thus, as at the gate of the Province, shutting out the entry of the barbarous nations. He must be ever on the alert who seeks to keep out the Barbarians. For fear alone checks these men, whom honour will not keep back.'

[A singular letter to write in the name of one who was himself a Barbarian invader.]

6. KING THEODORIC TO AGAPITUS, ILLUSTRIS AND PATRICIAN.

Embassy to Constantinople.

'We have decided to send you on an embassy to the East (Constantinople). Every embassy requires a prudent man, but here there is need of especial prudence, because you will have to dispute against the most subtle persons —artificers of words, who think they can foresee every possible answer to their arguments. Do your best therefore to justify the opinion which I formed of you before full trial of your powers.'

7. KING THEODORIC TO SURA (OR SUNA), ILLUSTRIS AND COMES.

Embellishment of the City.

'Let nothing lie useless which may redound to the beauty of the City. Let your Illustrious Magnificence therefore cause the blocks of marble which are everywhere lying about in ruins to be wrought up into the walls by the hands of the workmen whom I send herewith. Only take care to use only those stones which have really fallen from public buildings, as we do not wish to appropriate private property, even for the glorification of the City.'

8. King Theodoric to Bishop Severus, Vir Venerabilis.

'None is more suitable than a member of the Priesthood to perform acts of justice towards his flock.

'We therefore send your Holiness, by Montanarius, 1,500 solidi (£900), for distribution among the Provincials, according to the amount of damage which each one has sustained this year by the passage of our army. See that the distribution is made systematically—not at random—so that it may reach the right persons.'

Compensation for damage done by troops on march.

9. King Theodoric to Faustus, Praepositus.

'We always enjoy being generous. Compassion is the one virtue to which all other virtues may honourably give way. Long ago we made the charioteer Sabinus a monthly allowance of a solidus [twelve shillings]. Now, as we learn from Histrius [or Historius] that this former servant of the public pleasures is afflicted with the most melancholy poverty, we have pleasure in adding *another* solidus to his monthly allowance. We are never so well pleased as when the accounts of our expenditure show these items of charitable disbursement.'

Allowance to a retired charioteer.

10. King Theodoric to Speciosus, Vir Devotus, Comitiacus [Officer of the Court].

'The laws guarding the sanctity of the marriage bed[1] must be carefully upheld.

'Agapita[2] has explained to us that she was tempted away from her husband by seducers, who promised to procure his death. From the time of her leaving his company let all revenues which came to her under

The abduction of Agapita.

---

[1] 'Illud Humani generis procreabile Sacramentum.'
[2] 'Foemina spectabilis.'

the marriage contract (invalidated by her unfaithfulness) be given up by her wrongful detainers[1] without any delay. It is too absurd that men who ought to be severely punished for their wrong-doing should even seek to make a profit out of it.'

11. KING THEODORIC TO PROVINUS (PROBINUS ?), ILLUSTRIS AND PATRICIAN.

Gift obtained from Agapita under undue influence.

[Refers to the same business of Agapita, who seems to have been a woman of feeble intellect as well as an unfaithful wife.] The petition of her husband Basilius (vir Spectabilis) sets forth that, influenced by seducers, and from the levity so natural to woman, she for no good reason quitted her own home. Her own petition confirms this; and she states that, while taking refuge within the precincts of the Church, she by deed of gift bestowed on Provinus the 'Casa Areciretina,' a most preposterous gift from a poor woman to a rich man; from one whose reputation was gone to a chaste man; from a half-crazy creature to one who knew fully what he was about. This gift Agapita [and Basilius] now seek to annul. Provinus is exhorted at once to throw up a possession which cannot possibly bring him any credit, and the loss of which has brought the poor woman to destitution. Alienation of property should be the act of a person having 'solidum judicium,' which this poor creature evidently had not, or she would not have left her husband causelessly.

'This is the second time of writing. Let there be no further delay in complying.'

[Probably, therefore, Probinus really is one of the 'Retentatores' referred to in Letter 10, though this letter does not distinctly identify him with them.]

---

[1] 'Retentatores.' So the Gepid Prince is called the *Retentator* of Sirmium (Ennodius, Panegyric. Theod. 178. Ed. Migne).

12. KING THEODORIC TO THE COUNT OF THE SILIQUATARII (CUSTOMS OFFICERS), AND TO HIM WHO HAS THE CARE OF THE HARBOUR (OF PORTUS?).

Prohibition of export of lard.

'Italy ought to enjoy her own products, and it is monstrous that anything which she produces should be wanting to her own children.

'Therefore let no lard be exported to foreign parts, but let it by God's grace be all kept for consumption at home.

'Now take care not to incur the slightest blame in this matter. It is a very serious fault even in trifles to disobey orders. Sin consists in quality, not in quantity; and injustice cannot be measured. A command, if it be despised in one part, is violated in the whole.'

13. KING THEODORIC TO THE SAJO[1] FRUINARITH.

Dishonest conduct of Venantius.

'We are always especially touched by the prayers of petitioners who complain that they are forced to pay unjustly. Ulpianus in his lamentable petition informs us that on the request of Venantius he bound himself as a guarantor (fidei jussionis vinculo) to pay over to the public Treasury at the time of his administration 400 solidi (£240). With the presumption of a truculent rustic Venantius despised his own promise, and Ulpianus has therefore been burdened with payment of the money. We therefore order that Venantius, who has been accused of many other crimes besides this, shall be summoned before you, and if found to be legally liable, shall be at once, and sharply, compelled to fulfil his promise.'

[1] The Sajo was an officer, not of very high rank, apparently always of Gothic nationality, who was charged with executing the King's mandates. Perhaps our word 'henchman' would be the best translation of his title. His conventional attribute was 'devotio.' See Dahn, 'Könige der Germanen' iii. 181-186, and my 'Italy and her Invaders' iii. 282-284.

14. KING THEODORIC TO SYMMACHUS, PATRICIAN.

Romulus the parricide.

'Parricide is the most terrible and unnatural of crimes. Even the cubs of wild beasts follow their sires; the offshoot of the vine serves the parent stem: shall man war against him who gave him being? It is for our little ones that we lay up wealth. Shall we not earn the love of those for whom we would willingly incur death itself? The young stork, that harbinger of spring, gives a signal example of filial piety, warming and feeding its aged parents in the moulting season till they have recovered their strength, and thus repaying the good offices received in its earlier years. So too, when the partridge, which is wont to hatch the young of other birds, takes her adopted brood forth into the fields, if these hear the cry of their genuine mother they run to her, leaving the partridge forsaken.

'Wherefore, if Romulus[1] have fouled the Roman name by laying violent hands on his father Martinus, we look to your justice (we chose you because we knew you would not spare the cruel) to inflict on him legitimate revenge.'

15. KING THEODORIC TO VENANTIUS, VIR ILLUSTRIS.

Promotion of Venantius to Comitiva Domesticorum Vacans.

'We always like to promote to office the sons of distinguished fathers. We therefore bestow on you the honour of Comes Domesticorum (Comitiva Vacans), in memory of your glorious father. He held at the same time the Praefecture [of Italy] and the command of the army, so that neither the Provinces lacked his ordering, nor did his wise care for the army fail. All was mastered by his skilled and indefatigable prudence; he inclined the manners of the Barbarians to peace, and governed so that all were satisfied with our rule.

---

[1] Quaere if named from the last Emperor.

'You are a zealous student of literature, illustrious by birth and eloquent by education. Go on as you have begun, and show yourself worthy of our choice.'

16. KING THEODORIC TO THE SENATE OF THE CITY OF ROME.

On the same subject.

This letter adds a little to the information contained in the preceding one, as to the career of Liberius, father of Venantius.

Praises of Liberius.

Liberius was a faithful servant of Odovacar, who adhered to his master to the last. 'He awaited incorruptly the Divine judgments, nor did he allow himself to seek a new King till he had first lost his old one. On the overthrow of his lord he was bowed by no terror; he bore unmoved the ruin of his Prince; nor did the revolution, at which even the proud hearts of the Barbarians trembled[1], avail to move him from his calm.

'Prudently did he follow the common fortunes, in order that while fixedly bearing the Divine judgments he might with the more approbation find the Divine favour. We approved the faith of the man; he came over in sadness to our allegiance as one who being overcome changes his mind, not like one who has contrived [treacherously] that he should be conquered. We made him Praefectus Praetorio. He administered the finances admirably. By his economical management we felt the increased returns, while you knew nothing of added tributes.

Apportionment of Tertiae.

'We especially like to remember how in the assignment of the [Gothic] Thirds (in Tertiarum deputatione) he joined both the possessions and the hearts of Goths and Romans alike. For whereas men are wont to come into collision on account of their being neighbours, with these men the common holding of their farms proved in

[1] 'Quam etiam ferocitas gentilis expavit.'

practice a reason for concord. Thus it has happened that while the two nations have been living in common they have concurred in the same desires. Lo! a new fact, and one wholly laudable. The friendship of the lords has been joined with the division of the soil; amity has grown out of the loss of the Provincials, and by the land a defender has been gained whose occupation of part guarantees the quiet enjoyment of the whole. One law includes them: one equal administration rules them: for it is necessary that sweet affection should grow between those who always keep the boundaries which have been allotted them.

'All this the Roman Republic owes to Liberius, who to two such illustrious nations has imparted sentiments of mutual affection. See to it, Conscript Fathers, that his offspring does not go unrewarded.'

17. To the Possessors, Defensors, and Curials[1] of the City of Tridentum (Trient).

Immunity from Tertiae enjoyed by lands granted by the King.

'We do not wish to be generous at the expense of others, and we therefore declare that the *Sors* which in our generosity we have bestowed on Butilianus the Presbyter, is not to be reckoned in to the tax calculations; but as many solidi as are comprehended in that gift, so many are you to be relieved from, in the contribution of "Tertiae."'

[That is to say, the land given by the Gothic King to Butilian was to be itself, as a matter of course, free from Tertiae; but, in order that this might not throw a heavier burden on the other owners in the district, they were to be allowed to deduct the solidi of that portion from the gross amount payable by them on behalf of the whole district. Butilian's own immunity from Tertiae seems to be taken for granted as a result of the King's gift to him. (See Dahn, 'Könige der Germanen' iii. 145.)]

[1] Cf. iii. 9 for a similar heading.

18. KING THEODORIC TO BISHOP GUDILA.

An interesting but rather obscure letter on the condition of *Curiales*.

[Sidenote: Ecclesiastics as Curiales.]

Apparently some ecclesiastics were claiming as slaves some men whom the Curia of Sarsena (?) asserted to be fellow-curials of their own, whom they therefore wanted to assist them in performing curial obligations.

Cassiodorus argues that as the 'Sors nascendi' prevented the Curialis from rising to the higher honours of the State, it certainly ought also to prevent him from sinking into slavery[1]. 'Therefore we advise you to look well to your facts, and see whether these men are not justly claimed as Curials, in which case the Church should give them up before the matter comes to trial. It does not look well for the Bishop, who should be known as a lover of justice, to be publicly vanquished in a suit of this kind.'

[Did the alleged Curials, in such a case, wish to have their curiality or their quasi-ecclesiastical character established? Who can say?]

19. KING THEODORIC TO ALL THE GOTHS AND ROMANS, AND THOSE WHO KEEP THE HARBOURS AND MOUNTAIN-FORTRESSES (CLUSURAS).

[Sidenote: Domestic treachery and murder.]

'We hate all crime, but domestic bloodshed and treachery most of all. Therefore we command you to act with the utmost severity of the law against the servants of Stephanus, who have killed their master and left him unburied. They might have learned pity even from birds. Even the vulture, who lives on the corpses of other creatures, protects little birds from the attacks of

---

[1] 'Quod si eos vel ad honores transire jura vetuerunt, quam videtur esse contrarium, Curialem Reipublicae, amissâ turpiter libertate, servire? et usque ad conditionem pervenisse postremam quem vocavit antiquitas *Minorem Senatum*.'

the hawk. Yet men are found cruel enough to slay him who has fed them. To the gallows with them! Let *him* become the food of the pious vulture, who has cruelly contrived the death of his provider. That is the fitting sepulchre for the man who has left his lord unburied.'

20. KING THEODORIC TO THE SAJO UNIGILIS (OR WILIGIS).

[Provision-ships to follow movements of Theodoric's Court.]

'Let any provision-ships [*sulcatoriae?*] which may be now lying at Ravenna be ordered round to Liguria (which in ordinary times supplies the needs of Ravenna herself).

'Our presence and that of our Court (Comitatus) attracts many spectators and petitioners to those parts, for whose maintenance an extra effort must be made.' [See Dahn, 'Könige der Germanen' iii. 282.]

21. KING THEODORIC TO JOANNES THE APPARITOR.

[A concession too timidly acted upon.]

'The King has conceded to the Spectabiles Spes and Domitius a certain tract of land which was laid waste by wide and muddy streams, and which neither showed a pure expanse of water nor had preserved the comeliness of solid earth, for them to reclaim and cultivate.

'The petition of the *Actores* of Spes sets forth that the operation is put in jeopardy by the ill-timed parsimony of Domitius, which throws back the labourers to the point from which they set out at first[1]. Therefore let Domitius be stirred up to finish his part of the work, or if he thinks that too expensive, let him throw up his

---

[1] 'Cum jam in soli faciem paulatim mollities siccata duresceret, celatamque longâ voracitate tellurem sol insuetus afflaret.' I cannot understand these words. I suppose there was a hard cake of clay left when the water was drained off, which was baked by the sun, and that there should have been further digging to work through this stratum and get at the good soil beneath; but the wording is not very clear.

share of the concession and allow his partner to work it out.'

[We find in this letter a good motto for Theodoric's reign: 'Nos quibus cordi est in melius cuncta mutare.']

22. KING THEODORIC TO FESTUS, VIR ILLUSTRIS AND PATRICIAN.

'The sons of Ecdicius, whom at first we had ordered to reside in the city, are to be allowed to return to their own country in order to bury their father. That grief is insatiable which feels that it has been debarred from rendering the last offices to the dead. Think at what risk of his life Priam implored the raging Achilles to give him back the body of his son.' *[marginal: Ecdicius to be buried by his sons.]*

[Apparently the sons of Ecdicius, not Ecdicius himself, had fallen into disgrace with Theodoric, or incurred some suspicion of disloyalty, which led to the rigorous order for their detention in Rome. See Dahn iii. 279-280.]

23. KING THEODORIC TO AMPELIUS, DESPOTIUS, AND THEODULUS, SENATORS.

'It befits the discipline of our time that those who are serving the public interests shall not be loaded with superfluous burdens. Labour therefore diligently at the potteries (figulinae) which our Royal authority has conceded to you. Protection is hereby promised against the wiles of wicked men.' [What was the nature of the artifices to which they were exposed is not very clear.] *[marginal: Protection for owners of potteries.]*

24. KING THEODORIC TO THE SENATE OF THE CITY OF ROME.

'We hear with sorrow, by the report of the Provincial Judges, that you the Fathers of the State, who ought to set an example to your sons (the ordinary citizens), *[marginal: Arrears of taxation due from Senators.]*

have been so remiss in the payment of taxes that on this first collection [1] nothing, or next to nothing, has been brought in from any Senatorial house. Thus a crushing weight has fallen on the lower orders (*tenues, curiales*), who have had to make good your deficiencies and have been distraught by the violence of the tax-gatherers.

'Now then, oh Conscript Fathers, who owe as much duty to the Republic as we do, pay the taxes for which each one of you is liable, to the Procurators appointed in each Province, by three instalments (trinâ illatione). Or, if you prefer to do so—and it used to be accounted a privilege—pay all at once into the chest of the Vicarius. And let this following edict be published, that all the Provincials may know that they are not to be imposed upon and that they are invited to state their grievances [2].'

25. An Edict of King Theodoric.

[Referred to in the preceding letter.]

Evasion of taxes by the rich.

The King detests the oppression of the unfortunate, and encourages them to make their complaints to him. He has heard that the powerful houses are failing to pay their share of the taxes, and that a larger sum in consequence is being exacted from the *tenues* [3].

To 'amputate' such wickedness for the future, the letter last preceding has been addressed to the Senate; and the 'Possessores sive curiales' are now invited

---

[1] 'Primae transmissionis tempus.'

[2] See Dahn, 'Könige der Germanen' iii. 153 and 112, n. 5.

[3] Here follows a sentence which I am unable to translate: 'Superbia deinde conductorum canonicos solidos non ordine traditos, sed sub iniquo pondere imminentibus fuisse projectos nec universam siliquam quam reddere consueverant solemniter intulisse.' I think the meaning is, that the stewards of the Senators (conductores) arrogantly refused to allow the money paid to the tax-collectors (canonici solidi) to be tested, as in ordinary course it should have been, to see if it was of full weight. The 'imminentes' are, I think, the tax-collectors. I cannot at all understand the clause about 'universam siliquam.'

to state their grievances fully and frankly, or else ever after hold their peace and cultivate a habit of patience.

26. KING THEODORIC TO FAUSTUS, PRAETORIAN PRAEFECT.

A difficult letter about the corn-merchants of Apulia and Calabria.

Regulations for corn-traffic of Southern Italy.

1. The corn which they have collected by public sale is not to be demanded over again from them under the title of 'interpretium' [difference of price].

2. Similarly as to the Sextarius which the merchant of each Province imports. No one is to dare insolently to exact the prices which have been always condemned.

3. Fines of £1,200 on the Praefect himself, and £400 on his *officium* (subordinates), are to be levied if this order is disobeyed.

4. If the 'Siliquatarius' thinks right to withhold the monopoly (of corn) from any merchant, he must not also exact the monopoly payment from him.

5. As to the Aurarii [persons liable to payment of the *lustralis auri collatio* [1]], let the old order be observed, and those only be classed under this function whom the authority of antiquity chose to serve thereunder.

27. KING THEODORIC TO ALL THE JEWS LIVING IN GENOA.

The Jews are permitted to roof in the old walls of their synagogue, but they are not to enlarge it beyond its old borders, nor to add any kind of ornament, under pain of the King's sharp displeasure; and this leave is granted on the understanding that it does not conflict with the thirty years' 'Statute of Limitations.'

Rebuilding of Jewish Synagogue.

---

[1] This appears to have been a tax levied on all traders, otherwise known as the Chrysargyron. See Cod. Theod. xiii. 1. Aurarii is therefore equivalent to Licensed Traders.

'Why do ye desire what ye ought to shun? In truth we give the permission which you craved, but we suitably blame the desire of your wandering minds. *We cannot order a religion, because no one is forced to believe against his will.*'

28. KING THEODORIC TO STEPHANUS, 'SENATOR, COMES PRIMI ORDINIS, AND EX-PRINCEPS OF OUR OFFICIUM[1].'

Honours conferred on Stephanus on his retirement from the Civil Service.

Praises him for all the good qualities which have been recognised by successive Judges under whom he has served—his secrecy, efficiency, and incorruptibility.

He is therefore, on his retirement from active service, raised to the honour of a 'Spectabilis,' and rewarded with the rank of 'Comitiva Primi Ordinis.' As a substantial recompence he is to have all the privileges which by 'divalia constituta' belong to the 'ex-principes' of his Schola, and is guaranteed against all damage and 'sordid burdens[2],' with a hope of further employment in other capacities[3].

29. KING THEODORIC TO ADILA, SENATOR AND COMES.

Protection to dependents of the Church.

[Notice the Senatorial rank borne by a man with a Gothic name.]

'We wish to protect all our subjects[4], but especially the Church, because by so doing we earn the favour of Heaven. Therefore, in accordance with the petition of the blessed Eustorgius[5], Bishop of Milan, we desire you

---

[1] Are we to understand by this expression the Officium of the Praetorian Praefect?

[2] Curial obligations.

[3] '*Fixum tenuisti militiae probatae vestigium. Spectabilitatis honorem, quem militiae sudore detersis justa deputavit antiquitas praesenti tibi auctoritate conferimus ut laboris tui tandem finitas excubias ... intelligas ... Tibique utpote militiae munere persoluto.*' The term 'militia' is employed here, as in the Codes, of 'service in a bureau.'

[4] '*Quia Regnantes est gloria, subjectorum otiosa tranquillitas.*'

[5] For Eustorgius, cf. Letter i. 9.

to accord all necessary protection to the men and farms belonging to the Milanese Church in Sicily: always understanding, however, that they are not to refuse to plead in answer to any public or private suit that may be brought against them. They are to be protected from wrong, but are not themselves to deviate from the path of justice.'

30. KING THEODORIC TO FAUSTUS, PRAETORIAN PRAEFECT.

[Sequel to last letter.]

Freedom from taxation granted to Church of Milan.

'Our generosity to an individual does not harm the public, and there is no reason for putting any bounds to its exercise.

'The Defensores of the Holy Church of Milan want to be enabled to buy as cheap as possible the things which they need for the relief of the poor; and they say that we have bestowed this favour on the Church of Ravenna.

'Your Magnificence will therefore allow them to single out some one merchant who shall buy for them in the market, without being subject to monopoly, siliquaticum, or the payment of gold-fee[1].'

[It is easy to see how liable to abuse such an exception was. Who was to decide when this merchant was buying for the Church and when for himself; when the Church was buying for the poor and when for her own enrichment?]

31. KING THEODORIC TO THE DROMONARII [ROWERS IN EXPRESS-BOATS].

State Galleys on the Po.

'Those who claim the title of "militia" ought to serve the public advantage. We have therefore told the Count of Sacred Largesses that you are to assemble

---

[1] *Auraria pensio.* See note on ii. 26.

at Hostilia [on the Padus, about fifteen miles east of Mantua], there to receive pay from our Treasury, and then to relieve the land postal-service (veredarii) by excursions up and down the channel of the Padus. There is no fear of *your* limping; you walk with your hands. No fear of *your* carriages wearing out; they travel over liquid roads, and suffer no wear and tear because they are borne along upon the wave which itself runs with them.'

32. KING THEODORIC TO THE SENATE OF THE CITY OF ROME.

Drainage of marshes of Decennonium.

'We always enjoy rewarding public spirit. Decius, Magnificus and Patrician, has most nobly volunteered to drain the marsh of Decennonium, where the sealike swamp, accustomed to impunity through long licence, rushes in and spoils all the surrounding lands.

'We, in consideration of so great an undertaking, determine to secure to him the fruits of his labour, and we therefore wish that you, Conscript Fathers, should appoint a commission of two to visit the spot and mark out the ground, which is at present wasted by the inundations, that this land may be secured to Decius as a permanent possession when he has drained it.'

[The Palus Decennonii is undoubtedly connected with the Decennovial Canal mentioned by Procopius ('De Bello Gotth.' i. 11), and so called because it flowed for nineteen miles alongside the Appian Way. In the Piazza at Terracina there is a very interesting inscription, recording the fact that Theodoric had ordered that nineteen miles of the Appian Way should be cleared of the waters which had accumulated round it, and had committed the work to Caecina Maurus Basilius Decius, 'Vir Clarissimus et Illustris, Ex-Praefectus Urbi, Ex-Praefectus

Praetori, Ex-Consul Ordinarius et Patricius.' See 'Italy and her Invaders' iii. 348.]

33. KING THEODORIC TO DECIUS, ILLUSTRIS AND PATRICIAN.

The same subject.

The complement of the foregoing letter, about the drainage of the marshes of Decennonium, which are hereby granted to him, apparently 'sine fisco,' tax-free.

[But the meaning may be, 'the marshes which you drain *sine fisco*'—without help from the Treasury.]

The chief point of difference between this and the previous letter is that here Decius is allowed and encouraged to associate partners with him in the drainage-scheme, whom he is to reward according to their share of the work. Thus will he be less likely to sink under the enterprise, and he will also lessen men's envy of his success.

34. KING THEODORIC TO ARTEMIDORUS, PRAEFECT OF THE CITY.

Embezzlement of City building funds.

'The persons to whom money was entrusted for the rebuilding of the walls of Rome have been embezzling it, as was proved by your examination of their accounts (discussio). We are very glad that you have not hidden their misconduct from us (inclined as a generous mind is to cover up offences), since you would thereby have made yourself partaker of their evil deeds. They must restore that which they have dishonestly appropriated, but we shall not (as we might fairly do) inflict upon them any further fine. We are naturally inclined to clemency, and they will groan at having to give up plunder which they had already calculated upon as their own.'

35. KING THEODORIC TO TANCILA, SENATOR.

[We have here another Senator with a Gothic name].

Theft of brazen statue at Como.
'We are much displeased at hearing that a brazen statue has been stolen from the City of Como. It is vexatious that while we are labouring to increase the ornaments of our cities, those which Antiquity has bequeathed to us should by such deeds be diminished. Offer a reward of 100 aurei (£60) to anyone who will reveal the author of this crime; promise pardon [to an accomplice], and if this does not suffice, call all the workmen together "post diem venerabilem" [Does this mean on the day after Sunday?], and enquire of them "sub terrore" [by torture?] by whose help this has been done. For such a piece of work as moving this statue could only have been undertaken by some handicraftsman.'

36. EDICT ABOUT THE STATUE AT COMO.

[Refers to previous letter.]

The same subject.
'Though impunity for the crime should be sufficient reward, we promise 100 aurei, as well as forgiveness for his share in the offence, to anyone who will reveal the author of the theft of the statue at Como. A golden reward for a brazen theft. Anyone not accepting this offer and afterwards convicted will suffer the extreme penalty of the law.'

37. KING THEODORIC TO FAUSTUS, PRAETORIAN PRAEFECT.

Largesse to citizens of Spoleto.
'As our Kingdom and revenues prosper, we wish to increase our liberality. Let your Magnificence therefore give to the citizens of Spoletium another "millena" for extraordinary gratuitous admissions to the baths[1]. We

---

[1] 'Ad exhibitionem thermarum supra consuetudinem.'

wish to pay freely for anything that tends to the health of our citizens, because the praise of our times is the celebration of the joys of the people.'

[The 'millena' probably means 1,000 solidi, or £600.

38. KING THEODORIC TO FAUSTUS, PRAETORIAN PRAEFECT.

'We have no pleasure in gains which are acquired by the misery of our subjects. We are informed that the merchants of the city of Sipontum [in Apulia] have been grievously despoiled by hostile incursions [probably by the Byzantine fleet in 508]. Let your Magnificence therefore see to it that they are for two years not vexed by any claims for purveyance (coëmptio) on the part of our Treasury. But their other creditors must give them the same indulgence.' *Immunity from taxation. Hostile ravages.*

39. KING THEODORIC TO ALOISIUS THE ARCHITECT.

'The fountain of Aponus—so called originally in the Greek language as being the remover of pain [1]—has many marvellous and beneficial properties, for the sake of which the buildings round it ought to be kept in good repair. One may see it welling up from the bowels of the earth in spherical form, under a canopy of steam. From this parent spring the waters, glassy-clear and having lost their first impetuosity, flow by various channels into chambers prepared for them by nature but made longer by art. In the first, when the boiling element dashes against the rock, it is hot enough to make a natural sudatorium; then it cools sufficiently for the tepidarium; and at last, quite cold, flows out into a fish-pond like that of Nero. Marvellous provision of Nature, whereby the opposing elements, fire and water, are joined in harmonious union and made to *Hot springs of Aponum.*

---

[1] ἄπονος.

soothe the pain and remove the sickness of man! Yet more wonderful is the moral purity of this fountain. Should a woman descend into the bath when men are using it, it suddenly grows hotter, as if with indignation that out of its abundant supply of waters separate bathing-places should not be constructed for the two sexes, if they wish to enjoy its bounty[1]. Moreover, those secret caves, the bowels of the mountains from whence it springs, have power even to judge contentious business. For if any sheep-stealer presumes to bring to it the fleece of his prey, however often he may dip it in the seething wave, he will have to boil it before he succeeds in cleansing it.

'This fountain then, as we before said, deserves a worthy habitation. If there be anything to repair in the *thermae* themselves or in the passages (cuniculi), let this be done out of the money which we now send you. Let the thorns and briers which have grown up around it be rooted up. Let the palace, shaken with extreme old age, be strengthened by careful restoration. Let the space which intervenes between the public building and the source of the hot-spring be cleared of its woodland roughness, and the turf around rejoice in the green beauty which it derives from the heated waters.'

[The hot-springs of Abano, the ancient Aponum, are situated near the Euganean Hills, and are about six miles from Padua. The heat of the water varies from 77° to 185° (Fahr.). The chief chemical ingredients are, as stated by Cassiodorus, salt and sulphur. Some of the minute description of Cassiodorus (greatly condensed in the above abstract) seems to be still applicable; but he does not mention the mud-baths which now take a prominent place in the cure. On the other hand, the wonderful moral qualities of the spring are not mentioned by modern travellers.]

[1] I think this is Cassiodorus' meaning, but his language is obscure.

40. KING THEODORIC TO BOETIUS THE PATRICIAN.

Boetius to choose a harper for the King of the Franks.

'The King of the Franks [Clovis] has asked us to send him a harper. We felt that in you lay our best chance of complying with his request, because you, being such a lover of music yourself, will be able to introduce us to the right man.'

Reflections on the nature of music. She is the Queen of the senses; when she comes forth from her secret abiding place all other thoughts are cast out. Her curative influence on the soul.

The five tones: the Dorian[1], influencing to modesty and purity; the Phrygian to fierce combat; the Aeolian to tranquillity and slumber; the Ionian (Jastius), which sharpens the intellect of the dull and kindles the desire of heavenly things; the Lydian, which soothes the soul oppressed with too many cares.

We distinguish the highest, middle, and lowest in each tone, obtaining thus in all fifteen tones of artificial music.

The diapason is collected from all, and unites all their virtues.

Classical instances of music:
    Orpheus.
    Amphion.
    Musaeus.

The human voice as an instrument of music. Oratory and Poesy as branches of the art.

The power of song: Ulysses and the Sirens.

David the author of the Psalter, who by his melody three (?) times drove away the evil spirit from Saul.

---

[1] Cf. Milton:
'To the Dorian mood
Of flutes and soft recorders; such as rais'd
To highth of noblest temper heroes old
Arming to battle, and instead of rage
Deliberate valour breath'd, firm and unmov'd
With dread of death to flight or foul retreat.'

The lyre is called 'chorda,' because it so easily moves the hearts (corda) of men.

As the diadem dazzles by the variegated lustre of its gems, so the lyre with its divers sounds.

The lyre, the loom of the Muses.

Mercury, the inventor of the lyre, is said to have derived the idea of it from the harmony of the spheres. This astral music, apprehended by reason alone, is said to form one of the delights of heaven. 'If philosophers had placed that enjoyment not in sweet sounds but in the contemplation of the Creator, they would have spoken fitly; for there is truly joy without end, eternity abiding for ever without weariness, and the mere contemplation of the Divinity produces such happiness that nothing can surpass it. This Being furnishes the true immortality; this heaps delight upon delight; and as outside of Him no creature can exist, so without Him changeless happiness cannot be [1].

'We have indulged ourselves in a pleasant digression, because it is always agreeable to talk of learning with the learned; but be sure to get us that *Citharoedus*, who will go forth like another Orpheus to charm the beast-like hearts of the Barbarians. You will thus both obey us and render yourself famous.'

41. KING THEODORIC TO LUDUIN [CLOVIS], KING OF THE FRANKS.

Victories of Clovis over the Alamanni.

Congratulates him on his recent victories over the Alamanni. Refers to the ties of affinity between them (Theodoric having married the sister of Clovis). Clovis has stirred up the nation of the Franks, 'prisca aetate

---

[1] 'Bene quidem arbitrati, si causam celestis beatitudinis non in sonis sed in Creatore posuissent; ubi veraciter sine fine gaudium est, sine aliquo taedio manens semper aeternitas: et inspectio sola Divinitatis efficit, ut beatius esse nil possit. Haec veraciter perennitatem praestat: haec jucunditates accumulat; et sicut praeter ipsam creatura non extat, ita sine ipsâ incommutabilem laetitiam habere non praevalet.'

residem,' to new and successful encounters. 'It is a memorable triumph that the impetuous Alaman should be struck with such terror as even to beg for his life. Let it suffice that that King with all the pride of his race should have fallen: let it suffice that an innumerable people should have been doomed either to the sword or to slavery.'

He recommends (almost orders) Clovis not to touch the panic-stricken refugees who have fled to the territory of Theodoric. Theodoric himself has always found that those wars were prosperously waged which were ended moderately.

Theodoric sends 'illum et illum' as ambassadors, to take certain verbal counsels from himself, to bring this letter and carry back the reply, and also to introduce the Citharoedus of whom we heard in the preceding letter[1].

[The campaign of Clovis against the Alamanni, referred to in this letter, is not mentioned by Gregory of Tours. Ennodius, however, in his Panegyric on Theodoric, and Agathias in his History, make distinct allusions to this event, and to Theodoric's reception of the vanquished Alamanni in his own dominions, probably in the valleys of Raetia.

This letter is very fully discussed by Von Schubert, at pp. 32–43 of his 'Unterwerfung der Alamannen' (Strassburg, 1884). I may also refer to 'Italy and her Invaders' iii. 390–91.

The date of the letter is probably about 504.]

---

[1] There are two allusions to the relationship between the Kings: 'vestrae virtutis affinitate' (line 1), and 'ad parentum vestrorum defensionem confugisse' (line 10).

BOOK III.

CONTAINING FIFTY-THREE LETTERS WRITTEN BY CASSIODORUS IN THE NAME OF THEODORIC.

1. KING THEODORIC TO ALARIC, KING OF THE VISIGOTHS.

Dissuades Alaric the Visigoth from war with the Franks.

'SURROUNDED as you are by an innumerable multitude of subjects, and strong in the remembrance of their having turned back Attila[1], still do not fight with Clovis. War is a terrible thing, and a terrible risk. The long peace may have softened the hearts of your people, and your soldiers from want of practice may have lost the habit of working together on the battle-field. Ere yet blood is shed, draw back if possible. We are sending ambassadors to the King of the Franks to try to prevent this war between our relatives; and the ambassadors whom we are sending to you will go on to Gundibad, King of the Burgundians, to get him to interpose on behalf of peace. Your enemy will be mine also.'

[The battle of Vouglé, in which Alaric was overthrown by Clovis, was fought in 507; but the date of this letter is probably 506 (Dahn's date) rather than 507, as there were no doubt some premonitory symptoms before the war broke out.

---

[1] 'Quamvis Attilam potentem reminiscamini Visigothorum viribus inclinatum.'

Binding i. 181 (*n.* 608), and Pallmann ii. 55 *n.* 1, and 135 *n.* 2, incline to a date somewhat earlier even than 506, thinking that there may have been earlier threatenings of war, which Theodoric succeeded for the time in averting.

The earlier the date the better will it suit the allusion to Clovis (and Alaric) as 'Regii *Juvenes*' in the following letter. Clovis was born in 466, and was therefore 41 years of age at the battle of Vouglé.]

2. KING THEODORIC TO GUNDIBAD, KING OF THE BURGUNDIANS.

Repeats the arguments in iii. 1 about the ill effects of war on the fortunes of all, and says that it is Theodoric's part to moderate the angry impulses of 'regii juvenes.' It becomes them to reverence 'senes,' such as Theodoric and Gundibad, although they are themselves in the balmy vigour of the flower of their age. *Dissuades Gundibad from war.*

Sends two ambassadors ('illum atque illum') with letters and a verbal message, hoping that the wisdom of Gundibad may reflect upon what they say to him [perhaps too delicate a matter to be committed to writing], and find some way of preserving peace.

[It is remarkable that in this letter Theodoric, who was probably only 52, if the date of it be 506, and who may have been a year or two younger, speaks of himself along with Gundibad as a *senex*, and of Clovis, who could hardly be more than twelve years his junior, as *regius juvenis*. Perhaps this is partly due to the fact that Cassiodorus speaks from his own point of view. To him, now about 26 years of age, Theodoric might seem to be fitly described as 'senex.'

See Binding i. 181–183 on this letter and the reasons why it produced no effect on Gundibad. See also Dahn ii. 144.]

3. King Theodoric to the Kings of the Heruli, Warni (Guarni), and Thuringians.

Attempt to form a Teutonic coalition on behalf of Alaric.

[On the same subject.] If Clovis succeeds in his unprovoked aggression on Alaric, none of his neighbours will be safe. 'I will tell you just what I think: he who inclines to act without law is prepared to shake the kingdoms of all of us[1].'

'Remember how often Alaric's father Euric gave you presents and staved off war from your borders. Repay to the son the kindness of the father. I send you two ambassadors, and I want you to join your representations to mine and Gundibad's, calling on Clovis to desist from his attacks on Alaric and seek redress from the law of nations[2], or else expect the combined attack of all of us, for this quarrel is really the quarrel of us all.'

[The turn of the Thuringians to be swallowed up by the Frankish Monarchy came in 531.

See on this letter Dahn, 'Könige der Germanen' ii. 144 and 8 *n.* 2; Pallmann ii. 55.]

4. King Theodoric to Luduin (Ludwig, or Clovis), King of the Franks.

Desires Clovis to desist from war on Alaric.

[On the same subject.] 'The affinities of kings ought to keep their subjects from the plague of war. We are grieved to hear of the paltry causes which are giving rise to rumours of war between you and our son Alaric,

---

[1] Compare the state of Europe during the wars of the French Revolution, as expressed by Tennyson:

'Again their ravening eagle rose,
  In anger, wheel'd on Europe-shadowing wings,
  And barking for the thrones of kings.'

[2] 'Et leges gentium quaerat.' But how was the law of nations to be enforced?

rumours which gladden the hearts of the enemies of both of you. Let me say with all frankness, but with all affection, just what I think: "It is the act of a passionate man to get his troops ready for action at the first embassy which he sends." Instead of that refer the matter to our arbitration. It would be a delight to me to choose men capable of mediating between you. What would you yourselves think of me if I could hear unmoved of your murderous intentions towards one another? Away with this conflict, in which one of you will probably be utterly destroyed. Throw away the sword which you wield for *my* humiliation. By what right do I thus threaten you? By the right of a father and a friend. He who shall despise this advice of ours will have to reckon us and our friends as his adversaries.

'I send two ambassadors to you, as I have to my son Alaric, and hope that they may be able so to arrange matters that no alien malignity may sow the seeds of dissension between you, and that your nations, which under your fathers have long enjoyed the blessings of peace, may not now be laid waste by sudden collision. You ought to believe him who, as you know, has rejoiced in your prosperity. No true friend is he who launches his associates, unwarned, into the headlong dangers of war.'

5. KING THEODORIC TO IMPORTUNUS, VIR ILLUSTRIS AND PATRICIAN.

Importunus promoted to the Patriciate.

[Importunus was Consul in 509. This letter therefore probably belongs to the early part of 510.]

'Noble birth and noble deeds meet in you, and we are therefore bestowing on you an honour to which by age you are scarcely yet entitled. Your father and uncle were especially noteworthy, the glory of the Senate, men who adorned modern ages[1] with the antique virtues, men who were prosperous without being hated. The Senate felt their courage, the multitude their wisdom.

'Therefore, being descended from such ancestors, and yourself possessing such virtues, on laying down the Consular fasces, assume the insignia of the Patriciate. Bind those fillets, which are generally reserved for the hoary head, round your young locks, and by your future actions justify my choice of you.'

6. KING THEODORIC TO THE SENATE ON IMPORTUNUS' ACCESSION TO THE PATRICIATE.

[See preceding letter.]

The same subject.

'We delight to introduce new men to the Senate, but we delight still more when we can bring back to that venerable body, crowned with fresh honours, her own offspring[2]. And such is now my fortune in presenting to you Importunus, crowned with the honours of the Patriciate; Importunus, who is descended from the great stock of the Decii, a stock illustrated by noble names in every generation, by the favour of the Senate and the choice of the people. Even as a boy he had a countenance of serene beauty, and to the gifts of Nature he added the endowments of the mind. From his parents in household lays he learned the great deeds of the old Decii. Once, at a great spectacle, the whole school at the recitation of the Lay of the Decii turned their eyes on Importunus, discerning that he would one day rival his ancestors. Thus his widowed mother brought him up, him and all his troop of brothers, and gave to the Curia as many Consulars as she had sons[3]. All these

---

[1] Notice the use of the word *modernus* here, a post-classical word, which apparently occurs first in Cassiodorus.

[2] 'Origo ipsa jam gloria est: laus nobilitati connascitur. Idem vobis est dignitatis, quod vitae principium. Senatus enim honor amplissimus vobiscum gignitur, ad quem vix maturis aetatibus pervenitur.'

[3] 'Et quot edidit familiae juvenes, tot reddidit curiae consulares.'

private virtues I have discerned in him, and now seal them with promotion to the Patriciate. At this act I call on you specially to rejoice.'

7. KING THEODORIC TO THE VENERABLE JANUARIUS, BISHOP OF SALONA.

Extortion by the Bishop of Salona.

'The lamentable petition of John says that you have taken sixty tuns of oil from him, and never paid him for them. It is especially important that preachers of righteousness should be righteous themselves. We cannot suppose that God is ignorant whence come the offerings which we make before Him [and He must therefore hate robbery for a burnt offering]. Pray enquire into this matter, and if the complaint be well founded remedy it promptly. You who preach to us our duty in great things should not be caught tripping in little ones.'

8. KING THEODORIC TO VENANTIUS, SENATOR, CORRECTOR OF LUCANIA AND BRUTTII.

Remissness of Venantius in collection of public revenue.

[Venantius, son of Liberius, was, with many high commendations, made Comes Domesticorum in Letters ii. 15 and 16. See further as to his fall in iii. 36, also iii. 46.]

'Remissness in the collection of the public taxes is a great fault, and no kindness in the end to the taxpayer. For want of a timely caution you probably have to end by selling him up.

'The Count of Sacred Largesses tells us that you were long ago commissioned to get in the *Bina* and *Terna* [and have not done so]. Be quick about it, that the collection may be completed according to the registers of the Treasury. If you are not quick, and the Treasury suffers loss, you will have to make it good out of your private property. You have not shown proper respect to our orders, nor a due sense of the obligation of your own promise.'

[These 'Bina' and 'Terna' are a mystery; but Dahn[1] thinks they are not a specially Gothic tax, but an inheritance from the fiscal administration of Rome, having probably nothing to do with the Tertiae.]

9. KING THEODORIC TO THE POSSESSORES, DEFENSORES, AND CURIALES[2] DWELLING AT AESTUNAE[3].

Marbles for Ravenna.

'We wish to build new edifices without despoiling the old[4]. But we are informed that in your municipality there are blocks of masonry and columns formerly belonging to some building now lying absolutely useless and unhonoured. If it be so, send these slabs of marble[5] and columns[6] by all means to Ravenna, that they may be again made beautiful and take their place in a building there.'

10. KING THEODORIC TO THE ILLUSTRIOUS FESTUS, PATRICIAN.

The same subject.

A similar order, for the transport of marbles from the Pincian Hill to Ravenna, by Catabulenses[7]. 'We have ordered a "subvectus" [assistance from the public postal-service?], that the labourers may set to work at once.'

---

[1] iii. 145, *n.* 4.
[2] Note these three classes; as also in ii. 17.
[3] I have not been able to identify this place.
[4] 'Moderna sine priorum imminutione desideramus erigere.'
[5] 'Platonias.' This, which is the spelling found in Nivellius' edition, seems to be a more correct form than the 'platomas' of Garet. Ducange, who has a long article on the subject, refers the word to the Greek πλατύνιον.
[6] Possibly the columns in S. Apollinare Deutro may have been some of those here mentioned.
[7] 'Catabulenses,' or 'Catabolenses'—freighters, contractors, who effected the transport of heavy goods by means of draught-horses and mules.

11. KING THEODORIC TO ARGOLICUS, VIR ILLUSTRIS [A.D. 510].

Argolicus appointed Praefect of the City.

Announces to this young man his nomination to the Praefecture of the City (for the 4th Indiction). Enlarges on the dignity of the office, especially as involving the Presidency of the Senate, and calls upon him by a righteous and sober life to show himself worthy of the choice.

Argolicus is a great student [perhaps a literary friend of Cassiodorus], and he is exhorted to keep himself in the right path by musing on the great examples of antiquity.

[There is a sort of tone of apology for the appointment of Argolicus, which is perhaps accounted for by the fact, which comes out in the next letter, that his father was a comparatively poor man.

See a sharp rebuke of Argolicus for venal procrastination, iv. 29.]

12. KING THEODORIC TO THE SENATE OF THE CITY OF ROME.

The same subject.

Rehearses the usual sentiments about the dignity of the Senate and Theodoric's care in the choice of officials.

'It is easier, if one may say so, for Nature herself to err, than that a Sovereign should make a State unlike to himself.'

Recounts the ancestry of Argolicus. The older Senators will remember his eloquent and purely-living grandfather, a man of perfectly orthodox reputation, who filled the offices of Comes Sacrarum Largitionum and Magister Officiorum. His father never stained the dignity of 'Comes Privatarum' by cruelty, and was free from ill-gotten gains in an age when avarice was not accounted a crime[1].

---

[1] Tillemont understands this of the times of Odovacar, vi. 438.

'We may hope that the son will follow the example of such distinguished ancestors.'

13. KING THEODORIC TO SUNHIVAD, SENATOR.

Sunhivad, Governor of Samnium.

[Notice again the Roman title and Gothic name.]

'You who have ruled your own life in a long career so well should make a good governor of others. I therefore send you to Samnium as Governor, in reply to the complaints which reach me from that Province. Settle according to the law of justice the disputes which have arisen there between the Romans and the Goths.'

14. KING THEODORIC TO THE VENERABLE BISHOP AURIGENES.

Accusations against the servants of a Bishop.

'You as a Bishop will be especially grieved to hear of any offences against the sanctity of the married state. Julianus complains that his wife has been outraged and his goods wasted by some of your servants [probably slaves].

'Do you enquire into the matter, and if the complaint appears to be just, deal promptly and severely with the offenders.'

[Cf. Dahn, 'Könige der Germanen' iii. 193, on this letter. He shows that it has been improperly appealed to as proving the immunity of all ecclesiastical persons from a secular tribunal. What Theodoric really intended was to give the Bishop a chance of settling the affair himself, and so to prevent the scandal of its appearing in the secular Courts, which it assuredly would do if the Bishop were apathetic. But one sees how easily this would glide into something like immunity from secular tribunals.]

15. KING THEODORIC TO THEODAHAD, SENATOR[1].

A contumacious person handed over to Theodahad.

'It is the extreme of insolence in anyone not to execute our "sacred orders." A certain person whom we commanded to attend before the judgment-seat of the Illustrious Sona, has with inveterate cunning withdrawn himself therefrom. We therefore hand him over to you, that your fame may grow by your skilful management of a difficult case like this.'

16. KING THEODORIC TO GEMELLUS, SENATOR (509–510).

Appointment of Gemellus as Governor of Gaul.

'Having proved your worth by experience we are now going to send you to govern the Provinces of Gaul newly wrested [from Clovis], as Vicar of the Praefects[2].

'Think what a high opinion we must have formed of you to delegate to you the government of these Provinces, the conquest of which has added so much to our glory, and the good opinion of whose inhabitants we so particularly wish to acquire. Abhor turbulence; do not think of avarice; show yourself in all things such a Governor as "Romanus Princeps" ought to send, and let the Province feel such an improvement in her lot that she may "rejoice to have been conquered."'

[This is so like the words put by Sidonius into the mouth of Lyons, after Majorian's conquest of her, that I believe it to be intentionally imitated.]

---

[1] This is no doubt the nephew of Theodoric.

[2] 'Vicarius Praefectorum.' Vicar of what Praefects? Why the plural number? Had Theodoric a titular Praefect *of the Gauls*, to whom this Vicarius was theoretically subject while practically obeying the Praefect of Italy? Or, to prevent bickerings, did he give the 'Praefectus Italiae' and the 'Praefectus Urbis' conjoint authority over the new conquests? There is some mystery here which would be worth explaining.

17. KING THEODORIC TO ALL THE GAULISH PROVINCES (510).

Proclamation to the new Gaulish subjects.

'Obey the Roman customs. You are now by God's blessing restored to your ancient freedom; put off the barbarian; clothe yourselves with the morals of the toga; unlearn cruelty, that you may not be unworthy to be our subjects. We are sending you Spectabilis Gemellus as Vicarius Praefectorum, a man of tried worth, who we trust will be guilty of no crime, because he knows he would thereby seriously displease us. Obey his commands therefore. Do not dislike the reign of Law because it is new to you, after the aimless seethings of Barbarism (Gentilitas).

'You may now bring out your long-hidden treasures; the rich and the noble will again have a chance of suitable promotion. You may now enjoy what till now you have only heard of—the triumph of Public Right, the most certain solace of human life, the help of the weak, the curb of the strong. You may now understand that men are exalted not by their bodily strength, but by reason.'

[Some of these reflections on the past misgovernment of *Gentilitas* hit the Visigoths, Theodoric's friends, harder than the Franks. If the Gaulish nobles of the south-eastern Provinces (and these were all that Theodoric had conquered) had *long* been obliged to hide the treasures of their fathers, that surely was the fault rather of Euric and Alaric II than of Clovis.

Cf. Dahn, 'Könige der Germanen' iii. 261–2, on all this correspondence.]

18. KING THEODORIC TO GEMELLUS.

Magnus to be restored to his possessions.

[Probably during his government of Gaul].
'We wish that all who have elected to live under our Clemency should be the better for it.

'The Spectabilis Magnus, spurning the conversation of our enemies [Franks?], and remembering his own origin, has sought re-patriation in the Roman Empire; but during his absence his property has suffered loss. Let him therefore be restored to, and henceforward have unquestioned possession of, all that he can prove to be his own in the way of lands, urban or rural slaves.'

19. KING THEODORIC TO DANIEL [A 'COMMONITORIUM'].

'We wish the servants of our palace to have proper reward for their labours, though we might call on them to render them gratuitously. Therefore, being much pleased with your skill in preparing and ornamenting marbles, we concede to you the [sole] right of furnishing the marble chests in which the citizens of Ravenna bury their dead. *(Monopoly of supply of marble sarcophagi.)*

'They thus keep them above ground—no small consolation to the survivors, since the souls alone depart from this world's conversation; but they do not altogether lose the bodies which once were dear to them.

'Do not, however, impose upon their sadness; do not let a relative be forced to the alternative of wasting his substance in funeral expenses, or else throwing the body of his dear one into some well. Be moderate in your charges.'

[Odovacar was buried ἐν λιθίνῃ λάρνακι (Joann. Ant. fr. 214). The great stone coffins of Honorius and Valentinian will be remembered by every visitor to Ravenna.]

20. KING THEODORIC TO THE SAJO GRIMODA AND TO THE APPARITOR FERROCINCTUS.

[Cf. Dahn, 'Könige der Germanen' iii. 86 and 113.]

'We are determined to assist the humble, and to repress the violence of the proud. *(Oppression of Castorius by Faustus)*

'The lamentable petition of Castorius sets forth that he has been unjustly deprived of his property by the magnificent Praetorian Praefect Faustus. [The same, no doubt, to whom are addressed iii. 55, i. 35, and the immediately succeeding letter (iii. 21).]

'If it be so, let the invader (pervasor) restore to Castorius his property, and hand over, besides, another property of equal value.

'If Faustus have employed any intermediate person in the act of violence, let him be brought to us in chains; and if that well-known author of ill [Faustus] tries any further to injure Castorius, he shall pay £2,000, besides having the misery of seeing his would-be victim unharmed.

'No Powers of any kind, be they Praetorian Praefects or what they may, shall be permitted to trample on the lowly.'

21. KING THEODORIC TO FAUSTUS, VIR ILLUSTRIS.

Disgrace and temporary exile of Faustus.

'As all men require change, Faustus is allowed to absent himself from the sacred walls of Rome for four months, which he may spend at his own Penates. The King expects, however, that he will then return to the most famous (opinatissima) City, from which no Roman Senator can long be absent without grief.'

[Coupling this letter with its immediate predecessor it is difficult not to believe that Faustus is sent away in disgrace—notwithstanding the smooth words here used—for the act of injustice therein mentioned.

But why is he only addressed as Vir Illustris, and not also as Praefectus? Perhaps his term of office was expired; perhaps he was even dismissed from it.]

22. KING THEODORIC TO ARTEMIDORUS, VIR ILLUSTRIS.

An earnest invitation to the King's friend, Artemidorus.

'We hereby [by these oracles] invite your Greatness to behold us, which we know will be most agreeable to you, in order that you who have now spent a large portion of your life with us may be satisfied by the sweetness of our presence. He who is permitted to share our converse deems it a Divine boon. We believe that you will come gladly, as we shall entertain you with alacrity.'

[Cf. Dahn iii. 283–4. The ending of the letter (Venire te gaudentem credimus, quem alacriter sustinemus) is the common form, and 'sustineo' is a technical word for the King's reception of his subjects: see iii. 28. ad finem.]

23. KING THEODORIC TO COLOSSAEUS, VIR ILLUSTRIS AND COMES (CIR. A.D. 505).

Appointment of Colossaeus as Governor of Pannonia.

'We delight to entrust our mandates to persons of approved character.

'We are sending you "with the dignity of the illustrious belt" to Pannonia Sirmiensis, an old habitation of the Goths. Let that Province be induced to welcome her old defenders, even as she used gladly to obey our ancestors. Show forth the justice of the Goths, a nation happily situated for praise, since it is theirs to unite the forethought of the Romans and the virtue of the Barbarians. Remove all ill-planted customs[1], and impress upon all your subordinates that we would rather that our Treasury lost a suit than that it gained one wrongfully, rather that we lost money than the taxpayer was driven to suicide.'

[Cf. Muchar, 'Geschichte der Steiermark' iv. 131.]

---

[1] 'Consuetudines abominanter inolitas.' Fornerius thinks this means 'all extortionate taxes.' Compare the English use of the word 'customs.'

24. KING THEODORIC TO ALL THE BARBARIANS AND ROMANS SETTLED IN PANNONIA.

[Cf. Muchar, iv. 132.]

To the Pannonians, on the appointment of Colossaeus.

'Intent on the welfare of our subjects we are sending you Colossaeus for Governor. His name means a mighty man; and a mighty man he is, who has given many proofs of his virtue. Now we exhort you with patience and constancy to submit yourselves to his authority. Do not excite that wrath before which our enemies tremble. Acquiesce in the rule of justice in which the whole world rejoices. Why should you, who have now an upright Judge[1], settle your grievances by single combat? What has man got a tongue for, if the armed hand is to settle all differences? or where can peace be looked for, if there is fighting in a civilised State like ours[2]? Imitate then our Goths, who have learned to practise war abroad, to show peaceable dispositions at home. We want you so to live as you see that our subjects (parentes) have lived and flourished under the Divine blessing.'

25. KING THEODORIC TO SIMEON, VIR ILLUSTRIS AND COMES.

Tax-collecting and iron-mining in Dalmatia.

'We entrust to you the duty of collecting throughout the Province of Dalmatia the arrears of Siliquaticum for the first, second, and third Indictions [Sept. 1, 506, to Aug. 31, 509]. We do this not only for the sake of gain to our Treasury, but to prevent the demoralisation of our subjects.

'Also by careful mining (cuniculo veritatis) seek out the iron veins in Dalmatia, where the softness of earth is pregnant with the rigour of iron, which is cooked by fire that it may become hard.

---

[1] 'Cur ad monomachiam recurritis, qui venalem judicem non habetis?'
[2] 'Aut unde pax quaeritur si sub civilitate pugnetur.'

'Iron enables us to defend our country, is serviceable for agriculture and for countless arts of human life: yea, iron is master of gold, compelling the rich man, weaponless, to obey the poor man who wields a blade of steel.'

26. KING THEODORIC TO OSUN, VIR ILLUSTRIS AND COUNT.

Commands him to provide all the necessaries for the journey of 'Clarissimus' Simeon, setting off for Dalmatia on the aforesaid mission to collect Siliquaticum and develop the iron mines. *Simeon's journey to Dalmatia.*

[Why is Simeon not called Illustris, as in the previous letter? This seems to show that the titles 'Clarissimus' and 'Illustris' were not always used with technical exactness, as they would have been under Diocletian.]

27. KING THEODORIC TO JOANNES, SENATOR, CONSULAR OF CAMPANIA.

'You have not complained to us in vain that the Praetorian Praefect [perhaps again Faustus] is venting a private grudge against you under colour of the discharge of his public duty. We will wall you round with our protection. Go now and discharge the duties of Consular of Campania with the like devotion as your predecessors, and with this reflection: "If the King prevents my superior the Praetorian Praefect from doing me harm, with what unfailing rigour will he visit me if I do wrong."' *Promises protection against the Praetorian Praefect.*

28. KING THEODORIC TO CASSIODORUS, VIR ILLUSTRIS AND PATRICIAN[1].

'For your glorious services, and your incorruptible *An invitation to Cassiodorus Senior to come to Court.*

[1] Father of the writer.

administration, which has given deep peace to the nation, we reward you by summoning you to Court.

'Having endeavoured to check *another* [probably alluding to the disgrace of Faustus], we have bestowed our praises on you, as all the Palace knows. Come then, come eagerly, as he should do whom his Sovereign is going to entertain[1].'

29. KING THEODORIC TO ARGOLICUS, ILLUSTRIS AND PRAEFECT OF THE CITY.

Permission to Paulinus to repair certain granaries at Rome.

'The King should sow his gifts broadcast, as the sower his seeds—not put them all into one hole.

'The Patrician Paulinus represents to us that such and such granaries are falling into ruin and are of no use to anyone, and asks to be allowed to repair them and transmit them to his heirs. We consent to this, if you are of opinion that they are not wanted for the public, and if there is no corn in them belonging to our Treasury.

'It is especially fitting that all ruined buildings should be repaired in Rome. In Rome, praised beyond all other cities by the world's mouth, there should be nothing sordid or mediocre[2].'

30. KING THEODORIC TO ARGOLICUS, ILLUSTRIS AND PRAEFECTUS URBIS.

Repair of the Cloacae of Rome.

'We are ever vigilant for the repair and beautification of Rome.

'Let your Sublimity know that we have directed John to repair the Cloacae of the City, those splendid works

---

[1] There is an obscure sentence in this letter: 'Hinc omnibus factus notior, quia multi te positum in potestate nesciunt.' Possibly the meaning is that the elder Cassiodorus used his power so little for his own private aggrandisement, that many people did not even know that he possessed it.

[2] This letter is well illustrated by an inscription of the time of Severus Alexander, found at Great Chesters in Northumberland, and recording the repair of 'horreum vetustate conlabsum.' The words of Cassiodorus are 'horrea longi temporis vetustate destructa.'

which strike astonishment into the hearts of all beholders. There you see rivers as it were shut in by concave mountains, flowing down through mighty rafters[1] (?). There you see men steering their ships with the utmost possible care, lest they should suffer shipwreck. Hence may the greatness of Rome be inferred. What other city can compare with her in her heights when even her depths are so incomparable?

'See therefore, O Praefect, that John as a public officer receives his proper salary.'

31. King Theodoric to the Senate of the City of Rome.

Commission issued to John to check ruin of aqueducts and temples in Rome.

'Our care is for the whole Republic, "in which, by the favour of God, we are striving to bring back all things to their former state;" but especially for the City of Rome. We hear that great depredations are being committed on public property there.

'(1) It is said that the water of the aqueducts (formae) is being diverted to turn mills and water gardens— a thing which would not be suffered even in the country districts. Even in redressing this wrong we must be observant of law; and therefore if it should be found that those who are doing this can plead thirty years' prescription, they must be bought off, but the misuser must cease. If the diversion is of less ancient date[2], it must of course be at once stopped without compensation.

'(2) Slaves assigned by the forethought of previous rulers to the service of the formae have passed under the sway of private masters.

'(3) Great weights of brass and lead (the latter very easy to steal, from its softness) have been stripped off from the public buildings. Now Ionos, King of Thessaly,

---

[1] 'Per ingentia ligna decurrere.' Fornerius proposes to read 'stagna.'
[2] 'Si vero aliquid modernâ praesumptione tentatum est.' (Again 'modernus.')

is said to have first discovered lead, and Midas, King of Phrygia, brass. How grievous that we should be handed down to posterity as neglecting two metals which they were immortalised by discovering!

'(4) Temples and other public buildings, which at the request of many we have repaired, are handed over without a thought to spoliation and ruin.

'We have appointed the Spectabilis John to enquire into and set straight all these matters. *You* ought to have brought the matter before us yourselves: at least, now, support him with the necessary "solatia."'

[See preceding letter as to the commission entrusted to John, Theodoric's Clerk of the Works in Rome.]

32. KING THEODORIC TO GEMELLUS, SENATOR. A.D. 511.

[Appointed Governor of the Gaulish Province in Letter iii. 16.]

Remission of taxes to citizens of Arles.

'The men of Arles, who were reduced to penury in the glorious siege which they endured on our behalf, are freed from the obligation of taxes for the fourth Indiction [Sept. 1, 510, to Aug. 31, 511]. We ask for these payments from men at peace, not from men besieged. How can one claim taxes from the lord of a field when one knows he has not been able to cultivate it? They have already rendered a most precious tribute in their fidelity to us. After this year, however, the taxes will be collected as usual.'

Promotion of Armentarius and Superbus to post of Referendi Curiae.

33. KING THEODORIC TO ARGOLICUS, ILLUSTRIS, PRAEFECT OF THE CITY.

Armentarius (Clarissimus) and his son Superbus are to receive the privilege of *Referendi Curiae*[1]. Thus will the profession of the law be, as is most fitting, adorned with the honours of the Senate.

---

[1] Possibly Referendi is the same as Referendarii. See Var. vi. 17.

Praises of Rhetoric. The man who has swayed the judges by his eloquence is sure to have a favouring audience in the Senate.

34. KING THEODORIC TO THE INHABITANTS OF MASSILIA.

Marabad Governor of Marseilles.

'In accordance with our usual policy of sending persons of tried ability and moderation to govern the Provinces, we are sending Count Marabad [a Gothic name ?] to act as your Governor, to bring solace to the lowly and repress the insolent, and to force all into the path of justice, which is the secret of the prosperity of our Empire. As befits your long-tried loyalty, welcome and obey him.'

35. KING THEODORIC TO ROMULUS.

[It is surely possible that this is the dethroned Emperor. The name Romulus, which, as we know, he derived from his maternal grandfather, was not a very common one in Rome (it must be admitted there is another Romulus, ii. 14). And is there not something rather peculiar in the entire absence of all titles of honour, the superscription being simply 'Romulo Theodoricus Rex,' as if neither King nor scribe quite knew how to address an ex-Emperor?]

Gifts to Romulus shall not be revoked.

'The liberality of the Prince must be kept firm and unshaken by the arts of malignant men. Therefore any gift which shall be proved to have been given according to our orders by the Patrician Liberius, to you *or to your mother*, by written instrument (pictacium or pittacium), shall remain in full force, and you need not fear its being questioned.'

[For Liberius, see ii. 16. A man of that eminence, who was employed to arrange disputes between the

Goths and Romans at the first settlement of the former in Italy, was the very man to be also employed to arrange terms with Augustulus. There is some reason to think that the mother of the deposed Emperor was named Barbaria, and that she is mentioned in the history of the translation of the relics of St. Severinus. See 'Italy and her Invaders' iii. 190.]

36. KING THEODORIC TO THE ILLUSTRIOUS COUNT ARIGERN.

Complaints against Venantius.

'Firminus alleges that he has some cause of complaint against the Magnificent Venantius [son of Liberius, mentioned in the previous letter, and strongly commended in ii. 15], and that Venantius treats his claims with contempt. There is always a danger of justice being wrested in the interests of the great. We therefore desire you with all due reverence to address the aforesaid Magnificent person and desire him to appoint a representative, with proper credentials, to plead in our Court in answer to the claims of Firminus, who will be punished for his audacity if he have brought a false charge against so illustrious a person.'

[This and the preceding letter look as if the fortunes of the house of Liberius (so greatly extolled in ii. 15 and 16) were passing under a cloud. See also iii. 8, as to the disgrace of Venantius. This may have made the ex-Emperor anxious as to the validity of the settlement made through him.]

37. KING THEODORIC TO BISHOP PETER.

Alleged injustice of a Bishop.

[See the full explanation of this letter in Dahn, 'Könige der Germanen' iii. 193-4. Cf. also Var. iii. 14. Observe how the marginal note (in the edition of the Benedictine, Garet) strains the doctrine of this letter in favour of the clergy[1].]

'Germanus, in his "flebilis allegatio," informs us that you detain from him a part of the property of his father Thomas. As it is proper that causes which concern you should first be remitted to you (so often employed as judges to settle the disputes of others), we call upon you to enquire into this claim, and if it be a just one to satisfy it. Know that if you fail to do justice yourself to the petitioner, his cause will be carried through to our own audience-chamber.'

38. KING THEODORIC TO WANDIL [VUANDIL[2]].

The Gothic troops at Avignon to abstain from molesting the citizens.

'Our Piety wishes that there should be order and good government everywhere in our dominions, but especially in Gaul, that our new subjects there may form a good opinion of the ruler under whom they have come. Therefore by this authority we charge you to see that no violence happen in Avignon where you reside. Let our army live "civiliter" with the Romans, and let the latter feel that our troops are come for their defence, not for their annoyance.'

39. KING THEODORIC TO FELIX, ILLUSTRIS AND CONSUL (A.D. 511).

Largesse to charioteers of Milan.

'Those who minister to the pleasures of the public should be liberally treated, and the Consul must not belie the expectations of his generosity which have been formed when he was Senator. Therefore let your Sublimity enquire into the petition for largesse presented by the charioteers of Milan; and if their statements are correct, let them have whatever it has been cus-

---
[1] 'Causae sacerdotum a sacerdotibus debent terminari.'
[2] Probably a Gothic officer.

tomary for them to receive. In matters of this kind custom creates a kind of debt.'

40. KING THEODORIC TO ALL THE PROVINCIALS SETTLED IN GAUL.

Immunity from taxes for districts ravaged by war.

'We wish promptly to relieve all the distresses of our subjects, and we therefore at once announce to you that the districts ravaged by the incursions of the enemy will not be called upon to pay tribute at the fourth Indiction [Sept. 510, to Aug. 511]. For we have no pleasure in receiving what is paid by a heavy-hearted contributor. The part of the country, however, which has been untouched by the enemy will have to contribute to the expense of our army. But a hungry defender is a weak defender.'

41. KING THEODORIC TO GEMELLUS, SENATOR [Governor of Gothic Gaul[1]].

Corn for the garrisons on the Durance.

'A burden borne in common is lightened, since only the edge as it were of the whole rests on the shoulders of each individual. We have ordered the corn for the army to be carried from the granaries of Marseilles to the forts upon the Durance. Let all unite in this toil. The willing labour of many brings a speedy end to the work.'

[This letter, as showing that at least one if not both banks of the Durance were included in the Ostrogothic Monarchy in 511, has an important bearing on the geographical extent of the Burgundian Kingdom. See Exkurs vi. to Binding's 'Burgundisch-Romanische Königreich.' He makes the northern bank of the Durance belong to Burgundy, the southern to the Ostrogoths.]

[1] See Letters iii. 16 and 32.

42. King Theodoric to all the Provincials in Gaul.

No part of Gaul to be called on for military contributions.

'Because the generosity of the Prince should even outrun the petitions of his subjects we repeal that part of a previous letter [iii. 40] which says that the unravaged portion of the Province of Gaul must pay the expenses of our soldiers. We will transmit to the Duces and Praepositi sufficient money to provide "alimonia nostris Gothis."'

['Praebendae,' near the end of this letter, seems to be used in a technical sense, almost equivalent to stipendia or annonae.]

43. King Theodoric to Unigis, the Sword-bearer [Spatarius].

[No doubt a high officer in the Royal household.]

Runaway slaves to be restored to their owners.

'We delight to live after the law of the Romans, whom we seek to defend with our arms; and we are as much interested in the maintenance of morality as we can possibly be in war. For what profit is there in having removed the turmoil of the Barbarians, unless we live according to law? Certain slaves, on our army's entry into Gaul, have run away from their old masters and betaken themselves to new ones. Let them be restored to their rightful owners. Rights must not be confounded under the rule of justice, nor ought the defender of liberty to favour recreant slaves. [Probably an allusion to the office of the *Assertor Libertatis* in the *Liberalis Causa,* as set forth in the Theodosian Code iv. 8.] Let other kings desire the glory of battles won, of cities taken, of ruins made; our purpose is, God helping us, so to rule that our subjects shall grieve that they did not earlier acquire the blessing of our dominion.'

44. KING THEODORIC TO ALL THE LANDOWNERS [POSSESSORES] OF ARLES.

[Repair of walls of Arles, and supply of corn.]

'We wish to refresh men, but to repair cities also, that the renewed fortune of the citizens may be displayed by the splendour of their buildings.

'We have therefore directed that a certain sum of money be sent for the repair of the walls and old towers of Arles. But we are also going to send you, as soon as the time is favourable for navigation, provisions to supply the waste caused by the war. Be of good cheer, therefore! Grain for which our word is pledged is as good as grain already in your granaries.'

45. KING THEODORIC TO ARIGERN, ILLUSTRIS AND COUNT.

[Site disputed between Roman Church and Samaritans.]

'It is represented to us by the Defensors of the "sacrosanct" Roman Church that Pope Simplicius, of blessed memory, bought a house at Rome[1] of Eufrasius the Acolyte, with all proper formalities, and that now the people of the Samaritan superstition, hardened in effrontery, allege that a synagogue of theirs was built on that site, and claim it accordingly; whereas the very style of building, say their opponents, shows that this was meant as a private house and not as a synagogue. Enquire into this matter, and do justice accordingly. If we will not tolerate chicanery [calumniae] against men, much less will we against the Divinity Himself.'

46. KING THEODORIC TO ADEODATUS.

[Further charges of misgovernment against Venantius.]

'The crimes of subjects are an occasion for manifesting the virtues of princes. You have addressed to us your petition, alleging that you were compelled

---

[1] 'In sacratissimâ urbe.'

by the Spectabilis Venantius, Governor of Lucania and Bruttii, to confess yourself guilty of the rape of the maiden Valeriana.

'Overcome, you say, by the severity of your imprisonment and the tortures inflicted upon you, and longing for death as a release from agony; being moreover refused the assistance of Advocates, while the utmost resources of rhetoric were at the disposal of your opponents, you confessed a crime which you had never committed.

Illogical decision in the case of Adeodatus.

'Such is your statement. The Governor of Bruttii sends his *relatio* in opposition, saying that we must not give credence to a petitioner who is deceitfully seeking to upset a sentence which was given in the interests of public morality.

'Our decision is that we will by our clemency mitigate the severity of your punishment. From the date of this decree you shall be banished for six months; and on your return no note of infamy of any kind shall be attached to you; since it is competent for the Prince to wipe off all the blots on a damaged reputation. Anyone who offends against this decree [by casting your old offence in your teeth] shall be fined £120 (3lbs. of gold). And all who are accused of the same offence in any place or time, but who offended through ignorance, are to be freed from all fear of punishment.'

[A most illogical and unjust conclusion, by which the judgment of Venantius is in fact neither upheld nor reversed. And what the meaning of the concluding sentence may be it is impossible to conjecture. See Dahn, 'Könige der Germanen' iii. 107, on this absurd decision.

On the subject of the misgovernment and disgrace of Venantius, cf. Letters ii. 15, 16; iii. 8, 36. Cf. also Procopius, 'De Bello Gotthico' iii. 18 and 22, as to his son Tullianus. In connection with the alleged misgovernment of Bruttii and Lucania by Venantius,

47. KING THEODORIC TO FAUSTUS, PRAETORIAN PRAEFECT.

[Sidenote: Jovinus, for killing a fellow Curial, is banished to the islands of Lipari, the volcanoes of which are described.]

'Jovinus the Curialis, according to the report of the Corrector of Lucania and Bruttii, had an angry altercation with a fellow Curial (collega), and in his rage slew him.

'He then took refuge within the precincts of a church, and refused to surrender himself to justice. We decide that the capital punishment shall be remitted out of reverence for his place of refuge, but he shall be banished to the Vulcanian [Lipari] Islands, there to live away from the paternal hearth, but ever in the midst of burning, like a salamander, which is a small and subtile beast, of kin to the slippery worm, clothed with a yellow colour.

'The substance of volcanoes, which is perpetually destroyed, is by the inextricable power of Nature perpetually renewed.

'The Vulcanian Islands are named from Vulcan, the god of fire, and burst into eruption on the day when Hannibal took poison at the Court of Prusias. It is especially wonderful that a mountain kindling into such a multitude of flames, should yet be half hidden by the waves of the sea.'

48. KING THEODORIC TO ALL GOTHS AND ROMANS LIVING NEAR THE FORT OF VERRUCA [1].

[Sidenote: Fortification of Verruca in the Tyrol.]

'It is the duty and the glory of a ruler to provide with wise forethought for the safety of his subjects. We have therefore ordered the Sajo Leodifrid that

---

[1] The double 'r' seems to be the correct spelling, though the MSS. of the Variarum apparently have the single 'r.'

under his superintendence you should build yourselves houses in the fort Verruca, which from its position receives its most suitable name [1].

'For it is in the midst of the plains a hill of stone roundly arising, which with its tall sides, being bare of woods, is all one great mountain fortress. Its lower parts are slenderer (graciliora) than its summit, and like some softest fungus the top broadens out, while it is thin at bottom. It is a mound not made by soldiers [2], a stronghold made safe by Nature [3], where the besieger can try no *coup-de-main* and the besieged need feel no panic. Past this fort swirls the Adige, that prince of rivers, with the pleasant gurgle of his clear waters, affording a defence and an adornment in one. It is a fort almost unequalled in the whole world, "a key that unlocks a kingdom [4];" and all the more important because it bars the invasion of wild and savage nations. This admirable defence what inhabitant would not wish to share, since even foreigners delight to visit it? and though by God's blessing we trust that the Province [of Raetia] is in our times secure, yet it is the part of prudence to guard against evils, though we may think they will not arise.'

Examples of gulls, who fly inland when they foresee a storm; of dolphins, which seek the shallower waters; of the edible sea-urchin, 'that honey of flesh, that dainty of the deep,' who anchors himself to a little pebble to prevent being dashed about by the waves; of birds, who change their dwellings when winter draws nigh; of beasts, who adapt their lair to the time of year. And shall man alone be improvident? Shall he not

---

[1] 'Milites ad Verrucam illam—*sic enim M. Cato locum editum asperumque appellat*—ire jubeas' (Gell. 3. 7. 6). Verruca therefore means primarily a steep cliff, and only secondarily a wart. See White and Riddell, s.v.

[2] 'Agger sine pugna.'   [3] 'Obsessio secura.'

[4] 'Tenens claustra provinciae.'

imitate that higher Providence by which the world is governed?

[The fortress of Verruca does not seem to be mentioned in the 'Notitia,' in the Antonine 'Itinerary,' or by the geographer of Ravenna.

Maffei ('Verona Illustrata,' Book ix. Vol. 2, pp. 391-2 in ed. 1825) comments on this passage, and argues that *Verruca=Dos Trento*, a cliff about a mile from Trient, and this identification seems to have been accepted, for Ball ('Alpine Guide, Eastern Alps,' p. 404) says: 'In the centre of the valley, close to the city, rises a remarkable rock known as *Dos Trento, and also called La Verruca*, formerly frequented for the sake of the beautiful view which it commands. Since 1857 it has been strongly fortified, and permission to ascend to the summit is not easily obtained.'

Maffei says that the French bombarded Trient from this rock in 1703. He speaks of another 'Verruca, or Rocca,' on the other side of Aquileia, and thinks that the modern word 'rocca' (rock) may perhaps have been derived herefrom (?).

It is remarkable that there is a place called *Verrua* near the Po in Piedmont (about 20 miles east of Turin). 'Situated upon an abrupt and insulated hill, in a most defensible position, it opposed an obstinate resistance to the Emperor Frederick II. In more recent times (1704), the Duc de Vendôme attacked it without success' (Murray's 'Guide to Northern Italy,' p. 51). No doubt this was also originally called *Verruca*.]

49. KING THEODORIC TO THE HONOURED POSSESSORES, DEFENSORES, AND CURIALES OF THE CITY OF CATANA.

Repair of amphitheatre of Catana.

'It is a great delight to the Ruler when his subjects of their own accord suggest that which is for the good of the State. You have called our attention to the ruinous state of your walls, and ask leave to use for its repair the stones of the amphitheatre, which have fallen down from age and are now of no ornament to your town, in fact only show disgraceful ruins. You have not only our permission to do this, but our hearty approval. Let the stones, which can be of no use while they lie there, rise again into the fabric of the walls; and your improved defence will be our boast and confidence.'

[Some remains of the amphitheatre are still visible at Catania; not, however, so important as those of the theatre.]

50. King Theodoric to the Provincials of Noricum.

The Alamanni and Noricans to exchange their cattle.

'It is an admirable arrangement when a favour can be conferred by which giver and receiver are alike benefited.

'We therefore decree that you should exchange your oxen for those of the Alamanni.

'Theirs is the finer and larger breed of cattle, but they are worn out by the long journey. Thus will they get fresh beasts capable of doing the work which is required of them, and you will permanently improve your breed of cattle, and so be able to till your fields better. Thus, what does not often happen, the same transaction will equally benefit both parties to it.'

[Cf. ii. 41 as to these Alamannic exiles. Possibly this letter as well as that refers to their expulsion by Clovis (cir. 504); but it seems more probable, as von Schubert suggests (pp. 52-54), that we have here to do with a removal of some of the Alamannic subjects of Theodoric from Raetia to Noricum, in order to guard the north-east frontier of the kingdom.]

51. KING THEODORIC TO FAUSTUS, PRAETORIAN PRAEFECT.

[Sidenote: Stipend of Thomas the Charioteer. Description of the Circus.]

'Constancy in actors is not a very common virtue, therefore with all the more pleasure do we record the faithful allegiance of Thomas the Charioteer, who came long ago from the East hither, and who, having become champion charioteer, has chosen to attach himself to "the seat of our Empire[1];" and we therefore decide that he shall be rewarded by a monthly allowance. He embraced what was then the losing side in the chariot races and carried it to victory—victory which he won so often that envious rivals declared that he conquered by means of witchcraft.

'The sight of a chariot-race (spectaculum) drives out morality and invites the most trifling contentions; it is the emptier of honourable conduct, the ever-flowing spring of squabbles: a thing which Antiquity commenced as a matter of religion, but which a quarrelsome posterity has turned into a sport.

'For Aenomaus is said first to have exhibited this sport at Elis, a city of Asia (?), and afterwards Romulus, at the time of the rape of the Sabines, displayed it in rural fashion to Italy, no buildings for the purpose being yet founded. Long after, Augustus, the lord of the world, raising his works to the same high level as his power, built a fabric marvellous even to Romans, which stretched far into the Vallis Murcia. This immense mass, firmly girt round with hills, enclosed a space which was fitted to be the theatre of great events.

'Twelve *Ostia* at the entrance represent the twelve signs of the Zodiac. These are suddenly and equally opened by ropes let down by the *Hermulae* (little pilasters)[2]. The four colours worn by the four parties of

---

[1] 'Nostri sedes delegit fovere *Imperii*.'

[2] The Ostia are denoted by A and the Hermulae by H in the accompanying plan. (See page 230.)

charioteers denote the seasons: green for verdant spring, blue for cloudy winter, red for flaming summer, white for frosty autumn. Thus, throughout the spectacle we see a determination to represent the works of Nature. The *Biga* is made in imitation of the moon, the *Quadriga* of the sun. The circus horses (*Equi desultorii*), by means of which the servants of the Circus announce the heats (*Missos*) that are to be run, imitate the herald-swiftness of the morning star. Thus it came to pass that while they deemed they were worshipping the stars, they profaned their religion by parodying it in their games.

'A white line is drawn not far from the ostia to each *Podium* (balcony), that the contest may begin when the quadrigae pass it, lest they should interrupt the view of the spectators by their attempts to get each before the other [1]. There are always seven circuits round the goals (*Metae*) to one heat, in analogy with the days of the week. The goals themselves have, like the decani [2] of the Zodiac, each three pinnacles, round which the swift quadrigae circle like the sun. The wheels indicate the boundaries of East and West. The channel (*Euripus*) which surrounds the Circus presents us with an image of the glassy sea, whence come the dolphins which swim hither through the waters [3] (?). The lofty obelisks lift their height towards heaven; but the upper one is dedicated to the sun, the lower one to the moon: and upon them the sacred rites of the ancients are indicated with Chaldee signs for letters [4].

---

[1] 'Ut quadrigis progredientibus, inde certamen oriretur: ne dum semper propere conantur elidere, spectandi voluptatem viderentur populis abrogare.' In fact, to compel the charioteers to start fair.

[2] Each sign of the Zodiac was considered to have three decani, occurring at intervals of ten days.

[3] 'Unde illuc delphini aequorei aquas interfluunt.' The sentence is very obscure, but the allusion must be to the dolphins, the figures of which were placed upon the spina.

[4] 'Obeliscorum quoque prolixitates ad coeli altitudinem sublevantur: sed

'The *Spina* (central wall, or backbone) represents the lot of the unhappy captives, inasmuch as the generals of the Romans, marching over the backs of their enemies, reaped that joy which was the reward of their labours. The *Mappa* (napkin), which is still seen to give the signal at the games, came into fashion on this wise. Once when Nero was loitering over his dinner, and the populace, as usual, was impatient for the spectacle to begin, he ordered the napkin which he had used for wiping his fingers to be thrown out of window, as a signal that he gave the required permission. Hence it became a custom that the display of a napkin gave a certain promise of future *circenses*.

'The *Circus* is so called from "circuitus:" *circenses* is, as it were, *circu-enses*, because in the rude ages of antiquity, before an elaborate building had been prepared for the purpose, the races were exhibited on the green grass, and the multitude were protected by the river on one side and the swords (*enses*) of the soldiers on the other [1].

'We observe, too, that the rule of this contest is that it be decided in twenty-four heats [2], an equal number to that of the hours of day and night. Nor let it be accounted meaningless that the number of circuits round the goals is expressed by the putting up of *eggs* [3],

potior soli, inferior lunae dicatus est: ubi sacra priscorum Chaldaicis signis, quasi litteris indicantur.'

[1] I can extract no other meaning than the above from this extraordinary sentence: 'Circenses, quasi circu-enses; propterea quod apud antiquitatem rudem, quae necdum spectacula in ornatum deduxerat fabricarum, inter *enses* et flumina, locis virentibus agerentur.'

[2] *Missibus*. In a previous sentence Cassiodorus makes the acc. plural *missos*.

[3] The number of times that the charioteers had rounded the goal was indicated by large wooden *eggs*, which were posted up in a conspicuous place on the spina. It seems that in a corresponding place near the other end of the spina figures of *dolphins* were used for the same purpose. Upon the Cilurnum gem (figured on page 231) we can perceive four eggs near one end of the spina, and four creatures which may be dolphins near the other, indicating that four circuits out of the seven which constitute a missus have been accomplished by the quadrigae.

since that emblem, pregnant as it is with many superstitions[1], indicates that something is about to be born from thence. And in truth we may well understand that the most fickle and inconstant characters, well typified by the birds who have laid those eggs, will spring from attendance on these spectacles[2]. It were long to describe in detail all the other points of the Roman Circus, since each appears to arise from some special cause. This only will we remark upon as preeminently strange, that in these beyond all other spectacles men's minds are hurried into excitement without any regard to a fitting sobriety of character. The Green charioteer flashes by: part of the people is in despair. The Blue gets a lead: a larger part of the City is in misery. They cheer frantically when they have gained nothing; they are cut to the heart when they have received no loss; and they plunge with as much eagerness into these empty contests as if the whole welfare of the imperilled fatherland were at stake.

'No wonder that such a departure from all sensible dispositions should be attributed to a superstitious origin. We are compelled to support this institution by the necessity of humouring the majority of the people, who are passionately fond of it; for it is always the few who are led by reason, while the many crave excitement and oblivion of their cares. Therefore, as we too must sometimes share the folly of our people, we will freely provide for the expenses of the Circus, however little our judgment approves of this institution.'

[Notwithstanding some absurdities, the above description of the Circus Maximus (which I have attempted to translate in full) is of great value, being, after that given by Dionysius of Halicarnassus, our

---

[1] Alluding probably to the story of Castor and Pollux.
[2] 'Et ideo datur intelligi, volitantes atque inconstantissimos inde mores nasci, quos avium matribus aptaverunt.' *Ovium* would seem to give a better sense than *avium*.

chief authority on the subject. The accompanying plan (taken, with some slight variations, from Smith's 'Dictionary of Antiquities'), will, I trust, render it intelligible.

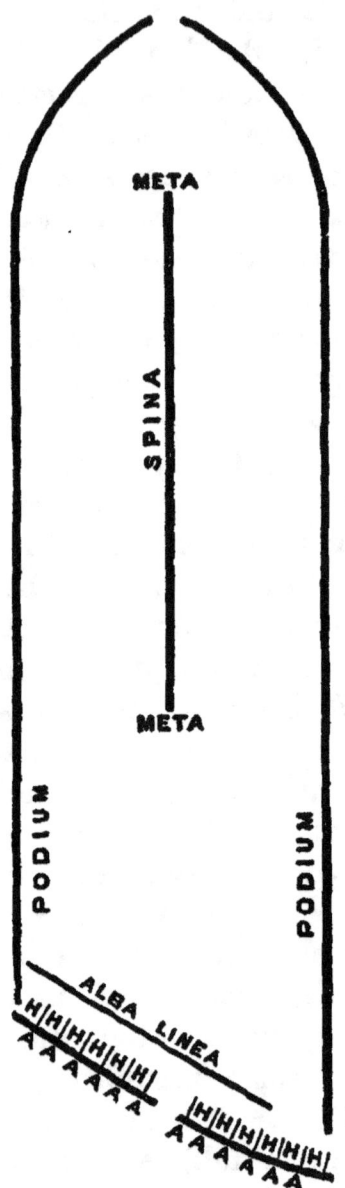

Plan of Ancient Circus.

It is well illustrated by the recently excavated 'Stadium of Augustus,' on the Palatine; but perhaps even better by a beautifully executed gem lately found at Chesters in Northumberland, on the site of the Roman station at Cilurnum. By the kindness of the owner, Mr. Clayton, I am able to give an enlarged copy of this gem, which is described in the 'Archaeologia Aeliana,' vol. x. pp. 133–137.

The Circus Maximus, a magnified engraving of an intaglio on a carnelian signet-ring found at Cilurnum (Chesters in Northumberland) in 1882.

The reader will easily discern the *Spina* with one obelisk (not two, as described by Cassiodorus) in the centre, the high tables supported by pillars on which the Ova and Delphini are placed, the three spindle-shaped columns which formed the *Meta* at each end, and the four quadrigae (four was the regular number for each missus) careering in front.]

52. KING THEODORIC TO THE ILLUSTRIOUS CONSULARIS.

On Roman land surveying.

'We are sorry to hear that a dispute (which is on the point of being settled by arms instead of by the law) has arisen between the Spectabiles Leontius and Paschasius as to the boundaries of their properties[1]. If they are so fierce against one another here in Italy, where there are mountains and rivers and the "arcaturae" [square turrets of the land surveyor] to mark the boundaries, what would they have done in Egypt, where the yearly returning waters of the Nile wash out all landmarks, and leave a deposit of mud over all?

'Geometry was discovered by the Chaldaeans, who perceived that its principles lay at the root of Astronomy, Music, Mechanics, Architecture, Medicine, Logic, and every science which deals with generals. This science was eagerly welcomed by the Egyptians, who perceived the advantage it would be to them in recovering the boundaries of estates obliterated by the wished-for deluge[2] of the Nile.

'Therefore let your Greatness send an experienced land surveyor (agrimensor) to settle this dispute by assigning fixed boundaries to the two estates.

'Augustus made a complete survey of the whole "Orbis Romanus," in order that each taxpayer should know exactly his resources and obligations. The results of this survey were tabulated by the author Hyrummetricus. The Professors of this Science [of land surveying] are honoured with a more earnest attention than falls to the lot of any other philosophers. Arithmetic, Theoretical Geometry, Astronomy, and Music are discoursed upon to listless audiences, sometimes to empty benches. But the land surveyor is like a judge; the deserted fields become his forum, crowded with eager spectators. You would fancy him a madman when you see him walking along the most devious paths. But in truth he is seeking for the traces of lost facts in rough woods and thickets[3].

---

[1] 'Casarum.' Casa is evidently no longer a cottage; perhaps the estate attached to a villa. There is probably still a flavour of rusticity about it.

[2] 'Votiva inundatione.'

[3] An excellent description of an antiquary walking along a Roman 'Limes Imperii.'

He walks not as other men walk. His path is the book from which he reads; he *shows* what he is saying; he proves what he hath learned; by his steps he divides the rights of hostile claimants; and like a mighty river he takes away the fields of one side to bestow them on the other.

'Wherefore, acting on our instructions, choose such a land surveyor, whose authority may be sufficient to settle this dispute, that the litigants may henceforth cultivate their lands in peace.'

53. KING THEODORIC TO THE ILLUSTRIOUS APRONIANUS, COUNT OF THE PRIVATE DOMAINS.

'Your Greatness tells us that a water-finder has come to Rome from Africa, where, on account of the dryness of the soil, his art is greatly in request. [*On Water-finders.*]

'We are glad to hear it. It is a very useful art.

'Signs of the existence of water are the greenness of the grass, the size of the trees, the nature of the plants, reeds, rushes, brambles, willows, poplars, &c. Some discover water by putting out dry wool under a bowl at night. So too, if you see at sunrise a cloud [or gossamer, 'spissitudinem'] of very small flies. A mist rising like a column shows water as deep below as the column rises high above.

'The water-finder will also predict the quality of the water, and so prevent you from wasting labour on a brackish spring. This science was ably treated of by ———[1], and by Marcellus among the Latins. They tell us that waters which gush forth towards the east and south are light and wholesome; that those which

---

[1] 'Apud Graecos *ille*.' Cassiodorus has left the name blank, and has either forgotten or been unable to fill it up; like the 'ille et ille' in his State documents.

emerge towards the north and west are too cold and heavy.

'So then, if the testimonials of the aforesaid water-finder and the results of his indications shall approve themselves to your wisdom, you may pay his travelling expenses and relieve his wants: he having to repay you by his future services. For though Rome itself is so abundantly supplied with aqueducts, there are many suburban places in which his help would be very useful. Associate with him also a mechanician who can sink for and raise the water when he has pointed it out. Rome ought not to lack anything which is an object of desire.'

BOOK IV.

CONTAINING FIFTY-ONE LETTERS WRITTEN BY CASSIODORUS IN THE NAME OF THEODORIC.

---

1. KING THEODORIC TO HERMINAFRID, KING OF THE THURINGIANS.

'DESIRING to unite you to ourselves by the bonds of kindred, we bestow upon you our niece [Amalabirga, daughter of Theodoric's sister; see 'Anon. Valesii' § 70], so that you, who descend from a Royal stock, may now far more conspicuously shine by the splendour of Imperial blood[1]'. [A remarkable passage, as showing that Theodoric did in a sense consider himself to be filling the place of the Emperors of the West.]

Marriage of Theodoric's niece to the King of the Thuringians.

The virtues and intellectual accomplishments of the new Queen of the Thuringians are described.

'We gladly acknowledge the price of a favour, in itself beyond price, which, according to the custom of the nations, we have received from your ambassadors: namely, a team of horses, silvery in colour, as wedding-horses should be. Their chests and thighs are suitably adorned with round surfaces of flesh. Their ribs are expanded to a certain width. They are short in the belly. Their heads have a certain resemblance to the stag, the swiftness of which animal they imitate. These horses are gentle from their extreme plumpness; very swift notwithstanding their great bulk; pleasant to look

---

[1] 'Nunc etiam longius claritate Imperialis sanguinis fulgeatis.'

at, still better to use. For they have gentle paces, not fatiguing their riders by insane curvetings. To ride them is repose rather than toil; and being broken-in to a delightful and steady pace, they can keep up their speed over long distances.

'We too are sending you some presents, but our niece is the fairest present of all. May God bless you with children, so that our lines may be allied in future.'

2. KING THEODORIC TO THE KING OF THE HERULI.
[Adopting him as his son by right of arms.]

<small>Herminafrid adopted as 'filius per arma' by Theodoric.</small>

'It has been always held amongst the nations a great honour to be adopted as "filius per arma." Our children by nature often disappoint our expectations, but to say that we esteem a man *worthy to be our son* is indeed praise. As such, after the manner of the nations and in manly fashion, do we now beget you [1].

'We send you horses, spears, and shields, and the rest of the trappings of the warrior; but above all we send you our judgment that you are worthy to be our son [2]. Highest among the nations will you be considered who are thus approved by the mind of Theodoric.

'And though the son should die rather than see his father suffer aught of harm, we in adopting you are also throwing round you the shield of our protection. The Heruli have known the value of Gothic help in old times, and that help will now be yours. A and B, the bearers of these letters, will explain to you in Gothic (patrio sermone) the rest of our message to you [3].'

---

[1] Notice the strong expression, 'Et ideo more gentium et conditione virili filium te praesenti munere *procreamus.*'

[2] 'Damus quidem tibi equos, enses clypeos, et reliqua instrumenta bellorum, sed quae sunt omnimodis fortiora, largimur tibi nostra judicia.'

[3] In 512, says Marcellinus Comes, 'Gens Erulorum in terras atque civitates Romanorum jussu Anastasii Caesaris introducta.' But what relation that entry of the Heruli into Roman territory may bear to this letter is a very difficult question. See Dahn, Könige der Germanen ii. 8, n. 2.

3. KING THEODORIC TO SENARIUS, VIR ILLUSTRIS, COMES.

[Conferring upon him the dignity of 'Comitiva Patrimonii.']

'The master's fame is enhanced by choosing the right persons for his servants. The Sovereign ought to promote such persons that whenever he condescends to behold them he may feel that his *judicia*[1] have been justified. We therefore hereby bestow upon you, for the fourth Indiction [Sept. 1, 510], the Illustrious dignity of Comes of our Patrimony.' *Senarius made Comes Patrimonii.*

Services of Senarius as a diplomatist, in standing up against Barbarian Kings and subduing their intellects to the moderate counsels of Theodoric[2].

His success as an advocate[3]. The charm of his pronunciation. His purity of morals; his popularity with high and low. He is exhorted still to cultivate these dispositions, and to win favour for his office by his affable demeanour.

4. KING THEODORIC TO THE SENATE OF THE CITY OF ROME.

[Announcing the promotion of Senarius, conferred in the preceding letter.]

Describes the merits of the new Comes, who when young in years but mature in merit had entered the service of the Palace; his diplomatic career[4] and his *On the same subject.*

---

[1] Same expression as in preceding letter.

[2] 'Subiisti saepe arduae legationis officium. Restitisti regibus non impar assertor, coactus justitiam nostram et illis ostendere, qui rationem vix poterant cruda obstinatione sentire. Non te terruit contentionibus inflammata regalis auctoritas,' etc.

[3] 'Usus es sub exceptionis officio eloquentis ingenio.' 'Exceptio' is a law term, the defendant's answer to the plaintiff's bill; but is it so used here?

[4] Again we have 'exceptiones' mentioned (see preceding letter). 'Nunc

moderation and reserve in the midst of success, although naturally 'joy is a garrulous thing,' and it is difficult for men who are carrying all before them to restrain the expression of their exaltation.

Compliments to the Senate, who are invited to give a hearty welcome to the new comer.

5. King Theodoric to Amabilis, Vir Devotus[1] and Comes.

Supply of provisions to famine-stricken Provinces of Gaul.

'Having heard that there is dearth in our Gaulish Provinces we direct your Devotion to take bonds from the shipmasters along the whole western coast of Italy (Lucania, Campania, and Thuscia) that they will go with supplies of food only to the Gauls, having liberty to dispose of their cargoes as may be agreed between buyer and seller. They will find their own profit in this, for there is no better customer for a corn-merchant than a hungry man. He looks on all his other possessions as dross if he can only supply the cravings of necessity. He who is willing to sell to a man in this condition almost seems to be *giving* him what he needs, and can very nearly ask his own price.'

[It will be seen that in this letter there is no attempt to fix a maximum price, only to prescribe the kind of cargo, 'victuales species,' which is to be carried to Gaul.]

6. King Theodoric to Symmachus, Vir Illustris, Patrician.

The sons of Valerian to be detained in Rome.

'The Spectabilis Valerian, who lives at Syracuse, wishes to return thither himself, but that his sons, whom he has brought to Rome for their education, may be detained in that City.

ad colloquia dignus, *nunc ad exceptiones aptissimus,* frequenter etiam in legationis honorem electus.'

[1] Probably this epithet means that Amabilis was a Sajo.

'Let your Magnificence therefore not allow them to leave the aforesaid City till an order has been obtained from us to that effect. Thus will their progress in their studies be assured, and proper reverence be paid to our command. And let none of them think this a burden, which should have been an object of desire[1]. To no one should Rome be disagreeable, for she is the common country of all, the fruitful mother of eloquence, the broad temple of the virtues: it is a striking mark of our favour to assign such a City as a residence to any of our subjects[2].'

7. KING THEODORIC TO SENARIUS, VIR ILLUSTRIS, COMES PRIVATARUM.

Losses by shipwreck to be refunded to those who were sending provisions to Gaul.

'Any calamity which comes upon a man from causes beyond his control ought not to be imputed to him as a fault. The pathetic petition of the Superintendents of Grain[3] informs us that the cargoes which they destined for Gaul have perished at sea.

'The framework of the timbers of the ships gaped under the violence of the winds and waves, and from all that overabundance of water nothing remains to them but their tears.

'Let your Sublimity therefore promptly refund to them the proportion (modiatio) which each of them can prove that he has thus lost. It would be cruel to punish them for having merely suffered shipwreck.'

---

[1] 'Non ergo sibi putet impositum quod debuit esse votivum. Nulli sit ingrata Roma, quae dici non potest aliena. Illa eloquentiae foecunda mater, illa virtutum omnium latissimum templum.'

[2] Cf. the very similar letter, i. 39.

[3] 'Prosecutores frumentorum.' It would seem that these are not merchants supplying the famine-stricken Provinces of Gaul as a private speculation (according to iv. 5), but public officers who have had certain cargoes of corn entrusted to them from the State magazines, and who, but for this letter, would be bound to make good the loss suffered under their management.

8. KING THEODORIC TO THE HONOURED POSSESSORES AND CURIALES OF FORUM LIVII (FORLI).

Transport of timber ordered for Alsuanum.

'You must not think anything which we order hard; for our commands are reasonable, and we know what you ought to do. Your Devotion is therefore to cut timber and transport it to Alsuanum[1], where you will be paid the proper price for it.'

9. KING THEODORIC TO OSUIN, VIR ILLUSTRIS AND COMES.

Tuitio regii nominis.

[This letter is quoted by Dahn ('Könige der Germanen' iii. 117) as an illustration of '*tuitio regii nominis.*']

'Maurentius and Paula, who are left orphans, inform us that their youth and helplessness expose them to the attacks of many unscrupulous persons.

'Let your Sublimity therefore cause it to be known that any suits against them must be prosecuted in our Comitatus, the place of succour for the distressed and of sharp punishment for tricksters.'

10. KING THEODORIC TO JOANNES, SENATOR AND CONSULARIS OF CAMPANIA.

The lawless custom of Pignoratio is to be repressed.

[A custom had apparently grown up during the lawless years of the Fifth Century, of litigants helping themselves, during the slow progress of the suit, to a 'material guarantee' from the fields of their opponents. This custom, unknown apparently at the time of the Theodosian Code, was called 'Pignoratio,' and was especially rife in the Provinces of Campania and Samnium.]

'How does peace differ from the confusion of war, if law-suits are to be settled by violence? We hear with displeasure from our Provincials in Campania and Sam-

[1] Where is this?

nium that certain persons there are giving themselves up to the practice of *pignoratio*. And so far has this gone that neighbours club together and transfer their claims to some one person who "pignorates" for the whole of them, thus in fact compelling a man to pay a debt to an entire stranger—a monstrous perversion of all the rules of law, which separates so delicately between the rights even of near relations, and will not allow the son to be sued for the father's debts unless he is the heir, nor the wife for the husband's unless she has succeeded to the estate. Hitherto our ignorance has allowed this lawless practice to exist. Now that we know of it we are determined to suppress it. Therefore, firstly, if any man lays violent hands on any property to secure an alleged claim, he shall at once forfeit that claim [and restore the *pignus*]. Secondly, where one has "pignorated" for another, he shall be compelled to restore twofold the value of that which he has taken. Thirdly, if any offender is so poor and squalid that restitution cannot be compelled from him, he shall be beaten with clubs.'

11. KING THEODORIC TO SENARIUS, VIR ILLUSTRIS AND COMES.

'Let your Magnitude enquire into and decide promptly the dispute between the Possessores and Curiales of Velia.' [A conjectural emendation for *Volienses*.]

Dispute between Possessores and Curiales.

12. KING THEODORIC TO MARABAD, VIR ILLUSTRIS AND COMES; AND GEMELLUS, SENATOR.

'It is our purpose not only to defend by arms but to govern by just laws the Provinces which God has subjected to us.

'Archotamia, an illustrious lady who has lost her grandson by death, complains that his widow Aetheria, having married again with a certain Liberius, is wasting

Archotamia's complaint against the extravagant widow of her grandson.

the property of her children in order to make her new home appear more splendid.

'Let your Sublimities enquire into this matter. After suppressing all violent action[1], placing the holy Gospels in the midst of the Court, and calling in three honourable persons agreed upon by the parties, as assessors, decide with their help upon the matter according to ancient law, due reference being had to the arrangements of modern times.'

[Theodoric says that in not hearing the case himself, but referring it to Marabad and Gemellus, he is following his usual practice, 'remittere ad statuta Divalium sanctionum;' that is, apparently, according to the Theodosian Code. See Dahn, 'Könige der Germanen' iv. 140, *n*. 2.]

13. KING THEODORIC TO SENARIUS, VIR ILLUSTRIS, COMES PRIVATARUM.

Supplies for Colossaeus and his suite.

'Let Colossaeus, who is sent as Governor to Pannonia Sirmiensis, have rations for himself and suite, according to ancient usage. [For his appointment, see Letters iii. 23 and 24.]

'A hungry army cannot be expected to preserve discipline, since the armed man will always help himself to that which he requires. Let him have the chance of buying, that he may not be forced to think what he can plunder. Necessity loves not a law[2], nor is it right to command the many to observe a moderation which even the few can barely practise.'

14. KING THEODORIC TO THE SAJO GESILA.

Evasion of land-tax by Goths in Picenum and Thuscia.

'It is a great offence to put off the burden of one's own debts upon other people. That man ought to pay the "tributum" for a property who receives the income of it.

---

[1] 'Omni incivilitate submotâ.'
[2] 'Necessitas moderamen non diligit.'

But some of the Goths in Picenum and the two Tuscanies[1] are evading the payment of their proper taxes[2]. This vicious practice must be suppressed at once, lest it spread by imitation. If anyone in a spirit of clownish stubbornness shall still refuse to obey our commands as expressed through you, affix the proper notice to his houses and confiscate them, that he who would not pay a small debt may suffer a great loss[3]. None ought to be more prompt in their payments to the exchequer than those [the Goths] who are the receivers of our donative. The sum thus given by our liberality is much more than they could claim as soldiers' pay. In fact *we* pay them a voluntary tribute by the care which we have of their fortunes.'

15. KING THEODORIC TO BENENATUS, SENATOR.

[Sidenote: New rowers to be selected. Their qualifications.]

'Being informed by the Illustrious and Magnificent Count of the Patrimony that twenty-one of the *Dromonarii* [rowers in the express-boats] have been removed by the inconvenient incident of death, we hereby charge you to select others to fill their places. But they must be strong men, for the toil of rowing requires powerful arms and stout hearts to battle with the stormy waves. For what is in fact more daring than with one's little bark to enter upon that wide and treacherous sea, which only despair enables a man successfully to combat?'

16. KING THEODORIC TO THE SENATE OF THE CITY OF ROME.

[Sidenote: Arigern entrusted with the charge of the City of Rome.]

'Some time ago we committed the government of our new Gaulish Provinces to Arigern, a member of your

---

[1] 'Gothi per Picenum sive Thuscias utrasque residentes.' What are the two Thusciae? [2] 'Debitas functiones.'
[3] 'Si quis ergo jussa nostra agresti spiritu resupinatus abjecerit, casas ejus appositis titulis fisci nostri juribus vindicabis; ut qui juste noluit parva solvere, rationabiliter videatur maxima perdidisse.'

body, that he might by his firmness and prudence bring about a settlement in that agitated country. This he has accomplished to our entire satisfaction, and, practising the lessons which he learned in your midst, he has also brought back warlike trophies from thence. We now decide to bestow upon him the charge of the Roman order.

'He is to see that the laws are vigorously administered, and that private revenge has no place.

'Receive, O Conscript Fathers, your honoured and venerable member back into your bosom.'

[It seems probable that Arigern was not appointed 'Praefectus Urbis,' because in Letter iv. 22 he is associated as Comes with Argolicus, 'Praefectus Urbis.' Was he 'Comes Urbis Romae?']

17. KING THEODORIC TO IDA, VIR SUBLIMIS AND DUX.

[Cf. the name of our own Northumbrian King.]

Possessions of the Church of Narbonne to be restored to it.

'We do not wish to disturb anything that has been well settled by a preceding King. Certain possessions of the Church of Narbonne, which were secured to it by grant of the late King Alaric of exalted memory, have been wrongfully wrested from it. Do you now restore these. As you are illustrious in war, so be also excellent in "civilitas." The wrong-doers will not dare to resist a man of your well-known bravery.'

18. KING THEODORIC TO ANNAS, SENATOR AND COMES.

A priestly Ghoul.

'Enquire if the story which is told us be true, namely that the Presbyter Laurentius has been groping for fatal riches among human corpses. An odious inversion of his functions, that he who should preach peace to the living has been robbing the dead, and that hands which have been touched with the oil of consecration should have been grasping at unholy gains, instead of distributing his own honestly acquired substance to the poor. If after diligent examination you find that the charge is true, you must make him disgorge the gold. As for punishment, for the sake of the honour of the priesthood we leave that to a higher Power[1].'

19. KING THEODORIC TO GEMELLUS, SENATOR.

[Sidenote: The Siliquaticum not to be levied on corn, wine, and oil.]

'The Prince should try to remedy the afflictions of his subjects. Therefore, for the present time [probably on account of the scarcity in Gaul], we decree that the tax of Siliquaticum, which Antiquity ordained should be levied on all buyings and sellings, shall not be levied on corn, wine, and oil. We hope thus to stimulate trade, and to benefit not only the Provincials, who are our chief care, but also the merchants. Let the ship that traverses the seas not fear our harbours. Often the sailor dreads the rapacity of the collector of customs more than the danger of shipwreck. It shall not be so now.'

20. KING THEODORIC TO GEBERICH, SENATOR.

[Sidenote: Land taken from the Church to be restored to it.]

'If we are willing to enrich the Church by our own liberality, à fortiori will we not allow it to be despoiled of the gifts received from pious princes in the past.

'The supplication of the Venerable Bishop Constantius informs us that a *jugum* [=jugerum, about two-thirds of an English acre] of land so bestowed on the "sacrosanct" Church has been taken away from her, and is unlawfully held by the despoiler.

'See that right is done, and that the Church has her own restored to her without any diminution.'

21. KING THEODORIC TO GEMELLUS, SENATOR.

[Sidenote: Promptness and integrity required.]

'Be prompt in the execution of our orders. No one should think our commands harsh, since they are ex-

---

[1] 'Scelus enim, quod nos pro sacerdotali honore relinquimus impunitum, majori pondere credimus vindicandum.' The words seem to be purposely vague, but I think they allude to the judgment of Heaven on the offender.

cused by the necessity of the times. [Reject the thought of all unjustly acquired gains, for] you are sure to receive from our favour all that you seem to lose by not yielding to temptation.'

22. KING THEODORIC TO ARGOLICUS, VIR ILLUSTRIS AND PRAEFECT OF THE CITY; AND

23. KING THEODORIC TO ARIGERN, VIR ILLUSTRIS AND COMES.

Roman Senators accused of magic.

These two letters relate to the affair of Basilius[1] and Praetextatus, men of high rank in Rome. They are accused of practising magical arts, and in the interval between the first and second letters they escape from prison by taking advantage of the insanity of the gaoler.

Theodoric, who says that he will not suffer any such acts of treason against the Divine Majesty, and that it is not lawful for Christian times to deal in magical arts, orders the recapture of the offenders, who are to be handed over to a Quinque-viral Board, consisting of the Patricians Symmachus, Decius, Volusianus, and Caelianus, with the Illustrious Maximian, and by them examined; if guilty to be punished (probably with confiscation and exile); if innocent, of course to be discharged[2].

---

[1] Basilius, the patron of Sidonius, was Consul in 463, and another Basilius, perhaps the father of the accused, was Consul in 480. The person here spoken of *may* be the same as the Basilius, 'olim regio ministerio depulsus,' whom Boethius (Phil. Cons. i. 4) mentions as one of his accusers; but it seems more likely that in that case this imputation of magical practices would also have been referred to by him. The name Basilius was a somewhat common one at this time.

[2] At the beginning of the first letter occurs the remarkable expression 'Abscedat ritus de medio jam profanus; conticescat *poenale murmur animarum*,' which the commentator interprets of the ventriloquistic sounds produced by soothsayers. Cf. Milton's Christmas Hymn:

'No voice or hideous hum
Runs through the arched roof in words deceiving.'

[The association of the Quinque-viri with the Praefectus Urbis is a mark of the high rank of the accused. The Praefectus Urbis could not adjudicate on the crimes of Senators without five Assessors chosen by lot from that body. Arigern, who was entrusted (it is not quite clear in what capacity) with the 'Disciplina Romanae Civitatis,' is commissioned to bring the accused to trial. Baronius says that we do not hear whether they were ever re-captured.]

24. KING THEODORIC TO ELPIDIUS, DEACON [of Spoleto].

Architectural restoration at Spoleto.

Gives leave to pull down a *porticus* behind the Baths of Turasius at Spoleto, and to build some new edifice [perhaps a church] on its site and on the site of a yard (areola) adjoining it, on condition only that the building thus pulled down is of no public utility.

Reflections on the duty of architectural restoration.

25. KING THEODORIC TO ARGOLICUS, VIR ILLUSTRIS, PRAEFECTUS URBIS.

Petrus to be inscribed as Senator.

[It is to be borne in mind that the Praefectus Urbis was the Official President of the Senate.]

'Ambition ennobles man, and he who has aimed when young at high honours is often stimulated to lead a worthy life by the fact of having obtained them. We therefore look favourably on the petition of Petrus, illustrious by descent, and in gravity of character already a Senator, to enter the Sacred Order (the Senate); and we authorise your Illustrious Magnificence to inscribe his name, according to ancient custom, in the album of that body.'

[A Petrus, probably the same as the subject of this letter, was Consul in 516.]

26. KING THEODORIC TO ALL THE CITIZENS OF MARSEILLES[1].

Taxes remitted for a year.

Confirms all privileges and immunities granted by previous Princes, and remits the taxes (censum) for one year, a boon which they had not dared to ask for. 'For that is perfect *pietas*, which before it is bent by prayer, knows how to consider the weary ones.'

[Here, as in many other passages of Cassiodorus, *pietas* shows signs of passing into the Italian *pietà* (=pity).]

27. KING THEODORIC TO THE SAJO TEZUTZAT, AND
28. KING THEODORIC TO DUDA, SENATOR AND COMES.

Petrus assaulted by the Sajo who was assigned for his protection.

[Duda was also a Sajo, as we see from Letter 32. Dahn ('Könige der Germanen' iv. 142, *n.* 3) thinks he was Comes Gothorum.]

Both letters relate to the affair of Petrus (a Vir Spectabilis, and probably the same whose admission to the Senate is ordered by iv. 25).

This Roman nobleman, according to a usage common under Theodoric's government, has had the Gothic Sajo Amara assigned to him as his Defensor. Amara, by an inversion of his functions, which the letter bitterly laments and upbraids, has turned upon his *protegé* and even used personal violence towards him. He has drawn a sword and wounded him in the hand; and nothing but the fact that Petrus was sheltered by a door saved him from losing his hand altogether.

Yet, notwithstanding this assault, Amara has had the audacity to claim from his victim 'commodi nomine,' the usual payment made by the defended to the defender.

The first letter decrees that this shall be refunded twofold, and assigns Tezutzat instead of Amara to the

---

[1] 'Universis Massiliae constitutis.' A curious expression.

office of Defender, warning him not to follow the evil example of his predecessor.

The second assigns to Duda the task of enquiring into the alleged assault and punishing it with the sword[1].

29. KING THEODORIC TO ARGOLICUS, VIR ILLUSTRIS, PRAEFECT OF THE CITY.

Official tardiness rebuked.

A sharp rebuke to him for having (if the *suggestio* of the Clarissimus Armentarius be correct) so long delayed, it is to be feared with a corrupt motive, complying with the instructions of the King to do justice in some case (not described) in which the honour of the Senate is concerned. As head of the Senate he ought to have been eager to examine into it, without any prompting from his master.

30. KING THEODORIC TO ALBINUS, VIR ILLUSTRIS AND PATRICIAN.

Workshops may be erected above the Porticus Curba, by the Roman Forum.

'Those whom the Republic has honoured should in their turn bring honour to the City. We are therefore gratified by receiving your supplication for leave to erect workshops[2] above the Porticus Curba, which being situated near the Domus Palmata, shuts in the Forum in comely fashion "in modum areae." We like the plan. The range of private dwellings will thereby be extended. A look of cheerful newness will be given to the old walls; and the presence of residents in the building will tend to preserve it from further decay. You have our permission and encouragement to proceed, if the proposed erections do not in

---

[1] The story of this assault is a typical specimen of the style of Cassiodorus, high-flown yet not really pictorial: 'Ita ut ictum gladii in se demersum, aliquatenus postium retardaret objectio: subjecta est vulneri manus, quae ut in totum truncata non caderet, januarum percussa robora praestiterunt: ubi lassato impetu corusca ferri acies corporis extrema perstrinxit.'

[2] Fabricae.

any way interfere with public convenience or the beauty of the City.'

[The MSS. of Cassiodorus waver between Curbae and Curiae in the above letter. Jordan ('Topographie der Stadt Rom.' i. 2. 258) inclines to the opinion that Porticus Curba denotes the Portico of the Secretarium of the Senate, on the site of the present Church of Sta. Martina. As the Curia immediately adjoined this building, there is practically but little difference between the two readings. In either case the fabricae were to be erected so as to overlook the north-west end of the Forum. It is admitted that the Domus Palmata was near the Arch of Septimius Severus.]

31. KING THEODORIC TO AEMILIANUS, VIR VENERABILIS, BISHOP.

An aqueduct to be promptly finished.

'Wise men should finish what they have begun, and not incur the reproach which attends half-done work.

'Let your Holiness therefore promptly complete what by our authority you so well began in the matter of the aqueduct, and thus most fitly provide water for your thirsting flock, imitating by labour the miracle of Moses, who made water gush forth from the flinty rock.'

32. KING THEODORIC TO DUDA THE SAJO.

The rights of the Crown to the property of the proscribed man, Tupha, to be asserted with moderation.

'We are anxious strictly to obey the laws, and to take no advantage over our subjects in courts of justice. If a man knows that he can get his own by legal process, even from the Sovereign, he is the less likely to seek it by the armed hand. The memorandum of Marinus informs us that the property of Tupha was long ago mortgaged to a certain Joannes[1]. But since it is quite clear that the property of a proscribed man belongs to our fiscus, we desire you to

---

[1] 'Marini relatione comperimus res Tuphae apud Joannem quondam sub emissione chirographi fuisse depositas.'

summon the widow of this Joannes and his secretary Januarius, "moderata executione."

'If they acknowledge that they have no right to the property let them at once restore it; but if not, let them come before the *Consularis* of Campania and establish their right according to course of law.

'But let all be done without loss or prejudice to the rights of innocent persons. If any such charge be established against you, *you* will become the offender in our eyes.'

[The description of Tupha as 'proscriptus' makes it probable that we are dealing with that officer of Odovacar whose double treachery (489-490) so nearly caused the failure of Theodoric's invasion of Italy, and who finally fell in battle against his fellow-rebel, Frederic the Rugian. The only difficulty is the lapse of time since those events, as this letter was probably written not earlier than about 511; but that is in some degree met by the word *quondam* in the sentence quoted (*n.* 1, p. 250).]

33. KING THEODORIC TO ALL THE JEWS OF GENOA.

Privileges of the Jews confirmed.

'The true mark of *civilitas* is the observance of law. It is this which makes life in communities possible, and which separates man from the brutes. We therefore gladly accede to your request that all the privileges which the foresight of antiquity conferred upon the Jewish customs shall be renewed to you [1], for in truth it is our great desire that the laws of the ancients shall be kept in force to secure the reverence due to us [2]. Everything which has been found to conduce to *civilitas* should be held fast with enduring devotion.'

---

[1] 'Privilegia debere servari quae Judaicis institutis legum provida decrevit antiquitas.'

[2] 'Quod nos libenter annuimus qui jura veterum ad nostram cupimus reverentiam custodiri.'

34. KING THEODORIC TO DUDA THE SAJO.

Buried treasure to be reclaimed for the State.

'It is the part of true prudence to recall to the uses of commerce "the talent hidden in the earth." We therefore direct you, by this "moderata jussio," where you hear of buried treasures to proceed to the spot with suitable witnesses and reclaim for the public Treasury either gold or silver, abstaining, however, from actually laying hands on the ashes of the dead[1]. The dead can do nothing with treasure, and it is not greedy to take away what the holder of it can never mourn the loss of.

'Eacus is said to have discovered the use of gold, and Indus, King of the Scythians, that of silver. They are extremely useful metals.'

35. KING THEODORIC TO THE REPRESENTATIVES (ACTORES) OF ALBINUS.

An extravagant minor. Restitutio in integrum.

'It has been wisely decided by Antiquity that minors cannot make a binding contract, for they are naturally the prey of every sharper. You allege that your *patronus* [Albinus] is under age, that he is heaping up expenses instead of property, and that his raw boyhood does not know what is really for his benefit. If this be correct, and be legally proved, he is entitled to a *restitutio in integrum*' [a suit commenced through these Actores for the quashing of the contracts which have been fraudulently made with the minor].

[For the *restitutio in integrum* see Cod. Theod. ii. 16. 1, and vi. 4. 16. Nothing seems to be expressly said in this letter about the appointment of a *Curator.*]

---

[1] How this was to be done is not quite clear, since it is plain that this letter is really and chiefly an order for rifling *sepulchres* in search of buried treasure.

36. King Theodoric to Faustus, Praetorian Praefect. A.D. 509–510.

Remission of taxes for Provincials of Cottian Alps.

'A wise ruler will always lessen the weight of taxation when his subjects are weighed down by temporary poverty. Therefore let your Magnificence remit to the Provincials of the Cottian Alps the *as publicum* for this year [the third Indiction], in consideration of their losses by the passage of our army. [The army of Ibbas, on its march in 408 to fight Clovis, after the fall of the Visigothic Monarchy.] True, that army went forth with shouts of concord to *liberate* Gaul. But so a river bursting forth may irrigate and fertilise a whole country, and yet destroy the increase of that particular channel in which its waters run.

'We have earned new subjects by that campaign: we do not wish them to suffer loss by it. Our own heart whispers to us the request which the subjects dare not utter to their Prince.'

37. King Theodoric to the Illustrious Woman Theodagunda.

Theodagunda is admonished to do justice to Renatus.

Warns Theodagunda [apparently a member of the royal family and governing some Province; but what place could she hold in the Roman official hierarchy?], that she must emulate the virtue of her ancestors and show prompt obedience to the royal commands. 'The lamentable petition of Renatus states that, after judgment given in his favour by the King's Court, he is still harassed by the litigation (not in the way of regular appeal) of Inquilina, who appears to be not so much desirous of victory as anxious to ruin his adversary.' [Notwithstanding the form of the name I think Inquilina is male, not female.]

'You must see that this is put right at once.'

38. KING THEODORIC TO FAUSTUS, PRAETORIAN PRAEFECT.

Taxes must be reduced to the figure at which they stood in the days of Odoacer.

'The inhabitants of Gravasi (?) and Ponto (?) complain that they have been overloaded with taxes by the Assessors (discussores) Probus and Januarius. They have bad land, and say that they really cannot cope with the taxes imposed upon them [at the last Indiction?]. The former practice is to be reverted to, and they are not to be called upon to pay more than they did in the days of Odoacer.' [An evidence that in one case at least the fiscal yoke of Odoacer was lighter than that of his successor.]

39. KING THEODORIC TO THEODAHAD, VIR ILLUSTRIS [AND NEPHEW OF THE KING].

The encroachments of Theodahad repressed.

'Avarice, which Holy Writ declares to be "the root of all evil," is a vulgar vice which you, our kinsman, a man of Amal blood, whose family is known to be royal, are especially bound to avoid[1].

'The Spectabilis Domitius complains to us that such and such portions of his property have been seized by you with the strong hand, without any pretence of establishing a legal claim to them.

'We send the Sajo Duda to you, and order you on his arrival[2], without any delay, to restore the property which you have taken possession of, with all the moveables of which you have despoiled it.

'If you have any claim to make to the lands in question, send a person fully informed of the facts to our Comitatus, and there let the case be fairly heard.

---

[1] 'Amali sanguinis virum nos decet vulgare desiderium: quia genus suum conspicit esse purpuratum.'

[2] 'Si momenti tempora suffragantur.' What is the meaning of this limitation?

'A high-born man should ever act according to well-ordered *civilitas*. Any neglect of this principle brings upon him odium, proportioned to the oppression which the man of humbler rank conceives himself to have suffered at his hands.'

40. KING THEODORIC TO THE REPRESENTATIVES (ACTORES) OF PROBINUS.

The affair of Agapeta, Basilius, her husband, ordered to plead.

Recurs to the case of the Possessio Areciretina, which Agapeta, the wife of Basilius, had given (or sold) to Probinus, and which Probinus was commanded to restore. (See Letters ii. 10 and 11.)

The petition, now presented by the representatives of Probinus, puts a somewhat different face upon the matter, and seems to show that the sale by Agapeta (notwithstanding her melancholy condition of fatuity and vice) was a *bonâ fide* one, for sufficient consideration.

Her husband Basilius is now ordered to reply to the pleadings of the opposite party, either at the King's Comitatus, or in some local court of competent jurisdiction. The King's Comitatus is meant to be a blessing to his subjects, and recourse to it is not made compulsory where, on account of distance, the suitor would rather be excused from resorting to it.

41. KING THEODORIC TO JOANNES, ARCH-PHYSICIAN.

An unjust judgment against Joannes reversed.

'A King should delight to succour the oppressed.

'You inform us that, by the devices of the Spectabilis Vivianus and his superior knowledge of the laws, an unjust judgment was obtained against you, in default, in the Court of the Vicarius of the City of Rome: that Vivianus himself has now renounced the world, repents of his injustice to you, and interposes no obstacle to the restitution of your rights. We therefore (if your statements shall prove to be correct) quash the sentence against you, restore you to your country and your property, and that you may be preserved from future molestation, founded on the old sentence against you, we assign you to the guardianship (tuitio) of the Patrician Albinus, without prejudice to the laws (salvis legibus).

'We wish that nothing contrary to *civilitas* should be done, since our daily labour is for the repose of all.' [I presume that this letter is in fact an edict for 'Restitutio in integrum.']

42. KING THEODORIC TO ARGOLICUS, PRAEFECT OF THE CITY.

The sons of Velusian to have their property restored to them.

'Under a good King the loss even of a father should be less felt than with a different ruler, for the King is the father of his people.

'The petition of Marcian and Maximius, sons of Velusian (Patrician and Magnificus), sets forth that they lost their father at Easter; that thus the time of joy to all Christians became to them a season of sorrow; that while they were immersed in their grief and incapable of attending to their affairs, "the tower of the circus and the place of the amphitheatre[1]," which had belonged to their illustrious father, were by some heartless intriguer wrested from them, under the authority of the Praefect.

'Be pleased to enquire into this matter, and if those places truly belonged to Velusian, restore them to his sons. We wish to cherish rather than oppress the sons of illustrious men, who are the germ of our future Senate.'

43. KING THEODORIC TO THE SENATE OF THE CITY OF ROME.

Punishment of incendiaries who have burned a Jewish Synagogue.

[On the burning of the Jewish synagogue. This synagogue of the Jews was in the Trastevere. See Gregorovius i. 296–298 for a description of it. I do

---

[1] Can this be the Amphitheatrum Castrense?

not know on what authority he assigns 521 for the date of the tumult in which it was burned.]

'The propriety of manners which is characteristic of the City of Rome must be upheld. To fall into the follies of popular tumult, and to set about burning their own City, is not like the Roman disposition [1].

'But we are informed by Count Arigern [2] that the populace of Rome, enraged at the punishment inflicted on some Christian servants who had murdered their Jewish masters, has risen in fury and burned their synagogue to the ground [3], idly venting on innocent buildings their anger against the men who used them.

'Be pleased to enquire into this matter, and severely punish the authors of the tumult, who are probably few in number.

'At the same time enquire into the complaints which are brought against the Jews, and if you find that there is any foundation for them, punish accordingly.'

44. KING THEODORIC TO THE VENERABLE ANTONIUS, BISHOP OF POLA.

Bishop Antonius called upon to do justice to Stephanus.

'It is an invidious task to have to listen to complaints against the revered ministers of the Church.

'But the petition of Stephanus sets forth that a property, which belonged to him before the time of your predecessor, has, within the last nine months, wrongfully, and in defiance of *civilitas*, been seized by the

---

[1] 'Levitates quippe seditionum et ambire propriae civitatis incendium, non est velle Romanum.'

[2] It happens that one of the letters addressed to Count Arigern also refers to a Jewish synagogue. See iii. 45.

[3] 'Quod in dominorum caede proruperit servilis audacia: in quibus cum fuisset pro districtione publica resecatum, statim plebis inflammata contentio synagogam temerario duxerunt incendio concremandam.' The above is Gregorovius' explanation of the somewhat enigmatical language of Cassiodorus.

S

officers of your church. If this be so, we desire you, as a matter of justice, to correct what your familiars have done amiss, and restore it to him without delay. But if you dispute his title, send a properly instructed person to plead the cause in our Comitatus.

'You will be better off by having the matter enquired into and settled, than if the complaints of Stephanus had never come to a hearing [1].'

45. KING THEODORIC TO THE COMITES, DEFENSORES, AND CURIALES OF TICINUM (PAVIA).

The Heruli to be forwarded on their way to Ravenna.

[It is not easy to see why this order should be addressed to the inhabitants of Ticinum. Had the Heruli crossed the Alps by some pass near the modern Simplon?]

'We have ordered the Heruli, who are suppliants to us, to come to our Comitatus at Ravenna.

'Provide them promptly with ships of provisions for five days, that they may at once see the difference between Italy and their own hungry country [2].'

46. KING THEODORIC TO MARABAD, VIR ILLUSTRIS.

The case of the wife of Liberius to be reheard.

'The Spectabilis Liberius [3] complains that his wife has had an unjust judgment given against her in your Court. Try the case over again, associating with yourself arbitrators chosen by both parties. If it cannot so be ended,

---

[1] There are some technical terms in this letter the meaning of which is not clear to me: 'Eam justitiae consideratione momenti jure rest e supplicanti ... Veruntamen si partibus vestris in *causa* possessionis *momentaria* vel *principali* justitiam adesse cognoscitis.'

[2] It is probably to the same transaction that Marcellinus Comes refers when he says, s. a. 512: 'Gens Erulorum in terras atque civitates Romanorum jussu Anastasii Caesaris introducta.' The words 'jussu Anastasii Caesaris' represent this chronicler's tendency to refer everything that is done in Italy to the initiation of Byzantium.

[3] Possibly a son of the Praefect Liberius.

let them appoint properly instructed persons to represent them at our Comitatus, if they cannot come themselves.'

47. KING THEODORIC TO GUDISAL THE SAJO.

'If the public post-horses (veredi) are not allowed proper intervals of rest they will soon be worn out.

'We are informed by our *legati* that these horses are constantly employed by persons who have no right to use them.

Abuses of the Cursus Publicus.

'You are therefore to reside in Rome, and to put yourself in constant communication with the officers of the Praefectus Praetorio and the Magister Officiorum, so as not to allow any to leave the City using the horses of the *Cursus Publicus* except the regularly commissioned agents of those two functionaries. Anyone transgressing is to pay a fine of 100 solidi (£60) per horse; not that the injury to the animal is represented by so high a figure, but in order to punish his impertinence. Our Sajones, when sent with a commission, are to go straight to the mark and return, not to make pleasure-tours at the public expense; and if they disobey this order, they are to pay the same fine as that just mentioned.

'Moreover, the extra horses (parhippi) are not to be weighted with a load of more than 100lbs. For we wish our messengers[1] to travel in light marching order, not to make of their journey a regular domestic migration.

'Cranes, when they are going to cross the sea, clasp little pebbles with their claws, in order to steady without overweighting themselves. Why cannot those who are sent on public errands follow so good an example? Every transport master[2] who violates this rule by loading a horse with more than 100lbs. shall pay 50 solidi (£30).

[1] 'Mittendarii.' A 'Scrinium Mittendariorum' formed part of the staff of the Count of Sacred Largesses. See Theodosian Code vi. 30. 7.
[2] 'Catabulensis.' See iii. 10.

'All fines levied under this edict are to go to the benefit of the postal-servants[1], and thus the evil will, as we so often see in human affairs, furnish its own remedy.'

48. KING THEODORIC TO EUSEBIUS, VIR ILLUSTRIS.

Honourable retirement of Eusebius.

'After the worries of the noisy City, and the heavy burden of your official duties, your Greatness is longing to taste the sweetness of country life. When therefore you have finished your present duties, we grant you by our authority a holiday of eight months in the charming recesses of Lucania [near Cassiodorus' own country], to be reckoned from the time when by Divine [royal?] favour you depart from the City. When those months are at an end, return with speed, much missed as you will be, to your Roman habitation, to the assembly of the nobles, and to social intercourse of a kind that is worthy of your character.'

49. KING THEODORIC TO ALL THE PROVINCIALS AND THE LONG-HAIRED MEN[2], THE DEFENSORES AND THE CURIALES RESIDING IN SUAVIA[3].

Fridibad to be Governor of Suavia, and to punish freebooters.

'The King's orders must be vigorously executed, that terror may be struck into the hearts of the lawless, and that those who have suffered violence may begin to hope for better days. Often the threat of punishment

---

[1] 'Mancipes mutationum.' The 'mutationes' were the places for changing horses; there are generally two of them between each 'mansio' (hostelry). Probably the horses were found by the 'Mancipes mutationum.' It was therefore a sort of *corvée*.

[2] *Capillati*. The only passage which throws a light on this name—and that is a doubtful one—is Jordanes, De Rebus Geticis xi. After describing the *pileati*, the tiara-wearing priests of the Getae, he says: 'Reliquam vero gentem capillatos dicere jussit [Diceneus] quod nomen Gothi pro magno suscipientes adhuc hodie suis cantionibus reminiscuntur.'

[3] *Suavia* is nearly equivalent to the modern Sclavonia, between the rivers Drave and Save.

does more to quiet a country than punishment itself. Therefore, under Divine guidance, we have appointed Fridibad to be your Governor.

'He will punish cattle-lifters with due severity, will cut off murderers, condemn thieves, and render you, who are now torn by presumptuous iniquity, safe from the daring attempts of villains. Live like a settled people; live like men who have learned the lessons of morality; let neither nationality nor rank be alleged as an excuse from these duties. If any man gives himself up to wicked courses, he must needs undergo chastisement.'

50. KING THEODORIC TO FAUSTUS, PRAETORIAN PRAEFECT.

Remission of taxes for Campanians who have suffered from an eruption of Vesuvius.

'The Campanians complain that their fields have been devastated by an eruption of Vesuvius, and ask in consequence for a remission of tribute. [This eruption is assigned—I do not know on what authority—to the year 512 [1].]

'Let your Greatness send men of proved integrity to the territories of Neapolis and Nola, who may examine the ravaged lands for themselves, and proportion the relief granted, to the amount of damage done in each case.

'That Province is visited at intervals by this terrible calamity, as if to mar its otherwise perfect happiness. There is one favourable feature in the visitation. It does not come wholly unawares. For some time before, the mountain groans with the strife of Nature going on inside it, and it seems as if an angry spirit within would terrify all the neighbourhood by his mighty roar. Then the air is darkened by its foul exhalations; hot ashes scudding along the sea, a shower of

---

[1] The passage in Marcellinus Comes, s. a. 512, which at first sight seems to describe an eruption taking place in that year, really describes the *commemoration* of the eruption of 472. See following note.

drops of dust upon the land, tell to all Italy, to the transmarine Provinces, to the world, from what calamity Campania is suffering[1].

'Go nearer: you will see as it were rivers of dust flowing, and glowing streams of barren sand moving over the country. You see and wonder: the furrows of the fields are suddenly lifted to a level with the tops of the trees; the country, which but now was dressed in a robe of gladsome greenness, is laid waste by sudden and mournful heat. And yet, even those sandy tracts of pumice-stone which the mountain vomits forth, dry and burnt up as they appear, have their promise of fertility. There are germs within them which will one day spring to life, and re-clothe the mountain side which they have wasted.

'How strange that one mountain alone should thus terrify the whole world! Other mountains may be seen with silently glowing summits; this alone announces itself to distant lands by darkened skies and changed air. So it still goes on, shedding its dusty dews over the land; ever parting with its substance, yet a mountain still undiminished in height and amplitude. Who that sees those mighty blocks in the plain would believe that they had boiled over from the depths of that distant hill, that they had been tossed like straws upon the wind by the angry spirit of the mountain?

'Therefore let your Prudence so manage the enquiry that those who have really suffered damage shall be relieved, while no room is left for fraud.'

---

[1] In the eruption of 472 (apparently the last great eruption previous to 512), the ashes were carried as far as Byzantium, the inhabitants of which city instituted a yearly religious service in memory of the event: 'Vesuvius mons Campaniae torridus intestinis ignibus aestuans exusta evomuit viscera, nocturnisque in die tenebris incumbentibus, *omnem Europae faciem minuto contexit pulvere*. Hujus metuendi memoriam cineris Byzantii annue celebrant VIII Idus Novembris.' The eruption was accompanied by widespread earthquake: 'In Asia aliquantae civitates vel oppida terrae motu collapsa sunt' (Marcellinus Comes, sub anno).

51. KING THEODORIC TO SYMMACHUS, PATRICIAN[1].

Commends the public spirit of Symmachus, as shown in the restoration of Pompey's theatre.

Commends him for the diligence and skill with which he has decorated Rome with new buildings—especially in the suburbs, which no one would distinguish from the City except for the occasional glimpses of pleasant fields; and still more for his restoration of the massive ruins of past days[2], chiefly the theatre of Pompeius.

As the letter is addressed to a learned man, it seems a suitable opportunity to explain why Antiquity reared this mighty pile. Accordingly a very long digression follows on the origin, progress, and decline of Tragedy, Comedy, and Pantomime.

It is remarked incidentally that Pompeius seems to have derived his appellation *Magnus* chiefly from the building of this wonderful theatre.

The expense which Symmachus has been put to in these vast works is to be refunded to him by the *Praepositus Sacri Cubiculi*, that he may still have the glory of the work, but that the King may have done his due part in preserving the memorials of Antiquity.

---

[1] The father-in-law of Boethius.
[2] We have here a striking description of the massive strength of the public buildings of Rome: '[Videmus] caveas illas saxis pendentibus apsidatas ita juncturis absconditis in formas pulcherrimas convenisse, ut cryptas magis excelsi montis crederes quam aliquid fabricatum esse judicares.'

BOOK V.

CONTAINING FORTY-FOUR LETTERS WRITTEN BY CASSIODORUS IN THE NAME OF THEODORIC.

---

1. KING THEODORIC TO THE KING OF THE VANDALS[1].

The King of the Vandals is thanked for his presents.

'The swords which you have sent us are most beautiful: so sharp that they will cut other weapons; so bright that they reflect with a sort of iron light[2] the face of the beholder; with the two blades descending to their edges with such absolute equality of slope, that you would fancy them the result of the furnace rather than of the whetstone[3]; in the middle, between the blades, channels carved which are filled in with beautiful enamel of various colours[4].

'Along with these arms you have also sent us musical instruments of ebony, and slave boys of beautiful whiteness.

---

[1] No doubt Thrasamund, who married Theodoric's sister. He reigned from 496 to 523.

[2] 'Ut speculum quoddam virorum faciat ferream lucem.'

[3] 'Quarum margines in acutum tali aequalitate descendunt, ut non limis compositae, sed igneis fornacibus credantur effusae.'

[4] 'Harum media pulchris alveis excavata, quibusdam videntur crispari posse vermiculis, ubi tanta varietatis umbra concludit, ut intextum magis credas variis coloribus lucidum metallum.'

'We thank you heartily, send by A and B, our ambassadors, presents of equal value; and hope that mutual concord will always unite our States.'

2. KING THEODORIC TO THE HAESTI.

[These are the Aestii of Tacitus, dwelling in or on the south border of the country which is still called Esthonia. Tacitus also mentions their quest of amber[1].]

The Haesti, dwellers by the Baltic. Their present of amber.

'It is gratifying to us to know that you have heard of our fame, and have sent ambassadors who have pressed through so many strange nations to seek our friendship.

'We have received the amber which you have sent us. You say that you gather this lightest of all substances from the shores of the ocean, but how it comes thither you know not. But, as an author named Cornelius [Tacitus] informs us, it is gathered in the innermost islands of the ocean, being formed originally of the juice of a tree (whence its name *succinum*[2]), and gradually hardened by the heat of the sun.

'Thus it becomes an exuded metal, a transparent softness, sometimes blushing with the colour of saffron, sometimes glowing with flame-like clearness[3]. Then, gliding down to the margin of the sea, and further purified by the rolling of the tides, it is at length transported to your shores to be cast up upon them. We have thought it better to point this out to you, lest you should imagine that your supposed secrets have escaped our knowledge.

---

[1] Germ. 45: 'Ergo jam dextro Suevici maris litore Aestiorum gentes alluuntur, quibus ritus habitusque Suevorum, lingua Britannicae propior ... Sed et mare scrutantur ac soli omnium sucinum quod ipsi glesum vocant, inter vada atque in ipso littore legunt.' Then follows an account of the nature of amber, and a history of its supposed origin, from which Cassiodorus has borrowed in this letter.

[2] Cassiodorus apparently spells this word with two c's. The more usual spelling is with one.

[3] 'Modo croceo colore rubens, modo flammea claritate pinguescens.'

'We send you some presents by our ambassadors, and shall be glad to receive further visits from you by the road which you have thus opened up, and to show you future favours.'

[The collection of amber is also noticed by Pliny ('Nat. Hist.' 37. 2). It is interesting to observe that he there, on the authority of Pytheas, attributes to the Guttones dwelling on the Baltic shore the collection of amber, and its sale to the Teutones. These Guttones were, if we are right in accepting Jordanes' account of the Gothic migrations, themselves ancestors of the Ostrogoths.]

3. KING THEODORIC TO HONORATUS, VIR ILLUSTRIS, QUAESTOR.

4. KING THEODORIC TO THE SENATE OF THE CITY OF ROME.

Honoratus, brother of Decoratus, is made Quaestor.

The usual pair of letters on the promotion of Honoratus to the Quaestorship. He succeeds his brother Decoratus, whose early death Theodoric regrets. The date of the letters is the Third Indiction, September 1, 509.

The writer remarks on the prophetic instinct[1] of the parents, who named these two sons, destined to future eminence, Decoratus and Honoratus. Decoratus was originally an advocate at Rome. His services were often sought by men of Consular rank, and before his admission to the Senate he had had a Patrician for his client in a very celebrated case[2].

---

[1] We have here a remark on unconscious prophecies: 'Loqui datur quod nos sensisse nescimus: sed post casum reminiscimur, quod ignorantes veraciter dixeramus.'

[2] 'Inferior gradu praestabat viris consularibus se patronum et cum honoribus vestris impar haberetur, Patricius ei dictus est in celeberrima cognitione susceptus.' The last part of this sentence is very obscure.

When he became Quaestor he distinguished himself by his excellent qualities. 'He stood beside us, under the light of our Genius, bold but reverent; silent at the right time, fluent when there was need of fluency. He kept our secrets as if he had forgotten them; he remembered every detail of our orders as if he had written them down. Thus was he ever an eminent lightener of our labours[1].'

The past career of the younger brother, Honoratus, who has been advocate at Spoleto, and has had to contend with the corrupt tendencies of Provincial judges, full of their little importance, and removed from the wholesome control which the opinion of the Senate exercised upon them at Rome, is then sketched; and the hope is expressed that, in the words of the Virgilian quotation[2], this bough upon the family tree will be found as goodly as that which it has untimely lost.

The letter to the Senate has an interesting passage on the duties and responsibilities of the Quaestor.

Duties of the Quaestorship.

'It is only men whom we consider to be of the highest learning that we raise to the dignity of the Quaestorship, such men as are fitted to be interpreters of the laws and sharers of our counsels. This is an honour which neither riches nor high birth by itself can procure, only learning joined with prudence. In granting all other dignities we confer favours, but from the holder of this we ever receive them. He is favoured to have a share in our anxieties; he enters in by the door

---

[1] Decoratus is called by Boethius, who was his colleague in some office, 'a wretched buffoon and informer' (nequissimus scurra et delator. Cons. Phil. iii. 4). But Ennodius addresses him in friendly and cordial language (Epist. iv. 17). His epitaph, which mentions his Spoletan origin, is of course laudatory:

'Nam fessis tribuit requiem, miseros que levavit,
Justitiae cultor, largus et hospes erat.'

(Quoted in the notes to Ennodius in Migne's Patrologia.)

[2] 'Primo avulso non deficit alter' (Aen. vi. 143).

of our thoughts; he is intimately acquainted with the breast in which the cares of the whole State are weighed. Think what judgment you ought to form of a man who is partaker of such a confidence. From him we require skill in the laws; to him flow together all the prayers of all suitors, and (a thing more precious than any treasure) to him is committed our own reputation for *civilitas*. Under a just Quaestor the mind of an innocent man is at rest: only the wicked become anxious as to the success of their evil designs; and thus the bad lose their hope of plunder, while more earnestness is shown in the practice of virtue. It is his to safeguard the just rights of all men: temperate in expenditure, lavish in his zeal for justice, incapable of deception, prompt in succour. He serves that Sovereign mind before which all bow: through his lips must he speak who has not an equal in the land.'

5. KING THEODORIC TO THE SAJO MANNILA.

Abuses of the Cursus Publicus. Repeats the injunctions given in Letter iv. 47 against improper use of the public post-horses, and overloading of the extra horses. The fines imposed are the same as in that letter [with the addition of a fine of two ounces of gold (about £6 10s.) for overloading]; the examples from Natural History are similar. 'The very bird when weighted with a load flies slowly. Ships though they cannot feel their toils, yet move tardily when they are filled with cargo. What can the poor quadruped do when pressed by too great burden? It succumbs.'

But apparently this rule against overloading is not to apply to Praepositi (Provincial Governors?), since 'reverenda antiquitas' has given them special rights over the *Cursus Publicus*.

6. KING THEODORIC TO STABULARIUS, COMITIACUS[1].

7. KING THEODORIC TO JOANNES, VIR CLARISSIMUS, ARCARIUS [TREASURER].

Default in payments to Treasury made by Thomas. His property assigned to his son-in-law Joannes.

'The *Vir Honestus*, Thomas, has long been a defaulter (reliquator) in respect of the Indictions payable for certain farms which he has held under the King's house in Apulia[2], and this default has now reached the sum of 10,000 solidi (£6,000). Repeatedly summoned to pay, he always procrastinates, and we can get no satisfaction out of him. The petition of Joannes, who is son-in-law to Thomas, informs us that he is willing to pay the 10,000 solidi due, if we will make over to him the said farms, and all the property of his father-in-law. This we therefore now do, reserving to Thomas the right to pay the debt at any time before the next Kalends of September, and thus to redeem his property. Failing such payment, the property is to pass finally into the hands of Joannes, on his paying the 10,000 solidi to the Illustrious Count of the Patrimony [possibly Stabularius].

'It may be some little consolation to Thomas to reflect that after all it is his son-in-law who enters into possession of his goods.'

[Dahn ('Könige der Germanen' iii. 277) remarks on this letter: 'But even the well-meaning Theodoric takes steps in the interests of substantial justice which from a juristic point of view it would be hard to justify.... Evidently here the King, in his consideration of what was practically just, has decided according to caprice, not

---

[1] Officer of the Court. See vi. 13.
[2] 'Thomatem domus nostrae certa praedia suscepisse sed eum male administrando suscepta usque ad decem millia solidorum de Indictionibus illa atque illa reliquatorem publicis rationibus extitisse.' It is not quite clear whether the debt is due as what we should call rent or as land-tax. Perhaps the debt had accumulated under both heads.

according to right; for the Fiscus could strictly only be repaid its debt out of the property of the defaulter, and hold the Arcarius (Joannes) responsible for the balance' (for which Dahn thinks he had already made himself liable). I do not quite agree with this view. It seems to me that Thomas was hopelessly bankrupt (the debt was 10,000 solidi, not 1,000, as stated by Dahn), and the Fiscus virtually sells the bankrupt's estate to his son-in-law, for him to make of it what he can.]

8. KING THEODORIC TO ANASTASIUS THE CONSULAR.

Transport of marble from Faenza to Ravenna.

'We rely upon your Sublimity's zeal and prudence to see that the required blocks of marble are forwarded from Faventia (Faenza) to Ravenna, without any extortion from private individuals; so that, on the one hand, our desire for the adornment of that city may be gratified, and on the other, there may be no cause for complaint on the part of our subjects.'

9. KING THEODORIC TO THE POSSESSORES OF FELTRIA.

New city to be built in district of Trient.

'We have ordered the erection of a new city in the territory of Tridentum (Trient). As the work is great and the inhabitants few, we order you all to assist and build each your appointed length (pedatura) of wall, for which you will receive suitable pay.'

[This use of the word *pedatura* is found in Vegetius, 'Epitoma Rei Militaris' iii. 8, and is illustrated by the centurial stones on the two great Roman walls in Britain, recording the number of feet accomplished by each century of soldiers (See 'Archaeologia Aeliana,' vol. ix. p. 28; paper by Mr. Clayton).]

'None, not even the servants of the royal house (divina domus), are excepted from this order.'

10. KING THEODORIC TO THE SAJO VERANUS.

11. KING THEODORIC TO THE GEPIDAE, ON THEIR MARCH TO GAUL.

Payment to Gepidae on their march to Gaul.

'We desire that our soldiers should always be well paid, and that they should never become the terror of the country which they are ordered to defend. Do you therefore, Sajo Veranus, cause the Gepid troops whom we have ordered to come to the defence of Gaul, to march in all peace and quietness through Venetia and Liguria.

'You Gepidae shall receive three solidi (£1 16s.) per week; and we trust that thus supplied you will everywhere buy your provisions, and not take them by force.

'We generally give the soldiers their pay in kind, but in this case, for obvious reasons, we think it better to pay them in money, and let them buy for themselves.

'If their waggons are becoming shaky with the long journey, or their beasts of burden weary, let them exchange for sound waggons and fresh beasts with the inhabitants of the country, but on such terms that the latter shall not regret the transaction.'

[Does this payment of three solidi mean per head? That would be an enormously high rate of pay. Sartorius (p. 289) feels the difficulty so strongly that he suggests that this was the pay given to the whole troop, whose number was not large; but 'multitudo' seems hostile to this hypothesis[1]. Possibly the high cost of provisions in the Alpine mountain-country may help to explain this unheard-of rate of pay to common soldiers.]

---

[1] 'Ut multitudinem Gepidarum quam fecimus ad Gallias custodiae causâ properare, per Venetiam atque Liguriam sub omni facias moderatione transire.'

12. KING THEODORIC TO THEODAHAD, VIR ILLUSTRIS [NEPHEW OF THE KING].

Avarice and injustice of Theodahad.

'If all are bound to seek justice and to avoid ignoble gains, most especially are they thus bound who pride themselves on their close relationship to us.

'The heirs of the Illustrious Argolicus [probably the Praefect of Rome] and the Clarissimus Amandianus complain that the estate[1] of Palentia, which we generously gave them to console them for the loss of the Casa Arbitana, has been by your servants, for no cause, unbecomingly invaded; and thus you, who should have shown an example of glorious moderation, have caused the scandal of high-handed spoliation. Wherefore, if this be true, let your Greatness at once restore what has been taken away; and if you consider that you have any claims on the land, come and assert them in our *Comitatus*. Even success yonder is injurious to your fame; but here, after full trial of the case and hearing of witnesses, no one will believe that any injustice has been done if your cause should triumph.'

[The republication of this letter at the close of his official life shows what was Cassiodorus' opinion of Theodahad, though he had served under him.]

13. KING THEODORIC TO EUTROPIUS AND ACRETIUS.

Commissariat.

'We rely upon you to collect the prescribed rations and deliver them to the soldiers. It is most important that they should be regularly supplied, and that there should be no excuse for pillage, so hard to check when once an army has begun to practise it.'

---

[1] 'Massa;' cf. the American 'block.'

14. KING THEODORIC TO SEVERI(A)NUS[1], VIR ILLUSTRIS (514–515).

'We send you to redress the long-standing grievances of the Possessores of the Province of Suavia, to which we have not yet been able to apply a remedy.

Financial abuses in Suavia.

'(1) It appears that some of the chief Possessores are actually making a profit out of the taxes, imposing heavy burdens on their poorer neighbours and not honestly accounting for the receipts to us. See that this is put right, that the land-tax (assis[2] publicus) is fairly and equitably reimposed according to the ability of each Possessor, and that those who have been oppressing their neighbours heal the wounds which they have made.

'(2) See also that a strict account is rendered by all Defensores, Curiales, and Possessores of any receipts on behalf of the public Treasury. If a Possessor can show that he paid his tax (tributarius solidus) for the now expired eighth Indiction (A.D. 514–515), and the money has not reached our Treasury, find out the defaulter and punish his crime.

'(3) Similarly with sums disbursed by one of the clerks of our Treasury[3], for the relief of the Province, which have not reached their destination.

'(4) Men who were formerly Barbarians[4], who have married Roman wives and acquired property in land, are to be compelled to pay their Indictions and other taxes to the public Treasury just like any other Provincials.

'(5) Judges are to visit each town (municipium) once in the year, and are not entitled to claim from such towns more than three days' maintenance. Our ancestors

---

[1] In the next letter the same official is called Severinus.
[2] Cassiodorus uses the rare nominative form 'assis.'
[3] 'Tabularius a cubiculo nostro.'
[4] 'Antiqui Barbari qui Romanis mulieribus elegerint nuptiali foedere sociari, quolibet titulo praedia quaesiverint, fiscum possessi cespitis persolvere, ac super indictitiis oneribus parere cogantur.'

wished that the circuits of the Judges should be a benefit, not a burden, to the Provincials.

'(6) It is alleged that some of the servants of the Count of the Goths and of the Vice-dominus (?) have levied black-mail on some of the Provincials. Property so taken must be at once restored and the offenders punished.

'(7) Enter all your proceedings under this commission in official registers (polyptycha), both for your own protection and for the sake of future reference, to prevent the recurrence of similar abuses.'

[A long and interesting letter, but with some obscure passages.]

15. KING THEODORIC TO ALL THE POSSESSORES IN SUAVIA.

On the same subject.

'Although our Comitatus is always ready to redress the grievances of our subjects, yet, on account of the length of the journey from your Province hither, we have thought good to send the Illustrious and Magnificent Severinus to you to enquire into your complaints on the spot. He is a man fully imbued with our own principles of government, and he has seen how greatly we have at heart the administration of justice. We therefore doubt not that he will soon put right whatever has been done wrong in your Province; and we have published our "oracles" [the previous letter, containing Severinus' patent of appointment], that all may know upon what principles he is to act, and that those who have grievances against the present functionaries may learn their rights.'

16. KING THEODORIC TO ABUNDANTIUS, PRAETORIAN PRAEFECT.

Formation of a navy.

'By Divine inspiration we have determined to raise a navy which may both ensure the arrival of the cargoes of public corn and may, if need be, combat the ships of an enemy. For, that Italy, a country abounding in timber, should not have a navy of her own hath often stricken us with regret.

'Let your Greatness therefore give directions for the construction of 1,000 *dromones* (swift cutters). Wherever cypresses and pines are found near to the sea-shore, let them be bought at a suitable price.

'Then as to the levy of sailors: any fitting man, if a slave, must be hired of his master, or bought at a reasonable price. If free, he is to receive 5 solidi (£3) as donative, and will have his rations during the term of service.

'Even those who were slaves are to be treated in the same way, "since it is a kind of freedom to serve the Ruler of the State[1];" and are to receive, according to their condition, two or three solidi (£1 4s. or £1 16s.) of bounty money[2].

'Fishermen, however, are not to be enlisted in this force, since we lose with regret one whose vocation it is to provide us with luxuries; and moreover one kind of training is required for him who has to face the stormy wind, and another for him who need only fish close to shore.'

17. KING THEODORIC TO ABUNDANTIUS, PRAETORIAN PRAEFECT.

On the same subject.

'We praise you for your prompt fulfilment of the orders contained in the previous letter. You have built a fleet almost as quickly as ordinary men would sail one. The model of the triremes, revealing the number of the rowers but concealing their faces, was first furnished by the Argonauts. So too the sail, that flying sheet[3] which wafts idle men to their destination quicker than swiftest

---

[1] 'Quando libertatis genus est servire Rectori.'
[2] 'Arrharum nomine.'
[3] 'Linum volatile.'

birds can fly, was first invented by the lorn Isis, when she set off on her wanderings through the world to find her lost son Apochran.

'Now that we have our fleet, there is no need for the Greek to fasten a quarrel upon us, or for the African [the Vandal] to insult us[1]. With envy they see that we have now stolen from them the secret of their strength.

'Let all the fleet be assembled at Ravenna on the next Ides of June. Let our own Padus send his home-born navy to the sea, his river-nurtured firs to battle with the winds of Ocean.

'But there is one suggestion of yours of great importance, and which must be diligently acted upon, namely the removal of the nets whereby the fishermen at present impede the channels of the following rivers: Mincius, Ollius (Oglio), Anser (Serchio), Arno, Tiber. Let the river lie open for the transit of ships; let it suffice for the appetite of man to seek for delicacies in the ordinary way, not by rustic artifice to hinder the freedom of the stream.'

18. KING THEODORIC TO UVILIAS [WILLIAS?], VIR ILLUSTRIS AND COUNT OF THE PATRIMONY.

19. KING THEODORIC TO GUDINAND, A SAJO.

20. KING THEODORIC TO AVILF, A SAJO.

On the same subject. These three letters all relate to the same subject as the two preceding ones—the formation of a navy, and the *rendezvous* of ships and sailors at Ravenna on the Ides of June.

The Count of the Patrimony is courteously requested to see if there is any timber suitable for the purposes of the navy, growing in the royal estates along the banks of the Po.

[1] 'Non habet quod nobis Graecus imputet aut Afer insultet.'

The Sajones are ordered in more brusque and peremptory fashion: Gudinand to collect the sailors at Ravenna on the appointed day; and Avilf to collect timber along the banks of the Po, with as little injury to the Possessors as possible (not, however, apparently paying them anything for it), to keep his hands clean from extortion and fraud, and to pull up the stake-nets in the channels of the five rivers mentioned in Letter 17; 'for we all know that men ought to fish with nets, not with hedges, and the opposite practice shows detestable greediness.'

21. KING THEODORIC TO CAPUANUS, SENATOR.

22. KING THEODORIC TO THE SENATE OF THE CITY OF ROME.

[On the appointment of Capuanus to the office of Rector of the Guilds (Rector Decuriarum). The Guilds (Decuriae) of the City of Rome—not to be confounded with the Provincial *Curiae*, membership in which was at this time a burden rather than an advantage—enjoyed several special privileges. We find from the Theodosian Code, Lib. xiv. Tit. 1, that there were Decuriae of the *Librarii, Fiscales, Censuales*. The *Decuria Scribarum* is perhaps the same as the *Decuria Librariorum*. I use the word Guilds, which seems best to describe a body of this kind; but it will be seen from their names that these Guilds are not of a commercial character, but are rather concerned with the administration of justice. Some of them must have discharged the duties of attorneys, others of Inland Revenue officers, others acted as clerks to register the proceedings of the Senate, others performed the mere mechanical work of copying, which is now undertaken by a law stationer.

It was ordained by a law of Constantius and Julian (357) that no one should enter the first class in these

Capuanus appointed Rector Decuriarum.

Decuriae[1] unless he were a trained and practised literary man.

The office which in the Theodosian Code is called *Judex Decuriarum* seems here to be called *Rector*.]

The young Capuanus has distinguished himself as an advocate both before the Senate and other tribunals. There has been a certain diffidence and hesitation in his manner, especially when he was dealing with common subjects; but he always warmed with his peroration, and the same man who even stammered in discussing some trifling detail became fluent, nay eloquent, when the graver interests of his client were at stake. When he saw that the Judge was against him he did not lose heart, but, by praising his justice and impartiality, gradually coaxed him into a more favourable mood. On one memorable occasion, when a certain document was produced which appeared hostile, he boldly challenged the accuracy of the copy [made probably by one of the *Decuria Librariorum*] and insisted on seeing the original. This young advocate is now appointed *Rector Decuriarum*, and thus accorded the privilege of seniority over many men who are much older than himself. He is exhorted to treat them with all courtesy, to remember the importance of accuracy and fidelity in the execution of his duties and those of the *Decuriales* under him, on whose correct transcription of documents the property, the liberty, nay even the life of their fellow-subjects may depend. Especially he is exhorted to remember his own challenge of the accuracy of a copied document, that he may not ever find that memorable oration of his brought up against himself.

The Senate is exhorted to give the young official a kindly welcome. It will now devolve upon him to report with praiseworthy accuracy the proceedings of that body, the most celebrated in the whole world. He who has often pleaded before them the cause of the

---

[1] 'Locum primi ordinis.'

humble and weak, will now have to introduce Consulars to their assembly. It is expected that his eloquence will grow and his stammer will disappear, now that he is clothed with a more dignified office. 'Freedom nourishes words, but fear frequently interrupts their plenteous flow.'

23. KING THEODORIC TO ABUNDANTIUS, PRAETORIAN PRAEFECT.

'Tata the Sajo is ordered to proceed to the Illustrious Count Julian, with the young archers whom he has drilled, that they may practise on the field the lessons which they have learned in the gymnasium. Let your Greatness provide them with rations and ships according to custom.' [The place to which this expedition was directed does not seem to be stated.] *(marginal note: Archery drill.)*

24. KING THEODORIC TO THE SENATOR EPIPHANIUS, CONSULARIS OF DALMATIA.

'We are informed that Joanna, the wife of Andreas, having succeeded to her husband's estate, has died intestate without heirs. Her property ought therefore to lapse to our Treasury[1], but it is being appropriated, so we are informed, by divers persons who have no claim to it. *(marginal note: Property of a widow dying intestate and without heirs to be claimed for the State.)*

'Enquire into this matter; and if it be as we are informed, reclaim for our Treasury so legitimate a possession. We should consider ourselves guilty of negligence if we omitted to take possession of that which, without harming anyone, so obviously comes in to lighten the public burdens.

'But if you find the facts different to these, by all means leave the present owners in quiet possession. The secure enjoyment by our subjects of that which is lawfully theirs we hold to be our truest patrimony.'

---

[1] 'Quia caduca bona fisco nostro competere legum cauta decreverunt.'

25. KING THEODORIC TO BACAUDA[1], VIR SUBLIMIS.

Bacauda receives the office of Tribunus Voluptatum for life.

'By way of support for your declining years we appoint you, for life, *Tribunus Voluptatum* [Minister of Public Amusement] at Milan.

'It is a new principle in the public service[2] to give any man a life-tenure of his office; but you will now not have to fear the interference of any successor, and your mind being at ease about your own future, you will be able to minister to the pleasures of the people with a smiling face.'

26. KING THEODORIC TO ALL THE GOTHS SETTLED IN PICENUM AND SAMNIUM.

The Goths summoned to the royal presence.

'The presence of the Sovereign doubles the sweetness of his gifts, and that man is like one dead whose face is not known to his lord[3]. Come therefore by God's assistance, come all into our presence on the eighth day before the Ides of June (June 6th), there solemnly to receive our royal largesse. But let there be no excesses by the way, no plundering the harvest of the cultivators nor trampling down their meadows, since for this cause do we gladly defray the expense of our armies that *civilitas* may be kept intact by armed men.'

27. KING THEODORIC TO GUDUIM, SAJO.

The same.

'Order all the captains of thousands[4] of Picenum and Samnium to come to our Court, that we may bestow the

---

[1] The name is a peculiar one, reminding us of the Bacaudae, who for more than a century waged a sort of servile war in Gaul against the officers of the Empire. It is not probable, however, that there is any real connection between them and the receiver of this letter.

[2] 'Quod est in Reipublicae *militiâ* novum.' Observe the use of militia for civil service.

[3] 'Nam pene similis est mortuo qui a suo Dominante nescitur.' A motto more suited to the presence-chamber of Byzantium than the camp-fires of a Gothic King.

[4] 'Millenarii.' Cf. the χιλίαρχοι, who, as Procopius tells us, were appointed by Gaiseric over the Vandals; also the *thusundifaths* of Ulfilas.

wonted largesse on our Goths. We enquire diligently into the deeds of each of our soldiers, that none may lose the credit of any exploit which he has performed in the field. On the other hand, let the coward tremble at the thought of coming into our presence. Even this fear may hereafter make him brave against the enemy.'

28. KING THEODORIC TO CARINUS, VIR ILLUSTRIS.

Invitation to Court.

'Granting your request, and also satisfying our own desire for your companionship, we invite you to our Court.'

29. KING THEODORIC TO NEUDES, VIR ILLUSTRIS.

A blind Gothic warrior enslaved.

'Our pity is greatly moved by the petition of Ocer, a blind Goth, who has come by the help of borrowed sight to *feel* the sweetness of our clemency, though he cannot see our presence.

'He asserts that he, a free Goth, who once followed our armies, has, owing to his misfortune, been reduced to slavery by Gudila and Oppas. Strange excess of impudence to make that man their servant, before whose sword they had assuredly trembled had he possessed his eyesight! He pleads that Count Pythias has already pronounced against the claims of his pretended masters. If you find that this is so, restore him at once to freedom, and warn those men not to dare to repeat their oppression of the unfortunate.'

30. KING THEODORIC TO GUDUI[M], VIR SUBLIMIS [AND DUX].

Servile tasks imposed on free Goths by a Duke.

'We expect those whom we choose as Dukes to work righteousness. Costula and Daila, men who by the blessing of God rejoice in the freedom of our Goths, complain that servile tasks are imposed upon them by you. We do not do this ourselves, nor will we allow

31. King Theodoric to Decoratus, Vir Devotus (?).

[For the career of Decoratus see v. 3 and 4.]

Arrears of Siliquaticum to be enforced.

'Thomas, Vir Clarissimus, complains that he cannot collect the arrears of Siliquaticum from certain persons in Apulia and Calabria.

'Do you therefore summon Mark the Presbyter, Andreas, Simeonius, and the others whose names are set forth in the accompanying schedule, to come into your presence, using no unnecessary force[1] in your summons. If they cannot clear themselves of this debt to the public Treasury, they must be forced to pay.'

[The arrears are said to be for the 8th, 9th, 11th, 1st, 2nd, and 15th Indictiones; i.e. probably for the years 500, 501, 503, 508, 509, 507. I cannot account for this curious order in which the years are arranged, which seems to suggest some corruption of the text. Probably this letter was written about 509.]

32. King Theodoric to Brandila (cir. 508–9).

[See remarks on this letter in Dahn ('Könige der Germanen' iv. 149–152); he claims it as a proof that Gothic law still existed for the Goths in Italy.]

Assault of the wife of Brandila on the wife of Patzenes.

'Times without number has Patzenes laid his complaint upon us, to wit that while he was absent on the recent successful expedition[2] your wife Procula fell upon his wife [Regina], inflicted upon her three murderous blows, and finally left her for dead, the victim having only escaped by the supposed impossibility of her living. Now therefore, if you acknowledge the fact to be so,

---

[1] 'Servata in omnibus civilitate.'   [2] Into Gaul; see next letter.

you are to consult your own honour by inflicting summary punishment as a husband on your wife, that we may not hear of this complaint again[1]. But if you deny the fact, you are to bring your said wife to our Comitatus and there prove her innocence.'

33. KING THEODORIC TO DUKE WILITANCH.

[Containing the explanation of Procula's violence to Regina].

'Patzenes brings before us a most serious complaint: that during his absence in the Gaulish campaign, Brandila dared to form an adulterous connection with his wife Regina, and to go through the form of marriage with her.

<small>Adulterous connection between Brandila and the wife of Patzenes.</small>

'Whose honour will be safe if advantage is thus to be taken with impunity of the absence of a brave defender of his country? Alas for the immodesty of women! They might learn virtue even from the chaste example of the cooing turtle-dove, who when once deprived by misfortune of her mate, never pairs again with another.

'Let your Sublimity compel the parties accused to come before you for examination, and if the charge be true, if these shameless ones were speculating on the soldier of the Republic not returning from the wars, if they were hoping, as they must have hoped, for general collapse and ruin in order to hide their shame, then proceed against them as our laws against adulterers dictate[2], and thus vindicate the rights of all husbands.'

[If these laws were, as is probable, those contained in the *Edictum Theodorici*, the punishment for both the guilty parties was death, § 38, 39.]

---

[1] 'Atque ideo decretis te praesentibus admonemus, ut si factum evidenter agnoscis, delatam querimoniam, pudori tuo consulens, *maritali districtione redarguas;* quatenus ex eâdem causâ ad nos querela justa non redeat.'

[2] 'Et rerum veritate discussâ *sicut jura nostra praecipiunt*, in adulteros maritorum favore resecetur.'

34. King Theodoric to Abundantius, Praetorian Praefect.

Endless evasions of Frontosus. The nature of the chameleon.

'Frontosus, acting worthily of his name [the shameless-browed one], confessed to having embezzled a large sum of public money, but promised that, if a sufficient interval were allowed him, he would repay it. Times without number has this interval expired and been renewed, and still he does not pay. When he is arrested he trembles with fear, and will promise anything; as soon as he is liberated he seems to forget every promise that he has made. He changes his words, like the chameleon, that little creature which in the shape of a serpent is distinguished by a gold-coloured head, and has all the rest of its body of a pale green. This little beast when it meets the gaze of men, not being gifted with speed of flight, confused with its excess of timidity, changes its colours in marvellous variety, now azure, now purple, now green, now dark blue. The chameleon, again, may be compared to the Pandian gem [sapphire?], which flashes with all sorts of lights and colours while you hold it still in your hand.

'Such then is the mind of Frontosus. He may be rightly compared to Proteus, who when he was laid hold of, appeared in every shape but his own, roared as a lion, hissed as a serpent, or foamed away in watery waves, all in order to conceal his true shape of man.

'Since this is his character, when you arrest him, first stop his mouth from promising, for his facile nature is ready with all sorts of promises which he has no chance of performing. Then ascertain what he can really pay at once, and keep him bound till he does it. He must not be allowed to think that he can get the better of us with his tricks.'

35. KING THEODORIC TO COUNT LUVIRIT, AND AMPELIUS.

Fraudulent shipowners to be punished.

'When we were in doubt about the food supply of Rome, we judged it proper that Spain should send her cargoes of wheat hither, and the Vir Spectabilis Marcian collected supplies there for this purpose. His industry, however, was frustrated by the greed of the shipowners, who, disliking the necessary delay, slipped off and disposed of the grain for their own profit. Little as we like harshness, this offence must be punished. We have therefore directed Catellus and Servandus (Viri Strenui) to collect from these shipmasters the sum of 1,038 solidi (£622 16s.), inasmuch as they appear to have received:

'From the sale of the corn . . . . 280 solidi.
'And from the fares of passengers . 758 „
                                    ─────
                                   '1,038 „

'Let your Sublimity assist in the execution of this order.'

36. KING THEODORIC TO STARCEDIUS, VIR SUBLIMIS.

Honourable discharge.

'You tell us that your body, wearied out with continual labour, is no longer equal to the fatigues of our glorious campaigns, and you therefore ask to be released from the necessity of further military service. We grant your request, but stop your donative; because it is not right that you should consume the labourer's bread in idleness. We shall extend to you our protection from the snares of your adversaries, and allow no one to call you a deserter, since you are not one[1].'

---

[1] This is perhaps a specimen of the 'honesta missio' of which we read in the Theodosian Code xii. 1. 43, 45.

37. KING THEODORIC TO THE JEWS OF MILAN.

Rights of the Jewish Synagogue not to be invaded by Christians.

'For the preservation of *civilitas* the benefits of justice are not to be denied even to those who are recognised as wandering from the right way in matters of faith.

'You complain that you are often wantonly attacked, and that the rights pertaining to your synagogue are disregarded[1]. We therefore give you the needed protection of our Mildness, and ordain that no ecclesiastic shall trench on the privileges of your synagogue, nor mix himself up in your affairs. But let the two communities keep apart, as their faiths are different: you on your part not attempting to do anything *incivile* against the rights of the said Church.

'The law of thirty years' prescription, which is a world-wide custom[2], shall enure for your benefit also.

'But why, oh Jew, dost thou petition for peace and quietness on earth when thou canst not find that rest which is eternal[3]?'

38. KING THEODORIC TO ALL CULTIVATORS[4].

Shrubs obstructing the aqueduct of Ravenna to be rooted up.

'The aqueducts are an object of our special care. We desire you at once to root up the shrubs growing in the Signine Channel[5], which will before long become big trees scarcely to be hewn down with the axe, and which interfere with the purity of the water in the aqueduct of Ravenna. Vegetation is the peaceable overturner of buildings, the battering-ram which brings them to the ground, though the trumpets never sound for siege.

---

[1] 'Nonnullorum vos frequenter causamini praesumptione laceratos et quae ad synagogam vestram pertinent perhibetis jura rescindi.'

[2] 'Tricennalis humano generi patrona praescriptio vobis jure servabitur; nec conventionalia vos irrationabiliter praecipimus sustinere dispendia.' I do not know what is meant by 'conventionalia dispendia.'

[3] 'Sed quid, Judaee, supplicans temporalem quietem quaeris si aeternam requiem invenire non possis.'

[4] 'Universis Possessoribus.'

[5] Where was this? Signia in Latium is, of course, not to be thought of.

'We shall now again have baths that we may look upon with pleasure; water which will cleanse, not stain; water after using which we shall not require to wash ourselves again; drinking-water such that the mere sight of it will not take away all our appetite for food[1].'

39. KING THEODORIC TO AMPELIUS AND LIVERIA[2].

Sundry abuses in the administration of the Spanish government to be rectified.

'That alone is the true life of men which is controlled by the reign of law.

'We regret to hear that through the capricious extortions of our revenue-officers anarchy is practically prevailing in Spain. The public registers (polyptycha), not the whim of the collector, ought to measure the liability of the Provincial.

'We therefore send your Sublimity to Spain in order to remedy these disorders.

'(1) Murder must be put down with a strong hand; but the sharper the punishment is made the more rigid we ought to be in requiring proof of the crime[3].

'(2) The collectors of the land-tax (assis publicus) are accused of using false weights [in collecting the quotas of produce from the Provincials]. This must cease, and they must use none but the standard weights kept by our Chamberlain[4].

'(3) The farmers[5] of our Royal domain must pay the rent imposed on them, otherwise they will get to look on the farms as their own property; but certain salaries may be paid them for their trouble, as you shall think fit[6]. [Dahn suggests that the salary was to reimburse

---

[1] The scarcity of water at Ravenna was proverbial.

[2] Cf. the somewhat similar letter to Severinus, Special Commissioner for Suavia (v. 14).

[3] 'Homicidii scelus legum jubemus auctoritate resecari: sed quantum vehementior poena est tanto ejus rei debet inquisitio plus haberi: ne amore vindictae innocentes videantur vitae pericula sustinere.'

[4] 'Libra cubiculi nostri.'   [5] 'Conductores domus Regiae.'

[6] 'Et ne cuiquam labor suus videatur ingratus, salaria eis pro qualitate locatae rei, vestrâ volumus aequitate constitui.'

them for their labours as a kind of local police, but is not himself satisfied with this explanation.]

'(4) Import duties[1] are to be regularly collected and honestly paid over.

'(5) The officers of the mint are not to make their private gains out of the coinage.'

(6) An obscure sentence as to the 'Canon telonei' [from the Greek τελώνης, a tax-gatherer. Garet reads 'Tolonei,' which is probably an error].

(7) The same as to the *Actus Laeti*, whose conscience is assailed by the grossest imputations. [Laetus is perhaps the name of an official.]

'(8) Those concerned in *furtivae actiones*, and their accomplices, are to disgorge the property thus acquired.

'(9) Those who have received *praebendae* [apparently official allowances charged on the Province] are, with detestable injustice, claiming them *both* in money and in kind. This must be put a stop to: of course the one mode of payment is meant to be alternative to the other.

'(10) The Exactores (Collectors) are said to be extorting from the Provincials more than they pay into our chamber (*cubiculum*). Let this be carefully examined into, and let the payment exacted be the same that was fixed in the times of Alaric and Euric.

'(11) The abuse of claiming extortions (*paraveredi*) by those who have a right to use the public posts must be repressed.

'(12) The defence of the Provincials by the *Villici* is so costly, and seems to be so unpopular, that we remove it altogether. [For this *tuitio villici*, see Dahn iii. 131; but he is not able to throw much light on the nature of the office of the *Villicus*.]

'(13) Degrading services (servitia famulatus) are not to be claimed of our free-born Goths, although they may be residents in cities[2].'

---

[1] 'Transmarinorum canon.'   [2] Cf. the 30th letter of this book.

[This very long letter is one of great importance, but also of great difficulty.]

40. KING THEODORIC TO CYPRIAN, COUNT OF THE SACRED LARGESSES.

[This Cyprian is the accuser of Albinus and Boethius.]

41. KING THEODORIC TO THE SENATE OF THE CITY OF ROME.

[On Cyprian's appointment to the above office, 524.]

Promotion of Cyprian to the Comitiva Sacrarum Largitionum.

The usual pair of letters setting forth the merits of the new official. The Senate is congratulated on the fact that the King never presents to a place in that body a mere tyro in official life, but always himself first tests the servants of the State, and rewards with a place in the Senate only those who have shown themselves worthy of it.

Cyprian is the son of a man of merit, Opilio, who in the times of the State's ill-fortune was chosen to a place in the royal household[1]. He was not able, owing to the wretchedness of the times, to do much for his son. The difference between the fortunes of father and son is the measure of the happy change introduced by the rule of Theodoric.

In some subordinate capacity in the King's final Court of Appeal (probably as *Referendarius*[2]) Cyprian has hitherto had the duty of stating the cases of the hostile litigants. He has shown wonderful dexterity in suddenly stating the same case from the two oppo-

---

[1] 'Vir quidem abjectis temporibus ad excubias tamen Palatinas electus.' The time of Odovacar's government is here alluded to (see viii. 17). An Opilio, probably father of the one here mentioned, was Consul under Valentinian III in 453.

[2] Anonymus Valesii says: 'Cyprianus, qui tunc Referendarius erat postea Comes Sacrarum et Magister,' § 85.

site points of view[1], and this so as to satisfy even the requirements of the litigants themselves.

Often the King has transacted business in his rides which used of old to be brought before a formal Consistory. He has mounted his horse, when weary with the cares of the Republic, to renew his vigour by exercise and change of scene. In these rides he has been accompanied by Cyprian, who has in such a lively manner stated the cases which had come up on appeal, that an otherwise tedious business was turned into a pleasure. Even when the King was most moved to wrath by what seemed to him a thoroughly bad cause, he still appreciated the charm of the Advocate's style in setting it before him. Thus has Cyprian had that most useful of all trainings, action, not books.

Thus prepared he was sent on an embassy to the East, a commission which he discharged with conspicuous ability. Versed in three languages (Greek, Roman, Gothic ?), he found that Greece had nothing to show him that was new; and as for subtlety, he was a match for the keenest of the Greeks. The Emperor's presence had nothing in it to make him hesitating or confused. Why should it, since he had seen and pleaded before Theodoric[2]?

In addition to all these other gifts he possesses *faith*, that anchor of the soul amidst the waves of a stormy world.

He is therefore called upon to assume at the third Indiction [524-525] the office of Count of the Sacred Largesses, and exhorted to bear himself therein worthily

---

[1] 'Nam cum oratoribus sit propositum diu tractata unius partis vota dicere, tibi semper necesse fuit repentinum negotium utroque latere declarare.'

[2] 'Talibus igitur institutis edoctus, Eoae sumpsisti legationis officium, missus ad summae quidem peritiae viros: sed nulla inter eos confusus es trepidatione *quia nihil tibi post nos potuit esse mirabile.* Instructus enim trifariis linguis, non tibi Graecia quod novum ostentaret invenit; nec ipsâ quâ nimium praevalet, te transcendit argutiâ.'

of his parentage and his past career, that the King may afterwards promote him to yet higher honour.

[For further remarks on this letter—a very important one, as bearing on the trial of Boethius—see viii. 16. The third Indiction might mean either 509-510 or 524-525; but the statement of 'Anomymus Valesii,' that Cyprian was still only Referendarius at the time of his accusation of Albinus, warrants us in fixing on the later date. This makes the encomiums conferred in this letter more significant, since they must have been bestowed *after* the delation against Albinus and Boethius. Probably it was during Cyprian's embassy to Constantinople (described in this letter) that he discovered these intrigues of the Senators with the Byzantine Court, which he denounced on his return.]

42. KING THEODORIC TO MAXIMUS, VIR ILLUSTRIS, CONSUL.

[Flavius Anicius Maximus was Consul A.D. 523.]

Rewards to performers in the Amphitheatre.

'If singers and dancers are to be rewarded by the generosity of the Consul, *à fortiori* should the *Venator*, the fighter with wild beasts in the amphitheatre, be rewarded for *his* endeavours to please the people, who after all are secretly hoping to see him killed. And what a horrible death he dies—denied even the rites of burial, disappearing before he has yet become a corpse into the maw of the hungry animal which he has failed to kill. These spectacles were first introduced as part of the worship of the Scythian Diana, who was feigned to gloat on human gore. The ancients called her the triple deity, Proserpina-Luna-Diana. They were right in one point; the goddess who invented these games certainly reigned *in hell*.'

The Colosseum (the Amphitheatre of Titus) is described.

The combats with wild beasts are pourtrayed in a style of pompous obscurity. We may dimly discern the form of the *bestiarius*, who is armed with a wooden spear; of another who leaps into the air to escape the beast's onset; of one who protects himself with a portable wall of reeds, 'like a sea-urchin;' of others who are fastened to a revolving wheel, and alternately brought within the range of the animal's claws and borne aloft beyond his grasp. 'There are as many perilous forms of encounter as Virgil described varieties of crime and punishment in Tartarus. Alas for the pitiable error of mankind! If they had any true intuition of Justice, they would sacrifice as much wealth for the preservation of human life as they now lavish on its destruction.' ['A noble regret,' says Gregorovius ('Geschichte der Stadt Rom.' i. 286), 'in which in our own day every well-disposed Minister of a military state will feel bound to concur with Cassiodorus.']

43. KING THEODORIC TO TRANSMUND [THRASAMUND], KING OF THE VANDALS (CIR. 511).

Complains of the protection given by Thrasamund to Gesalic.

'Having given you our sister, that singular ornament of the Amal race, in marriage, in order to knit the bonds of friendship between us, we are amazed that you should have given protection and support to our enemy Gesalic [natural son of Alaric II]. If it was out of mere pity and as an outcast that you received him into your realm, you ought to have kept him there; whereas you have sent him forth furnished with large supplies of money to disturb the peace of our Gaulish Provinces. This is not the conduct of a friend, much less of a relative. We are sure that you cannot have taken counsel in this matter with your wife, who would neither have liked to see her brother injured, nor the fair fame of her husband tarnished by such doubtful intrigues. We send you A and B as our ambassadors, who will speak to you further on this matter.'

44. King Theodoric to Transmund [Thrasamund], King of the Vandals.

Reconciliation between Theodoric and Thrasamund.

'You have shown, most prudent of Kings, that wise men know how to amend their faults, instead of persisting in them with that obstinacy which is the characteristic of brutes. In the noblest and most truly kinglike manner you have humbled yourself to confess your fault in reference to the reception of Gesalic, and to lay bare to us the very secrets of your heart in this matter. We thank you and praise you, and accept your purgation of yourself from this offence with all our heart. As for the presents sent us by your ambassadors, we accept them with our minds, but not with our hands. Let them return to your Treasury (cubiculum), that it may be seen that it was simply love of justice, not desire of gain, which prompted our complaints. We have both acted in a truly royal manner [1]. Let your frankness and our contempt of gold be celebrated through the nations. It is sweeter to us to return these presents to you, than to receive much larger ones from anyone else. Your ambassadors carry back with them the fullest salutation of love from your friend and ally.'

---

[1] 'Fecimus utrique regalia.'

BOOK VI.

CONTAINING TWENTY-FIVE FORMULAE[1].

1. FORMULA OF THE CONSULSHIP.

Consul-ship.

'In old days the supreme reward of the Consulship was given to him who, by his strong right hand, had delivered the Republic. The mantle embroidered with palms of victory[2], the privilege of giving his name to the year and of enfranchising the slave, even power over the lives of his fellow-citizens, were rightly given to a man to whom the Republic owed so much. He received the axe—the power of life and death—but bound up in the bundle of rods, in order that the necessary delay in undoing these might prevent him from striking the irrevocable stroke without due consideration. Whence also he received the name of Consul, because it was his duty to *consult* for the good of his country. He was bound to spend money freely; and thus he who had shed the blood of the enemies of Rome made the lives of her children happy by his generosity.

'But now take this office under happier circumstances, since we have the labours of the Consul, you the joys of his dignity. Your palm-embroidered robes therefore

---

[1] For the reasons which induced Cassiodorus to compile the two books of Formulae, see his Preface (translated, p. 138).

[2] 'Palmata vestis.'

are justified by our victories, and you, in the prosperous hour of peace, confer freedom on the slave, because we by our wars are giving security to the Romans. Therefore, for this Indiction, we decorate you with the ensigns of the Consulship.

'Adorn your broad shoulders[1] with the variegated colours of the palm-robe; ennoble your strong hand with the sceptre of victory[2]. Enter your private dwelling having even your sandals gilded; ascend the curule chair by the many steps which its dignity requires: that thus you, a subject and at your ease, may enjoy the dignity which we, the Ruler, assumed only after mightiest labours. You enjoy the fruit of victory who are ignorant of war; we, God helping us, will reign; we will consult for the safety of the State, while your name marks the year. You overtop Sovereigns in your good fortune, since you wear the highest honours, and yet have not the annoyances of ruling. Wherefore pluck up spirit and confidence. It becometh Consuls to be generous. Do not be anxious about your private fortune, you who have elected to win the public favour by your gifts. It is for this cause [because the Consul has to spend lavishly during his year of office] that we make a difference between your dignity and all others. Other magistrates we appoint, even though they do not ask for the office. To the Consulship we promote only those who are candidates for the dignity, those who know that their fortunes are equal to its demands; otherwise we might be imposing a burden rather than a favour. Enjoy therefore, in a becoming manner, the honour which you wished for. This mode of spending money is a legitimate form of canvassing[3]. Be illustrious in the world, be prosperous in your own life, leave an example for the happy imitation of your posterity.'

[1] 'Pinge vastos humeros vario colore palmatae.'
[2] 'Validam manum victoriali scipione nobilita.'
[3] 'Hic est ambitus qui probatur;' or, 'allowable bribery.'

2. Formula of the Patriciate.

Patriciate.

'In olden times the Patricians were said to derive their origin from Jupiter, whose priests they were. Mythology apart, they derived their name from *Patres*, the dignity of priest having blended itself with that of Senator.

'The great distinction of the Patriciate is that it is a rank held *for life*, like that of the priesthood, from which it sprang. The Patrician takes precedence of Praefects and all other dignities save one (the Consulship), and that is one which we ourselves sometimes assume.

'Ascend then the pinnacle of the Patriciate. You may have yet further honours to receive from us, if you bear yourself worthily in this station.'

3. Formula of the Praetorian Praefecture.

[On account of the importance of the office a translation of the whole formula is here attempted, though with some hesitation on account of its obscure allusions.]

Praetorian Praefecture.

'If the origin of any dignity can confer upon it special renown and promise of future usefulness, the Praetorian Praefecture may claim this distinction, illustrated as its establishment was by the wisdom of this world, and also stamped by the Divine approval. For when Pharaoh, King of Egypt, was oppressed by strange visions of future famine, there was found a blessed man, even Joseph, able to foretell the future with truth, and to suggest the wisest precautions for the people's danger. He first consecrated the insignia of this dignity; he in majesty entered the official chariot[1], raised to this height of honour, in order that his wisdom might confer bless-

---

[1] 'Ipse carpentum reverendus ascendit.' The *carpentum* was one great mark of the dignity of the Praetorian Praefect, as of his inferior, the Praefectus Urbis.

ings on the people which they could not receive from the mere power of the Ruler.

'From that Patriarch is this officer now called *Father of the Empire*; his name is even to-day celebrated by the voice of the crier, who calls upon the Judge to show himself not unworthy of his example. Rightly was it felt that he to whom such power was committed should always be thus delicately reminded of his duty.

'For some prerogatives are shared in common between ourselves and the holder of this dignity. [The next sentence[1] I leave untranslated, as I am not sure of the meaning. Manso (p. 343) translates it, 'He forces fugitives from justice, without regard to the lapse of time, to come before his tribunal.'] He inflicts heavy fines on offenders, he distributes the public revenue as he thinks fit, he has a like power in bestowing rights of free conveyance[2], he appropriates unclaimed property, he punishes the offences of Provincial Judges, he pronounces sentence by word of mouth [whereas all other Judges had to read their decisions from their tablets].

'What is there that he has not entrusted to him whose very speech is Judgment? He may almost be said to have the power of making laws, since the reverence due to him enables him to finish law-suits without appeal.

'On his entrance into the palace he, like ourselves, is adored by the assembled throng[3], and an office of such high rank appears to excuse a practice which in other cases would be considered matter for accusation[4].

'In power, no dignity is his equal. He judges everywhere as the representative of the Sovereign[5]. No

[1] 'Exhibet enim sine praescriptione longinquos.'
[2] 'Evectiones,' free passes by the *Cursus Publicus*.
[3] 'Ingressus palatium nostra consuetudine frequenter adoratur.' We know from Lydus (De Mag. ii. 9) that the highest officers of the army *knelt* at the entrance of the Praetorian Praefect. Perhaps we need not infer from this passage that Oriental *prostration* was used either towards Theodoric or his Praefect.
[4] 'Et tale officium morem videtur solvere, quod alios potuit accusare.'
[5] 'Vice sacrâ ubique judicat.'

soldier marks out to him the limits of his jurisdiction, except the official of the Master of the Soldiery. I suppose that the ancients wished [even the Praefect] to yield something to those who were to engage in war on behalf of the Republic.

'He punishes with stripes even the Curials, who are called in the laws a Lesser Senate.

'In his own official staff (officium) he is invested with peculiar privileges; since all men can see that he lays his commands on men of such high quality that not even the Judges of Provinces may presume to look down upon them. The staff is therefore composed of men of the highest education, energetic, strong-minded[1], intent on prompt obedience to the orders of their head, and not tolerating obstruction from others. To those who have served their time in his office, he grants the rank of Tribunes and Notaries, thus making his attendants equal to those who, mingled with the chiefs of the State, wait upon our own presence.

'We joyfully accomplish that which he arranges, since our reverence for his office constrains us to give immediate effect to his decrees. He deserves this at our hands, since his forethought nourishes the Palace, procures the daily rations of our servants, provides the salaries even of the Judges themselves[2]. By his arrangements he satiates the hungry appetites of the ambassadors of the [barbarous] nations[3]. And though other dignities have their specially defined prerogatives, by him everything that comes within the scope of our wisely-tempered sway is governed.

'Take therefore, from this Indiction, on your shoulders the noble burden of all these cares. Administer it with

---

[1] 'Officium plane geniatum, efficax, instructum et totâ animi firmitate praevalidum.'

[2] 'Humanitates quoque judicibus ipsis facit.'

[3] 'Legatos gentium voraces explet ordinationibus suis.' *Voraces* seems to give a better sense than the other reading, *veraces*.

vigour and with utmost loyalty, that your rule may be prosperous to us and useful to the Republic. The more various the anxieties, the greater your glory. Let that glory beam forth, not in our Palace only, but be reflected in far distant Provinces. Let your prudence be equal to your power; yea, let the fourfold virtue [of the Platonic philosophy] be seated in your conscience. Remember that your tribunal is placed so high that, when seated there, you should think of nothing sordid, nothing mean. Weigh well what you ought to say, seeing that it is listened to by so many. Let the public records contain nothing [of your saying] which any need blush to read. The good governor not only has no part nor lot in injustice; unless he is ever diligently doing some noble work he incurs blame even for his inactivity. For if that most holy author [Moses?] be consulted, it will be seen that it is a kind of priesthood to fill the office of the Praetorian Praefecture in a becoming manner.'

4. Formula of the Praefecture of the City.

Praefecture of the City.

'You, to whose care Rome is committed, are exalted by that charge to a position of the highest dignity. The Senate also is presided over by you; and the Senators, who wield full power in that assembly, tremble when they have to plead their own cause at your tribunal. But this is because they, who are the makers of laws, are subject to the laws; and so are we too, though not to a Judge.

'Behave in a manner worthy of your high office. Treat the Consulars with deference. Put away every base thought when you cross the threshold of every virtue. If you wish to avoid unpopularity, avoid receiving bribes. It is a grand thing when it can be said that Judges will not accept that which thousands are eager to offer them.

'To your care is committed not only Rome herself

(though Rome includes the world[1]), but, by ancient law, all within the hundredth milestone.

'You judge, on appeal, causes brought from certain Provinces defined by law. Your staff is composed of learned men; eloquent they can hardly help being, since they are always hearing the masters of eloquence. You ride in your *Carpentum* through a populace of nobles[2]; oh, act so as to deserve their shouts of welcome! How will you deserve their favour? By seeing that merchandise is sold without venality[3]; that the fires kindled to heat the wholesome baths are not chilled by corruption; that the games, which are meant for the pleasure of the people, are not by partisanship made a cause of strife. For so great is the power of glorious truth, that even in the affairs of the stage justice is desired[4]. Take then the robe of Romulus, and administer the laws of Rome. Other honours await you if you behave worthily in this office, and above all, if you win the applause of the Senate.'

5. FORMULA OF THE QUAESTORSHIP.

[This letter is particularly interesting, from the fact that it describes Cassiodorus' own office, that which he filled during many years of the reign of Theodoric, and in virtue of which he wrote the greater part of his 'Various Letters.']

Quaestorship.

'No Minister has more reason to glory in his office than the Quaestor, since it brings him into constant and intimate communication with Ourselves. The Quaestor has to learn our inmost thoughts, that he may utter

---

[1] 'Quamvis in illa contineantur universa.'

[2] 'Carpento veheris per nobilem plebem.'

[3] i.e. probably, 'that you are not bribed by monopolists.' Perhaps there is a reference to the *Annona Publica*.

[4] 'Tanta est enim vis gloriosae veritatis, ut etiam in rebus scenicis aequitas desideretur.'

them to our subjects. Whenever we are in doubt as to any matter we ask our Quaestor, who is the treasure-house of public fame, the cupboard of laws; who has to be always ready for a sudden call, and must exercise the wonderful powers which, as Cicero has pointed out, are inherent in the art of an orator. He should so paint the delights of virtue and the terrors of vice, that his eloquence should almost make the sword of the magistrate needless.

'What manner of man ought the Quaestor to be, who reflects the very image of his Sovereign? If, as is often our custom, we chance to listen to a suit, what authority must there be in his tongue who has to speak the King's words in the King's own presence? He must have knowledge of the law, wariness in speech, firmness of purpose, that neither gifts nor threats may cause him to swerve from justice. For in the interests of Equity we suffer even ourselves to be contradicted, since we too are bound to obey her. Let your learning be such that you may set forth every subject on which you have to treat, with suitable embellishments.

'Moved therefore by the fame of your wisdom and eloquence, we bestow upon you, by God's grace, the dignity of the Quaestorship, which is the glory of letters, the temple of *civilitas*, the mother of all the dignities, the home of continence, the seat of all the virtues.

'To you the Provinces transmit their prayers. From you the Senate seeks the aid of law. You are expected to suffice for the needs of all who seek from us the remedies of the law. But when you have done all this, be not elated with your success, be not gnawed with envy, rejoice not at the calamities of others; for what is hateful in the Sovereign cannot be becoming in the Quaestor.

'Exercise the power of the Prince in the condition of a subject; and may you render a good account to the Judges at the end of your term of office.'

6. Formula of the Magisterial Dignity, and its Excellency (Magister Officiorum).

[The dignity and powers of the Master of the Offices were continually rising throughout the Fourth and Fifth Centuries at the cost of the Praetorian Praefect, many of whose functions were transferred to the Master.]

Mastership of the Offices.

'The Master's is a name of dignity. To him belongs the discipline of the Palace; he calms the stormy ranks of the insolent Scholares [the household troops, 10,000 in number, in the palace of the Eastern Emperor, according to Lydus (ii. 24)]. He introduces the Senators to our presence, cheers them when they tremble, calms them when they are speaking, sometimes inserts a word or two of his own, that all may be laid in an orderly manner before us. It rests with him to fix a day for the admission of a suitor to our *Aulicum Consistorium*, and to fulfil his promise. The opportune velocity of the post-horses [the care of the *Cursus Publicus*] is diligently watched over by him[1].

'The ambassadors of foreign powers are introduced by him, and their *evectiones* [free passes by the postal-service] are received from his hands[2].

'To an officer with these great functions Antiquity gave great prerogatives: that no Provincial Governor should assume office without his consent, and that appeals should come to him from their decisions. He has no charge of collecting money, only of spending it. It is his to appoint *peraequatores*[3] of provisions in the capital, and a Judge to attend to this matter. He also superintends the pleasures of the people, and is

---

[1] According to Lydus (ii. 10), the Cursus Publicus was transferred from the Praefect to the Master, and afterwards, in part, retransferred to the Praefect.

[2] 'Per eum nominis nostri destinatur evectio.' The above is a conjectural translation.

[3] Are these Superintendents of the Markets, charged with the regulation of prices?

bound to keep them from sedition by a generous exhibition of shows. The members of his staff, when they have served their full time, are adorned with the title of *Princeps*, and take their places at the head of the Praetorian cohorts and those of the Urban Praefecture [the officials serving in the bureaux of those two Praefects]—a mark of favour which almost amounts to injustice, since he who serves in one office (the Master's) is thereby put at the head of all those who have been serving in another (the Praefect's)[1].'

[We learn from Lydus how intense was the jealousy of the grasping and aspiring *Magistriani* felt by the Praefect's subordinates; and we may infer from this passage that Cassiodorus thought that there was some justification for this feeling.]

'The assistant (Adjutor) of the Magister is also present at our audiences, a distinguished honour for his chief.

'Take therefore this illustrious office and discharge it worthily, that, in all which you do, you may show yourself a true Magister. If *you* should in anywise go astray (which God forbid), where should morality be found upon earth?'

7. Formula of the Office of Comes Sacrarum Largitionum.

'Yours is the high and pleasing office of administering the bounty of your Sovereign[2]. Through you we dispense our favours and relieve needy suppliants on New Year's Day. It is your business to see that our face

(margin: Office of Count of Sacred Largesses.)

---

[1] 'Miroque modo inter Praetorianas cohortes et Urbanae Praefecturae milites videantur invenisse primatum, a quibus tibi humile solvebatur obsequium. Sic in favore magni honoris injustitia quaedam a legibus venit, dum alienis excubiis praeponitur, qui alibi militasse declaratur.'

[2] 'Regalibus magna profecti felicitas *militare* donis ... Laetitia publica *militia* tua est.' Observe the continued use of military terms for what we call the Civil Service.

is imprinted on our coins, a reminder to our subjects of our ceaseless care on their behalf, and a memorial of our reign to future ages.

'To this your regular office we also add the place of *Primicerius* [*Primicerius Notariorum* ?], so that you are the channel through which honours as well as largesses flow. Not only the Judges of the Provinces are subject to you, even the *Proceres Chartarum* (?) have not their offices assured to them till you have confirmed the instrument. You have also the care of the royal robes. The sea-coasts and their products, and therefore merchants, are under your sway. The commerce of salt, that precious mineral, rightly classed with silken robes and pearls, is placed under your superintendence.

'Take therefore these two dignities, the Comitiva Sacrarum Largitionum and the Primiceriatus. If some of the ancient privileges of your office have been retrenched [some functions, probably, taken from the Comes Sacrarum Largitionum and assigned to the Comes Patrimonii], comfort yourself with the thought that you have two dignities instead of one.'

8. Formula of the Office of Comes Privatarum, and its Excellency.

Office of Count of Private Domains.

'Your chief business, as the name of your office implies, is to govern the royal estates by the instrumentality of the *Rationales* under you.

'This work alone, however, would have given you a jurisdiction only over slaves [those employed on the royal domains]; and as a slave is not a person in the eye of the law, it seemed unworthy of the dignity of Latium to confine your jurisdiction to these men. Some urban authority has therefore been given you in addition to that which you exercise over these boors: cases of incest, and of pollution or spoliation of graves, come before you. Thus the chastity of the living and the security of the dead are equally your care. In the Provinces you superintend the tribute-collectors (Canonicarios), you admonish the cultivators of the soil (Possessores), and you claim for the Royal Exchequer property to which no heirs are forthcoming[1]. Deposited monies also, the owners of which are lost by lapse of time, are searched out by you and brought into our Exchequer, since those who by our permission enjoy all their own property ought willingly and without sense of loss to offer us that which belongs to other men.

'Take then the honour of *Comes Privatarum*: it also is a courtly dignity, and you will augment it by your worthy fulfilment of its functions.'

9. FORMULA OF THE OFFICE OF COUNT OF THE PATRIMONY, AND ITS EXCELLENCY.

'To our distant servants we send long papers with instructions as to their conduct; but you, admitted to our daily converse, do not need these. You are to undertake the care of our royal patrimony.

Office of Count of the Patrimony.

'Do not give in to all the suggestions of our servants on these domains, who are apt to think that everything is permitted them because they represent the King; but rather incline the scale against them. You will have to act much in our sight; and as the rising sun discloses the true colours of objects, so the King's constant presence reveals the Minister's character in its true light. Avoid loud and harsh tones in pronouncing your decisions: when we hear you using these, we shall know that you are in the wrong. External acts and bodily qualities show the habit of the mind. We know a proud man by his swaggering gait, an angry one by his flashing eyes, a crafty one by his

---

[1] 'Caduca bona non sinis esse vacantia.'

downcast look, a fickle one by his wandering gaze, an avaricious one by his hooked nails.

'Take then the office of Count of the Patrimony, and discharge it uprightly. Be expeditious in your decisions on the complaints of the tillers of the soil. Justice speedily granted is thereby greatly enhanced in value, and though it is really the suitor's right it charms him as if it were a favour.

'Attend also to the provision of suitable delicacies for our royal table. It is a great thing that ambassadors coming from all parts of the world should see rare dainties at our board, and such an inexhaustible supply of provisions brought in by the crowds of our servants that they are almost ready to think the food grows again in the kitchen, whither they see the dishes carried with the broken victuals. These banqueting times are, and quite deservedly, your times for approaching us with business, when no one else is allowed to do so.'

10. FORMULA BY WHICH MEN ARE MADE PROCERES PER CODICILLOS VACANTES.

[Bestowal of Brevet-rank on persons outside the Civil Service.]

Codicilli Vacantes.

'There are cases in which men whom it is desirable for the Sovereign to honour are unable, from delicate health or slender fortunes, to enter upon an official career. For instance, a poor nobleman may dread the expenses of the Consulship; a man illustrious by his wisdom may be unable to bear the worries of a Praefecture; an eloquent tongue may shun the weight of a Quaestorship. In these cases the laws have wisely ordained that we may give such persons the rank which they merit by *Codicilli Vacantes*. It must always be understood, however, that in each dignity those who thus obtain it rank behind those who have earned it by actual service. Otherwise we should have all men flocking into these quiet posts, if the workers were not preferred to men of leisure [1].

'Take therefore, by these present codicils, the rank which you deserve, though you have not earned it by your official career.'

11. Formula by which the Rank of an Illustris and the Title of a Comes Domesticorum are Conferred, without Office.

'The bestowal of honour, though it does not change the nature of a man, induces him to consider his own reputation more closely, and to abstain from that which may stain it [2].

'Take therefore the rank (without office) of an Illustrious Count of the Domestics [3], and enjoy that greatest luxury of worthy minds—power to attend to your own pursuits.

'For what can be sweeter than to find yourself honoured when you enter the City, and yet to be able to cultivate your own fields; to abstain from fraudful gains, and yet see your barns overflowing with the fruit of your own sweet toil?

'But even as the seed and the soil must co-operate to produce the harvest, so do we sow in you the seed of this dignity, trusting that your own goodness of heart will give the increase.'

Illustratus Vacans.

12. Formula for the Bestowal of a Countship of the First Order, without Office.

[A similar honour to that which is conferred on an English statesman who, without receiving any place in the Ministry, is 'sworn of the Privy Council.']

---

[1] 'Alioqui omnes ad quietas possunt currere dignitates, si laborantes minime praeferantur ociosis.'

[2] 'Noblesse oblige.'

[3] 'Cape igitur ... Comitivae Domesticorum Illustratum Vacantem.'

Comitiva Primi Ordinis.

'It is a delightful thing to enjoy the pleasures of high rank without having to undergo the toils and annoyances of office, which often make a man loathe the very dignity which he eagerly desired.

'The rank of *Comes* is one which is reached by Governors (Rectores) of Provinces after a year's tenure of office, and by the Counsellors of the Praefect, whose functions are so important that we look upon them as almost Quaestors.

'Their rank[1] gives the holder of it, though only a *Spectabilis*, admission to our Consistory, where he sits side by side with all the Illustres.

'We bestow it upon you, and name you a *Comes Primi Ordinis*, thereby indicating that you are to take your place at the head of all the other Spectabiles and next after the Illustres. See that you imitate the latter, and that you are not surpassed in excellence of character by any of those below you.'

13. Formula for Bestowing the [Honorary] Rank of Master of the Bureau [Magister Scrinii] and Count of the First Order, on an Officer of the Courts (Comitiacus) in Active Service.

Honorary promotion for a Comitiacus.

'Great toils and great perils are the portion of an officer of the Courts in giving effect to their sentences. It is easy for the Judge to say, "Let so and so be done;" but on the unhappy officer falls all the difficulty and all the odium of doing it. He has to track out offenders and hunt them to their very beds, to compel the contumacious to obey the law, to make the proud learn their equality before it. If he lingers over the business assigned to him, the plaintiff complains; if he is energetic, the defendant calls out. The very honesty with which he addresses himself to the work is sure

---

[1] Betokened by the expression 'Ociosum cingulum.'

to make him enemies, enemies perhaps among powerful persons, who next year may be his superiors in office, and thus subjects him to all sorts of accusations which he may find it very hard to disprove. In short, if we may say it without offence to the higher dignitaries, it is far easier to discharge without censure the functions of a Judge than those of the humble officer who gives effect to his decrees.

'Wherefore, in reward for your long and faithful service, and in accordance with ancient usage, we bestow on you the rank of a Count of the First Order, and ordain that if anyone shall molest you on account of your acts done in the discharge of your duties, he shall pay a fine of so many [perhaps ten = £400] pounds of gold.'

[This letter will be found well worth studying in the original, as giving a picture of the kind of opposition met with by the men who were charged with the execution of the orders of the Rectores Provinciarum, and whose functions were themselves partly judicial, varying between those of a Master in Chancery and those of a Sheriff's officer. Throughout, the Civil Service is spoken of in military language. The officer is called *miles*, and his duty is *excubiae*.]

14. FORMULA BESTOWING RANK AS A SENATOR.

Senatorial rank. 'We desire that our Senate should grow and flourish abundantly. As a parent sees the increase of his family, as a husbandman the growth of his trees with joy, so we the growth of the Senate. We therefore desire that Graius should be included in that virtuous and praiseworthy assembly[1]. This is a new kind of graft-

---

[1] A conjectural translation of 'Sic nos virtutum jucundissimas laudes incinctum Graium desideramus includere.' Perhaps 'incinctum' means, 'though *not* girded with the belt of office.' Graium must surely be a proper name, and this document is therefore, strictly speaking, not a 'Formula.'

ing, in which the less noble shoot is grafted on to the nobler stock. As a candle shines at night, but pales in the full sunlight, so does everyone, however illustrious by birth or character, who is introduced into your majestic body. Open your Curia, receive our candidate. He is already predestined to the Senate upon whom we have conferred the dignity of the Laticlave.'

15. FORMULA OF THE VICARIUS OF THE CITY OF ROME.

Vicariate of the City of Rome.

'Though nominally only the agent of another [the Praefectus Urbi] you have powers and privileges of your own which almost entitle you to rank with the Praefects. Suitors plead before you in causes otherwise heard only before Praefects[1]; you pronounce sentence in the name of the King[2] [not of the Praefect]; and you have jurisdiction even in capital cases. You wear the chlamys, and are not to be saluted by passers-by except when thus arrayed, as if the law wished you to be always seen in military garb. [The chlamys was therefore at this time a strictly military dress.] In all these things the glory of the Praefecture seems to be exalted in you, as if one should say, "How great must the Praefect be, if his Vicar is thus honoured!" Like the highest dignitaries you ride in a state carriage[3]. You have jurisdiction everywhere within the fortieth milestone from the City. You preside over the games at Praeneste, sitting in the Consul's seat. You enter the Senate-house itself, that palace of liberty[4]. Even Senators and Consulars have to make their request to you, and may be injured by you.

'Take therefore this dignity, and wield it with moderation and courage.'

---

[1] 'Partes apud te sub Praetoriana advocatione confligunt' (?).
[2] 'Vice sacrâ sententiam dicis.'
[3] 'Carpentum.'
[4] 'Aula libertatis.'

16. Formula of the Notaries.

'It is most important that the secrets of the Sovereign, Notaries. which many men so eagerly desire to discover, should be committed to persons of tried fidelity. A good secretary should be like a well-arranged *escritoire*, full of information when you want it, but absolutely silent at other times. Nay, he must even be able to dissimulate his knowledge, for keen questioners can often read in the face what the lips utter not. [Cf. the description of the Quaestor Decoratus in v. 3.]

'Our enquiries, keen-scented as they are for all men of good life and conversation, have brought your excellent character before us. We therefore ordain that you shall henceforth be a Notary. In due course of service you will attain the rank of Primicerius, which will entitle you to enter the Senate, "the Curia of liberty." Moreover, should you then arrive at the dignity of Illustris or at the [Comitiva] Vacans, you will be preferred to all who are in the same rank but who have not acquired it by active service[1].

'Enter then upon this duty, cheered by the prospect of one day attaining to the highest honours.'

17. Formula of the Referendarii.

[We have no word corresponding to this title. Registrar, Referendarii. Referee, Solicitor, each expresses only part of the duties of the Referendarius, whose business it was, *on behalf of the Court*, to draw up a statement of the conflicting claims of the litigants before it. See the interesting letters (v. 40 and 41) describing the useful services rendered in this capacity by Cyprian in the King's

---

[1] I think this must be the meaning of the sentence: 'Additur etiam perfuncti laboris aliud munus, ut si quo modo ad Illustratum vel Vacantem meruerit pervenire, omnibus debeat anteponi, qui Codicillis Illustratibus probantur ornari.'

Court of Appeal. His duties seem to have been very similar to those which in the Court of the Praetorian Praefect were discharged by the officer called *Ab Actis* (See p. 107).]

'Great is the privilege of being admitted to such close converse with the King as you will possess, but great also are the responsibilities and the anxieties of the Referendarius. In the midst of the hubbub of the Court he has to make out the case of the litigant, and to clothe it in language suitable for our ears. If he softens it down ever so little in his repetition of it, the claimant declares that he has been bribed, that he is hostile to his suit. A man who is pleading his own cause may soften down a word or two here and there, if he see that the Court is against him; but the Referendarius dares not alter anything. Then upon him rests the responsibility of drawing up our decree, adding nothing, omitting nothing. Hard task to speak *our* words in our own presence.

'Take then the office of Referendarius, and show by your exercise of it to what learning men may attain by sharing our conversation. Under us it is impossible for an officer of the Court to be unskilled in speech. Like a whetstone we sharpen the intellects of our courtiers, and polish them by practice at our bar[1].'

18. FORMULA OF THE PRAEFECTUS ANNONAE, AND HIS EXCELLENCY.

Praefectus Annonae.

'If the benefit of the largest number of citizens is a test of the dignity of an office yours is certainly a glorious one. You have to prepare the Annona of the sacred City, and to feed the whole people as at

---

[1] 'Sub nobis enim non licet esse imperitos; quando in vicem cotis ingenia splendida reddimus, quae causarum assiduitate polimus.' Strange words to put into the mouth of a monarch who could not write.

one board. You run up and down through the shops of the bakers, looking after the weight and fineness of the bread, and not thinking any office mean by which you may win the affections of the citizens.

'You mount the chariot of the Praefect of the City, and are displayed in closest companionship with him at the games. Should a sudden tumult arise by reason of a scarcity of loaves, you have to still it by promising a liberal distribution. It was from his conduct in this office that Pompey attained the highest dignities and earned the surname of the Great.

'The pork-butchers also (Suarii) are subject to your control.

'It is true that the corn is actually provided by the Praetorian Praefect, but you see that it is worked up into elegant bread[1].

'Even so Ceres discovered corn, but Pan taught men how to bake it into bread; whence its name (*Panis*, from Pan).

'Take then this office: discharge it faithfully, and weigh, more accurately than gold, the bread by which the Quirites live.'

19. Formula of the Count of the Chief Physicians.

'The doctor helps us when all other helpers seem to fail. By his art he finds out things about a man of which he himself is ignorant; and his prognosis of a case, though founded on reason, seems to the ignorant like prophecy. (Comes Archiatrorum.)

'It is disgraceful that there should be a president of the lascivious pleasures of the people (Tribunus Voluptatum) and none of this healing art. Excellent

---

[1] 'Quando in quavis abundantia querela non tollitur, si panis elegantia nulla servetur.'

too may your office be in enabling you to control the squabbles of the doctors. They ought not to quarrel. At the beginning of their exercise of their art they take a sort of priestly oath to hate wickedness and to love purity. Take then this rank of Comes Archiatrorum, and have the distinguished honour of presiding over so many skilled practitioners and of moderating their disputes.

'Leave it to clumsy men to ask their patients "if they have had good sleep; if the pain has left them." Do you rather incline the patient to ask you about his own malady, showing him that you know more about it than he does. The patient's pulse, the patient's water, tell to a skilled physician the whole story of his disease.

'Enter our palace unbidden; command us, whom all other men obey; weary us if you will with fasting, and make us do the very opposite of that which we desire, since all this is your prerogative.'

20. FORMULA OF THE OFFICE OF A CONSULAR, AND ITS EXCELLENCY.

Consularis.

'You bear among your trappings the axes and the rods of the Consul, as a symbol of the nature of the jurisdiction which you exercise in the Provinces.

'In some Provinces you even wear the *paenula* (military cloak) and ride in the *carpentum* (official chariot), as a proof of your dignity.

'You must not think that because your office is allied to that of Consul any lavish expenditure by way of largesse is necessary. By no means; but it is necessary that you should abstain from all unjust gains. Nothing is worse than a mixture of rapacity and prodigality.

'Respect the property of the Provincials, and your tenure of office will be without blame.

'Receive therefore, for this Indiction, the office of Consular in such and such a Province, and let your moderation appear to all the inhabitants.'

21. Formula of the Governor (Rector) of a Province.

[The distinction between the powers of a Rector and those of a Consularis seems to have been very slight, if it existed at all; but the dignity of the latter office was probably somewhat the greater.]

'It is important to repress crime on the spot. If all criminal causes had to wait till they could be tried in the capital, robbers would grow so bold as to be intolerable. Hence the advantage of Provincial Governors. Receive then for this Indiction the office of Rector of such and such a Province. Look at the broad stripe (laticlave) on your purple robe, and remember the dignity which is betokened by that bright garment, which poets say was first woven by Venus for her son Priapus, that the son's beautiful robe might attest the mother's loveliness. *[Rector Provinciae.]*

'You have to collect the public revenues, and to report to the Sovereign all important events in your Province. You may judge even Senators and the officers of Praefects. Your name comes before that of even dignified Provincials, and you are called Brother by the Sovereign. See that your character corresponds to this high vocation. Your subjects will not fear you if they see that your own actions are immoral. There can be no worse slavery than to sit on the judgment-seat, knowing that the men who appear before you are possessors of some disgraceful secret by which they can blast your reputation.

'Refrain from unholy gains, and we will reward you all the more liberally.'

22. Formula of the Count of the City of Syracuse.

Comitiva Syracusana.

'We must provide such Governors for our distant possessions that appeals from them shall not be frequent. Many men would rather lose a just cause than have the expense of coming all the way from Sicily to defend it; and as for complaints against a Governor, we should be strongly inclined to think that a complaint presented by such distant petitioners must be true.

'Act therefore with all the more caution in the office which we bestow upon you for this Indiction. You have all the pleasant pomp of an official retinue provided for you at our expense. Do not let your soldiers be insolent to the cultivators of the soil (possessores). Let them receive their rations and be satisfied with them, nor mix in matters outside their proper functions. Be satisfied with the dignity which your predecessors held. It ought not to be lowered; but do not seek to exalt it.'

23. Formula of the Count of Naples.

Comitiva Neapolitana.

'As the sun sends forth his rays so we send out our servants to the various cities of our dominions, to adorn them with the splendour of their retinue, and to facilitate the untying of the knots of the law by the multitude of jurisconsults who follow in their train. Thus we sow a liberal crop of official salaries, and reap our harvest in the tranquillity of our subjects. For this Indiction we send you as Count to weigh the causes of the people of Naples. It is a populous city, and one abounding in delights by sea and land. You may lead there a most delicious life, if your cup be not mixed with bitterness by the criticisms of the citizens on your judgments. You will sit on a jewelled tribunal, and the Praetorium will be filled with your officers; but you will also be surrounded by a multitude of fastidious spectators, who assuredly, in their conversation, will judge the Judge. See then that you walk warily. Your power extends for a certain distance along the coast, and both the buyer and seller have to pay you tribute. We give you the chance of earning the applause of a vast audience: do you so act that your Sovereign may take pleasure in multiplying his gifts.'

24. FORMULA ADDRESSED TO THE GENTLEMEN-FARMERS (OR THE TITLED CULTIVATORS) AND COMMON COUNCILMEN[1] OF THE CITY OF NAPLES [AND SURROUNDING DISTRICT].

'You pay us tribute, but we have conferred honours upon you. We are now sending you a Comes [the one appointed in the previous formula], but he will be a terror only to the evil-disposed. Do you live according to reason, since you are reasonable beings, and then the laws may take holiday. Your quietness is our highest joy[2].' *Honorati Possessores et Curiales Civitatis Neapolitanae.*

25 is entitled, 'FORMULA DE COMITIVA PRINCIPIS MILITUM;' but this is evidently an inaccurate, or at least an insufficient title.

The letter, though very short, is obscure. *Doubtful.*
It starts with the maxim that every staff of officials ought to have its own Judge[3], and then, apparently,

---

[1] An attempt to translate 'Honoratis possessoribus et curialibus civitatis Neapolitanae.'

[2] 'Erit nostrum gaudium vestra quies . . . Degite moribus compositis, ut vivatis legibus feriatis.'

[3] 'Omnes apparitiones decet habere judices suos. Nam cui praesul adimitur et militia denegatur.'

proceeds to make an exception to this rule by making the persons addressed—the civil or military functionaries of Naples—subject to the Comes Neapolitanus who was appointed by the Twenty-third Formula. No reason is given for this exception, except an unintelligible one about preserving the yearly succession of Judges[1]; but the persons are assured that their salaries shall be safe[2].

[1] 'Ut judicibus annuâ successione reparatis, vobis solennitas non pereat actionis.'
[2] 'Vos non patimur emolumentorum commoda perdere.'

BOOK VII.

CONTAINING FORTY-SEVEN FORMULAE.

---

1. FORMULA OF THE COUNT OF A PROVINCE.

Comitiva Provinciae.

'YOUR dignity, unlike that of most civil officers, is guarded by the sword of war. See however that this terrible weapon is only drawn on occasions of absolute necessity, and only wielded for the punishment of evil-doers. Anyone who is determining a case of life and death should decide slowly, since any other sentence is capable of correction, but the dead man cannot be recalled to life. Let the ensigns of your power be terrible to drivers-away of cattle, to thieves and robbers; but let innocence rejoice when she sees the tokens of approaching succour. Let no one pervert your will by bribes: the sword of justice is sheathed when gold is taken. Receive then for this Indiction the dignity of Count in such and such a Province. So use your power that you may be able to defend your actions when reduced to a private station, though indeed, if you serve us well in this office, we are minded to promote you to yet higher dignities.'

2. FORMULA OF A PRAESES.

[The Praeses had practically the same powers as the Consularis (v. 20) and the Rector (v. 21), but occupied a less dignified position, being only a 'Perfectissimus,' not a 'Clarissimus[1].']

Praesidatus. 'It has been wisely ordered by the Ancients that a Provincial Governor's term of office should be only annual. Thus men are prevented from growing arrogant by long tenure of power, and we are enabled to reward a larger number of aspirants. Get through one year of office if you can without blame: even that is not an easy matter. It rests then with us to prolong the term of a deserving ruler[2], since we are not keen to remove those whom we feel to be governing justly. Receive then for this Indiction the Praesidatus of such and such a Province, and so act that the tiller of the soil (possessor) may bring us thanks along with his tribute. Follow the good example of your predecessors: carefully avoid the bad. Remember how full your Province is of nobles, whose good report you may earn but cannot compel. You will find it a delightful reward, when you travel through the neighbouring Provinces, to hear your praises sounded there where your power extends not. You know our will: it is all contained in the laws of the State. Govern in accordance with these, and you shall not go unrewarded.'

3. FORMULA OF THE COUNT OF THE GOTHS IN THE SEVERAL PROVINCES.

Comitiva Gothorum per singulas Provincias. [Dahn remarks ('Könige der Germanen' iv. 157): 'We must go thoroughly into the question of this office. The *Comes Gothorum* is the most important, in fact almost the only new dignity in the Gothic State, and the formula of his installation is the chief proof of the coexistence of Roman and Gothic law in this kingdom.' I have therefore translated this formula at full length.]

---

[1] See p. 92.

[2] 'Nostrum est merentibus tempus augere.' The limit of one year might therefore be exceeded by favour of the Sovereign.

'As we know that, by God's help, Goths are dwelling intermingled among you, in order to prevent the trouble (indisciplinatio) which is wont to arise among partners (consortes) we have thought it right to send to you as Count, A B, a sublime person, a man already proved to be of high character, in order that he may terminate (amputare) any contests arising between two Goths according to our edicts; but that, if any matter should arise between a Goth and a born Roman, he may, after associating with himself a Roman jurisconsult[1], decide the strife by fair reason[2]. As between two Romans, let the decision rest with the Roman examiners (cognitores), whom we appoint in the various Provinces; that thus each may keep his own laws, and with various Judges one Justice may embrace the whole realm. Thus, sharing one common peace, may both nations, if God favour us, enjoy the sweets of tranquillity.

'Know, however, that we view all [our subjects] with one impartial love; but he may commend himself more abundantly to our favour who subdues his own will into loving submission to the law[3]. We like nothing that is disorderly[4]; we detest wicked arrogance and all who have anything to do with it. Our principles lead us to execrate violent men[5]. In a dispute let laws decide, not the strong arm. Why should men seek by choice violent remedies, when they know that the Courts of Justice are open to them? It is for this cause that we pay the Judges their salaries, for this that we maintain such large official staffs with all their privileges, that we may not allow anything to grow up among you which may tend towards hatred. Since you see that one lordship (imperium)

---

[1] 'Adhibito sibi prudente Romano.'   [2] 'Aequabili ratione.'
[3] 'Qui leges moderatâ voluntate dilexerit.' To translate this literally might give a wrong idea, because with us 'to love the law' means to be litigious.
[4] 'Non amamus aliquid incivile.'
[5] 'Violentos nostra pietas execratur.'

is over you, let there be also one desire in your hearts, to live in harmony.

'Let both nations hear what we have at heart. You [oh Goths!] have the Romans as neighbours to your lands: even so let them be joined to you in affection. You too, oh Romans! ought dearly to love the Goths, who in peace swell the numbers of your people and in war defend the whole Republic[1]. It is fitting therefore that you obey the Judge whom we have appointed for you, that you may by all means accomplish all that he may ordain for the preservation of the laws; and thus you will be found to have promoted your own interests while obeying our command.'

4. Formula of the Duke of Raetia.

Ducatus Raetiarum.

'Although promotion among the *Spectabiles* goes solely by seniority, it is impossible to deny that those who are employed in the border Provinces have a more arduous, and therefore in a sense more honourable, office than those who command in the peaceful districts of Italy. The former have to deal with war, the latter only with the repression of crime. The former hear the trumpet's clang, the latter the voice of the crier.

'The Provinces of Raetia are the bars and bolts of Italy. Wild and cruel nations ramp outside of them, and they, like nets, whence their name[2], catch the Barbarian in their toils and hold him there till the hurled arrow can chastise his mad presumption.

'Receive then for this Indiction the *Ducatus Raetiarum*. Let your soldiers live on friendly terms with the Provincials, avoiding all lawless presumption; and at

---

[1] 'Vos autem, Romani, magno studio Gothos diligere debetis, qui et in pace numerosos vobis populos faciunt, et universam Rempublicam per bella defendunt.'

[2] Raetia, from *rete*, a net.

the same time let them be constantly on their guard against the Barbarians outside. Even bloodshed is often prevented by seasonable vigilance.'

5. Formula of the Palace Architect.

'Much do we delight in seeing the greatness of our Kingdom imaged forth in the splendour of our palace. *Cura Palatii.*

'Thus do the ambassadors of foreign nations admire our power, for at first sight one naturally believes that as is the house so is the inhabitant.

'The Cyclopes invented the art of working in metal, which then passed over from Sicily to Italy.

'Take then for this Indiction the care of our palace, thus receiving the power of transmitting your fame to a remote posterity which shall admire your workmanship. See that your new work harmonises well with the old. Study Euclid—get his diagrams well into your mind; study Archimedes and Metrobius.

'When we are thinking of rebuilding a city, or of founding a fort or a general's quarters, we shall rely upon you to express our thoughts on paper [in an architect's design]. The builder of walls, the carver of marbles, the caster of brass, the vaulter of arches[1], the plasterer, the worker in mosaic, all come to you for orders, and you are expected to have a wise answer for each. But, then, if you direct them rightly, while theirs is the work yours is all the glory.

'Above all things, dispense honestly what we give you for the workmen's wages; for the labourer who is at ease about his victuals works all the better.

'As a mark of your high dignity you bear a golden wand, and amidst the numerous throng of servants walk first before the royal footsteps [i.e. last in the procession

---

[1] 'Camerarum rotator.'

and immediately before the King], that even by your nearness to our person it may be seen that you are the man to whom we have entrusted the care of our palaces.'

6. Formula of the Count of the Aqueducts.

<small>Comitiva Formarum Urbis.</small>
'Though all the buildings of Rome are wonderful, and one can scarce for this reason say which are the chief among them, we think a distinction may be drawn between those which are reared only for the sake of ornament and those which also serve a useful purpose. Thus, however often one sees the Forum of Trajan, it always seems a wonder[1]. To stand on the lofty Capitol is to see all other works of the human intellect surpassed. And yet neither of these great works touches human life, nor ministers to health or enjoyment. But in the Aqueducts of Rome we note both the marvel of their construction and the rare wholesomeness of their waters. When you look at those rivers, led as it were over piled up mountains, you would think that their solid stony beds were natural channels, through so many ages have they borne the rush of such mighty waters. And yet even mountains are frequently undermined, and let out the torrents which have excavated them; while these artificial channels, the work of the ancients, never perish, if reasonable care be taken of their preservation.

'Let us consider how much that wealth of waters adds to the adornment of the City of Rome. Where would be the beauty of our *Thermae*, if those softest waters were not supplied to them?

'Purest and most delightful of all streams glides along the *Aqua Virgo*, so named because no defilement ever stains it. For while all the others, after heavy rain

---

[1] 'Trajani Forum vel sub assiduitate videre miraculum est.'

show some contaminating mixture of earth, this alone by its ever pure stream would cheat us into believing that the sky was always blue above us. Ah! how express these things in words worthy of them? The *Aqua Claudia* is led along on the top of such a lofty pile that, when it reaches Mount Aventine, it falls from above upon that lofty summit as if it were watering some lowly valley. It is true that the Egyptian Nile, rising at certain seasons, brings its flood of waters over the land under a cloudless sky; but how much fairer a sight is it to see the Roman Claudia flowing with a never-failing stream over all those thirsty mountain tops, and bringing purest water through a multitude of pipes to so many baths and houses. When Nile retreats he leaves mud behind him; when he comes unexpectedly he brings a deluge. Shall we not then boldly say that our Aqueducts surpass the famous Nile, which is so often a terror to the dwellers on his banks either by what he brings or by what he leaves behind him? It is in no spirit of pride that we enumerate these particulars, but in order that you may consider how great diligence should be shown by you to whom such splendid works are entrusted.

'Wherefore, after careful consideration, we entrust you for this Indiction with the *Comitiva Formarum*, that you may zealously strive to accomplish what the maintenance of such noble structures requires. Especially as to the hurtful trees which are the ruin of buildings, [inserting their roots between the stones and] demolishing them with the destructiveness of a battering-ram: we wish them to be pulled up by the roots, since it is no use dealing with an evil of this kind except in its origin. If any part is falling into decay through age, let it be repaired at once: the first expense is the least. The strengthening of the Aqueducts will constitute your best claim on our favour, and will be the surest means of establishing your own fortune.

Act with skill and honesty, and let there be no corrupt practices in reference to the distribution of the water.'

7. FORMULA OF THE PRAEFECT OF THE WATCH OF THE CITY OF ROME.

Praefectus Vigilum Urbis Romae.

'Your office, exercised as it is in the City itself, and under the eyes of Patricians and Consuls, is sure to bring you renown if you discharge its duties with diligence. You have full power to catch thieves, though the law reserves the right of punishing them for another official, apparently because it would remember that even these detestable plunderers are yet Roman citizens. Take then for this Indiction the *Praefectura Vigilum*. You will be the safety of sleepers, the bulwark of houses, the defence of bolts and bars, an unseen scrutineer, a silent judge, one whose right it is to entrap the plotters and whose glory to deceive them. Your occupation is a nightly hunting, most feared when it is not seen. You rob the robbers, and strive to circumvent the men who make a mock at all other citizens. It is only by a sort of sleight of hand that you can throw your nets around robbers; for *it* is easier to guess the riddles of the Sphinx than to detect the whereabouts of a flying thief. He looks round him on all sides, ready to start off at the sound of an advancing footstep, trembling at the thought of a possible ambush. How can one catch him who, like the wind, tarries never in one place? Go forth, then, under the starry skies; watch diligently with all the birds of night, and as they seek their food in the darkness so do you therein hunt for fame.

'Let there be no corruption, no deeds of darkness which the day need blush for. Do this, and you will have our support in upholding the rightful privileges of yourself and your staff.'

8. Formula of the Praefect of the Watch of the City of Ravenna.

Praefectus Vigilum Urbis Ravennatis.

Contains the same topics as the preceding formula, rather less forcibly urged, and with no special reference to the City of Ravenna.

An exhortation at the end not to be too hasty, nor to shed blood needlessly, even when dealing with thieves.

9. Formula of the Count of Portus.

Comitiva Portus Urbis Romae.

'It is a service of pleasure rather than of toil to hold the dignity of Comes in the harbour of the City of Rome, to look forth upon the wide sail-traversed main, to see the commerce of all the Provinces tending towards Rome, and to welcome travellers arriving with the joy of ended peril. Excellent thought of the men of old to provide two channels by which strangers might enter the Tiber, and to adorn them with those two stately cities [Portus and Ostia], which shine like lights upon the watery way!

'Do you therefore, by your fair administration, make it easy for strangers to enter. Do not grasp at more than the lawful dues; for the greedy hand closes a harbour, and extortion is as much dreaded by mariners as adverse winds. Receive then for this Indiction the *Comitiva Portus*; enjoy the pleasures of the office, and lay it down with increased reputation.'

10. Formula of the Tribunus Voluptatum.

Tribunus Voluptatum.

[Minister of public amusements, the Roman equivalent to our 'Lord Chamberlain' in that part of his office which relates to the control of theatres.]

'Though the wandering life of the stage-player seems

as if it might run to any excess of licence, Antiquity has wisely provided that even it should be under some sort of discipline. Thus respectability governs those who are not respectable, and people who are themselves ignorant of the path of virtue are nevertheless obliged to live under some sort of rule. Your place, in fact, is like that of a guardian; as he looks after the tender years of his ward, so you bridle the passionate pleasures of your theatrical subjects.

'Therefore, for this Indiction, we appoint you Tribune of [the people's] Pleasures. See that order is observed at the public spectacles: they are not really popular without this. Keep your own high character for purity in dealing with these men and women of damaged reputation, that men may say, "Even in promoting the pleasures of the people he showed his virtuous disposition."

'It is our hope that through this frivolous employment you may pass to more serious dignities.'

11. Formula of the Defensor of any City.

Defensor cujuslibet Civitatis. [Observe that the Defensor has power to fix prices, in addition to his original function of protecting the commonalty from oppression.]

'The number of his clients makes it necessary for the representative of a whole city to be especially wary in his conduct.

'At the request of your fellow-citizens we appoint you, for this Indiction, Defensor of such and such a city. Take care that there be nothing venal in your conduct. Fix the prices for the citizens according to the goodness or badness of the seasons, and remember to pay yourself what you have prescribed to others. A good Defensor allows his citizens neither to be oppressed by the laws nor harassed by the dearness of provisions.'

12. Formula of the Curator of a City.

[The Defensor and Curator had evidently almost equivalent powers, but with some slight difference of dignity. They cannot both have existed in the same city. It would be interesting to know what decided the question whether a city should have a Defensor or a Curator.]

Curator Civitatis.

This formula differs very little from the preceding, except that the new officer is told 'wisely to govern the ranks of the Curia.' Stress is again laid on the regulation of prices: 'Cause moderate prices to be adhered to by those whom it concerns. Let not merchandise be in the sole power of the sellers, but let an agreeable equability be observed in all things. This is the most enriching kind of popularity, which is derived from maintaining moderation in prices[1]. You shall have the same salary (consuetudines) which your predecessors had in the same place.'

13. Formula of the Count of Rome.

'If even bolts and bars cannot secure a house from robbery, much more do the precious things left in the streets and open spaces of Rome require protection. I refer to that most abundant population of statues, to that mighty herd of horses [in stone and metal] which adorn our City. It is true that if there were any reverence in human nature, it, and not the watchman, ought to be the sufficient guardian of the beauty of Rome[2]. But what shall we say of the marbles, precious both by material and workmanship, which many a hand longs, if it has opportunity, to pick out of their settings? Who

Comitiva Romana.

---

[1] 'Opulentissima siquidem et hinc gratia civium colligitur, si pretia sub moderatione serventur.'

[2] 'Si esset humanis rebus ulla consideratio Romanam pulchritudinem non vigiliae sed sola deberet reverentia custodire.'

when entrusted with such a charge can be negligent? who venal? We entrust to you therefore for this Indiction the dignity of the Comitiva Romana, with all its rights and just emoluments. Watch for all such evil-doers as we have described. Rightly does the public grief[1] punish those who mar the beauty of the ancients with amputation of limbs, inflicting on them that which they have made our monuments to suffer. Do you and your staff and the soldiers at your disposal watch especially by night; in the day the City guards itself. At night the theft looks tempting; but the rascal who tries it is easily caught if the guardian approaches him unperceived. Nor are the statues absolutely dumb; the ringing sound which they give forth under the blows of the thief seems to admonish their drowsy guardian. Let us see you then diligent in this business, that whereas we now bestow upon you a toilsome dignity, we may hereafter confer an honour without care.'

14. Formula of the Count of Ravenna.

Comitiva Ravennatis.

'High is your honour, to be the means of taking away all slowness from the execution of our orders. Who knows not what a quantity of ships you can muster at the least hint from us! Scarcely is the ink dry on the *evectio* [permission to use the public post] prepared by some palace dignitary, when already with the utmost speed it is by you being carried into effect. Do not exact too much service from merchants[2], nor yet from corrupt motives let them off too easily. Be very careful in your judicial capacity, and especially when trying the causes of the poor, to whom a small error in your judgment may be far more disastrous than to the rich.'

---

[1] 'Quia juste tales persequitur publicus dolor.'

[2] 'Negociatorum operas consuetas nec nimias exigas, nec venalitate derelinquas.' Apparently then a certain amount of forced labour could be claimed from the owners of merchant-vessels by the Count of Ravenna.

15. Formula addressed to the Praefect of the City on the Appointment of an Architect.

Architectus Publicorum.

'It is desirable that the necessary repairs to this forest of walls and population of statues which make up Rome should be in the hands of a learned man who will make the new work harmonise with the old. Therefore for this Indiction we desire your Greatness to appoint A B Architect of the City of Rome. Let him read the books of the ancients; but he will find more in this City than in his books. Statues of men, showing the muscles swelling with effort, the nerves in tension, the whole man looking as if he had grown rather than been cast in metal. Statues of horses, full of fire, with the curved nostril, with rounded tightly-knit limbs, with ears laid back—you would think the creature longed for the race, though you know that the metal moves not. This art of statuary the Etruscans are said to have practised first in Italy; posterity has embraced it, and given to the City an artificial population almost equal to its natural one. The ancients speak of the wonders of the world [here enumerated and described], but this one of the City of Rome surpasses them all. It had need to be a learned man who is charged with the care of upholding all these works; else, in his despair, he will deem himself the man of stone, and the statues about him the truly living men.'

16. Formula of the Count of the Islands of Curritana and Celsina.

Comitiva Insulae Curritanae et Celsinae.

[Celsina, from the place in which it is mentioned in the 'Itinerary' of Antonine (516), was probably one of the Lipari Islands. Curritana must have been near it, but is not further identified.]

'The presence of a ruler is necessary; and it is not desirable that men should live without discipline, according to their own wills. We therefore appoint you Judge of these two islands. For it is right that someone should go to the habitations of these men, who are shut out from converse with the rest of their kind, and settle their differences by fair reason.

'Oh ye inhabitants of these islands, ye now know whom our Piety has set over you, and we shall expect you to obey him.'

17. FORMULA CONCERNING THE PRESIDENT OF THE LIME-KILNS.

Praepositus Calcis.

'It is a glorious labour to serve the City of Rome. It cannot be doubted that lime (coctilis calx), which is snow-white and lighter than sponge, is useful for the mightiest buildings. In proportion as it is itself disintegrated by the application of fire does it lend strength to walls; a dissolvable rock, a stony softness, a sandy pebble, which burns the best when it is most abundantly watered, without which neither stones are fixed nor the minute particles of sand hardened.

'Therefore we set you, well known for your industry, over the burning and distribution of lime, that there may be plenty of it both for public and private works, and that thereby people may be put in good heart for building. Do this well, and you shall be promoted to greater things.'

18. FORMULA CONCERNING ARMOURERS.

Armorum Factores.

'Good arms are of the utmost importance to a community. By means of them man, the frailest of creatures, is made stronger than monstrous beasts. Phoroneus is said to have first invented them, and brought them to Juno to consecrate them by her divinity.

'For this Indiction we set you over the soldiers and workmen in our armouries. Do not presume in our absence to pass bad workmanship. We shall find out by diligent search all that you do, and in such a matter as this consider no mistake venial.'

19. Formula addressed to the Praetorian Praefect concerning the Armourers.

Announces to the Praefects the appointment conferred in the preceding letter, and repeats that to supply inferior arms to soldiers is an act of treason. The workmen are to receive their just *consuetudines* [wages].

Ad Praefectum Praetorio de Armorum Factoribus.

20 and 21. Formula as to the Collection of Bina and Terna:

(1) *If collected by the Judge himself;*
(2) *If collected by his Officium.*

These *Bina* and *Terna*, as stated in the note to iii. 8, are a mystery. All that can be positively stated about them is that they were a kind of land-tax, collected from the cultivators (possessores), and that they had to be brought into the Treasury by the first of March in each year. Under the first formula the Judex himself, under the second two *Scriniarii* superintend the collection, reporting to the Count of Sacred Largesses. As in the previous letter (iii. 8), the Judex is reminded that if there is any deficiency he will have to make it good himself. Cf. Manso, ' Geschichte des Ostgothischen Reiches' 388; and Sartorius, 'Regierung der Ostgothen' 207 and 347.

Binorum et Ternorum: (xx.) si per Judicem aguntur; (xxi.) si per Officium aguntur.

22. Formula of Exhortation addressed to the two Scriniarii referred to in Formula 21.

'Your day of promotion is come. Proceed to such and such a Province, in order that you may assist the Judex and his staff in collecting the *Bina* and *Terna* before the first of March, and may forward them without delay

Commonitorium illi et illi Scriniariis.

to the Count of Sacred Largesses. Let there be no extortion from the cultivator, no dishonest surrender of our rights.'

23. FORMULA OF THE VICARIUS OF PORTUS.

Vicarius Portus.
'Great prudence is necessary in your office, since discords easily arise between two nationalities. Therefore you must use skill to soothe those [the Greek merchants and sailors from the Levant] whose characters are unstable as the winds, and who, unless you bring their minds into a state of calm, will, with their natural quickness of temper, fly out into the extremity of insolence.'

24. FORMULA OF THE PRINCEPS OF DALMATIA.

Princeps Dalmatiarum.
[The Princeps, as observed on p. 96, seems to have practically disappeared from the Officium of the Praefectus Praetorio. Here, however, we find a Provincial Princeps whose rank and functions are not a little perplexing. It seems probable that, while still nominally only the chief of a staff of subordinates, he may, owing to the character of the superior under whom he served, have practically assumed more important functions. That superior in this case was a Comes, whose military character is indicated by the first letter of this book. The Princeps was therefore virtually the Civil Assessor of this officer.

The Comes under Theodoric would generally be a Goth; the Princeps must be a Roman and a Jurisconsult. The business of the former was war and administration; that of the latter, judgment, though his decisions were apparently pronounced by the mouth of the Comes, his superior in rank.]

'Whosoever serves while bearing the title of Princeps has high pre-eminence among his colleagues. To the

Consul of the Provinces power is given, but to you the Judge himself is entrusted. Without you there is no access to the Secretarium, nor is the ceremony of salutation[1] [by subordinate officers] performed. You hold the vine-rod[2] which menaces the wicked; you have the right, withheld from the Governor himself, of punishing the insolence of an orator pleading in his Court. The records of the whole suit have to be signed by you, and for this your consent is sought after the will of the Judge has been explained.'

25. FORMULA RECOMMENDING THE PRINCIPES[3] TO THE COMES.

Ad Commendandos Comiti Principes.

'It is our glory to see you [a Goth, one of our own nation] accompanied by a Roman official staff. Acting through such Ministers, your power seems to be hallowed by the sanction of Antiquity.

'For to this point, by God's help, have we brought our Goths, that they should be both well-trained in arms and attuned to justice. It is this which the other races cannot accomplish; this that makes you unique among the nations, namely, that you, who are accustomed to war, are seen to live obedient to the laws side by side with the Romans. Therefore from out of our *Officium* we have decided to send A and B to you, that according to ancient custom, while forwarding the execution of your commands they may bring those commands into conformity with the mind of past ages[4].'

---

[1] 'Pompa osculationis.' Another reading is 'Pompa postulationis.'

[2] 'Tu vitem tenes improbis minantem.' The allusion is to the vine-bough, which was used in scourging. The alternative reading, *vitam*, does not seem to give so good a sense.

[3] Plural. Apparently, therefore, each Count had more than one Princeps, perhaps one for each large city in his Province.

[4] 'Rationabili debeant antiquitate moderari.' Perhaps we might translate, 'with the Common Law.'

26. Formula of the Countship of the Second Rank in Divers Cities [1].

Comitiva diversarum civitatum.

For the sentences, more than usually devoid of meaning, in which Cassiodorus dilates on Free-will, Justice, and the mind of man, it may be well to substitute Manso's description of this dignity (p. 379):

'By the title of a Count of the Second Order the Judges in little towns appear chiefly to have been rewarded and encouraged. Those named for it, however, can hardly have received any great distinction or especial privileges, for Cassiodorus not only enumerates no civic advantages thus secured to them, but expressly says, "We intend to bestow better things than this upon you, if you earn our approbation in your present office." He does not use this language to those adorned with the *Comitiva Primi Ordinis*.'

27. Formula addressed to the Dignified Cultivators and Curiales [2].

Honorati Possessores et Curiales.

'As one must rule and the rest obey, we have for this Indiction conferred the Countship of your City on A B, that he may hear your causes and give effect to our orders.'

[Apparently this letter and the preceding relate to the same appointment. The words 'secundi ordinis' are not added to the title of the new Count when his fellow-citizens are informed of it.]

28. Formula announcing the Appointment of a Comes to the Chief of his Staff [3].

Princeps Militum Comitivae.

'Judge and Court Officer (Praesul and Miles) are terms which involve one another. The officers of the

---

[1] The title runs thus (in Nivellius' Edition): 'Formula Comitivae Honorum Scientiae Ordinis diversarum Civitatum.' I do not know what is meant by 'Honorum Scientiae.' Can 'Scientiae' be a transcriber's blunder for 'secundi?'   [2] Cf. vi. 24.

[3] This must, I think, be the meaning; but it is hard to extract it from the words 'Formula Principis Militum Comitivae.'

Court have no right to exist, without the Judge; he is powerless without them to execute his commands. We therefore think it well to inform you of our appointment of A B as Count over your body[1]. It is no light benefit that so long as you attend to your duty[2] you are allowed to elect the examiners.'

29. Formula concerning the Guard at the Gates of a City.

De Custodiendis Portis Civitatis.

'We entrust to you an important office, the care of the gate of such and such a city. Do not keep it always shut—that were to turn the city into a prison; nor let it always lie open—then the walls are useless. Use your own judgment, but remember that the gate of a city is like the jaws of the human body, through which provisions enter to nourish it.'

30. Formula of the Tribunate in the Provinces.

Tribunatus Provinciarum.

'It is right that one who has served his time in civil employment should receive his reward, and we therefore appoint as your Tribune the man who has a right to the office by seniority. You are to obey him, since officers of this kind partake of the nature of Judges [governors], as they are called to account for any excesses committed by you.'

[Who this Tribune was—since the *Tribunus Voluptatum* is apparently out of the question—and how

---

[1] 'Comitem Militiae Vestrae.'

[2] 'Nec istud leve credatis beneficium, ut cum vos scitis obsequium, vobis occurrat electio cognitorum.' For Cognitores, see vii. 3. These Cognitores had virtually the decision of all 'issues of fact,' and consequently their nomination was a very important matter. I think the meaning of this passage is: 'I, the King, appoint the *Comes* (= Judex), and graciously inform you of my decision. But you (the Officium) have the privilege—and it is no small one—of electing the *Cognitores*.'

his jurisdiction fitted in to that of other officers, Manso (p. 362) deems it impossible to decide, nor can I offer any suggestion.]

31. Formula of the Princeps of the City of Rome.

Formula Principatus Urbis Romae.

'As there must be the *Officium* of a Count in Rome, and as we want to have our chief Princeps[1] near us [in Ravenna], we wish you to take his place and wield power as his *Vicarius* in Rome.

'If you think that any of the *Comitiaci* ought to be sent to attend our Comitatus [at Ravenna], do so at your own discretion, retaining those whom you think proper to retain at Rome. Let there be an alternation, however, that one set of men be not worn out with continuous labour, while the others are rusting in idleness.'

32. Formula of the Master of the Mint.

Formula qua Moneta Committitur.

'Great is the crime of tampering with the coinage; a crime against the many—whose buying and selling is disturbed by it; and a crime and a sacrilege against us, whose image is impressed on the coins.

'Let everything be pure and unalloyed which bears the impress of our Serenity. Let the flame of gold be pale and unmixed, let the colour of silver smile with its gracious whiteness, let the ruddy copper retain its native glow.

'Coins are to keep their full weight. They used to pass current by weight, not by tale, whence the words for profit and expenditure[2]. *Pecunia* was named from cattle (pecus). You must see that our money does not return to this low condition. King

---

[1] 'Principem nostrum *cardinalem*' (observe this use of the word).
[2] 'Compendium et dispendium' (from *pendere*, to weigh).

Servius first used stamped money. Take then the care of the mint; hold it for five years, and be very careful how you administer it.'

33. Formula respecting the Ambassadors of Various Nations.

'Since it is important that when ambassadors return to their country they should feel that they have been well treated in ours, hand the enclosed *douceur* (humanitas), and a certain quantity of fodder for their horses, to the ambassadors of such and such a nation. Nothing pleases those who have commenced their return journey better than speeding them on their way.' Formula Legatorum Gentium Diversarum.

34. Formula of Summons to the King's Court (unsolicited).

'We summon you by these presents to our Comitatus, that you may have an extraordinary pleasure. Be brisk therefore, and come on such a day to such a city. Our Palace longs for the presence of good men, and God puts it into our hearts to give them a cordial reception.' Formula Evocatoria quam Princeps dirigit.

35. Formula of Summons to the Court (solicited).

'It is a sign of a good conscience to seek the presence of a just ruler; it is only good deeds that crave the light of the sun. Come then speedily. We consider our own glory augmented when we see noble men flocking to our obedience.' Formula Evocatoria quae petenti conceditur.

36. Formula granting temporary Leave of Absence.

'All men require change: even honey cloys after a time. We therefore give you leave to visit such Formula Commeatalis ad tempus.

a Province and remain there so many months, with the understanding that when they are over you return to the City. If it be tedious to live always in the City, how much more to live long in the country! But we gladly give you this holiday, not that Rome should be deserted, but that absence from her may commend her to you all the more.'

37. FORMULA CONFERRING THE RANK OF A SPECTABILIS.

Spectabilitas.

'Wishing to bestow the right honours on the right man among our subjects, we decorate you with the splendour of a *Spectabilis*, that you may know that your opinion is duly respected[1] at all public meeting-places, when you take your honoured seat among the nobles.'

38. FORMULA CONFERRING THE RANK OF A CLARISSIMUS.

Clarissimatus.

'The desire of praise is a good thing, and leads to the increase of virtue. Receive the honour of the *Clarissimatus*, as a testimony to the excellence of your past life and a pledge of your future prosperity. Observe, you are not called *Clarus*, but *Clarissimus*. Everything that is most excellent may be believed of him who is saluted by such a splendid superlative.'

39. FORMULA BESTOWING 'POLICE PROTECTION.'

Tuitio Regii nominis.

'Though it seems superfluous to grant special protection to any of our subjects, since all are shielded by the laws, yet moved by your cry for help we are willing to relieve you and to give you as a strong

---

[1] 'Spectandam,' an allusion to the derivation of *spectabilis*.

tower of defence the shelter of our name[1], into which you may retire when wounded by the assaults of your enemies. This defence will avail you alike against the hot-headed onslaughts [of the Goths] and the ruinous chicanery [of the Romans][2]; but you must beware that you, who have thus had to solicit the help of the law, do not yourself set law at defiance by refusing to appear in answer to a summons.

'That our royal protection be not a mere name, we appoint A and B to protect you by their fidelity and diligence, the former against the Goths, and the latter against the Romans[3]. If any one hereafter attempt any act of *incivilitas* against you, you will see your desire upon your enemies.'

[This important letter is commented upon at some length by Dahn ('Könige der Germanen' iii. 125–127). I am not sure that he is right in stating that *Tuitio* against a Goth would *necessarily* be given by means of a Sajo, though evidently this was often the rank of the officer employed.]

40. Formula for the Confirmation of Marriage and the Legitimation of Offspring.

De Matrimonio confirmando et liberis legitime constituendis.

'An eternal benefit is that which is bestowed on a man's offspring; and hard is the lot of him who, born with a stain on his name, finds his troubles prepared as soon as he comes forth to the light of day.

'You pray that the woman whom you have loved but not married may receive the honour of wedlock, and that your children by her may attain the name of heirs. We grant your request, and ordain that your mistress

---

[1] 'Tuitio nostri nominis.'
[2] 'Validissimam turrem contra inciviles impetus et conventionalia detrimenta.'
[3] 'Praesentis beneficii jussione adversus Gothis illa, adversus Romanos illa, facile te fides et diligentia custodiet' ('custodivit' is surely an error).

shall be your lawful wife, and the children whom you love and whom Nature has given you, your successors.'

[Some of the maxims of this letter can hardly have obtained the approval of the author after he 'entered religion.']

41. Formula conferring the Rights of Full Age.

Aetatis venia.

'An honourable boast is contained in the suit for "venia aetatis." In it a young man says, "Give me those rights which my stability of character warrants, though my age does not as yet entitle me to them."

'Thus you refuse the protection which the law throws round the years of weakness, and this is as bold a thing as any man can do. We grant your request; and if you can prove that you have come to the age at which "venia aetatis" should be asked for, we ordain that, with the proper formalities which have been of old provided in this matter [1], you shall be admitted to all the rights of an adult, and that your dispositions of property, whether in city or country, shall be held valid [2]. You must exhibit that steadfastness of character which you claim. You say that you will not be caught by the snares of designing men; and you must remember that now to deny the fulfilment of your promise will become a much more serious matter than heretofore.'

42. Formula of an Edict to the Quaestor ordering the Person who asks for the Protection of a Sajo to give Bail.

Edictum ad Quaestorem, ut ipse spondere debeat qui Sajonem meretur.

'Heavy charges are sometimes brought against the Sajones whom with the best intentions we have granted for the protection of our wealthy subjects. We are told that the valour of the Sajo is employed not merely for

---

[1] 'Ut in foro competenti ea quae in his causis reverenda legum dictat Antiquitas solenniter actitentur.'

[2] 'Ita ut in alienandis rusticis vel urbanis praediis constitutionum servitus auctoritas.'

the protection of him to whom he is assigned, but for illegal violence and rapine against that person's enemies. Thus our remedy becomes itself a disease. To guard against this perversion of our beneficent designs we ordain that anyone asking for the guardianship of a brave Sajo against violence with which he feels himself unable to cope, shall give a penal bond to our Officium, with this condition, that if the Sajo[1] who is assigned to him shall exceed our orders by any improper violence, he himself shall pay by way of fine so many pounds of gold, and shall make satisfaction for the damage sustained by his adversary as well as for the expenses of his journey [to obtain redress]. For our wish is to repress uncivil dispositions, not to injure the innocent. As for the Sajo who shall have wilfully transgressed the limit of our commands, he shall lose his donative, and —which is the heaviest of all punishments—our favour also. Nor will we entrust any further duty to him who has been the violator rather than the executor of our will.'

43. Formula approving the Appointment of a Clerk in the Record-Office.

Probatoria Cartariorum.

'At the suggestion of the Tribune of the Cartarii—to whom the whole office pays fitting reverence—we bestow upon you the title of a Cartarius. Flee avarice and avoid all unjust gains.'

[This letter gives no information as to the duties of a Cartarius, or, as he is called in the Codes, Cartularius.]

44. Formula for the Grant of Public Property on Condition of Improvement[2].

De Competitoribus.

'He who seeks to become owner of public property can only justify his claim by making the squalid beau-

---

[1] 'Sajus' in the original, and so in the next place where it occurs.

[2] Formula de Competitoribus is the somewhat obscure title of this document, which might perhaps be compared to our Commons' Enclosure Acts.

tiful, and by adorning the waste. Therefore, as you desire it, we confer upon you as your full property such and such a place, reserving all mineral rights—brass, lead, marbles—should any such be found therein; but we do this on the understanding that you will restore to beauty that which has become shabby by age and neglect. It is the part of a good citizen to adorn the face of his city, and you may securely transmit to your posterity that which your own labour has accomplished[1].'

45. FORMULA OF REMISSION OF TAXES WHERE THE TAXPAYER HAS ONLY ONE HOUSE, TOO HEAVILY ASSESSED.

Formula qua census relevetur ei qui unam casam possidet praegravatam.

'You complain that the land-tax (tributum) levied upon your holding (possessio) in such a Province is so heavy that all your means are swallowed up in the swamp of indebtedness, and that more is claimed by the tax-collectors than can be obtained from the soil by the husbandman. You might, by surrendering the property altogether, escape from this miserable necessity which is making you a slave rather than a landowner; but since the Imperial laws (sacratissimae leges) give us the power to relieve a man of moderate fortune in such circumstances, our Greatness, which always hath the cause of justice at heart, decrees by these presents that if the case be as you say, the liability for the payment of so many solidi on behalf of the aforesaid property shall be cancelled in the public archives, and that this shall be done so thoroughly that there shall be no trace of it left in any copy of the taxing-rolls by which the charge may be revived at a future day[2].'

[1] 'Securus etiam ad posteros transmissurus, quod proprio fuerit labore compositum.'

[2] 'Decernimus ut, si ita est, tot solidos tributario supradictae possessionis ... ita faciatis de vasariis publicis diligenter abradi ut hujus rei duplarum vestigium non debeat inveniri.' Cf. what is said by Evagrius (iii. 39) of the proceedings of Anastasius at the time of the abolition of the Chrysargyron.

46. Formula legitimating Marriage with a First Cousin.

Formula qua consobrina legitima fiat uxor.

'After the laws of the two tables, Moses adds the laws wherein God forbids marriages between near kindred, to guard against incest and provide for a wise admixture of divers strains of blood[1].

'These commands have been extended to remoter degrees of relationship by the wise men of old, who have however reserved to the Prince the power of granting dispensations from the rule in the cases (not likely to be frequent) where first cousins (by the mother's side) seek to intermarry.

'Acting on this wise principle we permit you to marry C D, if she is of no nearer kinship to you than first cousin. By God's favour may you have legitimate heirs from this marriage, which, our consent having been obtained, is not blameable but praiseworthy.'

47. Formula addressed to the Praetorian Praefect directing the Sale of the Property of a Curialis.

Formula ad Praefectum, ut sub decreto Curialis praedia vendat.

'It is the hard lot of human nature often to be injured by the very things which were intended as remedies. The prohibition against the sale of the property of a Curialis was intended for his protection, and to enable him fearlessly to discharge his share of the public burdens. In some cases, however, where he has contracted large debts, this prohibition simply prevents him from saving anything out of the gulf of indebtedness. You have the power, after making due enquiry into the circumstances, to authorise the sale of such a property. You have the power; but as the proceeding is an unusual one, to guard you against any odium to which it may expose you, we fortify your Eminence by this our present

---

[1] 'Ne dilationem providam in genus extraneum non haberent.'

command. Let the Curialis who petitions for this relief satisfy you as to the cause of his losses, that it may be shown that they are really the result of circumstances beyond his own control, not due to his own bad character.

'Wisely has Antiquity laid upon *you* the responsibility of deciding cases of this kind, you whose advantage lies in the maintenance of the Curia. For by whom could its burdens be borne, if the nerves of the communities should everywhere be seen to be severed [1]?'

---

[1] 'Quapropter provide vobis permisit antiquitas de illâ causa decernere, cui est utile Curiam custodire. A quibus enim munia petuerunt sustineri, si civitatum nervi passim videantur abscidi.'

BOOK VIII.

CONTAINING THIRTY-THREE LETTERS, ALL WRITTEN IN THE NAME OF ATHALARIC THE KING, EXCEPT THE ELEVENTH, WHICH IS WRITTEN IN THE NAME OF TULUM.

1. KING ATHALARIC TO THE EMPEROR JUSTIN
(A.D. 526).

The accession of Athalaric announced to the Emperor Justin.

[SOME MSS. read Justiniano, but there can be no doubt that Justino is the right reading. Athalaric's accession took place August 30, 526; the death of Justin, August 1, 527. Justinian was associated with his uncle in the Empire, April 1, 527.]

'Most earnestly do I seek your friendship, oh most clement of Princes, who are made even more illustrious by the wide extension of your favours than by the purple robe and the kingly throne. On this friendship I have an hereditary claim. My father was adorned by you with the palm-enwoven robe of the Consul [Eutharic, Consul 519] and adopted as a son in arms, a name which I, as one of a younger generation, could more fittingly receive[1]. My grandfather also received curule honours from you[2] in your city. Love and friendship

---

[1] The text is evidently corrupt here: 'Genitor meus desiderio quoque concordiae factus est per arma filius, quia unis nobis pene videbatur aequaevus.' The suggested reading, 'quamvis vobis,' does not entirely remove the difficulty.

[2] That is, of course, not from Justin himself but from his predecessors.

should pass from parents to their offspring, while hatred should be buried in the tomb; and therefore with confidence, as one who by reason of my tender years cannot be an object of suspicion to you, and as one whose ancestors you have already known and cherished, I claim from you your friendship on the same compacts and conditions on which your renowned predecessors granted it to my lord and grandfather of Divine memory[1]. It will be to me something better than dominion to have the friendship of so excellent and so mighty a ruler. My ambassadors (A and B) will open the purport of their commission more fully to your Serenity.'

2. KING ATHALARIC TO THE SENATE OF THE CITY OF ROME ON HIS ACCESSION (A.D. 526).

To the Senate.

'Great must be the joy of all orders of the State at hearing of the accession of a new ruler, above all of a peaceful succession, without war, without sedition, without loss of any kind to the Republic.

'Such has been our succession to our grandfather. On account of the glory of the Amal race, which yields to none[2], the hope of our youth has been preferred to the merits of all others. The chiefs, glorious in council and in war, have flocked to recognise us as King so gladly, so unmurmuringly, that it seems like a Divine inspiration, and the kingdom has been changed as one changes a garment.

'The institution of royalty is consolidated when power thus passes from one generation to another, and when a good prince lives again, not in statues of brass but in the lineaments and the character of his descendants.

'The general consent of Goths and Romans [at

---

[1] 'Ut amicitiam nobis illis pactis, illis conditionibus concedatis, quas cum divae memoriae domino avo nostro inclytos decessores vestros constat habuisse.'

[2] 'Quoniam quaevis claritas generis Amalis cedit.'

Ravenna] has crowned us King, and they have confirmed their allegiance by an oath. You, though separated from us by space, are, we know, as near to us in heart as they; and we call upon you therefore to follow their example. We all know that the most excellent fathers of the Senate love their King more fervently than other ranks of the State, in proportion to the greater benefits which they have received at his hand.

'And since one should never enter your Curia empty-handed, we have sent our Count, the Illustrious Sigismer, with certain persons to administer the oath to you. If you have any requests to make to us which shall be for the common benefit of the Republic, make them through him, and they are granted beforehand.'

3. KING ATHALARIC TO THE ROMAN PEOPLE (A.D. 526).

To the citizens of Rome.

'If a stranger to the royal line were succeeding to the throne, you might doubt whether the friendship between him and you would endure, and might look for a reversal of the policy of his predecessors. But now the person of the King only, not his policy, is changed. We are determined to follow the revered maxims of our predecessor, and to load with even more abundant benefits those whom he most kindly defended.

'Everything was so ordered by our glorious grandfather that on his death the glad consent of Goths called us to our kingdom; and that no doubt might remain upon the matter they pledged themselves by an oath most cordially taken, to accept us as their ruler. We invite you to follow their example, and like Trajan, we, the Sovereign, in whose name all oaths are made, will also swear to you. The bearers of this letter will receive your sworn promise, and will give you ours, "by the Lord's help to observe justice and fair clemency, the nourisher of the nations; that Goths and Romans shall meet with impartial treatment at our hands; and that there shall be no other division between the two nations, except that *they* undergo the labours of war for the common benefit, while *you* are increased in numbers by your peaceable inhabitancy of the City of Rome[1]." Raise then your spirits, and hope for even better things and more tranquillity, under God's blessing, from our reign than from that of our predecessor.'

4. KING ATHALARIC TO ALL THE ROMANS SETTLED IN ITALY AND THE DALMATIAS (A.D. 526).

To the Romans in Italy and Dalmatia.

'He who hears of a change in the ruler is apt to fear that it may be a change for the worse; and a new King who makes no kind promises at his accession is supposed to be harbouring designs of severity. We therefore inform you that we have received the oaths of Goths and Romans and are ready to receive yours, which we doubt not you will willingly offer.' [The rest as in the preceding letters.]

5. KING ATHALARIC TO ALL THE GOTHS SETTLED IN ITALY (A.D. 526).

To the Goths.

'Gladly would we have announced to you the prolonged life of our lord and grandfather; but inasmuch as he has been withdrawn by hard fate from us who loved him, he has substituted us, by Divine command, as heirs of his kingdom, that through us his successors in blood, he might make the benefits which he has conferred on you perpetual. And in truth we hope not only to defend but to increase the blessings wrought by him. All the

---

[1] 'Justitiam nos et aequabilem clementiam, quae populos nutrit, juvante domino, custodire et *Gothis Romanisque apud nos jus esse commune*, nec aliud inter vos esse divisum, nisi quod illi labores bellicos pro communi utilitate subeunt, vos autem civitatis Romanae habitatio quieta multiplicat.' I do not consider that the words in Italics, taken with the context, are irreconcilable with Dahn's view that the Goths were still, to a certain extent, under Gothic law.

Goths in the Royal City [Ravenna] have taken the oaths to us. Do you do the same by this Count whom we send to you.

'Receive then a name which ever brought prosperity to your race, the royal offshoot of the Amals, the sprout of the Balthae [1], a childhood clad in purple. Ye are they by whom, with God's help, our ancestors were borne to such a height of honour, and obtained an ever higher place amid the serried ranks of kings [2].'

6. KING ATHALARIC TO LIBERIUS, PRAETORIAN PRAEFECT OF THE GAULS (A.D. 526).

'You will be grieved to hear of the death of our lord and grandfather of glorious memory, but will be comforted in learning that he is succeeded by his descendant. Thus, by God's command, did he arrange matters, associating us as lords in the throne of his royalty, in order that he might leave his kingdom at peace, and that no revolution might trouble it after his death.'

[Invitation to take the oath, as in previous letters.]

To the Governor of Gaul.

7. KING ATHALARIC TO ALL THE PROVINCIALS SETTLED IN GAUL (A.D. 526).

'Our grandfather of glorious memory is dead, but we have succeeded him, and will faithfully repay, both on his account and our own, the loyalty of our subjects.

'So unanimous was the acclamation of our [Italian] subjects when we succeeded to the throne, that the thing seemed to be of God rather than of man.

To the Gaulish subjects of Athalaric.

---

[1] 'Amalorum regalem prosapiem, Baltheum germen.' I know not how Athalaric had any blood of the Balths in his veins. The other reading, 'blatteum,' gives the same idea as the following clause, 'infantiam purpuratam.'

[2] 'Inter tam prolixum ordinem Regum susceperunt semper augmenta.' Perhaps we should translate 'by such a long line of (Amal) kings obtained advancement for their nation;' but the meaning is not very clear.

'We now invite you to follow their example, that the Goths may give their oath to the Romans, and the Romans may confirm it by a *Sacramentum* to the Goths, that they are unanimously devoted to our King.'

'Thus will your loyalty be made manifest, and concord and justice flourish among you.'

[There is an appearance of mutuality about this oath of allegiance as between Goths and Romans, not merely by both to Athalaric, which we have not had in the previous letters.]

8. KING ATHALARIC TO VICTORINUS, VIR VENERABILIS AND BISHOP[1] (A.D. 526).

To Bishop Victorinus.

'Saluting you with all the veneration due to your character and office, we inform you with grief of the death of our lord and grandfather. But your sadness will be moderated when you hear that his kingdom is continued in us. Favour us with your prayers, that the King of Heaven may confirm to us the kingdom, subdue foreign nations before us, forgive us our sins, and propitiously preserve all that He was pleased to bestow on our ancestors. Let your Holiness exhort all the Provincials to concord.'

9. KING ATHALARIC TO TULUM, PATRICIAN.

Praises of Tulum, who is raised to the Patriciate.

'As our grandfather used to refresh his mind and strengthen his judgment by intercourse with you, so, *à fortiori*, may we in our tender years do the same. We therefore make you, by this present letter, Patrician, that the counsels which you give us may not seem to proceed from any unknown and obscure source.

'Greece adorned our hero [Tulum] with the chlamys and the painted silken buskin; and the Eastern peoples

---

[1] Baronius says (vii. 121): 'Cujusnam Ecclesiae Antistes fuerit Victorinus ignoratur.' From the tone of the letter one may conjecture that Victorinus was a Bishop in Gaul.

yearned to see him, because for some reason civic virtues are most prized in him who is believed to be of warlike disposition[1]. Contented with this repayment of honour he laboured with unwearied devotion for foreign countries (?), and with his relations (or parents) he deigned to offer his obedience to the Sovereign, who was begotten of the stock of so many Kings[2].

[After some very obscure sentences, in which the writer appears to be celebrating the praises of Theodoric, he turns to Tulum, of whom he has hitherto spoken in the third person, and addresses him as *you.*]

'His toil so formed your character that we have the less need to labour. With you he discussed the sure blessings of peace, the doubtful gains of war; and—rare boon from a wise King—to you, in his anxiety, he confidently opened all the secrets of his breast. You, however, responded fully to his trust. You never put him off with doubtful answers. Ever patient and truthful, you won the entire confidence of your King, and dared even, hardest of all tasks, to argue against him for his own good.

'Thus did your noble deeds justify your alliance with the Amal race [apparently he has received an Amal princess in marriage], and thus did you become worthy to be joined in common fame with Gensemund, a man whose praises the whole world should sing,

---

[1] Probably Tulum had gone on some embassy to Constantinople.

[2] 'Hac igitur honoris remuneratione contentus, pro exteris partibus indefessa devotione laboravit: et praestare cum suis parentibus principi dignabatur obsequium, qui tantorum regum fuerat stirpe procreatus.' This sentence is full of difficulties. What can he mean by the labour 'pro exteris partibus?' Who is the 'Princeps' whom Tulum deigns to serve: the Eastern Emperor or Theodoric? Above all, who is 'tantorum regum stirpe procreatus?' I think the turn of the sentence requires that it should be Tulum; but Dahn has evidently not so understood it, for in his Könige der Germanen (iii. 29, 30) he makes Tulum a conspicuous example of a man not of noble birth raised to high dignity, and says that the two long letters about him in the Variae contain no allusion to illustrious descent.

a man only made son by adoption in arms to the King, yet who exhibited such fidelity to the Amals that he transferred it even to their heirs, although he was himself sought for to be crowned[1]. Therefore will his fame live for ever, so long as the Gothic name endures.

'We look for even nobler things from you, because you are allied to us by race.'

[A singularly obscure, vapid, and ill-written letter. The allusion to Gensemund seems introduced on purpose to bewilder the reader.]

10. KING ATHALARIC TO THE SENATE OF THE CITY OF ROME.

[On the elevation of Tulum to the Patriciate.]

The same subject.

'We are conferring new lustre on your body by the promotion of Tulum. A man sprung from the noblest stock[2] he early undertook the duties of attendance in the King's bedchamber[3], a difficult post, where the knowledge that you share the secret counsels of royalty itself exposes you to enmity.

'In the dawn of manhood he went forth with our army to the war of Sirmium [A.D. 504], showed what one of our young nobles bred in peace could do in war, triumphed over the Huns[4], and gave to slaughter the Bulgarians, terrible to the whole world. Such warriors do even our nurseries send forth: thus does the prepa-

---

[1] 'Exstat gentis Gothicae hujus probitatis exemplum: Gensemundus ille toto orbe cantabilis, solum armis filius factus, tanta se Amalis devotione conjunxit ut haeredibus eorum curiosum exhibuerit famulatum, quamvis ipse peteretur ad regnum.' Dahn (ii. 61 and iii. 309) and Köpke (p. 142) refer this mysterious affair of Gensemund's renunciation to the interval after the death of Thorismund (A.D. 416). But this is mere conjecture. See Italy and her Invaders iii. 8-10.

[2] 'Primum, quod inter nationes eximium est, Gothorum nobilissima stirpe gloriatur.'

[3] 'Statim rudes annos ad sacri cubiculi secreta portavit.'

[4] We do not hear from the other authorities of Huns being engaged in this war. In 505 Mundo the Hun was in alliance with Theodoric against the Empire.

ration of a courageous heart supersede the necessity for martial training [1].

'Returned to the Court he became the most intimate counsellor of the King, who arranged with him all his plans for campaign, and so admitted him to his most secret thoughts that Tulum could always anticipate how Theodoric would act in every fresh conjuncture of events; and it may be said "by offering him counsel he ruled the King [2]."

'He then distinguished himself in the Gaulish campaign [A.D. 508], where he was already enrolled among the generals, directing the campaign by his prudence, and bravely sharing its dangers. In the fierce fight which was waged at Arles for the possession of the covered bridge across the Rhone [3], the bravery of our *candidatus* was everywhere conspicuous, and he received many honourable wounds, those best and most eloquent champions of a soldier's courage.

'But a general ought not to be always fighting. I have pleasure in relating his next success, which was brilliant yet achieved without bloodshed. When the Frank and Burgundian again fell out, he was sent to Gaul [A.D. 523] to defend our frontier from hostile incursion. He then obtained for the Roman Republic, without any trouble, a whole Province while others were fighting. It was a triumph without a battle, a palm-branch without toil, a victory without slaughter.

'So great were his services in this campaign that Theodoric considered that he ought to be rewarded by the possession of large lands in the district which he had added to our dominions.

'A storm overtook him on his return to Italy: the

---

[1] 'Tales mittunt nostra cunabula bellatores: sic paratae sunt manus, ubi exercetur animus.'

[2] 'Et ministrando consilium regebat ipse Rectorem.'

[3] 'Arelate est civitas supra undas Rhodani constituta, quae in Orientis prospectum tabulatum pontem per nuncupati fluminis dorsa transmittit.'

remembrance of the vanished danger of that storm is sweet to us now[1]. In the wide, foaming sea his ship was swallowed up. He had to save himself by rowing; the sailors perished; he alone with the dear pledge of his love [one child?] escaped. Theodoric rushed to the shore, and would have dashed into the waves to save his friend, but had the delight of receiving him unharmed, saved manifestly by Divine protection for his present honours.

'Favour then, Conscript Fathers, the ambition of our *candidatus*, and open for the man of our choice the Hall of Liberty[2]. The race of Romulus deserves to have such martial colleagues as Tulum.'

11. TULUM, ILLUSTRIS AND PATRICIAN, TO THE SENATE OF THE CITY OF ROME.

[Note that Cassiodorus has to provide an elegant oration not only for his master, but for this Gothic fellow-minister of State. See Dahn's remarks on the writer of this letter, 'Könige der Germanen' iii. 273.]

Tulum's address to the Senate.

'I pray you to receive favourably the order of the King which makes me a member of your body.

'I have ever favoured the dignity of the Senate, as if with a prescience that I should one day hold it. When I shared the counsels of Theodoric, that chief of Kings, of glorious memory, I often by my intercessions obtained for members of your body Consulships, Patriciates, Praefectures; and now, behold, I am similarly honoured myself. Reflect, I pray, that by my accepting it, the genius of the Patriciate is exalted, since none of my fellow-countrymen will hold cheaply that rank in you which he sees honoured in

---

[1] 'Discrimina dum feliciter cedunt, suavissimae memoriae sensum relinquunt.' Compare Claudian (De Bello Getico 207-8):

'An potius meminisse juvat semperque vicissim
Gaudia praemissi cumulant inopina dolores.'

[2] 'Favete nunc auspiciis candidati, et viris nostris libertatis atria reserate.'

me. Live in security, by the blessing of God; enjoy your prosperity with your children; and strive, now as always, to show forth the true Roman type of character. I shall defend those with whom I am now associated.'

12. KING ATHALARIC TO ARATOR, VIR ILLUSTRIS.

[Bestowing on him the rank of Comes Domesticorum.]

[I have altered the order of subjects in this letter, to make it correspond with that of time. There cannot be much doubt that Arator's *pomposa legatio* from Dalmatia was his first introduction to the Court of Theodoric, and preceded his employment as Advocatus.]

'By raising Tulum to the Patriciate we have provided for the military strength of the State. Now must we see to it that she is equally adorned by the glory of letters, and for this purpose we raise you, still in the prime of life, to the rank of *Comes Domesticorum*. By your example it was seen that eloquence could be acquired elsewhere than at Rome, since in your own Province [probably Dalmatia] your father, who was an extremely learned man, taught you to excel in this art: a happy lot for you, who obtained from your father's love that accomplishment which most youths have to acquire with terror from a master. *(Arator made Count of the Domestics.)*

'That I may say something here of a very *recherché* character[1], I may mention that, according to some, letters were first invented by Mercury, who watched the flight of cranes by the Strymon, and turned the shapes assumed by their flying squadron into forms expressive of the various sounds of the human voice.

'You were sent upon a stately embassy[2] by the Provincials of Dalmatia to our grandfather; and there, not in commonplace words but with a torrent of elo-

---

[1] 'Ut aliquid studiose exquisitum dicere videamur.'
[2] 'Juvat repetere pomposam legationem.'

quence, you so set forth their needs and the measures which would be for the advantage of the public, that Theodoric, a man of cautious temperament, listened to your flow of words without weariness, and all men desired still to listen, when you ceased speaking.

'[Since then] you have filled the office of Advocate in our Court. You might have been a trier of causes (Cognitor): you have preferred to be a pleader, though to all your advocacy you have brought so fair and judicial a mind that your eloquence and your zeal for your client have never exceeded the bounds of truth.'

13. KING ATHALARIC TO AMBROSIUS.

[Conferring on him the Quaestorship.]

[This Ambrosius, son of Faustinus, is apparently the same to whom Ennodius addressed his 'Paraenesis Didascalica,' containing some important notices of Festus, Symmachus, Boethius, Cethegus, and their contemporaries. (In Migne's 'Patrologia' lxiii. 250.)]

Ambrosius appointed Quaestor.

'A steady gradation of honours secures good servants for the State. You have already served with credit the office of Count of the Private Largesses. And you have also filled satisfactorily the place of a high official who was dismissed in disgrace[1]. We now therefore promote you to the office of Quaestor, and expect you to be the Pliny to the new Trajan. Let your eloquent tongue adorn all that we have to say, and be fearless in suggesting to us all that is for the welfare of the State. A good Sovereign always allows his ministers to speak to him on behalf of justice, while it is the sure mark of a tyrant to refuse to listen to the voice of the ancient maxims of law. Remember that celebrated saying of

---

[1] 'Gratiam quoque loci alterius invenisti. Dictationibus enim probaris adhibitus, cum sit offensionibus alter expulsus: et ita suspensum honorem tuum sustinebat ingenium, ut Palatio non sineres decesse Judicem, cujus ad tempus abrogatam cognovimus dignitatem.' I do not think we can say from this what the office temporarily filled by Arator was.

Trajan to an orator: "Plead, if I am a good ruler, for the Republic and me; if I am a bad one, for the Republic against me[1]." But remember, that if we are thus severe upon ourselves we are equally strict with regard to you, and expect you to follow the example of your noble ancestors, and to abstain from everything like an infraction of the laws. We confer upon you the insignia of the Quaestorship for this fifth Indiction' [Sept. 1, 526—Sept. 1, 527].

14. KING ATHALARIC TO THE SENATE OF THE CITY OF ROME.

[On the elevation of Ambrosius to the Quaestorship].

The same subject.

'As a kind of door to our royal favour do we appoint Ambrosius to be our Quaestor. You know his merits of old: but, to speak only of recent matters[2], we may remind you that when your hearts were wrung with grief for the death of our glorious grandfather, it was by his mouth that we assured you of our determination to continue to you the blessings of good government.

'The presence of Ambrosius is full of dignity, and has a soothing influence which the words of his speech do but confirm[3]. It is unfortunate for an orator to have eloquence for his only gift, and to have to obliterate by his oration the unfavourable effect produced on the multitude by his appearance.

'We consider it not necessary to praise his eloquence. Of course a Quaestor is eloquent. While some have the government of a Province committed to them, others

---

[1] 'Sume dicationem, si bonus fuero, pro Republica et me: si malus, pro Republica in me.'

[2] 'Quando et moderna quae loquimur.' (Notice again *moderna*.)

[3] So the contemporary poet Maximian, speaking of his own past successes as an orator, and a good-looking one, says:

'Nec minor his aderat sublimis gratia formae
Quae vel si decent cetera, muta placet.'
Elegiae i. 17–18.

the care of the Treasury, he receives the ensigns of his dignity in order that by him his Sovereign's fame may be spread abroad through the whole world.'

15. KING ATHALARIC TO THE SENATE OF THE CITY OF ROME.

[On the election of Pope Felix III, 526.]

[As this letter has an important bearing on the royal rights in connection with Papal elections, it is translated in full.]

Election of Pope Felix III (or IV).

'We profess that we hear with great satisfaction that you have responded to the judgment of our glorious lord and grandfather in your election of a Bishop. It was right in sooth to obey the will of a good Sovereign, who, handling the matter with wise deliberation, although it had reference to a form of faith alien from his own[1], thought fit to select such a Pontiff as could rightfully be displeasing to none. You may thus recognise that his one chief desire was that Religion might flourish by good priests being supplied to all the churches.

'You have received then a man both admirably endowed with Divine grace and approved by royal scrutiny. Let no one any longer be involved in the old contention. There is no disgrace in being conquered when the King's power has helped the winning side. That man makes him [the successful candidate] his own, who manifests to him pure affection. For what cause for regret can there be, when you find in this man, those very qualities which you looked for in the other when you embraced his party?

'These are family quarrels[2], a battle without cold

---

[1] 'Qui sapienti deliberatione pertractans quamvis in aliena religione.'

[2] The words of Cassiodorus are, 'crinea sunt ista certamina.' No one seems able to suggest a meaning for *crinea*. The editors propose to read *civica*, which however is very flat, and not exactly in Cassiodorus' manner. I suspect some recondite classical allusion, which has been missed by the transcribers, has led to the corruption of the text.

steel, a contest without hatred: by shouts, not wounds, a matter like this is decided.

'For even though the person who is desired be taken from you, yet naught is lost by the faithful, since the longed-for priesthood is possessed by them. [They have a Pope, if not just the Pope whom they wished for.] Wherefore on the return of your Legate, the Illustrious Publianus, we have thought it right to send to your assembly these letters of salutation. For we taste one of our highest pleasures when we exchange words with our nobles; and we doubt not that this is very sweet to you also, when you reflect that what you did by our grandsire's order is personally agreeable to ourselves.'

[For remarks on this important letter see Dahn's 'Könige der Germanen' iii. 239. He makes it a simple appointment of the Pope by the bare will of Theodoric, afterwards confirmed by Athalaric. To me it seems more probable that there had been a contest, threatening the election of an antipope (as in 498 in the case of Symmachus and Laurentius), and that the matter had been, as on that occasion, referred to the arbitration of Theodoric.]

16. KING ATHALARIC TO OPILIO, COUNT OF THE SACRED LARGESSES (527).

Opilio appointed Comes Sacrarum Largitionum.

'It is generally necessary to weigh carefully the merits of a new aspirant to the honours of the Court (aulicas dignitates); but in your case the merits of your family render this examination needless. Both your father and brother held the same office[1] which we are now entrusting to you, and one may say that this dignity has taken up its abode in your house.

'You learned the duties of a subordinate in the office under your brother; and often did he, leaning upon

---

[1] 'Pater his fascibus praefuit sed et frater eadem resplenduit claritate.'

you as on a staff, take a little needful repose, knowing that all things would be attended to by you. The crowds of suppliants who resorted to him with their grievances, shared the confidence which the people had in you, and saw that you were already assuming the character of a good judge.

'Most useful also were your services to the throne at the commencement of the new reign, when men's minds were in trouble as to what should happen next. You bore the news of our accession to the Ligurians, and so strengthened them by your wise address that the error into which they had been betrayed by the sun-setting was turned into joy at the rising of our empire[1].'

'We therefore confer upon you the dignity of Count of the Sacred Largesses from this sixth Indiction (Sept. 1, 527). Enjoy all the privileges and emoluments which belonged to your predecessors. God forbid that those whose own actions are right should be shaken by any machinations of calumny. There was a time when even Judges were harassed by informers (delatores); but that time is over. Lay aside then all fear, you who have no errors to reproach yourself with, and freely enjoy the advantages of your dignity. Imitate your brother: even though a little way behind him you will still be before most holders of the office. He was a man of the highest authority and of proved constancy, and the highest testimony to his merits was afforded by the fact that even under a successor who was hostile to him the whole official staff of the palace was loud in his praises[2].'

[This letter is of great importance, as containing indirectly the expression of Cassiodorus' opinion on the

---

[1] 'Nam cum ... auspicia nostra Liguribus felix portitor nuntiasti, et sapientiae tuae allocutione firmasti, in errorem *quem de occasu conceperant*, ortum nostri imperii in gaudia commutabant.' Does this obscure passage indicate some revolutionary movements in Liguria after the death of Theodoric, perhaps fomented by the Frankish neighbours of Italy?

[2] 'Quando sub ingrato successore palatinum officium praeconia ejus tacere non potuit.'

trial of Boethius, and the tendency of that opinion seems to be against him and in favour of his accusers. Comparing this letter with v. 40, addressed to Cyprian, Comes Sacrarum Largitionum and *son of Opilio*, we may with something like certainty construct this genealogical table:

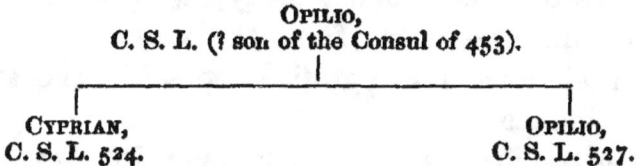

Now Cyprian, whose ready wit and ingenious eloquence had rendered him a favourite with Theodoric, is represented to us in the 'Philosophiae Consolatio' of Boethius (I. iv.) and in the 'Anonymus Valesii' (85) as the informer by whom Albinus and Boethius were accused of high treason. Opilio too (no doubt the same as the receiver of this letter) is described by Boethius (loc. cit.) as a man who on account of his numberless frauds had been ordered by the King to go into banishment, had taken refuge at the altar, and had been sternly bidden to leave Ravenna before a given day, and then had purchased pardon by coming forward as a *delator* against Boethius.

Against all this passionate invective it is fair to set this remarkable letter of Cassiodorus, written it is true in the young King's name and presenting the Court view of these transactions, but still written after the death of Theodoric, and perhaps republished by Cassiodorus in the 'Variarum' after the downfall of the Gothic Monarchy. In any case the allusions to *delatores* in this letter, considering the history of Opilio and his brother, are extraordinary.]

17. KING ATHALARIC TO THE SENATE OF THE CITY OF ROME.

[The same subject.]

This letter, though it does not mention the name of Opilio, is evidently written on his promotion to the office of Comes Sacrarum Largitionum. It enumerates his good qualities, and declares that it is marvellous and almost fortunate for Athalaric that so suitable a candidate should not have been promoted in the reign of his grandfather. The father of Opilio was a man of noble character and robust body, who distinguished himself by his abstinence from the vices of the times and his preference for dignified repose in the stormy period of Odovacar[1].

'He was reputed an excellent man in those times, when the Sovereign was not a man of honour[2]. But why go back to his parentage, when his brother has set so noble an example. The friendship, the rivalry in virtue of these two brothers, is worthy of the good old times. Both are true to their friends; both are devoid of avarice. Both have kept their loyalty to their King unspotted, and no marvel, since they have first shown themselves true to their friends and colleagues.

'Distinguished by these virtues, our candidate has been fittingly allied by marriage with the noble family of Basilius[3].

'He has managed his private affairs so as to avoid the two extremes of parsimony and extravagance. He has become popular with the Goths by his manner of life, and with the Romans by his righteous judgments[4]; and has

---

[1] 'Adjectis saeculi vitiis, ditatus claris honoribus.' The text is evidently corrupt. 'Abjectis' seems to be required; but some MSS. instead of 'vitiis' read 'Odovacris.' In any case Odovacar's government is evidently alluded to. Cf. the words used of the same man in the letter announcing the elevation of his other son, Cyprian (v. 41): 'Nam pater huic, sicut meministis, Opilio fuit, vir quidem *abjectis temporibus* ad excubias tamen Palatinas electus.'

[2] 'His temporibus habitus est eximius, cum princeps non esset erectus.'

[3] This is probably the Basilius who was concerned in the accusation of Boethius (Phil. Cons. I. iv.); possibly the Consul of 541, who fled to Constantinople when Totila took Rome in 546 (Procop. De Bello Gotthico iii. 20, and Anastasius Lib. Pontif. apud Murator. iii. 132); and perhaps the Basilius whom we find in trouble in Variarum iv. 22, 23; scarcely the Basilius of Variarum ii. 10, 11.]

[4] 'Gentiles victu (?), Romanos sibi judiciis obligabat.'

been over and over again chosen as a referee (Judex privatus), thus showing the high opinion in which his integrity is held.

'The Conscript Fathers are exhorted to endorse the favourable judgment of the King, by welcoming the new Count of Sacred Largesses into their body.'

[In view of these letters I do not understand what Gibbon means by saying (cap. xxxix. *n.* 95), 'The characters of the two delators, Basilius ('Var.' ii. 10, 11; iv. 22) and Opilio (v. 41; viii. 16), are illustrated, not much to their honour, in the Epistles of Cassiodorus.' This is quite true of Basilius, if the person alluded to in the references given by Gibbon be the same as the informer against Boethius, of which there may be a doubt; but Opilio is mentioned, as we see, with the highest honour by Cassiodorus. So, too, is Decoratus, whom in the same note Gibbon too hastily stigmatises as 'the worthless colleague of Boethius.']

18. KING ATHALARIC TO FELIX, QUAESTOR (527).

[This cannot be the same as the Consul of 511, nor even his son; for that Felix was of Gaulish extraction, and came from beyond the Alps.]

'It is desirable that those who are appointed as Judges should know something of law, and most unfitting that he whom so many officials (*milites*) obey should be seen to be dependent for his law on some one of his subordinates. Promotion of Felix to the Quaestorship.

'You long ago, when engaged in civil causes as an Advocate, were marked out by your Sovereign's eye[1]. He noted your eloquence, your fidelity, your youthful beauty, and your maturity of mind. No client could ask for more devotion than you showed in his cause; no Judge found in you anything to blame.

'Receive then now the dignity of Quaestor for this

---

[1] 'Dudum te forensibus negociis insudantem, *oculus imperialis* aspexit'—an expression which goes very near to styling Theodoric Imperator.

sixth Indiction (Sept. 1, 527), and judge in the Courts where hitherto you have pleaded.

'You are called Felix; act so as always to merit that name; for it is absurd to have a name which denotes one thing and to display the opposite in one's character. We think we have now said enough for a man of your good conscience. Many admonitions seem to imply a doubt of the character of him who receives them.' [A maxim often forgotten by Cassiodorus.]

19. KING ATHALARIC TO THE SENATE OF THE CITY OF ROME.

[On the promotion of Felix.]

The same subject.

'As the sky with stars, or the meadow with flowers, so do we wish the Senate to be resplendent with the men of eminence whom we introduce into it. It is itself a seminary of Senators; but our favour and the dignities of our Court also rear them.

'The Quaestorship is the true mother of the senatorial dignity, since who can be fitter to take his seat in the Curia than he who has shared the counsels of his Sovereign?

'You know the eloquence of our candidate [Felix], his early triumphs, his modesty, his fidelity. To leave such a man unpromoted were a public loss; and he will always love the laws by the practice of which he has risen to eminence.

'Nor is he the first of his race to earn rhetorical distinction. His father shone so brilliantly in the Forum of Milan, that he bloomed forth with undying fruits from the soil of Cicero[1]. He stood against Magnus Olybrius, he was found equal in fluency to Eugenius[2]

---

[1] 'Pater ita in Mediolanensi foro resplenduit, ut aeterno fructu e Tulliano cespite pullularet.'

[2] 'Is palmarum Eugenetis linguae ubertate suffecit.' Possibly this is the Magister Officiorum of Var. i. 12, and the person to whom is addressed a letter of Ennodius (iv. 26). The form Eugenetis, instead of Eugenii, belongs to the debased Latinity of the age.

and many others whom Rome knew as foremost in their art. If the transmission of material wealth by long descent makes men noble, how much more should the inheritance of the treasures of the intellect give nobility.'

20. KING ATHALARIC TO ALBIENUS, VIR ILLUSTRIS AND PRAEFECTUS PRAETORIO[1] (527).

Albienus made Praetorian Praefect.

'Your predecessor has been the model of a bad governor. As the North wind clears the face of the sky from the rain and clouds brought by the South wind, so do we look to you to repair the evils wrought by his misgovernment. In all things your best maxim will be to do exactly the opposite of what he did. He made himself hateful by his unjust prosecutions: do you become popular by your righteous deeds. He was rapacious: be you moderate. Soothe and relieve the harassed people entrusted to your charge. Receive for this sixth Indiction [Sept. 1, 527–528] the fasces of the Praefecture, and let the office of Praetorian Praefect return to its ancient fame, an object of praise to the whole world[2]. This office dates from Joseph, and rightly is he who holds it called by our laws Father of the Provinces, Father of the Empire.

'See that you avoid all unjust exactions. We cannot bear that our Treasury should be filled by unrighteous means.

'Your descent from a father who has held the same high office, and your intimate knowledge of the *Dicta prudentum*, warrant us in believing that you will make a good judge.'

[I have not been able to find any hint of the name

---

[1] In Nivellius' edition the title of this office is given as *Praepositus*.

[2] 'Redeat ad nomen antiquum Praefectura illa Praetorii, toto orbe laudabilis.' Is it possible that there had been some attempt to change the *title* of the Praefect, which accounts for the *Praepositus* which in some MSS. we find in the heading of this letter?

of the Praefectus Praetorio for 526–527, so bitterly condemned in this letter. As he may have held office for some years, his misgovernment may have been connected with the death of Boethius (524). Can we connect him with the Trigguilla 'Regiae Praepositus Domus' whose injustice is denounced by Boethius ('Phil. Cons.' i. 4)?]

21. KING ATHALARIC TO CYPRIAN, PATRICIAN.

22. KING ATHALARIC TO THE SENATE OF THE CITY OF ROME.

Cyprian's elevation to the Patriciate.

In these two letters the high character and distinguished services of Cyprian are commemorated. 'Under Theodoric he distinguished himself both in war and peace. At the time of the war of Sirmium he was conspicuous both in his resistance to the fiery onslaught of the Bulgarians and in his active pursuit of them when their ranks were broken[1]. He then filled, with great credit to himself, the office of Referendarius[2]. Great was the responsibility of exercising peaceful as well as warlike offices under such a master as Theodoric. In fact the training for one was helpful for the other, since it required a soldier's courage and promptness to be always ready with a truthful and accurate reply to that keen, firm-minded ruler of men[3].

'Thence he was promoted to the dignity of Count of the Sacred Largesses, a post well suited to his pure,

---

[1] 'Vidit te adhuc gentilis' (still under the dominion of the Gepidae) 'Danubius bellatorem: non te terruit Bulgarorum globus, qui etiam nostris erat praesumptione certaminis obstaturus. Peculiare tibi fuit et renitentes Barbaros aggredi, et conversos terrore sectari. Sic victoriam Gothorum non tam numero quam labore juvisti.'

[2] For a description of his services in this function, see Var. v. 40.

[3] This is evidently the meaning; but something seems to have dropped out of the text.

self-restrained character[1]. He is now growing old in body, but ever young in fame, and the King heartily wishes him increase of years to enjoy his renown.

'Rightly, too, is there now conferred upon him the dignity of *Patricius*, since he is the father of such noble sons, men whose childhood was passed in the palace under the very eye of Theodoric (thus like young eagles already learning to gaze upon the sun), and who now cultivate the friendship of the Goths, learn from them all martial exercises, speak their language, and thus give evident tokens of their future fidelity to the Gothic nation[2].

'The Senate is therefore exhorted to welcome its thus promoted colleague, who at each accession of rank has shown himself yet worthier of his high place, and whom grandfather and grandson have both delighted to honour. Thus will it renew the glories of the Decii and the Corvini, who were its sons in the days of old.'

[The subject of these letters is indisputably the same Cyprian whom the 'Anonymus Valesii' speaks of as suborning false witnesses against Albinus and Boethius, and of whom the latter says ('Phil. Cons.' i. 4): 'Ne Albinum, Consularem virum praejudicatae accusationis poena corriperet, odiis me Cypriani delatoris opposui.' Compare the remarks made on Letters 16 and 17; and remember that this letter was composed three years after the death of Boethius, when Theodoric also was dead, and his daughter was only too willing to retrace his steps, in all that concerned the severities of the latter years of his reign. For the pedigree of Cyprian see p. 363.]

---

[1] 'Hoc est laborum tuorum aptissimum munus: quam sic castâ sic moderatâ mente peregisti ut majora tibi deberi faceres, quamvis eam in magna praemia suscepisses.'

[2] 'Relucent etiam gratia gentili, nec cessant armorum imbui fortibus institutis. *Pueri stirpis Romanae nostrâ linguâ loquuntur; eximie indicantes exhibere se nobis futuram fidem, quorum jam videntur affectasse sermonem . . . Variis linguis loquuntur egregie,* maturis viris communione miscentur.'

23. KING ATHALARIC TO BERGANTINUS, VIR ILLUSTRIS AND COMES PATRIMONII.

Gifts to Theodahad.

'Kings should always be generous, but especially to those of their own family.

'Therefore we desire your Greatness to transfer the farms herein described, to the exalted and most honourable Theodahad, weighing out to him so many solidi, out of that which was formerly the patrimony of his magnificent Mother; and we guarantee to him the absolute ownership of such farms, free from any claims to the inheritance on our part[1].

'We trust to his sincerity and good faith, that in the future he will deserve the remainder of the above-mentioned patrimony, with the addition of the whole quantity[2].

'What can we deny to such a man, whose obedience might claim a higher reward even were he not our cousin—a man who is not puffed up by any pride of his noble birth, humble in his modesty, always uniform in his prudence? Therefore instruct the Cartarii of your office to make over the aforesaid farms to his Actores without delay[3].'

[1] 'Atque ideo illustrem magnitudinem tuam praecelso atque amplissimo viro Theodahado massas subter annexas, tot solidos pensitantes, ex patrimonio quondam magnificae foeminae matris ipsius, praecipimus reformari, ejus feliciter dominio plenissime vendicandas, cujus successionis integrum jus in ea qua praecipimus parte largimur.' According to Dahn (Könige der Germanen iv. 60–61), these lands had been given in her lifetime by Theodahad's mother to the King, and are now begged for by Theodahad. But why 'tot solidos pensitantes?' Why should Theodahad receive both land and money? There seems no authority for translating 'pensitantes' receiving. Probably the solidi thus paid to him are mesne rents received by the King and accounted for to Theodahad. On the whole affair of. Procopius, De Bello Gotthico i. 4.

[2] 'De cujus fide ac synceritate praesumimus, ut sequenti tempore reliqua supra memorati patrimonii cum omni adjecta quantitate mereatur.' This sentence is to me quite unintelligible.

[3] Cf. the formalities connected with Odovacar's deed of gift to Pierius (Marini, Pap. Diplom. 82, 83), quoted in Italy and her Invaders iii. 165.

24. King Athalaric to the Clergy of the Roman Church.

Ecclesiastical immunities.

'For the gift of kingly power we owe an infinite debt to God, whose ministers ye are.

'Ye state in your tearful memorial to us that it has been an ordinance of long custom that anyone who has a suit of any kind against a servant of the sacrosanct Roman Church should first address himself to the chief Priest of that City, lest haply your clergy, being profaned by the litigation of the Forum, should be occupied in secular rather than religious matters. And you add that one of your Deacons has, to the disgrace of religion, been so sharply handled by legal process that the Sajo[1] has dared actually to take him into his own custody.

'This dishonour to the Ministers of holy things is highly displeasing to our inborn reverence, yet we are glad that it gives us the opportunity of paying part of our debt to Heaven.

'Therefore, considering the honour of the Apostolic See, and wishing to meet the desires of the petitioners, we by the authority of this letter decree in regular course[2]:

'That if anyone shall think he has a good cause for going to law with a person belonging to the Roman clergy, he shall first present himself for hearing at the judgment-seat of the most blessed Pope, in order that the latter may either decide between the two in his own holy manner, or may delegate the cause to a Jurisconsult to be ended by him. And if, perchance, which it is impiety to believe, the

---

[1] In the text, 'Sajus.'

[2] 'Praesenti auctoritate moderato ordine definimus.' Dahn interprets 'moderato ordine,' 'not so absolutely as the Roman clergy desires.' Is not this to attribute rather too much force to the conventional language of Cassiodorus?

reasonable desire of the petitioner shall have been evaded, then may he come to the secular courts with his grievance, when he can prove that his petitions have been spurned by the Bishop of the aforesaid See[1].

'Should any litigant be so dishonest and so irreverent, both towards the Holy See and our authority, as to disregard this order [and proceed first in our tribunals against one of the Roman clergy], he shall forfeit 10lbs. of gold [£400], to be exacted by the officers of the Count of Sacred Largesses and distributed by the Pope to the poor; and he shall lose his suit in addition, notwithstanding any decree which he may have gained in the secular court.

'Meanwhile do you, whom our judgments thus venerate, live according to the ordinances of the Church. It is a great wickedness in you to admit such crimes as do not become the conversation even of secular men. Your profession is the heavenly life. Do not condescend to the grovelling wishes and vulgar errors of ordinary mortals. Let the men of this world be coerced by human laws; do you obey the precepts of righteousness.'

[See Dahn, 'Könige der Germanen' iii. 191-2, Sartorius 145, and Bauer's 'History of the Popes' ii. 323-4, for remarks on this important *privilegium*.

It is clear that it relates to civil, not criminal procedure, and that it does leave a right of final appeal from the Papal Courts to the dissatisfied secular litigant. At the same time, that such an appeal would be prosecuted with immense difficulty is clear even from the words of the decree. The appellant

---

[1] 'Definimus, ut si quispiam ad Romanum Clerum aliquem pertinentem, in quâlibet causâ probabili crediderit actione pulsandum, ad beatissimi Papae judicium prius conveniat audiendus. Ut aut ipse inter utrosque more suae sanctitatis agnoscat, aut causam deleget aequitatis studio terminandam: et si forte, quod credi nefas est, competens desiderium fuerit petitoris elusum, tunc ad saecularia fora jurgaturus occurrat, quando suas petitiones probaverit a supradictae sedis praesule fuisse contemptas.'

will have to satisfy the King's Judges of a thing which it is almost impiety to believe, that the occupant of the Roman See has spurned his petitions.]

25. KING ATHALARIC TO JOANNES, VIR SPECTABILIS, REFERENDARIUS.

Confirmation of Tulum's gift of property in the Lucullanum.

'It is a very fitting thing to confirm the generosity of others towards persons who might well have received gifts from oneself. We therefore declare that in your case the gift is another's but the will to give is our own, and the King has only been anticipated by the rapid bounty of the subject[1].

'Everyone knows that our grandfather wished to give you the house of Agnellus in the Castrum Lucullanum, but could not do so having already given it to the Patrician Tulum[2]. Tulum, however, with his usual generosity, seconding the wishes of his master, formally conveyed the property to you; and that conveyance we now confirm, guaranteeing the quiet possession of it to you and your heirs for all time to come. If any doubt exist as to your title, by any mischance, or by reason of any enquiry, such doubt is exploded by the authority of this letter of ours[3].

'And should any envious person, in contempt of our royal will, dare to raise any question in this matter hereafter, either on behalf of the Fiscus or of any private individual, we declare that he shall pay to you, or to the person to whom you may have assigned the said house, 100lbs. of gold (£4,000) by way of penalty.'

---

[1] 'Profitemur itaque alterius quidem donum, sed nostrum esse judicium, et modernam principis mentem praevenisse tantum velocissimam largitatem.' Observe again the use of Cassiodorus' favourite word *modernam*.

[2] Tholuit, or Tholum, in some MSS., but no doubt the same as the Tulum of Letters 9 and 10.

[3] 'Ubi et si quid esset quolibet casu, qualibet inquisitione fortassis ambiguum, hujus auctoritatis nostrae judicio constat explosum.'

[Why should there be the necessity of this royal confirmation of a transaction between two private individuals, Tulum and Joannes, and this tremendous penalty on all future impugners of it?

Evidently because the property had been impressed with the character of State domain, and it was doubtful how far Tulum's alienation of it might stand good against the claims of future Sovereigns.

This becomes quite clear when we reflect what is the property to which this letter refers. It is either the whole or a part of the Lucullanum, to which the deposed Emperor, Romulus Augustulus, was banished in 476. On his death, as we may conjecture, this property, one of the most delightful places of residence in Italy, has been given by Theodoric to Tulum, perhaps just after he had distinguished himself in the Gaulish campaign of 508. For some reason or other, Tulum has alienated it (ostensibly, given it) to the Reporter Joannes, no doubt a Roman, who is apparently nervous lest his title to it should hereafter be impugned on the ground that the palace of the last Roman Emperor was national property. Hence this letter. There is some difficulty and variation between the MSS. in the words describing the property: 'Saepe dicta domus paternae recordationis Agnelli, in Lucullano castro posita.' For *paternae*, Migne's editor reads *patriciae*. The forthcoming critical edition of the 'Variae' will show whether there is any support in the MSS. for a conjecture which I cannot help entertaining that *Agnelli* is an error for *Augustuli*.]

Gothic settlers in the Sabine territory exhorted to obedience to their Prior, Quidila.

26. KING ATHALARIC TO ALL THE INHABITANTS OF REATE AND NURSIA.

'Our glorious grandfather had arranged that, in accordance with your desire, Quidila, son of Sibia, should be your Captain (Prior). We confirm this appointment, and desire you to obey him in all things. You are so far moulded by the character of our grandfather that you willingly obey both the laws and the Judges. Our enemies are best vanquished, and the favour both of Heaven and of other nations is best conciliated for us, by our obeying the principles of justice. If anyone is in need of anything, let him seek to obtain it from the generosity of his Sovereign rather than by the strength of his own right hand, since it is for your advantage that the Romans be at peace, who, in filling our Treasury, at the same time multiply your donatives.'

[This letter is evidently addressed to Goths, and Quidila the *Prior*, who is set over them, is also a Goth. We can only conjecture what the office of Prior was: probably to some extent it involved civil as well as military authority. The conjecture of Dahn ('König der Germanen' iv. 173) that it corresponds to the Gothic *Hundafath* (Centenarius), seems to me extremely probable. The title of the letter is curious. It is addressed 'Universis Reatinis et Nursinis.' Are we then to suppose that strong military colonies of Goths had been settled in these places, the Roman inhabitants having been extruded? The fact that St. Benedict was born in Nursia, some fifty-seven years before the writing of this letter, gives an additional interest to this question.]

27. KING ATHALARIC TO DUMERIT THE SAJO, AND TO FLORENTINUS, A ZEALOUS OFFICER OF THE COURT[1].

Robbery in the district of Faenza to be suppressed.

'Justice must be shown upon the wicked. Different diseases require different remedies.

'Let your Devotion speed instantly through the territory of Faventia, and if you find any persons, either Goths or Romans, concerned in the plunder of the pos-

[1] 'Florentino viro devoto Comitiaco.'

sessors, punish them severely. How much better it would be for those misguided persons to live according to our will, and earn the reward of pleasing us.' [The last sentence is obscure, and perhaps the text is corrupt.]

28. KING ATHALARIC TO CUNIGAST, VIR ILLUSTRIS.

[No doubt the same as the Conigast attacked by Boethius in the 'Philosophiae Consolatio' i. 4[1].]

Possessores (or Coloni?) forced to become slaves.

'Our Serenity has been moved by the grievous petition of Constantius and Venerius, who complain that Tanca [probably a Goth] has wrested from them the farm which is called Fabricula, which belonged to them in their own right, together with the stock upon it[2], and has compelled them, in order to prevent similar forcible demands upon their property in future, to allow the worst lot of all—the condition of slavery—to be imposed upon them, who are really free[3].

'Let your Greatness therefore summon Tanca to your judgment-seat, and, after hearing all parties, pronounce a just judgment and one accordant to your character. For though it is a serious matter to oust a lord from his right, it is contrary to the feelings of our age to press down free necks under the yoke of slavery.

'Let Tanca therefore either establish his right to the slaves and their property, or, if they are proved free, let him give them up, whole and unharmed: in which case we will inflict upon him no further penalty.'

---

[1] 'Quoticus ego Conigastum in inbecillis cujusque fortunas impetum facientem obvius excepi!'

[2] 'Cum suo peculio.' If they were not slaves they could not have *peculium* in the technical sense. I therefore understand 'peculio' to be simply equivalent to *cattle*, a sense which is confirmed by 'Calabri peculiosi' in Letter 33.

[3] 'Adjicientes ne rerum suarum repetitionibus imminerent [? imminuerent] liberis sibi conditionem ultimae servitutis imponi.' Cf. Salvian, De Gubernatione Dei v. 8, 9, for a description of similar occurrences in Gaul.

29. King Athalaric to the Dignified Cultivators[1] and Curials of the City of Parma.

Sanitary measures needed in Parma.

'You ought willingly to co-operate in that which is being done for the advantage of your town. When it was suffering from a long drought, our grandfather, with God's help, watered it with the life-giving wave. Cleanse out then the mouths of your sewers, lest otherwise, being checked in its flow by the accumulated filth, it should surge back into your houses, and bring into them the pollution which it was meant to wash away.

'The Spectabilis Genesius is appointed to superintend this work, and to quicken your zeal regarding it.'

30. King Athalaric to Genesius, Vir Spectabilis.

[Relating to the same subject as the preceding.]

The same subject.

'Through love of your city our grandfather, with royal generosity, constructed an aqueduct of the ancient type[2] for you. But it is of no use to provide a good water-supply unless your sewers are in good order. Therefore let your Sublimity set the citizens of Parma diligently to work at this business, that all ancient channels, whether underground or those which run by the sides of the streets, be diligently repaired[3], in order that when the longed-for stream flows into your town it be not hindered by any obstacle.

'How fair is water in a running stream, but how ugly in puddles and swamps; it is good then neither for man nor beast. Without water city and country alike languish; and rightly did the ancients punish one who was unfit for human society by forbidding all men to give him water. Therefore you ought all heartily to combine

---

[1] 'Honoratis Possessoribus.'   [2] 'Antiqui operis formam.'
[3] 'Quatenus antiquos cuniculos, sive subterraneos, sive qui junguntur marginibus platearum diligenter emendent.'

for this most useful work, since the man who is not touched by the comeliness of his city has not yet the mind of a citizen.'

31. KING ATHALARIC TO SEVERUS, VIR SPECTABILIS.

[Is Severus *Vicarius Urbis*? His title Spectabilis seems to require some such rank as this, otherwise he seems more like a *Corrector* (Clarissimus) *Bruttiorum et Lucaniae*. Perhaps already the strict gradation established by Diocletian and Constantine was somewhat broken down, and governors received higher titles than strictly belonged to them.]

Dissuasions from a country life, and praises of Cassiodorus' native land of Bruttii.

'Since you, when on the staff of the Praefect, have learned the principles of statesmanship, we are sure that you will agree with us that cities are the chief ornament of human society. Let the wild beasts live in fields and woods: men ought to draw together into cities. Even among birds we see that those of gentle disposition—like thrushes, storks, and doves—love to flock together, while the greedy hawk, intent on its bloody pastime, seeks solitude.

'Now we say that the man who shuns human society becomes at once an object of suspicion. Let therefore the Possessores and Curiales of Bruttii return to their cities. The Coloni may cultivate the soil—that is what their name denotes[1]; but the men whom we decorate with civic honours ought to live in cities.

'In truth it is a lovely land. Ceres and Pallas have crowned it with their respective gifts (corn and oil); the plains are green with pastures, the slopes are purple with vineyards. Above all is it rich in its vast herds of horses[2], and no wonder, since the dense shade of its

---

[1] 'Coloni sunt qui agros jugiter colunt.'

[2] Cf. what is said (i. 4) as to the large present of horses made by the father of Cassiodorus to Theodoric for the use of the Gothic army.

forests protects them from the bites of flies, and provides them with ever verdant pasture even in the height of summer. Cool waters flow from its lofty heights; fair harbours on both its shores woo the commerce of the world.

'There the countryman enjoys the good food of the citizen, the poor man the abundance of the wealthy[1]. If such then be the charms even of the country in your Province, why should you shirk living in its cities[2]?

'Why should so many men refined by literature skulk in obscurity? The boy goes to a good school, becomes imbued with the love of letters, and then, when he is come to man's estate and should be seeking the Forum in order to display his talents, he suddenly changes into a boor, unlearns all that he has learned, and in his love for the fields forgets what is due to a reasonable love for himself. And yet even birds love human fellowship, and the nightingale boldly rears her brood close to the haunts of men.

'Let the cities then return to their old splendour; let none prefer the charms of the country to the walls reared by the men of old. Why should not everyone be attracted by the concourse of noble persons, by the pleasures of converse with his equals? To stroll through the Forum, to look in at some skilful craftsman at his work, to push one's own cause through the law courts, then between whiles to play with the counters of Palamedes (draughts), to go to the baths with one's acquaintances, to indulge in the friendly emulation of the banquet—these are the proper employments of a Roman noble; yet not one of them is

---

[1] 'Vivunt illic rustici epulis urbanorum, mediocres autem abundantia praepotentium.' 'Mediocres' and 'tenues' are technical words with Cassiodorus for the poor.

[2] Cassiodorus must have felt the weakness of his logic here. He patriotically praises the rural beauty of Bruttii, yet the conclusion which by main force he arrives at is, 'Leave the country and live in towns.'

tasted by the man who chooses to live always in the country with his farm-servants [1].

'We order therefore that all Possessores and Curiales shall, according to their relative means, find bail and give bonds, promising that they will for the larger part of the year reside in some city, such as they may choose [2]. And thus, while not wholly debarred from the pleasures of the country, they will furnish to the cities their proper adornment of citizens.'

32. KING ATHALARIC TO SEVERUS, VIR SPECTABILIS.

The Fountain of Arethusa.

'Nimfadius (Vir Sublimis) was journeying to the King's Comitatus on some affair of his own, when, wearied with his journey, he lay down to rest, and let his beasts of burden graze round the fountain of Arethusa.

'This fountain, situated in the territory of Squillace [3], at the foot of the hills and above the sand of the sea, makes a green and pleasant place all round it, fringed with rustling reeds as with a crown. It has certain marvellous properties: for let a man go to it in silence and he sees it calmly flowing, more like a pond than a fountain. But let him cough or speak with a loud voice, and it becomes violently agitated, heaving to and fro like a pot boiling. Strange power this of a fountain to answer a man. I have read that some

---

[1] 'Cui enim minus grata nobilium videatur occursio. Cui non affectuosum sit cum paribus miscere sermonem, forum petere, honestas artes invisere, causas proprias legibus expedire, interdum Palamediacis calculis occupari, ad balneas ire cum sociis, prandia mutuis apparatibus exhibere? Caret profecto omnibus his, qui vitam suam vult semper habere cum famulis.'

[2] 'Datis fidejussoribus jam Possessores quam Curiales, sub aestimatione virium, poenâ interpositâ, promittant anni parte majore se in civitatibus manere, quas habitare delegerint.'

[3] 'In Scyllatino territorio.' Transcribers, thinking of the Arethusa at Syracuse, have tried to alter this into *Siciliano;* but there can be little doubt that the above reading is right. As to the situation of the Fountain of Arethusa, see Introduction, p. 72.

fountains can change the colours of the animals that drink at them; that others can turn wood dropped into them to stone. The human reason is altogether unable to understand such things as these.

'But let us return to the complaint of our suppliant. Nimfadius asserts that, while he was resting, the country people artfully drove off his beasts of burden.

'This kind of crime brings our times into disgrace, and turns the charm of that quiet resting-place into disgust. Diligently enquire into it, for the credit of our Comitatus is involved in our subjects being able to journey to it in safety. At first, no doubt, the offenders will lie close, and seem as silent as the unmoved Arethusa. But begin your investigations, and they will soon break forth, like that fountain, with angry exclamations, in the midst of which you will discover the truth. Punish the offenders severely; for we should regret that owing to the excesses of robbers that wonderful and joy-bringing fountain should be deserted.'

33. KING ATHALARIC TO SEVERUS, VIR SPECTABILIS.

The Feast of St. Cyprian.

'We hear that the rustics are indulging in disorderly practices, and robbing the market-people who come from all quarters to the chief fair of Lucania on the day of St. Cyprian. This must by all means be suppressed, and your Respectability should quietly collect a sufficient number of the owners and tenants of the adjoining farms[1] to overpower these freebooters and bring them to justice. Any rustic or other person found guilty of disturbing the fair should be at once punished with the stick[2], and then exhibited with some mark of infamy upon him[3].

[1] 'Spectabilitas vestra praedicto tempore, unâ cum Possessoribus atque Conductoribus diversarum massarum ad quietem convenientium ... reos inveniat,' &c.

[2] 'Inter ipsa initia comprehensus fustuariae subdatur ultioni.'

[3] 'Pompatus mala nota.'

'This fair, which according to the old superstition was named Leucothea [after the nymph], from the extreme purity of the fountain at which it is held, is the greatest fair in all the surrounding country. Everything that industrious Campania, or opulent Bruttii, or cattle-breeding Calabria[1], or strong Apulia produces, is there to be found exposed for sale, on such reasonable terms that no buyer goes away dissatisfied. It is a charming sight to see the broad plains filled with suddenly-reared houses formed of leafy branches intertwined: all the beauty of the most leisurely-built city, and yet not a wall to be seen. There stand ready boys and girls, with the attractions which belong to their respective sexes and ages, whom not captivity but freedom sets a price upon. These are with good reason sold by their parents, since they themselves gain by their very servitude. For one cannot doubt that they are benefited even as slaves [or servants?], by being transferred from the toil of the fields to the service of cities[2].

'What can I say of the bright and many-coloured garments? what of the sleek and well-fed cattle offered at such a price as to tempt any purchaser?

'The place itself is situated in a wide and pleasant

---

[1] 'Calabri peculiosi.'

[2] 'Praesto sunt pueri ac puellae, diverso sexu atque aetate conspicuo, quos non facit captivitas esse sub pretio sed libertas: hos merito parentes vendunt, quoniam de ipsa famulatione proficiunt. Dubium quippe non est servos posse meliorari qui de labore agrorum ad urbana servitia transferuntur.' With almost any writer but Cassiodorus this would prove that in the Sixth Century free Italians were selling their children into actual slavery. But I doubt whether he really means more than that the children of the country people were for hire as domestic servants in the cities. If so, the scene is not unlike our own 'statute fairs' or 'hirings' in the north of England. It appears from § 94 of the Edictum Theodorici that parents could sell their children, but that the latter did not lose their *status ingenuus*. Must they then claim it on coming of age? 'Parentes qui cogente necessitate filios suos alimentorum gratia vendiderint ingenuitati eorum non praejudicant. *Homo enim liber pretio nullo aestimatur.*' Cf. also § 95: 'Operas enim tantum parentes filiorum quos in potestate habuerint, locare possunt.'

plain, a suburb of the ancient city of Cosilinum, and has received the name of Marcilianum from the founder of these sacred springs[1].

'And this is in truth a marvellous fountain, full and fresh, and of such transparent clearness that when you look through it you think you are looking through air alone. Choice fishes swim about in the pool, perfectly tame, because if anyone presumes to capture them he soon feels the Divine vengeance. On the morning which precedes the holy night [of St. Cyprian], as soon as the Priest begins to utter the baptismal prayer, the water begins to rise above its accustomed height. Generally it covers but five steps of the well, but the brute element, as if preparing itself for miracles, begins to swell, and at last covers two steps more, never reached at any other time of the year. Truly a stupendous miracle, that streams of water should thus stand still or increase at the sound of the human voice, as if the fountain itself desired to listen to the sermon.

'Thus hath Lucania a river Jordan of her own. Wherefore, both for religion's sake and for the profit of the people, it behoves that good order should be kept among the frequenters of the fair, since in the judgment of all, that man must be deemed a villain who would sully the joys of such happy days.'

---

[1] Marcilianum is now Sala, in the valley of the Calore (Tanager). Padula is thought by some to mark the site of Cosilinum. The Island of Leucosia, now Licosa, a few miles from Paestum, evidently does not represent the Leucothea of this letter.

BOOK IX.

CONTAINING TWENTY-FIVE LETTERS, ALL WRITTEN IN THE NAME OF ATHALARIC THE KING.

1. KING ATHALARIC TO HILDERIC, KING OF THE VANDALS (A.D. 527).

Murder of Amalafrida, widow of King Thrasamund and sister of Theodoric.

'FRIENDSHIP and relationship are turned to bitterness by the tidings that Amalafrida, of divine memory, the distinguished ornament of our race, has been put to death by you[1]. If you had any cause of offence against her, you ought to have sent her to us for judgment. What you have done is a species of parricide. If the succession, on the death of her husband, passed to another [yourself], that was no reason why a woman should be embroiled in the contest. It was really an addition to your

[1] With reference to this event Victor Tunnunensis writes: 'Cujus (Trasamundi) uxor Amalafrida fugiens ad barbaros congressione facta Capsae juxta Heremum capitur, et in custodia privata moritur.' Procopius (De B. Vandalico i. 9) says: Καὶ σφίσι (τοῖς Βανδίλοις) ξυνηνέχθη Θευδερίχῳ τε καὶ Γότθοις ἐν Ἰταλίᾳ ἔκ τε συμμάχων καὶ φίλων πολεμίοις γενέσθαι· τήν τε γὰρ Ἀμαλαφρίδαν ἐν φυλακῇ ἔσχον καὶ τοὺς Γότθους διέφθειραν ἅπαντας ἐπενεγκόντες αὐτοῖς νεωτερίζειν ἔς τε Βανδίλους καὶ Ἰλδέριχον. Both Victor and Procopius seem to place the conflict before the death of Theodoric; Victor says A.D. 523. Probably therefore the fighting, the capture of Amalafrida, and the death of her countrymen, took place in that year, the year of her husband's death and Hilderic's accession. Three or four years later (526 or 527), when her brother Theodoric was dead, the imprisoned princess was murdered—a grievous insult to the young Sovereign of the Goths, her great-nephew.

nobility to have the purple dignity of the Amal blood allied to the lineage of the Hasdingi.

'Our Goths keenly feel the insults conveyed in this deed, since to slay the royal lady of another race is to despise the valour of that race and doubt its willingness to avenge her.

'We send you two ambassadors to hear what your excuses are. We hear that you pretend that her death was natural. And you also must send ambassadors in return to us to explain the matter, without war or bloodshed, and either pacify us or acknowledge your guilt. If you do not do this, all ties of alliance between us are broken, and we must leave you to the judgment of the Divine Majesty, which heard the blood of Abel crying from the ground.'

2. EDICT OF KING ATHALARIC.

Oppression of the Curiales.

'The body of the Republic is so tempered together that if one member suffers all the members suffer with it. The Curiales, whose name is derived from their care (cura) and forethought, are, we are told, molested by hostile proceedings, so that what was bestowed upon them as an honour turns out rather to their injury. What scandalous injustice! What an insupportable evil! that he who ought to have benefited the Republic by his services, should often lose both fortune and liberty.

'Wherefore by this edict we decree that if any Curialis suffer oppression, if anyone, without the express warrant of ourselves or the high officers of State whose business it is, inflict upon a Curialis any injury or loss of property, he shall pay a fine of 10lbs. of gold (£400), to go to the benefit of the person thus oppressed; or, if his property be insufficient to pay this fine, he shall be beaten with clubs. The Curialis must then give additional diligence to the discharge of his public duties, since his debt to the

State is, as it were, increased by the protection which we are thus affording him. As for the farms of Curiales, in connection with which the greatest frauds are practised on poor men, let no one seek to obtain them by an unlawful purchase; for a contract cannot be called a contract when it is in violation of the law[1]. The Judges must help the Curiales against the molestations of Sajones and other officials. It is a grievous offence, when the very person to whom is entrusted the duty of defending the weak, himself turns oppressor.

'Raise your heads in hope, oh ye oppressed ones! lift up your hearts, ye who are weighed down with a load of evils! To each citizen his own city is his Republic. Administer justice in your cities in conformity with the general will. Let your various ranks live on a footing of justice. Do not oppress the weak, lest you in your turn be deservedly oppressed by the strong. This is the penalty of wrong-doing, that each one suffers in his own person what he has wantonly inflicted on another.

'Live then in justice and moderation. Follow the example of the cranes, who change the order of their flight, making foremost hindmost, and hindmost foremost, without difficulty, each willingly obeying its fellow—a commonwealth of birds.

'You have, according to the laws, power over your citizens. Not in vain has Antiquity conceded to you the title of Curia: not vainly did it call you the Lesser Senate, the nerves and vital organs of the State[2]. What is not contained of honour and power in that title! For that which is compared to the Senate is excluded from no kind of glory.'

---

[1] 'Praedia Curialium, unde maximae mediocribus parantur insidiae, nullus illicita emptione pervadat. Quia contractus dici non potest nisi qui de legibus venit.'

[2] 'Non enim incassum vobis Curiam concessit Antiquitas, non inaniter appellavit Minorem Senatum, nervos quoque vocitans ac viscera civitatum.'

3. KING ATHALARIC TO BERGANTINUS, VIR ILLUSTRIS, COMES [PATRIMONII], AND PATRICIAN[1].

Gold-mining in Italy.

'Gold, as well as many other fair fruits of Nature which gold can buy, is said to be produced by our generous Italy. Theodorus, who is an expert in such matters, asserts that gold will be found on the farm Rusticiana in Bruttii[2]. Let your Greatness therefore send a *Cartarius* to commence mining operations on that spot. The work of a miner resembles that of a mole. He burrows underground, far from the light of day. Sometimes the sides of his passages fall in and his way is closed up behind him; but if he emerge safely with his treasure, how happy is he! Then the gold-miner proceeds to immerse his ore in water, that the heavy metal may be separated from the lighter earth; then to submit it to a fervent heat, that it may thence derive its beautiful colour[3].

'Let then the land of Bruttii pay her tribute in gold, the most desired of all treasure. To seek gold by war is wicked, by voyages dangerous, by swindling shameful; but to seek it from Nature in its own home is righteous. No one is hurt by this honest gain. Griffins are said to dig for gold and to delight in the contemplation of this metal; but no one blames them, because their proceedings are not dictated by criminal covetousness. For it is not the act itself, but the motive for the act, that gives it its moral quality.'

---

[1] Cf. viii. 23.

[2] Have we any clue to the geographical position of this farm? The only Rusticiana known to the Itineraries is in Spain.

[3] 'Origo quidem nobilis, sed de flamma suscipit vim coloris, ut magis credas inde nasci, cujus similitudine videtur ornari. Sed cum auro tribuat splendidum ruborem, argento confert albissimam lucem. Ut mirum sit, unam substantiam tradere, quod rebus dissimilibus possit aptari.' Have we here a hint of 'the transmutation of metals?' Cassiodorus seems to think that it is only the furnace that makes the difference between the colours of gold and of silver.

4. KING ATHALARIC TO ABUNDANTIUS, PRAETORIAN PRAEFECT.

A family of Curiales permitted to step down into the ranks of the Possessores.

'The *pietas* of the King is happily shown in moderating the sentence of the law, where for certain reasons it bears with especial hardness on anyone. The Curiales have peculiar advantages in their opportunity of being thus liberated by the Sovereign from the performance of their duties [1]. It is reasonable to release a Curialis whose health prevents him from fulfilling his appointed task; and a numerous Curia will never miss a few names out of so large a number.

'Therefore let your Illustrious Magnificence remove Agenantia, wife [or widow?] of the most eloquent man Campanianus, dwelling in Lucania, from the album of her Curia, and her sons also, so that posterity may never know that they were formerly liable to Curial duties.

'Remitted to the ranks of [mere] Possessores they will now be liable to the same demands which formerly [as members of the Curia] they made upon others. They will now dread the face of the tax-collector (compulsor), and will begin to fear the mandates by which formerly they made themselves feared [2]. Still this is a sign of their past good life, that they are willing to live without office *among* a population whose dislike they are not conscious of having incurred, and *under* old colleagues whom they know that they have not incited to an abuse of their powers.'

---

[1] 'Neque enim ob aliud Curiales leges sacratissimae ligaverunt, nisi ut cum illos soli principes absolverent, indulgentiae praeconia reperirent.'

[2] 'Formidare delegata incipient, per quae antea timebantur.' To translate by an analogy, 'And will tremble at the rate-summonses, their signatures to which used to make other men tremble.'

5. KING ATHALARIC TO THE BISHOPS AND FUNCTIONARIES OF ———[1].

Forestalling and regrating of corn prohibited.

'We learn with regret by the complaint of the Possessores of your district that the severity of famine is being increased by the conduct of certain persons who have bought up corn and are holding it for higher prices. In a time of absolute famine there can be no "higgling of the market;" the hungry man will submit to be cheated rather than let another get the food before him[2].

'To stop this practice we send to you the present messengers, whose business it is to examine all the stores of corn collected for public distribution[3] or otherwise, to leave to each family sufficient for its needs, and to purchase the remainder from the owners at a fair market price. Co-operate with these orders of ours cheerfully, and do not grumble at them. Complain not that your freedom is interfered with. There is no free-trade in crime[4]. If you work with us you will earn good renown for yourselves; if against us, the King's reputation will gain by your loss. It is the sign of a good ruler to make men act righteously, even against their wills.'

6. KING ATHALARIC TO ———, PRIMISCRINIUS.

A furlough granted for a visit to Baiae.

'You complain that your health is failing under the long pressure of your work, and that you fear, if you absent yourself, you may lose the emoluments of your

---

[1] 'Episcopis et Honoratis.' Perhaps it is from motives of delicacy that Cassiodorus has not added the name of the Province.

[2] 'In necessitate siquidem penuriae pretii nulla contentio est: dum patitur quis induci ne possit aliquâ tarditate percelli.'

[3] 'Sive in gradu [panis gradilis?] sive in aliis locis.'

[4] A paraphrase, confessedly anachronistic, of 'Ne quis ergo venditionem sibi impositam conqueratur, sciat libertatem in crimine non requiri.'

office. At the same time you ask leave to visit the Baths of Baiae. Go then with a mind perfectly at rest as to your emoluments, which we will keep safe for you. Seek the Sun, seek the pure air and smiling shore of that lovely bay, thickly set with harbours and dotted with noble islands—that bay in which Nature displays all her marvels and invites man to explore her secrets. There is the Lake of Avernus, with its splendid supply of oysters. There are long piers jutting out into the sea; and the most delightful fishing in the world is to be had in the fish-ponds—open to the sky—on either side of them. There are warm baths, heated not by brick-work flues and smoky balls of fire, but by Nature herself. The pure air supplies the steam and softly stimulates perspiration, and the health-giving work is so much the better done as Nature is above Art. Let the Coralli [in Moesia, on the shore of the Euxine] boast their wonderful sea, let the pearl fisheries of India vaunt themselves. In our judgment Baiae, for its powers of bestowing pleasure and health, surpasses them all. Go then to Baiae to bathe, and have no fear about the emoluments.'

7. KING ATHALARIC TO REPARATUS, PRAEFECT OF THE CITY.

[We learn from Procopius ('De Bello Gotthico' i. 26) that Reparatus was brother of Pope Vigilius; that in 537 he escaped from the captivity in which the other Senators were kept at Ravenna by Witigis, and fled to Milan. In 539 Reparatus, who was then Praefectus Praetorio, was captured at Milan by the Goths, hewn in pieces, and his flesh given to the dogs (Ibid. ii. 21).]

Reparatus appointed Praefectus Urbis.

'The son of a high official naturally aspires to emulate his father's dignities. Your father had a distinguished career, first as Comes Largitionum, then as Praefectus Praetorio. While holding the latter office, he repaired the Senate-house, restored to the poor the gifts (?) of which they had been deprived[1], and though not himself a man of liberal education, pleased all by the natural charm of his manner.

'You have those advantages of mental training which were denied to your father. Education lifts an obscure man on to a level with nobles, but also adorns him who is of noble birth. You have moreover been chosen as son-in-law by a man of elevated character, whose choice is in itself a mark of your high merit. You are coming young to office[2]; but, with such a man's approbation, you cannot be said to be untried.

'We therefore confer upon you for this Indiction the dignity of Praefect of the City. The eyes of the world are upon you. The Senate, that illustrious and critical body, the youngest members of which are called *Patres*, will listen to your words. See that you say nothing which can displease those wise men, whose praise, though hard to win, will be most sweet to your ears. Diligently help the oppressed. Hand on to your posterity the renown which you have received from your ancestors.'

8. KING ATHALARIC TO COUNT OSUIN (OR OSUM), VIR ILLUSTRIS[3].

Osuin made Governor of Dalmatia and Savia.

'We reward our faithful servants with high honours, hoping thereby to quicken the slothful into emulation, when they ask themselves why, under such an impartial rule, they too do not receive promotion.

'We therefore again entrust to your Illustrious Great-

---

[1] 'Curiam reparans, pauperibus ablata restituens.'
[2] 'Licet primaevus venias ad honorem.'
[3] Cf. iii. 26 and iv. 9. In the former letter he is called Osun.

ness the Provinces of Dalmatia and S(u)avia. We need not hold up to you t] examples of others. You have only to imitate yourself, and to confer now again in your old age the same blessings on those Provinces which, as a younger man, you bestowed on them under our grandfather.'

9. KING ATHALARIC TO ALL THE GOTHS AND ROMANS (IN DALMATIA AND SAVIA).

The same subject.

'We send back to you the Illustrious Count Osuin, whose valour and justice you already know, to ward off from you the fear of foreign nations, and to keep you from unjust demands. With him comes the Illustrious Severinus[1], that with one heart and one mind, like the various reeds of an organ, they may utter their praiseworthy precepts.

Remission of Augmentum.

'As an act of grace on the commencement of our reign, we direct the Count of the Patrimony to remit to you all the super-assessment (augmentum) which was fixed for your Province at the fourth Indiction[2].

'We also grant that when the aforesaid person [Severinus] returns to our presence, you may send suitable men with him to inform us of your financial position, that we may, by readjustment of the taxes, lighten your load if it be still too heavy. Nothing consolidates the Republic so much as the uninjured powers of the taxpayer.'

---

[1] We are not told in what capacity Severinus came. Probably it was on account of Osuin's age that Severinus was associated with him.

[2] 'Per quartam Indictionem quod a nobis augmenti nomine quaerebatur illustrem virum Comitem Patrimonii nostri nunc jussimus removere.' As the fourth Indiction began Sept. 525, in the lifetime of Theodoric, it is clear that that date belongs to the imposition, not to the removal of the 'augmentum.'

10. KING ATHALARIC TO ALL THE PROVINCIALS OF THE CITY OF SYRACUSE.

Remission of Augmentum to Syracusans.

'Lately we announced to you our accession: now we wish to confer upon you a benefit in the matter of taxes. For we look on that only as our revenue which the cultivator pays cheerfully. Our grandfather, considering the great increase in wealth and population which his long and peaceful reign had brought with it, thought it prudent to increase the taxes to be paid by the Province of Sicily[1]. He was quite right in doing this, but he thereby prepared for us, his young successor, an opportunity of conferring an unexpected favour, for we hereby remit to you all the augmentum which was assessed upon you at the fourth Indiction. And not only so, but all that you have already paid under this head for the fifth Indiction (526-7) we direct the tax-collectors to carry to your credit on account[2].

'Besides this, if anyone have to complain of oppression on the part of the Governors of the Province, let him seek at once a remedy from our Piety. Often did our grandfather of glorious memory grieve over the slowness of the Governors to obey their letters of recall, feeling sure that they were lingering in the Provinces neither for his good nor yours.

'We however, with God's help, shall go on in the good work which we have begun. You have a Prince who, the older he grows, the more will love you. We send to you our Sajo Quidila, who will convey to you our orders on this matter.'

---

[1] 'Avus noster de suis beneficiis magna praesumens (quia longa quies et culturam agris praestitit et populos ampliavit) intra Siciliam provinciam sub consueta prudentiae suae moderatione censum statuit subflagitari ut vobis cresceret devotio, quibus se facultas extenderat.'

This must be the meaning of ' quicquid a discursoribus novi census per quintam Indictionem probatur affixum, ad vestram eos fecimus deferre notitiam.'

11. KING ATHALARIC TO GILDIAS, VIR SPECTABILIS, COUNT OF SYRACUSE.

12. KING ATHALARIC TO VICTOR AND WITIGISCLUS (OR WIGISICLA), VIRI SPECTABILES, CENSITORES[1] OF SICILY.

Oppressions exercised by the King's officers in Sicily rebuked.

Victor and Witigisclus are sharply rebuked for their delay in desisting from the oppression of the Provincials and coming to the Court of Theodoric when called for[2], a delay which is made more suspicious by their not having presented themselves to welcome Athalaric on his accession. Both they and Count Gildias are informed of the King's decision to remit the increased tax imposed at the fourth Indiction (Sept. 525); and the two Censitores are recommended, if they are conscious of having oppressed or injured any of the Provincials, to remedy the matter themselves, as the King has given all the Sicilians leave to appeal to himself against their oppressions: and the complaints of the Sicilians, though distant, will certainly reach his ears.

13. KING ATHALARIC TO WILLIAS, VIR ILLUSTRIS, COMES PATRIMONII.

Increase of emoluments of Domestici.

'Your Greatness informs us of cases that have come to your knowledge, in which the Guards (Domestici) attending the Counts who are appointed [to the government of various Provinces] have oppressed the Provincials by their exactions. As we believe that there is some excuse for this in the smallness of their *emolumenta*, which at present consist of only 200 solidi (£120) and ten rations (Annonae), we direct that you henceforth

---

[1] Tax-collectors. The word is unknown to the *Notitia*, but *Censuales* occurs once in it (Not. Occ. iv.).

[2] 'Quos etiam seris praeceptionibus credidit esse admonendos, ut *relicto tandem provincialium gravamine* ad ejus deberetis justitiam festinare.'

pay them, as from the fifth Indiction (Sept. 526), 50 solidi (£30) annually, in addition to the above, charging this further payment to our account. By taking away Necessity, the mother of crimes, we hope that the practice of sinning will also be removed. If, after this, any-one is found oppressing the Provincials, let him lose his *emolumenta* altogether. Our gifts ennoble the receiver, and are given in order to take away from him any pretext for begging from others.'

[The Domestici were a very select corps of Life-guardsmen; probably only a very small number of them would accompany a Provincial Governor to his charge. This may explain what seems an extraordinarily high rate of pay. Perhaps it is the Comes himself, not his Domestici, who is to receive the emolumenta here specified; but, if so, the letter is very obscurely expressed.]

14. KING ATHALARIC TO GILDIAS, VIR SPECTABILIS, COUNT OF SYRACUSE.

Oppressive acts charged against Gildias, Comes of Syracuse.

'We hear great complaints of you from the Sicilians; but, as they are willing to let bye-gones be bye-gones, we accede to their request, but give you the following warning:

'(1) You are said to have extorted large sums from them on pretence of rebuilding the walls, which you have not done. Either repay them the money or build up their walls. It is too absurd, to promise fortifications and give instead to the citizens hideous desolation[1].

'(2) You are said to be claiming for the Exchequer (under the name of "Fiscus Caducus") the estates of deceased persons, without any sort of regard for justice, whereas that title was only intended to apply to the case of strangers dying without heirs, natural or testamentary.

---

[1] 'Nimis enim absurdum est, spondere munitiones et dare civibus execrabiles vastitates.'

'(3) You are said to be oppressing the suitors in the Courts with grievous charges[1], so that you make litigation utterly ruinous to those who undertake it.

'We order therefore that when *our*[2] decrees are being enforced against a beaten litigant, the gratuity claimed by the officer shall be the same which our glorious grandfather declared to be payable—according to the respective ranks of the litigants—to the Sajo who was charged with the enforcement of the decree; for gratuities ought not to be excessive[3].

'But if *your* decrees are being enforced—and that must be only in cases against persons with whom the edicts allow you to interfere[4]—then your officer must receive half the gratuity allowed to him who carries our decrees into execution. It is obviously improper that the man who only performs *your* orders should receive as much as is paid out of reverence for *our* command. Anyone infringing this constitution is to restore fourfold.

'(4) The edicts of our glorious grandfather, and all the precepts which he made for the government of Sicily, are to be so obediently observed that he shall be held guilty of sacrilege who, spurred on by his own beastly disposition, shall try to break down the bulwark of our commands[5].

'(5) It is said that you cite causes between two Romans, even against their will, before your tribunal. If you are conscious that this has been done by you, do not so presume in future, lest while seeking the office of

---

[1] 'Conventiones.' I think the complaint here is of the expenses of 'executing process.' It is not as Judge but as the functionary who carries the Judge's orders into effect that Gildias is here blamed.

[2] 'Nostra' (the reading of Nivellius) seems evidently a better reading than 'vestra' (which Migne has adopted).

[3] 'Commodum debet esse *cum modo*.' A derivation or a pun.

[4] 'Duntaxat in illis causis atque personis, ubi te misceri edicta voluerunt.'

[5] 'Quisquis belluinis moribus excitatus munimen tentaverit irrumpere jussionum.'

Judge, for which you are incompetent, you wake up to find yourself a culprit. You, of all men, ought to be mindful of the Edictum, since you insist on its being followed by others. If not, if this rule is not observed by you, your whole power of decreeing shall be taken from you. Let the administration of the laws be preserved intact to the *Judices Ordinarii*. Let the litigants throng, as they ought to do, to the Courts of their *Cognitores*. Do not be gnawed by envy of their pomp. The true praise of the Goths is *law-abidingness*[1]. The more seldom the litigant is seen in your presence the greater is your renown. Do you defend the State with your arms; let the Romans plead before their own law courts in peace.

'(6) You are also accused of insisting on buying the cargoes of vessels that come to the port at your own price [and selling again at a higher]—a practice the very suspicion of which is injurious to an official, even if it cannot be proved against him in fact[2]. Wherefore, if you wish to avoid the rumour of this deed, let the Bishop and people of the city come forward as witnesses on behalf of your conscience[3]. Prices ought to be fixed by the common deliberation [of buyer and seller]; since no one likes a commercial transaction which is forced upon the unwilling.

'Wherefore we have thought it proper to warn your Sublimity by these presents, since we do not like those whom we love to be guilty of excess, nor to hear evil reports of those who are charged with reforming the morals of others.'

[This is an important letter, especially when taken in connection with the words of Totila (Procopius, 'De

---

[1] 'Gothorum laus est civilitas custodita.'

[2] This seems a possible interpretation of a dark sentence: 'Navigiis vecta commercia te suggerunt occupare, et ambitu cupiditatis exosae solum antiqua pretia definire, quod non creditur a suspicione longinquum etiam si non sit actione vicinum.'

[3] Is this a kind of compurgation which is here proposed?

Bello Gotthico' iii. 16), as to the exceptional indulgence with which the Gothic Kings had treated Sicily, 'leaving, at the request of the inhabitants, very few soldiers in the island, that there might be no distaste to their freedom or to their general prosperity.'

Gildias is evidently a Goth, and though a *Vir Spectabilis* and holding a Roman office—the Comitiva Syracusanae Civitatis—still it is essentially a military office, and he has no business to divert causes from the Judices Ordinarii to his tribunal, though probably a Roman Comes might often do this without serious blame. But by his doing so, the general principle, that in purely Roman causes a Goth is not to interfere, seems to be infringed, and therefore he receives this sharp reprimand to prevent his doing it again.]

15. KING ATHALARIC TO POPE JOHN II (532).

Against Simony at Papal elections.

'The Defensor of the Roman Church hath informed us in his tearful petition that lately, when a President was sought for the Papal chair, so much were the usual largesses to the poor augmented by the promises which had been extorted from the candidate, that, shameful to say, even the sacred vessels were exposed to sale in order to provide the necessary money[1].

'Therefore let your Holiness know that by this present decree, which relates also to all the Patriarchs and Metropolitan Churches [the five Metropolitan Churches in Rome, and such Sees as Milan, Aquileia, Ravenna], we confirm the wise law passed by the Senate in the time of the most holy Pope Boniface [predecessor of John II]. By it any contract or promise made by any person in order to obtain a Bishopric is declared void.

---

[1] 'Quosdam nefariâ machinatione necessitatem temporis aucupatos, ita facultates pauperum extortis promissionibus ingravasse, ut quod dictu nefas est, etiam sacra vasa emptioni publicae viderentur exposita.'

'Anyone refusing to refund money so received is to be declared guilty of sacrilege, and restitution is to be enforced by the Judge.'

'Should a contention arise as to an election to the Apostolic See, and the matter be brought to our Palace for decision, we direct that the maximum fee to be paid, on the completion of the necessary documents (?), shall be 3,000 solidi [£1,800][1]; but this is only to be exacted from persons of sufficient ability to pay it.

'Patriarchs [Archbishops of the other great Italian Sees] under similar circumstances are to pay not more than 2,000 solidi [£1,200].

'No one is to give [on his consecration] more than 500 solidi [£300] to the poor.

'Anyone professing to obtain for money the suffrage of any one of our servants on behalf of a candidate for Papacy or Patriarchate, shall be forced to refund the money. If it cannot be recovered from him, it may be from his heirs. He himself shall be branded with infamy.

'Should the giver of the money have been bound by such oaths, that, without imperilling his soul, he cannot disclose the transaction, anyone else may inform, and on establishing the truth of his accusation, receive a third part of the money so corruptly paid, the rest to go to the churches themselves, for the repair of the fabric or for the daily ministry. Remember the fate of Simon Magus. We have ordered that this decree be made known to the Senate and people by the Praefect of the City.'

[I think the early part of this letter gives us the clue to the pretext under which these simoniacal practices were introduced. It was usual for the Pope on his elec-

---

[1] 'Et quia omnia decet sub ratione moderari, nec possunt dici justa quae nimia sunt, cum de Apostolici consecratione Pontificis intentio fortasse pervenerit, et ad Palatium nostrum producta fuerit altercatio populorum, suggerentes (?) nobis intra tria millia solidorum, cum collectione cartarum censemus accipere.'

tion to give a certain sum of money to the poor. Then at a vehemently contested election certain of the voters—perhaps especially the priests of the different *tituli* of Rome—claimed to be distributors of the Papal bounty, a large part of which they no doubt kept for themselves.]

16. KING ATHALARIC TO SALVANTIUS, VIR ILLUSTRIS, PRAEFECT OF THE CITY.

The same subject. Rehearses the motives of the previous edict, and directs that both it and the Senatus Consulta having reference to the same subject [and framed two years previously], be engraved on marble tablets, and fixed up in a conspicuous place, before the Atrium of St. Peter the Apostle.

17. KING ATHALARIC TO THE SAME (BETWEEN 532 AND 534).

Release of two Roman citizens accused of sedition. 'We cannot bear that there should be sadness in Rome, the head of the world. We hear with regret from the Apostolic Pope John, and other nobles, that A and B, who are Romans, on a mere suspicion of sedition are being macerated by so long imprisonment that the whole city mourns for them; no gladness of a holyday and no respect for the Papal name[1] (which is most dear to us) availing to mitigate their confinement. This treatment of persons against whom no crime has been proved distresses us much, and we admonish your Greatness, wherever you may succeed in finding them, to set them free. If, confident in their innocence, they think that they have been unjustly tormented, we give them liberty to make their appeal to the laws. Judges

---

[1] 'Nec ulla—quae apud nos est gratissima—nominis sui dignitas subveniret.' I think *sui* must refer to the recently-mentioned *Papa Johannes*.

were raised to their high estate, not to oppress but to defend the innocent.

'Now let the Romans return to their ancient gladness; nor let them think that any [rulers] please us but those who seek to act with fairness and moderation. Let them understand that our forefathers underwent labours and dangers that *they* might have rest; and that we are expending large sums in order that they may rejoice with garrulous exultation. For even if they have before now suffered some rough and unjust treatment, let them not believe that that is a thing to be neglected by our Mildness. No; for we give ourselves no rest, that they may enjoy secure peace and calm gladness. Let them understand at once that *we* cannot love the men whose excesses have made them terrible to our subjects. Whose favour do those men expect to win who have earned the dislike of their fellow-citizens? They might have reaped a harvest of the public love, and instead thereof they have so acted that their names are justly held in execration.'

18. THE EDICT OF ATHALARIC.

[This edict is minutely examined by Dahn ('Könige der Germanen' iv. 123-135). I have adopted his division of paragraphs, though rather disposed to think that the 'De Donationibus' should be broken up into two, to prevent counting the Epilogue as a section. See also Manso ('Geschichte der Ostrogothen' 405-415).]

'*Prologue.* This edict is a general one. No names are mentioned in it, and those who are conscious of innocence need take no offence at anything contained therein.

Edict of Athalaric.

'For long an ominous whisper has reached our ears that certain persons, despising *civilitas*, affect a life of beastly barbarism[1], returning to the wild beginnings of

---

[1] 'Affectare vivere belluinâ saevitiâ.'

society, and looking with a fierce hatred on all human laws. The present seems to us a fitting time for repressing these men, in order that we may be hunting down vice and immorality within the Republic at the same time that, with God's help, we are resisting her external foes. Both are hurtful, both have to be repelled; but the internal enemy is even more dangerous than the external. One, however, rests upon the other; and we shall more easily sweep down the armies of our enemies if we subdue under us the vices of the age. [This allusion to foreign enemies is perhaps explained by the hint in Jordanes ('De Reb. Get.' 59) of threatened war with the Franks. But he gives us no sufficient indication of time to enable us to fix the date of the Edictum.]

'I. *Forcible Appropriation of Landed Property*[1] (Pervasio). This is a crime which is quite inconsistent with *civilitas*, and we remit those who are guilty of it to the punishment[2] provided by a law of Divus Valentinianus [Valentinian III. Novell. xix. 'De Invasoribus'], adding that if anyone is unable to pay the penalty therein provided he shall suffer banishment (deportatio). He ought to have been more chary of disobeying the laws if he had no means to pay the penalty. Judges who shrink from obeying this law, and allow the *Pervasor* to remain in possession of what he has forcibly annexed, shall lose their offices and be held liable to pay to our Treasury the same fine which might have been exacted from him. If the *Pervasor* sets the Judge's official staff (officium) at defiance, on the report of the Judge our Sajones will make *him* feel the weight of the royal vengeance who refused to obey the [humbler] *Cognitor*.

[1] 'Praedia urbana vel rustica.'

[2] The punishment consisted in loss of all claim to the property—which was generally seized by someone who had some kind of ostensible claim to it—and a penalty of equal value with that of the property wrongfully seized.

'II. *Affixing Titles to Property*. [When land had from any cause become public property, the Emperor's officers used to affix *tituli*, to denote the fact and to warn off all other claimants. Powerful men who had dispossessed weaker claimants used to imitate this practice, and are here forbidden to do so.]

'This offence shall subject the perpetrator to the same penalties as *pervasio*. It is really a kind of sacrilege to try to add the majesty of the royal name to the weight of his own oppression. Costs are to be borne by the defeated claimant.

'III. *Suppression of Words in a Decree*. Anyone obtaining a decree against an adversary is to be careful to suppress nothing in the copy which he serves upon him. If he does so, he shall lose all the benefits that he obtained. We wish to help honest men, not rogues.

'IV. *Seduction of a Married Woman*. He who tries to interfere with the married rights of another, shall be punished by inability to contract a valid marriage himself. [This punishment of compulsory celibacy is, according to Dahn, derived neither from Roman nor German law, but is possibly due to Church influence.] The offender who has no hope of present or future matrimony[1] shall be punished by confiscation of half his property; or, if a poor man, by banishment.

'V. *Adultery*. All the statutes of the late King (divalis commonitio) in this matter are to be strictly observed. [Edict. Theodorici, § 38, inflicted the penalty of death on both offenders and on the abettors of the crime.]

'VI. *Bigamy* is to be punished with loss of all the offender's property.

'VII. *Concubinage*. If a married man forms a connection of this kind with a free woman, she and all her

---

[1] 'Illis quos spes non habet praesentis conjugii vel futuri.' It is not easy to see how the Judge could ascertain whether a man belonged to this class or not.

children shall become the slaves of the injured wife. If with a woman who is a slave already, she shall be subjected to any revenge that the lawful wife likes to inflict upon her, short of blood-shedding[1].

'VIII. *Donations* are not to be extorted by terror, nor acquired by fraud, or as the price of immorality. Where a gift is *bonâ fide*, the document conveying it is to be drawn up with the strictness prescribed by Antiquity, in order to remove occasions of fraud.

'IX. Magicians and other persons practising nefarious arts are to be punished by the severity of the laws. What madness to leave the Giver of life and seek to the Author of death! Let the Judges be especially careful to avoid the contagion of these foul practices.

'X. *Violence Exercised towards the Weak.* Let the condition of mediocrity be safe from the arrogance of the rich. Let the madness of bloodshed be avoided. To take the law into your own hands is to wage private war, especially in the case of those who are fortified by the authority of our *tuitio*. If anyone attempts with foul presumption to act contrary to these principles, let him be considered a violator of our orders.

'XI. *Appeals* are not to be made twice in the same cause.

'XII. *Epilogue.* But lest, while touching on a few points, we should be thought not to wish the laws to be observed in other matters, we declare that all the edicts of ourself and of our lord and grandfather, which were confirmed by venerable deliberation[2], and the whole body of decided law[3], be adhered to with the utmost rigour.

[1] 'Quod si ad tale flagitium ancilla pervenerit, excepta poena sanguinis, matronali subjaceat ultioni: ut illam patiatur judicem, quam formidare debuisset absentem.' These provisions are probably of Germanic origin.

[2] 'Quae sunt venerabili deliberatione firmata.' Is it possible that we have here a reference to a theoretical right of the *Senate* to concur in legislation?

[3] 'Et usualia jura publica.' Dahn expands: 'All other juristic material,

'And these laws are so scrupulously guarded that our own oath is interposed for their defence. Why enlarge further? Let the usual rule of law and the honest intent of our precepts be everywhere observed.'

19. KING ATHALARIC TO THE SENATE OF THE CITY OF ROME.

Promulgation of the Edict.

'Good laws are called forth by evil manners. If no complaints were ever heard, the Prince might take holiday. Stirred up by many and frequent complaints of our people, we have drawn up certain regulations necessary for the Roman peace, in our edict which is divided into twelve chapters, after the manner of the civil law[1]. We do not thereby abrogate, but rather confirm, the previously existing body of law.

'Let this edict be read in your splendid assembly, and exhibited for thirty days by the Praefect of the City in the most conspicuous places. Thus shall our *civilitas* be recognised, and truculent men lose their confidence. What insolent subjects[2] can indulge in violence when the Sovereign condemns it? Our armies fight that there may be peace at home. Let the Judges do their duty fearlessly, and avoid foul corruption.'

20. KING ATHALARIC TO ALL THE JUDGES OF THE PROVINCES.

The same subject.

'It is vexatious that, though we appoint you year by year to your duties, and leave no district without its Judge, there is yet such tardiness in administering justice that suitors come by preference to our distant Court.

---

all sources of law—Roman *leges* and *jus*, and Gothic customary law—the whole inheritance of the State in public and private law.'

[1] 'Necessaria quaedam Romanae quieti edictali programmate duodecim capitibus sicut jus civile legitur institutum in aevum servanda conscripsimus, quae custodita residuum jus non debilitare, sed potius corroborare videantur.'

[2] Evidently aimed at the Goths.

'To take away all excuse from you, and relieve the necessity of our subjects, we have drawn up an edict which we desire you to exhibit for thirty days in the wonted manner at all places of public meeting.'

21. KING ATHALARIC TO THE SENATE OF THE CITY OF ROME.

Increase of salaries of grammarians.

'You who are called Fathers should be interested in all that concerns the education of your sons. We hear by certain whisperings that the teachers of eloquence at Rome are not receiving their proper reward, and that the sums appointed to be paid to the masters of schools are lessened by the haggling of some persons.

'Grammar is the noble foundation of all literature, the glorious mother of eloquence. As a virtuous man is offended by any act of vice, as a musician is pained by a discordant note, so does the grammarian in a moment perceive a false concord.

'The grammatical art is not used by barbarous kings: it abides peculiarly with legitimate sovereigns[1]. Other nations have arms: the lords of the Romans alone have eloquence. Hence sounds the trumpet for the legal fray in the Forum. Hence comes the eloquence of so many chiefs of the State. Hence, to say nothing more, even this discourse which is now addressed to you[2].

'Wherefore let the teacher of grammar and of rhetoric, if he be found suitable for his work and obey the decrees of the Praefect of the City, be supported by your authority, and suffer no diminution of his salary[3].

'To prevent his being dependent in any way on the caprice of his employer, let him receive half his salary at the end of half a year, and his *annonae* at the

---

[1] 'Hac non utuntur barbari reges: apud legales dominos manere cognoscitur singularis.'

[2] 'Et, ut reliqua taceamus, hoc quod loquimur inde est.'

[3] 'Et semel Primi Ordinis vestri ac reliqui Senatus amplissimi auctoritate firmatus.' What is the meaning of 'Primi Ordinis vestri?'

customary times. If the person whose business it is to pay him neglects this order, he shall be charged interest on the arrears.

'The Grammarian is a man to whom every hour unemployed is misery, and it is a shame that such a man should have to wait the caprice of a public functionary before he gets his pay. We provide for the salaries of the play-actors, who minister only to the amusement of the public; and how much more for these men, the moulders of the style and character of our youth! Therefore let them henceforward not have to try the philosophical problem of thinking about two things at once, but, with their minds at ease about their subsistence, devote themselves with all their vigour to the teaching of liberal arts.'

22. KING ATHALARIC TO PAULINUS, VIR CLARISSIMUS AND CONSUL (533).

[Flavius Theodorus Paulinus Junior was Consul with the Emperor Justinian in 534. This letter was written in Sept. 533, about thirteen months before the death of Athalaric. Paulinus was son of Venantius and grandson of Liberius.]

Paulinus chosen as Consul.

'The absent from our Court need not fear that they will be disregarded in the distribution of honours, especially when they are sprung from an illustrious stock, the offspring of the Senate.

'In your family Rome recognises the descendants of her ancient heroes the Decii, who, in a great crisis, alone saved their country.

'Take then for the twelfth Indiction the ensigns of the Consulship[1]. It is an arduous honour, but one which your family is well used to. The Fasti are studded with

---

[1] The twelfth Indiction began Sept. 1, 533. The Consul would enter office Jan. 1, 534. Was he *designated* when the great Imperial officers were *appointed* at the beginning of the Indiction?

its names, and nearly all the Senate is of kin to you. Still, presume not too much on the merits of your ancestors, but rather seek to emulate their noble deeds.'

23. KING ATHALARIC TO THE SENATE OF THE CITY OF ROME.

On the Consulship of Paulinus.

'Judge of our esteem for your honourable body, Conscript Fathers, when, without any hesitation, we appoint your sons whom we have never seen to high office, because they are your sons.

'We admire the Patrician Venantius, blessed as he has been with such an abundant progeny, and found equal to the weight of so many Consulships. His sons have been all temperate and lively; worthy members of the same distinguished family. They have been trained in arms, their minds have been formed by letters, their bodies by the exercises of the gymnasium. They have learned to show constancy to their friends, loyalty to their lords; and they have succeeded to the virtues of their ancestors, as they will to their patrimony. Wisely husbanding his own fortune, Venantius has been able to support the honour—gratifying, but burdensome—of seeing so many of his sons made Consuls. But this is an honour not strange to his family, sprung from the ancient Decii. His hall is full of laurelled Fasces, and in his line one might almost say that each one is born a Consular.

'Favour our candidate then, Conscript Fathers, and cherish him with that care which the name of your body [1] signifies.'

24. KING ATHALARIC TO SENATOR [CASSIODORUS HIMSELF], PRAETORIAN PRAEFECT (SEPT. 1, 533).

Cassiodorus appointed Praetorian Praefect.

'If you had been hitherto an obscure person we might feel some doubt how you would bear yourself in your

---

[1] *Curia,* from *cura.*

new office, but your long and glorious career under our grandfather relieves us from any such anxieties. *His* choice of you is a thing to be not discussed but reverently accepted. It was by him that we ourselves were chosen; and the Divine favour so conspicuously followed him that no General whom he selected was other than victorious, no Judge whom he appointed was other than just. In short, one might almost deem him to have been endowed with the gift of prophecy.

'In your early manhood he received you into the office of Quaestor, and soon found you to be a conscientious man, learned in the law beyond your years[1]. You were the chief ornament of your times, inasmuch as you, by your blameless service sustaining the weight of that royal intellect by all the force of your eloquence, enabled him, with his keen interest in all public affairs, to await the result with confidence. In you he possessed a counsellor pleasant in the transaction of business, rigid in his sense of justice, free from all taint of avarice. You never fixed a scandalous tariff for the sale of his benefits; and thus you reaped your reward in a wealth of public opinion, not in gold. It was because that just Prince proved you to be averse from all these vices that he selected you for his glorious friendship. A wise judge, he threw upon you the weight of listening to the arguments of contending parties; and so high was his opinion of your tried sagacity that he at once uttered your decision as the greatest benefit that he could confer on the litigants. How often did he rank you among the oldest chiefs of his Council! How often was it seen that your young beginnings were more than a match for them, who had the experience of long years behind them! What he found to praise in you was your excellent disposition, wide open for useful work, tight closed against

<small>His Quaestorship.</small>

---

[1] 'Primaevum recipiens ad Quaestoris Officium, mox reperit conscientia praeditum, et legum eruditione maturum.'

the vices of avarice. Whereas, for some reason, it is rare to find amongst men, the hand closed and justice open.

His career as Master of the Offices.

'Let us pass on to the dignity of *Magister Officiorum*, which all men knew that you obtained, not from the reputation of wealth, but as a testimony to your character. In this place you were always ready to help the [successive] Quaestors; for, when pure eloquence was required, the case was always put in your hands. The benignant Sovereign claimed from you the fulfilment of duties which he knew that he had not formally laid upon you; and such was the favour that he had for you, while others laboured you received the reward of his abundant praises[1]. For under your administration no dignity kept its exact limits; anything that was to be honestly done by all the chiefs of the State together, you considered to be entrusted to *your* conscience for its performance.

'No one found occasion to murmur anything to your disadvantage, though you had to bear all the weight of unpopularity which comes from the Sovereign's favour. The integrity of your life conquered those who longed to detract from your reputation, and your enemies were obliged to utter the praises which their hearts abhorred; for even malice leaves manifest goodness unattacked, lest it be itself exposed to general hatred.

His friendship for Theodoric.

'To the Monarch you showed yourself a friendly Minister and an intimate Noble[2]. For when he had laid aside the cares of State, he would seek in your conversation the opinions of wise men of old, that by his own deeds he might make himself equal to the

---

[1] 'Et quadam gratia praejudiciali vacabat alios laborare, ut te sententiae suae copiosa laude compleret.' One would have expected Cassiodorus to say, 'You had the special privilege of doing other people's work and being praised for it, while they enjoyed their leisure;' but I hardly see how we can get this meaning out of ' vacabat alios laborare.'

[2] 'Egisti rerum domino judicem familiarem et internum procerem.'

ancients[1]. Into the courses of the stars, into the gulfs of the sea, into the marvels of springing fountains, this most acute questioner enquired, so that by his diligent investigations into the nature of things he seemed to be a Philosopher wearing the purple.

'It were long to narrate all your merits in the past. Let us rather turn to the future, and show how the heir of Theodoric's Empire proposes to pay the debts of Theodoric.

'Therefore, with the Divine help, we bestow on you from the twelfth Indiction [Sept. 1, 533] the authority and insignia of Praetorian Praefect. Let the Provinces, which we know to have been hitherto wearied by the administration of dishonest men, fearlessly receive a Judge of tried integrity.

'Though you have before you the example of your father's Praefecture[2], renowned throughout the Italian world, we do not so much set before you either that or any other example, as your own past character, exhorting you to rule consistently with that. You have always been averse from bribery; now earnestly help the victims of injustice. We have purposely delayed your accession to this high office that you might be the more heartily welcomed by the people, who expected to see you clothed with it long ago. Diligently seek out anything belonging to the titles of the Praetorian Praefecture, of which it has been defrauded by the cupidity of others. We send you as a light into a dark chamber, and expect that your sagacity and loyalty will discover many hidden things.

'We know that you will work not so much for the sake of honour as in order to satisfy your con-

---

[1] 'Nam cum esset publica cura vacuatus, sententias prudentum a tuis fabulis exigebat; ut factis propriis se aequaret antiquis.'

[2] 'Quamvis habeas paternam Praefecturam, Italico orbe praedicatam.' This is one of the many proofs that Senator (now first advanced to the office of Praefectus Praetorio) is the *son* of the Cassiodorus to whom the letter (i. 3) is addressed on his retirement from that office.

science; and work so done knows no limit to its excellence.'

25. KING ATHALARIC TO THE SENATE OF THE CITY OF ROME (ON THE PROMOTION OF CASSIODORUS SENATOR TO THE PRAETORIAN PRAEFECTURE).

Eulogy of Cassiodorus on his appointment as Praetorian Praefect.

'We have loaded Senator with our benefits, Conscript Fathers, because he abounds in virtue, is rich in excellence of character, and is already full of the highest honours. But, in fact, we are his debtors. How shall we repay that eloquent tongue of his, with which he set forth the deeds of the Prince, till he himself who had wrought them wondered at his story? In praising the reign of the wearer of the purple, he made it acceptable to your nation. For taxes may be paid to a tyrant; praise, such as this, is given only to a good Prince.

His Gothic History.

'Not satisfied with extolling living Kings, from whom he might hope for a reward, he drew forth the Kings of the Goths from the dust of ages, showing that the Amal family had been royal for seventeen generations, and proved that the origin of the Gothic people belonged to Roman history[1], adorning the whole subject with the flowers of his learning gathered from wide fields of literature.

'In the early days of our reign what labour he gave to the settling of our affairs! He was alone sufficient for all. The duty of making public harangues, our own private counsels, required him. He laboured that the Empire might rest.

---

[1] 'Tetendit se etiam in antiquam prosapiem nostram, lectione discens, quod vix majorum notitia cana retinebat. Iste Reges Gothorum longa oblivione celatos, latibulo vetustatis eduxit. Iste Amalos cum generis sui claritate restituit, evidenter ostendens in decimam septimam progeniem stirpem nos habere regalem. Originem Gothicam historiam fecit esse Romanam, colligens quasi in unam coronam germen floridum quod per librorum campos passim fuerat ante dispersum.'

'We found him Magister; but he discharged the duties of Quaestor, and willingly bestowed on us, the heir, the experience which he had gained in the counsels of our grandfather. His official career.

'And not only so, he helped the beginning of our reign both with his arms and his pen. For when the care of our shores[1] occupied our royal meditation, he suddenly emerged from the seclusion of his cabinet, boldly, like his ancestors, assumed the office of General[2], and triumphed by his character when there was no enemy to overcome. For he maintained the Gothic warriors[3] at his own charges, so that there should be no robbery of the Provincials on the one hand, no too heavy burden on the exchequer on the other. Thus was the soldier what he ought to be, the true defender, not the ravager of his country. Then when the time for victualling the ships was over, and the war was laid aside, he shone as an administrator rather than a warrior, healing, without injury to the litigants, the various suits which arose out of the sudden cessation of the contracts[4]. His military services.

'Such was the glory of the military command of a Metellus in Asia, of a Cato in Spain—a glory far more durable than any that can be derived from the varying shock of war.

'Yet with all these merits, how humble he has been, how modest, how benevolent, how slow to wrath, how generous in the distribution of that which is his own, His religious character.

[1] Probably from some expected descent of the Vandals, in connection with the affair of Amalafrida.

[2] 'Par suis majoribus ducatum sumpsit intrepidus.'

[3] 'Deputatos.'

[4] A conjectural translation of a difficult sentence: 'Mox autem ut tempus clausit navium commeatum, bellique cura resoluta est, ingenium suum legum potius ductor exercuit: sanans sine damno litigantium quod ante sub pretio constabat esse laceratum.' I conjecture that by the sudden stoppage of the warlike preparations several of the contractors were in danger of being ruined, and there was a general disposition to repudiate all purchases.

how slow to covet the property of others! All these virtues have been consolidated by his reading of the Divine Book, the fear of God helping him to triumph over baser, human motives. Thus has he been rendered humble towards all, as one imbued with heavenly teaching.

'Him therefore, Conscript Fathers, we make, under God's blessing, Praetorian Praefect from the twelfth Indiction [Sept. 1, 533], that he may repress by his own loyalty the trafficking of knaves, and may use his power for the good of the Republic, bequeathing eternal renown to his posterity.'

BOOK X.

CONTAINING THIRTY-FIVE LETTERS WRITTEN BY CASSIODORUS:

FOUR IN THE NAME OF QUEEN AMALASUENTHA.
TWENTY-TWO IN THAT OF KING THEODAHAD.
FOUR IN THAT OF HIS WIFE GUDELINA.
FIVE IN THAT OF KING WITIGIS.

1. QUEEN AMALASUENTHA TO JUSTINIAN THE EMPEROR (A.D. 534).

Association of Theodahad in the Sovereignty.

'I HAVE hitherto forborne to distress you with the sad tidings of the death of my son of glorious memory, but now am able to mingle a joyful announcement with this mournful message. We have promoted to the sceptre a man allied to us by a fraternal tie, that he may wear the purple robes of his ancestors, and may cheer our own soul by his prudent counsels. We are persuaded that you will give us your good wishes on this event, as we hope that every kind of prosperity may befall the kingdom of your Piety. The friendship of princes is always comely, but your friendship absolutely ennobles me, since that person is exalted in dignity who is united by friendship to your glory [1].

[1] 'Nam licet concordia Principum semper deceat, vestra tamen absolute me nobilitat; quoniam ille redditur amplius excelsus, qui vestrae gloriae fuerit unanimiter conjunctus.'

'As we cannot in the short space of a letter express all that we desire to say on such an occasion, we have entrusted certain verbal messages to the ambassadors who bear this epistle.'

2. THEODAHAD THE KING TO JUSTINIAN THE EMPEROR.

The same subject.

'It is usual for newly-crowned Kings to signify their accession to the different nations round them. I, in making this communication to you, am greatly favoured by Providence, feeling secure of your favour, because I know that my most excellent Lady and Sister has already attained it. I feel confident that I shall justify the choice of one who shines in such a light of wisdom that she both governs her own kingdom with admirable forethought and keeps firmly the vows of friendship which she has plighted to her neighbours. Partner of her cares, I desire also to be a partner of her wisely-formed friendships, those especially which she has contracted with you, who have nothing like unto you in the whole world. This alliance is no new thing: if you will look back upon the deeds of our ancestors you will find that there is a custom which has obtained the force of a law, that the Amals should be friendly with the Empire. So old a friendship is likely to endure; and if, in obedience to it and to my Sister's choice, I have your love, I shall feel that I am indeed a King.

'The ambassadors who have charge of this letter will further express my sentiments.'

3. QUEEN AMALASUENTHA TO THE SENATE OF THE CITY OF ROME.

The same subject.

'After the death of our son of blessed memory[1] our love for the common weal overcame the yearnings of a

---

[1] 'Divae recordationis.'

mother's heart and caused us to seek your prosperity rather than an opportunity to indulge in our own sorrow. We have considered by what solace we should strengthen ourselves for the cares of royalty. The same Providence which has deprived us of a son in the dawn of manhood, has reserved for us the affection of a brother in mature age. Under the Divine auspices we have chosen Theodahad[1] as the fortunate partner of our throne. We two, with conjoined counsels, shall now labour for the common welfare, *two* in our meditations, *one* in the action which results from them. The stars give one another mutual help in ruling the heavens, and God has bestowed on man two hands, two ears, two eyes, that each one of these members should assist the other.

'Therefore exult, Conscript Fathers, and commend our deed to the blessing of the Almighty. Our sharing our power with another is a pledge of its being wisely and gently exercised. By God's help we have opened our palace to a man of our own race, conspicuous by his illustrious position, who, born of the Amal stock, has a kingly dignity in all his actions, being patient in adversity, moderate in prosperity, and, most difficult of all kinds of government, long used to the government of himself. Moreover, he possesses that desirable quality, literary erudition, lending a grace to a nature originally praiseworthy. It is in books that the sage counsellor finds deeper wisdom, in books that the warrior learns how he may be strengthened by the courage of the soul, in books that the Sovereign discovers how he may weld nations together under his equal rule. In short, there is no condition in life the credit whereof is not augmented by the glorious knowledge of literature.

Praises of Theodahad.

'Your new Sovereign is moreover learned in ecclesiastical lore, by which we are ever reminded of the things which make for our own true honour, right judgment, wise discretion, reverence for God, thought

[1] Is there any authority for the reading of Nivellius, '*Theobaldum*?'

of the future judgment. For the remembrance that we shall one day stand at the bar to answer for ourselves compels us to follow the footprints of Justice. Thus does religious reading not only sharpen the intellect but ever tend to make men scrupulous in the performance of their duties.

'Let me pass on to that most generous frugality of his private household[1] which procured the means of such abundance in his gifts, of such plenty at his banquets, that even the kingdom will not call for any new expenditure in this respect greater than the old. Generous in his hospitality, most pitiful in his compassions, while he was thus spending much, his fortune, by a heavenly reward, was ever on the increase.

'The wish of the people should coincide with our choice of such a man, who, reasonably spending his own goods, does not desire the goods of others[2]. For moderation in his own expenditure takes away from the Sovereign the temptation to transgress the precepts of justice and to abandon the golden mean.

'Rejoice then, Conscript Fathers, and give thanks to the Most High, that I have chosen such a ruler, who will supplement my justice by the good deeds which spring from his own piety. For this man is both admonished by the virtue of his ancestors and powerfully stimulated by the example of his uncle Theodoric.'

4. KING THEODAHAD TO THE SENATE OF THE CITY OF ROME.

The same subject.

'We announce to you, Conscript Fathers, the Divine favour which has been manifested unto us, in that our

---

[1] 'Veniamus ad illam privatae Ecclesiae (?) largissimam frugalitatem.' 'Ecclesiae,' if it means here 'the Church,' seems to spoil the sense. Can Cassiodorus mean to compare the household of Theodahad to a 'private Ecclesia?'

[2] 'Talem universitas debuit optare, qualem nos probamur elegisse, qui rationabiliter disponens propria, non appetat aliena.' And this of Theodahad!

sovereign Lady[1], who is renowned throughout the whole world, has with generous affection made me partaker of her throne, so that she may not lack loyal support and I may be fittingly clothed with the purple of my ancestors.

'I know that this elevation of mine was the object of the wishes of the community. Your whispers in my favour might have been a source of danger, but now your openly expressed acclamations are my proudest boast. You wished that God should bestow upon me this honour, to which I for my part should not have ventured to aspire. But if I have, as I trust I have, any influence with you, let me prevail upon you to join with me in perpetually hymning the glorious praises of our Lady and Sister. She has wished to strengthen the greatness of our Empire by associating me therein, even as the two eyes of a man harmoniously co-operate towards a single act of vision. Divine grace joins us together: our near relationship cements our friendship. Persons of diverse character may find it an arduous matter thus to work in common; but, to those who resemble one another in the goodness of their intentions, the difficulty would rather be *not* to work in harmony. The man devoid of forethought may fear the changing of his purposes; but he who is really great in wisdom eagerly seeks wisdom in another.

'But of all the gifts which with this regal dignity the Divine favour has bestowed upon me, none pleases me more than the fact that I should have been thus chosen by that wisest Lady who is herself a moral balance of the utmost delicacy, and who made me first feel her justice before advancing me to this high dignity. For, as you know, she ordained that I should plead my cause against private persons in the common judgment-hall[2]. Oh wonderful nobility of her mind! Oh admir-

---

[1] 'Dominam rerum.'

[2] 'Cujus prius ideo justitiam pertuli ut prius [posterius?] ad ejus provectionis gratiam pervenirem. Causas enim, ut scitis, jure communi nos fecit

able justice, which the world may well tell of! She hesitated not first to subject her own relation to the course of public justice, even him whom, a little after, she would raise above the laws themselves. She thoroughly searched the conscience of him to whom she was about to hand over the dignity of kingship, that she might be recognised as sovereign Lady of all, and that I, when tested, might be advanced by her to the throne.

Praises of Amalasuentha.

'When shall I be able to repay her for all these favours: her who, having reigned alone during the minority of her son, now chooses me as the partner of her realm? In her is the glory of all kingdoms, the flower of all our family. All our splendour is derived from her, and she reflects a lustre not only on our ancestors, but on the whole human race. Her dutiful affection, her weight of character, who can set forth? The philosophers would learn new lessons if they knew her, and would acknowledge that their books fail to describe all her attributes. Acute she is in her powers of reasoning; but with royal taciturnity she knows how to veil her conclusions in secrecy. She is mistress of many languages; and her intellect, if suddenly tested, is found so ready for the trial that it scarcely seems like that of a mortal. In the Books of Kings the Queen of the South is said to have come to learn the wisdom of Solomon: but here a woman speaks, and Sovereigns listen to her with admiration. Infinite depths of meaning are fathomed by her in few words, and she, with utmost ease, expresses what others can only after long deliberation embody in language[1].

---

dicere cum privatis.' We have here, no doubt, an allusion to the punishment which, as we learn from Procopius, Amalasuentha inflicted on her cousin for his various acts of injustice towards his Tuscan neighbours.

[1] 'Et summâ felicitate componitur quod ab aliis sub longâ deliberatione componitur.' 'Ab aliis' probably refers to Cassiodorus himself. The contrast between his elaborate and diffuse rhetoric, and the few, terse, soon-moulded sentences of his mistress is very fairly drawn.

'Happy the commonwealth which boasts the guidance of such a mistress. It was not enough that already liberty and convenience were combined for the multitude[1]: her merits have secured the fitting reverence for the person of the Sovereign. In obeying *her* we obey all the virtues. I, too, with such a counsellor, fear not the weight of the crown; and I know that whatever is strange to me in my new duties I shall learn from her as the safest of teachers.

'Acknowledge, noble Sirs, that all my power of increased usefulness to the State comes from this our most wise Lady, from whom I may either gain wisdom by asking questions, or virtue by following her example.

'Live happily: live in harmony by God's help, and emulate that grace of concord which you see prevailing between your Sovereigns.'

5. KING THEODAHAD TO HIS MAN THEODOSIUS[2].

'By my accession to the throne I have become lord of the whole nation and guardian of the general welfare. I therefore command that all who belong to my private household shall vindicate their rights only in the courts of law, and shall abstain from all high-handed modes of obtaining redress. Only that man must henceforward be called mine who can live quietly subject to the laws. My new dignity has changed my purpose; and if before I have defended my rights with pertinacity, I shall now temper all my acts with clemency[3]; since there is nothing exceptional about a Sovereign's household, but

The followers of the new King must live justly.

---

[1] 'Minus fuit ut generalitas sub libertate serviret.'

[2] 'Theodosio homini suo Theodahadus rex.' Does 'homo suus' mean a member of his Comitatus? We seem to have here an anticipation of the 'homagium' of later times.

[3] 'Mutavimus cum dignitate propositum, et si ante justa districte defendimus, nunc clementer omnia mitigamus.' A pretty plain confession of Theodahad's past wrong-doing, and one which was probably insisted upon by Amalasuentha in admitting him to a share in the kingship.

wheresoever, by the grace of God, our rule extends, there, as we fully confess, is something which it is our duty to defend. Augment therefore my renown by your patience, and let me hear praises rather than complaints of the actions of my servants.'

6. KING THEODAHAD TO PATRICIUS, VIR ILLUSTRIS AND QUAESTOR.

Patricius appointed Quaestor.

'In conferring upon you the office of Quaestor we look first to character, and we find in you that love of justice which is all important in a representative of the Prince. Then we look at the qualities of your intellect, and we find in you that flow of eloquence which among all mental accomplishments we value most highly. What does it profit to be a philosopher, if one cannot worthily set forth the results of one's investigations? To discover is natural to man; but to set forth one's discoveries in noble language, that is indeed a desirable gift. Therefore we bestow on you for this thirteenth Indiction[1] the fasces of the Quaestorship, desiring you to consecrate your time to the study of the laws and the *responsa prudentum*, and to spread abroad our fame by the eloquent manner in which you shall communicate our decrees to the Cities and Provinces under our sway, and speak in our name to the representatives of foreign nations.'

7. KING THEODAHAD TO THE SENATE OF THE CITY OF ROME.

The same subject.

'After announcing to you our own accession, one of our first cares was to choose a Judge whose style of speaking might dignify the State. Such a Judge have we found in Patricius (Patrician by his name already), whom we hereby appoint to the office of Quaestor. He

---

[1] 534–535. As Athalaric died Oct. 2, 534, the appointment of Patricius cannot have taken place on the usual day, Sept. 1.

studied eloquence at Rome. Where could he have studied better? For while other parts of the world have their wine, their balm, their frankincense, which they can export, the peculiar product of Rome is eloquence.

'Having thus learned his art, he practised it at the bar with singular moderation. No heat of strife hurried him into abuse of his competitors. Seeking only to win his client's cause, he calmly and courteously set forth that client's rights without sacrificing his own dignity of demeanour.

'Thinking that this man has pleaded long enough, we now appoint that he shall sit as Judge, having made diligent enquiry as to his character. In this, and in all other matters, we wish to follow the example of the Emperors who have gone before us, in so far as they followed the paths of justice[1].'

8. QUEEN AMALASUENTHA TO JUSTINIAN, AUGUSTUS.

'Delighting to receive from your Piety some of those treasures of which the heavenly bounty has made you partaker, we send the bearer of the present letter to receive those marbles and other necessaries which we formerly ordered Calogenitus to collect on our behalf. All our adornments, furnished by you, redound to your glory. For it is fitting that by your assistance should shine resplendent that Roman world which the love of your Serenity renders illustrious.'

Present of marbles from Justinian to Amalasuentha.

9. KING THEODAHAD TO JUSTINIAN, AUGUSTUS.

[On the same subject as the previous letter, and in nearly the same words. Calogenitus apparently is dead.]

The same subject.

'We have directed the bearer of this letter to exhibit (?) those things for which Calogenitus was previously des-

---

[1] 'Velle nostrum antiquorum principum est voluntas, quos in tantum desideramus imitari quantum illi justitiam sunt secuti.'

tined; so that, although that person is withdrawn from this life, your benefits, by God's help, may still be brought unto us.'

10. QUEEN AMALASUENTHA TO THEODORA, AUGUSTA[1].

Salutation to Theodora.

'We approach you with the language of veneration, because it is agreed on all hands that your virtues increase more and more. Friendship exists not for those only who are in one another's presence, but also for the absent. Rendering you therefore the salutation of august reverence, I hope that our ambassadors, whom we have directed to the most clement and most glorious Emperor, will bring me news of your welfare. Your prosperity is as dear to me as my own; and as I constantly pray for your safety, I cannot hear without pleasure that my prayers have been answered.'

11. KING THEODAHAD TO MAXIMUS[2], VIR ILLUSTRIS AND DOMESTICUS.

Maximus appointed to office of Primicerius (Domesticorum?)

'It is the glory of a good Sovereign to confer office on the deserving descendants of illustrious families. Such are the Anicii, an ancient family, almost on an equality with princes[3], from whom you are descended. Gladly would we decorate the descendants of the Marii and Corvini if time had permitted their progeny to survive to our own day. But it were inconsistent to regret the

---

[1] There is something in the tone of this letter which suggests that Theodora was known to be pregnant when it was written.

[2] This Maximus does not appear to be mentioned by Procopius. He may be the same Maximus who took refuge in one of the churches after Totila's capture of Rome in 546 (De Bello Gotthico iii. 20), and who was slain by order of Teias in 552 (Ibid. iv. 34); but that person was grandson of an Emperor, and it seems hardly probable that Cassiodorus would have spared us such a detail in the pedigree of Theodahad's kinsman. We seem also to be entirely without information as to the Amal princess who was the bride of Maximus.

[3] 'Anicios quidem pene principibus pares aetas prisca genuit.'

impossibility of enjoying this privilege if we neglected the opportunity which we do possess in your case.

'Therefore we bestow upon you from this fourteenth Indiction[1] the office of Primicerius, which is also called Domesticatus. This office may appear somewhat less than you are entitled to by your pedigree, but you have re-received an honour which is greater than all the *fasces* in being permitted to marry a wife of our royal race, a distinction which you could not have hoped for even when you sat in the curule chair. Comport yourself now with mildness, patience, and moderation, that you may show yourself worthy of your affinity with us. Your ancestors have hitherto been praised, but they were never dignified with such an alliance. Your nobility has now reached a point beyond which it can climb no further. All that you do henceforward of a praiseworthy kind will but have the effect of rendering you more worthy of the matrimonial alliance which you have already achieved[2].'

12. KING THEODAHAD TO THE SENATE OF THE CITY OF ROME.

The same subject.

'We do not think that the fact of a man's having received the Consulship early in life should shut him out from holding office of lower rank in his maturer years[3]. As the Tiber receives the water of smaller rivers which merge their names in his, so a man of Consular rank can serve the State in less conspicuous ways, yet still be Consular. Therefore we have thought fit to bestow on the Illustrious and Magnificent Patrician Maximus, the Primiceriatus which is also called Domesticatus, from this fourteenth Indiction, that the

---

[1] 535 to 536.
[2] 'Laudati sunt hactenus parentes tui, sed tantâ non sunt conjunctione decorati. Nobilitas tua non est ultra quod crescat. Quicquid praeconialiter egeris, proprio matrimonio dignissimus aestimaris.'
[3] Flavius Anicius Maximus was Consul in 523.

lowliness of the honour may be raised by the merit of the wearer. He is an Anicius, sprung from a family renowned throughout the whole world. He is also honoured with the affinity of our own illustrious race. Receive him, welcome him, rejoice at these nuptials, which bind me closer to you, now that you have in your ranks one whom I can truly call a relation.'

13. KING THEODAHAD TO THE SENATE OF THE CITY OF ROME.

[This letter may probably be referred to the Spring or Summer of 535. Theodahad, soon after the deposition or death of Amalasuentha, has apparently invited the Senate to Ravenna, an invitation which they have respectfully declined. He chides their suspicions of him.]

Summons to Ravenna. Suspicions of the Senators.

'After we had dismissed the venerable Bishops who brought your message, without taking exception to your requests, though there were some things blameworthy among them, we received tidings that the City of Rome was agitated by certain foolish anxieties, from which real evil would grow unless the suspicion which caused them could be laid to rest.

'I fear that I cannot complain of "popular levity" if your illustrious body, which should set an example to all others, should give way to such fond imaginings. If Rome, which should govern the Provinces, be so foolish, what can we expect of *them*?

'Divine grace, however, prompts us both to pardon your faults and to grant your requests. We owe you nothing, and yet we pay you[1]; but we trust to be rewarded by hearing not our own praises but yours. Put away these unworthy, these childish suspicions, and behave as becomes the fathers of the people.

'In desiring your presence at our Court, we sought

---

[1] 'Nihil debemus et solvimus.' Have we here an echo of St. Augustine's thought, 'Reddis debita nulli debens?'

not your vexation but your advantage. It is certainly a great privilege to see the face of the Sovereign, and we thought to bestow on you, for the advantage of the State, that which used to be counted as a reward. However, not to deal harshly with you, we shall be satisfied with the attendance of certain individuals from your body, as occasion may require, so that on the one hand Rome may not be denuded of her citizens, and on the other that we may not lack prudent counsellors in our chamber. Now return to your old devotion, and serve us, not as a matter of fear, but of love. The rest shall the bearer of this letter explain unto you.'

14. KING THEODAHAD TO THE ROMAN PEOPLE.

[The occasion of writing this letter, which we may perhaps refer to the early part of 535, is apparently that some Gothic troops have been sent to Rome, and the people have broken out into clamours against them, or petitioned for their removal.]

Dissensions between citizens of Rome and Gothic troops.

'Your predecessors have always been distinguished by the loyal love which they bore to the Chief of the State; and it is only right that he [the Sovereign] who is defended with so much toil, he, for whom, as the representative of public order, daily precautions are taken[1], should in return love that people above all others whose loyalty gives him a right to rule the world[2].

'Oh! let there be nothing in you in our days which may justly move our indignation. Still show forth your older loyalty. It is not fitting that the Roman people should be fickle, or crafty, or full of seditions.

'Let no fond suspicions, no shadow of fear sway you. You have a Sovereign who only longs to find opportunities to love you. Meet with hostile arms your enemies, not your own defenders.

---

[1] 'Qui maximo labore defenditur, cujus per dies singulos civilitas custoditur.'
[2] 'Ut illos diligat super omnia, per quos habere probatur universa.'

'You ought to have invited, not to have shut out the succour which we sent you. Evidently you have been misled by counsellors who care not for the public weal. Return to your own better minds.

'Was it some new and strange nation whose faces forsooth thus terrified you? No: the very men whom hitherto you have called your kinsmen, the men who in their anxiety for your safety have left their homes and families in order to defend you. Strange return on your part for their devotion!

'As for you, you should know this, that night and day our one ceaseless desire is to perfect, with God's help, the security which was fostered in the times of our relations [Theodoric and Amalasuentha]. Where, indeed, would our credit as a Sovereign be if anything happened to your hurt? Dismiss all such thoughts from your minds. If any have been unjustly cast down, we will raise him up again. We have sent you some verbal messages by the bearer of this letter, and hope that from henceforth we may rely on your constant obedience.'

15. KING THEODAHAD TO THE EMPEROR JUSTINIAN.

Letter of introduction for an ecclesiastic.

'It is always a delight to us to have an opportunity of directing our letters of salutation[1] to your Piety, since he is filled with happy joy who converses with you with sincere heart. I therefore recommend to your Clemency the bearer of this letter, who comes on the affairs of the Church of Ravenna. There can be no doubt that if you grant his request you will earn a just reward.'

16. KING THEODAHAD TO THE SENATE OF THE CITY OF ROME.

Assurances of good-will. Oath of concord.

'It is worthy of a ruler to do good of his own freewill, not under compulsion. By God's favour we *can* do

---

[1] 'Salutiferos apices.'

anything, but we choose to do only things that are praiseworthy. Recognise now, oh prudent counse'lors, that clemency of mine which ye might always have reckoned upon. Ye feared that I was your enemy; far from that, I cannot even bear that ye should be racked by the fear of evil[1]. And therefore, though I change no purpose of mine, since I never had thoughts of evil towards you, I have ordained that A and B, the bearers of this letter, should take unto you the oaths which you solicited[2]. I do this thing for God's sake, not for man's; for how could I, who have run through the story of ancient realms in Holy Writ, wish to do anything else but that which is well-pleasing to God, who will assuredly recompense me according to my works. Henceforward, then, serve me loyally, and in the full security which you have thus acquired: yea, your love will be now the repayment of a debt rather than a freewill offering.'

17. KING THEODAHAD TO THE ROMAN PEOPLE.

'Since your security is our highest ornament, and since our love wishes to remove every shade of anxiety from your minds, we have ordered A and B to take oaths to you in our name, whereby you may know the mind of your King towards you. Though this act might seem not to consort with our dignity, we willingly perform it for your sakes, and add the sanction of an oath, though we have learned from the Sacred Scriptures that a mere promise ought to be kept. Now it is for you to show your devotion, and with assiduous prayers to implore of the Majesty on high that the tranquil times which we long that you may enjoy may be granted by the gift of Heaven.'

The same subject.

---

[1] 'Ecce nec sollicitos patimur, quibus infensi esse putabamur.'
[2] 'Postulata siquidem sacramenta vobis, ab Illo atque Illo praestari nostra decrevit auctoritas.'

18. KING THEODAHAD TO THE SENATE OF THE CITY OF ROME.

A Gothic garrison for Rome.

'Anxious that what we are devising for your safety should not be misinterpreted by bitter suspicion, we do you to wit that the army which is marching to Rome is intended for your defence, in order that they who covet your possessions may by Divine help be resisted by the arms of the Goths. If the shepherd is bound to watch over his flock, the father of the family to see that no crafty deceiver enters therein, with what anxious care ought not we to defend the City of Rome, which by universal consent is unequalled in the world[1]. So precious a possession must not be staked upon any throw. But that the defence of the City may be in no wise burdensome to you, we have ordered that the soldiers shall pay at the ordinary market rate for the provisions which they require; and we have desired Vacco, the steward of our house, to superintend these purchases. He is a man of valour and integrity, whose character will secure him the obedience of the troops, and enable him to prevent any excesses.

'As for the soldiers, we have told them to take up their quarters in fitting places [outside the City?], that without there may be armed defence, within for you, tranquil order[2].

'God forbid that in our days that City should seem to be protected by walls, the very name of which hath been of old a terror to the nations[3]. We hope for this from the aid of Heaven, that she who hath always been free may never be stained by the insult of any blockade[4].'

---

[1] 'Quâ nos convenit cautelâ Romam defendere, quam constat in mundo simile nihil habere?'

[2] 'Quos tamen locis aptis praecipimus immorari, ut foris sit armata defensio, intus vobis tranquilla civilitas.'

[3] 'Absit enim ut nostris temporibus Urbs illa muris videatur protegi, quam constat gentibus vel sola opinione fuisse terrori.'

[4] 'Ut quae semper fuit libera, nullius inclusionis decoloretur injuria.'

19. KING THEODAHAD TO THE EMPEROR JUSTINIAN.

Embassy of Peter.

'We thank the Divine Being, who loves to see Kings at peace with one another, that you expressed such joy at our elevation to the throne. Continue to set to the world this example of benignity; continue to show your interest in one who recommends himself by his pure affection for you. For you do not seek to pick shabby quarrels with other Sovereigns; you do not delight in unjust contests, which are contrary to sound morality[1], since you seek for nothing but what may increase the good opinion which men have of you. How could you throw away that peace which it is the glory of your Piety to have imposed even on angry nations[2]?

'Even you, glorious Sovereigns! [Justinian and Theodora] gain somewhat when all other realms revere you. It is a common thing for the ruler to be praised in his own land, but to receive the unforced praise of foreign lands, that is indeed desirable. You are loved, most pious Emperor, in your own dominions; but how much grander a thing to be yet more loved in the regions of Italy, from whence the glory of the Roman name was diffused over the whole world! It behoves you therefore to continue that peaceful disposition which you showed towards us at the commencement of our reign.

'We have desired the most blessed Pope and the most honourable Senate of the City of Rome to give their answers to the eloquent and worthy Peter, your ambassador, with as little delay as possible; and we have joined with him that venerable person our ambassador[3],

---

[1] 'Non enim rixas viles per regna requiritis: non vos injusta certamina quae sunt bonis moribus inimica, delectant.' No doubt this was meant to be taken as a hint of the censure which it professes to deny.

[2] 'Pacem quam et iracundis gentibus consuevistis imponere.' An allusion, perhaps, to the peace concluded with Persia.

[3] The name of 'virum illum venerabilem' is not given, but we learn from Procopius (De Bello Gotthico i. 6) that it was Rusticus, a priest, a Roman, and an intimate friend of Theodahad.

that you may know our mind from our own messenger.'

20. QUEEN GUDELINA[1] TO THEODORA AUGUSTA.

Embassy of Rusticus.

'I have received with thanks the earnestly-desired letters of your Piety, and reverently prize the report of your spoken words as better than all gifts. You exhort us first of all to impart to your hearing whatever requests we wish to make to your triumphant lord and consort[2]. Backed by such patronage as yours, how can there be any doubt as to the success of our petitions? It is an addition to our joy that your Serenity has chosen such a man for your ambassador, one whom it is equally fitting for your glory to send and for our obedience to receive[3]. There can be no doubt that it is by constant observation of your character that his own has become so excellent, since it is by good maxims that the mind of man is cleansed from impurity[4]. According to the warning of your Reverence we have given orders that both Pope and Senate shall give their answers to your messengers quickly, so that there may be no delay.

Possible reference to death of Amalasuentha.

'For moreover, concerning that person about whom something came to our ears with tickling speech, know that that has been ordained which we believed would suit your intentions[5]; for it is our desire that by the

---

[1] Wife of Theodahad.

[2] 'Hortamini enim ut quidquid expetendum a triumphali principe domino jugali nostro (?) credimus vestris ante sensibus ingeramus.' It seems to me that the sense requires *vestro* instead of *nostro*, and I have translated accordingly. (Dahn also makes this correction.)

[3] 'Et vestra decet obsequia retinere.' Here 'nostra' seems to give a better sense than 'vestra.'

[4] 'Dubium enim non est illam mores dare cui observatur assidue, dum constat defaecari animum bonis praeceptionibus institutum.' Rather hazardous praise to address to a Theodora.

[5] 'Nam et de illâ personâ, de quâ ad nos aliquid verbo titillante pervenit, hoc ordinatum esse cognoscite, quod vestris credidimus animis convenire.'

interposition of our good offices your will should be law as much in our kingdom as in your empire [1].

'We therefore inform you that we had caused our messenger [Rusticus the priest] to be despatched by the Pope before your ambassador could possibly have left Rome. So saluting you with all the veneration which is your due, we assign the office of ambassador to a man eminent both by his character and learning, and venerable by reason of his office; since we believe that those persons are acceptable to you whom we have thought suitable to be entrusted with the Divine ministry.'

21. QUEEN GUDELINA TO THEODORA, AUGUSTA.

Soliciting Theodora's friendship.

'Oh, wisest of Augustas, both I and my wedded lord earnestly desire your friendship. The love of so great

---

[1] These mysterious sentences, according to Gibbon, cap. xli. n. 56 (following Buat), refer to Amalasuentha, and thus lend probability to the story in the Anecdota of Procopius that Theodora, out of jealousy, intrigued with Theodahad to have Amalasuentha put to death. But whatever may be the truth of that story, this sentence can hardly by any possibility refer to it. For (1) it is clear that this letter was written at the same time as Theodahad's, which precedes it, therefore after the arrival of Peter in Italy. But Procopius is clear that Amalasuentha was put to death before Peter had crossed the Hadriatic, whereas this event, whatever it be, is evidently a piece of news which Gudelina has to communicate to Theodora. (2) This letter, though purporting to be from Gudelina, is confessedly written by Cassiodorus, and published by him at the end of his official career. It is hardly conceivable that he would deliberately publish to the world his connection with the murder of Theodoric's daughter and his own friend and benefactress. It is remarkable, on the contrary, how complete (but for this passage) is the silence of the Variae as to Amalasuentha's deposition and death: as if Cassiodorus had said, 'If you do anything to harm *her*, you may get other apologists for your deeds; I will be no champion of such wickedness.' It is scarcely necessary to remark that there is nothing in the wording of the sentence 'de illa persona,' &c. which makes it more applicable to a woman than to a man. As Peter's embassy was ostensibly connected with ecclesiastical affairs, there is perhaps an allusion in this sentence to some scheme of Theodora's with reference to the Papacy. It is possible that she may have been already working for the election of Vigilius to the chair of St. Peter, and therefore that *he* is meant by 'illa persona.'

F f

a lady seems to raise me higher than royalty. Shed on us the lustre of your glory, for one light loses nothing by imparting some of its brilliancy to another. With affectionate presumption I commend myself to the favour of the Emperor and yourself, desiring that, as is fitting, there should be no discord between the two Roman realms[1].'

22. KING THEODAHAD TO THE EMPEROR JUSTINIAN[2].

Entreaties for peace.

'Our own ambassadors, and that most excellent person Peter, whom your Piety despatched to us, will both have informed you how earnestly we desire concord with your august Serenity. We now send two more ambassadors charged with the same commission. We certainly with all sincerity plead for peace who have no cause of quarrel with you. Consider also, oh learned Sovereigns, and consult the archives of your great grandfather[3], that you may see how large a part of their own rights your predecessors were willing to relinquish for the sake of an alliance with our ancestors[4]. Think how fortunate you are in having that friendship willingly offered to you for which they had humbly to sue. Yet, we may say it without arrogance, we know ourselves to be better than those ancestors of ours with whom the treaty was made[5]. We send

---

[1] 'Nullam inter Romana regna decet esse discordiam.'

[2] This letter seems as if it was written on precisely the same occasion as x. 19. Again Peter is sent back, and with him a 'venerable man' to represent Theodahad. We learn from Procopius (i. 6) that Theodahad, in his fear of war, recalled Peter when he had already got as far as Albano, and gave him another set of propositions for Justinian. It seems possible that these fresh letters (22 and 23) from Theodahad and his Queen were given him when he set out the *second* time.

[3] Zeno (not of course an ancestor in natural relationship, but predecessor in the third degree).

[4] 'Considerate etiam, principes docti, et abavi vestri historica monumenta recolite, quantum decessores vestri studuerint de suo jure relinquere ut eis parentum nostrorum foedera provenirent.'

[5] 'Nunc illi vestram gratiam ultro quaerunt, qui suis parentibus me-

you on this embassy a venerable man, made illustrious by his priestly office, and conspicuous by the renown of his learning. We pray the Divine goodness to bring our wishes to pass; and as not even a series of letters can contain all that we have to say, we have given some verbal messages to be conveyed to your sacred ears, that you may not be wearied by the reading of too diffuse a letter.'

23. QUEEN GUDELINA TO THEODORA, AUGUSTA[1].

The same subject.

'We learn with satisfaction from that most eloquent man Peter, that what has happened in this State is acceptable to you[2]. You show your love of justice when, all suspicion by God's providence having been wiped away, you desire that there should be lasting agreement between us. Let there then be definite promises on both sides, and lasting concord as the result. We therefore send that venerable man to secure the peace of our most serene husband with yours in the sight of all men. If there be anything in the Emperor's terms so hard that it ought not to be imposed on us, we trust to your wise moderation to mitigate the same,

---

liores se esse cognoscunt.' Dahn remarks that Theodahad's asserted superiority to Theodoric probably consisted in his philosophical culture.

[1] See note on the preceding letter.

[2] 'Ut per eum disceremus acceptum vobis esse quod in hac republicâ constat evenisse.' At first sight this seems to refer to the death of Amalasuentha or to the accession of Theodahad. Dahn thinks that those events have been disposed of in previous letters. Perhaps it is a general expression for 'the whole course of recent events in Italy.' Though upon the whole rejecting the story of Theodora's complicity in the death of Amalasuentha, I am bound to admit that this passage lends a certain amount of probability to the charge. At the same time, the words in the next sentence, 'per divinam providentiam omni suspicione detersâ,' are susceptible of an honourable meaning, even if the death of Amalasuentha be alluded to. 'You and your husband accused us of that crime. Now by God's providence we have been able to show that we were guiltless of it [that it was done without our privity by the relations of the three Gothic nobles whom she had put to death]. Nothing therefore remains to hinder peace between us.'

that the love which we have begun to feel towards your kingdom be not chilled by harsh terms of peace.

'Claim this palm of concord between the two States as your own especial crown, that as the Emperor is renowned for his successful wars, so you may receive the praises of all men for this accomplished peace. Let the bearer of these letters see you often and confidentially. We hope for just, not onerous, conditions of peace, although in truth nothing seems impossible to us if we know that it is asked for by such a glorious person as yourself.'

24. QUEEN GUDELINA TO THE EMPEROR JUSTINIAN[1].

The same subject.

A short letter of compliments to the Emperor, and earnest desire for the preservation of peace. Peter and 'ille vir venerabilis' are still the messengers.

25. KING THEODAHAD TO THE EMPEROR JUSTINIAN.

The same subject.

'The august page written by your Serenity, and brought to us by the venerable presbyter Heracleanus, has gleamed upon us, bringing us the grace of your salutation. Oh, what a great benefit for us is this sweet converse with so mighty a prince!

'May we ever hear of your safety, and of the increase of the happiness of your kingdom. We have no other wish but this. According to your desire we have addressed letters to the Pope of the City of Rome[2], telling him to reply to the letter brought by the present messenger with the least possible delay, since anyone

---

[1] Apparently sent at the same time as the two preceding letters.

[2] Negotiations were evidently still going on between the Emperor and the Pope, probably with reference to the election of Anthimus, who, though accused of Monophysitism, had been made Patriarch of Constantinople in 535 by Theodora's influence, and whom the Pope apparently refused to recognise. He was afterwards deposed by Pope Agapetus when he visited Constantinople.

who comes from you should be attended to with utmost celerity. We hope for many future opportunities of thus obeying your desires and earning your love in return.'

26. KING THEODAHAD TO THE EMPEROR JUSTINIAN.

A monastery too heavily taxed.

'Richer than all other gifts bestowed by your Serenity is this, when you exhort us to do that which will profit for our own salvation and recommend us to the Divine Power. We hear that it has been brought to the knowledge of your Glory that a monastery of God's servants is too heavily oppressed with tribute, and we point out that this is owing to an inundation which has smitten their land with the curse of barrenness. However, we have given orders to the most eminent Senator[1] to appoint a careful inspector to visit the farm in question, weigh the matter carefully, and make such reasonable reduction as may leave a sufficient profit to the owners of the soil. We consider that anything which we thus concede to the desire of your Mildness will be to us the most precious of all gains.

Alleged losses of a convert from Arianism.

'In the matter of Veranilda, too, about which your Serenity has deigned to admonish me, though it happened long ago under the reign of my relations, I thought it right to make good her loss by my own generosity, that she might not repent her change of religion[2]. For seeing that the Deity suffers many religions, we should not seek to impose one on all our subjects. He who tries to do otherwise flies in the face of the Divine commands. Your Piety, therefore, fittingly invites me to these acts of obedience to God.'

---

[1] Cassiodorus.

[2] Apparently Veranilda had in the reign of Theodoric become a convert from Arianism to Orthodoxy, and had suffered some pecuniary losses in consequence, which Theodahad now proposes to make up to her. See Dahn, Könige der Germanen iii. 199, *n.* 4.

27. KING THEODAHAD TO SENATOR[1], PRAEFECTUS PRAETORIO.

Corn distributions in Liguria and Venetia.

'In succouring his subjects, the payers of tribute, the King does not seem to give, so much as to restore what he has received. The cultivator of the soil is abandoned to future famine, unless he is helped in the day of his necessity. Therefore let the corn which has been received by the government from industrious Liguria and loyal Venetia, though it has been taken from their fields, be born again to them in our granaries, since it is too outrageous that the cultivator should starve while our barns are full. Therefore let your Illustrious Greatness (whose office is said to have been instituted for the express purpose of feeding the people from the accumulated stores of the State[2]) sell to the impoverished Ligurians the third part of the grain warehoused at Ticinum and Dertona, at the rate of 25 modii to the solidus[3]. Similarly distribute the third part of the stores in the warehouses of Tarvisium and Tridentum to the Venetians, at the same rate, that pitying Heaven, seeing men's bounty to one another, may give us fruitful harvests. Take care that this distribution is so managed that our indulgence shall reach those persons chiefly, who are least able to depend on their own resources.'

28. KING THEODAHAD TO SENATOR[4], PRAEFECTUS PRAETORIO.

Grant of monopolies.

'The King ought to confirm whatever has been wisely ordered by the Judges, especially those who are known to be above suspicion of bribery.

---

[1] Cassiodorus.

[2] 'Quorum dignitas ad hoc legitur instituta, ut de repositis copiis populum saturare possetis.' Probably an allusion to Joseph, whom Cassiodorus celebrates as the first Praefectus Praetorio.

[3] Six bushels for twelve shillings, or sixteen shillings a quarter.

[4] Cassiodorus.

'Therefore we confirm in their offices[1] the stewards[2], purveyors[3] of wheat, wine, and cheese, the meat sellers, vintners, farmers of the revenue derived from granaries and taverns[4], hay merchants, and general provision dealers[5], who belong to the City of Rome or the royal residence of Ravenna[6]; also those who hold public charges of this description along the river banks of Ticinum or Placentia[7], or in any other places, whom we know to have been appointed by you, whose judgments we willingly embrace and desire to hold fast exactly as if they were our own; nor will we allow the malice of any to prevail against those persons who by your choice have assumed these public functions. If therefore they acquit themselves to your satisfaction, they shall hold their office for five years without fear of disturbance during that period. On account of the present barrenness of the land you should cause them to fix such prices for the different kinds of grain as shall seem reasonable to your Eminence[8].

'As human ambition requires to be checked by fear of punishment, anyone who by petitioning or canvassing seeks to obtain the place of one of these lawfully appointed purveyors shall be visited with a fine of 30lbs. of gold[9], to be exacted from him by you. If unable to pay this fine he shall suffer corporal punishment and be noted as infamous. Nothing can be considered safe or stable if men are to be perpetually exposed to the snares of envious competitors like these.

[1] The sentence is so long that Cassiodorus seems to have forgotten its construction, and these important words are in fact omitted.
[2] 'Arcarios.'
[3] 'Prorogatores.'
[4] 'Capitularios horreariorum et tabernariorum.'
[5] 'Cellaritas.'
[6] 'Mansionem Ravennatem.'
[7] 'Ripam Ticinensem vel Placentinam.'
[8] Here follows, 'Ut hi quibus commissum est exercere singulos apparatus de injusto gravamine non querantur,' which I do not venture to translate, as I am not sure whether it relates to buyers or sellers.
[9] £1,200.

Your Greatness is to bring this law to the knowledge of all men.'

[It is clear that this letter refers to an office greatly coveted, and one in which there was a possibility of making great gains, but also one in which, owing to the regulation of prices by the government, there might be temporary losses; to guard against which it was considered reasonable that the holder should be guaranteed in his office for five years.

The office is the supply of the staple articles of food to the King's household at Rome and Ravenna, and to the garrisons probably of Pavia and Piacenza and the neighbouring country. Did this right carry with it an absolute monopoly as far as the other inhabitants of those places are concerned? This seems probable; but I do not know that we can positively state it.

The term used, 'Arcarii,' is applied in the Theodosian Code (xii. 6, 14) to the bailiffs by whom the rents on the Imperial domain were collected. Here it has manifestly altered its meaning.]

29. KING THEODAHAD TO COUNT WINUSIAD.

An old soldier receives furlough for a visit to the baths of Bormio.

'Your noble birth and tried fidelity induced us to commit to you the government of the City of Ticinum, which you had defended in war: but now, being deluged with a sudden inundation of muddy gout[1], you ask leave to resort to the waters of Bormio, which by their drying influences are of healing power for this malady.

'We permit, nay earnestly encourage, you to undertake this journey; for we cannot bear that one of our warriors should fall a victim to the tyranny of this cruel disease, which, like the Barbarians, when it has once claimed by force hospitality in the owner's body,

---

[1] 'Limosae podagrae subitâ inundatione complutus.'

ever after defends its right thereto by cruelty. It seeks out all the hollow places of the system, makes stones out of its moisture, and deposits them there, destroying all the beautiful arrangements of Nature for free and easy movement. It loosens what ought to be tight, it contracts the nerves, and so shortens the limbs that a tall man finds all the comeliness of his stature taken from him while he is still unmutilated. It is in truth a living death; and when the excruciating torment is gone, it leaves an almost worse legacy behind it—inability to move. Even debtors in the torture chamber have the weights sometimes removed from their feet; but this cruel malady, when it has once taken hold of a man, seems never to relinquish possession. A disease of this kind, bringing with it weakness and helplessness, is especially terrible to a warrior, who after overcoming the foes that came against him in battle, finds himself thus struck down by an enemy within.

'Go then, in Heaven's name, to the healing springs. We cannot bear the thought that you the warrior should be carried on men's shoulders, instead of bestriding your war-horse. We have painted all these evils in somewhat exaggerated style in order to stir you up to seek an early cure.

'Use then these waters, soothing to the taste, and in the hot bath able to dry up the gouty humours. God has given us this ally wherewith to overcome that enemy of the human race; and under its double influence, within and without, the malady, which ten years of regimen and endless medicines cannot lessen, is put to flight by remedies which are in themselves delightful.

'May God grant that this far-famed place may restore your body to health[1].'

---

[1] The nature-heated springs of Bormio are still resorted to; and some pedestrian travellers, who have crossed the Stelvio from Trafoi, have a grateful remembrance of their soothing waters.

30. KING THEODAHAD TO HONORIUS, PRAEFECT OF THE CITY.

The elephants in the Via Sacra.

'We regret to learn from your report that the brazen elephants placed in the Via Sacra[1] (so called from the many superstitions to which it was consecrated of old) are falling into ruins.

'This is to be much regretted, that whereas these animals live in the flesh more than a thousand years, their brazen effigies should be so soon crumbling away. See therefore that their gaping limbs be strengthened by iron hooks, and that their drooping bellies be fortified by masonry placed underneath them.

Natural history of the elephant.

'The living elephant, when it is prostrate on the ground, as it often is when helping men to fell trees, cannot get up again unaided. This is because it has no joints in its feet; and accordingly you see numbers of them lying as if dead till men come to help them up again. Thus this creature, so terrible by its size, is really not equally endowed by Nature with the tiny ant.

'That the elephant surpasses all other animals in intelligence is proved by the adoration which it renders to Him whom it understands to be the Almighty Ruler of all. Moreover it pays to good princes a homage which it refuses to tyrants.

'It uses its proboscis[2], that nosed hand which Nature has given it to compensate for its very short neck, for the benefit of its master, accepting the presents which will be profitable to him. It always walks cautiously, mindful of that fatal fall [into the hunter's pit] which was the beginning of its captivity. At its master's bidding it exhales its breath, which is said to be a remedy for the human headache.

---

[1] I have not found any other mention of these brazen elephants. Nardini (Roma Antica i. 295) cites this passage, and illustrates it by quotations from Suetonius, Pliny, and the Historia Augusta, showing that it was the custom to erect to Emperors and Empresses statues of elephants drawing triumphal chariots.

[2] Cassiodorus calls it 'promuscis.'

'When it comes to water it sucks up in its trunk a vast quantity, which at the word of command it squirts forth like a shower. If anyone have treated it with contempt, it pours forth such a stream of dirty water over him that one would think a river had entered his house. For this beast has a wonderfully long memory, both of injury and of kindness. Its eyes are small, but move solemnly. There is a sort of kingly dignity in its appearance, and while it recognises with pleasure all that is honourable, it seems to despise scurrilous jests. Its skin is furrowed by deep channels, like that of the victims of the foreign disease named after it [1], *elephantiasis*. It is on account of the impenetrability of this hide that the Persian Kings used the elephant in war.

'It is most desirable that we should preserve the images of these creatures, and that our citizens should thus be familiarised with the sight of the denizens of foreign lands. Do not therefore permit them to perish, since it is for the glory of Rome to collect all specimens of the process by which the art of workmen hath imitated the productions of wealthy Nature in all parts of the world.'

[This letter traverses the same ground as Pliny's 'Historia Naturalis' viii. 1–11, but supplies some new facts. Pliny makes the elephant live to the age of 200 or even 300 years. Cassiodorus boldly says 'more than a thousand.' The curious story of the elephant's religion is given with more detail by Pliny; but he knows nothing of the political sagacity which enables it to discern between a good king and a tyrant. Pliny mentions the fact that the elephant's breath is a cure for headache, but adds, 'especially if he sneeze [2].'

Upon the whole, though Cassiodorus had probably read Pliny's description, his own must be pronounced original.

---

[1] 'A quâ transportaneorum (?) nefanda passio nomen accepit.'
[2] Hist. Nat. xxviii. 8.

This marvellous letter is the last that we have, written in the name of Theodahad.]

31. KING WITIGIS[1] TO ALL THE GOTHS.

Elevation of Witigis.

'Though every advance in station is to be accounted among the good gifts of the Divinity, especially is the kingly dignity to be looked upon as coming by His ordinance through Whom kings reign and subjects obey. Wherefore, with liveliest satisfaction returning thanks to our Maker Christ, we inform you that our kinsmen[2] the Goths, amid a fence of circling swords, raising us in ancestral fashion upon a shield, have by Divine guidance bestowed on us the kingly dignity, thus making arms the emblem of honour to one who has earned all his renown in war. For know that not in the corner of a presence-chamber, but in wide-spreading plains I have been chosen King; and that not the dainty discourse of flatterers, but the blare of trumpets announced my elevation, that the Gothic people, roused by the sound to a kindling of their inborn valour, might once more gaze upon a Soldier King.

'Too long indeed have these brave men, bred up amid the shock of battle, borne with a Sovereign who was untried in war; too long have they laboured to uphold his dubious fame, though they might presume upon their own well-known valour[3]. For it is inevitable that the character of the ruler should in some degree influence the reputation of the whole people.

'But, as ye have heard, called forth by the dangers of my kindred, I was ready to undergo with them one common fate; but they would not suffer me to continue a

---

[1] Spelt 'Vitigis' by Cassiodorus.
[2] 'Parentes nostros Gothos.'
[3] 'Ut de ejus fama laboraret quamvis de propria virtute praesumeret.' I have translated as if 'laboraret' and 'praesumeret' were in the plural, and even so, find it difficult to get a satisfactory meaning out of these words.

mere General, feeling that they needed a veteran King. Wherefore now accept first the Divine decree, and then the judgment of the Goths, since it is your unanimous wish which makes me King. Lay aside then the fear of disaster: cast off the suspicion of further losses: fear no rude strokes of fate under our dominion. We who have ridden so oft to war have learned to love valiant men. Associated in all things with your labours, I have been myself a witness to the brave deeds of each of you, and need no other evidence of your worth. By no fraudulent variations between my public and private negotiations shall the might of the Gothic arms be broken[1]. Everything that we do shall have respect to the welfare of our whole people: in private we will not even love. We promise to follow those courses which shall adorn the royal name. Finally, we undertake that our rule shall in all things be such as becomes a Gothic King, the successor of the renowned Theodoric—that man who was so rarely and so nobly qualified by Nature for the cares of royalty; that man of whom it may be truly said that every other Sovereign is illustrious in so far as he loves *his* counsels. Therefore he who succeeds in imitating the deeds of Theodoric ought to be considered as belonging to his line. Thus then, manifest your anxious care for the welfare of our kingdom, while your hearts are at ease, through God's goodness, as to our internal security.'

32. KING WITIGIS TO THE EMPEROR JUSTINIAN.

Overtures for peace with the Empire.

'How much, oh most clement Emperor, we long for the sweetness of your favour, may be understood from this fact alone, that after such serious injuries and such grievous bloodshed as you have inflicted on us, we still come forward to ask for peace with you, as if none of your

[1] 'Arma Gothorum nullâ promissionum mearum varietate frangenda sunt.' An evident allusion to the treacherous and unpatriotic diplomacy of Theodahad, as described by Procopius.

servants had ever wronged us. We have suffered such things as might move the indignation even of our enemies, who must know that they have attacked us without our guilt, have hated us without our fault, have despoiled us without our owing them anything. Nor can it be said that the blow has been so slight that no account need be taken of it, since it has been struck not in the Provinces alone but in Rome [or Italy] herself, the Capital of the World[1]. Think how great must be our pain at this, which nevertheless we banish from memory in order that we may obtain justice at your hands. Such disturbance has been made as the whole world speaks of[2] [and condemns], and it deserves to be so composed by you that all men may admire your spirit of equity.

'If vengeance on King Theodahad be the thing required, I [who have put him to death] merit your love. If you desire to honour the blessed memory of Queen Amalasuentha, think of her daughter[3], who has reached [by our means] that royal station to which your soldiers might well have striven to exalt her, in order that all the nations might see how faithful you remained to the old friendship.

'This fact too ought to influence you, that by the ordering of Providence we were permitted to make your acquaintance before our accession to the throne, that the remembrance of our favourable reception at your Court, and the sight of your person in that splendid position, might move us to love and reverence.

'Even now you can undo all that has been misdone, since the continual expectation of favours to come, makes

---

[1] 'Non in provinciis tantum sed in ipso rerum capite probatur inflictum.'

[2] 'Talis res effecta est quam mundus loquatur.' The commentator Fornerius absurdly understands this of Mundus, the general of Justinian in Dalmatia, who had already fallen in battle before the accession of Witigis.

[3] Matasuentha, now wife of Witigis.

perseverance in affection easy[1]. Therefore, soliciting your Clemency with all due respect, we inform you that we have appointed A and B our ambassadors to the Wisdom of your Serenity, that you may, according to your custom, duly weigh all these considerations, that the two Republics may persevere in restored harmony, and that all which hath been settled in past times by Sovereigns of blessed memory may, by God's help, be increased and made more prosperous under your dominion.

'The rest of their commission will be more fully explained to your Serenity by the aforesaid ambassadors.'

33. KING WITIGIS TO THE MASTER OF THE OFFICES [AT CONSTANTINOPLE].

Embassy to Constantinople.

'In sending our two ambassadors to the most serene Emperor, it is fitting also to send letters of salutation[2] to your Greatness. May your prudence support our reasonable requests with the Emperor. You can easily correct those things [the war against the Gothic people] which you ought never to have allowed to take place; and all things can now be arranged in the most friendly manner, since a reconciliation between men who have fought out their quarrel is often the surest ground of friendship. An unknown man might possibly have been shunned by you; but I, who have seen the magnificence of your Republic, who have known the hearts of so many of your noble statesmen, have no desire to quarrel with your most pious Emperor, if he will only cherish thoughts of justice towards me. If another [Theodahad] deserved the anger of the Emperor, I ought to be looked upon with the highest favour, who have executed vengeance on that hateful predecessor. I have carried your

---

[1] 'Quando non est difficile illum in affectu retinere, qui gratiam constat desideranter expetere.' Very nearly, but not quite, the modern proverb which says that gratitude is 'a lively sense of favours to come.'

[2] 'Salutiferos apices.' See x. 15.

intentions into effect, and therefore I deserve reward, not punishment. Let all hatred be buried in the grave of the sinner; and even if you think nothing of our deservings, think of the liberty of the Romans, which is everywhere suffering amid the clash of arms. A few words to a man of your wisdom are sufficient.'

34. KING WITIGIS TO HIS BISHOPS.

The same subject.

'If we owe honour to Priests even when unknown to us, how much more so to you whom we have seen and spoken to, and with whom we have had frequent and familiar intercourse.

'By the ambassadors who are bearing our letters to the most serene Emperor we send a message of reverence to your Holiness, hoping that you will pray for us and set them forward on their journey with all necessary assistance, since you are bound to wish well to those whom you know to be united to you by the ties of religion.'

35. KING WITIGIS TO THE PRAEFECT OF THESSALONICA.

The same subject.

'We are sending two ambassadors to the most serene Emperor, who will salute your Greatness. We earnestly hope that your Excellency will speed them on their journey.'

BOOK XI.

PREFACE.

'THE necessity for a Preface often arises from some contrariety in an Author's position which prevents him from writing as he would wish to write. It is admitted that it is not fair to expect the same degree of excellence from a busy man which we may reasonably look for in a man of leisure. But a man in high official position cannot be a man of leisure. It would be the highest disgrace to him if he were, since even his so-called privy-chamber[1] resounds with the noise of clamorous litigants.

'I can well understand that a man of few occupations will object against me, here that a word has been thrown out with ill-considered haste, there that a commonplace sentiment has not been dressed up in sufficiently ornamental language, or there that I have not complied with the rules of the Ancients by making my persons speak "in character." But the busy man, hurried from one cause to another, and constantly under the necessity of dictating to one man and replying to another, will not make these objections, because the consciousness of his own literary perils will make him tender in his judgments. And yet there is something even in the

[1] 'Secretum.'

pressure of business which sometimes promotes briskness of mind, since the art of speaking is one which is placed very much in our own power [1].

'If anyone objects that I, placed in the height of the Praetorian dignity, should have dictated so few decisions of a legal kind, let him know that this was the result of my associating with myself that most prudent man Felix [2], whose advice I have followed in every case. He is a man of absolute purity of character, of surpassing knowledge of the law, of distinguished accuracy of speech; a young man with the gravity of age, a sweet pleader, a measured orator; one who by his graceful discharge of his official duties has earned the favourable opinion of the public.

'Had it not been for his help, overwhelmed by so great a multitude of causes, I must either have been found unequal to the burden, or else perchance have seemed arrogant [in my disregard of previously settled decisions]. But, what was more important still, relieved by his labours from this duty, I was able to give such attention to the higher affairs of the State, that I could not fail to win approbation even in those arduous duties.

'I have therefore subjoined two books, in which I myself speak in my capacity as Praefect, to the ten in which I have spoken by the mouth of the King; for it seemed absurd to me to be silent in my newly-acquired dignity, who had so often spoken on behalf of others.

'Then, after these twelve books had been brought to their long-desired end, my friends compelled me to discuss the substance and the powers of the Soul, that

---

[1] Here follows a sentence which I do not understand: 'Remanet itaque ad excusandum brevitas insperata librorum, quam nemo purgat diutius, nisi qui bene creditur esse dicturus.'

[2] This can hardly be the Consul of A.D. 511, since he is called in the next sentence 'senilis juvenis.'

I might say something *about* that faculty *through* which I had already said so much[1].

'Now then, learned men! view these letters with indulgence. If there be no eloquence in them, attribute it to my many occupations, which have prevented my reading as much as I would gladly have done. Cicero, that fountain of eloquence, when he was one day asked to speak, excused himself on the ground that he had read nothing the day before. The barn must be constantly refilled if it is not to become empty. All that is good in our minds is the fruit of study, and soon withers if it be separated from reading, which is the parent stem. Great indulgence therefore should be shown to us if we have often had to write when we were busy, to be read by others when we had no leisure to read, ourselves. And now enough of excuses, lest too elaborate a defence should rather injure our cause.'

[1] 'De Animae substantiâ vel de virtutibus ejus amici me disserere coëgerunt: ut per quam multa diximus, de ipsa quoque dicere videremur.'

BOOK XI.

CONTAINING THIRTY-NINE LETTERS WRITTEN BY CASSIODORUS IN HIS OWN NAME AS PRAEFECTUS PRAETORIO, AND ONE ON BEHALF OF THE ROMAN SENATE.

1. SENATOR, PRAETORIAN PRAEFECT, TO THE SENATE OF THE CITY OF ROME (A.D. 534)[1].

Cassiodorus on his promotion to the Praefecture.

'IF I can only be sure that my advancement is acceptable to you, Conscript Fathers, I shall not doubt of its being approved by God and popular with all good men.

'It is in the nature of things to love a colleague, and you are in fact exalting your own honour when you approve of a dignity given to a *Senator*[2].

'After our Sovereigns there is none to whom I so much desire to commend myself as you. To me honour will ever be the sole test of advantage. Justice, like a

---

[1] This letter, which was not composed immediately after Cassiodorus' accession to office, must have been written after the death of the Frankish King Theodoric, which occurred, according to Clinton, early in 534, and before October 2 of the same year, the date of the death of Athalaric. Notwithstanding the obscurity of many of the allusions in it, this document is one of our best authorities for the history of Amalasuentha's regency, and is therefore translated almost verbatim.

[2] Partly a pun on his name, partly an allusion to his rank.

handmaid, will wait upon my actions; and the power, which I have not myself bought from our virtuous Sovereign, I in my turn shall sell to no man. You have heard, noble Sirs, the panegyrics[1] passed upon me at my entrance into office. These praises I will not dare to call false, but I will say that they lay upon me a heavy responsibility to show that they are not unmerited.

'Happy fortune of our time in which, while the Sovereign himself takes holiday, the love of his mother rules and covers us all with the robe of her universal charity! Happy for the young Ruler, who in this difficult position learns first to triumph over his impetuous impulses, and attains in the springtime of his life that self-control which hoary age with difficulty acquires!

'As for the Mother whom he so dutifully obeys, her most fittingly do all kingdoms venerate, whom to behold is to adore, to listen to is to witness a miracle. Of what language is she not a perfect mistress? She is skilled in the niceties of Attic eloquence; she shines in the majesty of Roman speech; she glories in the wealth of the language of her fathers. She is equally marvellous in all these, and in each the orator in his own especial tongue feels himself surpassed by her. A great safeguard and a great excellence is this in the ruler of so many nationalities. None needs an interpreter with his accomplished mistress. No ambassador need wait, or hear his words slowly filtered through the mind of a go-between. Everyone feels that his own words are listened to, and receives his answer from her lips in the language of his forefathers.

Praises of Amalasuentha.

'To these accomplishments, as a splendid diadem, is added that priceless knowledge of Literature, by which

---

[1] The letter written by Cassiodorus himself, in the name of Athalaric, to announce his elevation to the Praefecture (Var. ix. 25).

the treasures of ancient learning are appropriated, and the dignity of the throne is ever enhanced.

'Yet, while she rejoices in such perfect mastery of language, on public occasions she is so taciturn that she might be supposed to be indolent. With a few words she unties the knots of entangled litigations, she calmly arranges hot disputes, she silently promotes the public welfare. You do not hear her announce beforehand what will be her course of action in public; but with marvellous skill she attains, by feigning, those points which she knows require to be rapidly gained[1].

Comparison to Placidia.

'What case like this can be produced from the annals of revered Antiquity? Placidia's care for her purple-clad son has often been celebrated; but by Placidia's lax administration of the Empire its boundaries were unbecomingly retrenched. She gained for him a wife and for herself a daughter-in-law[2] by the loss of Illyricum; and thus the union of Sovereigns was bought by a lamentable division of the Provinces[3]. The discipline of the soldiers was relaxed by too long peace; and, in short, Valentinian, under the guardianship of his mother, lost more than he could have done if he had been a helpless orphan.

[1] 'Et temperamento mirabili dissimulando peragit quod accelerandum esse cognoscit.'

[2] 'Eudoxia.'

[3] 'Nurum denique sibi amissione Illyrici comparavit: factaque est conjunctio Regnantis, divisio dolenda provinciis.' On this alleged loss of Illyricum by the Western Empire, see Gibbon, cap. xxxiii. note 6. One may doubt, however, whether Cassiodorus has been correctly informed concerning it. Noricum and Pannonia at the time of Valentinian's marriage must have been entirely in the possession of the Huns; and on the dissolution of their monarchy Noricum at any rate seems to be connected with the Western rather than the Eastern Empire. As for Dalmatia, or the *Province* (as distinct from the *Praefecture*) of Illyricum, the retirement thither of the Emperor Nepos in 475, and the previous history of his uncle Marcellinus, point towards the conclusion that this Province was then considered as belonging *de jure* to the Caesar of Rome rather than to him of Constantinople.

'But under this Lady, who can count as many Kings as ancestors in her pedigree, our army by Divine help is a terror to foreign nations. Being kept in a prudent equipoise it is neither worn away by continual fighting nor enervated by unbroken peace. In the very beginnings of the reign, when a new ruler's precarious power is apt to be most assailed, contrary to the wish of the Eastern Emperor she made the Danube a Roman stream. Well known is all that the invaders suffered, of which I therefore omit further mention, that the shame of defeat may not be too closely associated with the thought of the Emperor, our ally. Still, what he thought of your part of the Empire is clear from this, that he conceded to our attack that peace which he has refused to the abject entreaties of others. Add this fact, that though we have rarely sought him he has honoured us with so many embassies, and that thus his unique majesty has bowed down the stately head of the Orient to exalt the lords of Italy[1].

Relations with the East.

'The Franks also, overmighty by their victories over so many barbarous tribes—by what a great expedition were they harassed! Attacked, they dreaded a contest with our soldiers; they who had leaped unawares upon so many nations and forced them into battle. But though that haughty race declined the offered conflict, they could not prevent the death of their own King. For Theodoric[2], he who had so often availed himself of the name of our glorious King as an occasion for triumph, now fell vanquished in the struggle with disease—a stroke of Divine Providence surely, to prevent us from staining ourselves with the blood of our kindred, and yet to grant some revenge to the army which had

Expedition against the Franks.

---

[1] 'Et singularis illa potentia, ut *Italicos Dominos*, erigeret, reverentiam Eoi culminis ordinavit.' This somewhat favours the notion that Theodoric and his successors called themselves Kings of Italy.

[2] Theodoric I, son of Clovis, King of the Franks, reigning at Metz, died, as before stated, in 534.

been justly called out to war. Hail! thou Gothic array, happy above all other happiness, who strikest at the life of a Royal foe, yet leavest us not the poorer by the life of one of the least of our soldiers[1].

League with the Burgundians.

'The Burgundian too, in order to receive his own again, crouched in devotion, giving up his whole self that he might receive a trifle. For he chose to obey with unimpaired territories, rather than to resist with these cut short; and thus, by laying aside his arms, he most effectually defended his kingdom, recovering by his prayers what he had lost by the sword[2].

'Happy Princess, whose enemies either fall by the hand of God, or else by your bounty are united with your Empire! Rejoice, Goths and Romans alike, and hail this marvel, a being who unites the excellences of both the sexes! As woman she has given birth to your illustrious King, while with manly fortitude of mind she has maintained the bounds of your Empire.

'And now, if leaving the realm of war we enter the inner courts of her moral goodness, a hundred tongues will not suffice to sound forth all her praises. Her justice is as great as her goodwill, but even greater is her kindness than her power. You, Senators, know the heavenly goodness which she has shown to your order, restoring those who had met with affliction to a

---

[1] 'Et nobis nec unius ultimi facta subducis (?).'

[2] 'Burgundio quinetiam, ut sua reciperet, devotus effectus est: reddens se totum dum accepisset exiguum. Elegit quippe integer obedire, quam imminutus obsistere: tutius tunc defendit regnum quando arma deposuit. Recuperavit enim prece, quod amisit in acie.' The meaning of these mysterious words, as interpreted by Binding (268-270) and Jahn (ii. 252), is that Godomar, King of the Burgundians, received back from Amalasuentha (probably about 530, or a little later) the territory between the Durance and the Isere, which Theodoric had wrested from his brother in 523. The occasion of this cession was probably some league of mutual defence against the Franks, which Cassiodorus could without dishonesty represent as a kind of vassalage of Burgundy to Ostrogothia. If so, it availed Godomar little, as his territories were overrun by the Frankish Kings in 532, and the conquest of them was apparently completed by 534 (Jahn ii. 68-78).

higher state than that from which they had fallen[1], and exalting to honour those who were still uninjured.

'Look at the case of the Patrician Liberius[2], Praefect of the Gauls—a man of charming manners, of distinguished merit, a soldier with honourable scars—who even while absent in his Praefecture has received the *fasces* and a patrimony from her.

'What can I say of her strength of mind and tenacity of purpose, in which she excels even philosophers? I speak of this from my own experience. You know, oh Conscript Fathers, what influences were arrayed against me[3]. Neither gold nor the prayers of great men availed: all things were tried, and tried in vain, to prove the glorious constancy of that wisest Lady.

'And here the rules of rhetoric would require me to compare her with a long line of Empresses in the past. But if men cannot vie with her glory, what is the use of adducing female examples? If we look at the Royal Cohort of her ancestors, we shall see that she, like a pure mirror, reflects all their excellences. For Amal[4] was conspicuous for his good fortune, Ostrogotha for his patience, Athal for mildness, Munitarius [Winithar] for justice, Unimund for beauty, Thorismuth for chastity, Unalamer [Walamir] for faith, Theudimer for warmth of heart[5], and Theodoric, the renowned

Virtues of the Amal Kings.

---

[1] 'Afflictos statu meliore restituit.' An allusion, probably, to her kindness to the families of Boethius and Symmachus.

[2] No doubt the same Liberius who nobly defended the character of Amalasuentha at the Court of Justinian (Procopius, De Bello Gotthico i. 4). Apparently he was made Consul, but his name does not appear in the Fasti at this time.

[3] Probably to prevent his obtaining the Praefecture.

[4] This and the following names belong to the ancestors of Amalasuentha, and are found with slight variations in the treatise of Jordanes on the History of the Goths, which was founded on a similar treatise by Cassiodorus.

[5] 'Pietate Theudimer.'

father of Amalasuentha, as ye have all seen, for patience. Each of these would recognise in her his own special attribute, but all would acknowledge that in these very attributes they are excelled by her.

'You will now perhaps expect me to praise our young King, but in extolling the author of his being, I have abundantly extolled him, her offspring. You will remember that excellent saying of the eloquent Symmachus; "I hesitate to praise the beginning of his career because I am confidently hoping for his advance in virtue[1]." Come to my help, Conscript Fathers, and render to your Lords and mine your united thanks for my promotion.'

2. SENATOR, PRAETORIAN PRAEFECT, TO POPE JOHN[2].

Salutations to the Pope.

'Your prayers are assuredly the cause of our promotion. Your fastings have procured plenty for the citizens. Saluting you therefore with all due reverence, we pray you to continue your prayers for long life to our rulers, for peace and plenty to the State, and for an increase of heavenly wisdom to me. Let the Judge in public life be such as the Catholic Church has trained her son to be. I am indeed a Judge of the Palace, but I shall not cease to be your disciple[3]. Cast not off upon me the whole care of this City, which you watch over with a father's love, but take thought both for its bodily and spiritual wants, and admonish me whenever

---

[1] 'Specto feliciter virtutis ejus augmenta, qui differo laudare principia.' The annotator says that these words are not to be found in the extant writings of Symmachus [the orator]. It was probably the younger Symmachus, the father-in-law of Boethius, who uttered them. At this time Athalaric was killing himself by his debaucheries.

[2] Pope John II (a Roman, son of Projectus, and originally named Mercurius) succeeded Boniface II Jan. 1, 533. His pontificate lasted till May 26, 535. His successor was Agapetus. This letter appears to have been written at a time of scarcity in Rome.

[3] 'Sum quidem Judex Palatinus, sed vester non desinam esse discipulus.'

you think I am erring. Your See is an object of admiration through all lands, and your charity is worldwide; but yet you have also an especial, local love for the sheep of your own flock.

'Rome has in her own borders those shrines of martyrdom[1] of the Apostles [Peter and Paul] which the whole world longs to behold. With such patrons, if only your prayers ascend, we need fear no evil.'

3. SENATOR, PRAETORIAN PRAEFECT, TO DIVERS BISHOPS.

Salutations to the Bishops.

'Fathers after the flesh delight in the advancement of their sons. Even so do ye, my spiritual fathers, diligently pray to the Holy Trinity that He may make my candle to give light to all that are in the house; yea, and that He may so purge and enlighten mine own conscience that I may not, while an accurate Judge over other men, be a deceiver of mine own self.

'I beg of you to declare a fast, and supplicate the Lord that He will prolong the life of our Sovereigns[2], for the happiness of the realm; that He will defend our State from the assaults of its enemies, will give us all tranquillity in our time, and will deign to make me worthy of your love.

'Watch narrowly the acts of the subordinates whom I send among you, and inform me of anything which they do amiss. I cannot be held responsible for deeds of which I know nothing. And if they take bribes they at least cannot justify themselves by saying that they have first had to pay money for their offices.

'Continue to afford your wonted solace to the widow and orphan; yet beware that your pity does not lead you to seek to set aside the laws even for these. Oh, most holy men, banish to the home of all other unclean spirits violence, avarice, hatred, rapine; and root out from

---

[1] 'Confessiones.'

[2] This was written, no doubt, when Athalaric was on his deathbed.

among your people luxury, which is the depopulator of the human race. Let the Bishop teach, that the Judge may have a maiden assize[1]. If only your preaching be continued, the penal course of law must necessarily come to an end.

'I therefore commend my dignity to your prayers, and end my letter with a salutation of love and honour to your Holinesses.'

4. Senator, Praetorian Praefect, to his Deputy[2] Ambrosius, an Illustris.

Functions of the Praefect's Deputy.

'We have formed a high opinion of you from long observation of your career as an Advocate, and feel sure that you will justify that opinion by your conduct in the office to which we are now calling you. The Forum has long resounded to your eloquence: now your turn is come to sit upon the magistrate's bench. Hitherto you have assisted the officers of the court: now you are yourself called upon to play the part of a Judge. Even when you are absent from me, you will be deemed to be sitting by my side; but whatever credit you may earn when hearing a case by yourself will be reckoned to you alone.

'We therefore ordain that the official staff which waits upon our orders shall be at your disposal, to carry your decisions into effect, and to see that none treat them with contempt.

---

[1] 'Episcopus doceat, ne judex possit invenire quod puniat.'

[2] 'Agenti vices.' Bethmann Hollweg (Gerichtsverfassung des sinkenden römischen Reichs, pp. 49–50) remarks: 'The relation of the *Vices Magistratuum agentes* does not belong to the *Jurisdictio mandata*. They are lieutenants (Stellvertreter) who are substituted provisionally in the room of an ordinary official of the Empire or of a Province, on account of his being temporarily disqualified or suspended from office by the Emperor or Praetorian Praefect. The municipal magistrates were also represented by *vices agentes*. But the extant authorities give us no very clear information as to their position.' Unfortunately this letter, relating to a *vices agens* of the Praetorian Praefect himself, does not add much to our information.

'If you shall think it necessary to hand over any [insolvent] persons to those who have become security for them, assume that right with confidence, because that will most effectually relieve my mind when I shall learn that this matter has been finally disposed of by you[1]. For if I were present you might give me words only; but now in my absence you owe me, rather, deeds.

'Think, then, of all that is involved in your high office. Let your toil procure me rest from all men. Avoid the rocks on either side of you. These warnings come rather from my over-particularity[2] than from any distrust of you, for I believe that with God's help you will order all things as shall be best for our fame and for the Republic.'

5. THE SAME TO THE SAME.

[On the occasion of a scarcity in Rome, either existing or dreaded. See the letter to Pope John II (xi. 2).]

Grain distributions for Rome.

'I am sure that you will rejoice with me if the needs of the Roman people can be satisfied by our means, and thus we can testify our gratitude for the hospitality which we have both received from that City. To this end have we endured the discomforts of travel, for this purpose have we racked our brains with anxious thought, that that people, which tasted such delights of old in the happy days of its former rulers, may now see its necessities relieved and again enjoy its former prosperity.

---

[1] I suggest this with hesitation as the translation of a difficult sentence: 'Si quos etiam fidejussoribus committere necessarium aestimaveris, confidenter assume: quia illud magis relevare potest animum nostrum, si aliquid per vos cognoscimus impletum.' Cassiodorus seems to be urging his deputy not to shrink from the exercise of even the most stringent rights inherent in his office, in order that causes may be terminated without reference to him. But is there authority for such a translation of the words 'fidejussoribus committere?'

[2] 'Curiositas.'

'Their poverty and hunger we make our own. Therefore, with all speed, let stores of grain in good condition be at once collected, so that the bread cooked therefrom may be a delight and not a horror. Let just weight be given. Flee all thought of unholy profit from this source. My own soul is wounded if anyone dares to transgress in this matter of the food-supply of the people. Not favour nor popular applause is my aim; but to be permitted, by God's help, to accomplish my own heart's desire.

'I love all my fellow-countrymen, but the Roman citizens deserve more than ordinary love from me. Theirs is a City adorned with so many illustrious Senators, blest with such a noble commonalty, a City so well fitted to celebrate the victories of our glorious rulers. When the question of my promotion hung in suspense, it was the good wishes of these citizens which turned the scale in my favour with the lords of the world[1], who complied with the universal desire of the Roman people. Come, then; so act that this goodwill of theirs to me may continue. Let us all beseech the mercy of the Most High to bless us with an abundant harvest; and let us resolve that, if we are thus favoured, no negligence of ours shall diminish, no venality divert from its proper recipients, the bounty of Heaven[2].'

6. SENATOR, PRAETORIAN PRAEFECT, TO JOANNES, CANCELLARIUS.

[An interesting letter, as showing the lowly original of the office from whence have sprung the mediaeval and modern Chancellors.]

Functions of the Cancellarius.

'Your rare merit causes you to enjoy a position beyond

---

[1] Athalaric and Amalasuentha.

[2] In the last sentence but one, 'Fidem meam promitto: sed cum ipsis Divinitatis dona sustineo, cautelam offero,' I would suggest *ipsius* for 'ipsis,' making *cum* = 'when,' not 'with.' There does not seem to be any antecedent plural to which 'ipsis' can refer.

that which of right belongs to you in the official hierarchy[1]. Those who are above you cheerfully manifest to you a deference which you might be required to show to them; and thus you, while keeping your inferiors in their proper place, take without presumption precedence of many of your superiors.

'This laudable prejudice has assigned to you, from the twelfth Indiction[2], the dignity of Cancellarius[3].

'Guard then the secrets of our Consistory with incorruptible fidelity. Through your intervention the petitioner for justice has to approach me. On your acts depends in great measure the opinion which men shall form of me; for as a house is judged by its front towards the street, and men by the trimness or shabbiness of their raiment, so are we high officials judged by the demeanour of our subordinates who represent us to the crowd. Therefore, if such officials do anything which redounds to their master's dishonour, they put themselves altogether outside the pale of his clemency.

'Remember your title, *Cancellarius*. Ensconced behind the lattice-work (cancelli) of your compartment, keeping guard behind those windowed doors, however studiously you may conceal yourself, it is inevitable that you be the observed of all observers[4]. If you step forth, *my* glances range all over you: if you return to your shelter, the eyes of the litigants are upon you. This is where Antiquity ruled that you should be placed, in order that your actions should be visible to all.

'Attend now to this advice which I have given you, and let it not merely filter through your mind, like water through a pipe, but let it sink down into your

---

[1] 'Transgressio matriculae actio tua est.'

[2] September 1, 533.

[3] 'Hoc igitur laudabili praejudicium a duodecima Indictione cancellorum tibi decus attribuit.'

[4] 'Respice quo nomine nuncuperis. Latere non potest quod inter cancellos egeris. Tenes quippe lucidas fores, claustra patentia, fenestratas januas; et quamvis studiose claudas, necesse est ut te cunctis aperias.'

heart, and, safely stored up there, let it influence the actions of your life.'

7. SENATOR, PRAETORIAN PRAEFECT, TO ALL THE JUDGES OF THE PROVINCES.

Duties of the Collectors of Taxes.

'It is an excellent thing that the yearly taxes should be regularly paid. What confidence does the consciousness of this give to the taxpayer, who can march boldly through the Forum, feeling that he owes nothing to anybody and need not fear the face of any official! One can only enjoy an estate if one has no fear of the process-server making his appearance upon it.

'Therefore, in the Diocese of your Excellency[1], we desire you and your staff at the beginning of this twelfth Indiction[2], with all proper gentleness, to impress upon the cultivator of the soil that he must pay his land-tax[3] and end those long arrears, which were introduced not for the assistance of the taxpayer, but for the corrupt profit of the tax-collector. For the officials who in this way professed to relieve the burdens of the people, really imposed upon them a heavier and more hateful weight in the shape of douceurs[4] to themselves.

'Let then this hateful swindling be henceforth banished. Let the cultivator pay nothing more than his lawful debt to the Treasury, and let him pay it at the appointed time, thus removing the confusion in which the slowness of collection has involved our accounts.

'Make up, therefore, the abstracts of accounts[5] at the stated times, and forward them to the proper bureaux[6],

---

[1] 'Dicationis tuae.' A peculiar and untranslatable form of respect.

[2] September 1, 533.

[3] 'Trina illatio' (See Var. ii. 24). So called because it was collected three times in the year. See Dahn, Könige der Germanen iii. 140; and Sartorius, Regierung der Ostg. 200. The latter seems however to confuse it with the 'tertiae,' from which Dahn very properly distinguishes it.

[4] 'Nundinationes.'

[5] 'Breves.'   [6] 'Scrinia.'

according to old law and the authority of this present edict; and if you neglect any of these injunctions, know that you do so at your peril. To quicken your diligence we have appointed A and B, persons of tried merit in the past, to supervise the proceedings of yourself and your staff, that this double check may prevent the possibility of negligence.

'Act then with justice if you wish to receive further promotion. Only those gains are to be sought for which the cultivator gladly offers and which the public servant can securely accept. If you take bribes you will be miserable ever after, through fear of discovery; but if you act uprightly, you will have in me a willing spectator and rewarder of your merits. I am most anxious to be your friend; do not force me against my will to become your enemy.'

8. Edict Published through the Provinces by Senator, Praetorian Praefect.

Edict announcing Cassiodorus' principles of administration.

'The custom of the ancients was for a new ruler to promulgate a new set of laws to his subjects, but now it is sufficient praise to a conscientious ruler that he adheres to the legislation of Antiquity.

'Do you all study to perform good actions, and shrink from deeds of lawlessness and sedition, and you will have nothing to fear from your Governors. I know that some fear, however irrational, is felt in the presence of the Judge; but as far as my purpose can avail, with the help of God and the rulers of the State[1], I can promise you that all things shall be done with justice and moderation.

'Venality, that greatest stain upon a Judge's character, will be unknown in me; for I should think scorn to sell the words that go out of my lips, like clothes in the market-place.

---

[1] 'Juvante Deo, rerumque Dominis regnantibus.'

'In exercising the right of pre-emption we shall be solely guided by the wants of the State, buying nothing at a forced price in order to sell it again[1].

'Be cheerful and of good courage, therefore, with reference to the new administration. No soldier or civil servant shall harass you for his own pleasure. No tax-collector shall load you with burdens of his own imposition. We are determined to keep not only our own hands clean, but also those of our officials. Otherwise, vainly does a good Judge guard himself from receiving money, if he leaves to the many under him licence to receive it on their own account. But we, both by precept and example, show that we aim at the public good, not at private and fraudulent gains.

'We know what prayers you put up for us, how anxiously you watched for our elevation, and we are determined that you shall not be disappointed. Our Praetorium, which no base action has ever defiled, shall be open to all. No servile throng shall lord it over you. You shall come straight to us, making your requests known to us through no hired interpreter, and none shall leave our presence poorer than he entered it. With God's help we trust we shall so act as to conform to the instructions which we have received from our Sovereign[2]; and we trust that you, by your loyalty, will enable us to be rather the Father of our Provinces than their Judge. You have patiently obeyed governors who fleeced you; how much more ought you to obey one who, as you know, loves you mightily! Pay the regular fees to the officials who are labouring in your midst; for there is no such excuse for high-handed oppression as the fact that a man is not receiving his covenanted salary. Obey the rule of reason, and you will not have to fear the armed man's wrath.

[1] 'Sperari a vobis aliquid sola specierum indigentia faciet, non malitiosa venalitas ... nec ad taxationem trahimus quae necessaria non habentur.'
[2] 'Quemadmodum a rerum Dominis mandata suscepimus.'

'We wish that you should enjoy the privileges conceded to you by former rulers without any encroachment by violent men.

'And now be of good heart; I pledge myself for your righteous government. Had I been present with you face to face, ye could not have seen my mind; but ye can read it in this letter, which is the mirror of my heart, the true image of my will, and ye can see that it desires only your prosperity.'

9. SENATOR, PRAETORIAN PRAEFECT, TO THE JUDGES OF THE PROVINCES.

Exhortation to the Judges to govern in conformity with the Edict.

'Knowing that past suffering makes men anxious and timid as to the future, we have put forth an edict [the preceding document] in order to reassure the minds of the Provincials, and to deliver them from the torment of ever-present fear.

'Therefore we call upon your Excellency[1] to cause this edict to be exposed in all the places which are most resorted to. Thus let the love and devotion of all classes be excited towards our happy Sovereigns[2], that as our thoughts towards the people are entirely thoughts of goodwill, so their dispositions towards the rulers who govern them in righteousness may be only loyal[3].

'It now rests with you, by your just government of the Provincials, to carry our promises into effect.

'Remember that the official staff standing by, is a witness of the acts of every one of you; and so comport yourselves, that both they and all others may see that you in your own conduct obey the laws which you administer.

---

[1] 'Dicatio tua.' [2] 'Circa Dominos felices.'
[3] 'Ita se et illi devotos debent *pie regnantibus* exhibere.' Compare again Claudian's words:

'Nunquam libertas gratior exstat,
Quam sum *rege pio*.'

'Be more anxious to remedy the poverty of the Provincials than to inflict punishment upon them. So act that when you are giving an account of your stewardship your year of office may be felt to have been all too short[1]. If you have acted justly, and earned the good-will of your Provincials, you will have no need of gifts to stave off accusations.

'We do not appoint any spies upon your actions, and we pray you so to act that this most humiliating expedient may not be necessary.

'If you meet with any who pertinaciously set themselves up against the authority of your *fasces*, send us at once a messenger with your report; or, if you cannot spare such an one, send the report alone, as you have authority to use the public postal-service[2]. Thus all excuse for remissness on your part is taken away, since you can either wield your power or explain to us the hindrances which beset you.'

10. SENATOR, PRAETORIAN PRAEFECT, TO BEATUS, VIR CLARISSIMUS AND CANCELLARIUS.

Davus is invalided to the Mons Lactarius.

'Our lord the King[3] (whose prayer it is that he may ever rejoice in the welfare of all his subjects), when he reflected upon the impaired health of his servant Davus[4], ordered him to seek to the healing properties of the Mons Lactarius[5], for the cure which medical aid seemed powerless to bestow. A frequent cough resounded from

---

[1] 'Sic agite ut cum justitia probata quaeritur, annus vester brevis esse videatur.'

[2] 'Quando et evectiones publicas accepistis et nobis gratum sit audire de talibus.'

[3] 'Rerum Domini clementia.'

[4] Or David, according to some MSS.

[5] This is no doubt the mountain on whose skirts was fought the decisive battle between Narses and Teias in 553, now known as Monte Lettere. It is a spur of the range reaching from Sorrento to Salerno, which attains its highest elevation in Monte San Angelo (4,690 feet high). It rises opposite to Mount Vesuvius on the south-east, the ruins of Pompeii and the valley of the Sarno (formerly the Draco) lying between the two.

his panting chest, his limbs were becoming emaciated, and the food which he took seemed to have lost all power to nourish his frame. Persons in this state can neither feed nor endure to fast, and their bodies seem like leaky casks, from which all strength must soon dribble away.

'As an antidote to this cruel malady Heaven has given us the Mons Lactarius, where the salubrious air working together with the fatness of the soil has produced a herbage of extraordinary sweetness. The cows which are fed on this herbage give a milk which seems to be the only remedy for consumptive patients who have been quite given over by their physicians. As sleep refreshes the weary limbs of toil, so does this milk fill up the wasted limbs and restore the vanished strength. Strange is it to see the herds feeding on this abundant pasture. They look as if it did not profit them at all. Thin and scraggy, as they wander through the thickets they look like the patients who seek their aid; yet their milk is so thick that it sticks to the milker's fingers. The milk-cure, a remedy for consumption.

'Do you therefore supply the invalid when he arrives, with the appointed rations and pecuniary allowance, that he may be suitably maintained in that place while he is recreating his exhausted energies with the food of infancy.

'And, oh! all ye who are suffering under the like grievous malady, lift up your hearts. There is hope for you. By no bitter antidote, but by a delicious draught, you shall imbibe life—life, in itself the sweetest of all things.'

11. Edict concerning Prices to be Maintained at Ravenna.

'The price at which provisions are sold ought to follow, in a reasonable way, the circumstances of the times, that Prices at Ravenna.

there may be neither cheapness in a dear season, nor dearness in a cheap one, and that the grumblings of both buyers and sellers may be avoided, by fairness being observed towards both.

'Therefore, after careful consideration, we have fixed in the subjoined schedule the prices of the various articles of produce, which prices are to remain free from all ambiguity.

'If any vendor does not observe the prices named in the present edict, he will be liable to a fine of six solidi (£3 12s.) for each violation of the law, and may be visited by corporal punishment[1].'

[The schedule mentioned in this letter is unfortunately not preserved. Few documents that Cassiodorus could have handed down to posterity would have been more valuable. If we could have compared it with the celebrated Edict of Stratonicea (cir. A.D. 301), we should have seen what changes had been wrought in the value of the precious metals and the distribution of wealth during the two centuries of disturbance and barbaric invasion which had elapsed since the reign of Diocletian. But, unfortunately, Cassiodorus believed that his rhetoric and his natural history would be more interesting to us than these vulgar facts.]

12. EDICT CONCERNING PRICES ALONG THE FLAMINIAN WAY.

Prices per Viam Flaminiam.

'If prices need to be fixed for the leisurely inhabitant of a town, much more for the traveller, whose journey may otherwise become a burden instead of a pleasure. Let strangers therefore find that they are entertained by you at fixed prices. To fawn upon them with feigned politeness and then terrify them with enormous charges

---

[1] 'Per singulos excessus sex solidorum mulctam a se noverit exigendam et fustuario posse subjacere supplicio.'

is the act of a highway robber. Do you not know how much better moderate prices would suit your own purpose? Travellers would gladly flock to your accommodation-houses[1] if they found that you treated them fairly.

'Let no one think that because he is a long way off, his extortion will escape notice, for people are arriving here every day with tales of your rapacity.

'An official despatched for the purpose will, after deliberation with the citizens and Bishops of each place, decide what prices are to be charged there; and then whosoever dares to ask higher prices will have to pay a fine of six solidi (£3 12s.) and will be afflicted by the laceration of his body.

'Honest gains at the expense of your fellow-citizens ought to suffice for all of you. One would think that the highways were beset with brigands.'

13. THE SENATE OF THE CITY OF ROME TO THE EMPEROR JUSTINIAN.

Supplications of the Senate to Justinian.

'It seems a right and proper thing that we should address our prayers for the safety of the Roman Republic to a dutiful Sovereign[2], who can only desire what will benefit our freedom. We therefore beseech you, most clement Emperor, and from the bosom of the Curia we stretch forth our two hands to you in prayer, that you will grant a most enduring peace to our King. Spurn not us, who ever seemed certain of your love. It is in truth the Roman name that you are commending, if you grant gracious terms to our lords. May your league with them assure the peace of Italy; and if our prayers be not sufficient to accomplish this thing, imagine that you hear our country break forth with

---

[1] This is, I believe, the expression used in some of the Australian colonies for what Cassiodorus calls *commoda vestra*.

[2] 'Pio Principi.'

these words of supplication: "If ever I was acceptable to thee, love, oh most dutiful Sovereign, love my defenders! They who rule me ought to be in harmony with thee, lest otherwise they begin to do such deeds towards me as thou least of all men wouldest desire. Be not to me a cause of death, thou who hast ever ministered unto me the joys of life. Lo, while at peace with thee I have doubled the number of my children, I have been decked with the glory of my citizens. If thou sufferest me to be wounded, where is thy dutiful name of Son? What couldest even thou do more for me [than these rulers], seeing that my religion and thine thus flourish under their rule?

'"My Senate grows in honour and is incessantly increasing in wealth. Do not dissipate in quarrels what thou oughtest rather to defend with the sword. I have had many Kings; but none so trained in letters as this one. I have had foreseeing statesmen, but none so powerful in learning and religion. I love the Amal, bred up as he has been at my knees, a strong man, one who has been formed by my conversation, dear to the Romans by his prudence, venerable to the nations by his valour. Join rather thy prayers to his; share with him thy counsels: so that any prosperity which I may earn may redound to thy glory. Do not woo me in the only fashion in which I may not be won. Thine am I already in love, if thou sendest none of thy soldiers to lacerate my limbs. For if Africa has deserved through thee to recover freedom, it were hard that I should from the same hand lose that freedom which I have ever possessed. Control the emotions of anger, oh illustrious conqueror! The claims urged upon thee by the general voice of the people ought to outweigh the offence which the ingratitude of any private individual may have occasioned to thy heart."

'Thus Rome speaks while, through her Senators, she makes supplications to you. And if that be not enough, let the sacred petition of the blessed Apostles Peter and Paul be also taken into your account. For surely they, who are proved to have so often defended the peace of Rome from her enemies, deserve that your Sovereignty should yield everything to their merits. The venerable man, our most pious King's ambassador to your Clemency, will further set forth our prayers.'

[It is not easy to fix the exact occasion on which this petition was likely to be sent from the Senate to the Emperor. The allusion to the conquest of Africa shows that it was after the Vandal War, which ended in March, 534. On the other hand, the language put into the mouth of the Senate implies that the Imperial troops had not yet landed in Italy or Sicily, and the petition is therefore of an earlier date than the summer of 535. During the whole of these fourteen months the relations between Empire and Kingdom were more or less strained, the causes of complaint on the part of Constantinople beginning with the occupation of Lilybaeum and ending with the murder of Amalasuentha. I fear that the flattering portrait drawn of 'the Amal' can apply to no one but Theodahad, the terms used being hopelessly inapplicable to a boy like Athalaric. Who then are 'our lords' ('nostri Domini'), in whose name peace is besought. The best that we can hope, for the sake of the reputation of Cassiodorus, is that they are Amalasuentha and Theodahad, the letter being written between October 2, 534 (when Athalaric died), and April 30, 535 (when Amalasuentha was imprisoned). Upon the whole this seems the most probable conclusion. If written after Amalasuentha's death, in the few months or weeks which intervened between that event and the landing of Belisarius in Sicily, the language employed reflects deep discredit on the writer. In that case, 'nostri Domini' must mean Theodahad and Gudelina.]

14. SENATOR, PRAETORIAN PRAEFECT, TO GAUDIOSUS, CANCELLARIUS OF THE PROVINCE OF LIGURIA.

Praises of Como. Relief of its inhabitants.

'The City of Como[1] is visited by so many travellers that the cultivators of the soil declare that they are quite worn out with requisitions for post-horses[2]. Wherefore we direct that by Royal indulgence they be favoured in this matter[3], that this city, so beautifully situated, do not become a solitude for want of inhabitants.

'Como, with its precipitous mountains and its vast expanse of lake, seems placed there for the defence of the Province of Liguria; and yet, again, it is so beautiful that one would think it was created for pleasure only. To the south lies a fertile plain with easy roads for the transport of provisions; on the north a lake sixty miles long, abounding in fish, soothing the mind with delicious recreation.

'Rightly is it called *Como*, because it is adorned (compta) with such gifts. The lake lies in a shell-like valley, with white margins. Above rises a diadem of lofty mountains, their slopes studded with bright villas[4], a girdle of olives below, vineyards above, while a crest of thick chestnut-woods adorns the very summit of the hills. Streams of snowy clearness dash from the hill-sides into the lake. On the eastern side these unite to form the river Addua, so called because it contains the *added* volume of two streams. It plunges into the lake with such force that it keeps its own colour[5] (dark among the

---

[1] Thus called by Cassiodorus; not Comum.

[2] 'Se possessores paraveredorum assiduitate suggerunt esse fatigatos.'

[3] 'Quibus indultu Regali beneficium praecipimus jugiter custodiri.' These words do not make it clear how the inhabitants were relieved by the Royal decree; but it was probably by some gift of money like that which is announced in the next letter.

[4] 'Praetoriorum luminibus decenter ornata.'

[5] So Claudian (De VI Consolata Honorii 196), 'et Addua visu caerulus.'

whiter waters) and its own name far along the northern shore[1], a phenomenon often seen with rivers flowing into the ocean, but surely marvellous with one flowing into an inland lake. And so swift is its course as it moves through the alien waves, that you might fancy it a river flowing over the solid plains.

'So delightful a region makes men delicate and averse to labour. Therefore the inhabitants deserve especial consideration, and for this reason we wish them to enjoy perpetually the royal bounty.'

15. SENATOR, PRAETORIAN PRAEFECT, TO THE LIGURIANS.

[Announcing the despatch of money to relieve the necessities of the Province, possibly after some incursions of the Franks. This would fit in pretty well with the mention of *Astensis Civitas* as having suffered the most.]

Relief of the necessities of Liguria.

'It is the privilege of a King to increase the happiness of his subjects. Not to postpone your joy by too long a preface, I will come to the point at once, and inform you that our most glorious Lords, taking the necessities of their loyal Liguria into account, have sent 100lbs. of gold [£4,000] by the hands of A and B, officers of the Royal Bedchamber. *You* are to say how the money is to be spent, indicating the persons who are in the greatest necessity; but as we are informed that the city of Asti has been more heavily weighted than others, it is our wish that it should be chiefly helped by this disbursement. Now, do you who are tributaries, reflect upon the clemency of your lords, who are inverting the usual order of things, and paying out to you from the Treasury what they are accustomed to receive. Let us know at once

---

[1] 'Ut nomen retinens et colorem in Septentrionem obesiore alvei ventre generetur.'

how much you think each taxpayer ought to receive, that we may deduct it from his first instalment of land-tax[1].

'And put up your prayers for your most affectionate Sovereigns, that they may receive back again from Heaven the favour which they are conferring on you.'

16. SENATOR, PRAETORIAN PRAEFECT, TO THE LIGURIANS.

Oppressions practised on the Ligurians to be remedied.

'In thanking me so earnestly for a recent benefit [probably the present mentioned in the preceding letter] you invited me to further favours, and the implied promise which I then gave you I now fulfil.

'You complain that you are burdened with unjust weights and measures, and I therefore declare that this iniquity shall cease, and that no tax-collector or tithe-collector[2], shall dare to use too long a measure or too heavy a weight [in the collection of the King's revenue].

'Also that their accounts shall be promptly balanced, and that any overcharge that may be detected shall be at once repaid.

'Now then, your minds being freed from anxiety on this score, turn your attention to the supply of the wants of our most flourishing army, and show your zeal for the public good, since we have satisfied you that it is not for private and fraudulent gains that you are to pay your contributions.'

---

[1] 'Sed ut beneficia Dominorum *subtractis exactionum incommodis* augeantur, celerius relatio vestra nos instruat, quid unicuique de hac summâ relaxandum esse judicetis, ut tantum de *primâ illatione* faciamus *suspendi* quantum ad nos notitia directa vulgaverit.' The meaning of Cassiodorus seems quite clear, though it is not easy to understand how far the actual gift of money was supplemented by, or independent of, remission of land-tax.

[2] 'Exactores atque susceptores.' For the latter office, see Cod. Theod. xii. 6.

17. ON THE PROMOTIONS IN THE OFFICIAL STAFF OF THE PRAETORIAN PRAEFECT, MADE ON CHRISTMAS DAY[1].

Promotions in Officium of Praefectus Praetorio.

'On this day of general rejoicing, when by the kindness of Heaven the way of salvation was opened to all mankind, we wish that the members of our staff should also be glad. For to rejoice, ourselves, when those around us are mourning, is a kind of sacrilege. Hence some philosophers have held that the whole human race is one being, the various members of which are constrained to share one another's feelings of joy or sadness. Therefore let every official in our staff according to his grade[2] get promotion on this day, not only rising himself, but creating a vacancy which enables those below him to rise also.'

[All the Letters from 18 to 35 are documents, for the most part very short ones, relating to these promotions.

For an explanation of the terms used in these letters, and of the whole subject of the staff of the Praetorian Praefect, see chapter iv. of the Introduction.]

In Letter 18, Antianus, who is vacating the office of CORNICULARIUS, receives the rank of *Spectabilis*, and has a place assigned him among the Tribuni and Notarii, where he may 'adore the presence of his Sovereign[3].'

In Letter 19 the successor of Antianus in the office of CORNICULARIUS receives his appointment.

In Letter 20 the retiring PRIMISCRINIUS also receives the rank of *Spectabilis*, and takes his place among

---

[1] This letter was probably addressed to the Princeps, the highest person in the whole Officium, as it contains the words '*unus* quisque ... *tuâ designatione vulgetur.*'

[2] '*Juxta matriculae seriem.*'

[3] '*Inter Tribunos et Notarios ad adorandos aspectus properet Principales.*'

the Tribuni and Notarii, 'to adore the Purple of Royalty.'

In Letter 21 Andreas is rewarded for his faithful service on the Praetorian staff[1], by being promoted to the office of PRIMISCRINIUS.

In Letter 22 Catellus, who stands next in grade for this promotion[2], obtains the post of SCRINIARIUS ACTORUM.

In Letter 23 Constantinian, to whose virtues Cassiodorus himself bears witness, receives the charge of letters relating to the collection of Land-Tax (CURA EPISTOLARUM CANONICARUM).

In Letter 24 Lucillus is appointed a clerk in the War-Office (SCRINIARIUS CURAE MILITARIS).

In Letter 25 Patricius is appointed chief of the short-hand writers (PRIMICERIUS EXCEPTORUM).

In Letter 26 Justus obtains a place as member of the Sixth Schola (SEXTUS SCHOLARIS[3]).

In Letter 27 Joannes, whom we saw in the Sixth Letter of this Book entrusted with the duties of Cancellarius, is rewarded for his faithful discharge of those duties by receiving the place of PRAEROGATIVARIUS[4].

In Letter 28 Cheliodorus[5] is appointed to the place of COMMENTARIENSIS (Magistrates' clerk).

---

[1] 'Qui Praetorianis fascibus inculpabiliter noscitur obsecutus.'

[2] 'Quem matriculae series fecit accedere.'

[3] I am unable to suggest any explanation of this title.

[4] I have not found any explanation of this title, which is apparently unknown to the Notitia, to Lydus, and to the Theodosian Code.

[5] Note the corrupt form of the name Heliodorus.

In Letter 29 Cart(h)erius is promoted to the office of REGERENDARIUS (Secretary of the Post-Office), in the hope that this promotion will render him yet more earnest in the discharge of his Praetorian labours.

In Letter 30 Ursus is appointed PRIMICERIUS DEPUTATORUM, and Beatus (probably the Cancellarius addressed in Letter 10) is made PRIMICERIUS AUGUSTALIUM.

In Letter 31 Urbicus, on vacating the post of PRIMICERIUS SINGULARIORUM (Chief of the King's Messengers), is placed among the Body-guards (Domestici et Protectores), where he may adore the Royal Purple, that, being made illustrious by gazing on the Sovereign, he may rejoice in his liberation from official harassment.

[As the Singularii did not form part of the learned staff (Militia Litterata), their chief on retiring receives a guardsman's place, but still one which gives him access to royalty.]

In Letter 32 Pierius receives the post of PRIMICERIUS SINGULARIORUM which is thus vacated.

In Letter 33 Cassiodorus, expanding the proverb 'Bis dat qui cito dat,' agrees that the *Delegatoria*[1] (or Delegatiorius), the letter conferring on the receiver the right to receive the increase of rations due to his promotion, should not be long delayed. *Delegatoria.*

In Letter 34 Antianus, the retired Cornicularius of Letter 18, receives a somewhat evasive answer to a petition which apparently affected the rights of those below him in the official hierarchy[2].

---

[1] We get this sense of Delegatio in Cod. Theod. vii. 4. 35 : '*Annonas omnes,* quae universis officiis atque Sacri Palatii Ministeriis et Sacris Scriniis ceterisque cunctarum adminiculis dignitatum adsolent *delegari.*'

[2] In this letter occurs a sentence of tantalising obscurity : 'Sola nos Alpha complectitur ubi ea littera non timetur.'

In Letter 35 we have an example of the *Delegatoria* alluded to in Letter 33. It is concerned with a PRINCEPS, apparently the Princeps of the AGENTES IN REBUS; and, after extolling the zeal and alacrity of those officers, who are constantly intent on enforcing obedience to the Imperial decrees and reverence for the authority of the Praetorian Praefect, he observes that it would be impiety to delay the reward of such labour.

'Therefore let your Experience[1] pay, out of the third instalment of land-tax[2] from such and such a Province, those monies which the wisdom of Antiquity directed should be paid to the Princeps Augustorum[3]. Let this be done at once to those who are chargeable on the accounts of the thirteenth Indiction (Sept. 1, 534—Sept. 1, 535). Let there be no venal delays. Behave to the out-going public servant as you would wish that others should behave to you on your retirement from office. All men should honour the veteran, but especially they who are still toiling in the public service.'

36. SENATOR, PRAETORIAN PRAEFECT, TO ANAT(H)OLIUS, CANCELLARIUS OF THE PROVINCE OF SAMNIUM.

The retirement of a Cornicularius on a superannuation allowance justified on astronomical grounds.

'As all things else come to an end, so it is right that the laborious life of a civil servant should have its appointed term.

'The heavenly bodies have their prescribed time in which to complete their journeyings. Saturn in thirty years wanders over his appointed portion of space. Jupiter in twelve years finishes the survey of his kingdom. Mars, with fiery rapidity, completes his course in eighteen months. The Sun in one year goes through all the signs of the Zodiac. Venus accomplishes her circuit in fifteen months; the rapid Mercury in thirteen months. The Moon, peculiar in her

---

[1] It is not clear to whom the letter is addressed.
[2] 'Ex illatione tertiâ.'
[3] The marginal note says: 'i.e. Agentium in Rebus.'

nearer neighbourhood, traverses in thirty days the space which it takes the Sun a year to journey over[1].

'All these bodies, which, as philosophers say, shall only perish with the world, have an appointed end to their journeyings. But they complete their course that they may begin it again: the human race serves that it may rest from its ended labours. Therefore, since the Cornicularius in my Court has completed his term of office, you are to pay him without any deduction this 1st September 700 solidi (£420) from the revenues of the Province of Samnium, taking them out of the third instalment of land-tax[2]. He commanded the wings of the army of the Praefect's assistants, from whence he derived his name[3]. When he handed us the inkstand, we wrote, unbribed, those decrees which men would have paid a great price to obtain[4]. We gratified him whom the laws favoured, we frowned on him who had not justice on his side. No litigant had cause to regret his success, since it came to him unbought. You know all this that we are saying to be true, for our business was all transacted in the office, not in the bedchamber. What we did, the whole troop of civil servants knew[5]. We were private

---

[1] As might be expected from an observer who did not understand the earth's motion in its orbit, the periods assigned to the *inferior* planets in this paragraph are all wrong, while those assigned to the *superior* planets are pretty nearly right.

	Periods according to Cassiodorus.			*True Periods.*	
Saturn	30 years			29 years	174 days.
Jupiter	12 "			11 "	317 "
Mars	1 year	182 days		1 year	321 "
Venus	1 "	91 "			224 "
Mercury	1 "	30 "			88 "

[2] 'Per illam Indictionem de Samnii provinciâ ex illatione tertiâ sine ambiguitate contrade.'

[3] 'Praefuit enim Cornibus Secretarii Praetoriani, unde ei nomen est derivatum.'

[4] 'Eo ministrante caliculum scripsimus inempti quod magnis pretiis optabatur impleri.'

[5] 'Quod egimus cohortes noverunt.' Observe the military character of the service, 'cohortes.'

persons in our power of harming, Judges in our power of doing good. Our words might be stern, our deeds were kindly. We frowned though mollified; we threatened though intending no evil; and we struck terror that we might not have to strike. You have had in me, as you were wont to say, a most clean-handed Judge: I shall leave behind in you my most uncorrupted witnesses.'

37. SENATOR, PRAETORIAN PRAEFECT, TO THE CLARISSIMUS LUCINUS, CANCELLARIUS OF CAMPANIA.

Payment of retiring Primiscrinius.

'It was well ordered by Antiquity that the servants of the Public should receive a due reward for their labours; and who of all these are more deserving than the officers of the Praetorian Praefect (Praetoriani). Theirs is the difficult task of waiting on the necessities of the army. They must demand accounts, often minute and intricate, from great officers whom they dare not offend. They must collect the stores of food for the Roman people from the Provincials without giving them cause for complaint[1]. Their acts constitute our true glory; and in the formation of their characters, work, hard work, that stern and anxious pedagogue[2], is better than all literary or philosophic training.

'Such men ought assuredly to receive their stipulated rewards; and therefore we order you to pay regularly so many solidi of the third instalment, from the land-tax of the Province of Campania[3], to such and such a person, who has now just completed his term of service as Primiscrinius.'

---

[1] 'Eorum est etiam sudoribus applicandum, quod victuales expensae longe quidem positae, *sed tamquam in urbe Regiâ natae* [I do not quite understand this antithesis] sine querelâ Provincialium congregantur.'

[2] 'Labores, violenti magistri, solliciti paedagogi, per quos cautior quis efficitur dum incurri pericula formidantur.'

[3] 'Ex canone provinciae Campaniae tertiae illationis tot solidos solenniter te dare censemus.'

38. SENATOR, PRAETORIAN PRAEFECT, TO JOANNES, CANONICARIUS[1] OF THUSCIA.

'Rightly did Antiquity ordain that a large store of paper should be laid in by our Bureaux (Scrinia), that litigants might receive the decision of the Judge clearly written, without delay, and without avaricious and impudent charges for the paper which bore it[2].

Praises of paper.

'A wonderful product in truth is this wherewith ingenious Memphis has supplied all the offices in the world. The plants of Nile arise, a wood without leaves or branches, a harvest of the waters, the fair tresses of the marshes, plants full of emptiness, spongy, thirsty, having all their strength in their outer rind, tall and light, the fairest fruit of a foul inundation.

'Before Paper was discovered, all the sayings of the wise, all the thoughts of the ancients, were in danger of perishing. Who could write fluently or pleasantly on the rough bark of trees, though it is from that practice that we call a book *Liber?* While the scribe was laboriously cutting his letters on the sordid material, his very thought grew cold: a rude contrivance assuredly, and only fit for the beginnings of the world.

'Then was paper discovered, and therewith was eloquence made possible. Paper, so smooth and so continuous, the snowy entrails of a green herb; paper which can be spread out to such a vast extent, and yet be folded up into such a little space; paper, on whose white expanse the black characters look beautiful; paper which keeps the sweet harvest of the mind, and restores it to the reader whenever he chooses to consult it; paper which is the faithful witness of all human actions, eloquent of the past, a sworn foe to oblivion.

---

[1] Tax-collector.

[2] Lydus (De Magistratibus iii. 14) makes a similar remark, but says that in his time the copying clerks (Exceptarii, or Exceptores) supplied disgracefully bad paper made of grass, and charged a fee for doing so.

'Therefore for this thirteenth Indiction[1] pay so many solidi from the land-tax of the Tuscan Province to our Bureau, that it may be able to keep in perpetuity a faithful record of all its transactions.'

39. SENATOR, PRAETORIAN PRAEFECT, TO THE CLARISSIMUS VITALIAN, CANCELLARIUS OF LUCANIA AND BRUTTII.

Payment by Province of Bruttii of commuted cattle-tax.

'The vast numbers of the Roman people in old time are evidenced by the extensive Provinces from which their food supply was drawn, as well as by the wide circuit of their walls, the massive structure of their amphitheatre, the marvellous bigness of their public baths, and the enormous multitude of mills, which could only have been made for use, not for ornament.

'It was to feed this population, that mountainous Lucania paid her tribute of swine, that fertile Bruttii furnished her droves of oxen. It was a glorious privilege for them thus to feed the Roman people: yet the length of roads over which the animals had to be driven made the tribute unnecessarily burdensome, since every mile reduced their weight, and the herdsman could not possibly obtain credit at the journey's end for the same number of pounds of flesh which he possessed at its beginning. For this reason the tribute was commuted into a money payment, one which no journeyings can diminish and no toil can wound. The Provinces should understand and respond to this favourable change, and not show themselves more slack than their ancestors were, under far more burdensome conditions. Your Diligence has now collected both these taxes[2] at the appointed periods; and I am glad of it, that my

---

[1] Sept. 1, 534. The reading 'de tertiae decimae Indictionis rationibus' seems required by the sense, instead of 'tertiam de decimae Indictionis rationibus.' It is quite clear that Cassiodorus was not Praetorian Praefect at the tenth Indiction.

[2] 'Ambos titulos.'

countrymen, who have served alien magistrates with praiseworthy diligence, might not seem negligent under my rule. These Provinces, which I, my grandfather, and my great-grandfather have benefited as private persons, I have endeavoured to help yet more earnestly while I bore the majesty of the *fasces*, that they who have rejoiced in my exaltation might see that I still retained my love for our common country. Let them pay the tax then, not from fear but from love. I have prevailed on the royal generosity to limit its amount; for whereas it used to be 1,200 solidi [£720] annually, it is henceforward to be 1,000 [£600][1].'

40. AN INDULGENCE [OR AMNESTY TO PRISONERS ON SOME GREAT FESTIVAL OF THE CHURCH, PROBABLY EASTER].

'All the year we are bound to tread in the path of Justice, but on this day we secure our approach to the Redeemer by the path of Forgiveness. Therefore we forswear punishments of all kinds, we condemn the torture, and thus feel ourselves, in forgiving, to be more truly than ever a Judge. *General Amnesty.*

'Hail to thee, O Clemency[2], patroness of the human race! thou reignest in the heavens and on the earth: and most fitting is it that, at sacred seasons like this, thou shouldest be supreme.

'Therefore, O Lictor, thou who art allowed to do with impunity the very thing for which other men are punished, put up thy axe; let it be henceforth bright, not bloody. Let the chains which have been so often wet with tears now grow rusty. The prison— that house of Pluto, in which men suffer a living death, from its foul odours, from the sound of groaning which

---

[1] This sum seems ridiculously small for the Province of Bruttii. Can it be the sum assessed on each district?

[2] 'Indulgentia.'

assails their ears, from the long fastings which destroy their taste, from the heavy weights which weary their hands, from the endless darkness which makes their eyes grow dim—let the prison now be filled with emptiness. Never is it so popular as when it is seen to be deserted.

'And you, its denizens, who are thus in a manner transplanted to Heaven from Hell, avoid the evil courses which made you acquainted with its horrors. Even animals shun the things which they have once found harmful. Cattle which have once fallen into a pit seek not again the same road. The bird once snared shuns bird-lime. The pike buries himself in deep sand, that he may escape the drag-net, and when it has scraped his back leaps nimbly into the waves and expresses by his gambols his joy for his deliverance. When the wrasse [1] finds that he is caught in an osier trap, he moves himself slowly backwards till he can leave his tail protruding, that one of his fellows, perceiving his capture, may pull him out from his prison.

'So too the Sauri (?), a clever race of fish, named from their speed, when they have swum into a net, tie themselves together into a sort of rope; and then, tugging backwards with all their might, seek to liberate their fellow-prisoners.

'Many facts of the same kind would be discovered on enquiry. But my discourse must return to thee, O Gaoler. Thou wilt be miserable in the general joy, because thou art wont to derive thy gladness from the affliction of many. But as some consolation for thy groans, we leave to thee those prisoners whom the Law, for very pity's sake, cannot set free—the men found guilty of outrageous crimes, whose liberation would make barbarous deeds frequent. Over these thou mayest still exert thy power.'

[1] 'Scarus.'

BOOK XII.

CONTAINING TWENTY-EIGHT LETTERS WRITTEN BY CASSIODORUS IN HIS OWN NAME AS PRAETORIAN PRAEFECT.

---

1. SENATOR, PRAETORIAN PRAEFECT, TO THE VARIOUS CANCELLARII OF THE SEVERAL PROVINCES.

General instructions to the Cancellarii.

'IT is generally supposed that long attendance at the Courts of Law increases the love of justice. The character of the Judge also is in some degree estimated by that of his officers[1], as that of a philosophical teacher by his disciples. Thus your bad actions might endanger our reputation, while, on the other hand, with no effort on our part, we earn glory from all that you do well. Beware, therefore, lest by any misconduct of yours, which is sure to be exaggerated by popular rumour, you rouse anger in us, who as your Judge will be sure to exact stern recompence for all the wrong you have done to our reputation. Study this rather, that you may receive praise and promotion at our hands, and go forth, with Divine help, on this Indiction, to such and such a Province, adorned with the pomp of the Cancelli, and girt about with a certain proud gravity. Remember the honour of the *fasces* which are borne before you, of the Praetorian seat whose commands you execute.

[1] 'Per milites suos judex intelligitur.'

'Fly Avarice, the Queen of all the vices, who never enters the human heart alone, but always brings a flattering and deceiving train along with her. Show yourself zealous for the public good; do more by reason than by terror. Let your person be a refuge for the oppressed, a defence of the weak, a stronghold for him who is stricken down by any calamity. Never do you more truly discharge the functions of the Cancelli than when you open the prison doors to those who have been unjustly confined.'

2. SENATOR, PRAETORIAN PRAEFECT, TO ALL THE JUDGES OF THE PROVINCES (A.D. 534-535).

General instructions to the Provincial Governors.

'God be thanked, the Provincials have attended to all my admonitions, and I have kept all my promises to them. You, as Judges, have admirably copied my own freedom from corruption, and I can only desire that you will go on as you have begun.

'Let the peasant pay cheerfully his share of the public taxes, and I on my part will guarantee him the administration of justice in the courts [1].

'It was evidently the intention of the legislators that you should be imitators of our dignity, since they have given you almost the same jurisdiction in the Provinces as ourselves.

'What avails the reputation of being a rich man? It confers no glory. But to be known as a just man wins the praise of all. Nothing mean or avaricious is becoming in a Judge. All his faults are made more conspicuous by his elevation. Better were it to be absolutely unknown, than to be marked out for the scorn of all men. Let us keep our own brows clear from shame; then can we rebuke the sins of others.

---

[1] 'Possessor mihi publicas pecunias libens inferat: ego illi in conventus justitiae tributa persolvam.'

A terrible leveller is iniquity: it makes the Judge himself feel like the culprit who is tried before him. All these considerations, according to my custom, I bring before you in this my yearly address, since it is impossible ever to have too much of a good thing[1].

'Now, to proceed to business. Do you and your official staff impress upon all the cultivators of the soil the absolute necessity of their paying their land-tax[2] for this thirteenth Indiction[3] at the appointed time. Let there be no pressing them to pay before the time, and no venal connivance at their postponement of payment after the time. What kindness is there in delay? The money must be paid, sooner or later.

'Prepare also a full and faithful statement of the expenditure for every four months[4], and address it to our bureaux[5], that there may be perfect clearness in the public accounts.

'In order to help you, we send A and B, members of our official staff, to examine your accounts. See that you come up to the standard of duty here prescribed for you.'

3. SENATOR, PRAETORIAN PRAEFECT, TO ALL THE SAJONES WHO HAVE BEEN ASSIGNED TO THE CANCELLARII.

General instructions to the Sajones.

'There must be fear of the magistrate in the heart of the citizen, else the laws would never be obeyed. But as in medicine various remedies are required by various constitutions, so in the administration of the laws sometimes force and sometimes gentleness has to be used.

---

[1] 'Haec nos annuo sermone convenit loqui: quia bonarum rerum nulla satietas est.'

[2] 'Trina Illatio.'

[3] Sept. 1, 534, to Sept. 1, 535.

[4] 'Expensarum fidelem notitiam quaternis mensibus comprehensam.' As the receipts of the *Trina Illatio* had to be gathered in every four months, the account of Provincial expenditure covered the same period.

[5] 'Ad scrinia nostra dirigere maturabis.'

Wisdom is required to decide which is the best mode of dealing with each particular case.

'Therefore we despatch your Devotion[1] to attend upon A B, Clarissimus Cancellarius. Be terrible to the lawless, but to them alone. Above all things see to the punctual collection of the taxes. Do not study popularity. Attend only to those cases which are entrusted to your care, and work them thoroughly. No greater disgrace can attach to an officer of Court than that a Judge's sentence should be left unexecuted[2]. Do not swagger through the streets exulting in the fact that nobody dares meet you. Brave men are ever gentle in time of peace, and there is no greater lover of justice than he who has seen many battles. When you return to your parents and friends let it not be brawls that you have to boast of, but good conduct. We also shall in that case welcome you back with pleasure, and not leave you long without another commission. And the King too, the lord of all[3], will entrust higher duties to him who returns from the lower with credit and the reward of a good conscience.'

4. SENATOR, PRAETORIAN PRAEFECT, TO THE CANONICARIUS[4] OF THE VENETIAE.

Praise of Acinaticium, a red wine of Verona.

'A well furnished royal table is a credit to the State. A private person may eat only the produce of his own district; but it is the glory of a King to collect at his table the delicacies of all lands. Let the Danube send us her carp, let the *anchorago* (?) come from the Rhine, let the labour of Sicily furnish the *exormiston*[5], let the sea of Bruttii send its sweet *acerniae* (?); in short, let

---

[1] 'Devotio tua' was the technical way of addressing the *fortis Sajo*.
[2] 'In executore illud est pessimum, si judicis relinquat arbitrium.'
[3] 'Rerum Dominus.'
[4] Revenue-officer.
[5] 'Perhaps a kind of lamprey' (White and Riddle's Latin-English Dictionary).

well-flavoured dishes be gathered from all coasts. It becomes a King so to regale himself that he may seem to foreign ambassadors to possess almost everything.

'And therefore, not to neglect home-produce also, as our fertile Italy is especially rich in wines, we must have these also provided for the King's table. Now the report of the Count of the Patrimony informs us that the stock of *Acinaticium*[1] has fallen very low in the royal cellars. We therefore order you to visit the cultivators of Verona, and offer them a sufficient price for this product of theirs, which they ought to offer without price to their Sovereign.

'It is in truth a noble wine and one that Italy may be proud of. Inglorious Greece may doctor her wines with foreign admixtures, or disguise them with perfumes. There is no need of any such process with this liquor. It is purple, as becomes the wine of kings. Sweet and strong[2], it grows more dense in tasting it, so that you might doubt whether it was a liquid food or an edible drink[3].

'I have a mind to describe the singular mode of manufacturing this wine. The grape cluster, gathered in autumn, is hung up under the roof of the house to dry till December. Thus exuding its insipid humours it becomes much sweeter. Then in December, when everything else is bound by the frost of winter, the chilly blood of these grapes is allowed to flow forth. It is not insultingly trodden down by the feet, nor is any foul admixture suffered to pollute it; its stream of gem-like clearness is drawn forth from it by a noble provocation. It seems to shed tears of joy, and delights the eye by its beauty as much as the palate by its flavour. Collect this wine as speedily as possible, pay a sufficient price for it, and

---

[1] Apparently a kind of raisin wine; from *acina*, a grape or berry.

[2] What are we to make of 'Stipsis nescio quâ firmitate roboratur?'

[3] 'Tactus ejus densitate pinguescit: ut dicas esse aut carneum liquorem aut edibilem potionem.' Questionable praise, according to the ideas of a modern wine-grower.

hand it over to the *Cartarii* who are charged with this business.

'And this point is not to be forgotten, that it is to be served up in goblets of a milky whiteness. Lilies and roses thus unite their charms, and a pleasure is ministered to the eye, far beyond the mere commonplace facts that the wine has a pleasant taste, and that it restores the strength of the drinker.

'We rely on you to provide both the wine and the drinking vessels[1] with all despatch.'

5. SENATOR, PRAETORIAN PRAEFECT, TO VALERIAN, VIR SUBLIMIS.

[Written probably in the autumn or winter of 535, when Belisarius was in Sicily threatening the Southern Provinces of Italy.]

Measures for relief of Lucania and Bruttii.

'The ruler's anxiety for the common good of all over whom he is placed, may allowably show itself in an especial manner towards the dwellers in his own home, and that pre-eminently at a time when they need his succour from peril.

'The numerous army which was destined for the defence of the Republic is said to have laid waste the cultivated parts of Lucania and Bruttii, and to have diminished the abundance of those regions by its love of rapine.

'Now since they must take and you must give, and since the cultivator must not be robbed nor the army starved, know that the prices of provisions are fixed by the order of the Lord of the State at a much lower figure than you have been wont to sell at[2].

---

[1] We might have expected to find wine-bottles rather than wine-glasses thus requisitioned; but I think the words of Cassiodorus, 'quod lacteo poculo relucescit,' oblige us to adopt the latter translation.

[2] 'Pretia quae antiquus ordo constituit ex jussione rerum Domini cognoscite temperata, ut multo arctius quam vendere solebatis in assem publicum praebita debeant imputari.'

'Be not therefore anxious. You have escaped the hands of the tax-collector. The present instrument takes away from you the liability to tribute. In order that your knowledge may be made more complete, we have thought it better that the amounts of the provisions for which you are held responsible should be expressed in the below-written letters [1], that no one may sell you a benefit which you know to be conferred by the public generosity.

'Repress, therefore, the unruly movements of the cultivators [2]. While the Gothic army is fighting, let the Roman peasant enjoy in quiet the peace for which he sighs. According to the King's command, admonish the several tenants on the farms, and the better sort of peasants, not to mingle in the barbarism of the strife, lest the danger to public tranquillity be greater than any service they can render in the wars [3]. Let them lay hands to the iron, but only to cultivate their fields; let them grasp the pointed steel, but only to goad their oxen.

'Let the Judges be active: let the tribunals echo with their denunciations of crime. Let the robber, the adulterer, the forger, the thief, find that the arm of the State is still strong to punish their crimes. True freedom rejoices when these men are made sad. Here, in this civil battle, is full scope for your energies: attend to this, and enjoy the thought that others are fighting the battle with the foreign foe for you.

---

[1] 'Sed quo facilius instrueretur vestra notitia, *imputationum summas infra scriptis brevibus credidimus exprimendas.*' Apparently the ordinary taxes for the two Provinces are remitted, but a certain quantity of provisions has to be furnished to the army, perhaps by each township; and besides this, the commissariat officers have a right of pre-emption at prices considerably below the market rate.

[2] 'Continete ergo possessorum intemperantes motus.'

[3] 'Ex Regiâ jussione singulos conductores massarum et possessores validos admonete, ut nullam contrahant in concertatione barbariem: ne non tantum festinent bellis prodesse quantum quiete confundere.' Evidently the rustics are dissuaded from taking up arms lest they should use them on the side of Belisarius.

'Exercise great care in calculating the rations of the soldiers, that no trickery may succeed in defrauding the soldier of his due.

'The officers of the army are by the rulers of the State placed under my authority, and you are therefore to admonish them if they go wrong, while redressing all their real grievances. They, in their turn, must uphold discipline, which is the most powerful weapon of an army. Rise to the dignity of the occasion, and show that you are able to govern a Province in a disturbed condition of public affairs, since anyone can govern it while all things are quiet.

'The royal household is specially ordered to pay the same obedience to this rescript as all the rest of the Province; and as for my own dependants, I say expressly that, though I wish them well, I ask for no favour for them which I would not grant to all the other inhabitants of the Province.'

6. SENATOR, PRAETORIAN PRAEFECT, TO ALL THE SUBORDINATE GOVERNORS OF THE PRAEFECTURE[1].

General instructions to subordinate Governors.

'The exhortations addressed to you by the inborn piety of our Lords ought to suffice; but nevertheless, that we may be doubly assured, we will address to you our threats against all who shall wield their power unrighteously. Cease from avarice, from arrogance, from venality. What will your money avail you when the day of inquisition comes? *We* shall not be tempted by it. Let it be clearly understood that we shall not sell pardons to unjust Judges, but shall hunt them to their ruin.

'But all you, good and honest rulers, continue to serve the State without fear. No rival will buy your offices over your heads; you are secure in your seats so long as

---

[1] 'Universis Praefecturae titulos administrantibus.'

you do well, until the time fixed by our Lords expires. Be earnest, therefore, that my good deeds may be imitated and receive their due meed of praise in your persons.'

7. SENATOR, PRAETORIAN PRAEFECT, TO THE TAX-COLLECTOR OF THE VENETIAN PROVINCE [1].

Remission of taxes on account of invasion by the Suevi.

'A good Sovereign will always exert himself to repair fortuitous disasters, and will allow those who have paid their taxes punctually in prosperity, considerable liberty in times of barbaric invasion. On this ground, and on account of the incursions of the Suevi, the King grants for this year, the fifteenth Indiction [2], a discharge of all claims by the Fiscus preferred against A and B. And in all similar cases where you shall be satisfied that the property has really been laid waste by those Barbarians, you are at liberty to remit the taxes for this Indiction. Afterwards you will use all the ordinary methods, in order that you may be able to pay over the stipulated sum to the Royal Treasurer. But meanwhile the poor cultivator has the best of all arguments against paying you, namely, that he has nothing left him wherewith to pay. Thus is his calamity his best voucher for payment [3]; and we do not wish that he who has been already alarmed by the arms of the robber should further tremble at the official robe of the civil servant [4].'

8. SENATOR, PRAETORIAN PRAEFECT, TO THE CONSULARIS OF THE PROVINCE OF LIGURIA.

Permission to pay taxes direct to Royal Treasury.

'It is a new and delightful kind of profit to be able to grant the request of a petitioner without feeling any loss oneself. The present suitor, complaining that he is

---

[1] 'Canonicario Venetiarum.'
[2] Sept. 1, 536, to Sept. 1, 537.
[3] 'Validas contra te apochas invenerunt.'
[4] 'Chlamydes non pavescant, qui arma timuerunt.'

vexed by the exactions of the tax-gatherer on account of certain farms mentioned in the subjoined letter, offers to bring the amount due from them himself to our Treasurers[1]. We are willing to grant this request, on condition that the Fiscus does not suffer thereby; and therefore desire your Respectability to warn all *Curiales, Compulsores,* and all other persons concerned, to remove for this Indiction every kind of legal process from the before-mentioned properties; the condition of this immunity being that he shall, before the kalends of such and such a month produce the receipts[2] of the *Arcarius*, showing that he has discharged his debt to the State. Otherwise the debt must be exacted by ordinary process. But it is delightful to us whenever the tax is paid without calling in the aid of the *Compulsor*. Would that the peasant would always thus freely anticipate the needs of the Treasury!'

9. SENATOR, PRAETORIAN PRAEFECT, TO PASCHASIUS, PRAEFECT OF THE CORN-DISTRIBUTIONS[3].

African claims to succeed to estate of an intestate countryman.

[To make this letter intelligible we must presuppose a custom, certainly a very extraordinary one, by which on the death of an African without heirs, any other African in Italy was allowed to claim the inheritance. By 'African,' no doubt, we must understand one of the indigenous inhabitants of Africa, perhaps a man of Negro race. The custom certainly cannot have applied to African Provincials of Roman descent. It was perhaps based on some old tribal notions of joint possession and mutual inheritance.]

'It is a work of wondrous kindness to oblige a foreign race with public benefits, and not only to invite blood relations to enjoy the advantages of property, but to permit even strangers to share them. This kind of heirship is independent of the ties of kindred, independent

---

[1] 'Arcarii.' [2] 'Apochae.' [3] 'Praefectus Annonae.'

of succession from parents, and requires nothing else save only power to utter the speech of the fatherland.

'This is the privilege which, as the African asserts, was of old bestowed on his race. By virtue thereof they lawfully demand the inheritance of others, and thus obtain a right which the Roman in a similar case could never claim. Nor have they this benefit in their own land; but here they are for this purpose looked upon as all related to one another.

'The whole nation, in what relates to the advantages of succession, is regarded as one family.

'Your Experience is therefore to submit the subject of this man's petition to a diligent examination, and if it shall turn out, as he alleges, that the deceased has left no sons nor other persons who might reasonably claim to succeed him, your official staff is to induct him into the aforesaid property according to the established usage.

'He will thus cease to be a foreigner, and will acquire the status of a native possessor, and therewith the usual liability to pay tribute. He is inferior to other owners only in this one point, that he lacks the power of alienating his property. Let him who has derived so much benefit from our commiseration now relieve others. Fortunate and enviable has turned out his captivity[1], which enables him at one and the same time to enjoy the citizenship of Rome and the privileges of the African.'

10. SENATOR, PRAETORIAN PRAEFECT, TO DIVERS CANCELLARII IN THE PROVINCES.

Taxes to be punctually enforced.

'Arrears of tribute are like bodily diseases, serious and enfeebling when they become chronic. A man

---

[1] 'Felix illi contigit et praedicanda captivitas.' A little before, we read, 'Resumat facultatem quam se suspiraverat amisisse.' These sentences suggest the idea that the petitioner had been brought over in the train of the lately deceased person as a slave. This a little lessens the difficulty of his being admitted to the inheritance. Compare Gen. xv. 3, where Abraham, before the birth of a son, says, 'And one born in my house' (i.e. a slave) 'is mine heir.'

who is under a load of debt cannot be called free: he has abandoned the power of controlling his actions to another. Your supposed indulgence to the taxpayer is no real kindness. There comes a time when the whole arrear of debt has to be claimed, and then these venal delays of yours make the demand seem twice as heavy in the eyes of the unfortunate taxpayer. Cease then to trade upon the peasants' losses. Exact the whole amount of taxes for the coming Indiction, and pay them in on the appointed day to the Treasurer[1] of the Province; or else it will be the worse for you, and you will have to return, stripped of all official rank[2], into the Province which you are conscious of having badly administered.

'I shall not *speak* again on this subject, but shall, if necessary, extract the sums from you by an irrevocable act of distraint.'

11. SENATOR, PRAETORIAN PRAEFECT, TO PETER, VIR CLARISSIMUS, DISTRIBUTOR OF RELISHES[3].

Distribution of relishes to Roman citizens.

'The liberality of a good Sovereign must not be discredited by fraud and carelessness in the person charged with its distribution. Even molten gold contracts a stain if not poured into an absolutely clean vessel. How sweet is it to see a stream flowing clear and unpolluted over a snow-white channel! Even so must you see that the gifts of the Sovereign of the State reach the Roman people as pure and as copious as they issue forth from him.

'All fraud is hateful; but fraud exercised upon the people of Romulus is absolutely unbearable. That quiet and easily satisfied people, whose existence you might forget except when they testify their happiness by their shouts; noisy without a thought of sedition; whose

---

[1] 'Arcarius.'   [2] 'Degeniatus.'
[3] 'Erogatori obsoniorum.'

only care is to shun poverty without amassing wealth; lowly in fortune but rich in temper—it is a kind of profanation to rob such people as these.

'We therefore entrust to you the task of distributing the relishes[1] to the Roman people from this Indiction. Be true to the citizens, else you will become as an alien unto us. Do not be bribed into allowing anyone to pass as a Latin who was not born in Latium.

'These privileges belong to the Quirites alone: no slave must be admitted to share them. That man sins against the majesty of the Roman people, who defiles the pure river of their blood by thrusting upon them the fellowship of slaves.'

12. Senator, Praetorian Praefect, to Anastasius, Cancellarius of Lucania and Bruttii.

Praise of the cheese and wine of Bruttii.

'When we were dining, according to our wonted custom, with the Sovereign of the State[2], the conversation happened to turn upon the delicacies of various Provinces, and we praised the wines of Bruttii and the cheese of the district around Mount Sila[3].

'The *cheese*, which retains in its pores the milk which has been collected there, recalls by its taste the fragrant herbs upon which the cattle have fed; by its texture it reminds us of the softness of oil, from which it differs in colour by its snowy whiteness. Having been carefully pressed into a wide cask and hardened therein,

---

[1] 'Obsonia.'

[2] 'Cum apud rerum Dominum solemni more pranderemus.'

[3] 'Silanum.' Mount Sila is a range of hills in Calabria immediately to the north of Squillace, forty miles from north to south, and twenty miles from east to west, and occupying the whole of the projecting portion of the south-east side of Italy between the Gulf of Squillace and the Bay of Taranto. The highest peaks, which are about 5,700 feet high, are covered with snow during half the year. It is said that from the beginning of June till far on into October, 15,000 head of cattle and 150,000 sheep, besides horses and mules, graze in these uplands. (See Gsel-Fells: Unter Italien, p. 721.)

it retains permanently the beautiful round shape which has thus been given to it[1].

'The *wine*, to which Antiquity gave the name of praise, Palmatiana, must be selected not of a rough but sweet kind[2]. Though last [in geographical position] among the wines of Bruttii, it is by general opinion accounted the best, equal to that of Gaza, similar to the Sabine, moderately thick, strong, brisk, of conspicuous whiteness, distinguished by the fine aroma, of which a pleasant after-taste is perceived by the drinker[3]. It constrains loosened bowels. dries up moist wounds, and refreshes the weary breast.

'Let it be your care to provide as speedily as possible a stock of both these products of our country, and send them in ships to the Royal residence. For a temporary supply we have drawn on our own cellars, but we look to you to choose specimens of the genuine quality for the King. We cannot be deceived, who retain the true taste in our patriotic memory; and at your peril will you provide any inferior article to that which our cellars will have supplied[4].'

Frauds committed by the revenue officers on the Churches of Bruttii and Lucania.

13. AN EDICT.

'The generous gifts of Kings ought to be respected by their subjects.

'Long ago the constitutions of the Emperors enriched

---

[1] From the description of Cassiodorus, it seems to have been a kind of cream cheese.

[2] 'Non stipsi asperum sed gratum suavitate perquire.' The same peculiar word, *stipsis*, which we had in Letter xii. 4. What meaning are we to assign to the word?

[3] 'Magnis odoribus singulare:—quod ita redolet ore ructatum ut merito illi a palma nomen videatur impositum.'

[4] 'Baronius (Ad Ann. 591) quotes this letter of Cassiodorus to explain an allusion in the life of Pope Gregory the Great, who refused to receive a present of 'Palmatianum' from the Bishop of Messina, and insisted on paying for it.

the holy Churches of Bruttii and Lucania with certain gifts. But since the sacrilegious mind is not afraid of sinning against the Divine reverence, the Canonicarii (officers of the Exchequer) have robbed these ecclesiastical positions of a certain portion of their revenue in the name of the Numerarii of the Praetorian Praefect's staff; but these latter, with righteous indignation, declare that they have received no part of the spoils thus impiously collected in their name.

'Thus have the Canonicarii turned the property of the clergy into a *douceur* for the laity[1]. Oh, audacity of man! what barriers can be erected against thee? Thou mightest have hoped to escape human observation, but why commit crimes which the Divinity cannot but notice?

'Therefore we ordain by this edict that anyone who shall hereafter commit this kind of fraud shall lose his own private gains, and shall forfeit his place in the public service[2].

'Let the poor keep the gifts which God has put it into the heart of Kings to bestow upon them. It is cruel above all other cruelty to wish to become rich by means of the scanty possessions of the mendicant.'

14. SENATOR, PRAETORIAN PRAEFECT, TO ANASTASIUS, CANCELLARIUS OF LUCANIA AND BRUTTII.

Plea for gentle treatment for citizens of Rhegium.

'The citizens of Rhegium (so called from the Greek word ῥηγνύμι, to break, because their island has been broken off from Sicily by the violence of the waves) complain that they are being unfairly harassed by the tax-gatherers. I, as an eyewitness, can confirm the truth

---

[1] 'Facientes laicum commodum substantiam clericorum.'
[2] 'Edictali programmate definimus, ut qui in hac fuerit ulterius fraude versatus et militiâ careat et compendium propriae facultatis amittat.' The last clause is perhaps purposely vague. We should have expected to hear something about restitution, but the words will not bear that meaning.

of their statement that their territory does not bring forth the produce which is claimed at their hands. It is a rocky and mountainous country, too dry for pasture, though sufficiently undulating for vineyards; bad for grain-crops, though well suited for olives. The shade has to be all provided by the industry of man, who has planted there the tree of Pallas [the olive], which prospers in even the driest soil, because it sends its roots down into the very depths of the earth.

'The corn has to be watered by hand, like pot-herbs in a garden. You seldom see the husbandman bending beneath his load as he returns from the threshing-floor. A few bushels full are all that he can boast of, even in an abundant harvest [1].

'Contrary to the opinion of Virgil [who speaks of the bitter roots of the endive [2]], the fibres of endive are here extremely sweet, and encircled by their twisting leaves are caked together with a certain callous tenderness [3].

'In the treasures of the deep that region is certainly rich; for the Upper and Lower Sea meet there. The *exormiston* [4], a sort of king among fishes, with bristly nostrils and a milky delicacy of flavour, is found in these waters. In stormy weather it is tossed about on the top of the waves, and seems to be too tired or too indolent to

---

[1] I do not understand the following sentences: 'In hortis autem rusticorum agmen habetur operosum: quia olus illic omne saporum est marinâ irroratione respersum. Quod humanâ industriâ fieri consuevit, hoc cum nutriretur accepit.' Can they have watered any herbs with salt water?

[2]   'Nec tamen, haec quum sint hominumque boumque labores
      Versando terram experti, nihil improbus anser,
      Strymoniaeque grues, et *amaris intuba fibris*
      Officiunt.'—Georgic i. 118-121.

[3] I must renounce the attempt to translate the rest of the sentence: 'Unde in morem nitri aliquid decerptum frangitur, dum a fecundo cespite segregatur.' There is an alternative reading, *vitri* for *nitri*; but I am still unable to understand the author's meaning.

[4] Apparently a kind of lamprey. See the fourth letter of this book.

Book XII. Letters 14–15. 503

seek a refuge in the deeper water[1]. No other fish can be compared to it in sweetness[2].

'These are the products—I speak from my own knowledge—of the Rhegian shore. Therefore you must not seek to levy a tribute of wheat or lard from the inhabitants under the name of "coemptio."

'I may add that they are so troubled by the constant passage of travellers entering Italy or leaving it, that it would have been right to excuse them even if those products had been found there in abundance[3].'

15. SENATOR, PRAETORIAN PRAEFECT, TO MAXIMUS, VIR CLARISSIMUS, CANCELLARIUS OF LUCANIA AND BRUTTII[4].

'Scyllacium, the first city of Bruttii, which Ulysses the destroyer of Troy is believed to have founded, is said to be unreasonably vexed by the exorbitant demands of purveyors[5]. These injuries grieve us all the more on account of our patriotic love for the place.

Praises of the author's birthplace, Scyllacium.

'The city of Scyllacium, which is so placed as to look down upon the Hadriatic Gulf, hangs upon the hills like a cluster of grapes: not that it may pride itself upon their difficult ascent, but that it may voluptuously gaze on verdant plains and the blue back of the sea. The city beholds the rising sun from its very cradle, when the day that is about to be born sends forward

---

[1] Perhaps Cassiodorus means to say this makes it more easy of capture, but he does not say so.

[2] The praises of the exormiston are not only foreign to the main subject of the letter, but to a certain extent weaken the writer's argument on behalf of his countrymen; but, as a good Bruttian, he cannot help vaunting the products of his country.

[3] The passage to and fro of travellers no doubt brought with it burdensome duties for the inhabitants in connection with the *Cursus Publicus*. It was therefore a reason for mitigating other taxes.

[4] This letter, being the description by Cassiodorus of his native place, is translated entire.

[5] 'Irrationabiliter dicitur praesumentium nimietate vexari.'

no heralding Aurora; but as soon as it begins to rise, the quivering brightness displays its torch. It beholds Phoebus in his joy; it is bathed in the brightness of that luminary, so that it might be thought to be itself the native land of the sun, the claims of Rhodes to that honour being outdone.

'It enjoys a translucent air, but withal so temperate that its winters are sunny, and its summers cool; and life passes there without sorrow, since hostile seasons are feared by none. Hence, too, man himself is here freer of soul than elsewhere, for this temperateness of the climate prevails in all things.

'In sooth, a hot fatherland makes its children sharp and fickle, a cold one slow and sly; it is only a temperate climate which composes the characters of men by its own moderation. Hence was it that the ancients pronounced Athens to be the seat of sages, because, enriched with an air of the greatest purity, it prepared with glad liberality the lucid intellects of its sons for the contemplative part of life. Assuredly for the body to imbibe muddy waters is a different thing from sucking in the transparency of a sweet fountain. Even so the vigour of the mind is repressed when it is clogged by a heavy atmosphere. Nature herself hath made us subject to these influences. Clouds make us feel sad; and again a bright sky fills us with joy, because the heavenly substance of the soul delights in everything that is unstained and pure.

'Scyllacium has also an abundant share of the delicacies of the sea, possessing near it those gates of Neptune which we ourselves constructed. At the foot of the Moscian Mount we hollowed out the bowels of the rock, and tastefully[1] introduced therein the eddying waves of Nereus. Here a troop of fishes, sporting in free captivity, refreshes all minds with delight, and charms all eyes with admiration. They run greedily to

[1] 'Decenter.'

the hand of man, and before they become his food seek dainties from him. Man feeds his own dainty morsels, and while he has that which can bring them into his power, it often happens that being already replete he lets them all go again.

'The spectacle moreover of men engaged in honourable labour is not denied to those who are sitting tranquilly in the city. Plenteous vineyards are beheld in abundance. The fruitful toil of the threshing-floor is seen. The face of the green olive is disclosed. No one need sigh for the pleasures of the country, when it is given him to see them all from the town.

'And inasmuch as it has now no walls, you believe Scyllacium to be a rural city, though you might judge it to be an urban villa; and thus placed between the two worlds of town and country, it is lavishly praised by both.

'This place wayfarers desire frequently to visit, and as they object to the toil of walking, the citizens, called upon to provide them with post-horses, and rations for their servants, have to pay heavily in purse for the pleasantness of their city. Therefore to prevent this, for the future we decide that all charges for providing post-horses and rations shall be debited to the public account. We cut up, root and branch, the system of paying *Pulveratica*[1] to the Judge; and we decide, according to ancient custom, that rations for three days only shall be given on their arrival to the great Dignitaries of the State, and that any more prolonged delay in their locomotion be provided for by themselves.

'To relieve your city of its heaviest burdens will be, according to our injunctions, an act of judicial impartiality, not of laxity. Live, by God's help, a mirror of the justice of the age, delighting in the security of all. Some people call the Isles of the Atlantic 'Fortunate:' I

[1] Dust-money.

16. SENATOR, PRAETORIAN PRAEFECT, TO A REVENUE OFFICER[1].

[This interesting letter is one of the few written by Cassiodorus as Praetorian Praefect which we can date with certainty. It is written apparently at the beginning of the first Indiction, i.e. Sept. 1, 537. Witigis and the Goths have been for nearly six months besieging Rome, and are beginning to be discouraged as to its capture. Cassiodorus is probably at Ravenna, directing the machine of government from that capital.]

Payment of Trina Illatio.

'Time, which adapts itself incessantly to the course of human affairs, and reconciles us even to adversity[2], has brought round again the period for collecting the *Trina Illatio* from the taxpayer. Let the peasant (*possessor*) pay in your Diocese, for this first Indiction, his instalment of the tax freely, not being urged too soon nor allowed to postpone it too late, so that he may plead that he has been let off from payment[3]. Let none exceed the fair weight, but let him use a just pound: if once the true weight is allowed to be exceeded, there is no limit to extortion[4].

'Let a faithful account of the expenses of collection be rendered every four months to our office[5], that, all error and obscurity being removed, truth may be manifest in the public accounts.

'That you may, with God's help, be the better able to fulfil our instructions, I have ordered A and B, ser-

---

[1] 'Canonicario.'

[2] 'Dum res nobis etiam asperas captatâ semper opinione conciliat.' Apparently a veiled allusion to the disasters of the Goths.

[3] 'Nec iterum remissione lentatâ quisquam se dicat esse praeteritum.'

[4] This mention of the just weight of course suits a tax paid in kind, not in money.

[5] 'Expensarum quoque fidelem notitiam per quaternos menses ad scrinia nostra solemniter destinabis.'

vants of our tribunal, who are mindful of their own past responsibilities, to assist you and your staff[1]. Beware therefore, lest you incur the blame of corruptly discharging the taxpayer, or of sluggish idleness in the discharge of your duties, in which case your own fortunes will suffer from your neglect.'

17. SENATOR, PRAETORIAN PRAEFECT, TO JOHN, SILIQUATARIUS[2] OF RAVENNA.

Defence of Ravenna.

'In times of peace, by contact with foreigners who swarm in our cities, we learn what will be our best defence in war. Who can tell with what nation we may be next at war? Therefore, to be on the safe side, make such preparations as our future enemies, whosoever they may be, will dislike to hear of. Accordingly you are to order the peasants to dig a series of pits with wide mouths near the mountains of Caprarius and the parts round about the walls[3]; and let such a chasm yawn there that there shall be no possibility of entrance that way.

'If strangers want to enter the city, why do they not enter it in the right way—by the gates—instead of going skulking about these bye-paths? Henceforth, anyone trying to take any such short cut to our city will probably find that he loses his life in consequence[4].'

18. SENATOR, PRAETORIAN PRAEFECT, TO CONSTANTIAN, VIR EXPERIENTISSIMUS.

Repair of Flaminian Way.

'Great is the reward of those who serve Kings

---

[1] 'Illum atque illum sedis nostrae milites, tibi officioque tuo periculorum suorum memores praecipimus imminere.'

[2] Collector of the Siliquaticum, or tax of one twenty-fourth on sales. See ii. 30, iii. 25, iv. 19.

[3] No doubt the walls of Ravenna. I cannot identify the Mons Caprarius. The name Caprera is a common one in Italy.

[4] One may conjecture that this letter was written in 535, when war with the Empire was imminent, but before it was actually declared.

efficiently; as severe is the punishment of those who neglect their duties towards them.

'How delightful is it to journey without obstacles over a well-made road[1], to pass doubtful places without fear, to ascend mountainous steeps by a gentle incline, to have no fear of the planking of a bridge when one crosses it[2], and in short to accomplish one's journey so that everything happens to one's liking!

'This is the pleasure which you can now prepare for your Sovereign. Therefore, as the Flaminian Way is furrowed by the action of torrents, join the yawning chasms by the broadest of bridges; clear away the rough woods which choke the sides of the highway; procure the stipulated number of post-horses, and see that they have all the points which are required in a good steed; collect the designated quantities of provisions without plundering the peasants. A failure in any one of these particulars will ruin your whole service.

Supply of delicacies for the King's table.
'Collect, too, with the utmost diligence the spices which are needed for the King's table. What avails it to have satisfied the army, if the King's own board lack proper care. Let all the Provincials attend to your admonitions: let the cities furnish the stores set forth in the accompanying letters. Then, when they have put the Sovereign in a good humour, they may ask him for benefits to some purpose.

'Think of me as present and as judging of all your deeds. I shall have to bear the blame of your failures at Court; so act rather as to set my mind at rest, to cover me and yourselves with glory, and to entitle me to receive on your behalf the thanks of the whole army.'

[This letter was probably written in the autumn of 535, when Theodahad was preparing to march to Rome.

---

[1] 'Videre judicia diligentia.' I leave this clause untranslated, as I cannot understand it.

[2] 'In pontibus contrabium non tremere.'

The mention of the delicacies for the royal table suggests that that King, in addition to the other excellencies of his character, was probably an epicure.]

19. SENATOR, PRAETORIAN PRAEFECT, TO MAXIMUS, VICARIUS OF THE CITY OF ROME.

Bridge of boats across the Tiber.

'As all great events in Nature have their heralding signs, so is the approaching visit of the King announced to you even by the concourse of wayfarers to your City. We, however, have to order you to clothe the waves of Tiber with a bridge [of boats]. The boat, thus used, is no longer moved by slowly hauled ropes, as it is wont to be. Fixed itself, it affords a means of transit to others. The joining of its planks gives the desired appearance of solidity; all the terror of the waves is removed by its likeness to the land, and the traveller passing over it unharmed only wishes that the bridge were longer.

'Let a safe bulwark of lattice-work shield the bridge on the right side and on the left. See that you give no cause for misadventure of any kind. You have a noble opportunity of distinguishing yourself in the presence of so many Senators and of the King himself, the rewarder of every well-done work. On the other hand, if you do it badly and put him out of humour, woe be unto you!

'We send A B, a servant of our Praefecture[1], to assist you and your staff and bring us report of the accomplishment of the work; for so heavy is our responsibility in this matter that we dare not leave anything to chance.'

[The King whose advent to Rome is here announced may be Witigis, after his election in the plains of Regeta (August, 536). But the fact that he is apparently approaching Rome by the northern bank of the Tiber,

---

[1] 'Illum sedis nostrae militem.'

coupled with the directions in the preceding letter for the repair of the Flaminian Way, makes it more probable that some visit of Theodahad (probably in the year 535), when he would come from Ravenna to Rome, is here in prospect.]

20. SENATOR, PRAETORIAN PRAEFECT, TO THOMAS AND PETER, VIRI CLARISSIMI AND ARCARII.

Sacred vessels mortgaged by Pope Agapetus to be restored to the stewards of the Papal See.

'You will remember, most faithful Sirs, that when the holy Agapetus, Pope of the City of Rome, was sent as ambassador to the Sovereign of the East[1], he received so many pounds of gold from you for the expenses of the journey, for which he gave his bond[2] and deposited some of the Church plate as security[3]. The provident ruler thus lent him money in his necessity, and now, far more gloriously, returns as a free gift those pledges which the Pope might well have thanked him for taking.

'Therefore, in obedience to these instructions of ours, and fortified by the Royal order, do you return without any delay to the stewards[4] of the holy Apostle Peter the vessels of the saints together with the written obligation, that these things may be felt to be profitably restored and speedily granted, that the longed-for means of performing their world-famous ministrations may be replaced in the hands of the Levites. Let that be given back which was their own, since that is justly received back by way of largesse which the Priest had legally mortgaged.

'Herein is the great example of King Alaric surpassed. He, when glutted with the spoil of Rome, having received the vessels of the Apostle Peter from his men, when he

---

[1] He was sent by Theodahad; entered Constantinople February 20, 536, and died there 21st April of the same year.

[2] 'Facto pictacio.'

[3] 'Vasa sanctorum.' One would think this must refer to the vessels used in celebrating mass; but I do not quite see how the meaning is to be got out of the words.

[4] 'Actoribus.'

heard the story of their seizure, ordered them to be carried back across the sacred threshold, that so the remembrance of the cupidity of their capture might be effaced by the generosity of their restoration.

'But our King, with religious purpose, has restored the vessels which had become his own by the law of mortgage. In recompense for such deeds frequent prayer ought to ascend, and Heaven will surely gladly grant the required return for such good actions [1].'

[There are in this letter several extremely obscure sentences as to the generosity of Theodahad. As the Papal journey was undertaken by Theodahad's orders, it was a piece of meanness, quite in keeping with that King's character, to treat the advance of money for the journey as a loan, and to insist on a bond and the deposit of the Church plate as a security for repayment. Cassiodorus evidently feels this; and very probably the restoration of the vessels and the quittance of the debt had been insisted on by him. But the more he despises his master's shabbiness, the more he struggles through a maze of almost nonsensical sentences, to prove that he has committed some very glorious action in lending the money and then forgiving the debt.]

21. SENATOR, PRAETORIAN PRAEFECT, TO DEUSDEDIT, A SCRIBE OF RAVENNA.

'The Scribe's office is the great safeguard of the rights of all men. The evidence of ownership may be destroyed by fire or purloined by dishonest men, but the State by making use of the Scribe's labours is able to make good the loss so sustained. The Scribe is more diligent in other men's business than they are in their own. His

Duties of a Scribe.

---

[1] Baronius not unfairly argues that if the Roman See was so poor that the Church plate had to be pawned to provide for the Pope's journey to Constantinople, the *wealth* of the Pope cannot have largely contributed to that great increase of his influence which marked the early years of the Sixth Century.

muniment-chest is the refuge of all the oppressed, and the repository of the fortunes of all men[1].

'In testimony of your past integrity, and in the hope that no change will mar this fair picture, we appoint you to this honourable office. Remember that ancient Truth is committed to your keeping, and that it often really rests with you, rather than with the Judge, to decide the disputes of litigants. When your indisputable testimony is given, and when the ancient voice of charters proceeds from your *sanctum*, Advocates receive it with reverence, and suitors, even evil-intentioned men, are constrained into obedience.

'Banish, therefore, all thoughts of venality from your mind. The worst moth that gets into papers and destroys them is the gold of the dishonest litigant, who bribes the Scribes to make away with evidence which he knows to be hostile. Thus, then, be ready always to produce to suitors genuine old documents; and, on the other hand, transcribe only, do not compose ancient proceedings[2]. Let the copy correspond to the original as the wax to the signet-ring, that as the face is the index of the emotions[3] so your handwriting may not err from the authentic original in anything.

'If a claimant succeed in enticing you even once from the paths of honesty, vainly will you in any subsequent case seek to obtain his credence for any document that you may produce; for he will always believe that the trick which has been played once may be played again. Keep to the line of justice, and even his angry exclamations at the impossibility of inducing you to deviate therefrom, will be your highest testimonial. Your whole career is public, and the favour or disgrace which awaits you must be public also.'

[1] 'Armarium ipsius fortuna cunctorum est.'

[2] 'Translator esto, non conditor antiquorum gestorum.'

[3] Compare Cassiodorus' treatise De Anima, chapters x. and xi., in which he enumerates the various points in which the faces of good men and bad men differ from one another.

22. SENATOR, PRAETORIAN PRAEFECT, TO THE PROVINCIALS OF ISTRIA.

[This letter was written Sept. 1, 537, probably in consequence of the scarcity which the operations of Belisarius were already causing at Ravenna. Apparently the whole taxes levied from a Province at an Indiction were divided into two heads: so much for the central authority, and so much for the Province. Cassiodorus in this and the following letter says in effect: 'All the State's share of the taxes we will take not in money, but in your staple products, corn, wine, and oil. The rest goes as usual to the Province; but owing to the scarcity at Ravenna we shall be glad to buy all that can be spared either by the authorities of the Province or by individuals, whether farmers or merchants.']

'The true way to prevent the requirements of the public revenue from becoming oppressive, is to order each Province to supply those products in which it is naturally most fertile.

'Now I have learned by conversation with travellers that the Province of Istria is this year especially blessed in three of its crops—wine, oil, and corn. Therefore let her give of these products the equivalent of . . . solidi, which are due from you in payment of tribute for this first Indiction[1]: while the remainder we leave to that loyal Province for her own regular expenses. But since we require a larger quantity of the above-mentioned products, we send . . . solidi from our state chest for the purchase of them, that these necessaries may be collected for us with as little delay as possible. Often when you are desirous to sell you cannot find a purchaser, and suffer loss accordingly. How much better is it to obey the requirements of

Requisition from Province of Istria.

---
[1] The first Indiction was from September 1, 537, to September 1, 538.

your Lords than to supply foreigners; and to pay your debts in the fruits of the soil, rather than to wait on the caprices of a buyer!

'We will ourselves out of our love of justice state a fact of which you might otherwise remind us, that we can afford to be liberal in price because we are not burdened by the payment of freights [on account of your nearness to the seat of government]. For what Campania is to Rome, Istria is to Ravenna—a fruitful Province abounding in corn, wine, and oil; so to speak, the cupboard of the capital. I might carry the comparison further, and say that Istria can show her own Baiae in the lagunes with which her shores are indented[1], her own Averni in the pools abounding in oysters and fish. The palaces, strung like pearls along the shores of Istria, show how highly our ancestors appreciated its delights[2]. The beautiful chain of islands with which it is begirt, shelter the sailor from danger and enrich the cultivator. The residence of the Court in this district delights the nobles and enriches the lower orders; and it may be said that all its products find their way to the Royal city. Now let the loyal Province, which has often tendered her services when they were less required, send forward her stores freely.

'To guard against any misunderstanding of our orders, we send Laurentius, a man of great experience, whose instructions are contained in the annexed letter.

'We will publish a tariff of moderate prices when we next address you, and when we have ascertained what is the yield of the present crops; for we should be deciding quite at random before we have received that information.'

[1] Here follows this sentence: 'Haec loca garismatia plura nutriunt.' Garum seems to have been a sauce something like our anchovy-sauce. Garismatium is evidently a garum-supplying place.

[2] We have a special allusion in Martial (iv. 25) to the villas of Altinum, and he too compares them to those of Baiae.

23. SENATOR, PRAETORIAN PRAEFECT, TO LAURENTIUS, VIR EXPERIENTISSIMUS[1].

The same subject.

'Anyone can discharge the duties of the Commissariat in a time of abundance. It is a mark of our high appreciation of your experience and efficiency, that we select you for this service in a time of scarcity. We therefore direct you to repair to the Province of Istria, there to collect stores of wine, oil, and corn, equivalent to ... solidi, due from the Province for land-tax[2], and with ... solidi which you have received from our Treasurer to buy these products either from the merchants or from the peasants directly, according to the information prepared for you by the Cashiers[3]. Raise your spirits for this duty, and discharge it in a manner worthy of your past reputation. Make to us a faithful report of the yield of the coming harvest, under these three heads[4], that we may fix a tariff of prices which shall be neither burdensome to the Provincials nor injurious to the public service.'

24. SENATOR, PRAETORIAN PRAEFECT, TO THE TRIBUNES OF THE MARITIME POPULATION[5].

First historical notice of Venice.

'We have previously given orders that Istria should send wine and oil, of which there are abundant crops

---

[1] Evidently 'the annexed letter' referred to in No. 22.

[2] 'Ut in tot solidos vini, olei, vel tritici species de tributario solido debeas procurare.'

[3] 'Sicut te a Numerariis instruxit porrecta Notitia.' Note this use of the word 'Notitia,' as illustrating the title of the celebrated document bearing that name.

[4] Corn, wine, and oil.

[5] Written shortly after Sept. 1, 537. This is the celebrated letter to which Venetian historians point as evidence of the existence of their city (or at least of the group of settlements out of which their city sprang) in the Sixth Century. We may set side by side with it the words of the Anonymous Geographer of Ravenna (in the Seventh Century), 'In patria vero Venetiae sunt aliquantae insulae, quae hominibus habitantur.'

The address, *Tribunis Maritimorum*, looks as if there were something like a municipal government established in these islands. Tribunus was this year, to the Royal residence at Ravenna. Do you, who possess numerous ships on the borders of the Province, show the same devotion in forwarding the stores which they do in supplying them.

'Be therefore active in fulfilling this commission in your own neighbourhood, you who often cross boundless distances. It may be said that [in visiting Ravenna] you are going through your own guest-chambers, you who in your voyages traverse your own home[1]. This is also added to your other advantages, that to you another route is open, marked by perpetual safety and tranquillity. For when by raging winds the sea is closed, a way is opened to you through the most charming river scenery[2]. Your keels fear no rough blasts; they touch the earth with the greatest pleasure, and cannot perish however frequently they may come in contact with it. Beholders from a distance, not seeing the channel of the stream, might fancy them moving through the meadows. Cables have been used to keep them at rest: now drawn by ropes they move, and by a changed order of things men help their ships with their feet. They draw their drawers without labour, and instead of the capricious favour of sails they use the more satisfactory steps of the sailor.

'It is a pleasure to recall the situation of your dwellings as I myself have seen them. Venetia the praiseworthy[3], formerly full of the dwellings of the nobility,

at this time generally, but not exclusively, a military title. Compare the Tribunus Fori Suarii and Tribunus Rerum Nitentium of the Notitia (Occidens iv. 10 and iv. 17). But there can be no doubt, from the tone of this letter, that the islanders were subjects of the Ostrogothic King.

[1] An obscure sentence: 'Per hospitia quodammodo vestra discurritis qui per patriam navigatis.' The idea seems to be: 'You have to sail about from one room to another of your own house, and therefore Ravenna will seem like a neighbouring inn.'

[2] The next four sentences describe the movement of the ships when towed along the channels of the streams (Brenta, Piave, Tagliamento, &c.) the deposits from which have made the lagunes.

[3] 'Venetiae praedicabiles.' An allusion, no doubt, as other commentators have suggested, to the reputed derivation of Venetia from Αἰνετοί, 'the laudable.'

touches on the south Ravenna and the Po, while on the east it enjoys the delightsomeness of the Ionian shore, where the alternating tide now discovers and now conceals the face of the fields by the ebb and flow of its inundation. Here after the manner of water-fowl have you fixed your home. He who was just now on the mainland finds himself on an island, so that you might fancy yourself in the Cyclades[1], from the sudden alterations in the appearance of the shore.

'Like them[2] there are seen amid the wide expanse of the waters your scattered homes, not the product of Nature, but cemented by the care of man into a firm foundation[3]. For by a twisted and knotted osier-work the earth there collected is turned into a solid mass, and you oppose without fear to the waves of the sea so fragile a bulwark, since forsooth the mass of waters is unable to sweep away the shallow shore, the deficiency in depth depriving the waves of the necessary power.

'The inhabitants have one notion of plenty, that of gorging themselves with fish. Poverty therefore may associate itself with wealth on equal terms. One kind of food refreshes all; the same sort of dwelling shelters all; no one can envy his neighbour's home; and living in this moderate style they escape that vice [of envy] to which all the rest of the world is liable.

'Your whole attention is concentrated on your salt-works. Instead of driving the plough or wielding the sickle, you roll your cylinders. Thence arises your whole crop, when you find in them that product which you have not manufactured[4]. There it may be said is your

---

[1] Alluding probably to the story of the floating island of Delos.

[2] 'Earum similitudine.' Does Cassiodorus mean 'like the water-fowl,' or 'like the Cyclades?'

[3] The reading of Nivellius (followed by Migne), 'Domicilia videntur sparsa, quae Natura non protulit sed hominum cura fundavit,' seems to give a better sense than that of Garet, who omits the 'non.'

[4] 'Inde vobis fructus omnis enascitur, quando in ipsis, et quae non facitis possidetis.'

subsistence-money coined[1]. Of this art of yours every wave is a bondservant. In the quest for gold a man may be lukewarm: but salt every one desires to find; and deservedly so, since to it every kind of meat owes its savour.

'Therefore let your ships, which you have tethered, like so many beasts of burden, to your walls, be repaired with diligent care: so that when the most experienced Laurentius attempts to bring you his instructions, you may hasten forth to greet him. Do not by any hindrance on your part delay the necessary purchases which he has to make; since you, on account of the character of your winds, are able to choose the shortest sea-track[2].'

25. SENATOR, PRAETORIAN PRAEFECT, TO HIS DEPUTY[3] AMBROSIUS, AN ILLUSTRIS.

[This letter appears to have been written in the early autumn of 538, about a year after the three last letters, and also after Letters 27 and 28, which precede it in order of date, though they follow it in this collection. For an account of the terrible famine in Italy, the beginning of which is here described, see Procopius, De Bello Gotthico ii. 20.]

Famine in Italy. 'Since the world is not governed by chance, but by a Divine Ruler who does not change His purposes at random, men are alarmed, and naturally alarmed, at the extraordinary signs in the heavens, and ask with anxious hearts what events these may portend. The Sun, first of stars, seems to have lost his wonted light, and appears of a bluish colour. We marvel to see no shadows of our

---

[1] 'Moneta illic quodammodo percutitur victualis.' Some have supposed that these words point to a currency in salt; but I think they are only a Cassiodorian way of saying 'By this craft ye have your wealth.'

[2] This is the only translation I can suggest of 'quatenus expensas necessarias nulla difficultate tardetis, qui pro qualitate aeris compendium vobis eligere potestis itineris.'

[3] 'Agenti vices.' See note on xi. 4.

bodies at noon, to feel the mighty vigour of his heat wasted into feebleness, and the phenomena which accompany a transitory eclipse prolonged through a whole year.

'The Moon too, even when her orb is full, is empty of her natural splendour. Strange has been the course of the year thus far. We have had a winter without storms, a spring without mildness, and a summer without heat. Whence can we look for harvest, since the months which should have been maturing the corn have been chilled by Boreas? How can the blade open if rain, the mother of all fertility, is denied to it? These two influences, prolonged frost and unseasonable drought, must be adverse to all things that grow. The seasons seem to be all jumbled up together, and the fruits, which were wont to be formed by gentle showers, cannot be looked for from the parched earth. But as last year was one that boasted of an exceptionally abundant harvest, you are to collect all of its fruits that you can, and store them up for the coming months of scarcity, for which it is well able to provide. And that you may not be too much distressed by the signs in the heavens of which I have spoken, return to the consideration of Nature, and apprehend the reason of that which makes the vulgar gape with wonder.

'The middle air is thickened by the rigour of snow and rarefied by the beams of the Sun. This is the great Inane, roaming between the heavens and the earth. When it happens to be pure and lighted up by the rays of the sun it opens out its true aspect[1]; but when alien elements are blended with it, it is stretched like a hide across the sky, and suffers neither the true colours of the heavenly bodies to appear nor their proper warmth to penetrate. This often happens in cloudy weather for a time; it is only its extraordinary prolongation which has produced these disastrous effects,

[1] 'Vestros (?) veraciter pandit aspectus.'

causing the reaper to fear a new frost in harvest, making the apples to harden when they should grow ripe, souring the old age of the grape-cluster.

'All this, however, though it would be wrong to construe it as an omen of Divine wrath, cannot but have an injurious effect on the fruits of the earth. Let it be your care to see that the scarcity of this one year does not bring ruin on us all. Even thus was it ordained by the first occupant of our present dignity[1], that the preceding plenty should avail to mitigate the present penury.'

26. SENATOR, PRAETORIAN PRAEFECT, TO PAULUS, VIR STRENUUS[2].

Remission of taxes for Province of Venetia in consequence of the famine.

'We are glad when we can reconcile the claims of the public service with the suggestions of pity. The Venerable Augustin, a man illustrious by his life and name, has brought under our notice the lamentable petition of the Venetians, to the effect that there have been in their Province no crops of wine, wheat, or millet, and that they must be ruined unless the Royal pity succours them.

'In these circumstances it would be cruel to exact the customary supplies from them, and we therefore remit the contributions of wine and wheat for the use of the army which we had ordered from the cities of Concordia, Aquileia, and Forojulii[3], exacting only the meat, as shown by the accompanying letter[4].

'We shall send from hence a sufficient supply of wheat when the time comes; and as we are told that there is a plentiful crop of wine in Istria, you can buy there the wine that would have been furnished by the three

---

[1] Joseph, Praetorian Praefect of Egypt under Pharaoh.

[2] Paulus was probably a Sajo.

[3] Now Cividale in Friuli. Notice the terminations of these names: 'ex Concordiense, Aquileiense, et Forojuliense civitatibus' ('e,' not 'i').

[4] The letter here alluded to does not appear to be preserved.

cities. Be sure that you ask for no fee in this matter. This remission of taxes is absolutely gratuitous on our part.'

27. SENATOR, PRAETORIAN PRAEFECT, TO DATIUS[1], BISHOP OF MILAN.

Relief of famine-stricken citizens of Ticinum and Dertona.

'It is most fitting that good and holy men should be made the stewards of the Royal bounty. We therefore request your Holiness, in accordance with the King's commands, to open the granaries at Ticinum[2] and Dertona[3], and sell millet thereat to the starving people at the rate of 20 modii per solidum[4]. We are anxious that you should do this, lest the work should fall into venal hands which would sell the King's bounty to those who are able to provide for themselves. It is the poor, not the rich, that we wish to help: we would pour our bounty into empty vessels. Let not then your Holiness think this work of compassion unworthy of your sacred office. In order to assist you we have sent A and B, who will simply obey the orders of your Holiness, doing nothing of their own motion.

'Send us an account of the solidi received in payment for the said millet, that they may be stored up with our Treasurer[5], in order to replace the before-mentioned grain, and thus provide a reserve for future times of scarcity; like a garment taken to pieces that it may be made up again as good as new.'

---

[1] Cassiodorus, like Procopius, spells this name with a 't.' Some of the ecclesiastical writers spell it with a 'c.'

[2] Pavia.   [3] Tortona.

[4] Twelve shillings for twenty pecks, or about nineteen shillings and twopence a quarter; not a very low price, one would think, for such a grain as millet.

Datius is ordered to sell *tertiam portionem* of this millet. Probably this expression has the same meaning as the 'tertia illatio' of xi. 37.

In the similar letter, x. 27, 'tertia portio' (whether of wheat or millet is not stated) is to be sold at 25 modii per solidum.

[5] 'Arcarius.'

[It is not very easy to assign a date to this letter. The mention of the famine would incline us to assign it to 538, as that seems to have been the year when the full force of the famine was felt in Italy (see Procopius, De Bello Gotthico ii. 20, where 538 and 539 seem to be marked as the two great famine years). But very early in 538 the Bishop of Milan, the same Datius to whom this letter is addressed, visited Rome to entreat Belisarius to send a small garrison to occupy Milan, which had already revolted, or was on the verge of revolting, from the Gothic King. As soon as the siege of Rome was raised Belisarius complied with this request, and sent 1,000 men, under Mundilas, to escort Datius back to Milan. This expedition set forth probably in April 538, and as soon as it arrived at Milan that city openly proclaimed its defection from Witigis and its allegiance to the Emperor. It was soon besieged by Uraias, nephew of Witigis, by whom in the following year (539) it was taken. The city, we are informed, was rased to the ground, and Bishop Datius escaped to Constantinople. Evidently we have here a continuous chain of events, which makes it impossible for us to date this letter in 538 or any subsequent year.

We ought probably therefore to assign it to the autumn of 537, and to look upon it as an attempt (unsuccessful, as it proved) to retain Datius and the citizens of Milan on the side of the Goths. We know from the Twenty-second Letter of this book that signs of scarcity had already shown themselves in Italy by the 1st September, 537; and in an interesting passage of the 'Historia Miscella' (Book xvi.), famine in Liguria, the year 537, and the name of Datius are all combined. 'Praeter belli instantiam angebatur insuper Roma famis penuriâ: tanta siquidem per universum mundum eo anno [the year of the siege of Rome], *maxime apud Liguriam* fames excreverat, ut *sicut vir sanctissimus Datius Me-*

diolanensis antistes retulit, pleraeque matres infelicium natorum membra comederent.' I owe this reference to Baronius.]

28. AN EDICT [ADDRESSED TO THE LIGURIANS].

Relief of inhabitants of Liguria.

'Divine Providence uses adversity as a means of testing our characters. Famine has afflicted the Provinces, but the result of it has been that they have proved more fully than before the bounty of their King. Rejoice herein, oh ye Ligurians! For when, as you will remember, on a previous occasion the savage temper of your neighbours was aroused, and Aemilia and your Liguria were shaken by an incursion of the Burgundians, who waged a sneaking campaign by reason of their nearness to your territory, suddenly the renown of the insulted Empire[1] arose like the sun in his strength. The enemy mourned the ruin which was caused by his own presumption, when he learned that that man was Ruler of the Gothic race whose rare valour he had experienced when he was still a private soldier[2]. How often did the Burgundian wish that he had never left his own frontiers to be compelled to fight with such an adversary as our Sovereign; for though he found with relief that he escaped his actual presence in the field, none the less did his rashness bring him in contact with the good fortune of his arms. For when with redoubled

---

[1] Literally, 'of the present Empire:' 'subito praesentis Imperii tanquam solis ortus fama radiavit.' I avoid the word 'present,' because of its ambiguity. Observe the use of 'Imperii' applied to the Gothic Kingdom.

[2] 'Quando illum cognovit nominatae (?) gentis esse Rectorem, quem sub militis nomine probaverat esse singularem.' This evident allusion to Witigis obliges us to place the date of this Burgundian invasion not much earlier than the summer of 536, when Witigis was raised to the throne. Apparently the Burgundians were already in Italy when they heard the news of that event.

fortitude[1] the Goths turned to the prosecution of the war, with such successfully combined operations did they strike the bands of the rebels, that you would have thought those were all armed men, these were all defenceless[2]. Such was the just judgment of God, that the robber should perish in those very plains which he had presumed to desolate. Exult now, oh Province, adorned with the carcases of thine adversaries! rejoice, oh Liguria, at the heap of dead bodies! If the harvest of corn is denied thee, the harvest of dead enemies shall not be wanting. Tribute thou mayest not be able to offer to thy King, but the triumphs which are won in thy land thou canst offer with pride.

'[3] To these triumphs must be added the lately foiled plunder-raid of the Alamanni, so checked in its very first attempts that their entrance and exit were almost one event, like a wound well and opportunely cauterised. Thus were the excesses of the presumptuous invader punished, and the subjects of our King were saved from absolute ruin. I might indeed enumerate to you what crowds of the enemy fell in other places, but I turn rather—such is human nature—to more joyful themes, and revert to the point with which I at first commenced, namely that the Sovereign who has saved you from the hostile sword is determined now to avert from your Province the perils of famine.

'In this new war the citadels are well-stored granaries; Starvation is the dreaded foe: if they are closed she

---

[1] 'Ut Gothi ad belli studium geminâ se fortitudine contulerunt.' These words perhaps allude to the necessity of fighting two enemies at once, Belisarius and the Burgundians; or perhaps to the existence of two Gothic armies, whose combined operations are indicated by the following words, 'prospera concertatione.'

[2] 'Quasi inde nudos hinc stare contigisset armatos.' 'Hinc' and 'inde' refer to geographical position, not to the order of the words in the sentence.

[3] See von Schubert's 'Unterwerfung der Alamannen,' pp. 57-59, for a careful analysis of the following paragraph.

enters; by opening them wide she is put to flight. I know not what the world in general may think of the relative merit of these two campaigns of our King. For my part, though I recognise it as the mark of a brave man to have fought a winning battle, I think it is something above mere human valour to have conquered penury.

'In addition to these benefits the King has remitted one-half of the taxes of the Province, that he might not sadden with the one hand those whom he was gladdening with the other. Herein he compares favourably with Joseph, who sold corn to the Egyptians, but on such terms that they lost their personal freedom. Doubtless that holy man was placed in a dilemma between the necessity of satisfying a covetous King on the one hand, and that of rescuing a starving people on the other. Still I must think that the Egyptian, whose life was preserved, groaned over the loss of his liberty; and if I may say so, with all respect to so great a patriarch[1], far nobler is it to sell corn to freemen who remain freemen, and to lighten their taxes on account of poverty. This is really a gratuitous distribution, when both the money with which to buy is handed over to you [by the abatement of tribute], and a price is fixed on purpose to please you.

'The generosity of the State therefore will sell 25 modii, when the peasant has lost his crops, at the price at which 10 are usually sold[2]. Humanity has altered the usual course of affairs, and by a strange kind of chaffering, but one which truly becomes a King, just when the famished peasant is willing to offer us an

---

[1] 'Pace tanti patris dixerim.'

[2] Probably one solidus: making the largesse price 15s. 4d. a quarter (about four shillings less than the price named in the preceding letter for millet); while the market price was 38s. 4d. a quarter. I read these sentences thus: 'Vendit itaque largitas publica vicenos quinque modios, dum possessor invenire non possit, ad denos. Ordinem rerum saeculi mutavit humanitas.' The construction is harsh and elliptical, but this makes sense, which the ordinary punctuation, throwing 'ad denos' into the following sentence, does not.

enhanced price for food, we are directed to offer it to him for a smaller one.

'The King himself had seen your calamity, and thereupon bestowed on you previously one favour. Now, on hearing of its continuance, he adds to it a second. Happy calamity, which forced itself on the notice of such an eye-witness!

'Now, oh Ligurian, rejoice in the good fortune which has come to thee. Compare thy lot with the Egyptian's and be happy. He was fed, but lost his freedom; thou art fed, and at the same time defended from thy enemies. Joseph gave back the purchase-money to his brethren in their sacks, showing a greater kindness to his kindred than to his subjects. Our King shows no such partiality, but bestows on all the taxpayers larger benefits than he did on his brethren. Happy age! in which Kings may be likened, not to Kings, but to Prophets, and yet bear away the palm.

'But that we may not longer detain you from the desired enjoyment of the Royal benefits, know that our commands have been given to those whose business it is to attend to this affair, that, according to the tenour of this edict, the generosity of the Sovereign may penetrate into your homes.'

[The same considerations which were applied to the date of the preceding letter seem to require that this also be dated in 537. After the raising of the siege of Rome (March, 538), by the despatch of Imperial troops into Liguria, and the enthusiastic adherence of that Province to the Imperial cause, a new state of things was established, and one to which the language of this letter would have been utterly inapplicable.

There are two events of which we have no other knowledge than that furnished by this letter: the invasion of the Burgundians, and the ravages of the Alamanni in the Province of Liguria.

(1) The invasion of the Burgundians seems, as stated

in a previous note, to have occurred in the spring or early summer of 536; so that Cassiodorus could represent the invaders as surprised and disheartened by learning of the elevation of Witigis. It no doubt formed part of those hostile operations of the Frankish Kings described by Procopius (De Bello Gotthico i. 13), the termination of which was purchased by Witigis by the cession of Provence and the payment of a subsidy. It is interesting to observe, however, that the Burgundians, notwithstanding their subjugation in 534, and their incorporation in the Frankish monarchy, are still spoken of as conducting an invasion on their own account. This is just like the invasion of Italy in 553 by the Alamannic brethren, and is quite in keeping with the loosely compacted character of the Merovingian monarchy, in which it was copied by the Anglian and Saxon Kingdoms.

(2) For the ravages of the Alamanni consult, as before stated, von Schubert's monograph. This passage quite confirms his view of the events connected with the overthrow of the Alamannic Kingdom by Clovis. A remnant of the people, settled as refugees in Raetia under Theodoric's protection, now, in the decline of the Ostrogothic monarchy throw off their allegiance to his successors, and press forward over the Alps to share the spoil of Italy. Witigis, however, notwithstanding his struggle with Belisarius, is still able promptly to repel this incursion; but it co-operates with the Burgundian invasion and the inclement spring and summer of 537 to bring about the famine in Liguria in the autumn of that year.]

THE END.

INDEX OF PERSONS

TO WHOM THE LETTERS ARE ADDRESSED.

A.

Abundantius, Praetorian Praefect, v. 16, 17, 23, 34; ix. 4.
Acretius, *see* Eutropius.
Adeodatus, iii. 46.
Adila, Vir Spectabilis, Comes, ii. 29.
Aemilianus, Vir Venerabilis, Bishop, iv. 31.
Aestunae, Possessores, Defensores, and Curiales dwelling at, iii. 9.
Agapitus, Praefectus Urbis, Vir Illustris atque Patricius, i. 6, 23, 32, 33, 41; ii. 6.
Alaric (II), King of the Visigoths (484-507), iii. 1.
Albienus, Vir Illustris atque Patricius, i. 20; Praefectus Praetorio, viii. 20.
Albinus and Albienus, Viri Illustres atque Patricii, i. 20.
Albinus, Vir Illustris, Patricius, iv. 30.
Albinus, Actores of, iv. 35.
Aloisius, Architect, ii. 39.
Amabilis, Exsecutor, i. 8; Vir Devotus (? Sajo) and Comes, iv. 5.
Ambrosius, Quaestor, viii. 13; Vir Illustris Agens Vices (Praefecti Praetorio), xi. 4, 5; xii. 25.
Ampelius, Despotius, and Theodulus, Viri Spectabiles, ii. 23.
Ampelius, Count Luvirit and, v. 35.
Ampelius and Liveria, v. 39.
Anastasius, Emperor (491-518), i. 1; ii. 1.
Anastasius, Consularis, v. 8.
Anastasius, Cancellarius of Lucania and Bruttii, xii. 12, 14.
Anat(h)olius, Cancellarius of Province of Samnium, xi. 36.
Andreas, Primiscrinius, xi. 21.
Andreas, *see* Maximian.
Annas, Vir Spectabilis and Comes, iv. 18.

Antianus, Vir Spectabilis, ex-Cornicularius, xi. 18, 34.
Antonius, Vir Venerabilis, Bishop of Pola, iv. 44.
Apronianus, Vir Illustris, Comes Privatarum, iii. 53.
Arator, Vir Illustris, Comes Domesticorum, viii. 12.
Arelate (*Arles*), Possessores of, iii. 44.
Argolicus, Vir Illustris, Praefectus Urbis, iii. 11, 29, 30, 33; iv. 22, 25, 29, 42.
Arigern, Vir Illustris, Comes, iii. 36, 45; iv. 23.
Artemidorus, Vir Illustris atque Patricius, Praefectus Urbis, i. 42; ii. 34; iii. 22.
Assuin (Assius, or Assum), Vir Illustris, Comes, i. 40.
Aurigenes, Vir Venerabilis, Bishop, iii. 14.
Avilf, Sajo, v. 20.

B.

Baion (Coion, or Goinon), Vir Spectabilis, i. 38.
Beatus, Vir Clarissimus and Cancellarius, xi. 10; Primicerius Augustalium, xi. 30.
Benenatus, Vir Spectabilis, iv. 15.
Bergantinus, Vir Illustris and Patrician, Comes Patrimonii, viii. 23; ix. 3.
Boetius, Vir Illustris atque Patricius, i. 10, 45; ii. 40.
Brandila, v. 32.

C.

Cancellarii diversi Provinciarum Singularum, xii. 1, 10.
Canonicarius Venetiarum, xii. 4, 7.
Capuanus, Vir Spectabilis, v. 21.

Index of Persons

Carinus, Vir Illustris, v. 28.
Cart(h)erius, Regerendarius, xi. 29.
Cassiodorus, Vir Illustris atque Patricius (father of Cassiodorus Senator), i. 3; iii. 28.
Catana, City of, Honorati Possessores, Defensores, and Curiales of, iii. 49.
Catellus, Scriniarius Actorum, xi. 22.
Cheliodorus, Commentariensis, xi. 28.
Clovis, see Luduin.
Coelianus and Agapitus, Viri Illustres et Patricii, i. 23.
Colossaeus, Vir Illustris, Comes, Governor of Pannonia, iii. 23.
Comes Siliquatariorum et Portus Curas Agens, ii. 12.
Constantian, Vir Experientissimus, xii. 18.
Constantinian, Cura Epistolarum Canonicarum, xi. 23.
Consularis, Vir Illustris, iii. 52.
Consularis Liguriae, xii. 8.
Crispianus, i. 37.
Cunigast, Vir Illustris, viii. 28.
Cyprian, Comes Sacrarum Largitionum and Patrician, v. 40; viii. 21.

D.

Dalmatia and S(u)avia, all the Goths and Romans in, ix. 9.
Daniel, iii. 19.
Datius, Bishop of Milan, xii. 27.
Decius, Vir Illustris, Patricius, ii. 33.
Decoratus, Vir Devotus, v. 31.
Dertona (*Tortona*), all Goths and Romans abiding (consistentes) at, i. 17.
Despotius, see Ampelius.
Deusdedit, Scriba Ravennas, xii. 21.
Domitianus and Willias, i. 18.
Dromonarii, the, ii. 31.
Duda, Vir Spectabilis and Comes, iv. 28; Sajo, iv. 32, 34.
Dumerit, Sajo, viii. 27.

E.

Ecdicius (or Benedictus), Vir Honestus, ii. 4.
Elpidius (or Hespidius), Deacon, iv. 24.
Epiphanius, Vir Spectabilis, Consularis of Dalmatia, v. 24.
Episcopi et Honorati (?), ix. 5.
Episcopi sui, x. 34; diversi, xi. 3.
Eugenius (Eugenites, or Eugenes), Vir Illustris, Magister Officiorum, i. 12.

Eusebius, Vir Illustris, iv. 48.
Eustorgius, Vir Venerabilis, Bishop of Milan, i. 9.
Eutropius and Acretius, v. 13.

F.

Faustus, Praefectus Praetorio (in the edition of Nivellius his title is given as Praepositus), i. 14, 26, 34, 35; ii. 5, 9, 26, 30, 37, 38; Vir Illustris, iii. 21; Praefectus Praetorio, iii. 47, 51; iv. 36, 38, 50.
Felix, Vir Clarissimus, i. 7; Vir Illustris, Consul (511), ii. 2; iii. 39.
Felix, Quaestor, viii. 18.
Feltria (*Feltre*), Possessores of, v. 9.
Ferrocinctus, see Grimoda.
Festus, Vir Illustris atque Patricius, i. 15, 39; ii. 22; iii. 10.
Florentinus (or Florentianus), Vir Devotus, Comitiacus, viii. 27.
Florianus, Vir Spectabilis, i. 5.
Forum Livii (*Forlì*), Honorati, Possessores, and Curiales of, iv. 8.
Fruinarith, Sajo, ii. 13.

G.

Gaudiosus, Cancellarius of Province of Liguria, xi. 14.
Gaul, all the Provincials of, iii. 17, 42; viii. 7.
Geberich, Vir Spectabilis, iv. 20.
Gemellus, Vir Spectabilis, Governor of Gaul, iii. 16, 18, 32; iv. 12, 19, 21.
Genesius, Vir Spectabilis, viii. 30.
Gepidae, ad Gallias destinati, v. 11.
Gesila, Sajo, iv. 14.
Gildias, Vir Spectabilis, Count of Syracuse, ix. 11, 14.
Goths, all the, i. 24; x. 31; settled in Italy, viii. 5.
Goths, all the, and Romans, i. 28.
Goths, all the, and Romans, and those who hold the harbours and mountain-passes, ii. 19.
Grimoda, Sajo, and Ferrocinctus, Apparitor, iii. 20.
Gudila, Bishop, ii. 18.
Gudinand, Sajo, v. 19.
Gudisal, Sajo, iv. 47.
Guduim, Sajo, v. 27; Vir Sublimis and Dux, v. 30.
Gundibad, King of the Burgundians (473-516), i. 46; iii. 2.

H.

Haesti, the, v. 2.
Herminafrid, King of the Thuringians, iv. 1.
Heruli, King of the, iv. 2.
Heruli, Warni, and Thoringi, Kings of the, iii. 3.
Hilderic, King of the Vandals (523–531), ix. 1.
Honoratus, Vir Illustris, Quaestor, v. 3.
Honorius, Praefectus Urbis, x. 30.

I.

Ida (perhaps Ibbas), Vir Sublimis and Dux, iv. 17.
Importunus, Vir Illustris, Patricius, iii. 5.
Istria, Provincials of, xii. 22.

J.

Januarius, Vir Venerabilis, Bishop of Salona, iii. 7.
Jews, all the, residing in Genoa, ii. 27; iv. 33.
Joannes, Vir Spectabilis, Consularis Campaniae, iii. 27; iv. 10.
Joannes, Vir Spectabilis, Referendarius, viii. 25.
Joannes, Vir Clarissimus, Arcarius, v. 7.
Joannes, Canonicarius of Thuscia, xi. 38.
Joannes, Cancellarius, xi. 6; Praerogativarius, xi. 37.
Joannes, Siliquatarius of Ravenna, xii. 17.
Joannes, Apparitor, ii. 21; Arch-Physician, iv. 41.
John II, Pope (533–535), ix. 15; xi. 2.
Judges, all the, of the Provinces, ix. 20; xi. 7, 9; xii. 2.
Julianus, Comes Patrimonii, i. 16.
Justin, Emperor (518–527), viii. 1.
Justinian, Emperor (527–566), x. 1, 2, 8, 9, 15, 19, 22, 24, 25, 26, 32; xi. 13.
Justus, Sextus Scholaris, xi. 26.

L.

Laurentius, Vir Experientissimus, xii. 23.
Liberius, Praetorian Praefect of the Gauls, viii. 6.

Ligurians, the, xi. 15, 16; xii. 28.
Liveria, see Ampelius.
Lucillus, Scriniarius Curae Militaris, xi. 24.
Lucinus, Vir Clarissimus, Cancellarius of Campania, xi. 37.
Lucristani (Lustriani?), the, settled (constituti) on the river Sontius (Isonzo), i. 29.
Luduin (Clovis), King of the Franks (481–511), ii. 41; iii. 4.
Luvirit, Count, and Ampelius, v. 35.

M.

Magister Officiorum (at Constantinople), x. 33.
Mannila, Sajo, v. 5.
Marabad, Vir Illustris and Comes, iv. 12, 46.
Marcellus, Vir Spectabilis, Advocatus Fisci, i. 22.
Massilia (Marseilles), citizens of, iii. 34; iv. 26.
Maximian, Vir Illustris, and Andreas, Vir Spectabilis, i. 21.
Maximus, Vir Illustris, Consul, v. 42; Vir Illustris and Domesticus, x. 11.
Maximus, Vir Clarissimus, Cancellarius of Lucania and Bruttii, xii. 15.
Maximus, Vicarius Urbis Romae, xii. 19.
Milan, the Jews of, v. 37.

N.

Neudes, Vir Illustris, v. 29.
Noricum, Provincials of, iii. 50.
Nursia, see Reate.

O.

Opilio, Comes Sacrarum Largitionum, viii. 16.
Osun (Osuin, or Osum), Vir Illustris, Comes, iii. 26; iv. 9; ix. 8.

P.

Pannonia, all the Barbarians and Romans settled in, iii. 24.
Parma, Honorati Possessores, and Curiales of, viii. 29.
Paschasius, Praefectus Annonae, xii. 9.
Patricius, Vir Illustris and Quaestor, x. 6.
Patricius, Primicerius Exceptorum, xi. 25.

Paulinus, Vir Clarissimus and Consul, ix. 22.
Paulus, Vir Strenuus, xii. 26.
Peter, Bishop, iii. 37.
Peter, Vir Clarissimus, Erogator Obsoniorum, xii. 11; Arcarius, xii. 20.
Picenum and Samnium, all the Goths settled in, v. 26.
Pierius, Primicerius Singulariorum, xi. 32.
Possessores, universi, v. 38.
Provinus (Probinus), Vir Illustris, Patricius, ii. 11; Actores of, iv. 40.

R.

Reate and Nursia, all the inhabitants of, viii. 26.
Reparatus, Praefectus Urbis, ix. 7.
Roman Church, Clergy of, viii. 24.
Romans, all the, i. 28; in Italy and the Dalmatias, viii. 4.
Roman people, the, i. 31; viii. 3; x. 14, 17.
Rome, people of the City of, i. 44.
Romulus (? ex-Emperor), iii. 35.

S.

Sabinianus, Vir Spectabilis, i. 25.
Sajones, universi, qui sunt Cancellariis deputati, xii. 3.
Salvantius, Vir Illustris, Praefectus Urbis, ix. 16, 17.
Samnium, *see* Picenum.
Saturninus and Verbusius, Viri Illustres, Senatores, i. 19.
Senarius, Vir Illustris, Comes Patrimonii, iv. 3; Comes Privatarum, iv. 7, 11, 13.
Senate of the City of Rome, i. 4, 13, 30, 43; ii. 3, 16, 24, 32; iii. 6, 12, 31; iv. 4, 16, 43; v. 4, 22, 41; viii. 2, 10, 11, 14, 15, 17, 19, 22; ix. 19, 21, 23, 25; x. 3, 4, 7, 12, 13, 16, 18; xi. 1.
SENATOR (MAGNUS AURELIUS CASSIODORUS), Praetorian Praefect, ix. 24; x. 27, 28.
Servatus, Dux Raetiarum, i. 11.
Severianus (or Severinus), Vir Illustris, v. 14.
Severus, Vir Venerabilis, Bishop, ii. 8.
Severus, Vir Spectabilis, viii. 31, 32, 33.
Simeon, Vir Illustris, Comes, iii. 25.
Speciosus, i. 27; Vir Devotus, Comitiacus, ii. 10.
Stabularius, Comitiacus, v. 6.
Starcedius, Vir Sublimis, v. 36.

Stephanus, Vir Spectabilis, Comes Primi Ordinis et ex-Princeps nostri Ordinis, ii. 28.
S(u)avia, all the Provincials and Capillati, Defensores and Curiales, residing in, iv. 49; all the Possessores in, v. 15; all the Goths and Romans in, ix. 9.
Sunhivad, Vir Spectabilis, iii. 13.
Sura (or Suna), Vir Illustris, Comes, ii. 7.
Symmachus, Vir Illustris and Patricius, ii. 14; iv. 6, 51.
Syracuse, all the Provincials of the City of, ix. 10.

T.

Tancila, Vir Spectabilis, ii. 35.
Tezutzat, Sajo, iv. 27.
Theodagunda, Illustris Femina, iv. 37.
Theodahad, Vir Spectabilis, iii. 15; Vir Illustris, iv. 39; v. 12.
Theodora, Augusta, x. 10, 20, 21, 23.
Theodosius, Homo Theodahadi (?), x. 5.
Theodulus, *see* Ampelius.
Theon (or Theonius), Vir Sublimis, i. 2.
Theriolus, Vir Spectabilis, i. 36.
Thessalonica, Praefect of, x. 35.
Thomas, Vir Clarissimus, Arcarius, xii. 20.
Thoringi (Thuringians), *see* Heruli.
Ticinum (*Pavia*), Comites, Defensores, and Curiales of, iv. 45.
Transmund (or Thrasamund), King of the Vandals, v. 43, 44.
Tribuni Maritimorum, xii. 24.
Tridentinae Civitatis, Honorati Possessores, Defensores, et Curiales, ii. 17.
Tulum, Patrician, viii. 9.

U.

Unigis, Spatarius, iii. 43.
Uniligis (or Wiligis), Sajo, ii. 20.
Urbicus, ex-Primicerius Singulariorum, xi. 31.
Ursus, Primicerius Deputatorum, xi. 30.

V.

Valerian, Vir Sublimis, xii. 5.
Vandals, King of the, v. 1, 43, 44; ix. 1.
Venantius, Vir Illustris, ii. 15; Spectabilis, Corrector of Lucania and Bruttii, iii. 8.

Veranus, Sajo, v. 10.
Verbusius, *see* Saturninus.
Verruca, fort of, all Goths and Romans living near, iii. 48.
Victor, Vir Spectabilis, Censitor of Sicily, ix. 12.
Victorinus, Vir Venerabilis, Bishop, viii. 8.
Vitalian, Vir Clarissimus, Cancellarius of Lucania and Bruttii, xi. 39.

W.

Wandil (Vuandil), iii. 38.
Warni (Guarni), *see* Heruli.
Wilitanch, Duke, v. 33.
Willias, i. 18; v. 18; Vir Illustris, Comes Patrimonii, ix. 13.
Winusiad, Count, x. 29.
Witigisclus (or Wigisicla), Vir Spectabilis, Censitor of Sicily, ix. 12.

GENERAL INDEX.

[NOTE.—*The references to the Introduction and to the Notes are by the page (thus, 106-108); references to the 'Variae' are by the numbers of the Book and Letter (thus, v. 16, 17). The FORMULAE are printed in small capitals.*]

A

Ab Actis (Registrar), officer in Court of Praetorian Praefect, 106-108; origin of the name, 107; compared to Referendarius, 312.

Abundantius, Praetorian Praefect, instructions to, as to forming a navy, v. 16, 17; to provide ships, and rations for young recruits, v. 23; instructions to, in the case of Frontosus, v. 34; to allow a family of Curials to degrade into Possessores, ix. 4.

Acinaticium, red wine of Verona, praises of, and account of its manufacture, xii. 4.

Actores (Representatives, Attorneys), of Albinus, iv. 35; of the holy Apostle Peter, xii. 20; of Probinus, iv. 40; of Spes, ii. 21; of Theodahad, viii. 23.

Addua, River (*Adda*), derivation of the name, xi. 14.

Adeodatus, forced by torture to confess himself guilty of rape, iii. 46; the sentence against him partially cancelled, iii. 46.

Adjutores, general word for assistants, 97, 102-104; is Adjutor equivalent to Primiscrinius? 103; a lower class of Exceptores seem to have been called Adjutores, 111; of Magister Officiorum, vi. 6.

Admissionales, Ushers of the Praefectoral Court, 112.

Adriana, petition of Curiales of, as to taxation, i. 19.

Adulterer slain by the injured husband, case of, i. 37.

Adultery, punishment of (Edictum Athalarici), ix. 18.

Aemilia, Province of, invaded by Burgundians, xii. 28.

Aemilianus, Bishop, ordered to finish the aqueduct which he has begun, iv. 31.

Aestii, *see* Haesti.

Aestunae (?), inhabitants of, ordered to send marbles to Ravenna, iii. 9.

AETATIS VENIA, FORMULA GRANTING, vii. 41; letter relating to, i. 38.

Aetheria, a widow, re-married, accused of wasting her children's property, iv. 12.

African. Singular custom by which an African was allowed to claim estate of a fellow-countryman dying without heirs, xii. 9.

Agapetus, Pope (June 3, 535—April 21, 536), Cassiodorus seeks to persuade him to found a School of Theology at Rome, 56; ordered by Theodahad and Gudelina to give his answer to Justinian's ambassador promptly, x. 19, 20, 25; mortgaged the Church plate to defray expenses of his journey to Constantinople, xii. 20.

Agapita (or Agapeta), Foemina Spectabilis, wife of Basilius, and a person of feeble intellect, ii. 11; affair of her abduction, ii. 10, 11; further light on this affair, iv. 40.

Agapitus, with Coelianus, seems to have had special jurisdiction in cases affecting Patricians, i. 23, 27.

Agathias on Theodoric's protection of the Alamanni, 195.

Agenantia, widow of Campanianus, ix. 4.

Agens Vices (Deputy), functions of, 460 n; xii. 25.

Agentes in Rebus, Schola of, emissaries of the Magister Officiorum, 36; Princeps of, xi. 35.

Agnellus, Patrician, chooses Festus to defend his interests in his absence, i. 15.

Agnellus, fidei-jussor of Crispianus, i. 37.

Agnellus, house of, in Castrum Lucullanum given to Joannes, viii. 25.

Agrimensor, a Roman, description of, iii. 52.

Alamanni, date of Clovis' victory over, 23, 24, 195; Theodoric congratulates Clovis on his victory over, ii. 41; directed to exchange their cattle with Noricans, iii. 50; plundering incursion of, into Liguria, xii. 28; 527.

Alaric I, clemency of, at siege of Rome, 28; xii. 20.

Alaric II, letters intended to avert war between Alaric and Clovis, iii. 1-4; possessions granted by, to Church of Narbonne, iv. 17; taxation in the time of, v. 39; reception of his son Gesalic by Thrasamund, v. 43, 44.

Albienus, Vir Illustris and Patrician, deputed to select a Pantomimist, i. 20, 33; appointed Praetorian Praefect (527), viii. 20.

Albinus, Vir Illustris and Patrician, deputed to select a Pantomimist, i. 20, 33; allowed to erect 'fabricae' overlooking the Forum, iv. 30; accused by Cyprian of treason, 289, 291.

Albinus, an extravagant minor, case of, iv. 35.

Allecticii, Symmachus' oration on behalf of, 74; probable explanation of the term, 78.

Alpes Cottiae, Provincials of, to be relieved from taxation, iv. 36.

Alsuanum (?), transport of timber to, iv. 8.

Altinum, villas of, 514 n.

Amal race, glorified by Cassiodorus in his Gothic History, 29, 30, 33; 'Amali sanguinis purpurea dignitas,' ix. 1.

Amal race, glory of, viii. 2, 5; 'consuetudinis est lex, cum imperio [Romano] amicitiam Amalos semper habuisse,' x. 11.

Amalus (according to Jordanes, Amala), ancestor of Theodoric, 'felicitate enituit,' xi. 1.

Amalabirga, niece of Theodoric, married to Herminafrid, King of the Thuringians, iv. 1.

Amalafrida, Queen of the Vandals, sister of Theodoric, wife of King Thrasamund, put to death by his successor Hilderic, ix. 1.

Amalasuentha, daughter of Theodoric, mother of Athalaric, her regency, 38, 42-43; associates Theodahad in the kingship on the death of her son, 44; x. 1-4; dethroned and put to death by Theodahad, 45; praises of her character, x. 4; xi. 1; sends present of marbles to Justinian, x. 8; writes warmly to Theodora, x. 10; a doubtful allusion to her death, x. 20 (see note on p. 433).

Amandianus, Clarissimus, heirs of, defrauded by Theodahad, v. 12.

AMBASSADORS, FORMULA RESPECTING, vii. 33.

Amber, nature of, described, v. 2.

Ambrosius, son of Faustinus, addressed by Ennodius in 'Paraenesis Didascalica,' 358; Count of the Sacred Largesses, viii. 13; appointed Quaestor, viii. 13, 14.

Ambrosius, Illustris (probably the same as preceding), appointed 'Vices Agens' to Cassiodorus as Praetorian Praefect, xi. 4; instructions to, xii. 25.

Amphitheatre, sports of, described and condemned, v. 42.

Anastasius, Emperor, date of letter to, in the 'Variae,' 23; his wrath against Apion and Macedonius, 105; relations between him and Theodoric, i. 1 n; informed of elevation of Felix to Consulship, ii. 1; as to introduction of Heruli into Italy, 258 n.

Anchorago, a fish caught in the Rhine, xii. 4.

Andreas, intestacy of widow of, v. 24.

Andreas, defaulting taxpayer in Apulia, v. 31.

'Anecdoton Holderi,' MS. containing information as to Cassiodorus and his friends, 73-84.

Anicii, dignity of the family of, x. 11.

Annonae, of soldiers stationed in passes near Aosta, ii. 5; of garrisons on the Durance, iii. 41, 42; is praelendae equivalent to? 219; to be regularly supplied, v. 13 (see Praefectus Annonae).

Anonymus Valesii (an unknown chronicler of the Sixth Century, whose fragments are generally edited along with the history of Ammianus Marcellinus), quoted, 291, 363, 369.

Anthimus, Patriarch of Constantinople (535-536), deposition of, by Pope Agapetus, 436 n.

Antianus, ex-Cornicularius, made a Spectabilis, xi. 18; evasive reply to, xi. 19.

Antiochus, apparently a tax-collector, ii. 4.

Antiquarius, transcriber of manuscripts, Cassiodorus on the functions of, 60.

Apion, anger of Anastasius against, 105.

Apocha, a voucher for payment of taxes, xii. 7, 8.

Aponus (*Abano*, six miles from Padua), marvellous qualities of hot-springs at, ii. 39.

Apparitores, attendants on the great Ministers of War, 114; Joannes, Apparitor, ii. 21; Ferrocinctus, Apparitor, iii. 20.

Applicitarii, officers of arrest, 114; under orders of Commentariensis, 104.

Apulia, Conductores of, despoiled by hostile invaders, i. 16; merchants similarly despoiled, ii. 38; crops from, not forwarded expeditiously, i. 35; corn-merchants of, ii. 26; farms of Thomas in, transferred to his son-in-law Joannes, v. 6, 7; arrears of Siliquaticum in, v. 31.

'Apuli idonei,' viii. 33.

Aqua Claudia, Roman aqueduct, description of, vii. 6.

Aqua Virgo, Roman aqueduct, description of, vii. 6.

Aqueducts of Rome, abuses connected with, iii. 31; glory of, vii. 6.

Aqueduct begun by Bishop Aemilianus must be finished by him, iv. 31.

Aqueduct of Ravenna protected, v. 38.

Aqueduct constructed by Theodoric for City of Parma, viii. 30.

Aquileia, contributions of wine and wheat from, remitted, xii. 26.

Arator, Vir Illustris, sent by Provincials of Dalmatia to Theodoric, viii. 12; made Comes Domesticorum, viii. 12.

Arcadius, Emperor (395–408), change effected by him in relation of Praetorian Praefect to Master of the Offices, 99.

Arcarius, Treasurer or Steward, v. 7; x. 28 (*see* p. 440); xii. 8, 11, 27.

Archery, practice in, for young soldiers, v. 23.

Archiatrus, Arch-Physician, iv. 41 (*see* Comes Archiatrorum).

Architect, duties of, vii. 5.

Architect, Public, Formula for the Appointment of, vii. 15.

Archotamia, 'Illustris Femina,' accuses her grandson's widow of wasting her children's property, iv. 12.

Arelate (*Arles*), remission of taxation to inhabitants of, iii. 32; 'glorious defence of,' iii. 32; its walls to be repaired and its citizens fed, iii. 44; fight for possession of covered bridge at, viii. 10.

Arethusa, Fountain of, site of, near Squillace, 72; qualities of, described, viii. 32.

Argolicus, Vir Illustris, made Praefect of the City of Rome, iii. 11, 12; his ancestry and character, iii. 11, 12; ordered to repair Cloacae of Rome, iii. 30; other references to, iii. 29, 30; iv. 22, 25; iv. 42; his tardiness rebuked, iv. 29; heirs of, defrauded by Theodahad, v. 12.

Arigern, Vir Illustris and Comes, Governor of the new Gaulish Provinces, iv. 16; appointed Comes Urbis Romae (?), iv. 16; instructions to, iii. 45; iv. 23; report by, iv. 43.

Armentarius, Clarissimus, appointed Referendus Curiae, iii. 33; informs against Argolicus, Praefect of the City, iv. 29.

Armourers (Armorum Factores), Formulae of, vii. 18, 19.

Arsenals of Italy, under the Magister Officiorum, 37.

Artemidorus, Illustris and Patrician, a relation of Emperor Zeno, and friend of Theodoric, i. 43; Tribunus Voluptatum (?), i. 43; Praefectus Urbis, i. 42, 44; detects embezzlement by persons employed for repair of walls of Rome, ii. 34; invited to Theodoric's Court, iii. 22.

Assertor Libertatis (of the Theodosian Code, iv. 8), a possible allusion to, iii. 43.

Astensis Civitas (*Asti*), to be especially helped in relief of necessities of Liguria, xi. 15.

Astronomy, reasons derived from, for pensioning off civil servants, xi. 36.

Athala, ancestor of Theodoric, 'mansuetudine enituit,' xi. 1.

Athalaric, grandson of Theodoric, date of birth of, 29 n; accession of (Aug. 30, 526), 37; manner of his education, 42; his death (Oct. 2, 534), 43; letters announcing his accession, viii.

1-7; edict of, ix. 2; his death announced to Justinian, x. 1; praises of, by Cassiodorus, xi. 1.
Athesis (*Adige*), flows past fort of Verruca, iii. 48.
Attila, defeat of, in Catalaunian plains, 28; iii. 1; embassy of Cassiodorus (grandfather of Senator) to, i. 4.
Augiensis, Codex, of 'Anecdoton Holderi,' 73.
Augmentum, super-assessment, remitted by Athalaric for Dalmatia and Suavia, ix. 9; for Syracuse, ix. 10.
Augusta (*Turin*, or *Aosta*), Bishop of, falsely accused of treason, i. 9; fastnesses (clusurae) of, soldiers stationed at, ii. 5.
Augustales, highest class of Exceptores (shorthand writers), 104 *n*, 110; xi. 30.
Augustin, Vir Venerabilis (probably a bishop), brings the scarcity in Venetia under the notice of the King, xii. 26.
Augustus, builder of the Circus Maximus, iii. 51; his survey of the 'Orbis Romanus,' iii. 52.
Aurarii, persons liable to payment of 'lustralis auri collatio,' ii. 26.
Auraria Pensio = probably 'lustralis auri collatio,' ii. 30.
Avenio (*Avignon*), Gothic troops not to molest citizens of, iii. 38.

B.

Bacauda, Vir Sublimis, Tribunus Voluptatum, v. 25.
Bacaudae, insurgent peasantry of Gaul, v. 25.
Baiae, baths of, praises of, ix. 6; xii. 22.
Balthae, royal house of the Visigoths, was Athalaric descended from? viii. 5.
Balzani, Ugo, on Cassiodorus, 121.
Barbarians, checked by fear, not honour, ii. 5.
Barbaria, probably the name of the mother of Romulus Augustulus, 216.
Barbarian Kings, intellects of, subdued by diplomacy, iv. 3; do not use the grammatical art, ix. 21.
Baronius, Cardinal, author of 'Annales Ecclesiae,' quoted, 500 *n*, 511 *n*.
Basilius (No. 1), Vir Spectabilis, claims restoration of his wife's property from Probinus, ii. 10, 11; iv. 40.
Basilius (No. 2), accused of magical practices, iv. 22, 23 (*see* note on p. 246).
Basilius (No. 3, possibly same as No. 2), Opilio connected with him by marriage, viii. 17; concerned in accusation of Boethius (?), 364 *n*.
Baths, gratuitous admission to, at Spoletium, ii. 37; of Turasius, at Spoletium, iv. 24; at Baiae, ix. 6.
Baudi de Vesme, fragments of oration of Cassiodorus (?), published by, 117.
Beatus, Vir Clarissimus and Cancellarius, ordered to supply rations to invalided officer, xi. 10; made Primicerius Augustalium, xi. 30.
Belisarius, Imperial general, his capture of Neapolis, 48; his campaign in Southern Italy, 492; his recovery and loss of Milan, 522; his entry into Ravenna, 51.
Bellum (war), derived from King Belus, i. 30.
Benedict, St., not alluded to by Cassiodorus, 55; relation of his rule to that of Cassiodorus, 57, 59.
Benedictus, a civil officer of some kind in the City of Pedon, guardianship of his children assigned to Theriolus, i. 36.
Bethmann Hollweg, his 'Gerichtsverfassung des sinkenden römischen Reichs,' 41, 95, 109 *n*.
Bigamy, punishment of, according to Edictum Athalarici, ix. 18.
Bina, a kind of tax, iii. 8.
BINA ET TERNA, FORMULAE FOR THE COLLECTION OF, vii. 20, 21, 22.
Birds, habits of, i. 21; the hawk's way of teaching her young to fly, i. 24; the eagle and her young, i. 38; filial piety of the stork, ii. 14; instinct of young partridges towards their mother, ii. 14; the vulture protects little birds from attacks of the hawk, ii. 19; gulls fly inland when they foresee a storm, iii. 48; cranes when about to cross the sea clasp pebbles with their claws, iv. 47; the turtle-dove once widowed never takes another mate, v. 33; flight of cranes suggested to Mercury shapes of letters, viii. 12; thrushes, storks, and doves gregarious, the greedy hawk loves solitude, viii. 31; orderly evolutions of cranes, ix. 2.
Bishops, King Witigis' exhortations to, x. 34; Cassiodorus' exhortations to, xi. 4.

Blue party in the Circus, rivalry of, with the Greens, iii. 51.
Bodily signs by which character may be discerned, vi. 9 (compare also Cassiodorus, 'De Anima,' capp. 10 and 11, referred to p. 53).
Boethius (or Boetius), Illustris and Patrician, receives orders to choose a harper to be sent to Clovis, 23, 24; ii. 40; information as to his life in the 'Anecdoton Holderi,' 74, 79-84; really author of the theological treatises which have passed current with his name, 74, 80-83; and of a 'Bucolic Poem,' 74, 83; difficulty caused by the non-Christian character of his 'Consolations of Philosophy,' 81, 83; consulted as to depreciation of currency, i. 10; ordered to prepare water-clock and sundial for King of Burgundians, i. 45.
Boethius, as to character of Basilius, 246 n; as to character of Decoratus, 267 n; character of his accuser Cyprian, v. 40, 41; viii. 21, 22; character of Opilio, viii. 17.
Boethus, Bishop of Byzacene Province in Africa, author, according to M. Jourdain, of the theological treatises attributed to Boethius, 82.
Bormiae Aquae (Baths of Bormio), Count Winusiad recommended to visit, x. 29.
Brandila, husband of Procula, story of his intrigue with Regina, wife of Patzenes, v. 32, 33.
Breones, a Raetian freebooting tribe living near the Brenner pass, i. 11.
Bribery repressed, xii. 2, 6, 21, 26.
Bridge of boats ordered to be built across the Tiber, xii. 19.
Brosse, Pierre, notes of, on Cassiodorus, 117.
Bruttii and Lucania, Venantius Corrector of, iii. 8, 46, 47; his misgovernment of, 221; the praises of, viii. 31; xii. 15; 'opulenti Bruttii,' viii. 33; gold-mining to be commenced in, ix. 3; abundance of cattle in, xi. 39; measures for relief of, during presence of Gothic army, xii. 5; praise of the wine of, xii. 12; Canonicarii of, rebuked for despoiling the churches, xii. 13.
Buat, Count, on the life and ancestry of Cassiodorus, 118; as to Theodora's share in the murder of Amalasuentha, 433 n.

Burgundians, King of (see Gundibad); cease to be 'Gentiles' under Gundibad, i. 46; boundary of, with Ostrogothic kingdom, iii. 41; dispute with Franks, viii. 10; league with Amalasuentha, xi. 1 (see 456 n); invasion of Liguria and Aemilia, xii. 28; 527.
Butilianus, Presbyter, land allotment given by Theodoric to, in neighbourhood of Trient, ii. 17.

C.

Caduca bona, property to which no heir is forthcoming, and which is therefore claimed by the State, v. 24; vi. 8.
Caelianus, one of the Quinque-viri appointed to try Basilius and Praetextatus, iv. 22, 23.
Calabria, crops from, not forwarded expeditiously, i. 35; regulations for corn-traffic in, ii. 26; arrears of Siliquaticum in, v. 31.
'Calabri peculiosi,' viii. 33.
Calogenitus, sent by Amalasuentha to Justinian with a present of marbles, x. 8, 9.
Campania, practice of *pignoratio* prevalent in, iv. 10; suffers from eruption of Vesuvius, iv. 50; 'industriosa Campania,' viii. 33; Cancellarius of, to pay pension to retiring Primiscrinius, xi. 37; the cupboard of Rome ('urbis regiae cella penaria'), xii. 22.
Campanianus, of Lucania, widow and family of, permitted to step down from rank of Curiales, ix. 4.
Cancellarius an officer of humble rank in the Court of the Praetorian Praefect, 111, 112; origin of the name, 112; his functions described, xi. 6; of Faustus, desired to forward corn from Apulia, i. 35; Beatus (Vir Clarissimus) ordered to supply rations to invalided officer, xi. 10; Gaudiosus, Cancellarius of Province of Liguria, xi. 14; Anatholius, Cancellarius of Samnium, xi. 36; Lucinus, Cancellarius of Campania, xi. 37; Vitalian, Cancellarius of Lucania and Bruttii, xi. 39; admonition to various Cancellarii, xii. 1, 10; Sajones ordered to wait upon Cancellarii, xii. 3; Anastasius, Cancellarius of Lucania and Bruttii, ordered to send cheese and wine for royal table, xii. 12; the same, ordered to be gentle with

the citizens of Rhegium, xii. 14; Maximus, Cancellarius of Lucania and Bruttii, xii. 15.

Canonicarii, tribute-collectors under Comes Rerum Privatarum, vi. 8; to collect the Trina Illatio, xii. 16; of Thuscia, xi. 38; of Venetia, xii. 4, 6; of Bruttii, rebuked for robbing the churches, xii. 13.

Candac, King of Alani, mentioned by Jordanes, 164.

Candax, apparently next of kin to a man slain by Crispianus, i. 37.

Capillati (?) of Suavia, iv. 49.

Capitularii horreariorum et tabernariorum, farmers of revenue derived from granaries and taverns, x. 28.

Caprarius, Mons (situation of doubtful, but near Ravenna), xii. 17; works of defence to be constructed near, xii. 17.

Capuanus, Senator, appointed Rector Decuriarum, v. 21, 22; his character, v. 22.

Cardinalis = chief officer of Court, vii. 31.

Carpentum, official chariot of Praetorian Praefect, vi. 3; of Praefect of the City, vi. 4; of Consularis of a Province, vi. 20.

CARTARIUS (or Cartularius), Clerk in the Record Office, FORMULA APPROVING APPOINTMENT OF, vii. 43.

Cartarii ordered to prepare transfers of property to Theodahad, viii. 23; to receive the wine collected for the royal table, xii. 4.

Casa Arbitana taken from heirs of Argolicus and Amandianus, v. 12.

Casa Areciretina, deed of gift of, from Agapita to Probinus, annulled, ii. 11; this decree revoked, iv. 40.

Cassian, one of the founders of Western Monachism, Cassiodorus' qualified praises of, 55.

Cassiodorus (1), an Illustris, great-grandfather of Cassiodorus Senator, 3; history of, i. 4.

Cassiodorus (2), grandfather of Cassiodorus Senator, Tribunus and Notarius under Valentinian III, his embassy to Attila, 3; history of, i. 4.

Cassiodorus (3), father of Cassiodorus Senator, Comes Privatarum Rerum and Comes Sacrarum Largitionum under Odovacar, 3; Consularis of Sicily, 4; Corrector of Bruttii and Lucania, 4; Praetorian Praefect (cir. 500), 4, 12; Patrician (cir. 504), 4; frequently confused with his son, 11; his praises, i. 3, 4; a man of tried integrity and pure fidelity, i. 26; invited to visit Court of Theodoric, iii. 28.

CASSIODORUS, MAGNUS AURELIUS SENATOR, his position in history, 1, 2; his name, Cassiodorus or Cassiodorius (?), 5; Senator not a title, 5; his birthplace, Scyllacium, 6; date of his birth (cir. 480), 9-12; his love of Natural History, 12; ix. 24; appointed Consiliarius under his father, 12; his panegyric on Theodoric, 13, 16; appointed Quaestor, 14; ix. 24; his special utility, as Quaestor, to Theodoric, 15; his official correspondence, the 'VARIAE,' 16-19, 22-24; statesmanlike insight which led him to second Theodoric's policy, 20, 21; his religious tolerance, 22; duration of his Quaestorship, 25; his Consulship (514), 25; restores harmony between clergy and people of Rome, 25; Patrician, 27; his 'Chronicon,' its defective character, 27-29; his Gothic History, 29-35; ix. 25; appointed Magister Officiorum, 36; ix. 24; his services to the regent Amalasuentha, 38; provides ships and soldiers for the state, 38; appointed Praefectus Praetorio, 39; ix. 24; letters during his Praefecture, 42; continues in office after murder of Amalasuentha, 46; announces the elevation of Witigis, 49; his position during the first five years of the Gothic War, 50; he retires from office (538 or 539 ?), 51; probably did not meet Procopius, 51; edits the 'Variae,' 51, 52; writes the treatise 'De Anima,' 53, 450, 512; his reasons for publishing the 'Variae,' 133-140; letter written by himself to himself on receiving the Praetorian Praefecture, describing his many virtues, ix. 24; letters to the Senate on the same subject, ix. 25; xi. 1; his account of his occupations as Praetorian Praefect, 450; issues his Edict, xi. 8, 9; his own and his ancestors' services to Bruttii and Lucania, xi. 39; his praises of Scyllacium, xii. 15; resides at Ravenna (?) during the war, 506; retires to Scyllacium and founds two monasteries there, 54; probably never Abbot, 56; devotes the leisure of his monks to literature, 57; his relation to the Benedictines, 59; his merits as a transcriber of the Scriptures, 60; his Commentary on the Psalms, 60; on the Epistles, 61; his Tripartite History, 61; his 'Institutiones Divinarum et Humanarum Lectionum,' 62-65; his 'De Orthographiâ,' 65, 66; his death, (575 ?), 66; his knowledge of Greek probably slight, 61; information derived from the 'Anecdoton Holderi' as to his life, 74, 84; editions of his works, 115-121; chronology of the life of, 122-130.

Castellius, Mons, near Scyllacium, monastery founded by Cassiodorus at, 55.

Castorius unjustly deprived of his property by Faustus, iii. 20.

Castrensis, Butler or Seneschal, 88, 91.

Catabulenses, freighters, transport masters, iv. 47; ordered to transport marbles from Pincian Hill to Ravenna, iii. 10.

Catana, walls of, to be repaired with stones of amphitheatre, iii. 49.

Cathalia (?), petition of inhabitants of, as to collection of Tertiae, i. 14.

Catos, the mob of the circus is not precisely a congregation of, i. 27; 'the father of Felix was the Cato of our times,' ii. 3.

Cellaritae, provision dealers (?), x. 28.

Celsina, see Curritana.

Censitores, tax-collectors, ix. 12.

Cethegus, Rufus Petronius Nicomachus, Consul (504), Magister Officiorum, Patrician, probably the person to whom the 'Anecdoton Holderi' was addressed, 76.

Chameleon, appearance and habits of, v. 34.

Chance, the world not governed by, xii. 25.

Chariot-race, effect of, on spectators, iii. 51; picture of, from Cilurnum gem, 231.

Cheese of Mount Sila described, xii. 12.

Chorda, the lyre so called 'quia facile corda moveat,' ii. 40.

Christmas Day (Natale Domini), promotions of Praefect's staff upon, xi. 17.

'Chronicon' of Cassiodorus, faulty character of the work, 28, 29.

Chrysargyron, tax on traders = 'lustralis auri collatio,' ii. 26 n.

Church, Dean, author of article on Cassiodorus, 121.

Cilurnum (*Chesters* in Northumberland), gem found at, representing chariot-race, 231.

Circus, factions of the, i. 20, 27, 30, 31; iii. 51.

Circus Maximus, description of, iii. 51; plan of, 227.

City and country life contrasted, viii. 31.

Civilitas, Theodoric's anxious care for, 20; description of, iv. 33; Theodahad exhorted to observe, iv. 39; for the sake of it even Jews are to be protected, v. 37; references to, iv. 41, 44; v. 31; vi. 5; ix. 14, 18, 19.

CLARISSIMUS, FORMULA CONFERRING RANK OF, vii. 38.

Clarissimus, title of ministers of the third rank, 91; epithet of Clarissimus conferred on all Senators, 91.

Clavicularii, gaolers, 114; under orders of Commentariensis, 104.

Climate, influence of, on character, xii. 15.

Cloacae of Rome, description of, iii. 30.

Clovis (Luduin), King of the Franks, date of letters to, 23, 24; Theodoric marches his troops against (508), i. 24; a harper sent to, chosen by Boethius, ii. 40; congratulated on victory over Alamanni, ii. 41; letter dissuading from war with Alaric II, iii. 3; called 'regius juvenis' by Theodoric, iii. 2; his overthrow of the Alamannic kingdom, 527.

Clusurae, mountain fastnesses, ii. 5, 19.

Codicilli Vacantes, vi. 10.

Coelianus, with Agapitus, seems to have had special jurisdiction in cases affecting Patricians, i. 23, 27.

Coemptio (purveyance) of wheat or lard not to be claimed from the citizens of Rhegium, xii. 14.

Cognitor, trier of causes, viii. 12; ix. 14, 18.

Cohortes, used of civil servants of Praetorian Praefect, xi. 36.

Coloni, apparent case of, reduced to slavery, viii. 28; 'coloni sunt qui agros jugiter colunt,' viii. 31.

Colossaeus, Illustris and Comes, appointed Governor of Pannonia Sirmiensis, iii. 23; pun on his name, iii. 24; rations ordered for him and his suite, iv. 13.

Colosseum described, v. 42.

COMES ARCHIATRORUM, FORMULA OF, vi. 19.
Comes, a Spectabilis, nature of his office (military), 90 n; relation of Comes to his Principes, vii. 25, 28.
COMES DOMESTICORUM (VACANS), FORMULA OF, vi. 11; Arator receives the rank of, viii. 12.
Comes Domorum, his functions, 88.
COMES FORMARUM, FORMULA OF, vii. 6.
COMES GOTHORUM, FORMULA OF, vii. 3; servants of, have oppressed Provincials of Suavia, v. 14; his dignity almost the only one peculiar to the Gothic state, 320.
COMES NEAPOLITANUS, FORMULA OF, vi. 23; reference to, vi. 24.
COMES PATRIMONII, FORMULA OF, vi. 9; references to, iv. 3, 15; Bergantinus as, ordered to transfer property to Theodahad, viii. 23; ordered to commence gold-mining in Bruttii, ix. 3; Willias (Comes Patrimonii) ordered to increase the pay of the Domestici, ix. 13.
COMES PORTUS URBIS ROMAE, FORMULA OF, vii. 9.
COMES PRIMI ORDINIS, FORMULA OF, vi. 12, 13; letter addressed to, ii. 28.
COMES PRINCIPIS MILITUM (?), FORMULA OF, vi. 25.
COMES PROVINCIAE, FORMULA OF, vii. 1.
COMES RAVENNAS, FORMULA OF, vii. 14.
COMES RERUM PRIVATARUM, FORMULA OF, vi. 8; an Illustris, 86; iv. 7; his functions, 89; office of, held by father of Argolicus, iii. 12; held by Senarius (510), iv. 13.
COMES ROMANUS, FORMULA OF, vii. 13.
Comes Sacrae Vestis, Keeper of the Wardrobe, 88.
COMES SACRARUM LARGITIONUM, FORMULA OF, vi. 7; an Illustris, 86; his functions, 88; orders given to, ii. 31; reports remissness of Venantius, iii. 8; office of, held by grandfather of Argolicus, iii. 12; Bina and Terna to be collected under his superintendence, vii. 21; Ambrosius held office of, viii. 13; Opilio, father and son, held office of, viii. 16; Cyprian held office of, v. 40.
COMES SECUNDI ORDINIS, FORMULA OF, vii. 26.
COMES SYRACUSANUS, FORMULA OF, vi. 22 (see also ix. 11, 14).
Comitatus of the King, litigants summoned to, i. 7; iv. 44, 45; v. 12, 32; presence of in Liguria requires extraordinary supply of provisions, ii. 20; the place 'ubi et innocentia perfugium et calumniatores jus possunt invenire districtum,' iv. 9; meant to be a blessing to his subjects, iv. 40; recourse to it by a distant suitor not compulsory, iv. 40; journey of the Heruli to, iv. 45; always ready for redress of grievances, v. 15; Nimfadius journeying to, viii. 32.
Comites of Pavia, iv. 45.
COMITIACUS (officer of the law courts), FORMULA BESTOWING HONORARY RANK ON, vi. 13; Stabularius, Comitiacus, v. 6; Florentinus, Vir Devotus, Comitiacus, viii. 27.
Commentariensis (or Commentarisius), officer in Court of Praetorian Praefect, nature of his functions, 104–106; Cheliodorus appointed, xi. 28.
Commonitorium, iii. 19; vii. 22.
Como, City and Lake of, the praises of, xi. 14.
COMPETITORES, FORMULA CONCERNING, vii. 44.
Compulsor, officer employed to compel payment of taxes, xii. 8.
Compurgation, evidences of a practice similar to, ix. 14 (p. 397).
Computus Paschalis, tract on determination of Easter, attributed to Cassiodorus, 10, 11.
Comum (*Como*), theft of brazen statue at, ii. 35, 36.
Concordia (*Caorle*), contributions of wine and wheat from, remitted, xii. 26.
Conductores, farmers of royal domain, losses of, in Apul'a, i. 16; in Spain, v. 39.
Confiscated property, manner of asserting claims of Crown to, iv. 32.
Consiliarius (Assessor), nature of the office, 12, 13; Cassiodorus appointed to office of, 12.
Constantinople, character of diplomatists of, ii. 6; Cyprian's mission to, v. 41.
Constantius, Bishop, his petition as to spoliation of the Church, iv. 20.
Constantius, a farmer, unjustly reduced to slavery by Tanca, viii. 28.
CONSULARIS, FORMULA OF, vi. 20; of Liguria, xii. 8.
CONSULSHIP, FORMULA OF, vi. 1; of Cassiodorus (514), 25–26; of reigning Emperors, 28 n; of Felix, ii. 1, 2, 3

of Maximus, not to prevent his filling lower offices afterwards, x. 12.

Consuls, Eastern and Western, order of precedence of, in the Fasti, 122.

Consumption cured by milk of the cows on Mons Lactarius, xi. 10.

Corn, restraints on exportation of, i. 34; traffic in, for Southern Italy, regulated, ii. 26; traffic in, from western coast of Italy to Gaul, iv. 5, 7; traffic in, from Spain to Rome, v. 35; forestalling and regrating of, prohibited, ix. 5; sale of, at reduced price, in Liguria and Venetia, x. 27; distribution of, in Rome, xi. 5; sale of, at reduced price, to citizens of Milan, xii. 27.

Cornicularius, his position on the official staff of the Praetorian Praefect, 97; nature of his functions, 97–102; must be chosen from the Augustales, 110; Antianus vacates office of, xi. 18, 19; retired, to be pensioned, xi. 36.

Corrector (lowest grade of Provincial Governor) of Bruttii and Lucania, iii. 8.

Cosilinum (? *Padula*), a city of Lucania, viii. 33.

Costula, a free Goth, complains that servile tasks are imposed on him by Guduim, v. 30.

Cubiculum = royal treasury, v. 44; 'libra cubiculi nostri' = the standard pound, v. 39.

Cunigast (or Conigast), Vir Illustris, evil character of, according to Boethius, 376; ordered to administer justice between Tanca and his poorer neighbours, viii. 28.

Cura Epistolarum, officer charged with copying letters on fiscal matters, 109.

Cura Epistolarum Canonicarum, Constantinian appointed, xi. 23.

CURA PALATII, FORMULA OF, vii. 5.

CURATOR OF A CITY, FORMULA OF, vii. 12.

Curia, called by Antiquity Minor Senatus, ii. 18; vi. 3; ix. 2.

CURIALIS, FORMULA DIRECTING SALE OF PROPERTY OF, vii. 47.

Curiales, condition of, ii. 18; conflict between Curial and Ecclesiastical obligations, ii. 18; have to make good the Senators' deficiencies in payment of taxes, ii. 24; 'sordid burdens' = Curial obligations (?), ii. 28; of Aestunae, iii. 9; penalty on Jovinus for killing a fellow-curial, iii. 47; might be punished with stripes by Praetorian Praefect, vi. 3; oppression of, forbidden by Edictum Athalarici, ix. 2; of Adriana, i. 19; of Catana, iii. 49; of Forum Livii, iv. 8; of Velia (?), iv. 11; of Ticinum, iv. 45; of Suavia, iv. 49; v. 14; of Neapolis, vi. 24; of Liguria, xii. 8; FORMULA ADDRESSED TO, vii. 27; family of, permitted to descend from the Curia, ix. 4.

Currency, wickedness of depreciating, i. 10; vii. 32.

CURRITANA INSULA ET CELSINA (two of the Lipari Islands), FORMULA FOR THE COMES OF, vii. 16.

Cursus Publicus, Postal-service, 37; transferred from Praetorian Praefect to Magister Officiorum, 99, 302; vi. 3, 6; under Regerendarius, 109; letter as to, i. 29; abuses of, to be reformed by the Sajo Gudisal, iv. 47; by Sajo Mannila, v. 5; abuses of, in Spain, v. 39; citizens of Scyllacium not to be harassed by, xii. 15.

Cyprian, Vir Illustris, Count of the Sacred Largesses (524–525), his character and appointment to above office, v. 40, 41; viii. 16; his services as Referendarius, v. 40; his mission to Constantinople, v. 40; his accusation of Albinus and Boethius, 289, 291, 363, 369; raised to honour of Patriciate, viii. 21, 22.

D.

Dahn, Felix (author of 'Könige der Germanen'), quoted, 119, 152, 155, 165, 177, 180, 182, 183, 184, 197, 198, 202, 204, 206, 207, 209, 216, 221, 236, 240, 242, 248, 269, 282, 287, 320, 341, 350 *n*, 353 *n*, 356, 361, 370 *n*, 372, 375, 401, 403, 435, 437 *n*.

Daila, a free Goth, complains that servile tasks are imposed on him by Duke Guduim, v. 30.

Dalmatia, Simeon appointed to collect arrears of taxation from, iii. 25; iron mining in, iii. 25; Epiphanius Consularis of, v. 24; address of Athalaric to Goths settled in, viii. 4; Arator sent on an embassy from Provincials of, to Theodoric, viii. 12; Osuin appointed Governor of, ix. 8, 9.

Danube, River, 'made a Roman stream by Amalasuentha, xi. 1.

Datius, Bishop of Milan, made steward of the King's bounty to the citizens, xii. 27. (For his history, see 522.)

Davus receives sick-leave to visit Mons Lactarius, xi. 10.

Death, the inconvenience of, 'comperimus dromonarios viginti et unum de constituto numero *mortis incommodo* fuisse subtractos,' iv. 15.

Decennonium, Marsh of, drained by Decius, ii. 32, 33.

Decennovial Canal mentioned by Procopius, 188.

Decii, Lay of the, recited at school, iii. 6; family of Liberius and Paulinus descended from, ix. 22, 23.

Decius, Caecina Maurus Basilius, Illustris, ex-Praefect of the City, and ex-Praetorian Praefect, undertakes to drain the Marsh of Decennonium, ii. 32, 33; one of the Quinque-viri appointed to try Basilius and Praetextatus (?), iv. 22, 23.

Decoratus (Vir Devotus), brother of Honoratus, appointed Quaestor, his character and early death, v. 3, 4; conflicting testimony of Boethius and Ennodius as to, 267 *n*; instructions to, as to arrears of Siliquaticum, v. 31.

Decuriae, guilds of copying-clerks, &c., connected with administration of justice, 277.

Defensor, Gothic soldier of a Roman noble, iv. 27, 28.

DEFENSOR OF A CITY, FORMULA OF, vii. 11.

Defensores of Church of Milan, ii. 30; of Aestunae, iii. 9; of the sacrosanct Roman Church, iii. 45; of Catana, iii. 49; of Ticinum, iv. 45; of Suavia, iv. 49; v. 14.

'Defloratis prosperitatibus,' meaning of this phrase, used by Cassiodorus of his Gothic History, 137 *n*.

Degeniatus = (apparently) stripped of official rank, xii. 10.

Delegatoria, warrant for increased rations consequent on promotion, xi. 33, 35.

Denarius, puzzling passage as to relation of to solidus, i. 10.

Deputati, fifteen shorthand writers of the highest class, appropriated to the Emperor's service, 111; xi. 30.

Dertona (*Tortona*), fortification of, i. 17; corn warehouse at, to be opened, x. 27; xii. 27.

Diceneus, philosopher-king of Dacia, perhaps Cassiodorus' ideal of a king, 32.

Dionysius 'Exiguus,' author of our present chronology, a colleague of Cassiodorus in his literary enterprises, 64.

Dionysius of Halicarnassus, chief authority on the Roman chariot-races, 230.

Discussores, assessors of taxes, iv. 38.

Documents not to be tampered with by the Scribe, xii. 21.

Domestici, life-guardsmen attached to the Provincial Governors, to receive larger pay, ix. 13.

Domitian, office of Master of the Horse abolished by, 99.

Domitius, Spectabilis, has received a concession for drainage of land which he is too parsimonious to take full advantage of, ii. 21; complains of seizure of his estates by Theodahad, iv. 39.

Domus Palmata, near the Forum, iv. 30.

Donativum, *see* Largesse.

Drainage concession to Spes and Domitius, ii. 21.

Drill, need of, exemplified, i. 40.

Dromonarii, rowers in express boats, ii. 31; twenty-one dead, iv. 15.

Dromones, express boats, one thousand to be built, v. 16.

Druentia (*Durance*), River, frontier of Ostrogothic and Burgundian Monarchies, 218; provisions for garrisons upon, iii. 41.

Dux, a military officer of the rank of Spectabilis, his relation to the Comes, 90 *n*.

DUX RAETIARUM, FORMULA OF, vii. 4.

E.

Eastern Empire, Amalasuentha's relations with, xi. 1.

Ecclesiastical privileges and immunities, i. 9, 26; ii. 29, 30; iii. 14, 37, 45; iv. 17, 20; viii. 24; ix. 15, 16; x. 26, 34; xii. 13, 20; conflict between Ecclesiastical and Curial obligations, ii. 18.

Ecdicius, sons of, allowed to leave Rome to bury their father, ii. 22.

Edictum Athalarici, ix. 2, 18, 19, 20.

Edictum Theodorici, published by Nivellius, from a MS. belonging to Pithou, 116; punishment for adulterers according to, 283, 403; permission to parents to sell their children, 382 *n*.

Egregii, fifth rank in Imperial service,

92; not mentioned by Cassiodorus, 92.

Elephant, natural history of the, x. 30; brazen images of, in Via Sacra, x. 30.

Eloquence the special product of Rome —'Aliae regiones vina, balsama et olentia thura transmittant: Roma tradit eloquium, quo suavius nil sit auditum,' x. 7.

Endive of Bruttii has not the bitter fibres spoken of by Virgil, xii. 14.

Ennodius, Magnus Felix, Bishop of Ticinum (died 516), information given by, as to Boethius, 79 n; information as to Alamannic refugees, 195; his testimony to character of Decoratus, 267 n; addressed his 'Paraenesis' to Ambrosius, 358.

Epiphanius employed by Cassiodorus to assist him in the compilation of 'Historia Tripartita,' 61.

Eufrasius the Acolyte sold a house at Rome to Pope Simplicius, iii. 45.

Eugenius, Vir Illustris, receives the dignity of Master of the Offices, i. 12, 13; possibly alluded to, viii. 19 (see note).

Euric, King of the Visigoths (466-485), father of Alaric II, taxation in his time, v. 39.

Eustorgius, Bishop of Milan, his petition for protection to Milanese Church granted, ii. 29.

Eutharic, husband of Amalasuentha, Consulship of (519), 27, 28; adopted as son in arms by Justin, viii. 1.

Evans, Arthur J., on the topography of Squillace, 9, 68-72.

Exceptores, shorthand writers, 104, 110, 111; xi. 25; charged a fee for the bad paper which they supplied to suitors, 483 n.

Exormiston, a kind of lamprey (?), xii. 4. 14.

Expeditio, derivation of, i. 17.

F.

Famine, provisions for relief of, x. 27; unusual appearances foreboding the famine of 538, xii. 25; in Liguria to be relieved, xii. 28.

Faustus, Praetorian Praefect, Illustris, rebuked for his delay in sending corn from south of Italy to Rome, 17-19; i. 35; embassy of, to Constantinople (493), 23; Consulship of, 122; severely censured for his oppression of Castorius, iii. 20, 28; sent into the country for change of air, iii. 21; oppression of Joannes (?), iii. 27.

Faustus the younger, son of the above, i. 41; enquiry into character of, on his admission to the Senate, i. 41.

Faventia (*Faenza*), blocks of marble to be forwarded to Ravenna from, v. 8.

Felix III, Pope (526-530), election of, in deference to recommendation of Theodoric, viii. 15.

Felix (apparently a native of Milan), appointed Quaestor (527), viii. 18, 19; his pedigree, viii. 19.

Felix, Vir Clarissimus, accused by Venantius of defrauding the minor Plutianus, i. 7, 8.

Felix, Consul with Secundinus (511), his character and elevation to the Consulship, ii. 1, 2, 3; ordered to give largesse to charioteers of Milan, iii. 39.

Felix, Consul with Taurus (428), 173.

Felix, an assistant (probably Vices Agens), to Cassiodorus in the discharge of his duties as Praetorian Praefect, 450.

Feltria (*Feltre*), inhabitants of, to assist in erection of new city in district of Tridentum, v. 9.

Festus, embassy of, to Constantinople (497), 23; chosen by Agnellus to defend his interests in his absence, i. 15; his claims against Paulinus, i. 23.

Fidei-jussor, guarantor, i. 37; ii. 13; xi. 4.

Filagrius, Vir Spectabilis, petition of, as to his nephew's detention in Rome, i. 39.

'Filius per arma,' adoption of, iv. 2.

Firminus, complaints of, against Venantius, iii. 36.

Fiscus Gothorum, rights of, i. 19; its claims not to be pressed unduly, i. 22.

Fiscus, rights of, as to Castrum Lucullanum, viii. 25; rights of, to estates of deceased persons (Fiscus Caducus), ix. 14.

Fishermen, not to be enlisted for the navy, v. 16; their nets not to be allowed to hinder navigation of rivers, v. 17, 20.

Fishes, natural history of: the echeneis or sucking-fish, 18; i. 35; shell-fish of Indian Ocean, their power of arresting vessels, 18; i. 35; torpedo, its numbing touch, 18; i. 35; dolphins, habits of, iii. 48; echinus, 'that honey of flesh, that dainty of the deep,' iii. 48; the strange habits of the pike and the wrasse, xi. 40; in the fishponds (vivaria) of Scyllacium, xii. 15; the anchorago, exormiston, &c., xii. 4, 14.

Flaminian Way, edict regulating prices upon the, xi. 12; to be put in order for the King's passage, xii. 18.

Flavianus, Virius Nicomachus, Consul Suffectus (394), ancestor of Symmachus, 78; a leader of the heathen party in the Senate, 78; author of a Roman History, 78.

Formulae, reasons given by Cassiodorus for composing, 138.

Fornerius, notes of, on Cassiodorus, 116.

Forojulii (*Cividale*), contributions of wine and wheat from, remitted, xii. 26.

Forum Livii (*Forlì*), inhabitants of, to transport timber to Alsuanum, iv. 8.

Franks, the, dispute of with Burgundians (523), viii. 10; war between Amalasuentha and, xi. 1.

Franz, Adolph, author of 'M. Aurel. Cassiodorius Senator,' 119.

Fraudulent shipowners punished, v. 35.

Frontinus (cir. A.D. 97), author of 'Strategematicon' and 'De Aquaeductibus,' quoted by Lydus, 97.

Frontosus has embezzled a large sum of public money, v. 34; his evasions and slippery character, v. 34.

'Furtivae actiones,' those concerned in, to be punished, v. 39.

Fuscus, appointed Praetorian Praefect by Domitian, 99.

G.

Garet, F. J., his edition of Cassiodorus, 117; his ecclesiastical bias, 217.

Garismatium, a place supplying garum, 514 *n*.

Garum, a kind of sauce, 514 *n*.

Gaul, summons to the Goths to take up arms for invasion of, i. 24; Gemellus appointed Governor of, iii. 16; address to Theodoric's subjects in, iii. 17; remission of taxation in, iii. 32, 40; iv. 19, 36; especial desire of Theodoric for good government of, iii. 38; famine in, to be relieved from Italy, iv. 5, 7; placed under government of Arigern (probably before Gemellus), iv. 16; Gepid troops ordered for defence of, v. 10, 11; peace of, disturbed by Gesalic, v. 43; Athalaric's accession announced to his subjects in, viii. 6, 7.

Gemellus, Senator, appointed Governor of Gaul, iii. 16, 17; instructions to, iii. 32, 41; iv. 12, 19, 21.

Genesius, Vir Spectabilis, directed to reform the sanitary condition of Parma, viii. 30.

Genoa, Jews living at, ii. 27.

Gensemund, an example of fidelity to the Amal race, viii. 9; his history mysterious, 354 *n*.

Gentilis, barbarian, i. 46; ii. 16; viii. 22.

Gentilitas, barbarism, misery of, iii. 17.

Geometry, origin of, iii. 52.

Gepidae, ordered for defence of Gaul, to march peaceably through Northern Italy, v. 10, 11; extraordinarily high rate of pay of (?), v. 11.

Germanus, his complaint against Bishop Peter, iii. 37.

Gesalic, natural son of Alaric II, sheltered by Thrasamund, King of the Vandals, v. 43, 44.

Getae, confusion of, with Goths, 31, 32.

Gibbon, on the 'Variae,' 120; as to character of accusers of Boethius, 365; as to Theodoric's participation in murder of Amalasuentha, 433 *n*.

Gildias, Vir Spectabilis, Count of Syracuse, rebuked for oppression of the Sicilians, ix. 14 (*see* also ix. 11).

Godomar, King of the Burgundians (524–534), 456 *n*.

Gold-mining in Bruttii, ix. 3.

Gothic History of Cassiodorus, estimate of, by its author, 29, 30, 137; ix. 25; purpose of, 30; Jordanes' abstract of, 34.

Gothic law for Gothic men (?), vii. 3; viii. 3; not for Romans, ix. 14.

Goths, delight of in war, i. 24; manner of training young, i. 38; disputes between, and Romans, in Samnium, to be settled by Sunhivad, iii. 13; Pannonia of old the dwelling of, iii. 23; in Picenum and Tuscia evading payment of taxes, iv. 14; ancestors of (Guttones), dealers in amber, 266; in Picenum and Samnium summoned to royal presence, v. 26, 27; free Gothic warriors enslaved, v. 29, 30; degrading services not to be claimed from, v. 39; disputes with Romans, how to be decided, vii. 3; relation of Gothic Comes to his Roman staff, vii. 25; oath between, and Romans on Athalaric's accession, viii. 7; settled at Reate and Nursia, viii. 26; indignant at the murder of Amalafrida, ix. 1; 'Gothorum laus est civilitas custodita,' ix. 14; dissensions between Gothic soldiers and Roman populace, x. 14; raise Witigis on the shield as King, 'indicamus parentes nostros Gothos inter procinctuales gladios, more majorum, scuto supposito, regalem nobis contulisse, praestante Deo, dignitatem,' x. 31.

Gout, a living death, x. 29.

Graius (?), Senatorial rank conferred on, vi. 14.

Grammarians, twelve eminent, quoted by Cassiodorus, 65; salaries of, to be increased, ix. 21.

Granaries in Rome, repair of, iii. 29.

Gravasiani (?), iv. 38.

Green party in the Circus, complaint made by, i. 20; complaint against Theodoric (the Patrician) and Importunus, i. 27; mentioned, i. 32, 33; rivalry of with the Blues, iii. 51.

Gregory of Tours, incompleteness of his history of Clovis, 24.

Gregory the Great, Pope (590-604), as to wine called Palmatiana, 500 n.

Griffins dig for gold, and delight in contemplation of that metal, ix. 3.

GUARD AT THE GATES OF A CITY, FORMULA RESPECTING, vii. 29.

Guardianship of orphans delegated by Theodoric, i. 36; of the young Hilarius not to be protracted, i. 38.

Gudelina, wife of Theodahad, letters of, to Theodora, x. 20, 21, 23; letter of, to Justinian, x. 24; doubtful allusion of, to murder of Amalasuentha, x. 20.

Gudila accused of enslaving Ocer, a blind Goth, v. 29.

Guduim, Sajo, v. 27; Vir Sublimis and Dux, v. 30; accused of imposing servile tasks on Costula and Daila, v. 30.

Gundibad (Gundobad), King of the Burgundians (473-516), Theodoric sends him a water-clock and sundial, i. 45, 46; Theodoric asks him to assist in reconciling Clovis and Alaric, iii. 2; called 'senex' by Theodoric, iii. 2.

H.

Haesti, or Aestii, inhabitants of Esthonia, send present of amber to Theodoric, v. 2.

Hannibal, death of, iii. 47.

Hasdingi (Hasdirigi?), or Asdingi, royal family of the Vandals, honoured by alliance with the Amals, ix. 1.

Heliodorus, a relative of Cassiodorus, Praefect in the Eastern Empire, i. 4.

Helladius, candidate for office of Pantomimist, i. 20; ordered to come forth and amuse the people, i. 32.

Heracleanus, Presbyter, messenger from Justinian to Theodahad, x. 25.

Herminafrid, King of the Thuringians, married to Amalaberga, niece of Theodoric, iv. 1.

Heruli, King of, appealed to by Theodoric to prevent war between Clovis and Alaric, iii. 3; King of, adopted as Theodoric's son by right of arms, iv. 2; to receive provisions at Ticinum on their journey to Ravenna, iv. 45.

Hilarius, a young Goth, grandson of Baion, i. 38; to be allowed to enter on enjoyment of his property, i. 38.

Hilderic, King of the Vandals (523-531), murders Amalafrida, widow of his predecessor, ix. 1.

Histrius (or Historius), ii. 9.

Homer quoted, as to travels of Ulysses, i. 39; as to Priam's request for the body of Hector, ii. 22.

Homo; Theodosius is addressed by Theodahad as *Homo suus*; meaning of the term (?), x. 5.

'Honesta missio' of the Theodosian Code illustrated by v. 36.

Honoratus, Vir Illustris, brother of Decoratus, appointed Quaestor; his character, v. 3, 4.

Hormisdas, Pope (514-523), election of during Consulship of Cassiodorus, 26.

Horses, description of, sent as a present by the King of the Thuringians, iv. 1.

Hostilia, on the Po, place of rendezvous for the dromonarii, ii. 31.

Hot-springs of Abano described, ii. 39.

Hydruntum, or Hydron (*Otranto*), chief seat of the purple manufacture, i. 2.

I.

Ibbas, General of Theodoric in Gaul (perhaps the person to whom iv. 17 is addressed), 253.

Ides of June (June 13th), sailors and ships to meet at Ravenna on, v. 19, 20; eighth day before (June 6th), Goths to come to Ravenna for their largesse upon, v. 26.

ILLUSTRATUS VACANS, FORMULA OF, vi. 11.

Illustres, highest class of Ministers; who belonged to it? 86-90; was an Illustris once, always an Illustris? 89; were the Consuls Illustres? 90.

Illyricum, alleged loss of, under Placidia, xi. 1.

Imperium, used of the Gothic kingdom, xii. 28.

Importunus, Illustris and Consul (509), accused of assaulting the Green party at the Circus, i. 27.

Importunus, Vir Illustris and Patrician, Consul (509), descended from the Decii, iii. 5; incident of the recitation of Lay of the Decii, iii. 5.

Indictions, mode of reckoning by, 123-125; remission of taxes at, i. 16.

Indulgentia, an amnesty to prisoners, xi. 40.

Inquilina persists in harassing Renatus with litigation, iv. 37.

Interpretium not to be exacted from Apulian corn-merchants, ii. 26.

Intestate property of widow claimed by the State, v. 24 (see also vi. 8); property of an African claimed by a fellow-countryman, xii. 9.

Iron, mines of, in Dalmatia, iii. 25; praises of, iii. 25.

Istria, Province of, large harvests of wine, oil, and corn in, xii. 22; extraordinary requisition from, xii. 22; plentiful yield of wine in, xii. 26.

Italy, ought to enjoy her own products, ii. 12; western coast of, exports corn to Gaul, iv. 5.

J.

Januarius, Secretary of Joannes, iv. 32.
Januarius, Assessor of taxes, iv. 38.
Jews, of Genoa, permitted to rebuild but not enlarge their synagogue, ii. 27; their privileges confirmed, iv. 33; synagogue of, at Rome, burned by the mob, iv. 43; Christian servants of, punished for murdering their masters, iv. 43; of Milan, protected from molestation, v. 37.

Joanna, widow of Andreas, intestacy of, v. 24.

Joannes, Vir Spectabilis, Referendarius, receives gift of property at Castrum Lucullanum from Tulum, confirmed by Athalaric, viii. 25.

Joannes, Cancellarius (533-534), xi. 6; appointed Praerogativarius, xi. 27.

Joannes, mortgagee of property of Tupha, iv. 32.

Joannes, Vir Clarissimus, Arcarius (perhaps same as preceding), pays off the debt of his father-in-law Thomas, and takes his property in Apulia, v. 6, 7.

Joannes, Arch-Physician, unjust judgment against, reversed, iv. 41.

John II, Pope (Jan. 1, 533—May 27, 535), letter to, against simony at Papal elections, ix. 15; report from, as to imprisonment of Roman citizens, ix. 17; Cassiodorus sends greeting to, on his promotion, xi. 2.

John complains that the Bishop of Salona has taken 60 tuns of oil from him, iii. 7.

John, Spectabilis, ordered to enquire into abuses connected with aqueducts of Rome, iii. 31.

Jordanes, relation of his book 'De Rebus Geticis' to the Gothic History of Cassiodorus, 34; his quotations from Symmachus' History, 78; as to 'Capillati' among the Getae, 260 n; as to Goths by the Baltic Sea, 266; as to threatened war between Goths and Franks, 402.

Joseph, the Patriarch, office of Praetorian Praefect derived from, vi. 3; alluded to, x. 27; precautions of, against Egyptian famine, xii. 25; his bargain with the starving Egyptians criticised, xii. 28.

Jovinus banished to the Lipari Islands for murder of a fellow-curial, iii. 47.

Judges to visit each town once in the year, and not to claim more than three days' maintenance, v. 14.

Julianus complains of injuries received from the servants of Bishop Aurigenes, iii. 14.

Julian, Count and Illustris, Tata is ordered to conduct recruits to, v. 23.

Justin, Emperor (518-527), Athalaric announces his accession to, viii. 1.

Justinian, Emperor (527-566), his negotiations with Amalasuentha, 43; with Theodahad, 46, 47; Amalasuentha announces her son's death and the association of Theodahad to, x. 1, 2; present of marbles from Amalasuentha to, x. 8, 9; letters of Theodahad to, x. 15, 19, 22, 25, 26; letter of Gudelina to, x. 24; letter of Witigis to, x. 32; his interference on behalf of a heavily taxed monastery, x. 26; on behalf of Veranilda, a Catholic convert, x. 26; petition of Senate to, xi. 13.

L.

Lactarius, Mons (*Monte Lettere*), description of, xi. 10; health-resort for consumptive patients, xi. 10.

Land surveying among the Romans, iii. 52.

Lard not to be exported from Italy, ii. 12.

Largesse (Regalia Dona, Donativum), Goths summoned to Court to receive, on the Ides of June, v. 26, 27; Starcedius' donative stopped on his retirement from service, v. 36.

Laurentius, Presbyter, accused of rifling graves, iv. 18.

Laurentius, Vir Experientissimus, ordered to collect in Istria stores of wine, oil, and corn for Ravenna, xii. 22, 23, 24.

Lawsuits not to be interminable, i. 5.

LEAVE OF ABSENCE, TEMPORARY, FORMULA COMMEATALIS AD TEMPUS, viii. 36.

Lenormant, his work 'La Grande Grèce' quoted, 7, 8, 71.

Leodifrid, *see* under Sajo.

Leontius, Vir Spectabilis, his dispute about boundaries with Paschasius, iii. 52.

Leontius, Praefecture of, 105.

Letters, origin of, from imitation of flight of cranes, viii. 12.

Leucothea, Fountain of, its marvellous qualities, viii. 33.

Liber, derivation of, xi. 38.

Liberius (1), Praetorian Praefect under Theodoric (493-500), 16; ii. 15, 16; his fidelity to Odovacar, ii. 16; conduct in assignment of 'Tertiae,' ii. 16; father of Venantius, ii. 15; arranged gift from Theodoric to ex-Emperor (?) Romulus. iii. 35.

Liberius (2), Spectabilis (possibly son of preceding), complains of unjust judgment by Marabad, iv. 47.

Liberius (3), Senator, sent as ambassador by Theodahad to Justinian, 45.

Liberius (4, probably same as No. 3), Patrician, Praetorian Praefect of the Gauls (526), viii. 6; xi. 1.

Liberius (5), second husband of Aetheria, iv. 12.

Lictor, apostrophised by Cassiodorus in his 'Indulgentia,' xi. 40.

Liguria, Province of, ships ordered from Ravenna to, ii. 20; the Gepidae on their way to Gaul to march peaceably through, v. 10, 11; obscure allusion to troubles in, viii. 16; famine in 'Liguria industriosa' to be relieved by corn-distribution, x. 27; relief of 'devota Liguria,' xi. 15, 16; Consularis of, addressed, xii. 8; invaded by the Burgundians, xii. 28; plunder-raid of Alamanni into, xii. 28; famine in, relieved, xii. 28.

Lime, the praises of, vii. 17.

Lime-kilns, President of, PRAEPOSITUS CALCIS, FORMULA OF, vii. 17.

Lucania, Province of, Ensebius is recommended to take holiday in, iv. 48; rustics of, at Feast of St. Cyprian, viii. 33; Campanianus, inhabitant of, ix. 4; 'Montuosa Lucania' abounded in swine, xi. 39; measures for relief of, during presence of Gothic army, xii. 5. (*See also* Bruttii.)

Lucrine Port (?) to furnish tiles for repair of walls of Rome, i. 25.

Lucullanum, Castrum (*Castel dell Ovo*, at Naples), property at, given by Theodoric to Tulum, and by Athalaric to Joannes, viii. 25 (*see* note, p. 374).

Lydus, Joannes, civil servant in Constantinople under Justinian, author of 'De Dignitatibus;' his account of the dignity of the Praetorian Praefect, 40; on the official staff of the Praetorian Praefect, 94-114; his disappointment with the emoluments of the Cornicularius, 101; as to salutation of Praetorian Praefect, 297; as to Scholares, 302; jealousy of Magistriani, 303; as to supply of paper for law courts, xi. 38.

M.

Maffei, Scipione, author of 'Verona Illustrata,' on situation of Verruca, 224.

Magic, trial of Roman Senators on accusation of practising, iv. 22, 23; punishment of, according to Edictum Athalarici, ix. 18.

MAGISTER OFFICIORUM, FORMULA OF, vi. 6; nature of his office, 36, 37; jealousy between his subordinates and those of the Praefectus Praetorio, 100, 302; Eugenius promoted to office of, i. 12, 13; office of, held by grandfather of Argolicus, iii. 12; as to Cursus Publicus, 99; iv. 47; vi. 6; letter of Witigis to M. O. at Constantinople, x. 33.

MAGISTER SCRINII, FORMULA OF, vi. 13.

Magistriani, officers under Magister Officiorum, jealousy of, felt by members of Praefectoral staff, 303.

Magistri Scriniorum, Spectabiles, 91.

Magnus, a Spectabilis, of Gaul (?), to be reimbursed for losses sustained from the Franks, iii. 18.

Major Domus, Steward of the Royal House; Theodahad calls Vacco 'majorem domus nostrae,' and orders him to superintend the purchase of provisions for Gothic garrison of Rome, x. 18.

Mancipes mutationum, servants at posting-stations, iv. 47.

Maniarius, complaint of, as to abstraction of his slaves by the Breones, i. 11.

Manso, author of 'Geschichte des Ostgothischen Reiches,' quoted, 333, 336, 401.

Mappa, why used to denote the signal for the races, iii. 51.

Marabad, Vir Illustris and Comes, appointed Governor of Marseilles, iii. 34; instructions to, iv. 12, 46.

Marcellinus Comes, chronicler in the reign of Justinian, as to introduction of Heruli into Italy, 258 *n*; as to eruption of Vesuvius, 261 *n*, 262 *n*.

Marcellus on water-finding, iii. 53.

Marcian, Vir Spectabilis, employed to collect grain for Italy in Spain, v. 35.

Marcilianum (*Sala*, in Lucania), viii. 33.

Marinus, his petition about the property of Tupha, iv. 32.

Mark the Presbyter summoned for arrears of Siliquaticum, v. 31.

MARRIAGE, CONFIRMATION OF, AND LEGITIMATION OF OFFSPRING, FORMULA FOR, vii. 40.

MARRIAGE, FORMULA LEGITIMATING WITH FIRST COUSIN, vii. 46.

Marriage law (Edictum Athalarici), ix. 18.

Martinus, his son Romulus accused of parricide, ii. 14.

Massa Palentiana, wrested from rightful owners by Theodahad, v. 12.

Massa, a farm, viii. 23.

Massilia (*Marseilles*), inhabitants of, to welcome Count Marabad, iii. 34; privileges confirmed to, and exemption from taxation granted to for one year, iv. 26.

Master of the Horse, office of, abolished by Domitian.

Matasuentha, granddaughter of Theodoric, married to Witigis, 49.

Maurentius, an orphan, taken under the King's guardianship, iv. 9.

Maximian, Vir Illustris, one of the Quinque-viri appointed to try Basilius and Praetextatus, iv. 22, 23.

Maximus, Flavius Anicius, Vir Illustris, Consul (523), encouraged to reward handsomely the *Venator* in the amphitheatre, v. 42; appointed Primicerius Domesticorum (535), x. 11, 12; married a wife of the Amal race, x. 11; discussion as to his subsequent history, 424 *n*.

Mercury, inventor of letters, viii. 12.

Milan, Church of, immunities granted to, ii. 29, 30; charioteers of, to receive largesse from Felix, iii. 39; Bacauda, Tribunus Voluptatum at, v. 25; Jews of, protected from molestation, v. 37; famine in, to be relieved by Datius, xii. 27; sieges and demolition of, 522.

Militia, used of the purely civil service of the staff of the Praetorian Praefect, 92; ii. 28; obligations of the title, ii. 31; used of service of Tribunus Voluptatum, v. 25; of functions of Count of Sacred Largesses, vi. 7; of functions of Comitiacus, vi. 13.

Militia Litterata, the learned staff, 479.

Millenarius (in Gothic, *thusundifaths*), captain of a thousand, v. 27.

Millet (panicum), to be sold to citizens of Milan at 20 modii per solidum, xii. 27.

Minors, protection of, from fraud, iv. 35.
MINT (MONETA), MASTER OF, FORMULA APPOINTING, vii. 32.
Mommsen, Theodor, severe judgment of, on 'Chronicon' of Cassiodorus, 29, 120.
Monopoly, letters relating to, ii. 26, 30; iii. 19; x. 28.
Montanarius, bearer of money to Bishop Severus, ii. 8.
Mosaic, description of, i. 6.
Moscius, Mons, near Scyllacium, xii. 15.
Mundus, General of Justinian, in Dalmatia, 446 n.
Munitarius (Winithar), ancestor of Theodoric, 'aequitate enituit,' xi. 1.
Music, dissertation on, ii. 40.

N.

Narbonne, Church of, possessions granted by Alaric, wrested from, iv. 17.
Navy, Theodoric's directions as to raising, v. 16, 17.
Neapolis (*Naples*), territory of, suffers from eruption of Vesuvius, iv. 50; FORMULA OF COUNT OF NAPLES, vi. 23; FORMULA addressed HONORATIS POSSESSORIBUS, ET CURIALIBUS CIVITATIS NEAPOLITANAE, vi. 24.
Neotherius, a spendthrift, and brother of Plutianus, i. 7, 8.
Nero, anecdote of, giving the signal for the chariot-race, iii. 51.
Nicephorus Phocas, Emperor of the East (963-969), his work of restoration at Squillace, 71.
Nicomachus, *see* Cethegus.
Nimfadius, Vir Sublimis, his adventure at the Fountain of Arethusa, viii. 32.
Nivellius, Sebastianus, his edition of Cassiodorus, 115, 116.
Nobilissimus, title given to nearest relatives of the Emperor, 85, 86.
Nola, territory of, suffers from eruption of Vesuvius, iv. 50.
Noricum, Provincials of, to exchange their cattle with the Alamanni, iii. 50.
NOTARII, FORMULA OF, vi. 16.
Notitia Utriusque Imperii, general correspondence of, with the 'Variae,' 85; on the official staff of the Praetorian Praefect, 94-114; illustration of the name, xii. 23.
Numerarii, cashiers in the Court of Praetorian Praefect, 96, 108; spoliation of churches of Bruttii alleged to be committed in their name, xii. 13; referred to, xii. 23.
Nursia, the birthplace of St. Benedict, 375; colony of Goths settled at, viii. 26.

O.

Oath, mutual, between Athalaric and his subjects on his accession, viii. 3; between Goths and Romans, viii. 7.
Obsonia (= relishes, anything eaten with bread, especially fish), to be distributed to the Roman people, xii. 11.
Ocer, a blind Gothic warrior, reduced to slavery by Gudila and Oppas, v. 29.
Odovacar (Odoacer), King (476-493), faithful service of Liberius to, ii. 16; possible allusion to times of, iii. 12; buried in a stone chest, 207; Tupha an officer of, 251; moderate taxation under, iv. 38; Opilio filled a place under (?), v. 41.
Officium (official staff) of Praetorian Praefect, 93-114; otherwise called Praetoriani, xi. 37; to be fined if they disobey the King's orders, ii. 26; duties of in collection of Bina and Terna, vii. 21; promotion of, on Christmas Day, xi. 17; their duties and rightful claims, xi. 37.
Opilio, Count of Sacred Largesses, father of Cyprian, viii. 16, 17; chosen for a place in household of Odovacar (?), v. 41.
Opilio, son of above, Count of Sacred Largesses, viii. 16, 17; ambassador from Theodahad to Justinian (535), 45; evil character of, given by Boethius, 363.
Oppas, accused of enslaving Ocer, a blind Goth, v. 29.
Orthography, difficulties of Latin, in Sixth Century, 66.
Ostrogotha, ancestor of Theodoric, 'patientiâ enituit,' xi. 1.
Osuin (or Osum), Vir Illustris and Comes, made Governor of Dalmatia and Suavia, ix. 8, 9.

P.

Padus (*Po*), timber for navy to be collected upon the banks of, v. 17, 20; stake-nets to be removed from mouth of, v. 17, 20.

Palamediaci calculi = draughts, citizens fond of playing at, viii. 31.

Palmatiana, wine of Bruttii, described, xii. 12.

Panis, derivation of, from Pan, vi. 18.

Pannonia Sirmiensis, Colossaeus appointed Governor of, iii. 23, 24; an old habitation of the Goths, iii. 23.

Pantomimist, dispute as to choice of, i. 20; his menstruum (monthly allowance), i. 32, 33.

Papal election, contested between Symmachus and Laurentius (498), 26; of Felix III (526), viii. 15.

Paper, praises of, xi. 38.

Paraveredi, extra horses, v. 39. (*See Errata.*)

Parhippi, extra horses, iv. 47.

Parma, sanitary measures in, viii. 29, 30.

Parricide, the horror of, ii. 14.

Paschasius, Vir Spectabilis, his dispute about boundaries with Leontius, iii. 52.

PATRICIATE, FORMULA OF, vi. 2.

Patricius, Vir Illustris, appointed Quaestor by Theodahad, x. 6, 7.

Patzenes, husband of Regina, story of his wife's intrigue with Brandila during his absence on Gaulish campaign, v. 32, 33.

Paula, an orphan, taken under the King's guardianship, iv. 9.

Paulinus, Illustris and Patrician, claims of Festus and Symmachus against, i. 23 [N.B. Compare the following passage from Boethius' 'Philosophiae Consolatio' i. 4: 'Paulinum consularem virum cujus opes palatini canes jam spe atque ambitione devorassent, ab ipsis hiantium faucibus traxi.' Considering the relationship between Boethius and Symmachus, it is impossible that Symmachus could be one of these 'palatini canes,' but perhaps not impossible that Festus may be here aimed at. Paulinus was Consul 498]; Felix is praised for cultivating the friendship of, ii. 3; allowed to repair and appropriate public granaries, iii. 29.

Paulinus (Flavius Theodorus Paulinus Junior), Vir Clarissimus, son of Venantius, grandson of Liberius, chosen Consul for 534, ix. 22.

Peace, praises of, i. 1.

Pedatura, length of wall assigned to be built by soldiers, v. 9.

Pedonensis Civitas (situation unknown), Benedictus a citizen of, i. 36.

Peraequatores, regulators of prices of provisions (?), vi. 6.

Perfectissimi, fourth grade in the Imperial service, 92, 320; not mentioned by Cassiodorus, 92.

Pervasio, forcible appropriation of landed property, condemned by Edict of Athalaric, ix. 18.

Peter, Consul (516) and rhetorician, ambassador from Justinian to Theodahad, 46, 47; x. 19, 22, 23, 24.

Petrus, Vir Spectabilis, illustrious by descent, allowed to enter the Senate, iv. 25; his troubles with the Sajo assigned to him as his Defensor, iv. 27, 28.

Physician, duty of a good, vi. 19.

Picenum, Province of, Goths resident in, iv. 14; v. 26, 27.

Pietas = pity (very nearly), iv. 26.

Pignoratio, lawless practice of, described and repressed, iv. 10.

Pincian Hill, *see* Rome.

Pithoeus (Pierre Pithou), editor of Cassiodorus, attributes to him the 'Computus Paschalis,' 11.

Placentia, provision dealers at, x. 28.

Placidia, unfavourable comparison of with Amalasuentha, xi. 1.

Planets, periods of, xi. 36.

Pliny, on amber, 266; on the elephant, 443.

Plutianus, a minor, Felix accused of defrauding, i. 7, 8.

Pola, Antonius, Bishop of, iv. 44.

Pollentia, battle of, represented as Gothic victory by Cassiodorus, 28.

Polyptycha, official registers, v. 14, 39.

Pompeius Magnus, theatre of, the origin of his epithet, iv. 51.

Pontonates (?), iv. 38.

Popes, *see* Agapetus, Felix III, Gregory the Great, John II, Symmachus, Vigilius.

Porticus Curba (or Curiae), near the Forum, 'fabricae' to be erected above, iv. 30.

Portus (*Porto*), quays and warehouses of, under the Praefectus Urbis Romae, 87; 'Portus Curas Agens,' ii. 12; Comes Portus, vii. 9; Vicarius Portus, vii. 23.

Possessores, ii. 25; vi. 8; of Aestunae, iii. 9; of Arles, iii. 44; of Velia, iv. 11.

Possessores Honorati, of Catana, iii. 49; of Forum Livii, iv. 8; of Feltria, v. 9; of Suavia, v. 14, 15; of neighbourhood of Ravenna (?), v. 38; of Sicily, vi. 22; of Neapolis, vi. 24.

POSSESSORES HONORATI, ET CURIALES, FORMULA ADDRESSED TO, vii. 27; of Parma, viii. 29; of Bruttii, exhorted to return to their cities, viii. 31.

Possessores, Curiales permitted to become, ix. 4; complain of abuses in corn-traffic, ix. 5.

Potteries (figulinae), owners of, safeguarded, ii. 23.

Praebendae, apparently = stipendia or annonae, 219; claimed both in money and kind, v. 39.

PRAEFECTUS ANNONAE, FORMULA OF, vi. 18; office of, held by Paschasius, xii. 9.

PRAEFECTUS PRAETORIO, FORMULA OF, vi. 3; FORMULA AS TO SUPERINTENDENCE OF ARMOURERS, vii. 19; dignity of the office, 39-41, 134; quotation from Lydus as to, 40; his functions described by Bethmann-Hollweg, 41 n; gradations of rank in his official staff, 93-114; fine on, for disobeying King's orders, ii. 26; not to be allowed to oppress men in humbler station, iii. 20, 27; as to Cursus Publicus, 99; iv. 47; vi. 3; Albienus appointed (527), viii. 20; was Trigguilla his predecessor? 368.

PRAEFECTUS URBIS ROMAE, FORMULA OF, vi. 4; an Illustris, 86; his functions described, 87, 88; to punish insults against the Senate, i. 30, 31; Artemidorus raised to dignity of, i. 42; Argolicus raised to dignity of (510), iii. 11; Quinque-viri associated with him for trial of Senators, iv. 22, 23; his close companionship with the Praefectus Annonae, vi. 18; Honorius ordered to see to preservation of brazen elephants at Rome, x. 30.

PRAEFECTUS VIGILUM URBIS ROMAE, FORMULA OF, vii. 7.

PRAEFECTUS VIGILUM URBIS RAVENNATIS, FORMULA OF, vii. 8.

Praepositus Sacri Cubiculi, an Illustris, 86; his functions, 88; to refund to Symmachus expense of restoration of Pompey's Theatre, iv. 51.

Praepositi (?) have special rights as to the Cursus Publicus, v. 5.

Praerogativarius (?), Joannes appointed, xi. 27.

PRAESES PROVINCIAE, FORMULA OF, vii. 2.

Praetextatus, a Roman Senator, accused of magical practices, iv. 22, 23.

Prescription, title by, i. 18; ii. 27; v. 37.

Prices, to be fixed by the Defensor of a city, vii. 11; by the Curator, vii. 12; tariff of, to be charged at Ravenna, xi. 11; regulated along the Flaminian Way, xi. 12; fixed in Bruttii and Lucania, xii. 5; tariff of, for Istria, xii. 22, 23; of corn sold for relief of Ligurians in time of famine, x. 27; xii. 27.

Primicerius Augustalium, Beatus appointed, xi. 30 (see Augustales).

Primicerius Cubiculariorum, a Spectabilis, 88; his functions, 88.

Primicerius Deputatorum, Ursus appointed, xi. 30; (see Deputati).

Primicerius Domesticorum, Maximus appointed, x. 11, 12.

Primicerius Exceptorum, chief of shorthand writers, Patricius appointed, xi. 25.

Primicerius Notariorum, vi. 16; a Spectabilis, 91; his office (apparently) joined to that of Count of Sacred Largesses, vi. 7.

Primicerius Singulariorum, Pierius appointed, in the room of Urbicus, xi. 31, 32 (see Singularii).

Primiscrinii, officers of Court of Praetorian Praefect, 96, 103; perhaps equivalent to Adjutores, 103; might be chosen from the ordinary Exceptores, 110; retiring Primiscrinius receives rank of Spectabilis, xi. 20; Andreas obtains rank of, xi. 21; retiring Primiscrinius to receive pension, xi. 37.

Princeps, head of the Officium of the Praefectus Praetorio, nature of his office, 96, 97, 477 n; ex-Princeps, ii. 28; title of, given to Magistriani, vi. 6; FORMULA RECOMMENDING PRINCIPES TO COMES, vii. 25; FORMULA ANNOUNCING APPOINTMENT OF COMES TO PRINCEPS, vii. 28.

Princeps Augustorum, 96; xi. 35.

Princeps Magistrianorum, 97, 99, 100.

PRINCEPS DALMATIAE, FORMULA OF, vii. 24.

PRINCEPS URBIS ROMAE, FORMULA OF, vii. 31.

Prior, a military officer among the Goths, viii. 26; perhaps equivalent to 'Hundafath,' 375.

Probinus (or Provinus), Illustris and Patrician (perhaps same as Consul

489), obtains property by undue influence from Agapita, ii. 11; the transfer declared to be bonâ fide, iv. 40.
Probus, Assessor of taxes, iv. 38.
PROCERES PER CODICILLOS VACANTES, FORMULA OF, vi. 10.
Proceres Chartarum (?), subordinate to Count of Sacred Largesses, vi. 7.
Procopius, his narrative of events in Italy in 534 and 535, 42–48; makes no mention of the name of Cassiodorus, 51; his statement of Justinian's argument as to the position of Theodoric, 143 n; his account of family of Venantius, 221; attributes the death of Amalasuentha to Theodora, 433 n; quoted, 370 n, 384 n, 390, 397, 431, 434, 518, 522, 527.
Procula, wife of Brandila, her assault on Regina, v. 32.
Prorogatores, purveyors (?), x. 28.
Prosecutores frumentorum, petition of, as to loss of cargoes, iv. 7.
Provincials, compensation to, for damage done by troops on march, ii. 8.
Publianus, Vir Illustris, messenger from the Senate to Court at Ravenna as to election of Pope (526), viii. 15.
Public property assigned on condition of improvement, vii. 44.
Pulveratica (dust-money) not to be paid to a Judge on his journeys, xii. 15.
Purple dye, history of the discovery of, i. 2.
Pyctacium (pictacium or pittacium), delegatoris, bond or document of title, i. 18; iii. 35; xii. 20.
Pythias, Count, pronounces decree in favour of liberty of Ocer, a blind Goth, v. 29.

Q.

QUAESTOR, FORMULA OF, vi. 5; duties of the office of, 14, 135; v. 4; vi. 5; other Quaestors besides Cassiodorus between 501 and 510, 25 n; Ambrosius appointed (526), viii. 13; Felix appointed (527), viii. 18; Patricius appointed (534), x. 6.
Quidila, son of Sibia, made 'Prior' of the Goths in Reate and Nursia, viii. 26.
Quinque-viri associated with Praefectus Urbis to try two Senators accused of magical arts, iv. 22, 23.

R.

Raetia (Grisons and Tyrol), Servatus, Duke of, i. 11; Alamannic refugees received in, ii. 41; guarded by fortress of Verruca, iii. 48; duties of the Duke of, vii. 4; derivation of the name from rete, vii. 4.
Rationales, bailiffs superintending the royal estates under the Comes Rerum Privatarum, vi. 8.
Rationalii, persons charged with distribution of the annona, 114.
Rations for three days only, to be given to Provincial Governors and others journeying to Scyllacium, xii. 15.
Ravenna, Basilica of Hercules (?) at, i. 6; mosaic ordered for, i. 6; ships ordered round from, to Liguria, ii. 20; favour bestowed on Church of, ii. 30; marbles to be transported to, iii. 9, 10; marble chests in which the citizens of Ravenna buried their dead, iii. 19; blocks of marble to be forwarded from Faventia to, v. 8; fleet to be mustered at, v. 17, 19; aqueduct of, to be kept clean, v. 38; drinking water of, de-appetising, v. 38; police of, vii. 8; elevation of Athalaric at, viii. 2, 5; provision dealers at, x. 28; tariff of prices at, xi. 11; siliquatarius of, xii. 17; defences of, to be strengthened, xii. 17; Deusdedit, a Scribe of, xii. 21; wine, oil, and corn to be furnished by Provincials of Istria to, xii. 22, 23, 24.
Reate (Rieti, in the Sabine territory), Goths settled at, viii. 26.
Rector Decuriarum, Governor of Guilds, v. 21, 22; same as Judex Decuriarum of Theodosian Code, 278.
RECTOR PROVINCIAE, FORMULA OF, vi. 21.
Referendi Curiae, Armentarius and his son Superbus appointed, iii. 33.
REFERENDARIUS, FORMULA OF, vi. 17; Cyprian's services as, v. 40, 41; viii. 22; Joannes, Vir Spectabilis, holds the post of, viii. 25.
Regerendarius (or Regendarius), officer charged with regulation of the postal-service, 109; Cartherius appointed, xi. 29.
Regina, wife of Patzenes, her intrigue with Brandila, v. 33; assaulted by Brandila's wife, v. 32.

Religious toleration practised by Theodoric, 21, 22; principle of, stated, ii: 27; v. 37; x. 26.

Remission of taxes, i. 16.

Renatus complains that he is harassed by litigation of Inquilina, iv. 37.

Reparatus, brother of Pope Vigilius, appointed Praefect of the City, ix. 7; his subsequent history, 390.

Restitutio in integrum, 252.

Retentator, a wrongful detainer, ii. 10.

Rhegium (*Reggio*), derivation of the name, xii. 14; the citizens of, to be exempt from 'coemptio' of wheat and lard, xii. 14.

Roccella, near Squillace, probable site of Scyllacium, 68.

Roman law only to be administered between Romans, ix. 14.

Roman citizens, release of, imprisoned on suspicion of sedition, ix. 17.

Rome, Theodoric's measures for embellishment of, i. 21; ii. 7; walls of, to be repaired, i. 25, 28; ii. 34; the nephews of Filagrius detained at, for their education, i. 39; 'everyone's country,' i. 39; blocks of marble lying about in, to be used, ii. 7; sons of Ecdicius detained at, ii. 22; marbles on the Pincian Hill to be transported to Ravenna, iii. 10; repair of granaries in, iii. 29; Cloacae of, iii. 30; repair of aqueducts and temples in, iii. 31; vii. 6; sons of Valerian detained at, iv. 6; new buildings overlooking Forum of, iv. 30; 'turris circi et locus amphitheatri' wrested from sons of Volusianus, iv. 42; burning of Jewish synagogue at, iv. 43; theatre of Pompey restored by Symmachus, iv. 51; to receive supplies of corn from Spain, v. 35; brazen elephants in Via Sacra, x. 30; police of, vii. 7; statues of, vii. 13, 15; dissensions between citizens of, and Gothic troops (535), x. 14; a Gothic garrison for, x. 18; owns the shrines of the Apostles, xi. 2; scarcity in, relieved by corn-distributions, xi. 5; Roman citizens, and they only, to receive *obsonia*, xii. 11; high character given to the Roman populace, xii. 11.

Romulus, assured that Theodoric's gift to him through the Patrician Liberius shall not be revoked, iii. 35; probably this is the ex-Emperor Romulus Augustulus, 216; subsequent disposal of his palace, the Lucullanum, 374.

Romulus accused of murder of his father, ii. 14.

Rufinus, Praetorian Praefect under Arcadius, his usurpation caused some of Praetorian Praefect's powers to be transferred to the Magister, 99.

Rusticiana, farm of, in Bruttii, gold discovered at, ix. 3.

Rusticus, a priest and a friend of Theodahad, sent on return embassy with Peter to Justinian, 431 *n*; x. 20, 24.

S.

Sabinus, ex-Charioteer, his pension increased, ii. 9.

Sacrilege, the folly of, xii. 13.

St. Cyprian's fair (in Lucania) described, viii. 33.

Sajo, Saio, or Sajus (henchman), description of his office, 177 *n*; to go straight to object of his mission, and not to make pleasure tours at the public expense, iv. 47; Nandius, sent to summon Goths to war, i. 24; to support Ecdicius in levying Siliquaticum, ii. 4; Fruinarith to enquire into conduct of Venantius, ii. 13; Grimoda ordered to redress the oppression of Faustus, iii. 20; Leodifrid ordered to superintend building of houses near fort Verruca, iii. 48; Amabilis (?) ordered to superintend grain traffic from Italy to Gaul, iv. 5; Gesila ordered to make Gothic defaulters in Picenum and Tuscia pay their taxes, iv. 14; Tezutzat assigned as Defensor to Petrus, iv. 27; Amara has wounded Petrus, whose Defensor he nominally was, iv. 27, 28; Duda (Vir Spectabilis and Comes), instructions to, iv. 28, 32, 34; Gudisal ordered to reform abuses of *Cursus Publicus*, iv. 47; Mannila receives like instructions, v. 5; Veranus to see that the Gepidae march peaceably through Liguria, v. 10; Gudinand and Avilf ordered to muster sailors and collect timber for navy, v. 19, 20; Tata ordered to conduct recruits to Count Julian, v. 23; Guduim ordered to summon Gothic captains to Court, v. 27; Catellus and Servandus (?), 'Viri Strenui,' to collect fines from fraudulent shipowners, v. 35; a Sajo (unnamed) accused of rough treatment of a deacon, viii. 24; Dumerit sent to repress robbery at Faventia, viii. 27; Quidila sent with Athalaric's orders to Sicily, ix. 10; to execute vengeance on Pervasores, ix. 18; BOND FOR PROPER USE OF SAJO'S SERVICES, FORMULA OF, vii. 42; was he necessarily the instrument by which 'tuitio regii nominis' was given? 341; Sajones assigned to various Cancellarii, xii. 3; their duties and temptations, xii. 3; Paulus, Vir Strenuus, perhaps a Sajo, xii. 26.

Salamander, nature of, iii. 47.

Salona (in Dalmatia), inhabitants of, to be armed and drilled, i. 40; Bishop of, takes 60 tuns of oil from one John, iii. 7.

Salt-works at Venice, xii. 24.

Samaritans contest possession of a house in Rome with the Roman Church, iii. 45.

Samnium, Province of, Sunhivad appointed Governor of, iii. 13; practice of *pignoratio* prevalent in, iv. 10; Goths resident in, v. 26, 27; Anatholius, Cancellarius of, xi. 36; retiring allowance of Cornicularius charged on revenues of, xi. 36.

Sarsena (?), Curia of, ii. 18.

Scholares, household troops, under Magister Officiorum, v. 6.

Scholaris, Sextus (?), Justus appointed, xi. 26.

Schubert, von, author of 'Unterwerfung der Alamannen,' 120, 524, 527.

Science, list of Greek men of, whose works were translated by Boetius, i. 45.

Scribe, importance of the office of, xii. 21.

Scrinia, the four, under the Magister Officiorum, 36, 112; to provide themselves with paper, xi. 38.

Scriniarii, vii. 21, 22.

Scriniarius, 106.

Scriniarius Curae Militaris, 109; Lucillus appointed, xi. 24.

Scrinium Memoriae, 102.

Scriniarius Actorum, Catellus obtains rank of, xi. 22.

Scyllacium (*Squillace*), birthplace of Cassiodorus, 6; the Greek colony, Scylletion, 6, 7; Roman colony, Minerva Scolacium, 7, 8; appearance of, 8; xii. 15; modern remains at, 9; Cassiodorus founds his monasteries at, 55; topography of, 68-72; citizens of, not to be called on to contribute to the *Cursus Publicus*, xii. 15.

Scythian, vagueness of the term, which was often applied to the Goths, 31, 32.

Senarius, Vir Illustris, appointed Comes Patrimonii, iv. 3, 4; instructions to, as Comes Privatarum Rerum, iv. 7, 11, 13.

Senate of Rome, attitude of Theodoric and Cassiodorus towards, 26, 27; flattery of, i. 13, 42; iii. 12; v. 41; not to degrade themselves by altercations with the mob in the Circus, i. 27, 30; enquiry into character of candidates for admission to, i. 41; iv. 25; Senators' taxes in arrear, ii. 24; Senators with Gothic names, ii. 29, 35; iii. 13; proceedings on trial of Senators, iv. 22, 23; vi. 21; addressed on election of Pope Felix III, viii. 15; Theodahad's elevation announced to, x. 4; chidden by Theodahad for not accepting his invitation to Ravenna, x. 13; Theodahad announces arrival of Gothic garrison to, x. 18; ordered by Theodahad to communicate with Justinian, x. 19; Cassiodorus writes to, on his elevation to the Praetorian Praefecture, xi. 1; petition of, to Justinian for peace, xi. 13.

SENATOR, FORMULA CONFERRING THE RANK OF, vi. 14.

Severinus (or Severianus), Vir Illustris, appointed a Commissioner for Province of Suavia, to remedy financial abuses, v. 14, 15; again sent to Suavia and Dalmatia with Osuin, ix. 9.

Severus, Vir Spectabilis, apparently Governor of Bruttii and Lucania, viii. 31-33.

Sextarius, corn measure, ii. 26.

Sicily, inhabitants of, suspicious, and with difficulty won over to the rule of Theodoric, i. 3; Filagrius, a citizen of Syracuse, asks leave to return to, i. 39; possessions of Milanese Church in, ii. 29; Valerian, a citizen of Syracuse, allowed to return thither, iv. 6; FORMULA OF COUNT OF SYRACUSE, vi. 22; *augmentum* imposed by Theodoric remitted by Athalaric, ix. 10, 11, 12; oppressive acts of Censitores and Count of Syracuse rebuked, ix. 11, 14.

Sidonius, Apollinaris, possible quotation from, iii. 16.

Sigismer, Illustris and Count, sent to administer to the Senate the oath of fidelity to Athalaric, viii. 2.

Signine Channel, near Ravenna (?), shrubs growing in, to be rooted up, v. 38.

Sila, Mount, in Bruttii, celebrated for its cheese, xii. 12.

Silentiarii, thirty life-guards, 88.

Siliqua, one-twenty-fourth of solidus, 173.

Siliquaticum, a tax of one-twenty-fourth on sales in open market, collection of, ii. 4; exemption from, ii. 30; iv. 19; collection of arrears of, in Dalmatia, iii. 25; collection of arrears of, in Apulia and Calabria, v. 31.

Siliquatarii, ii. 12, 26; xii. 17.

Simeon, Vir Illustris and Comes, appointed to collect arrears of taxation in Dalmatia, iii. 25, 26.

Simeonius (an Apulian or Calabrian), summoned for arrears of Siliquaticum, v. 31.

Simony practised at Papal elections, edict against, ix. 15, 16.

Simplicius, Pope (468–483), bought a house at Rome claimed by the Samaritans, iii. 45.

Singularii, servants charged with conveying the orders of the Praetorian Praefect into the Provinces, 113; origin of their name, 113. (See also, xi. 31, 32.)

Sipontum in Apulia, merchants of, despoiled by Byzantine fleet (?), ii. 38.

Sirmium, war of (504), Tulum's services in, viii. 10; Cyprian's services in, viii. 22.

Slave of a Senator, murderer of a freeborn citizen, to be surrendered, i. 30; as to levy of slaves for the navy, v. 16; Gothic soldier made a slave wrongfully, v. 29; degrading services (servitia famulatus) not to be claimed of freeborn Goths, v. 30, 39; Tanca is accused of unjustly enslaving two rustic neighbours, viii. 28.

Slaves, runaway, to be restored to their owners, iii. 43; did free Italians sell their children as? viii. 33 *n.*

Solidus, 'the ancients wished that it should consist of 6,000 denarii' (?), i. 10.

Sona, Illustris, iii. 15.

Sontius (*Isonzo*), River of, Theodoric's crossing of, made an era in lawsuits as to landed property, i. 18; the Lucristani (?) on, ordered to attend to the Cursus Publicus, i. 29.

Sors, land-allotment, ii. 17.

Sors nascendi of the Curialis, ii. 18.

Spain, to send corn-supplies to Rome, v. 35; abuses in administration of, to be repressed, v. 39.

Spatarius, sword-bearer, an officer in the royal household, iii. 43.

Spectabiles, second class of Ministers, who belonged to it? 90, 91; honour of, conferred on Stephanus, ii. 28; Comes Primi Ordinis, highest of, vi. 12; FORMULA CONFERRING RANK OF, vii. 37; Antianus, ex-Cornicularius, receives rank of, xi. 18; retiring Primiscrinius receives rank of, xi. 20.

Spes, Spectabilis, has a concession for draining land, ii. 21.

Spoletium (*Spoleto*), gratuitous admission to baths at, ii. 37; rebuilding behind the Baths of Turasius at, iv. 24; Honoratus, advocate at, v. 4.

Staletti, near Squillace, near the site of Vivarian Monastery, 71.

Starcedius, Vir Sublimis, allowed to retire from military service, but without a pension, v. 36.

Statue, theft of brazen, at Comum, ii. 35, 36.

Statues, care of, at Como, ii. 35, 36; at Rome, vii. 13, 15.

Ste Marthe, Denys de, author of 'Vie de Cassiodore,' 118.

Stephanus, killed by his servants and left unburied, ii. 19.

Stephanus, petition of, against Bishop of Pola, iv. 44.

Stratonicea, Edict of, by Diocletian, 'de pretiis venalium rerum,' 470.

Style, Cassiodorus on the different kinds of, 139.

Suarii, pork-butchers, subject to Praefectus Annonae, vi. 18.

S(u)avia (*Sclavonia*), Fridibad appointed Governor of, iv. 49; order to be maintained in, iv. 49; grievances of the Possessores of, to be redressed, v. 14; Osuin appointed Governor of, ix. 8, 9.

Subadjuvae, deputy cashiers (?), 109.

Sublimis, epithet used in the 'Variae,' 91 n; equivalent to Spectabilis (?), 91.
Suevi (perhaps here the same as Alamanni) invade the Venetian Province (536), xii. 7.
Sulcatoriae (?), some kind of merchant ships, ii. 20.
SUMMONS, LETTERS OF, TO THE KING'S COURT, FORMULAE EVOCATORIAE, vii. 34, 35.
Sundial, description of, to be made by Boetius for Gundibad, i. 45.
Superbus, son of Armentarius, appointed Referendus Curiae, iii. 33.
Sustineo, technically used of the King's reception of his guests, iii. 22 (and 28).
Swords, description of, sent by King of the Vandals to Theodoric, v. 1.
Symmachus, Pope (498-514), contested election with Laurentius, 26.
Symmachus the Elder, orator and leader of the Pagan party in the Senate, 78; was he also a historian? 78.
Symmachus, Q. Aurelius Memmius, Consul (485), Patrician, father-in-law of Boethius, information as to, in the 'Anecdoton Holderi,' 74, 77-79; his speech for the 'Allecticii,' 78; his Roman History, 78; his claims against Paulinus, i. 23; one of the Quinque-viri appointed to try Basilius and Praetextatus, iv. 22, 23; commended for his restoration of buildings in Rome, iv. 51; a saying of, xi. 1.

T.

Table of the King, provision of delicacies for, vi. 9; xii. 4, 18.
Tabularii, Cashiers of a municipality, a lower class of Numerarii, 108.
Tacitus, on amber, quoted, v. 2.
Tanca, a Goth (?), accused of unjustly enslaving free rustics, viii. 28.
Tarvisium (*Treviso*), corn-warehouse at, to be opened, x. 27.
Taxation, arrears of, ii. 24, 25; iv. 14; v. 31; immunity from, ii. 30; remissness in tax-collectors condemned, iii. 8; xii. 10; remission of, for citizens of Arles, iii. 32; remission of, for all Provincials of Gaul, iii. 40; iv. 19; remission of, for one year, for citizens of Marseilles, iv. 26; weight of, to be lessened, iv. 38; regulation of, for Province of Suavia, v. 14, 15; abuses of, in Spain, corrected, v. 39; collection of *Bina* and *Terna*, vii. 20-22; remission of super-assessment for Dalmatia, ix. 9; similar remission for Sicily, ix. 10, 11, 12; remission of, for a monastery, x. 26; proper manner of collecting, xi. 7; correction of abuses of, in Liguria, xi. 16; commutation of cattle-tax for Lucania and Bruttii, xi. 39; taxes to be paid punctually, xii. 2; in Lucania and Bruttii in time of war, xii. 5; remission of, for Venetia, on account of invasion of the Suevi, xii. 7; tax-gatherer allowed to make prepayment of his taxes, xii. 8; *Trina Illatio* to be collected regularly, xii. 16; special requisition from Istria, xii. 22, 23; contributions from Venetia remitted, xii. 26; remission of half of, for Liguria, xii. 28.
TAXES, FORMULA FOR REMISSION OF, WHERE THE TAXPAYER IS TOO HEAVILY ASSESSED, vii. 45.
Teias, King of the Goths (552-553), his battle with Narses on Monte Lettere, 468 n.
Tenues = the poor, ii. 24, 25.
Terna, a kind of tax (not to be confounded with the Tertiae or the Trina Illatio), iii. 8; collection of, vii. 20, 21, 22.
Terracina, inscription at, as to draining Marsh of Decennonium, 188.
Tertiae, probably either the land assigned to the Goths in Italy or the pecuniary equivalent paid by the Roman possessor for an undivided 'Sors Barbarica,' 152; (tax), to be collected at same time as ordinary tribute, i. 14; (land), demarcation of, by Liberius, ii. 16; (tax), immunity from, ii. 17.
Theodagunda, Illustris Foemina, apparently a Gothic princess, ordered to do justice to Renatus, iv. 37.
Theodahad, nephew of Theodoric, associated in the sovereignty by Amalasuentha, 44; x. 1-4; his character, 44; he dethrones Amalasuentha (April 30, 535), and puts her to death, 45; his negotiations with Justinian, 47; his deposition and death, 49; style of address in the 'Variae,' 86; ordered to undertake a case of contu-

macy, iii. 15; his avarice condemned, iv. 39; v. 12; to receive farms which had belonged to his mother, viii. 23; declares that his character has changed with his accession, x. 5; chides the Senate for their suspicions of him, x. 13; thinks himself much superior to Theodoric, x. 22; intended journey of, to Rome, xii. 18, 19; his questionable generosity in releasing his mortgage on the Church plate to the Pope, xii. 20.

Theodora, Augusta (married to Justinian 525, died 548), letter of Amalasuentha to, x. 10; letters of Gudelina to, x. 20, 21, 23; alleged complicity of, in murder of Amalasuentha, 433, 435.

Theodoric, King of the Goths and Romans (493-525), his position in Italy, 16, 19; story of his inability to write, 15; relation of Cassiodorus to, 16, 19; his religious tolerance, 21, 22; his persecution of the Orthodox, 35; condemnation of Boethius and Symmachus, 35; death of (Aug. 30, 526), 37; may *possibly* have called himself King of Italy, 62 *n*; 455 *n*; confusion between him and Theodoric II. the Visigoth, 116; letters written in the name of, 141-293; learned in the Roman Republic the art of governing Romans with equity, i. 1; relations between him and Anastasius, i. 1; allusion to his adoption by Zeno (?), i. 20; his intervention in Gaul (508), i. 24; his friendship for Artemidorus, i. 43; motto for his reign, ii. 21; inscription recording his drainage of Decennonial Marsh, 188; his attempts to prevent war between Alaric and Clovis, iii. 1-4; calls himself 'Romanus Princeps,' iii. 16; his high purpose in ruling, iii. 43; his alliance with the Thuringians, iv. 1; his alliance with the Heruli, iv. 2; his rides after the hours of business with Cyprian his *Referendarius*, v. 40; Cassiodorus speaks of his 'oculus imperialis,' viii. 18; praises of, by Witigis, x. 31; his especial characteristic was patience, xi. 1.

Theodoric I, King of the Franks (511-534), death of, xi. 1; 452 *n*, 455 *n*.

Theodoric, or more probably Theodorus, Patrician, accused of assaulting the Green party in the Circus, i. 27.

Theodorus, candidate for office of Pantomimist, i. 20.

Theodorus, report of, as to gold in Bruttii, ix. 3.

Theodosian Code, perhaps referred to in the words 'Statuta Divalium sanctionum,' iv. 12; as to Decuriae Librariorum, &c. 277; as to Delegatio, 479 *n*.

Theodosius, man of Theodahad (?), exhorted to abstain from violence, x. 5.

Thessalonica, Praefect of, entreated by Witigis to speed his ambassadors on their way to Justinian, x. 35.

Theudimer, father of Theodoric, 'pietate enituit,' xi. 1.

Thor..s, father of Germanus, iii. 37.

Tho..s, Vir Clarissimus, complains that he cannot collect arrears of taxes in Apulia, v. 31.

Thomas, Vir Honestus, hopelessly in debt for taxes on Apulian farms, v. 6, 7.

Thomas the Charioteer to receive a monthly allowance, iii. 51.

Thorbecke, August, author of 'Cassiodorus Senator,' 119.

Thorismuth, predecessor of Theodoric, 'castitate enituit,' xi. 1.

Thuringians, King of, appealed to by Theodoric to prevent war between Clovis and Alaric, iii. 3; Herminafrid, King of, married to Amalabirga, niece of Theodoric, iv. 1.

Tiber to be crossed by a bridge of boats, xii. 19.

Ticinum (*Pavia*), inhabitants of, ordered to provision the Heruli on their journey to King's Comitatus, iv. 45; corn warehouse at, to be opened, x. 27; xii. 27; provision dealers at, x. 28; Count Winusiad, Governor of, x. 29.

Tituli, practice of affixing to property, condemned, ix. 18.

Totila, words of, as to exceptional favour accorded to Sicily, 397.

Trajan, oath taken by, to the Roman people, viii. 3; noble saying of, to an orator, viii. 13.

Transmund (Thrasamund), King of the Vandals (496-523), complained of for sheltering Gesalic, Theodoric's enemy, v. 43; the reconciliation, v. 44.

Transmutation of metals (?), viii. 3.

Treasure, buried, search for, iv. 34.

TRIBUNATUS PROVINCIARUM, FORMULA OF, vii. 30.

Tribuni Maritimorum (in islands of Venetia), xii. 24.
TRIBUNUS VOLUPTATUM, MINISTER OF PUBLIC AMUSEMENT, FORMULA OF, vii. 10; Bacauda appointed, at Milan, v. 25; referred to, vi. 19.
Tridentum (*Trient*), proprietors in district of, ii. 17; new city to be erected in district of, v. 9; corn warehouse at, to be opened, x. 27.
Trigguilla, 'Regiae Praepositus Domus,' was he the Praetorian Praefect whose misgovernment is denounced, viii. 30?
Trina Illatio, three instalments for payment of taxes, ii. 24; x. 27 (?); xi. 7, 35, 36, 37; xii. 2, 16, 27 (?).
Trittheim, John (Trithemius), Abbot of Spanheim, his notice of date of Cassiodorus' birth, 9, 10, 66; as to office of Abbot held by Cassiodorus, 56 *n*.
TUITIO REGII NOMINIS, FORMULA BESTOWING, vii. 39; promised to owner of potteries, ii. 23; to Milanese Church, ii. 29; to Maurentius and Paula, iv. 9; alluded to in Edictum Athalarici, ix. 18 (p. 404).
Tullianus, son of Venantius, 221.
Tulum, Patrician, his early history and character, viii. 9, 10; embassy to Constantinople (?), viii. 9; share in the war of Sirmium, viii. 10; in the Gaulish wars (508 and 523), viii. 10; his escape from shipwreck, viii. 10; marriage with an Amal princess, viii. 9; letter written on his behalf to the Senate, viii. 11; declared Patrician, viii. 9, 10, 11, 12; receives Castrum Lucullanum from Theodoric and hands it over to Joannes, viii. 25.
Tupha (Tufa), an officer of Odovacar, who deserted to Theodoric and then betrayed him, 251; lawsuit about his property, confiscated to the Treasury, iv. 32.
Tusciae (Thusciae) utraeque, iv. 14; Goths resident in, iv. 14; Canonicarius of, to buy a fitting quantity of paper, xi. 38.

U.

Ulpianus, guarantor for Venantius, has lost 400 solidi by his default, ii. 13. (As this occurred 'administrationis suae tempore,' Ulpianus must have held some kind of public office.)
Ulysses, reputed founder of Scyllacium, xii. 15.

Unalamer (Walamir), uncle of Theodoric, 'fide enituit,' xi. 1.
Unimundus (Hunimund), collateral ancestor of Theodoric, 'forma enituit,' xi. 1.
Uraias, nephew of King Witigis, his capture of Milan (539), xii. 27.
Usener, Hermann, editor of 'Anecdoton Holderi,' 73–84, 119.

V.

Vacco, Major Domus to Theodahad, x. 18; to superintend purchase of provisions for Gothic garrison, x. 18.
Valentinian III, Emperor (425–455), quotation from Novellae of, ix. 18; Placidia's guardianship of, xi. 1.
Valerian, a Spectabilis, citizen of Syracuse, sons of, to be detained in Rome, iv. 6.
Valeriana, Adeodatus condemned for rape of, iii. 46.
Vandals, King of (Thrasamund), sends presents to Theodoric, v. 1. (*See* also *Transmund* and *Hilderic*.)
Vandals, allusion to, v. 17.
'VARIAE' of Cassiodorus, their style described, 16–19; not arranged in chronological order, 22; time and manner of their editing, 51, 52; reason of the name, 138, 139.
Velia (or Volia), dispute between Possessores and Curiales of, iv. 11.
Venantius (1), guardian of Plutianus, his accusation of Felix, i. 7, 8.
Venantius (2), by his dishonesty has caused his guarantor Ulpianus to forfeit 400 solidi, ii. 13.
Venantius (3), son of Liberius, Vir Illustris, praises of, ii. 15; made Comes Domesticorum, ii. 15, 16; rebuked for remissness in collection of taxes when Corrector of Bruttii and Lucania, iii. 8; complaints of Firminus against, iii. 36; his alleged unjust judgment of Adeodatus, iii. 46; descended from the ancient Decii, ix. 23; congratulated on Consulship of his son Paulinus (534), ix. 23.
Venerius, a farmer, unjustly reduced to slavery by Tanca, viii. 28.
Venetia, Province of, Gepidae on their way to Gaul to march peaceably through, v. 10, 11; famine in 'devotae Venetiae' to be relieved by corn distribution, x. 27; Canonicarius of, ordered to collect wine for

the King's table, xii. 4; taxes of, remitted, on account of invasion of the Suevi, xii. 7; 'Venetiae praedicabiles,' xii. 24; scarcity of crops in, xii. 26.

Venice, letter containing first historical notice of (537), xii. 24.

Veranilda, convert from Arianism to Catholic faith, interceded for by Justinian, x. 26.

Vercelli, grant of freedom from taxation made to Church of, i. 26.

Veredarii, drivers of the royal mail, ii. 31.

Veredi, post-horses, not to be overworked, iv. 47.

Verruca (perhaps *Dos Trento*), near Trient, description of the fort of, iii. 48; meaning of the word, 223, n 1.

Vesuvius, eruption of, iv. 50.

Vicarius, a Spectabilis and Governor of a Diocese, 90; i. 37.

Vicarius Praefectorum (?), title borne by Gemellus as Governor of Gaul, iii. 16.

VICARIUS PORTUS, FORMULA OF, vii. 23.

VICARIUS URBIS ROMAE, FORMULA OF, vi. 15; limits of his jurisdiction, 88.

Vice-dominus (?), servants of, have oppressed Provincials of Suavia, v. 14.

Victor Tunnunensis, chronicler (died in 569), as to the death of Amalafrida, 384 n.

Victor, Vir Spectabilis, Censitor of Sicily, severely rebuked for acts of oppression, ix. 12.

Vigilius, Pope (537–555), allusion to by Cassiodorus, 6; brother of Reparatus, 390; perhaps alluded to by Gudelina, x. 20 (see p. 433 n).

Villiciorum Tuitio (?), removed in Spain, as being costly and unpopular, v. 39.

Virgil quoted, 63 n; xii. 14.

Vivarian Monastery, founded by Cassiodorus, near Scyllacium, 55; site of, 71.

Vivianus, Spectabilis, renouncing the world, foregoes the benefit of an unjust decree which he has obtained against Joannes, iv. 41.

Volcanoes, nature of, iii. 47; iv. 50.

Volusianus, one of the Quinque-viri appointed to try Basilius and Praetextatus, iv. 22, 23; died at Easter, iv. 42; his sons robbed of their possessions by a heartless intriguer, iv. 42.

Vulcanian Islands (*Lipari*), a murderer banished to, iii. 47.

W.

Walamir (see Unalamer).

Warni (or Guarni), King of, appealed to by Theodoric to prevent war between Clovis and Alaric, iii. 3.

Water-clock, description of, to be made by Boetius for Gundibad, i. 45.

Water-finder has come from Africa to Rome, iii. 53; description of his art, iii. 53.

Wine, Acinaticium, xii. 4; Palmatiana, xii. 12; of Gaza, xii. 12; Sabine, xii. 12.

Winithar (see Munitarius).

Winusiad, Comes, Governor of Ticinum, recommended to visit baths of Bormio, x. 29.

Witigis (or Vitigis), King of the Goths (536–540), proclamation announcing his accession, 49; x. 31; letters written in the name of, x. 32–35; his vengeance on Theodahad, x. 32; his marriage with Matasuentha, x. 32; his siege of Rome, 506; possibly alluded to in xii. 19; 509; the Burgundians' fear of him, xii. 28.

Witigisclus (or Wigisicla), Vir Spectabilis, Censitor of Sicily, severely rebuked for acts of oppression, ix. 12.

Z.

Zeno, Emperor (474–491), his concessions to Theodoric, x. 22.